A Comprehensive History of Medieval India

Twelfth to the Mid-Eighteenth Century

Salma Ahmed Farooqui

Acquisitions Editor: Prasun Chatterjee
Development Editor: Yajnaseni Das
Senior Production Editor: Gaurav Jain
Composition: Serco India Pvt. Ltd.
Printer:

ISBN 978-81-317-3202-1

First Impression

Published by Dorling Kindersley (India) Pvt. Ltd, licensees of Pearson Education in South Asia.

Head Office: 7th Floor, Knowledge Boulevard, A-8(A), Sector–62, Noida, UP 201309, India.

Registered Office: 11 Community Centre, Panchsheel Park, New Delhi 110017, India.

Printed in India at Repro India Limited

Overview

Contents

Maps

Note: All maps used in this book can be accessed at www.pearsoned.co.in/salmaahmedfarooqui

Note: The spellings used in the maps are different from those used in the actual text. The maps have been sourced from *A Historical Atlas of South Asia* by Joseph E. Schwartzberg. Copyright © 1978 by the Regents of the University of Minnesota, assigned 1988 to Joseph E. Schwartzberg, additional material copyright © 1992 by Joseph E. Schwartzberg.

Images

Preface

The study of medieval Indian history has engaged both scholars and students over the last two hundred years in India and elsewhere. Its understanding and interpretation illustrates the nature of social forces, complexity of causation and the interdependence of change and continuity. Whenever a book on medieval Indian history is written and read, a connection needs to be established between the reading of the text and its multi-layered historical perspective that encompasses the political, social, economic and cultural contexts. *A Comprehensive History of Medieval India* assesses the entire medieval period—twelfth to the mid-eighteenth century—from multiple perspectives, enabling the reader to build connections and form new ideas. The primary objective of this book is to aid students in becoming active historians, and scholars to refresh their memory and generate fresh views on the progression of medieval Indian history. Keeping this in mind, the book has been designed to appeal to a wide audience and to give this crucial period of Indian history the attention it deserves.

Organized into eight parts, the thirty-three chapters of approximately equal length begin with an introductory part on the crucial transition from ancient to early medieval India. The parts on the Delhi Sultanate, Vijayanagar–Bahmani kingdoms and the Mughals proceed chronologically to the Marathas, and the advent of European companies to the establishment of the British in Bengal depicting the unfolding of the developments as they occurred during this entire period. In-between these parts, a section on religious thought provides an insight into the ideological–philosophical basis of the times, focusing on the Sufi and Bhakti movements. The chapters in themselves follow the course of medieval Indian history in chronological order so that the reader learns to grasp the essential direction of events as they led from one to another.

The history of medieval India as a topic for investigation may appear curiously anachronistic at a time when historians are less preoccupied with the history of personalities or the grand narrative of dynastic changes. History writing has now moved towards the analysis of institutions and structures. It often attempts to explain micro historical studies in certain regions at a given time. The ability of the medieval Indian state to adapt to the new forms of governance that emerged during a long span of time makes this task not without its benefits. It needs to be kept in mind that medieval India's history has not moved in a linear fashion. The resultant interface between the political, social, economic, religious and cultural elements has shaped the historical processes at work. Much of the period saw phases of expansion and realignment of political attributes lending the medieval Indian state a distinct character. In this light, this book seeks to integrate the general with the specific, thus contributing to a deeper understanding of the much misread and often bypassed period of Indian history.

About the Author

Salma Ahmed Farooqui is Associate Professor of History at the Directorate of Distance Education, Maulana Azad National Urdu University, Hyderabad. A gold medallist from the University of Hyderabad and an UGC-JRF/SRF awardee she completed the MPhil and PhD programmes in History from the same university. She then proceeded to finish a post-doctoral fellowship awarded by the K. K. Birla Academy, Division of Historical Research, New Delhi. She has also worked with ICFAI University. Her resolve to look at the past afresh with a questioning mind has led to several research publications which include two books, *Islam and the Mughal State* and *Multicultural Dimensions of Medieval Deccan,* and several papers. Her presentation of papers at many national and international seminars and conferences include one at the University of Cambridge, UK. She was also selected for the Study of the United States Institutes Program on Religious Pluralism hosted by the University of California, Santa Barbara, USA.

Acknowledgments

I have several people to thank, as the present study is the outcome of many years of learning and sharing. Here I wish to put on record my gratitude to all those who inspired and lent me support in completing this project. Among them are my teachers, colleagues, family members and friends. They helped me with the quiet space I needed, with new ideas and with the encouragement when I was facing the 'writer's block'. I sincerely value their reading of the drafts, brainstorming sessions, comments and allowing me to quote their remarks.

I start with my teachers—Prof. R.L. Hangloo, Prof. V. Ramakrishna and Prof. Suleman Siddiqui—who not only instilled the rigour for research from the beginning of my academic life but have also guided me at various phases of my career. I deeply acknowledge the constant encouragement I received from Prof. A.M. Pathan, Prof. Rila Mukherjee, Prof. Rekha Pande, Prof. K.R. Iqbal Ahmed and Prof. S.A. Wahab. I sincerely appreciate what I have learnt over the years from Dr. Ziauddin Ahmed Shakeb about the finer nuances of medieval Indian history. I convey a special word of gratitude to Mr. Mir Ayoob Ali Khan who fulfilled the role of a teacher when I needed to sort out difficult questions.

My thanks are particularly due to the staff of the libraries of the University of Hyderabad, Maulana Azad National Urdu University, Osmania University, Salarjung Museum and Henry Martyn Institute.

I earnestly express my gratitude to my publishers who assisted me at various stages of editing, proofreading and designing of the book. My special thanks are due to Debjani Dutta, Arani Banerjee, Yajnaseni Das, Saon Bhattacharya and Gaurav Jain who were always there with their quick response and ready help.

Lastly, I convey deep gratitude to my family members—Naveed Farooqui, Niloufer Ahmed, Naim Farooqui, Sania and Abdul Khan, Sameen and Saher—who have been a great source of strength and motivation. They always stood by me in my pursuit of excellence in academic life. My quest for research would not have borne fruit without their support.

Salma Ahmed Farooqui

Introduction

Conventionally, the history of medieval India comprises a timeline between the twelfth and the eighteenth centuries. But, there are some historians who include the time between the eighth and the eleventh centuries in the medieval period and term it as the early medieval period. The early medieval period, historians say, forms the entry point of certain significant trends into the Indian society that began leaving a noticeable impact on the Indian way of life.

In Indian history the entire 'medieval period' is often equated with the 'Muslim rule'. In such depictions the arrival of the Turks is regarded as the beginning of the Muslim conquests and the period starting from the twelfth century till the onset of the modern age is classified as the Muslim period. This kind of portrayal is the result of a number of misconceptions which historians now recognize as conventional and orthodox representations. Sadly, in spite of new insights into medieval history, such views continue to find place in the political parlance of modern religious nationalism and influence our perception of identities.

In the early medieval period, the Rajputs belonging to north India were floating around restlessly looking for a home before finally settling down in the Rajputana (mostly today's Rajasthan) area. Then, they pushed themselves into the political arena and established numerous small monarchical kingdoms. In addition to these fiefdoms, large states arose elsewhere in India between 750 CE and 1000 CE—the Palas in eastern India, the Pratiharas in western India and the upper Gangetic valley, and the Rashtrakutas in the Deccan. The feudatory pattern of relationships played a key role in the political and economic developments of those times and also in the rise and fall of small and big kingdoms. It also made these states incapable of withstanding the foreign invasions. In the absence of a paramount power in the country, it was comparatively easy, first, for the Arabs in 712 CE and a hundred years later for the Turks who had settled down in what is today known as Afghanistan to undertake expeditions into India. The Turks, a Central Asian people, later led conquests beyond the frontiers of India and from thence advanced into the Indian mainland.

By the beginning of the twelfth century, Delhi with its strategic location had begun to surface as the new power centre from where the fresh entrants marched into the fertile Punjab and the Ganges valley. What emerged from there was a period in Indian history that triggered prominent trends in thought and institutions. It is during this period that the Arabs, Afghans, Turks and Persians gained a firm foothold on the Indian soil and made it their permanent abode.

Islam's advent into India in the eighth century, first as a religion and then as military force, and its firm establishment by the eleventh century as a political power in the northern regions, gave rise to a culture as complex as the pressures exerted on it. This long period of advancement and interaction started to flourish and assume leadership making a mark by its intrusive centralization, novel institutions of statecraft and different norms of governance. The new leadership manifested itself through vital developments, such as the expansion of population, agriculture, trade and towns. Reforms in religion and the development of literature, art and architecture was to continue for the next several centuries.

The foreigners brought with them a new faith, hitherto unknown military practices, love for gardens and lakes, passion for building palaces, forts, mosques and other kinds of structures, fascination for delectable foods, ideas and philosophies, and traditions and customs that India had never been through in the past. In the beginning, the two sets of what broadly could be called civilizations resisted influence over each other, sometimes bitterly in wars. But with time this reluctance gave way to experiment, adjustment and then to understanding and acceptance of the inevitable progression of history.

Let us first analyse the changes that came up in the Indian society with the coming of Islam to India. Al-Beruni was perhaps the first historian to use the word Hindu to refer to the people living in Hindustan who comprised a religious group different from the Muslims. It is important to understand that the term 'Hindu' as referring to a religious denomination was rare until medieval times when it began to be used to refer to a community with its own way of living. Since the eighth century, Islamic traditions were introduced into India by traders, warriors, Sufis and travellers of different ethnicities.

Interaction between the two culturally diverse traditions has often been represented in terms of tension between the 'Turk' and the 'Hindu', both conceptualized as being monolithic and static with conflicting ways of life. But it was not so. The process was definitely difficult for a society that was witnessing a sudden transformation as a result of military, political, racial, religious and regional conflicts. However, the quotient of adaptability and resilience went beyond the skirmishes naturally evolving exchanges in cultural assimilation and synthesis.

The Arabs had been trading with the people of Malabar since the pre-Islamic days. After the revelation of the message to the Prophet, the Arabs became Muslims, and many of them married local women whose children went to live in different parts of the region. On the other hand, Islam came to North India through the invasion of Sind by Muhammad bin Qasim in 712 CE. Later, when Arab rule weakened in Sind, the Persianized Turks and Afghans uprooted by the Mongols from their homeland in Iran and Central Asia established their presence as rulers in much of north India from the twelfth century onwards.

The new military technology used by Mahmud of Ghazni and Muhammad of Ghur in the form of the crossbow while at the gallop gave them a decisive advantage over their Indian opponents, the Rajputs, who ultimately collapsed in the face of the swift cavalry of the Afghans and Turks. In the thirteenth century, Iltutmish, a former slave-warrior, established the Delhi Sultanate, which enabled future sultans to push their way forward in every direction. Within the next hundred years, the Delhi Sultanate extended its sway east to Bengal and south to the Deccan, while the Sultanate itself experienced repeated threats from the northwest and internal revolts from displeased, independent-minded nobles. The Sultanate was in a constant state of flux as five dynasties rose and fell—the Slaves or Mamluks, the Khiljis, the Tughlaqs, the Sayyids and the Lodis. The remains of these kingdoms are still visible in Delhi and elsewhere around North India.

Even as the upheaval in the North continued, other sultanates were being established in the Deccan and South India. The south had begun to exercise an increasing fascination over men from north India as well as those from Persia who got an opportunity to travel and survey areas hitherto unknown to them. Powerful states such as Vijayanagar, based on Brahmanical political traditions of *dharma*, the Bahmanis, and smaller Muslim sultanates emerged in the Deccan and Far South. Not surprisingly, there was travel and exchange of diverse ideas, traditions and cultures between the north and the south.

Medieval India was beginning to witness the many syncretic and inclusionist dimensions of Indian cultures. Those were times when Muslims fought against Muslims and Hindus against Hindus in their struggle for power.

The Delhi sultans were finally replaced by the Turko-Mongol reign of the Mughals in North India, under whom India once again achieved a large measure of political unity. The Mughal Empire set up by Babur in the sixteenth century continued to rule effectively till the eighteenth century. The Mughals brought about integration and harmony in the Indian society. They established a vast empire, which became the envy of the world in terms of power, prestige and prosperity.

Rising in the seventeenth century against the central authority of the Mughals in quest of autonomy were the Marathas under Shivaji. They succeeded in destabilizing, to a large extent, the Mughal Empire that continued to linger on till 1857.

Even before the Mughal-Maratha conflict gained intensity, the Europeans had already arrived on the Indian shores as merchants. Their presence dates back to the early sixteenth century. The Portuguese merchants were followed by the Dutch, the English and the French. Among them, the English and the French went on to become giant maritime powers. As the Mughal Empire began to disintegrate in the latter part of the seventeenth century it paved the way for regional powers to contest for supremacy. The turmoil in India provided the Europeans with the opportunity to play one regional power against the other, as it suited their vested interests. In those series of conflicts, the English emerged victorious, beginning their rule with the conquest of Bengal. British imperialist rise in India saw the Muslims standing shoulder to shoulder with their Hindu compatriots in a fight for freedom against the foreign rule.

While writing this book what came to mind is that there are a few simple yet thought provoking terms which need a re-look in terms of understanding and usage. Often one finds that certain terms have been used in medieval Indian history recklessly, sometimes giving one meaning and some giving yet another in different situations. Therefore, an attempt has been made to draw a distinction and correct the misusage that has gone unnoticed so far. For instance, in this book the term 'empire' has been used only to refer to the Mughals and the British. All the other powers, such as the Delhi Sultanate, Bahmanis, Vijayanagar and Marathas have been referred to as kingdoms. In doing so, the justification lies in the fact that an empire is the domain ruled by an emperor within which there are a group of countries under a single authority. The territory or countries under the jurisdiction and dominion of an emperor (rarely of a king) are usually of greater extent than a kingdom, always comprising a variety of nationalities and forms of administration in its constituent and subordinate portions. Here, it is important to remark that the kingdoms of Alauddin Khilji and Muhammad bin Tughlaq although stretching from the north to the south of India could not become empires as they merely unified India politically, but could not achieve the degree of potency that is necessary to keep it intact for long. A kingdom, on the other hand, was basically a monarchy, whether big or small, ruled by a king or queen who exercised control. A sultanate or a *rashtra* had the stature of a kingdom. But both the empires and the kingdoms in medieval Indian history were sovereign states having the same features that comprise statehood, such as population, territory, sovereignty and government.

The state in medieval India other than being a functional structure was made up of specific activities and ideas of individuals who comprised it. This encouraged an alternative approach to kingship that focused on the activities of the royal court. In view of this, the king's court not only symbolized the state but the activities of the court were the activities of the state.

Now, a small note of clarification on the terms English and British in Indian history. English is a term used for the people of England while British includes people from England, Scotland and Wales together forming Great Britain. The earliest Englishmen to come into India were the English merchants who had formed themselves into a company to trade with India. They obtained a charter from Queen Elizabeth, the ruler of England, and named their company 'The Company of Merchants of London trading in the East Indies'. From this small beginning the Company evolved into 'The English East India Company'. Similarly, more or less at the same time and a little before the formation of the English East India Company, the Portuguese, the Dutch and the French had formed their respective East India Companies. These companies were formed initially for pursuing trade with the East Indies, thus, deriving their name, but ended up trading with the Indian subcontinent and China. Until the conquest of Bengal, as a result of the battles of Plassey and Buxar in 1757 CE and 1764 CE, the English had not established themselves politically in India. It was only then that more people belonging to different stocks of Great Britain came into India as administrators and soldiers. This aspect makes the use of the term 'British' politically correct and suitable from then onwards in Indian history.

Setting aside clarifications, let us look at the generic evolution of interesting terminology in medieval Indian history whose usage has made them identifiable with the particular period alone. *Jiziya,* a term used to refer to a poll tax, was a tax made payable by non-Muslims known as *zimmis* living in a Muslim state. *Iqta,* the forerunner of the *jagir,* was the piece of land allotted by the Delhi sultans, in lieu of salary to the *iqtadar,* a nobleman, for collection of land revenue in the non-crown lands and for maintaining troops which could be utilized by the sultan. Almost all civil and military officers of the Sultanate were *iqtadars*. The *iqta* system was established to relieve the state treasury when insufficient tax revenue and little booty from campaigns made it difficult for the government to pay army salaries. Later, came the terms *mansabdari* and *jagirdari* which referred to the two main institutions of the Mughal Empire and embraced both civil and military sectors of administration. The system was developed to create a centralized administration as well as aimed at raising a large force. The large forces of the mansabdars were used to expand the empire and administer it effectively. Like the *iqtadars* during the Delhi Sultanate, the *mansabdars* were paid in Mughal India through the assignment of *jagirs*. The *jagirdari* system as an institution was used to appropriate the surplus from the peasantry. At the same time, it was used for distributing the revenue resources among the ruling classes. This military-fiscalism as an important feature in the political traditions of medieval India along with paternalism and absolutism formed the basis of medieval Indian statecraft. Akin to *jagirdars* in nature of responsibilities, were the *zamindars*, who invariably squeezed between the *jagirdars* and the rural peasantry and were the landowning class with full proprietary rights over land. More generally in north India, the *zamindar* denoted the cultivator of the soil or joint proprietors holding village lands. In Bengal, the word denoted a hereditary tax collector who could retain a percentage of the revenue he collected while in the Maratha territories the name was generally applied to all local hereditary revenue officers. In the late eighteenth century, the British government made these *zamindars* landowners, thus creating a landed aristocracy. A peculiar system put in place as a result of these manifestations was that of revenue farming—a system in which the right to collect revenue was given as a franchisee under license from the state to a category of persons known as revenue farmers.

Thus, the political map of medieval India was made up of myriad kingdoms with fluctuating boundaries during the long span of 700 years when the Hindus and Muslims mingled, created a new Indo-Islamic sub-civilization and left an indelible mark on South Asia, specially the Indian subcontinent.

A Comprehensive History of Medieval India

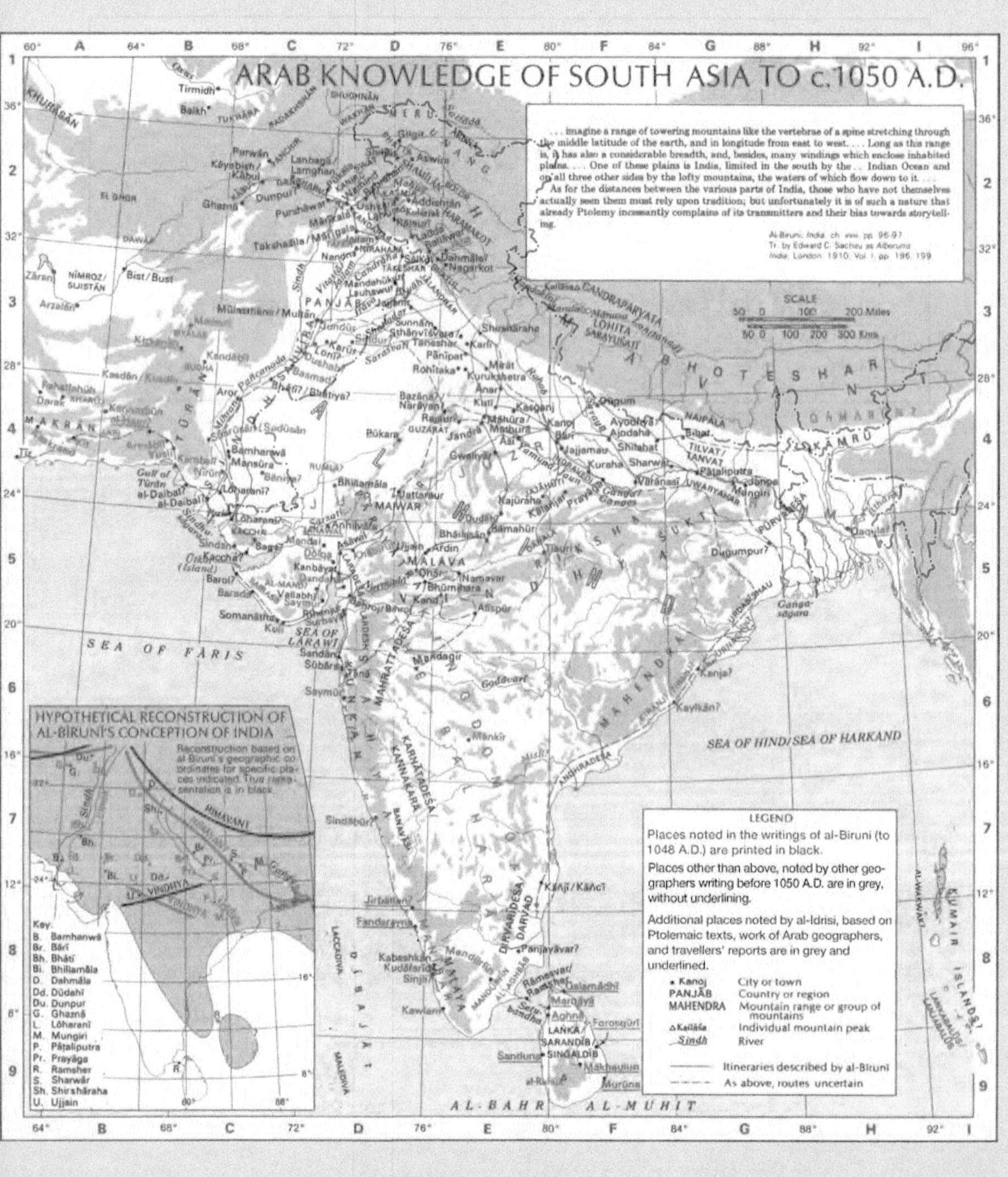

ARAB KNOWLEDGE OF SOUTH ASIA TO c.1050 A.D.
. . . imagine a range of towering mountains like the vertebrae of a spine stretching through the middle latitude of the earth, and in longitude from east to west. . . . Long as this range is, it has also a considerable breadth, and, besides, many windings which enclose inhabited plains. . . . One of these plains is India, limited in the south by the . . Indian Ocean and on all three other sides by the lofty mountains, the waters of which flow down to it. . . .
As for the distances between the various parts of India, those who have not themselves actually seen them must rely upon tradition; but unfortunately it is of such a nature that already Ptolemy incessantly complains of its transmitters and their bias towards storytelling.
SCALE
50 0 100 200 Miles
50 0 100 200 300 Kms
HYPOTHETICAL RECONSTRUCTION OF AL-BIRUNI'S CONCEPTION OF INDIA
Key:
B. Bamhanwā
Br. Bārī
Bh. Bhātī
Bi. Bhillamāla
D. Dahmāla
Dd. Dūdahī
Du. Dunpur
G. Ghaznā
L. Lōharanī
M. Mungiri
P. Pātaliputra
Pr. Prayāga
R. Ramsher
S. Sharwār
Sh. Shirshāraha
U. Ujjain
SEA OF FĀRIS
SEA OF HIND/SEA OF HARKAND
AL-BAHR AL-MUHIT
LEGEND
Places noted in the writings of al-Biruni (to 1048 A.D.) are printed in black.
Places other than above, noted by other geographers writing before 1050 A.D. are in grey, without underlining.
Additional places noted by al-Idrisi, based on Ptolemaic texts, work of Arab geographers, and travellers' reports are in grey and underlined.
Kanoj City or town
PANJĀB Country or region
MAHENDRA Mountain range or group of mountains
Kailāsa Individual mountain peak
Sindh River
Itineraries described by al-Biruni
As above, routes uncertain

PART I–Transition from Ancient to Medieval India

"We understand by witchcraft, making by some kind of delusion a thing appear to the senses as something different from what it is in reality. Taken in this sense, it is far spread among people. Understood, however as common people understand it, as the producing of something which is impossible, it is a thing which does not lie within the limits of reality. For as that which is impossible cannot be produced, the whole affair is nothing but a gross deception. Therefore, witchcraft in this sense has nothing whatever to do with science.

One of the species of witchcraft is alchemy, though it is generally not called by this name. But if a man takes a bit of cotton and makes it appear as a bit of gold, what would you call this but a piece of witchcraft? It is quite the same as if he were to take a bit of silver and make it appear as gold, only with this difference, that the latter is a generally known process, i.e. the gilding of silver, the former is not.

The Hindus do not pay particular attention to alchemy, but no nation is entirely free from it, and one nation has more bias for it than another, which must not be construed as proving intelligence or ignorance; for we find that many intelligent people are entirely given to alchemy, whilst ignorant people ridicule the art and its adepts. Those intelligent people, though boisterously exulting over their make-believe science, are not to be blamed for occupying themselves with alchemy, for their motive is simply excessive eagerness for acquiring fortune and for avoiding misfortune. Once a sage was asked why scholars always flock to the doors of the rich, whilst the rich are not inclined to call at the doors of scholars. "The scholars," he answered, "are well aware of the use of money, but the rich are ignorant of the nobility of science." On the other hand, ignorant people are not to be praised, although they behave quite quietly, simply because they abstain from alchemy, for their motives are objectionable ones, rather practical results of innate ignorance and stupidity than anything else.

The adepts in this art try to keep it concealed, and shrink back from intercourse with those who do not belong to them. Therefore I have not been able to learn from the Hindus which methods they follow in this science, and what element they principally use, whether a mineral or an animal or a vegetable one. I only heard them speaking of the process of sublimation, of calcination, of analysis, and of the waxing of talc, which they call in their language talaka, and so I guess that they incline towards the mineralogical method of alchemy."

Source: Alberuni, Muhammad ibn Ahmad, *Alberuni's India,* Vol I, London: Kegan Paul, Trench, Trübner and Co., 1910. Extract taken from Chapter XVII: On Hindu Sciences Which Prey on the Ignorance of People, pp.187–88.

Map: Arab Knowledge of South Asia to 1050 CE.

CHAPTER **1**

Survey of Sources in Medieval Indian History

Review and Discussion

- History Writing in Medieval India
- Contemporary Texts
- Travelogues
- Indigenous Literature
- Archaeological Sources

The writing of history, or historiography, is the methodology of scholarly historical research and presentation—based on a critical evaluation and selection of authentic source materials—of a narrative that stands up to methods of criticism. In this context, the importance of identifying and recognizing appropriate historical sources cannot be emphasized enough. For the creation of a clear and authentic narrative, a mere narration of events from any single historical source becomes inadequate; necessitating the cross-referencing of facts through a variety of other relevant sources.

Historical sources may be broadly categorized into *primary* and *secondary* categories, where the former are contemporary written records of the period under study and the latter are historical texts based on the primary sources. Primary sources are generally available in the form of documents or texts produced by eyewitnesses, participants or commentators of the event or period being researched upon; while secondary sources are usually articles, essays and other texts based on such first-person accounts. Both primary and secondary written records come in various forms: legal codes, annals, chronicles, biographies, public documents (such as financial, administrative, ecclesiastical, parliamentary and diplomatic papers), literature and private records such as newspapers, pamphlets and personal letters. Historians also have access to a vast corpus of oral sources (legends, ballads and folk tales), sociological and ethnographic sources (various customs and traditions), as well as archaeological sources (stone and clay inscriptions, coins, seals, tools, weapons, objects of art and articles of daily use).

Among all categories of historical source materials, however, it is the written or printed text that has enjoyed primacy over all the rest, since written chronicles have so far been understood to constitute the earliest records of any civil society. More recent academic traditions have, however, begun to recognize oral narratives as authentic historical evidence too. As an increasing amount of non-traditional source material is able to substantiate

NALANDA, MANUSCRIPT COVER, *11th century. Although the earliest remaining South Asian manuscripts date from the 11th century, the tradition of copying and illuminating manuscripts is considerably older. For example, Fa Hsien copied Buddhist* sutras *and drew images of deities while at Tamralipti. All early manuscripts were executed on palm leaf. Those from Western India generally treat Jaina subjects, while Northeastern manuscripts are almost all Buddhist. This scene from a cover of a Buddhist* Prajnaparamita *manuscript was executed at Nalanda during Ramapala's reign. It depicts the symbol of perfect wisdom, the Bodhisattva Prajnaparamita.*

existing historical data today, the term 'source' is often used interchangeably with 'evidence'. It is important to recognize that even though sources may sometimes be incomplete, or even prejudiced, they nevertheless form the basic units for recreating the past.

The use of different kinds of sources by historians has, over the years, led to the incorporation of several changes in the research techniques used in the study of history. In recent years, for instance, Indian kingship has received considerable academic attention, which has created various models for studying the structures of authority and functions of state in ancient and medieval India. Broadly speaking, Nationalist, Marxist and Revisionist models have dominated the academic arena with their specific interpretations of available historical data. These models generally view the state as an administrative or bureaucratic entity situated above society, which is composed of different groups. Major debates in historiography have revolved around the extent to which the state and its various administrative structures are centralized or decentralized. Such issues have transformed the way in which historians perceive concepts and theories or prioritize events and occurrences in medieval Indian history, bringing about a marked change in both the understanding and interpretation of facts and data.

History Writing in Medieval India

Assessing medieval India for its historical significance has led to the growth of new trends of looking at the basic concepts. This has in turn recorded a number of thematic changes over the last two hundred years, one among which is the history of historiography, an area that has attracted the attention of many historians of late. Scholars working in this area have recognized the arrival of Islam and its introduction to the people of India as the key factor in studying India's medieval period. The story of the contact between these culturally diverse traditions initiated a new chapter by the end of the eighth century, with Islam gradually making inroads into various quarters of the Indian sub-continent and leaving behind a significant influence on both the natives and their existent sociological systems.

The wealthy cities of northern and central India together with the rich ports along the western coast had started to attract the attention of the Arabs, who were now united under the newly acquired banner of Islam. Urban centres at Sind, Multan, Agra, Delhi, and Malwa developed as nodal points for the exchange of agrarian produce and other commodities. Thana, Goa, Bhatkal, Karwar, Mangalore, Kambath, Baruch, Visakapatnam, Ghantasala, Nellore, Kolikkodu and Kollam became important centres of maritime trade. Varanasi and Kanchipuram emerged as centres for textile manufacturing.

This cultural contact produced a huge amount of historical texts and archaeological evidence—coins, seals, monuments and inscriptions—that comprise important sources for researching on medieval India. The two main historiographical traditions that developed during this period were those of the Arabs and the Persians. The former laid emphasis on the entirety of human society, while the latter highlighted the feats of kings and courtiers, describing their opulent lifestyles in great detail. Though they differed in their focus, both traditions contributed to maintaining continuity in the historiography of medieval India. Much later a native tradition was to be developed by both Muslims and Hindus, writing primarily in Persian. Subsequently a European tradition was also to be developed during the British colonial period, with both British and Indian scholars writing in English.

Professor Harbans Mukhia, while talking about medieval Indian historiography, says that 'the association of history with date or chronology came as late as in the third century. Before that there was almost no concept of history except individual history or family history.' He further states that 'medieval Indian history has two sections: dynastic and individual narration that was based on human will or nature'. On the topic of the history of Muslim states in India, he states that 'historians divide it into two sections: before and after the rise of Islam'. While throwing light on medieval Indian history, he ranks Abul Fazl, the author of the *Akbar Namah,* as one of our greatest historians—one without any predecessors or successors. The point that caught the attention of Prof. Mukhia was that Abul Fazl was probably the only medieval historian to have desisted from compartmentalizing history into sections; thereby offering a well rounded account of historical facts. Methodologies aside, his elegant style leaves a lasting impression on scholars studying Mughal historiographical traditions.

Contemporary Texts

Studies on medieval India reflect various trends and methods of history writing, with many historians having contributed immensely to the writing of contemporary medieval Indian history. For the history of Central Asia and the rise of the Shansabani dynasty of Ghur, Ibn ul Asir's *Kamilut-Tawarikh* provides a lot of factual information about the twelfth and thirteenth centuries CE. The author has critically analysed his sources, supporting his descriptions of political events with dates and facts. The *Tarikh-i-Jahan Gusha-i-Juwaini* by Ata Malik Juwaini was also written in the thirteenth century, but it throws more light upon the history of Central Asia than it does on India. The text is, nevertheless, considered to give an accurate account of all the information that it does provide. The *Tarikh-i-Guzidah* by Hamdullah Mastaufi Qazwini was written in the early fourteenth century and is known for its impressive account of the general history of the East. It gives a brief but fairly accurate account of the Ghaznavids, Shansabanis, Ghurids and the sultans of Delhi. Interestingly, Nuruddin Muhammad Aufi's *Jawamiul-Hikayat* presents an eyewitness account of the military operations conducted by Iltutmish against Nasiruddin Qabacha in 1227 CE.

The *Chach Nama*, originally an Arabic work, was translated into Persian by Muhammad Ali bin Abu Bakr Kufi during the time of Nasiruddin Qabacha. It is considered to be the main source of information on the Arab conquest of Sind. The *Tabaqat-i-Nasiri* (1260 CE) of Minhaj us Siraj gives a complete account of Muhammad of Ghur's conquest of India and the history of the Delhi Sultanate up to 1260 CE, speaking in exemplary tones about Muhammad of Ghur, Iltutmish and Balban. The *Tarikh-i-Muhammadi* (1439 CE) by Muhammad Bihamad Khani provides valuable information on the rise of Islam in Arabia, the Prophet and Caliphs, Ummayads, Abbasids, Ghaznavids, Seljuqs, Sanjarids, Shansabanis of Ghazni and Ghur and the Shamsi sultans of Hind. It also throws light on the sultans of Delhi and on Timur Lang, besides presenting biographies of saints and the struggles of the sultans of Kalpi with their Hindu and Muslim neighbours. The work begins with a detailed military account of Arabia before shifting focus to Central Asia and India.

Ziauddin Barani's *Tarikh-i-Firuz Shahi* (1359 CE) is an important historical source for the Tughlaq dynasty, with detailed accounts of the reigns of Ghiyasuddin Tughlaq, Muhammad bin Tughlaq and Firuz Shah Tughlaq. Barani also provides a useful account of the reigns of the previous Delhi sultans (from Balban's rule) till the accession of the Tughlaqs, describing their systems of revenue administration elaborately. Having been highly placed in the administrative service of the Tughlaq sultans, the information provided by Barani may be considered to be authentic; but his accounts are not free from prejudice and his style is often difficult to understand. Ziauddin Barani also wrote the monumental *Fatawah-i-Jahandari*, a complementary volume to the *Tarikh-i-Firuz Shahi*, in the fourteenth century. The text gives an important insight into the administrative, political and religious policies of state.

Shams al-din Siraj Afif also wrote a *Tarikh-i-Firuz Shahi* (1398 CE), which deals with the reign of Firuz Shah Tughlaq. A courtier at the court of Firuz Shah Tughlaq, Afif's work is ranked among the best texts on medieval India. It reproduces accounts from various other sources that eulogize Alauddin Khilji, Ghiyasuddin Tughlaq, Muhammad bin Tughlaq and Firuz Shah Tughlaq. The text goes on to praise Firuz Shah Tughlaq as an ideal man, recounting his generosity and care towards his staff and his people, his respect for the Sufis and his accomplishments as an architect.

Presenting a comparatively more macro-level view, the *Taj ul Maasir*, written by Hasan Nizami, deals with the political events in North India from about 1192 CE to 1228 CE. It focuses upon the reign of Qutbuddin Aibak and the early rule of Iltutmish. Being a contemporary text, the work is regarded as an authentic account on the subject. Having migrated from Ghazni to Delhi, Hasan Nizami had written the *Taj ul Maasir* at the behest of the *sadr* of Delhi, who wanted to maintain an account of the Ghurid conquerors. The *Tarikh-i-Sind*, also known as the *Tarikh-i-Masumi*, was written by Mir Muhammad Masum. Based on the *Chach Nama*, it is an account of the history of Sind from the Arab conquest to the reign of the Mughal Emperor Akbar.

The acclaimed Arab scholar and scientist Alberuni (973–1048 CE), proficient in both Arabic and Persian, wrote the *Tahqiq-i-Hind* in the eleventh century. This monumental work, written when he had accompanied Mahmud of Ghazni in his Indian campaigns, gives an incisive account of the life and times of the people of India; their literature, religion and sciences prior to the introduction of Islam into India.

The *Tarikh-i-Yamini*, written by Utbi, deals with the reigns of Subuktagin and Mahmud of Ghazni till 1020 CE. Despite incorrect dates and details, it gives a fair amount of information on Mahmud of Ghazni. Another work that sheds light on Mahmud of Ghazni is *Zain-ul-Akbar* by Abu Said. The *Tarikh-i-Masudi* by Abul Fazl Muhammad bin Hussain al Baihaqi also deals

The Sadr

When Ghazni came under Ghurid control, the earlier administrative institutions developed by the Ghaznavids were adopted by the Ghurids. In India, therefore, the Ghaznavid, Ghurid and indigenous traditions of administration co-existed together. Under the Ghurids, the office of the *sadr-i-jahan,* also known simply as the *sadr,* looked after religious affairs of state. Later during the Mughal period, the *sadr* became more important as all persecution under the canon law required his sanction and letters of appointment for the *qazis, muhtasibs, imams* and *mutawallis* were all issued by him for stipends and charitable endowments.

with the history of Mahmud of Ghazni, describing in detail courtly life and the intrigues among nobles. The brilliant Sufi poet, Amir Khusrau, who was also a courtier at the courts of the Khiljis and Tughlaqs, composed the *Khazain ul Futuh* (1310 CE), which gives first hand information on the sultans. The poet presents a superlative account of Alauddin Khilji in his work, overlooking the sultan's faults and shortcomings. Amir Khusrau is also credited with the prose chronicles and verse compositions of the *Nuh Siphr, Tughlaq Nama, Mifta ul Futuh* and *Qiraan us Sadain*, among others.

The *Tarikh-i Mubarak Shahi* (1428–34 CE) by Yahya ibn Ahmad Sihrindi is valuable for its information on the Sayyid rulers of Delhi. Many later writers have used it as a primary text for their works, some even having reproduced it. The *Tabaqat-i-Akbari* of Nizamuddin Ahmad, for instance, is a mere narration from this same account. The *Sirat-i-Firuz Shahi* (1370 CE) is a contemporary account of the reign of Firuz Shah Tughlaq, while Khwaja Abu Malik Isami's *Futuh-al-Salatin* (consisting of almost 12,000 verses) is yet another elaborate account of the Delhi Sultanate.

Coming to the reign of the Afghan and Lodi rulers, Ahmad Yadgar's *Tarikh-i-Salatin-i-Afghan* is an important text on that period of history. Another general historical text to be found on the Afghans is Niamatullah's *Makhzan-i-Afghani.* The author was a contemporary of Ferishta, and his account deals primarily with the Mughal Emperor Jahangir's reign. Yet another text from this period is the *Tarikh-i-Daudi* of Abdullah, on the reigns of the Lodis and Surs; which, however, provides fragmentary information, unsupported by proper dates or accounts. Other contemporary texts include the *Tarikh-i-Shershahi* or *Tohfa-i-Akbarshahi*, a useful work on the Lodi dynasty, and Ferishta's *Tarikh-i-Ferishta* (also known as the *Gulshan-i-Ibrahimi*), a valuable historical source on medieval India.

During the Mughal era, a number of contemporary works were written on current events as well as the social, economic and cultural trends followed by the royalty and nobility. Most of these texts form invaluable sources for researching on the Mughal dynasty. Zahiruddin Muhammad Babur's autobiography, the *Baburnama*, and the *Tarikh-i Rashidi* by Mirza Muhammad Haidar Dughlat, an account composed by his cousin in 1545–46 CE, remain the most popular texts for studying Babur's reign. The *Baburnama,* also known as the *Tuzuk-i-Baburi* or the *Memoirs of Babur,* constitute a first rate account of Babur's own career and the history of his times. It describes the land, with its geography, trade and industry in evocative tones. The *Tarikh-i-Rashidi,* on the other hand, introduces the rise of the Mughals under Babur and also sheds light on Humayun. Both these works are valuable for the intricate political culture of Central Asia and Afghanistan during Babur's time.

For assessing Humayun's reign, the *Qanun-i Humayuni*, the *Tazkirat-ul-Vaqiat*, the *Tazkireh-i Humayun va Akbar* and Gulbadan Banu's *Ahval-i Humayun Badshah* are still extensively read. The *Qanun-i Humayuni* (also called *Humayun Namah*) was composed in 1534 CE under Humayun's patronage by Khvandamir, one of his officials. The memoir is an eyewitness account of Humayun's reign, describing court festivities, and buildings erected by the *padshah*. The *Tazkirat-ul-Vaqiat* (also called the *Humayun Shahi,* and the *Tarikh-i-Humayun*) was put together in 1587 CE by Jawhar Aftabchi, Humayun's ewer-bearer. This contemporary account by an attendant, which was later to be revised by Ilahabad Faizi Sarhindi, is a major source on the life and times of Humayun. Next in the corpus of source materials comes the *Tazkireh-i Humayun va Akbar* (1590–91 CE) by Bayazid Bayat, a history of the reigns of Humayun and Akbar from 1542 CE–1591 CE. Emperor Babur's daughter, Gulbadan Banu Begum also wrote her account of her brother's life, the *Ahval-i Humayun Badshah* or the *Humayun Nama*. Interestingly, the term *Ahval* in the title of her text, denotes conditions, circumstances or situations; and her unique account of the everyday lives of the royal family presents many aspects of Mughal life about which very little is known from other sources. The work reflects a feminist perspective and also raises questions on the genre of history writing.

Akbarnama (1596 CE), the first official history of the Mughal court, was commissioned by Emperor Akbar. Its official and equally voluminous appendix, the *Ain-i Akbari* (an administrative and statistical record of Akbar's government), was written by a close associate and minister of the emperor, Abul Fazl Allami. Still considered to be one of the most important sources for Emperor Akbar's reign, it holds forth on household administration, court ceremonials, coinage, salaries and ranks, literary and intellectual life. Abdul Qadir Badauni's three-volume *Muntakhab-ut-Tawarikh* is also considered to be a comprehensive account of Muslim rule in India from the Ghaznavids to Akbar. It is widely believed that Badauni, a severe critic of Akbar's policies, wrote this text in secrecy. It was to be subsequently found, copied and circulated after the death of Akbar. Historians have found this text useful for verifying facts portrayed by Abul Fazl; and also for a fuller picture of the political and religious climate of the time. The *Tabaqat-i Akbari,* written by another of Akbar's courtiers, Nizamuddin Ahmad, offers a more objective account of Akbar's reign; and is therefore considered to be one of the most reliable sources. Yet another text on the period, the *Tarikh-i-Akbar Shahi* of Muhammad Arif Qandahari presents a general survey of Muslim rule in India from Mahmud of Ghazni to the middle of the sixteenth century.

Emperor Jahangir's reign has been represented by Khwaja Kamgar Hussaini's *Maasir-i-Jahangiri* as well as by Jahangir's autobiography, the *Tuzuk-i-Jahangiri*. Another important text from this era was Mutamad Khan's *Iqbal Nama-i-Jahangiri,* which describes the general history of the Mughals in India.

A number of contemporary historiographers also captured accounts of Emperor Shahjahan's reign; of which Abdul Hamid Lahori's *Padshah Namah* is a comprehensive account of the emperor's life and times. Inayat Khan's *Shahjahan Nama* is another biography that archives Shahjahan's life till his thirtieth year.

Emperor Aurangzeb's rule has been compiled by his court historiographer, Mirza Muhammad Kazim, in the *Alamgir Nama*. Khafi Khan's *Muntakhab-ul-Lubab* also covers Aurangzeb's lifetime, besides proffering the results of his political measures. The *Maasir-i-Alamgiri* of Muhammad Saqi Mustaid Khan, based on the official accounts of Aurangzeb's rule, covers a major part of his reign; while Shahnawaz Khan's *Maasir-ul-Umara* and Ishwardas Nagaur's *Fatuhat-i-Alamgiri* give more detailed accounts of Aurangzeb's reign.

CHRONOLOGY	
1100 CE	Nuruddin Muhammad Aufi, *Jawamiul-Hikayat*
1100 CE	Ibn ul Asir, *Kamilut-Tawarikh*
1200 CE	Hasan Nizami, *Taj ul Maasir*
1200 CE	Muhammad Ali bin Abu Bakr Kufi, Persian translation of *Chach Nama*
1200 CE	Ata Malik Juwaini, *Tarikh-i-Jahan Gusha-i-Juwaini*
1260 CE	Minhaj us Siraj, *Tabaqat-i-Nasiri*
1300 CE	Shams al-din Siraj Afif, *Tarikh-i-Firuz Shahi*
1300 CE	Ziauddin Barani, *Fatawah-i-Jahandari*
1300 CE	Hamdullah Mastaufi Qazwini, *Tarikh-i-Guzidah*
1359 CE	Ziauddin Barani, *Tarikh-i-Firuz Shahi*
1428–1434 CE	Yahya ibn Ahmad Sihrindi, *Tarikh-i Mubarak Shahi*
1439 CE	Muhammad Bihamad Khani, *Tarikh-i-Muhammadi*
1534 CE	Khvandamir, *Humayun Namah*
1587 CE	Jawhar Aftabchi, *Tazkirat-ul-Vaqiat*
1590–91 CE	Bayazid Bayat, *Tazkireh-i Humayun va Akbar*

Travelogues

Apart from the works of contemporary historians and officials, the accounts of foreign travellers also constitute important historical sources for understanding India's socio-economic condition during the medieval age. The Moorish traveller, Ibn Batuta's *Kitab-ur-Rehlah* (1333 CE) gives valuable insights on the reign of Muhammad bin Tughlaq. The Venetian explorer Marco Polo's travelogues, on his visit to South India during the thirteenth century, gives an illuminating account of contemporary life. Abdur Razzak, the Persian ambassador, was to visit South India much later in the fifteenth century; and his writings leave behind social, economic, political, administrative and cultural accounts of the Vijayanagar court. Nicolo Conti, another Italian traveller, together with the two Portuguese travellers, Domingo Paes and Barbosa, also visited South India in the early sixteenth century and left behind vivid accounts of the era. Historical accounts of India left by Arab geographers and merchants also form an important reserve of information on medieval India.

Francois Bernier's *Travels in the Mogul Empire* (1656–1668), Pierre Du Jarric's *Akbar and the Jesuits*, Niccolao Manucci's *Storio do Mogor*, Tavernier's *Travels in India*, C.H. Payne's *Jahangir and the Jesuits*, Thevenot and Careri's *Travels in India*, Thomas Roe and John Fryer's *Travels in India in the Seventeenth Century* and Francisco Pelsaert's travelogues—all form significant historical sources for the times they represent.

Indigenous Literature

Since a description of the intellectual climate of any particular era is derived largely from a study of the creative artists of that age, indigenous literature forms an important part of any serious historical study. A vast repository of literary texts, such as chronicles, ballads, songs and verses, etc. composed in medieval India offer just such rare insights into the lives, beliefs and customs of the times. The *Rajatarangini* of Kalhana describes the history of Kashmir from the earliest times to 1149 CE. Kalhana used almost a dozen histories of Kashmir, besides other material, to write his celebrated chronicle, *Rajatarangini* (1149–50 CE). Kalhana's impact on later historians and chroniclers is evident in the works of some Sanskrit historians, who carried on with the tradition of recording the events of the rulers of their times.

Historical romances such as Chand Bardoi's *Prithviraj Raso* narrates the heroic exploits of Prithviraj Chauhan, the struggles between the Rajputs and Muhammad of Ghur, besides providing details on the political, military and socio-economic structure of the Rajputs. Jayanaka's *Prithviraj Vijaya* (1193–1200 CE) is another reliable source of the history of the Rajput Chauhans. The *Surjana Charita Kavya* of Chandrashekhar is also valuable for the light it throws on the particular dynasties that are depicted in its contents.

Though most of these chroniclers barely stated facts and did not as such authenticate their sources or the occurrences described in their texts, yet these works may not be termed as mere historical fiction. For the most part, the historical content of such texts would be limited to royal and/or noble births and deaths, wars and victories, and to the appointments and dismissals of important officials. It is significant to note that only the life of the ruling nobility was written about, while the life of their common subjects was left out of the purview of such historical accounts. Such an exclusivist attitude could have been born out of the royal/noble patronage enjoyed by most such chroniclers. Indigenous literature also helps in providing information about regional specificities, written as they were in the local dialect by local personages. The indigenous literature of medieval India, therefore, offers a complex and rich field of study with subjects ranging from the sacred to the profane—becoming an all encompassing source for reconstructing the history of the period.

Archaeological Sources

A substantial amount of information about medieval India may be gathered from various archaeological sources. The inscriptions of the Hindu rulers of Orissa, the Deccan and South India contain a lot of useful data on the history of these regions. The years of royal accession, the extent of a king's dominion, relations with neighbouring kingdoms and religious preferences may all be ascertained from the study of various archaeological sources, such as coins, seals, monuments and inscriptions.

KONARAK, SUN TEMPLE, *13th century. Special canons of architecture and a particular nomenclature for the parts of temples were developed in Orissa. One of the latest and most elaborately conceived Orissan shrines is the Sun Temple at Konarak, erected during the reign of the Eastern Ganga monarch, Narasimha I (1238–64). Built in the form of a solar chariot pulled by seven horses, this temple is an appropriate shrine for Surya, the Sun God, whose image was placed in the sanctum.*

ELLORA, KAILASA TEMPLE, *8th century.*
Earlier rock-cut shrines, especially in the Deccan and Southeast India provided the basis for the largest and most impressive rock-cut monument in the subcontinent, the Kailasa Temple at Ellora. Carved during the reign of the Rashtrakuta king, Krishna I (757–83), this is a full-scale Dravida-style temple sculptured from the rock of the cliff. The two-storeyed structure symbolizes Mount Kailasa, on whose summit Shiva dwells. The deity, in the form of a linga *is enshrined in the innermost sanctum, while relief panels illustrating stories of Shiva adorn the exterior walls.*

SOMNATHPUR, KESAVARA TEMPLE, *13th century.*
The distinctive Hoysala temples of Karnataka develop from the tradition of late Chalukya architecture. Typical of Hoysala design, as seen in the small but especially well preserved Kesavara Temple at Somnathpur erected in 1268, are multiple shrines. These are stellate in plan and grouped around a central hall or mandapa. *Each shrine is surmounted by a super-structure composed of horizontal tiers indicating that the Hoysala temples are part of the Dravida group. The rich, intricately sculptured decoration of the temples presents an extraordinarily ornate appearance.*

TAMIL NADU, SHIVA NATARAJA, *11th century. Bronze images, such as this one depicting Shiva as the Lord of the Dance, were made extensively in Southern India. Here Shiva marks time on a drum as he engages in the cosmic dance, symbolic of the movement of all forces in the cosmos. It occurs on the last night of the world, when all is destroyed before being renewed by Shiva's own power. A few bronze images of Pallava and earlier times are known, but from the Chola period onwards, many solid cast bronze images were made for placement in temple sanctums and used in religious processions.*

The Delhi sultans did not leave behind much epigraphic evidence of historical significance but the monumental evidence of the Sultanate period does provide an insight into the cultural trends of the times. They are a living testimony to the intermingling of Hindu and Muslim architectural traditions and structural designs. Such archaeological structures also reveal the lifestyles, faiths, beliefs and socio-cultural outlook of the sovereigns and nobility of their age.

A close study of the contemporary coinage system of the period also provides information about the political pursuits and economic conditions of the Delhi Sultanate. Although as a practice coins were also minted by provincial governors even before the establishment of the Sultanate, it was only after their reign that a serious attempt was made at a standardization of the monetary system. Beautiful coins started to be minted, with existing motifs gradually being replaced by Islamic calligraphy to a large extent. The unit of account came to be consolidated as the *tanka*, with *dirhams* and *jitals* forming smaller values. The silver coins of Mahmud of Ghazni are considered special in medieval Indian numismatics as they have his name inscribed on them in two different languages. Iltutmish's coins, on the other hand, describe him as a lieutenant of the *Khalifa*. Fine coins of silver, called the *tanka*, were also issued by Balban, while the Khilji rulers issued coins in abundance with pompous titles. Alauddin Khilji, for instance, struck coins assuming various honorific epithets including the title of *Sikandar al Sani*—meaning the second Alexander. The Delhi mint also bore elaborate titles such as *Hazrat Dar-al-Khilafat*. Though the coins of the Tughlaqs were superior in design and execution to those of the Khiljis, many of their monetary experiments were a failure—Muhammad bin Tughlaq's infamous experiments being a case in point. By the time of the Lodis, coins were struck almost exclusively in copper. The provinces of Bengal, Jaunpur, Deccan, Malwa, and Gujarat were also in the practice of striking coins. The southern kingdom of Vijayanagar, for example, had evolved a coinage system of a different metrology and design, which was to remain as a standard for the region, influencing the designs of coins till as late as the nineteenth century.

Coins of various eras serve as important sources of data other than being breathtaking examples of numismatic art. The coins minted

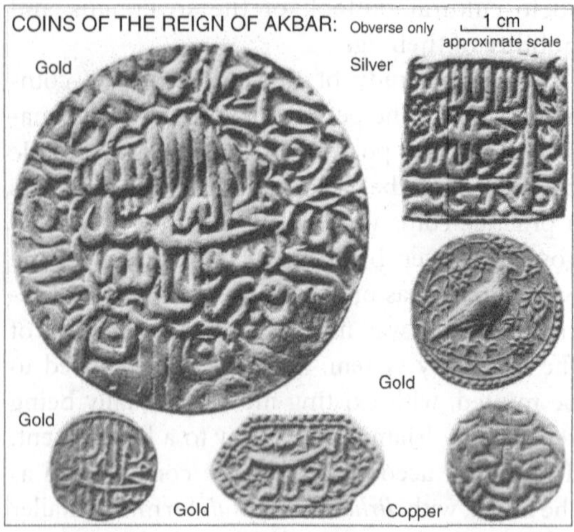

under Babur's reign, however, were largely regarded only for their monetary value, thus lacking in the beauty and elegance of the coins of his successors, Akbar and Jahangir. Mughal coinage is certainly unique among all Islamic monetary systems, since they depicted portraits of the emperors. Despite the prohibition imposed by Islam on displaying the images of humans or animals, both Akbar and Jahangir minted coins with their portraits. Coins in Jahangir's reign, however, were much finer and bolder than those issued before him. By an ordinance, these coins also had the impression of the queen, Begum Nur Jahan, on one side, with Jahangir's image on the other—indicating the sharing of power between the emperor and his queen.

While the focus of medieval historians remained largely on the military and political prowess of the rulers, socio-economic and cultural factors were not ignored either. Rethinking social and cultural relations, studying family and gender issues at the medieval courts in the light of new questions arising needed to be investigated. This led to the development of alternative historical models of medieval India studying aspects not probed before, those different from the political-administrative-institutional accounts, which began to be analyzed by historians. In doing so a fascination developed towards the achievements of medieval sultans, illustrative of India's historical greatness, its autonomous development and secular traditions.

These different traditions encompassed features that reflected upon varied aspects of historical importance—resulting in a great amount of historical literature that was sufficient enough to stimulate further studies on the subject.

SUMMARY

- Historical sources form the basic tools for recreating the past.
- The use of different kinds of sources by historians has, over the years, led to the incorporation of several changes in the research techniques of looking into the past.
- New trends have emerged in prioritizing events and occurrences in medieval Indian history.
- Historians have realized that the most vital factor in studying the medieval period in India has been the arrival of Islam and its introduction to the people of India.
- Contemporary historians, living under the patronage of medieval sultans, contributed immensely to the recording of historical events by producing a great amount of texts in Arabic and Persian.
- Accounts of foreign travellers are also valuable in providing socio-economic information about medieval India.
- Indigenous literature, ranging from Sufi poetry to historical romances, also provides rare insights into the customs and beliefs of the times.
- Archaeological sources in the form of coins, monuments and inscriptions offer data on the cultural trends of the era.

KEYWORDS

Historiography
Text
Travelogue
Coinage system
Source
Narrative

REVIEW QUESTIONS

1. Discuss the significance of historiography indicating the new trends that have emerged in historical research and how they differ from traditional methodologies.
2. What are the different kinds of sources for studying medieval Indian history? Give a brief description of each.
3. Briefly describe the contemporary literary accounts that provide information about the Tughlaqs.
4. What is the corpus of information available with reference to Humayun's reign?
5. Discuss the significance of studying the coinage system of the medieval sultans of India.
6. What kind of information is provided by Abul Fazl and Badauni about Akbar's reign?
7. Identify the important foreign travellers who visited India during the medieval period.
8. What, in your opinion, is the authenticity of indigenous historical literature?

CHAPTER 2

Early Medieval India

Review and Discussion

- The Rajputs of North India
- The Kingdoms of South India

The colossal monarchy of King Harshavardhana collapsed suddenly with his death in 647 CE, causing his dominions to gradually split into a number of petty principalities. There then followed a period of nearly two centuries of confusion and uncertainty until the appearance of the Rajputs on the political landscape, who established several small kingdoms. For nearly four centuries thereafter (800–1200 CE), most of these kingdoms remained under the control of Rajput families lending the age its name—the Rajput Age.

The Rajputs of North India

The origin of the Rajputs, who dominated the history of northern India from the eighth to the twelfth century CE, has always been debated. One group of historians (Todd, Kennedy and Bhandarkar) believe them to have descended from the foreign tribes of the Sakas, Pahlavas, Kushans and Huns who had miscegenated with the native population, to the extent of even following the native faith. This miscegenation gave rise to a new social clan with the warlike qualities of the sturdy Central Asian tribes; but one who adhered to Hindu religious and cultural practices. Another group of historians, lead by CV Vaidya, considers the Rajputs to be chivalrous representatives of ancient *kshatriya* families who drew their lineages from either *Suryavamshi, Chandravamshi* (royal bloodlines of the *itihasa-purana* tradition) or *Agnikula* (fire) forebearers. This theory is based on the strong belief that the waves of foreign conquerors who had invaded India at a time when the Indo-Aryans had long been established as an organized community *should* have been naturally absorbed into the prevalent social milieu. Yet another group of historians—VA Smith being principal among them—have, however, combined both views. Smith explains that while many of the distinguished Rajput clans—such as the Pratiharas, Paramaras, Chauhans and Chalukyas—descended mostly from foreign tribes, others—like the Rashtrakutas of the Deccan, the Rathors of Rajputana and the Chandelas of Bundelkhand—were descendents of ancient Hindu families.

Whatever their disputed origin, the term 'Rajput' merely denotes tribes or clans with warlike habits, who followed Hindu traditions and claimed aristocratic rank. Over time, the disparate Rajput clans became a homogeneous group through constant inter-marriages and adoption of common customs.

Despite the frequent quarrels between various Rajput chiefs, there was a high level of prosperity in India between the eighth and the twelfth centuries CE, when trade prospered, and the arts and the pursuit of knowledge were greatly encouraged. This was the age of Bhavabhuti, Rajashekhara, Raja Bhoja and the great Kalhana. This was also the era when Malwa, Nalanda and Vikramasila became important seats of learning, and magnificent works of public utility were constructed in cities adorned with splendid temples, buildings and tanks. Hinduism became still more popular, its progress being helped by the construction of temples and the organization of festivals and pilgrimages. The *Puranas* were re-edited and frequent recitations of the great epics were organized. All this resulted in even aboriginal tribes being quietly absorbed into the Hindu fold, which multiplied with castes and sub-sects.

Despite all their achievements, the Rajputs lacked the genius for political organization. The frequent squabbles amongst themselves only weakened them further; leading to the formation of several more Rajput states of varied sizes.

The Pratiharas of Kannauj

Kannauj, King Harshavardhana's capital, was considered to be the most important city of northern India during this period under discussion. Soon after the king's death, however, Kannauj fell into the hands of the Rajput clan of the Gurjara-Pratiharas, who were probably descendents of the Gurjaras who had settled in India in the sixth century CE. They remained independent rulers of a small Rajputana kingdom during Harsha's reign, increasing their power after his death by capturing Kannauj in the beginning of the eighth century CE. The first great ruler of this dynasty was Nagabhatta (725–40 CE), during whose reign the Arab Muslims—who had occupied Sind—invaded Central India, but were defeated and driven back.

Nagabhatta's successors, Devaraja, Vatsaraja and Nagabhatta II, increased the extent of the Pratihara kingdom, which included modern Agra, Awadh, Rajasthan, Gwalior and east Punjab. The most powerful ruler of this dynasty, Mihir Bhoj (840–90 CE), led successful campaigns against neighbouring kingdoms, soon causing the Pratiharas and Kannauj to reach the zenith of glory in northern India. Mihir Bhoj was not only a great warrior but also a great patron of the arts and learning.

Mihir Bhoj was succeeded by his worthy son, Mahendrapala (890–910 CE), who like his father maintained the dignity of his kingdom, while patronizing the arts. The Pratihara kingdom, however, began to decline after the death of Mahendrapala. His successors were weak and unable to protect their vast kingdom. The last blow came from Mahmud of Ghazni when he attacked and conquered Kannauj in 1018 CE. Though the Pratiharas re-occupied Kannauj after Mahmud's retreat, they had lost all their power and prestige by then, reducing Kannauj to a small principality. Later, yet another Rajput dynasty—the Rathors—would come to occupy Kannauj during 1090 CE.

The Rathors of Kannauj

The Rathors ruled over the great city of Kannauj and its neighbouring territories for about a hundred years. The first Rathor ruler was Chandradeva whose kingdom spread across Banaras, Ayodhya and Kannauj. His grandson, Govindachandra, would grow up to be the most powerful of the Rathor clan, ruling for about forty years and restoring the former glory and greatness of Kannauj to some extent. The last great ruler of this dynasty was Jayachandra, the principal enemy of Prithviraj Chauhan, the king of Delhi and Ajmer. Their legendary enmity provided ample opportunity to Muhammad of Ghur to conquer northern India.

The Chauhans of Ajmer and Delhi

The Chauhans established an independent kingdom in Ajmer after the downfall of the great Pratihara kingdom. The founder, Visalayadeva (1158–64 CE) is said to have conquered Delhi from a Tomara chief, Anandapala, before shifting his capital to Delhi. Prithviraj, the nephew

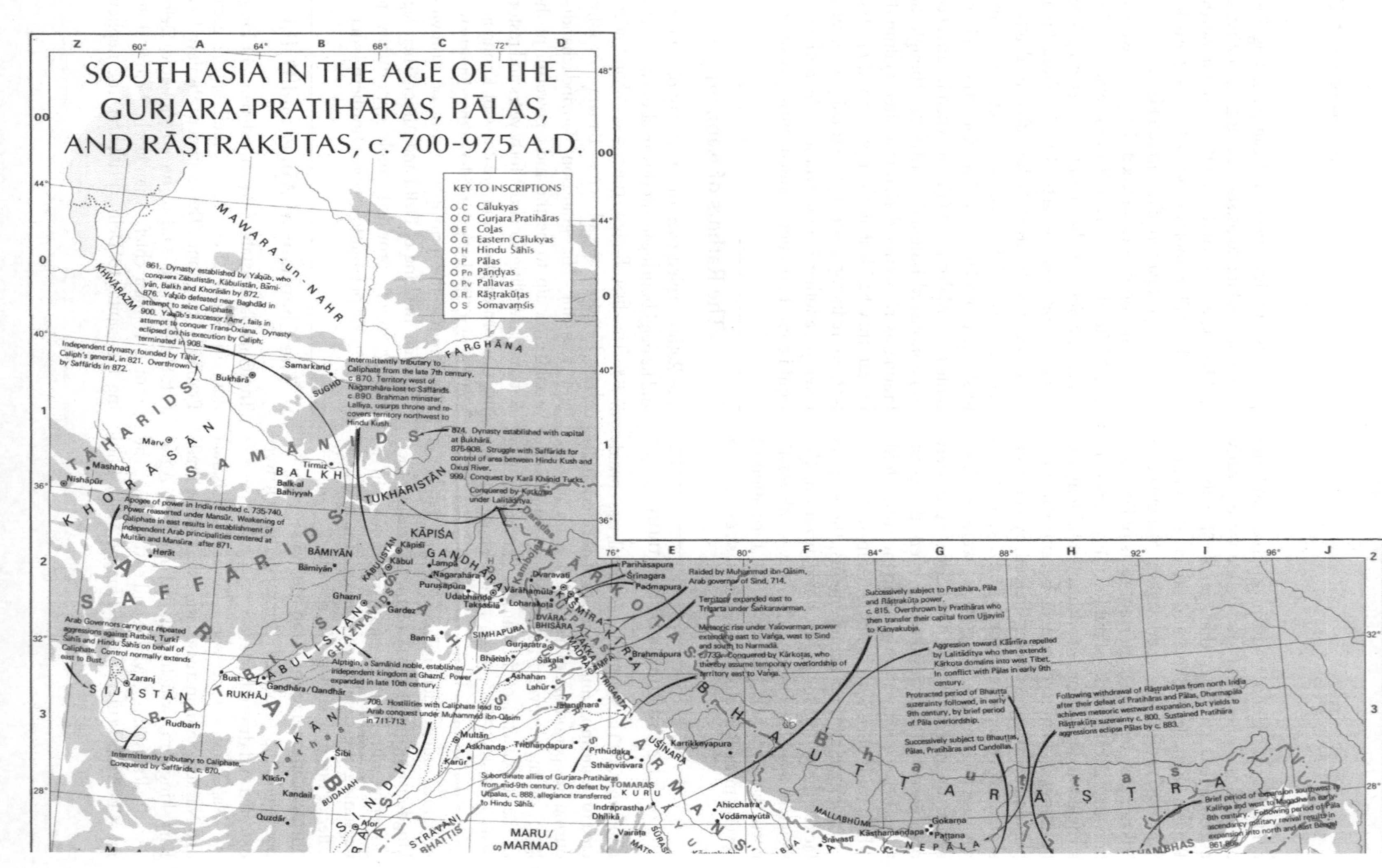
SOUTH ASIA IN THE AGE OF THE GURJARA-PRATIHĀRAS, PĀLAS, AND RĀṢṬRAKŪṬAS, c. 700-975 A.D.
KEY TO INSCRIPTIONS
C Cālukyas
Cl Gurjara Pratihāras
E Coḷas
G Eastern Cālukyas
H Hindu Śāhīs
P Pālas
Pn Pāṇḍyas
Pv Pallavas
R Rāṣṭrakūṭas
S Somavaṃśis
MAWARA-un-NAHR
KHWĀRAZM
FARGHĀNA
TĀHARIDS
SĀMĀNIDS
KHORĀSĀN
SAFFĀRIDS
TUKHĀRISTĀN
KĀPIŚA
GANDHĀRA
KĀRKOṬAS
GHAZNAVIDS
SIJISTĀN
SINDHU
UTTARĀPATHA
NEPĀLA
MARU / MARMAD
Independent dynasty founded by Tāhir, Caliph's general, in 821. Overthrown by Saffārids in 872.
Intermittently tributary to Caliphate from the late 7th century. c. 870. Territory west of Nagarahāra lost to Saffārids. c. 890. Brahman minister, Lalliya, usurps throne and recovers territory northwest to Hindu Kush.
874. Dynasty established with capital at Bukhārā. 875-908. Struggle with Saffārids for control of area between Hindu Kush and Oxus River. 999. Conquest by Karā Khānid Turks.
Conquered by Kārkoṭas under Lalitāditya.
Apogee of power in India reached c. 735-740. Power reasserted under Mansūr. Weakening of Caliphate in east results in establishment of independent Arab principalities centered at Multān and Mansūra after 871.
Arab Governors carry out repeated aggressions against Ratbils, Turkī Śāhis and Hindu Śāhis on behalf of Caliphate. Control normally extends east to Bust.
Alptigin, a Samānid noble, establishes independent kingdom at Ghaznī. Power expanded in late 10th century.
708. Hostilities with Caliphate lead to Arab conquest under Muhammed ibn-Qāsim in 711-713.
Intermittently tributary to Caliphate. Conquered by Saffārids, c. 870.
Subordinate allies of Gurjara-Pratihāras from mid-9th century. On defeat by Utpalas, c. 888, allegiance transferred to Hindu Śāhis.
Raided by Muhammad ibn-Qāsim, Arab governor of Sind, 714.
Territory expanded east to Trigarta under Śaṅkaravarman.
Meteoric rise under Yaśovarman, power extending east to Vaṅga, west to Sind and south to Narmadā. c. 733. Conquered by Kārkoṭas, who thereby assume temporary overlordship of territory east to Vaṅga.
Successively subject to Pratihāra, Pāla and Rāṣṭrakūṭa power. c. 815. Overthrown by Pratihāras who then transfer their capital from Ujjayinī to Kānyakubja.
Aggression toward Kāśmīra repelled by Lalitāditya who then extends Kārkoṭa domains into west Tibet. In conflict with Pālas in early 9th century.
Protracted period of Bhauṭṭa suzerainty followed, in early 9th century, by brief period of Pāla overlordship.
Successively subject to Bhauṭṭas, Pālas, Pratihāras and Candellas.
Following withdrawal of Rāṣṭrakūṭas from north India after their defeat of Pratihāras and Pālas, Dharmapāla achieves meteoric westward expansion, but yields to Rāṣṭrakūṭa suzerainty c. 800. Sustained Pratihāra aggressions eclipse Pālas by c. 883.
Samarkand
Bukhārā
Marv
Mashhad
Nishāpūr
Tirmiz
Herāt
Bāmiyān
Kābul
Kāpiśī
Lampā
Nagarahāra
Puruṣapūra
Udabhānda
Takṣaśilā
Ghaznī
Gardez
Bannā
Bust
Zaranj
Rudbarh
Gandhāra / Qandhār
Sibi
Kikān
Kandail
Quzdār
Alor
Multān
Askhanda
Karūr
Lahūr
Ashahan
Bhāṭiāh
Sākala
Jālandhara
Dvaravatī
Vārāhamūla
Loharakoṭa
Parihāsapura
Śrīnagara
Padmapura
Brahmāpura
Pṛthūdaka
Sthāṇvīśvara
Kartikkeyapura
Indraprastha / Dhillikā
Ahicchatra
Vodāmayūtā
Vairāṭa
Śrāvastī
Kāsthamaṇḍapa
Gokarṇa
Paṭṭana

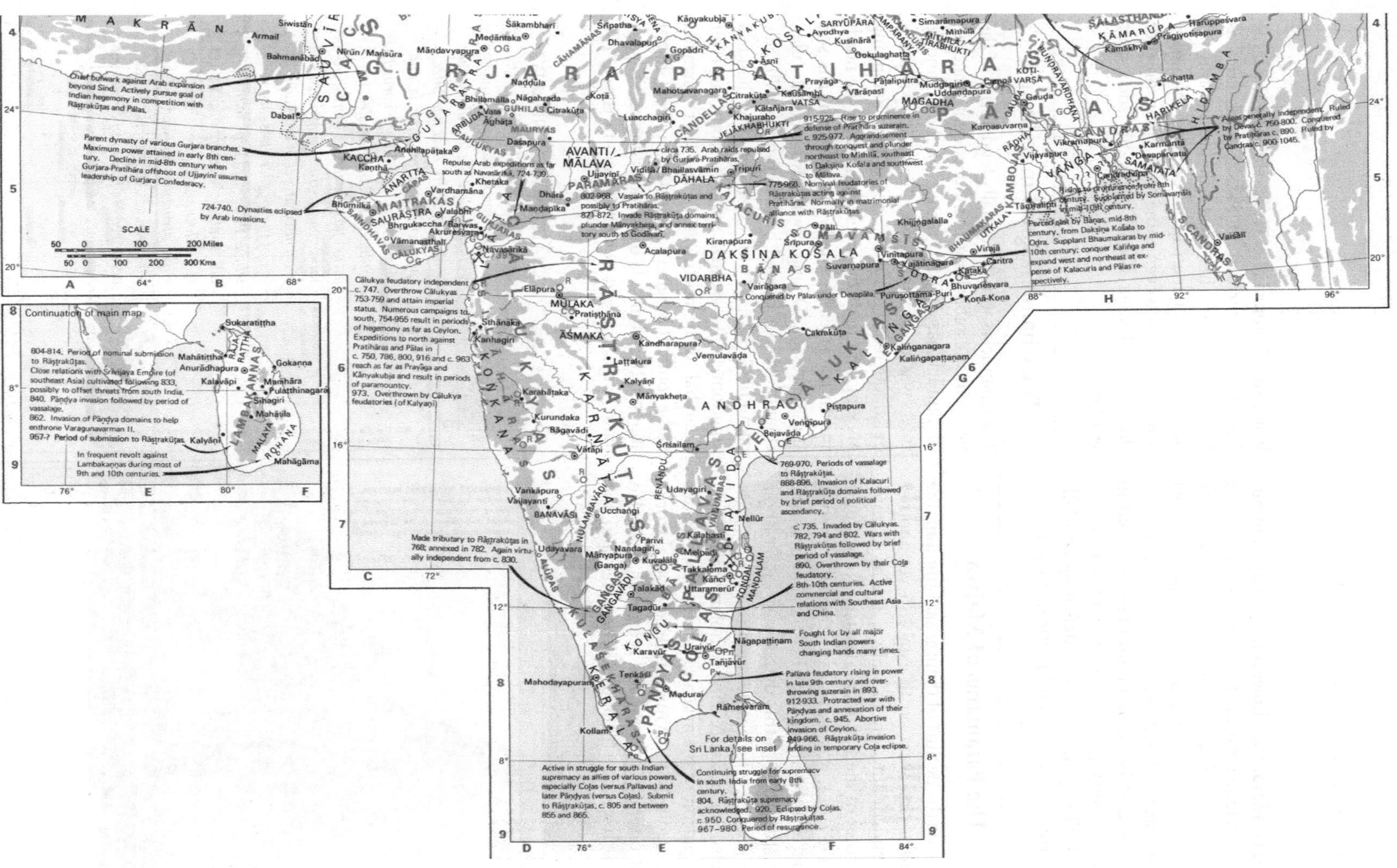

Map 2-1 *South Asia in the Age of the Gurjara-Pratiharas, Palas and Rashtrakutas, 700–975* CE

of Visalayadeva, was, however, the most famous of the Chauhan rulers. He was a warrior king whose military feats remain immortalized in the epic *Prithviraj Raso*, composed by his court poet Chand Bardoi. He defeated Muhammad of Ghur in in the first Battle of Tarain (1191 CE); but in the very following year, Muhammad of Ghur invaded Delhi again—this time defeating and killing Prithviraj in the second Battle of Tarain.

The Paramaras of Malwa

Following the decline of their great kingdom, the Pratihara clan went on to establish yet another independent kingdom in Malwa. The most powerful ruler of the Paramara dynasty, Raja Munja (c 974–97 CE), was a great warrior who carried on successful wars against his neighbours. Another great ruler of this dynasty was Raja Bhoja (1018–60 CE), who besides being a great warrior was also an accomplished scholar. Raja Bhoja was a patron of the arts and letters too. Besides being credited for having authored several works on astronomy, astrology and grammar, he is also said to have constructed 104 temples and the beautiful Bhojpur Lake. He is said to be the same Raja Bhoja described in Sanskrit literature as being famous for his great scholarship and for his patronage of men of letters. The Paramara line of kings, however, came to an end soon after the death of Raja Bhoja, since his successors were weak.

The Chandelas of Bundelkhand

The Chandelas were essentially feudatories of the Pratiharas, establishing an independent kingdom in Bundelkhand. The greatest of the Chandela rulers was Yasovarman. With his military abilities he conquered the hill fort of Kalinjar, extending his kingdom upto the river Yamuna in the north and to the river Narmada in the south. His son and successor, Dhanga, was also a great ruler. Dhanga was succeeded by his grandson Vidyadhara (1017–29 CE), who expanded the Chandela kingdom to its greatest extent—from the river Chambal in the northwest to the river Narmada in the south. It is believed that Mahmud of Ghazni attacked the Chandela dominions during Vidyadhara's reign, but did not retain any territory. The

KHAJURAHO, KENDARIYA MAHADEVA TEMPLE, *11th century. Ancient architectural texts, the Silpa Sastras divide the temples of South Asia into three categories: Nagara, Dravida, and Vasara, corresponding to northern, southern, and mixed styles. In actual form, however, there were numerous distinctive regional styles of architecture, each a subtype of one of the broader divisions. The temple illustrated here, with its tall parabolic shikhara over the main shrine and lower stepped super-structures over each of the three porches, represents the most developed Nagara form in the region ruled by the Chandella dynasty.*

Chandelas ruled Bundelkhand till the end of the twelfth century CE, when their last ruler, Parmal, was defeated by the Muslim general Qutbuddin Aibak. Following that defeat, Bundelkhand was to pass into the hands of the Delhi sultans.

The Chandelas are credited with having built the famous temple city of Khajuraho between the mid-tenth and mid-eleventh centuries CE. During this period, a flourishing Jain community lived in Bundelkhand and numerous Jain temples were also constructed then.

The Palas of Bengal

There was anarchy and confusion in Bengal for almost a hundred years following the death of Harshavardhana. To put an end to the anarchy, it is said that the people of Bengal elected a personage named Gopala to become their ruler. Gopala ruled for about five years (765–70 CE), but he successfully laid down the foundations of the Palas in Bengal. Gopala's son and successor, Dharmapala (770–815 CE), was a warrior king who waged successful wars against neighbours and extended the boundaries of his kingdom. He enjoyed a long reign of about forty five years before his death in 815 CE. Dharmapala's son and successor, Devapala, was also an able ruler. He was a patron of learning and a great architect, who built many Buddhist monasteries and temples. The Mahabodhi Temple at Bodh Gaya is said to have been constructed under his patronage. The successors of Devapala were, however, weak and unable to retain the glory of the Pala kingdom—resulting in a major part of Bengal passing off into the hands of the Senas towards the end of the eleventh century. Later, Muslim armies under their general, Bakhtiyar Khilji, conquered Bengal towards the end of the twelfth century CE.

The Senas of Bengal

The Senas were originally feudatories of the Palas, who took advantage of the weakness of the later Pala rulers to occupy a major portion of Bengal. Vijayasena, the founder king, ousted the Palas, conquered nearly the whole of Bengal and defeated the neighbouring provinces of Bihar, Assam and Orissa, before establishing a large kingdom. He was succeeded by his son, Ballalasena, who was the most popular ruler of his clan. He was a learned scholar and a patron of men of letters. The last ruler of the Senas was Lakshmansena, who was to be defeated by Bakhtiyar Khilji.

The Solankis of Gujarat

The Solankis were also feudatories of the Pratiharas like the Chandelas and the Paramaras,. Mularaja, who claimed descent from the Chalukya Rajput clan, founded an independent kingdom in Gujarat towards the middle of the tenth century, making Anhilwara his capital. But it is believed that his bloodline was different from the southern Chalukyas, and was better known as the Solankis. Mularaja was constantly threatened by his powerful neighbour, the Paramaras of Malwa, but he defended his newly established kingdom successfully. Another important ruler of this dynasty was Bhima I, during whose time Gujarat was invaded by Mahmud of Ghazni. The most important ruler of this dynasty, however, was Kumarapala (1143–74 CE), who was a great patron of the arts and learning, patronizing many scholars in his court. After Kumarapala's death the power of the Solankis declined. When Muhammad of Ghur invaded India, the last Solanki ruler was Karnadeva II. Later, Gujarat was to be added by the Khiljis into their dominions.

The Kingdoms of South India

After the downfall of the Satavahanas, the Deccan was again divided into small kingdoms and principalities. Some of these kingdoms even became powerful enough to establish their sway over a large part of the Deccan, yet none were able to

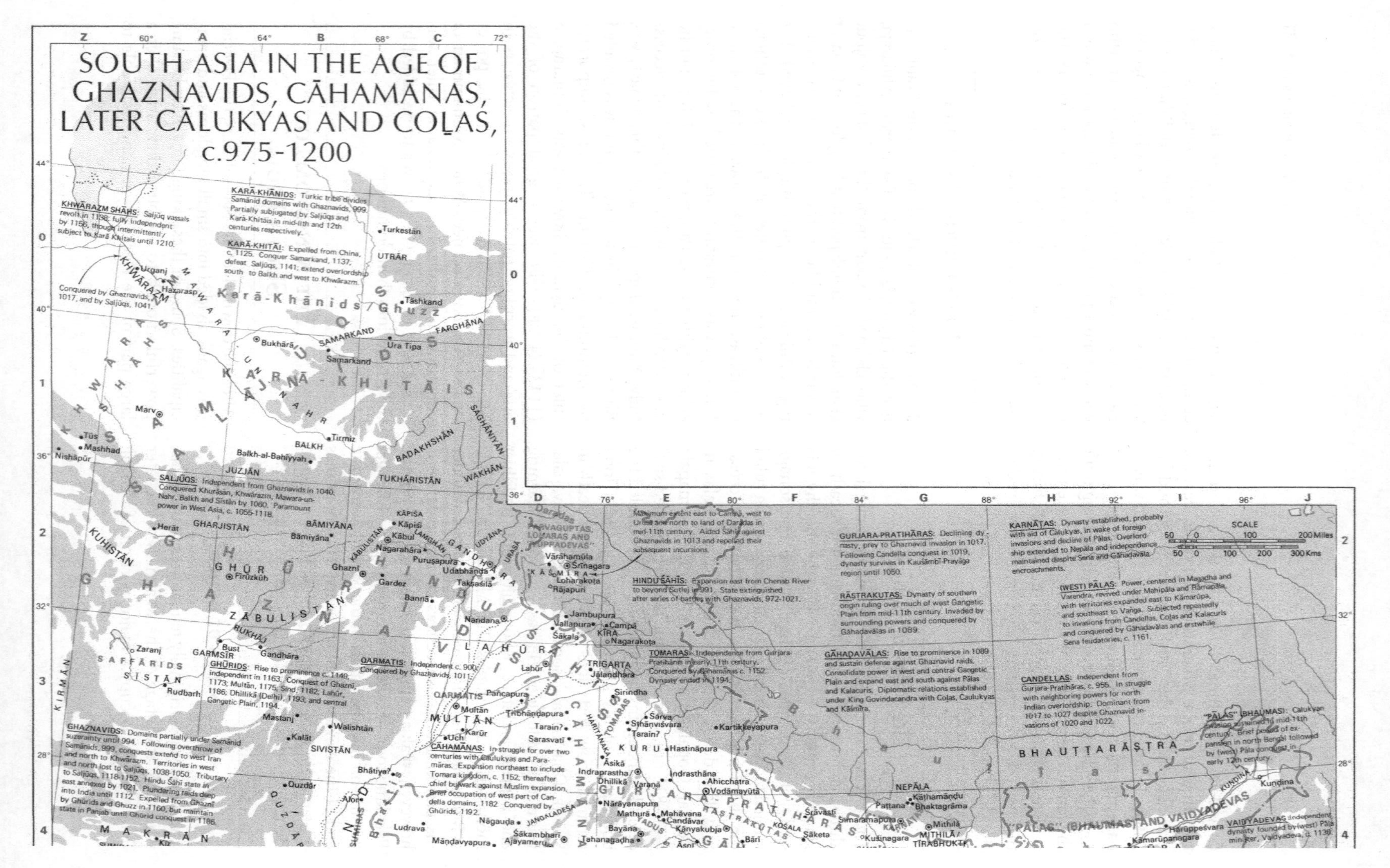
SOUTH ASIA IN THE AGE OF GHAZNAVIDS, CĀHAMĀNAS, LATER CĀLUKYAS AND COḺAS, c.975-1200
KHWĀRAZM SHĀHS: Saljūq vassals revolt in 1138; fully independent by 1156, though intermittently subject to Karā Khitais until 1210.
Conquered by Ghaznavids, 1017, and by Saljūqs, 1041.
KARĀ-KHĀNIDS: Turkic tribe divides Samānid domains with Ghaznavids, 999. Partially subjugated by Saljūqs and Karā-Khitāis in mid-11th and 12th centuries respectively.
KARĀ-KHITĀI: Expelled from China, c. 1125. Conquer Samarkand, 1137; defeat Saljūqs, 1141; extend overlordship south to Balkh and west to Khwārazm.
SALJŪQS: Independent from Ghaznavids in 1040. Conquered Khurāsān, Khwārazm, Mawara-un-Nahr, Balkh and Sīstān by 1060. Paramount power in West Asia, c. 1055-1118.
GHŪRIDS: Rise to prominence c. 1149; independent in 1163. Conquest of Ghaznī, 1173; Multān, 1175; Sind, 1182; Lahūr, 1186; Dhillikā (Delhi), 1193, and central Gangetic Plain, 1194.
GHAZNAVIDS: Domains partially under Samānid suzerainty until 994. Following overthrow of Samānids, 999, conquests extend to west Iran and north to Khwārazm. Territories in west and north lost to Saljūqs, 1038-1050. Tributary to Saljūqs, 1118-1152. Hindu Śāhī state in east annexed by 1021. Plundering raids deep into India until 1112. Expelled from Ghaznī by Ghūrids and Ghuzz in 1160, but maintain state in Panjab until Ghūrid conquest in 1186.
QARMATIS: Independent c. 900; Conquered by Ghaznavids, 1011.
CĀHAMĀNAS: In struggle for over two centuries with Caulukyas and Paramāras. Expansion northeast to include Tomara kingdom, c. 1152; thereafter chief bulwark against Muslim expansion. occupation of west part of Candella domains, 1182. Conquered by Ghūrids, 1192.
HINDU ŚĀHĪS: Expansion east from Chenab River to beyond Sutlej in 991. State extinguished after series of battles with Ghaznavids, 972-1021.
TOMARAS: Independence from Gurjara-Pratihāras in early 11th century. Conquered by Cāhamānas c. 1152. Dynasty ended in 1194.
GURJARA-PRATIHĀRAS: Declining dynasty, prey to Ghaznavid invasion in 1017. Following Candella conquest in 1019, dynasty survives in Kauśāmbī-Prayāga region until 1050.
RĀSTRAKUTAS: Dynasty of southern origin ruling over much of west Gangetic Plain from mid-11th century. Invaded by surrounding powers and conquered by Gāhaḍavālas in 1089.
GĀHAḌAVĀLAS: Rise to prominence in 1089 and sustain defense against Ghaznavid raids. Consolidate power in west and central Gangetic Plain and expand east and south against Pālas and Kalacuris. Diplomatic relations established under King Govindacandra with Coḷas, Caulukyas and Kāśmīra.
KARṆĀṬAS: Dynasty established, probably with aid of Cālukyas, in wake of foreign invasions and decline of Pālas. Overlordship extended to Nepāla and independence maintained despite Sena and Gāhaḍavāla encroachments.
(WEST) PĀLAS: Power, centered in Magadha and Varendra, revived under Mahipāla and Rāmapāla, with territories expanded east to Kāmarūpa, and southeast to Vaṅga. Subjected repeatedly to invasions from Candellas, Coḷas and Kalacuris and conquered by Gāhaḍavālas and erstwhile Sena feudatories, c. 1161.
CANDELLAS: Independent from Gurjara-Pratihāras, c. 955. In struggle with neighboring powers for north Indian overlordship. Dominant from 1017 to 1027 despite Ghaznavid invasions of 1020 and 1022.
VAIDYADEVAS: Independent dynasty founded by (west) Pāla minister, Vaidyadeva, c. 1138.
SCALE
50 0 100 200 Miles
50 0 100 200 300 Kms

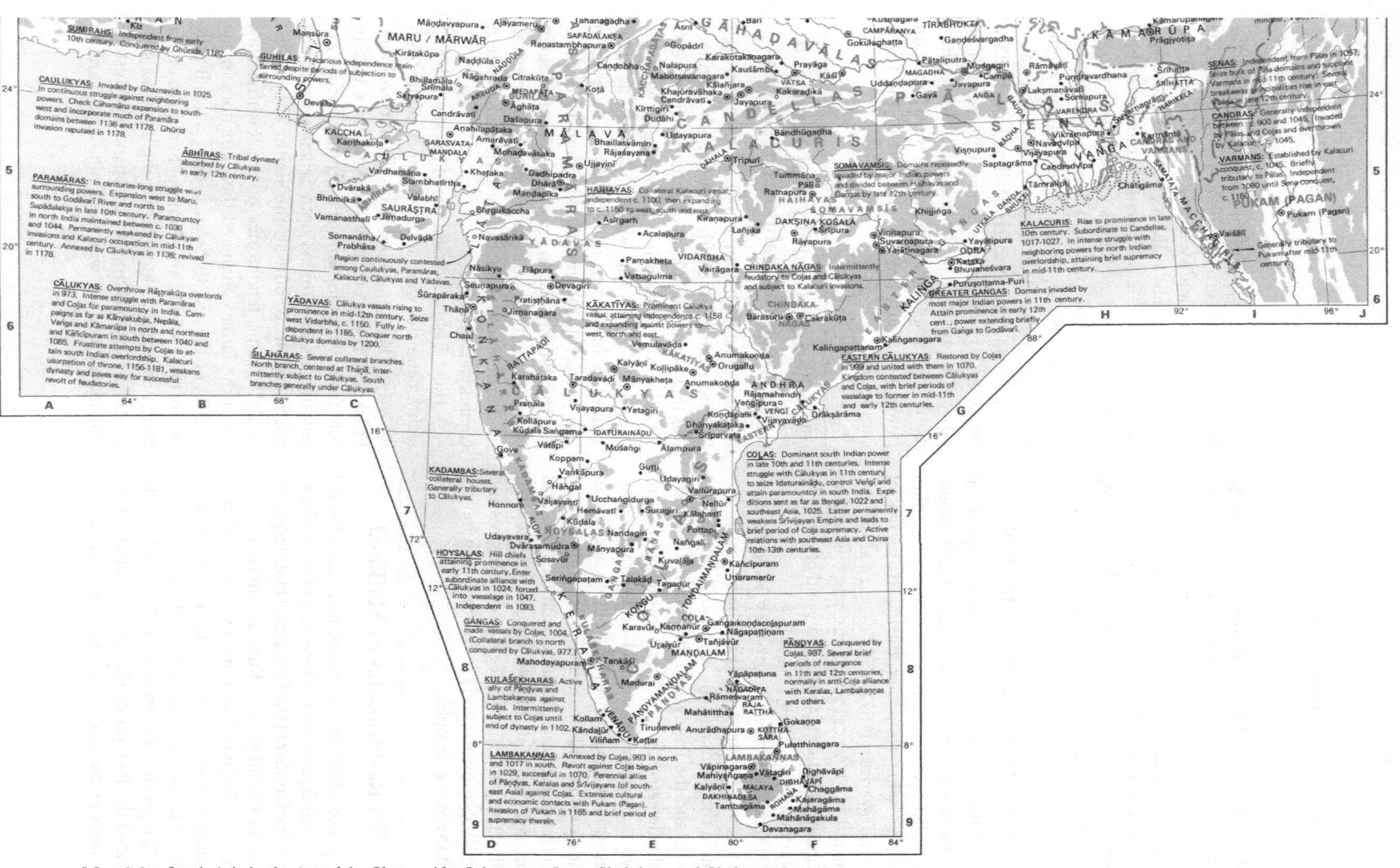

Map 2-2 *South Asia in the Age of the Ghaznavids, Cahamanas, Later Chalukyas and Cholas, 975–1200 CE*

achieve the glory of the Satavahanas. These kingdoms were often at war with one another, and there was constant rivalry amongst them. The Pallavas of Badami (Vatapi), Ellora and Kanchipuram and the Chalukyas of Badami were some of the more significant dynasties of southern India, reigning just before the onset of the eighth century.

The Pallavas of Kanchipuram

The Pallava dynasty, with their capital at Kanchipuram, were of Dravidian Tamil origin. They ruled over northern Tamil Nadu and Andhra Pradesh, rising to power during the reign of Mahendravarman I (571–630 CE) and Narasimhavarman I (630–68 CE) who dominated the region for about six hundred years till the end of the ninth century CE.

Throughout their reign they were in constant conflict with both the Chalukyas of Badami in the north and the Tamil kingdoms of the Cholas and the Pandyas to the south. They were finally defeated by the Cholas in the eighth century CE. Narasimhavarman I and Paramesvaravarman I are kings who stand out on account of their glorious achievements in both military and architectural spheres. Pallava architecture is still seen today at Mahabalipuram, where they left behind their magnificent legacy of sculptures and temples. Nandivarman II is credited with having built the Shore Temple.

The Rashtrakutas of Malkhed

The power which rose to prominence after the fall of the Chalukyas of Badami was that of the Rashtrakutas. The founder of the kingdom, Dantidurga, defeated the Chalukya ruler, Kirtivarman II in 753 CE, occupying Badami. Dantidurga was succeeded by his uncle, Krishna I, who is credited to have had the rock-cut Kailasa Temple built at Ellora.

The greatest Rashtrakuta ruler, Govinda III, defeated the Pallavas of Kanchi and repulsed the invasions of the Pratihara king, Nagabhatta II of Kannauj. While busy fighting his northern neighbours, his southern neighbours—including the Cholas, Pandyas and Pallavas—formed a coalition against him. Govinda III was, however, successful in defeating all his opponents. Amoghavarsha I (813–77 CE), his son and successor, was also an able ruler who enjoyed a long reign of sixty three years. He was also a great patron of the arts. Amoghavarsha founded his new capital at Manyakheta, the modern Malkhed of Andhra Pradesh. His successors, however, were not as powerful, resulting in the decline of the Rashtrakutas. Thereafter the Chalukyas were to regain power yet again towards the end of the tenth century CE.

The Eastern Chalukyas of Vengi and the Western Chalukyas of Kalyani

An important Deccan kingdom that emerged to power during the fifth to the eighth centuries was that of the Chalukyas of Badami. Their greatest ruler was Pulakesin II (608–42 CE), who was succeeded by his son Vikramaditya I—as great a ruler as his father. His successors were again less powerful, causing the kingdom to decline. But the dynasty was to arise to power once again between the tenth and the twelfth centuries CE, in the new avatar of the Eastern and Western Chalukya kingdoms.

These Eastern Chalukyas of the seventh and eighth centuries were another branch of the Chalukyas of Badami; founded by Vishnuvardhana, Pulakesin II's brother. Vishnuvardhana was to rule from Vengi for almost a century, before extending his dominions upto Srikakulam in the north and to Nellore in the south. They eventually became feudatories of the Rashtrakutas, when the latter conquered their kingdom in the middle of the eighth century. Only a small portion of their former kingdom was to remain under their possession. But yet again the clan was successful in establishing an independent Western Chalukya kingdom, with the capital at Kalyani, in

973 CE. After ruling for another 200 years, their last king, Somesvara IV, was defeated by the Yadavas of Devagiri in 1190 CE—finally ending their powerful reign.

The Cholas of Tanjore

From the very early ages, the territory south of the Krishna and Tungabhadra extending upto Cape Comorin, was divided into the three kingdoms of the Cholas, the Cheras and the Pandyas. The ancient Chola kingdom even finds mention in the accounts of Megasthenese (the Greek traveller and envoy sent by Seleucus to the court of Emperor Chandragupta Maurya) and the inscriptions of Emperor Ashoka. It was a small kingdom, however, and did not play an active political role till the eighth century. The Cholas rose to power under King Vijayalaya, who defeated the Pallavas in 870 CE, taking over Tanjore, which was to become the capital of the Chola kingdom. Under Vijayalaya and his able successors, Aditya and Parantaka I, the Cholas became a powerful kingdom to reckon with in southern India.

The greatest ruler of the Cholas, King Rajaraja I (985–1018 CE), was a great conqueror who established his sway by defeating the eastern Chalukyas of Vengi, the Pandyas of Madurai and the Gangas of Mysore. His vast kingdom extended from Kalinga in the north to Cape Comorin in the south. He also conquered Sri Lanka, then Ceylon, and other smaller islands of the Bay of Bengal. Rajaraja I is also said to have built a strong navy for the defense of his islands and coastal territories. He was an able administrator who excelled in administrating his vast dominions. The growth of the system of local self government was the main characteristic of Chola administration under Rajaraja I and his successors. Rajaraja I was also a great architect who built the magnificent temple at Tanjore, which is named after him.

The son and successor of Rajaraja I, King Rajendra Chola (1018–48 CE), was also a great and able ruler who not only consolidated his kingdom but also managed to extend its borders further. He suppressed the rebellions of the Gangas and Pallavas, and extended the territories of his kingdom upto the river Ganga by defeating and subduing many principalities along the way. King Rajendra Chola assumed the title of *Gangaikonda* (victor of the river Ganga) and named his new capital, Gangaikondacholapuram, to celebrate his conquest of northern India. The greatest achievement of Rajendra Chola was his conquest of the

THANJAVUR, BRIHADESVARA TEMPLE, *early 11th century. Perhaps the most impressive example of Dravida style architecture in the region ruled by the Cholas is this temple, also known as the Rajarajeshvara Temple for its royal patron, Rajaraja I (984 –1014). This form of temple evolved from the earlier Pallava style, but under the Cholas, a more cohesive form was developed, emphasizing the tall storeyed super-structure, here rising 190 feet. The walls of Chola temples are divides by pilasters to form niches occupied by sculptures. This feature, together with the storeyed super-structure and its massive crowning member, the* stupika, *characterizes the Dravida style.*

Andamans, Malavi and Nicobar islands. After his death, the power of the Cholas began to decline again, since his successors were weak rulers and could not check the disintegration of the mighty Chola kingdom. Feudatory states of the kingdom, such as the Hoysalas of Dwarasamudra, the Pandyas of Madurai and the Gangas of Mysore, revolted against them and asserted their independence, thereby causing the Cholas to eventually shrink into oblivion.

The Pandyas of Madurai

The Pandyas of Madurai had formed their own regional kingdom in southern India by the sixth century CE. After the close of the Sangam era, King Kadungon defeated the Kalabhras and established the first Pandya kingdom at Korkai, a seaport on the southernmost tip of the Indian peninsula. Their capital was to move to Madurai in later ages, as the Pandyas steadily grew in power and expanded their territories further.

There was, however, constant conflict between the Pandyas and the Cholas; and after Vijayalaya Chola conquered Thanjavur by defeating the Muttarayar chieftains around 850 CE, the Pandyas no longer remained a power to contend with. The Chola king, Parantaka I, also invaded the Pandyas and defeated King Rajasimha III. The Pandyas, however, refused to entirely submit to the Cholas despite their loss of power and territory. Thereafter the Pandyas frequently tried to form alliances with the Cheras and the Lanka kings to defeat the Cholas, who had already established their supremacy over the region by then. Despite all their efforts, the Pandyas failed to overpower the Cholas who was to remain the most powerful dominion in southern India from 880 CE to 1210 CE.

The later Pandyas (1150–1350 CE) were to enter into a new phase of expansion under their kings, Maravman Sundara Pandyan and Jatavarman Sundara Pandyan, who expanded into Telengana (part of modern Andhra Pradesh), conquered Kalinga (modern Orissa) and invaded Sri Lanka. During this period they also entered into extensive trade links with the southeast Asian maritime kingdoms of Srivijaya and their successors. After repeated conflicts with the Pallavas, Cholas and Hoysalas—and finally the Delhi sultans—the Pandya kingdom finally disappeared towards the sixteenth century CE.

The Hoysalas of Dwarasamudra

The Hoysalas of Dwarasamudra, originally feudatories of the Cholas, asserted their independence towards the close of the eleventh century as a result of the decline of the Chola kingdom. Their territories comprised roughly of parts of modern-day Tamil Nadu and Karnataka. Vishnuvardhana (1110–40 CE) was one of the greatest Hoysala kings, who is said to have defeated the Cholas, Pandyas and Kadambas in his time. Vira Ballala II (1172–1215 CE) was another prominent ruler who won great victories over his neighbours, and adopted the title of *Maharajadhiraja*. Not much is known about the successors of Vira Ballala II; though it is believed that they were probably weak rulers constantly at war with their neighbours. During the reign of the last ruler of the Hoysala dynasty, Vira Ballala III, Dwarasamudra was attacked and plundered by the Khilji general, Malik Kafur, sending the Hoysala dynasty into decline.

The Gangas of Kalinga

The Gangas had established their kingdom in Mysore in the fifth century CE; and sometime afterwards one of their branches was to establish its rule at Kalinga. The Gangas of Kalinga, or the Eastern Gangas as they were popularly known, had their capital at Kalinganagara. Their kingdom spread across the Ganjam district of modern-day Orissa and the Vizianagaram district of modern Andhra Pradesh. One of the most famous Ganga kings, Anantavarman Chodaganga (1078–1150 CE), conquered Orissa in 1118 CE. Although not very successful in his wars with the Paramaras of Malwa, he still left behind a vast kingdom extending from the Ganga to the Godavari. Anantavarman is also said to have constructed the famous temple of Jagannath Puri. The successors of Anantavarman were, however, weak rulers who were unable to keep Kalinga from passing off into the hands of Muslim rulers in the fourteenth century.

The Yadavas of Devagiri

Bhillama (1187–91 CE), a feudatory noble of the Chalukya kingdom, founded the line of the Yadavas of Devagiri, who regarded themselves to be descendants of Lord Krishna, Following his death during his battle with the Hoysala king, Tribhuvanamalla Vira Ballala II, his son Jaitrapala (1191–1210 CE) ascended his throne. The political struggle between the Yadavas and the Kakatiyas is said to have started during his reign. Jaitrapala is credited with having defeated the Kakatiya ruler, Rudradeva. Simhana (1210–47 CE), the successor of Jaitrapala, is said to have established a kingdom that rivalled the realms of the Chalukyas and Rashtrakutas in its extent during his reign and that of his grandson, Krishna. Simhana and Krishna were both patrons of education and learning. The author of *Sangeet Ratnakar*, Sarangadhara, was a prominent scholar in Simhana's court; while Krishna patronized the Kashmiri Pandit Jalhana who authored the *Sukti Muktavali*. Mahadeva (1260–71 CE), the brother and successor of Krishna, fought the Kakatiya queen, Rudramadevi, inflicting her with a crushing defeat. His court was also adorned by famous scholars, such as Hemadri who wrote several religious works including the *Chaturanga Chintamani*. Mahadeva was succeeded by his nephew, Ramachandra, the last independent raja of Devagiri. During his reign Devagiri was attacked by Alauddin Khilji who forced a treaty on Ramachandra, accessing the region of Elichpur into the Khilji sultanate. Ramachandra was to be succeeded by his son, Shankaradeva, the last ruler of the Yadava dynasty. Though his father had accepted the suzerainty of the Khiljis, he stopped paying the annual tribute to the Sultanate. On this pretext Malik Kafur attacked Devagiri in 1312 CE and and killed Shankaradeva—bringing an end to the Yadavas rule.

The Kakatiyas of Warangal

The Kakatiyas occupy an important place in the history of southern India in general, and that of the Deccan in particular. They were feudatories of the Western Chalukyas, when the early Kakatiya chiefs (Beta I, Prola I, Beta II and Prola II) ruled as subordinate chieftains. The disintegration of the Western Chalukyan kingdom during the reign of the Kakatiya ruler, Tailapa III, gave an opportunity to the Kakatiyas to assert their independence over the region. Rudradeva (1158–95 CE), the son and successor of Prola II, however, is considered to be the actual founder of the great Kakatiya dynasty who laid the foundation of the city of Warangal. His successor, Ganapatideva (1199–1262 CE), was also an important ruler of the dynasty, who is credited with conquests against the Latas, Yadavas, Kalinga and Cholas. It was Ganapatideva who shifted the Kakatiya capital from Hanamkonda to Warangal; finally to be defeated by the Pandya king, Jatavarman Sundara Pandya.

Rudramadevi (1262–89 CE), the daughter of Ganapatideva, successfully repulsed the Yadava invasion in her time; but was later killed by Ambadeva of Kayathas, a powerful feudatory family ruling the Cuddapah region. She was followed by Prataprudra (1289–1323 CE), the last ruler of the Kakatiya dynasty. He reorganized the administration and consolidated the army, before turning his attention to the enemies of the kingdom. He chastised Ambadeva, crushed the Telugu Chodas of Nellore, curbed the Yadavas of Devagiri and crumbled the power of the Pandyas of Madurai. The Kakatiya kingdom reached its zenith during his reign, its southern frontier extending till Kanchi. For nearly a decade after that he ruled in peace. The famous scholar, Vidyanatha, has immortalized the king's achievements in the *Prataprudra*

Yashobhushanam. In 1309 CE, Malik Kafur inflicted a crushing defeat on the Kakatiyas; and forced Prataparudra to accept the suzerainty of the Delhi sultans. The death of Alauddin Khilji in 1320 CE, however, prompted Prataprudra to become independent once again. But when the new Delhi sultans, the Tughlaqs, conducted a series of expeditions against the Kakatiyas—Prataprudra was captured. He killed himself by drowning in the Narmada, while being taken captive to Delhi. The Kakatiya dynasty too, thus came to an end.

All these numerous principalities and kingdoms which ruled from the eighth to the twelfth centuries CE, lent our ancient land a common culture, even though they failed to give it political unity.

CHRONOLOGY

Timeline	Northern Empires	Southern Dynasties	Northwestern Kingdoms
5th century		Pallavas	
		Chalukyas	
6th century			
	Pushyabhutis		
7th century			
8th century	Pratiharas	Rashtrakutas	
	Palas		Muslim Invasions
9th century		Pandyas	
		Cholas	
		Western Chalukyas	
10th century	Solankis		
	Paramaras		
		Hoysalas	
11th century	Senas	Kakatiyas	
	Chandelas		
12th century	Chauhans	Yadavas	Sultanate Rule

SUMMARY

- After the death of Harshavardhana there was confusion in northern India and a large number of small kingdoms were established on the ruins of his vast domain.
- The origin of the Rajputs, who dominated the history of northern India from the eighth to the twelfth century, has always been debated.
- It is believed that many of the distinguished Rajput clans—such as the Pratiharas, Paramaras, Chauhans and Chalukyas—descended mostly from foreign tribes; while the Rashtrakutas of the Deccan, the Rathors of Rajputana and the Chandelas of Bundelkhand were examples of Rajput clans who had descended from ancient Hindu families.
- Several Rajput states of varying sizes were formed during the early medieval period. The Pratiharas and Rathors of Kannauj, the Chauhans of Ajmer and Delhi, the Paramaras of Malwa, the Chandelas of Bundelkhand, the Palas and Senas of Bengal and the Solankis of Gujarat were some of the more prominent ruling dynasties of northern India during this time.
- After the downfall of the Satavahanas, the Deccan was again divided into small kingdoms and principalities. These kingdoms were often at war with

each other and there was constant rivalry amongst themselves.

- The Pallavas ruling from Badami (Vatapi), Ellora and Kanchipuram and the Eastern Chalukyas ruling from Badami were significant dynastic lines of southern India who ruled over the land till the turn of the seventh century.
- The more prominent Deccan and other far southern kingdoms in early medieval India were the Rashtrakutas of Malkhed, the Western Chalukyas of Kalyani, the Cholas of Tanjore, the Pandyas of Madurai, the Hoysalas of Dwarsamudra, the Gangas of Kalinga, the Yadavas of Devagiri and the Kakatiyas of Warangal.
- Despite the frequent quarrels between various Rajput and southern Indian states, there was a high level of prosperity in India between the eighth and the twelfth centuries. Trade prospered and a great amount of encouragement was given to the arts and learning.

KEYWORDS

Clan	Miscegenation	Consolidation	Suzerainty
Principality	Patronize	Dynasty	

REVIEW QUESTIONS

1. Write a short note on the origin of the Rajputs in medieval India.
2. How did the Gurjara-Pratiharas establish their kingdom in northern India?
3. What is the significance of kings Rajaraja I and Rajendra Chola in the history of the Chola kingdom?
4. What was the position of the Hoysala kingdom of Dwarasamudra in southern India?
5. Bring out the accomplishments of the Kakatiyas of Warangal.

CHAPTER 3

Conditions in India During the Pre-Sultanate Period

Review and Discussion

- Polity
- Society
- Economy
- Religion
- Culture
- Towards Transition

The numerous kingdoms and principalities that had mushroomed throughout the length and breadth of India owing to the lack of any centralized authority, continued to thrive for more than four centuries before the formal establishment of the sultanate rule in the Indian subcontinent. During this period, there was continuous intermingling amongst the Rajput clans, lending Indian society and culture a new shape. The glorious dynasties of both northern and southern India, which emerged in this era, contributed to the making of a common culture that had a direct impact on the political, socio-economic, religious and cultural life of the people of India.

Polity

Feudalism was the prominent socio-economic system that moulded developments in India during the period between the decline of Harshavardhana's dominions and the emergence of the Delhi Sultanate. As discussed in Chapter 2, several prominent states arose in northern India and the Deccan between 750 CE and 1000 CE. The Palas of eastern India, the Pratiharas of western India and the upper Gangetic valley, and the Rashtrakutas of the Deccan dominated the political scenario during this period. Owing to the prevalence of the feudal pattern of political relationships, many kingdoms rose and fell in the Deccan. A similar pattern was noticeable in northern India too, where although various Rajput kingdoms emerged on the political scene, they were unable to withstand the onslaught of the Turkish invaders.

Although most historians agree that feudalism as a system largely influenced the political, social and economic structures in medieval India, there is no unanimous agreement among historians on the nature of Indian feudalism, and whether the Indian model could be compared with its European counterpart. Some historians express the view that the feudal set-up in India—although not akin to the typical example of feudalism from Western Europe—had many characteristics that allow room for comparison between the two models. Others argue that the main difference between the two is the fact that in the Indian context there was no economic contract between the ruler, vassal and serf as it existed in Europe. The common feature found in the two models, however, was the presence of a dominant class who derived their income from the surplus produced by the peasant. While the peasants toiled, the dominant class did not contribute by working on the land themselves. This made the peasants dependent on the landlords in many ways. In any case, it was a system that changed the patterns of land dealings, social relations, political status and cultural affairs considerably.

A major change was evident in the very nature of the state during this age. In the absence of totally centralized states, the feudal form that the Indian subcontinent had begun to adopt included the decentralization of administration and revenue collection. Officials such as governors, *senapatis,* judges and other related state personnel were assigned land in lieu of salaries in cash. Epigraphic and literary sources indicate that in northern India, particularly in Uttar Pradesh, Central India, Rajasthan, Malwa and Gujarat, rulers assigned villages as grants to feudal chiefs. Grants of land were also made to individuals for distinguished acts of valour. Chieftains were also frequently reduced to submission after defeat in war, and forced into accepting the overlordship of the conqueror by paying tributes. Such chiefs came to be known as the *samantas, ranaks* or *rauttas,* who apart from paying annual tributes and rendering mandatory military aid, also had to pay homage in person to the victorious overlord. There were various categories of such *samantas* and *ranaks*—as long as the chief remained as a feudatory of the ruler, he called himself a *samanta, ranak* or *rautta,* acknowledging his overlord in official documents and charters. However, as soon as the chief became independent from the overlord, he discarded such titles and adopted others like *maharaja* and *maharajadhiraja.*

The revenue assignments, or *bhogas,* were temporarily granted by a ruler to his officers, and could be revoked whenever the ruler desired. Virtually in total control of the administration and fiscal supervision over the land granted to him, the feudatory still had certain obligations to perform towards his overlord. He had to pay a percentage of the revenue gained from his land grant to the ruler, besides maintaining a specified body of troops for him. He was often permitted to use certain symbols of authority on formal occasions, and was sometimes asked to give his daughter in marriage to the ruler too. Sometimes members of noble families as well as officers, who received land grants, made smaller grants to others with or without royal consent. This was known as the practice of sub-infeudation, which became more widespread with various categories of service providers—cooks, watchmen, metal workers, betel sellers and others attached to temples—being given land grants too. Such chiefs even went ahead and assumed grand titles that were out of proportion with their actual political status.

With the coming into effect of a system based on land rights, there came into existence a class of landed aristocracy who comprised powerful intermediaries vested with extensive economic and military powers vis-à-vis the overlord.

The grantees belonged to different quarters of the social strata: while most of them were nobles and secular officials, there were often examples of *brahman* beneficiaries who had been given land grants in return for religious services rendered to the state. As the number of such land owning *brahmans* increased, some of them left their priestly functions and concentrated on managing their lands which were a source of rich dividends. On account of these lucrative grants, the *brahmans* could also marry into the families of local chiefs, which explains how many non-*brahman* families claim to have had *brahman* ancestors. These major administrative and economic changes, although primarily concerning fiscal arrangements and revenue organization, also had their impact on the politics and culture of the time.

The southern Chola kingdom, for instance, was able to establish control over the Krishna, Godavari and Kaveri deltas, thereby establishing supremacy over a large part of the region. The kingdom was known for its administrative genius, the most remarkable feature being the organization of village administration through primary associations along democratic lines. Much information may be procured about their organization and highly systematized and efficient functioning of village assemblies and local bodies from the inscriptions on temple walls. Alongside the village assemblies, there were also a number of other groups and corporations of social, economic and religious character—each responsible for some specific local institution or interest. While these institutions took care of particular interests (like those of temples, castes and artisans), the village assembly had the ultimate responsibility of the general social welfare. Villages that had been donated to *brahmans* had assemblies called the *sabha*, while non-*brahman* villages had assembly known as the *ur*. Rules and regulations relating to age and ownership of property were fixed by these assemblies which were expected to be followed strictly. Among the primary responsibilities of the assembly were the collection of revenue and the supervision of irrigation.

There are examples of village bodies and local councils prevalent under the rule of the Pallavas and Pandyas too. Such an induction of a democratic set-up within the administrative functioning of the state in several regions of the country has helped to open up new dialogues among historians on the very nature of the state during the early medieval age.

Until the 1970s, most historians had characterized medieval kingdoms of India as either being bureaucratically-centralized unitary states or as decentralized feudal systems. In 1980, however, Burton Stein innovatively applied the segmentary state model—developed by anthropologist Aidan Southall in his study of the Alur society of East Africa—to the Chola and Vijayanagar kingdoms. According to this theory, the state that had evolved in southern India had a segmentary structure without any fixed boundaries, whose basic socio-political segment was a local territory grouped into zones. These zones comprised major sub-divisions which were again split into macro regions. All these segments together constituted the kingdom as a whole. The king's authority in such states had two forms—while smaller kings within their localities exercised direct authoritative control, the royal head at the helm of the segmentary structure used ritualistic or symbolic sovereignty to maintain a loose hegemony over all localities. As is evident from this model, a very limited area was under actual control of the central authority—the remaining peripheral zones owing only customary allegiance to the head of state. In other words, such kingdoms had a weak centre; and although the king had immense symbolic importance, he lacked coercive power.

Society

Politically, there were numerous large territorial divisions within the Indian subcontinent, each containing multiple independent kingdoms. These countless dominions, ill defended and situated in close proximity with each other, were torn by mutual jealousies and bitterness, and were seldom at peace with one another. Clannish sentiments ran so high that certain states would often look with satisfaction at the destruction of rivals by foreign invaders. Perpetual feuds prevented any meaningful union between these states and destroyed all chances of any effective resistance against Muslim invasions which were to soon follow.

This particular social aspect is now being viewed from another perspective by historians today. *Jati* or caste-based social hierarchy had become rigid in ancient India, leading to well-formed distinctions and social restrictions—particularly between the learned *brahman* group and other castes. Although this gradation was true to some extent, it was more an idea cultivated on a theoretical level rather than what was actually practiced. Given the dynamic and evolving nature of society, it could hardly be packed into water-tight compartments. Social mobility existed among castes and classes in society, where individuals and groups could rise and fall in the *varna* scale. *Brahmans* were not confined to their profession of learning and teaching alone, but were even rulers of particular territories sometimes. Most *kshatriya* groups denoting the warrior class had but recently acquired their status. Having gained political power, a person of any caste could also acquire a genealogy connecting him with traditional lineages. Especially in northern India where petty Rajput principalities were often unaware of their bloodlines, many saw great opportunity in tracing a prestigious pedigree for themselves that conferred *kshatriya* status. Social aspirations apart, the conscious reference to being a *kshatriya*, symbolizing the ruling class, was a particularly noticeable feature among the Rajput clans. The basic duty of the *kshatriyas* was to protect their people, a matter of great pride for the Rajputs.

Social mobility coupled with free intermingling between castes led to the formation of several new sub-castes, such as the *kayasthas* or scribes and *khatris* or traders. These castes assumed importance by getting bound to socially higher castes through inter-caste marriages, alliances seen as attempts to rationalize their rank in the social hierarchy.

In the traditional social hierarchy, the *brahmans* by and large enjoyed a superior position on account of their control over education and learning. Formal learning was virtually restricted to institutions attached with temples, while technical knowledge was available through various artisan guilds. By the onset of the medieval age, society had become extremely caste and class conscious, resulting in an inequitable social distribution throughout the country.

Women did not enjoy a high status in society; they remained subordinate in a dominant patriarchal social structure. They were married off early so did not get an adequate opportunity to devote time to educating themselves. No reference is made to women teachers; however, court ladies excelled in writing Sanskrit and Prakrit verses during this period.

Economy

Bestowing land grants for secular and religious purposes gradually gave rise to a class of prosperous landed aristocracy, whose power and influence depended upon the extent of lands they held and the privileges connected with it. Religious beneficiaries enjoyed perpetual right of occupation, and were exempted from all tax payments to the state. Secular donees owned the landed estates as long as they fulfilled their obligations and paid the prescribed tributes. Such land holders constituted important intermediaries between the ruler and the cultivators of the land, which resulted in the diffusion of income from land. In most cases, however, the major beneficiaries of this income were the feudatories alone. Tax-free land grants implied financial loss for the ruler, since revenues which should have filled the state treasury swelled the coffers of the donees instead. Such practices also compelled head of states to tap alternative sources of income. The tax burden, therefore, fell not only on peasants but on craftsmen too. Thus, while feudal lords became wealthy and influential, the financial and political power of the kings became vulnerable, forcing them to become increasingly dependent on the intermediaries.

Many feudatories often took advantage of such a situation by pushing the boundaries of their lands on the pretext of bringing more land under cultivation. Grantees were also sometimes given the right to take over lands that were not owned by anybody. In earlier ages these practices had the benefit of bringing uncultivated lands under cultivation, thereby increasing agricultural production. But when uncultivated arable land became scarce, such encroachments took place at the expense of the concerned peasants and villages.

The communal rights enjoyed by all villagers for using village resources became gradually undermined. Under the Palas and Pratiharas, for instance, all agrarian rights, such as use of pastures, forests, barren lands and water reservoirs, were transferred to the feudatories. With the growth of individual occupancy rights, such communal village rights were taken over by landlords, a factor that adversely affected rural communities. Additionally, landlords began to fleece peasants by levying taxes as high as nearly a third of the produce, while the earlier system of taxation levied a rate not more than one sixth of the produce.

The period was such that a static agricultural economy continued to persist from the ancient age; and variations to the norm, if any, were more of degree than of kind. Similar to preceding ages, an overwhelming majority of people lived in villages, leading a simple and frugal life. Cultivation was the mainstay of peasants, who generally belonged to the *shudra* caste, which gave them little choice but to remain tied to the land. Since the revenue was now paid to the landlord and not the ruler, the peasants naturally began to pay more attention to the former's requirements than before. Although landlords tried to emulate a royal lifestyle, by setting up their own miniature courts, the system also encouraged the development of regional artistic and cultural interests. Bilhana's *Vikramankadevacharita* illustrating the life of the Chalukya king, Vikramaditya VI, and Kalhana's *Rajatarangini,* based on the history of Kashmir, were fine examples of regional historical texts produced in the period.

The earlier decline in trade also gradually reversed gears during this era, with trading centres emerging along various parts of the subcontinent. Urban life picked up with the growth of cities and towns, which acted as nodal points for the exchange of agrarian produce even as other urban centres became involved in overseas trade. The ports of Baruch and Kambath along the Gujarat coast, for example, became important centres of maritime trade. While Indian traders often travelled to distant lands, in many cases foreign traders also settled in India—such as the Arabs along the Malabar Coast. Industrial and mercantile guilds continued to play, as in earlier centuries, a vital role in the economic life of the people—often enjoying political and military support, as was the case with the Cholas. Even rich Hindu temples of southern India invested their money in trade. Although trade relations were closely associated with the spread of Buddhist philosophy and contacts were still maintained with the monasteries of Nalanda and Vikramashila, by this time the Buddhist presence was visible only in eastern India. Old land routes continued to be used for trade by some kingdoms that gained revenue through the imposition of levies along established trading routes, such as the Aravalli Range, Malwa, and the Chambal and Narmada valleys.

The introduction of the *sakia* or Persian wheel was a major technological innovation that helped the agrarian community in northern India to augment their agricultural production. But any vagaries of nature had their impact over the people. There were occasional natural calamities like droughts, famines, floods and epidemics which completely ruined many rural families. While adequate seasonal rains resulted in good harvest and added to the prosperity of the people, the failure of the monsoons caused much misery. As a safeguard against such calamities, encouragement was given to the digging of wells and tanks, and part of the functions of village assemblies was to keep the tanks in good order. The main source of irrigation, however, was the wells. Dams were constructed across rivers to irrigate fields and prevent water wastage. The Cholas were especially renowned for undertaking major irrigation projects on a large scale, resulting in the formation of many branches of the Kaveri, and the overall prosperity of agricultural communities.

Religion

The pre-sultanate period was a time of social and religious erosion. An increasing number of complexities were beginning to set into existing systems, making life difficult and dogmatic for the common man. The new cultural milieu led to a great amount of religious expression, ranging from Vedic Brahmanism and the popular Bhakti movement to the even more widespread fertility cults. Though the distinctions between all three were not clearly demarcated in practice, there was a mutual flow of rites and concepts amongst each other.

It is sometimes believed that there were as many as forty two religions extant in India at this time. This may no doubt be an exaggeration, but it only implies the existence of a large number of religious sects. Hinduism in its modern form, as the *sanatana dharma,* emerged stronger by replacing the old simplicity of its early Vedic avatar. In its new form, Hinduism accepted different modes of worship within its ever increasing fold. Nature was now worshipped in a three-fold form—the Trinity of Brahma, Vishnu and Shiva. Although the Hindu *dharma* accepted the existence of several gods or deities, it accepted only one Supreme Being, symbolizing the Trinity. The Trinity represented the eternal processes of creation, sustenance and destruction, in that order. The formal worship of Vishnu and Shiva was liberally patronized by the elites, as numerous Vaishnavite and Shaivite temples cropped up all over the subcontinent.

To draw the common man, who had converted to Buddhism (attracted by its simplicity), back into the Hindu fold, popular epic heroes like Rama and Krishna were elevated to the status of gods. Each sub-sect tried to formulate elaborate rules and rituals by recomposing the *Puranas* to incorporate popular trends that would appeal to the masses. This was a time when the *Upapuranas* were written to place on record the new forms of rites and practices of worship for local deities. Krishna, as the cowherd deity, was worshipped as a popular incarnation of Vishnu. The Krishna cult that emerged during this period contained pastoral and erotic themes of worship. The love between Radha and Krishna became a popular theme that engendered a tradition of beautifully sensitive literature that survives to this day.

Along with the Trinity and demi-gods, many more deities connected with the fertility cults also emerged, where the mother goddess played an important role. The renewed emphasis on the primordial female power or *Shakti,* strengthened the status of female deities in the Hindu pantheon, giving rise to the worship of the Mother Goddess as Kali, Durga, Lakshmi and Saraswati. Tara, a popular goddess of Vajrayana Buddhism, was considered to be the Buddhist counterpart of Shakti.

Fertility cults and various Tantrik traditions, apart from giving rise to the element of erotism in Hinduism, also gave rise to several esoteric sub-sects. The Tantrik traditions, named after the *Tantra* scriptures, influenced both Hindu and Buddhist rituals of this time. What had begun as a form of folk religion later gained popularity among the elite, before being counted among the more sophisticated faiths of the times. Around the same time, Buddhism, which was hitherto popular with the masses, ceased to exist as an organized religion. The simplicity propagated by the Buddhist monks had lost much of its popular appeal. With declining trade, the patronage of Buddhism had also dwindled to a large extent. Since the Buddha was seen as an incarnation of Vishnu in the Hindu pantheon, his presence, however, continued to exist in some minor form. Vajrayana Buddhism, practiced in eastern India, Nepal and Tibet, was the only remnant left of this great religion in the land of its birth. But even this remaining tradition was devoid of its original form and reflected a strong Tantrik influence. In certain pockets of Rajasthan, Gujarat and Karnataka, however, Buddhism's earlier cousin, Jainism, has managed to survive to this day.

Tantrik and Bhakti cults emerged as major contenders to Brahmanism at this time. They continued on the same lines as Buddhism and Jainism, where opposition to Brahmanic orthodoxy was a major concern. The Tantriks expressed their protest through extreme rites and rituals, as did a few other of their sub-sects such as the Kalamukhas and Kapalikas. The Bhakti cult, on the other hand, was more of an emotional and puritanical expression of protest, based on pure devotion (*bhakti*). Though it began from urban roots, it spread to rural areas very soon. Pre-eminent among the Bhakti cults of this period were the Lingayats or Virashaivas, who became a powerful force in Karnataka; the Pandharpuris of Maharashtra, who attracted powerful preachers such as Namadeva and Jñaneshvara; and the Vaishnav followers of Chaitanya Mahaprabhu in medieval Bengal and Orissa.

As a natural consequence, the old atmosphere of religious harmony and tolerance yielded place to sectarian rivalries and bitterness. Tragically enough, religious animosity was so strong that the proponents of a sect would sometimes be delighted at the destruction of the temples of another, when the initial Muslim hoards began to arrive. The political and religious changes had a natural reaction on the social order too. Replacing the earlier four-fold division of *brahmans, kshatriyas, vaishyas* and *shudras,* a new order consisting of a number of castes and sub-castes sprang up instead. Birth, occupation and domicile decisions now all began to be based on divisions that harboured feelings of caste, class and clan. Members of each occupational group cared more for the interests of their own order, with the result that there was a great narrowing of social and political vision. This also led to a tightening of sectarian bonds and an increasing rigidity of caste associations. Most of the social forces at work during this time aimed more at dividing society than constructing it. All these factors taken together weakened the power of resistance of the natives of the subcontinent, making the Muslim conquest of India easier than it would have been otherwise.

Culture

It would be a mistake to say that the history of early medieval India consisted of a dismal record of political strife and social degeneration alone. Royal courts of immense magnificence sprang up during this age, promoting art, architecture and sculptures of great magnitude. Learned men enjoyed the liberal patronage of royal courts, while Hindi, Bengali, Gujarati and other regional language texts gradually attained the dignity of literature and began their journey of triumphant progress.

There was a remarkable development of art and architecture during this period, as immense wealth began to be accumulated by rulers and the nobility. Many kings diverted much of their wealth to the construction of temples. Three main styles of temple architecture emerged during this time—*nagara, dravida,* and *vasara*—which involved a particular ground plan of the temple and the *shikhar* (steeple or tower) in a distinct shape as it rose over the *garbhagrha* (inner sanctum sanctorum). These forms became the commanding features of temple architecture in this era. Northern temples were built along the typical *nagara* style, which had a curved tower that bulged in the middle and ended in almost a point—as demostrated by the temple structures at Osian (Rajasthan), Khajuraho (Madhya Pradesh), Konark, Bhubaneshwar and Puri (Orissa). The temples of Orissa, however, remain nearest to this original model. Southern temples were mostly constructed in the *dravida* style with a pyramidal structure made of storeys, each rung smaller than the one below, ending in a small round piece of stone at the very top. These temples had commanding *gopurams* (gateways) as may be seen at the temple complexes of Rajarajeshvara and Gangaikondacholapuram. The Deccan style, *vasara,* was a mix of both these northern and the southern architectural traditions. Many of its early examples existed at Vatapi, Aihole and Pattadakal; and later at the present temple complexes of Halebid, Belur and Somnathpura (Karnataka).

This period was rich in sculpture, of both stone and metal, each region registering a variant style of its own. Sculptures in western India and Rajasthan were highly ornate, with the Jain Dilwara temples of Mount Abu attaining a marvellous architectural perfection in stone. Nalanda was also the centre of striking, but less ornate, images in black stone, and Buddhist bronze icons. Central Indian craftsmen used the softer sandstone to create wonders. The profusely sculptured, rock-cut temples of the Kailasa at Ellora, constructed under Chalukya and Rashtrakuta patronage, created a style of their own. The dominant southern style was that of Chola sculptures, particularly in bronze. The beauty and elegance of these bronze images, mainly of Shiva, Vishnu and the saints, remains unsurpassed to this day.

A new genre of painting that rose to popularity in Nepal, eastern India and Gujarat during this age, was the designing of Buddhist and Jain manuscripts with exquisite miniature paintings. The mythological tales of Rama and Sita, Krishna and Radha were popular at this time, becoming the dominant themes for Rajput paintings. The subject matter of most of these works of art depicted the beloved in her various moods, seasonal landscapes, court scenes, kings, portraits and scenes of royal pursuits such as festivities, processions and hunting expeditions. The Pahari or Kangra school of painting was localized to Kashmir, Garhwal, Himachal Pradesh and Punjab, with themes that were mainly centred on Radha and Krishna.

Under the impact of the Bhakti movement, the *matha* and the *ghatika* attached to the temples emerged as centres where influential philosophical debates were conducted in Sanskrit. From the ninth to the thirteenth century, leading philosophers who contributed immensely to philosophical traditions in India were Shankaracharya, Ramanuja and Madhavacharya. They debated on several issues concerning the spiritual upliftment of human beings. Their discussions centred on religious issues, such as whether knowledge or devotion was the more effective means of salvation, and on metaphysical issues, including that of the nature of reality.

KASHMIR, AVALOKITESVARA IMAGE, *10th century. In northern India, the art of bronze sculpture flourished, especially in Kashmir and the Northeast. In northeast India, great hoards of bronzes have been found at monastic sites such as Nalanda and Kurkihur, while in Kashmir fewer bronze sculptures have been found. North Indian bronze sculptures continue the Gupta hollow casting technique. Those from Kashmir, such as this seated* bodhisâttva, *Avalokitesvara, have a higher copper content and therefore a brassy appearance. Avalokitesvara, one of the principal deities of later Buddhism, is identified by the small seated figure in the headdress.*

BIHAR, STANDING VISHNU, *11th century. Unlike temples of most other parts of South Asia, those of Bihar and Bengal generally bear little sculpture. Nevertheless, enormous numbers of sculptures were made in this area, especially during the centuries of Pala rule. Pala images, such as this Vishnu, are almost invariably carved from grey or black stone. Within the common general style, one may observe slight regional variations of style and iconography, indicating the independent traditions of local workshops. Here Vishnu holds his four characteristic emblems discus, conch, mace, and lotus.*

The literary activity of this period had its own significance too. Sanskrit and Prakrit were the two main languages used by scholars and common men, respectively. In the Rajput period, they regained their popularity as many scholars adopted them for their texts. Court literature, irrespective of any region, continued to be composed in Sanskrit, with many royal courts competing for the patronage of leading poets and the dramatists of the time. There was a revival of interest in earlier literature, generating abundant commentaries on prosody, grammar and technical texts. With the rising use of Sanskrit by non-Sanskrit speakers, there was also a marked increase in the number of lexicons for reference. There were no stylistic innovations in the literary works of the time, however, making the language dull and monotonous. The celebrated poet, Jayadeva's lyrical poem on the love of Radha and Krishna, the *Gitagovinda,* stands out as an exception to this rule at this juncture. During this period, the Bhakti preachers made extensive use of the local languages too, giving a tremendous fillip to regional literature. Adaptations of the *Ramayana, Mahabharata* and *Bhagavad Gita* were used regularly by the preachers. There was, thus, a gradual breaking away from Sanskrit and Prakrit and the eventual appearance and progression of languages such as Kannada, Telugu, Marathi, Gujarati, Bengali and Oriya, along with the local dialects of Bhojpuri, Maithili and Magadhi, among others.

Towards Transition

The history of India from the eighth to the twelfth century CE has been sometimes projected as a period of strife and stagnation, but a keen study of this period brings forth the less emphasized fact that this epoch, like any other era, was also a celebration in continuity. While it had its own phases of turmoil and depression, indicating transition, a wholesome look reveals the remarkable quality of resilience among the Indian people and its polity.

One of the main features of this age was the absence of any effective central authority in India. The period, also referred to as the pre-Sultanate age, witnessed a mushrooming of innumerable kingdoms, which appeared and disappeared from the scene, before reappearing again after a gap of a century or two. This pattern was witnessed in both northern and southern India.

Rather than forging alliances to keep major regional or external political threats in check, these kingdoms were more interested in protecting their own parochial interests. Torn as they were by mutual jealousies and the rigid caste system, they were seldom at peace with one another. As mentioned earlier, sectarian animosity ran high, taking pleasure in the destruction of rivals by invading foreign hoards—whether in matters religious or political.

This was also a time of social and religious rigidity. While the dominant class comprised the priestly *brahmans* and the martial *kshatriyas,* the majority of the population belonged to the lower social strata, consisting largely of *shudras* who were either artisans or peasants.

The socio-political situation had also become increasingly complex because of the growth of feudalism in the country. The Indian social scene had begun to take the shape of a conglomerate of small, enclosed and self contained units that demonstrated the inability to unite and forge common objectives together. The feudal lords benefited from the toil of peasants, at times declaring their autonomy and even independence. The polity had nosedived and the Indians had become self-centred in their social approach, seriously lacking a wider world view.

Such socio-political conditions made India vulnerable to foreign incursions that turned into major invasions with time. Gradually, Turkish hoards of various hues began to penetrate the country and settle down.

There were, however, some bright spots in such dark times too. The Cholas, for instance, are remembered for their remarkable system of village administration. Similar examples of village bodies and local councils working efficiently together could also be found under the rule of the Pallavas and Pandyas. The Cholas were especially famous for undertaking major irrigation projects. As discussed earlier, encouragement was given to the digging of wells and tanks and to the construction of dams across rivers, as a safeguard against the vagaries of nature.

This was also the time when trading centres emerged across the subcontinent; and emerging cities and towns acted as nodal points for the exchange of agrarian produce, even as other urban centres became involved in overseas trade. Royal courts of significant magnificence dedicated to the promotion of literature, art, architecture and sculpture, sprang up during this period.

In such a scenario, the coming of the Muslims to India acted as a catalyst for bringing about changes that led to the formation of large centralized kingdoms, while Islam began to influence Indian society at multiple levels. The arrival of the Muslims also initiated the advancement in arts and handicrafts, architecture, literature, music, cuisine, along with technological innovations in warfare, formation of new economic institutions, and the development of trading networks.

SUMMARY

- Till the conquest of northern India by Muslim invaders, there was no political unity in the country during the latter part of the twelfth century. Innumerable kingdoms would be formed and dissolved, before being formed yet again.
- For the most part these kingdoms belonged to the Rajputs who followed Hinduism and their people pursued the same culture despite differences of language. Yet, each kingdom was a separate unit and each contended to humiliate the other by forcefully bringing it under subjection.
- The feudal system of political relationships not only made dynasties to rise and fall but it also changed the patterns of land dealings, social relations, political status and cultural affairs considerably.
- In the absence of totally centralized states, the systems that the Indian subcontinent had begun to adopt in this period included decentralization of administration and revenue collection.
- With the coming into effect of a system based on land rights, there came into existence a landed

aristocracy, a class of powerful intermediaries vested with extensive economic and military powers.
- Caste-based social hierarchies became more rigid, leading to well-formed distinctions and social restrictions, particularly between the learned group of the *brahmans* and all other castes.
- In the new social milieu, however, there was also an opportunity to rise in the social system.
- There was a great amount of religious expression ranging from Vedic Brahmanism and the popular Bhakti movement to the even more widespread fertility cults.
- The old atmosphere of religious harmony and tolerance yielded place to sectarian rivalries and bitterness.
- The political and religious changes had a natural reaction on the social order too. Replacing the earlier four-fold division of *brahmans, kshatriyas, vaishyas* and *shudras,* a new order consisting of a number of castes and sub-castes sprang up instead.
- Birth, occupation and domicile decisions now all began to be based on divisions that harboured feelings of caste, class and clan.
- All these factors taken together weakened the power of resistance of the natives of the subcontinent, making the Muslim conquest of India easier than it would have been otherwise.
- Bestowing land grants for secular and religious purposes gave rise to a class of prosperous, landed aristocracy whose power and influence depended upon the extent of lands they held and the privileges connected with it.
- These land holders constituted important intermediaries in land relations between the king and the peasants, resulting in the diffusion of income from land, but the major beneficiaries of this income remained the feudatories alone.
- Tax-free land grants swelled the coffers of the donees, compelling rulers to tap alternative sources of income. The burden of taxes, therefore, fell equally on the peasants as well as the craftsmen.
- Royal courts of great magnificence sprang up, promoting art, architecture and sculptures of immense magnitude. Learned men enjoyed the liberal patronage of the royal courts. Hindi, Bengali, Gujarati and other regional languages gradually attained the dignity of literature and started their career of triumphant progress.

KEYWORDS

Feudalism	Feudatory	Segmentary	Fertility cults
Decentralization	Subinfeudation	Patriarchy	

REVIEW QUESTIONS

1. What were the main characteristics of the feudal society as present in India during the pre-Sultanate period?
2. How did the Rajput clans make use of social mobility to rise in society?
3. Analyze the new trends in religion that developed during the Rajput Age.
4. Explain how the feudatories emerged stronger after becoming recipients of landed estates.
5. Exemplify the cultural efflorescence in the Rajput Age.

PART II–Northern India Under the Delhi Sultanate

"While Firuz Shah was engaged at Dehli in arranging the affairs of government, Khudawandzada, daughter of Sultan Tughlik Shah, was also residing there with her husband, Khusru Malik, in a palace which had belonged to the late Sultan Muhammad. Sultan Firuz had made it his custom to go every Friday after prayers to pay a visit to Khudawandzada, and whenever he saw her he treated her with the greatest possible respect. She also, on her part, showed every mark of respect to him. The Sultan and Khudawandzada used to sit down together in the robe-room; Khusru Malik used to stand; and Dawar Malik to sit behind his mother, Khudawandzada. When their conversation was over, the princess used to present paan, and then the Sultan departed. So it went on every Friday. Under the decrees of God envy and rancour still lurk in the constitution of man, and so Khusru Malik and Khudawandzada conceived the idea of hastening the end of Sultan Firuz, and of killing him treacherously in the place where he was in the habit of visiting Khudawandzada on Fridays.

In the palace there was a long room, having two lateral chambers. These rooms Khusru Malik filled with men armed from head to foot, and gave them instructions that when Khudawandzada adjusted the garment round her head, they were to rush forth and cut off the Sultan's head. Khusru Malik also concealed some more armed men under the floor of the outer gateway, who were directed to fall upon the Sultan and despatch him should he succeed in escaping from the inside of the palace. When Friday came, the Sultan paid his accustomed visit, and sat down to converse as usual. Dawar Malik, son of Khudawandzada (but, as the author has been informed, by another husband than the base Khusru Malik), sat behind his mother. He took no part in the plot, and when he saw the Sultan, he made signs that he should depart quickly and secure himself in his own palace. The Sultan took the hint and rose to depart. Khudawandzada pressed him to wait until the paan was served, but he said that Fath Khan was sick, and he must hasten away, but that he would come another day. The armed men in concealment were not informed of what passed, and so the Sultan escaped from the room. The men who were hidden in the gateway knew the Sultan had gone in, but they were unaware of his having come out, and so, by the grace of God, the Sultan got away safe from the house of Khudawandzada.

As soon as he got outside the house (into the courtyard), the Sultan raised a loud cry for his followers, but as it was Friday most of the nobles had gone back; Rai Bhiru Bhatti remained in attendance. When the Sultan came forth very excited, he cried out in a fierce tone, "Rai Bhiru, give me the sword which thou hast in thine hand!" The Rai perceived that he was in a state of great excitement, and replied, "I will draw my sword and will follow your Majesty; will you not proceed home?" Without heeding what was said, the Sultan snatched the sword from the hands of the Rai, and drew it; then getting safely away from the buildings of Sultan Muhammad's harem, he mounted to the top of the kushk (palace). The princes and nobles were instantly summoned, and they surrounded the dwelling of Khusru Malik and Khudawandzada. The armed men were brought forth, and, on being questioned, told all the truth of the matter. The Sultan asked if they were not aware of what had passed. They replied with one voice that the Almighty had closed the eyes of their perception, so that they were aware of the Sultan's going into the house, but did not know of his coming out.

When the facts were proved, the Sultan ordered Khudawandzada into retirement and settled an allowance upon her. She had very great wealth, by the power of which Khusru Malik had hoped to affect his designs; all this was brought into the public treasury. Khusru Malik was banished, and Dawar Malik was directed to pay a visit to the Sultan at the beginning of every month, wearing an overcoat and slippers on his feet."

Source: Extract taken from Shams al-din Siraj Afif's *Tarikh-i-Firuz Shahi, Seventeenth Mukaddama—Perfidy of Khusru Malik and Khudawandzada* composed after 1398. Available at Persian Literature in Translation: The Packard Humanities Institute.

Image: Firuz Shah's Tomb and Adjoining Madrassa, Hauz Khas Complex, Delhi. Accessed at http://commons.wikimedia.org/wiki/File:Feroze_Sha's_tomb_with_adjoining_Madrasa.JPG on 29 May 2010.

CHAPTER 4

Early Muslim Invasions

Review and Discussion

- Arab Conquest of Multan and Sind
- Arab Interaction with the Indians
- Coming of the Turks
- Mahmud of Ghazni
- Muhammad of Ghur

The political situation of the subcontinent in the eighth century was such that in the absence of a paramount centre of authority there was widespread political disintegration, resulting in the frequent plundering of the land. The eastern expansion of the Arabs and their consequent conquest of Kabul had brought them to the very frontiers of India. Arab merchants relayed to their fellow countrymen accounts of the fabulous wealth and luxuries of India. As a result, many Arabs ventured abroad for trading ties with India, while others made repeated attempts to plunder the Indian coasts.

Arab Conquest of Multan and Sind

The first organized attempt at entering Indian territory was made in 711 CE, during the reign of caliph Al-Walid. When an Arab ship carrying Muslim pilgrims from Ceylon with valuable presents for the caliph was seized at Dewal—a sea port in Sind—Dahir, the Rajput ruler of Sind, refused to make amends on the grounds that Dewal was an independent province. This explanation was unacceptable for the Arabs; and at the special request of Hajaj, the governor of Iraq, an expedition was organized to discipline Dahir.

The difficult task of negotiating unknown territory was entrusted to a high spirited seventeen-year-old, Muhammad bin Qasim, a cousin of Hajaj. Qasim's adventurous journey to India was a feat in itself. Starting from the south of Persia to the Indus delta, he first took over the town of Dewal, and then marched up the river into the interiors, capturing many towns on the way. He then killed Dahir in a pitched battle near Alor, the capital of Sind. After Dahir's death, his widow, Rani Bai, along with other noble Rajput ladies immolated themselves to protect their honour. This custom of *Jauhar* or voluntary death through self-immolation was customary among Rajput women on being captured by the enemy. Thereafter Qasim advanced against Multan, capturing it and a few other regions of Dahir's kingdom. With this, the conquest of Sind by the Arabs was completed in 712 CE; and Muhammad bin Qasim was recalled towards the end of the expedition. Despite Qasim's return, however, the Arabs continued to hold sway over parts of Sind, with some Arab soldiers even settling down in Sind permanently and taking Indian wives. The success of the Arabs, nevertheless, was very limited because of the vigorous opposition that came from the Gurjara Pratiharas of Kannauj, a prominent Rajput dynasty of northern India.

Arab Interaction with the Indians

The regions around Sind formed part of the dominions of the caliphate for about a century. The resident Arabs gradually began to acquire land, on which they imposed the *jiziya* as well as other vexatious tolls on the natives of Sind. Over time the Arabs had to entrust natives with several administrative duties out of necessity; since on the one hand the Arabs conducted extensive trading activities under the patronage of the Rashtrakutas, and on the other they had the task of collecting taxes. Despite initial displays of religious fanaticism, the Arabs realized soon enough that they could not afford to take an exclusivist approach to the natives of the land. This led to a close working relationship between the two groups; but historical records indicate that acts of bigotry and cruelty were not entirely uncommon.

The Arab dominions were destroyed within a century of their establishment and nothing remained, except for a few remnants of the past. The Arabs were unable to sustain a long-term presence in India because their tribesmen differed widely from each other in their habits and sentiments,

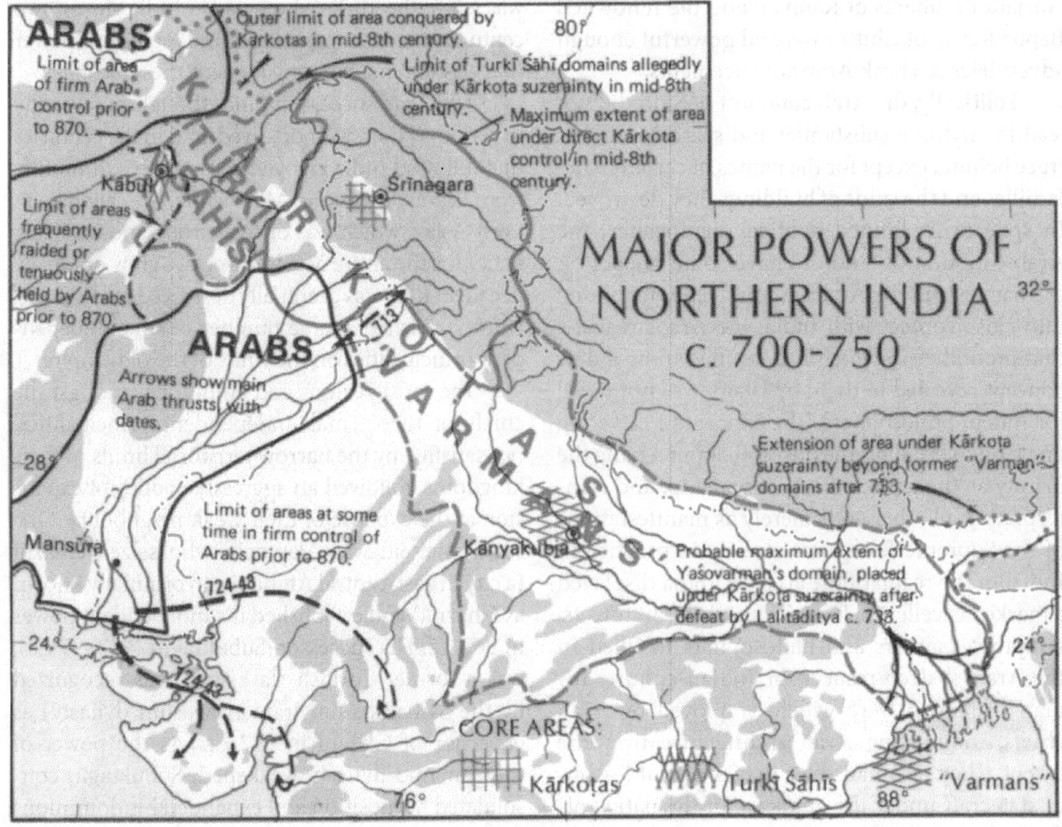

Map 4-1 *Major Powers of Northern India and Extent of Arab Control, 700–750 CE*

rendering any united action impossible. The hereditary feuds among various Arab tribes further weakened their position. Additionally, the Indians resented foreign intrusions on their sovereign status; thus, no firm bonds were forged between the two. Inadequate reinforcements from the caliphate for the maintenance of their Indian conquests, together with the declining power and influence of the caliphs further reduced the strength of the Arabs in a non-Islamic land. Above all, the Arabs had chosen to set base in an inhospitable and unproductive terrain that was cut off from the fertile Gangetic plains by an extensive desert. Having powerful Rajput chiefs for neighbours did not help matters much either, hardly allowing for any peaceful existence. The Karkotas of Kashmir, the Gurjara Pratiharas of Kannauj and the renowned Bappa Rawal of Chittor were all powerful enough adversaries to check Arab advancements.

Politically, the Arab conquest of Sind did not lead to anything substantial and scarcely left any trace behind, except for the names of certain Arab families and the ruins of buildings they destroyed. In spite of its limited political significance, the Arab conquest of Sind did have some impact on the natives and the Arabs themselves. On coming into close contact with India, the Arabs realised that monotheism which had seemed to be a new concept revealed to them by Islam, was not novel for Indian philosophers. The concept of elevating one God to the supreme position or perceiving the Trinity as the highest form of worship, and reinterpreting all other gods merely as manifestations of the Supreme Being was already in practice in India. In the realm of the arts too, India displayed a marked excellence. Indian musicians, architects, sculptors, painters and philosophers instilled in the Arabs a deep respect for Indian culture. Indian craftsmen were widely employed by Arab chiefs, influencing Arab architecture to some extent. They also had their first practical lessons in statecraft under the guidance of the native officials deployed in administering Sind, where they learnt to modify their crude patriarchal polity into a more developed system of government. Armed with an array of skills and knowledge picked up from their encounter with India, they merely presented to Europe the scientific knowledge which constituted Arab scholarship in philosophy, mathematics, astronomy, medicine and chemistry—borrowed from India, in a new garb.

Coming of the Turks

As we have seen, it was the Arabs who, in the eighth century, led the first Muslim foray through the western seacoast into the Indian subcontinent, establishing the presence of Islamic trading communities in India. The significant and permanent military movement of Muslims into northern India, however, was left to the Turks who invaded India almost two centuries later to amass riches and establish a power that was to remain strong for centuries to come.

The Arab success in Sind, though noteworthy in certain ways, was short-lived; and in the centuries that followed India enjoyed comparative immunity from Islamic invasions. Meanwhile, the caliphate in West Asia—which was once a strong and inspiring entity for the entire Muslim world—grew gradually decadent till it was eventually destroyed by the Turks who established a large number of small independent principalities on the ruins of the old empire.

The most zealous and ambitious amongst the chiefs of these small independent principalities, not satisfied by the narrow territorial limits of their kingdoms, followed an aggressive policy of expansion at the expense of their weak neighbours. One such chieftain was Alaptagin who seized Ghazni (a city in east-central Afghanistan originally known as Ghazna) and established his independent power in 962 CE. His successor, Subuktagin (977–97 CE), was a former Turkish slave who was recognized by the Samanids (an Iranian Muslim dynasty) as governor of Ghazni in 977 CE. As the power of the Samanid dynasty weakened, Subuktagin consolidated his position and expanded his dominions as far as the Indian border. A talented general of remarkable ability, he furthesr consolidated his position by strengthening the Ghazni kingdom

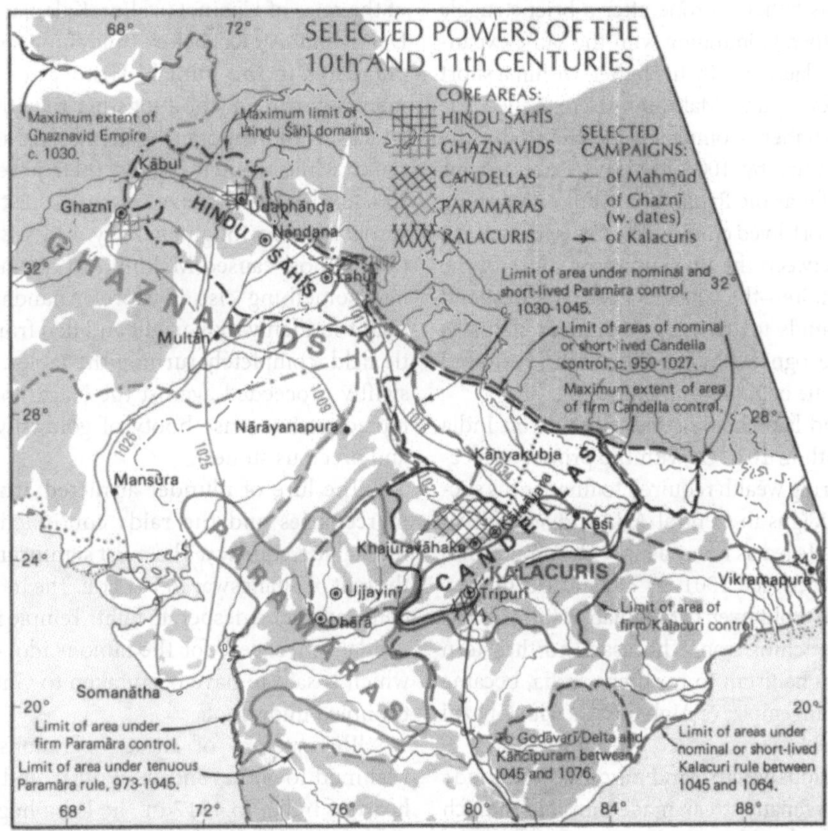

Map 4-2 *Selected Powers of the 10th and 11th Centuries*

through conquests and a sound administration. The eastward expansion of the Ghazni kingdom was, however, restricted by Jayapala, the Hindu raja of the Punjab who in the ninth century had taken over Gandhara and the Kabul Valley from a Turkish chieftain. During the time, there were extremely close political and economic ties between the Punjab and Afghanistan, with Afghanistan in turn being closely involved in Central Asian politics.

Understandably, a war ensued between the expanding power of the Turks and the north western frontier kingdom of the Punjab, in which Subuktagin led a huge army into the Indian terrain and advanced as far as Peshawar. After a stiff struggle, Jayapala, who did not have adequate resources to meet the invading hoards, was finally defeated. He was compelled to cede the territory around Kabul, pay a heavy tribute and recognize the Muslim ruler's sovereignty. After Subuktagin's death, his son, Mahmud, took over the principality of Ghazni—by then an extensive and well-established kingdom with a full treasury.

Mahmud of Ghazni

(997–1030 CE)

Mahmud, the eldest son of Subuktagin, had inherited his father's martial spirit and organizational abilities. Even while very young he had acquired military expertise by becoming his father's constant companion during wars. At the age of thirty, he succeeded his father's throne after a brief struggle with his brother. Continuing with the same expansionist policy launched by his father, within a short span of a few years, Mahmud strengthened the Northern Frontier—completely destroyed by the Samanid Empire by 1005 CE—and extended his kingdom as far as the River Oxus, thus establishing a large but short-lived empire. The Oxus formed the boundary between the two successor states of the Samanid Empire—the Ghaznavids to the west and the Qarakhanids to the east. Mahmud's status as sultan was recognized by the caliph who bestowed on him the title of *Yamin-ud-Daula*.

Mahmud launched a series of raids on India until his death in 1030 CE with the primary objective of acquiring wealth required to finance his successful campaigns in Central Asia and strengthen the empire. He led as many as seventeen raids into North India between 1001–27 CE, successfully establishing his hold over the Punjab. With this his kingdom, stretching from Khurasan (northeastern Iran) and Afghanistan to northern India, became the first Muslim empire of Afghanistan, with Ghazni as its capital.

The fabulous wealth of India aroused Mahmud's greed and his fanatic streak made him raid the rich temple towns of northern and western India in particular. These raids, though militarily successful, were primarily meant to plunder rather than conquer. In 1001 CE, he crossed the Indian frontier and in the following year he defeated Jayapala, the raja of Bhatinda and captured him. The captives were set free after an immense booty fell into the hands of Mahmud and his army. Following his release, it is said that Jayapala killed himself in order to uphold his Rajput dignity.

The rich spoils from this expedition encouraged Mahmud to repeat his raids; the second and third raids being directed against the Rai of Bhera on the River Jhelum in 1004 CE and the Muslim state of Multan in 1005 CE, respectively. The fourth raid was conducted against Anandapala, the son of Jayapala, who realizing the seriousness of the situation, organized a confederacy of the rajas of Ujjain, Gwalior, Kalanjar, Kannauj, Delhi and Ajmer before marching against the plunderer in the Punjab. History recounts that men and women stood together to withstand the attacks, with men offering themselves as army recruits while women offered their jewels for the war funds. The massive onslaught of the Indian warriors, who fought fiercely and with conviction, almost caused Mahmud to retreat, but fate had something else in store. Anandapala's elephant suddenly took fright and fled from the battle field, completely turning the tables. Mahmud swiftly proceeded against the Nagarkot fort and looted an immense booty of gold, silver, pearls and precious stones.

The lure of plunder attracted a number of mercenaries and the raids continued with remarkable frequency. The most significant one was the loot of Thaneswar in 1014 CE. The Indians were defeated after a desperate fight. Temple idols were vandalized, except for the famous idol of Vishnu which is said to have been taken to Ghazni to be trampled underfoot.

The success of these operations induced Mahmud to go beyond the Punjab and reach the heart of India. In 1017 CE, he led a huge force to the sacred Vaishnavite city of Mathura, whose shrines there were looted and razed to the ground. He then marched against Kannauj, where the ruler, Rajyapala, was taken by surprise and surrendered without resistance. The sultan returned after sacking the town, destroying temples and seizing immense wealth. The surrender of Rajyapala infuriated the Rajput chiefs who, under the leadership of the Chandela king of Kalanjar, defeated and slew him. Mahmud regarded Rajyapala as his vassal since he had surrendered to him. Upon seeing him slain, he marched against the Chandela prince and defeated him. On his journey back home, Mahmud captured Lahore after dispossessing Trilochanapala, the son of Anandapala, and annexed Lahore to Ghazni.

An important exploit of Mahmud's career was his attack on the great temple of Somnath

THE SOMNATH TEMPLE *at Somnath, Prabhas Patan, in Gujarat, from the west. From the Archaeological Survey of India, photograph taken by D.H. Sykes in 1869* CE.

in the Kathiawar district of Gujarat in 1024 CE. After a dangerous and skillful march across the Thar desert, he crushed and looted the city despite the valiant struggle put up by its residents, before destroying the sacred *shiva lingam,* and returning to his capital triumphant. His last expedition took place in 1027 CE against the Jats who had attacked his army on his return from Somnath. Weary with war and worn out with illness, he finally died in 1030 CE.

An Assessment of Mahmud of Ghazni

As mentioned earlier, Mahmud's objective in undertaking his Indian expeditions was primarily to plunder the land and not to establish any empire. Only the Punjab was annexed to the Ghazni sultanate in his encounters with India. Being a devout Muslim, Mahmud reshaped the Ghaznavids from their pagan Turkish origins into an Islamic state, spreading the philosophy of Islam across his conquered lands. While he was kind towards his family, fellow brethren and the poor, and though he displayed piety in worship, he could not rise above the social conditioning of the age he belonged to; and betrayed a basic dichotomy in his character through his religious fanaticism towards non-Islamic groups. With his dream of founding a Perso-Turkish empire, his expeditions were, interestingly, aimed more at financing his wars rather than enforcing Islam. From this perspective, it may be concluded that his raids were driven more by economics than by any zealous religious considerations. It is believed that he did not force the conquered races to accept Islam in all cases, and that he even extended toleration towards some Hindus settled at Ghazni. Whatever his primary motives might have been, it still does not exonerate Mahmud from the charges of idol destruction and plunder of Hindu temples.

Although Mahmud acquired the reputation of an iconoclast, his contribution to the socio-cultural development of his time was significant. He was responsible for sending to India the noted scholar, Alberuni, whose study *Tahqiq-i-Hind* is a source of valuable information on contemporary developments. Utbi, the historian, Baihaqi whose

AYAZ KNEELING BEFORE SULTAN MAHMUD OF GHAZNI. *A miniature painting from a fifteenth century manuscript of six poems by 'Attar. 'Six poems' by Farid al-Din 'Attar, Southern Iran, 1472, British Library, London.*

memoirs are of immense historical value, and the earliest poets of the Persian revival—Unsuri, Faruqi and Asjadi—all resided in his kingdom. The Persian poet, Firdausi, completed his epic *Shah Namah* (Book of Kings) at the court of Mahmud in about 1010 CE. Mahmud's patronage of these scholars and literary luminaries is evident from the huge grants of money that were given to them. He is also credited with building a university at Ghazni and equipping it with a library, museum and salaried teachers. He enhanced the image of Ghazni as a centre of civilization that rose from the shackles of lawlessness into a cultured city.

Ghaznavid power reached its zenith during Mahmud's reign. He created a colossal kingdom that stretched from the Oxus and the Indus Valley to the Indian Ocean. He also captured the Iranian cities of Rayy and Hamadan (from the Buyids) in the west. Despite his huge conquests, Mahmud could not consolidate them with a firm hand. He lacked the genius for civil administration, and neither did his reign create any lasting institutions. There were no enduring bonds between the conqueror and the conquered in a state that was built and maintained by force alone. Yet, it was no mean achievement to have developed a small mountain principality into a large and prosperous kingdom. His military genius, strategic planning abilities and undaunting courage helped in controlling his soldiers, who came from varied stocks, inspiring them with a passion for adventure.

CHRONOLOGY

962–977 CE	Alaptagin	1053 CE	Qiwam ud-Dawlah (Tughril)
977–997 CE	Subuktagin	1053–1059 CE	Jamal ud-Dawlah Farrukhzad
997–1030 CE	Mahmud of Ghazni	1059–1099 CE	Zahir ud-Dawlah Ibrahim
1030–1031 CE	Jalal ud-Dawlah Mohammed	1099–1115 CE	Ala ud-Dawlah Masud III
1031–1041 CE	Shihab ud-Dawlah Masud I	1115 CE	Kemal ud-Dawlah Shirzad
1041 CE	Jalal ud-Dawlah Mohammed (second time)	1115–1180 CE	Sultan ud-Dawlah Arslan Shah
1041–1050 CE	Shihab ud-Dawlah Mawdud	1118–1152 CE	Yamin ud-Dawlah Bahram Shah
1050 CE	Masud II	1152–1160 CE	Muizz ud-Dawlah Khusrau Shah
1050 CE	Baha ud-Dawlah Ali	1160–1187 CE	Taj ud-Dawlah Khusrau Malik
1053 CE	Izz ud-Dawlah Abd ul-Rashid		

Mahmud's son, Masud I (1031–41 CE), was unable to preserve the power and integrity of the Ghaznavids. In Khurasan and Khwarezm, Ghaznavid power was challenged by the Seljuq Turks. Masud also suffered a disastrous defeat at the Battle of Dandanqan (1040 CE), resulting in the loss of all Ghaznavid territories in Iran and Central Asia to the Seljuqs. In the end, the Ghaznavids were left in possession of only eastern Afghanistan and northern India, where they continued to rule until 1186 CE, when Lahore fell to the Ghurids.

Impact of the Ghaznavid Invasions

The economic and cultural impact of the Ghaznavid invasions on India is important for the bridges they built between clashing cultures. Following the invasions, Persian, Arab, and Indian traders were seen augmenting their trade network with various parts of South Asia, including China. It is believed that Asian traders entered Europe, and eventually Rome, via Central Asian trading routes. In the eleventh and twelfth centuries CE, international trade competition escalated, gradually paving the way for subjecting Asia to European encroachment. Interestingly, the game of chess made its way to Persia from India and was thence taken to Europe. By the eleventh century, chess had become known throughout Europe. It is also possible that it reached Central Europe via contemporary trading routes. Through trade and territorial conquests, language, and religious and cultural practices were being dispersed from one region to another. Mahmud of Ghazni was the only militarist sovereign of the era to maintain a large enough army over a considerable period of time to sufficiently develop a language. It is for the same reasons that the earliest surviving texts from this period are that of Sufi saints who accompanied the Ghaznavids on their expeditions. The language in which these texts were written was similar to Urdu, which was to develop much later. This assertion is based on the premise that this early Urdu-like language was derived from Ghaznavid Persian, which in turn was derived from Avestan via Sassanid Pahlavi. But trade and religion channeled through the Ghaznavid invasion could not spread sufficiently due to the advent of the Ghurids.

The Ghaznavid period is also important for its influence on the Seljuq Turks in Iran and on later Islamic art in India. Although little survives of Ghaznavid art, the introduction of the four *eyvan* ground plan in the palace at Lashkari Bazar, located on a plateau above the Helmond River just north of Qaleh-ye Best in Afghanistan, is noteworthy. An *eyvan* is a large vaulted hall, closed on three sides and open to a court on the fourth. The design of a court being surrounded by four *eyvans* dominated Seljuq mosque architecture, and was later used throughout the Timurid and Safavid periods in Persia. The victory tower of Masud III, built from 1099–1115 CE, has a complete floor covered with ornamental inscriptions. This tower is a precursor of the Seljuq tomb-tower. The excavations at the site of the palace at Lashkari Bazar have also uncovered figurative paintings with stylistic elements similar to early Seljuq work.

Muhammad of Ghur (1173–1206 CE)

The early history of the Ghurids is closely associated with the changing balance of power in Central Asia. The Ghurids, who inhabited the region between Ghazni and Herat, rose rapidly to power during the last half of the twelfth century. It was a time when the non-Muslim Karakitai Turks were moving westwards into the region dominated by the Seljuq Turks. Iran and parts of Afghanistan had already been under Seljuq control over the past fifty years, and the Seljuq defeat in 1141 CE led to a struggle for power among the Karakitai, the Khwarezm-Shahs and the Ghurids over parts of Central Asia and Iran. In 1149 CE there was a brief conflict between the last Ghaznavid ruler, Bahram Shah, and a local Ghurid leader,

Qutbuddin. The former poisoned the latter, who had taken refuge in the city of Ghazni following a family quarrel. In retaliation, the Ghurid chief, Alauddin Hussain, sacked and burned the city of Ghazni. The Ghaznavids regained control over Ghazni for a short period, assisted by the Seljuks. The struggle with the Ghurids continued in the subsequent years and eventually Ghazni was lost a group of Oguz Turks.

In 1152 CE Ghazni was again captured by Alauddin Hussain, who was unable to retain it under his control for long. His initial success, however, helped his nephews, Ghiyasuddin and Muizuddin, to once again capture the city in 1173 CE from the Oguz Turkmen nomads who had ruled it since the fall of the Ghaznavids. A cooperative relationship between the two brothers—unusual in Muslim dynastic annals—was to greatly contribute to the Ghurid success.

The first important ruler of this dynasty, Ghiyasuddin Muhammad, who ruled over Ghur from Firuz-Kuh, had ambitious plans of capturing Khurasan. He brought Ghazni under his control and appointed as governor his brother, Muizuddin Muhammad ibn Sam, popularly known as Shihabuddin Muhammad of Ghur. Shihabuddin began to try his luck over expanding the Ghurid kingdom into India. The Ghurid invasions of northern India were thus part of this Central Asian struggle for power.

Between 1173 and 1202 CE, Ghurid power rose to its peak under the rule of both Ghiyasuddin and Muizuddin. Ghiyasuddin struggled with the Khwarezm-Shah for control of the Seljuq Turks' former holdings in Khurasan (in northeastern Iran). He also occupied Herat in western Afghanistan (1176 CE) and then went on to establish control over most of Afghanistan, eastern Iran, and what is today known as Turkmenistan, by 1200 CE.

Meanwhile, Muhammad of Ghur and his lieutenant, Qutbuddin Aibak, were busy establishing Ghurid rule over Northern India—from Multan in Sind to Gaur in Bengal. Muhammad of Ghur's expansionist programme into northern India led to the country being subjected to Muslim invasions once again in the third quarter of the twelfth century, after an interval of nearly a hundred and fifty years. By this time, however, most of northern India was already in contact with Ghur through an extensive trading network, particularly that for horses. The Ghurids were well known as horse breeders and also had a reputation for supplying Indian and Turkish slaves to the markets of Central Asia. Muslim merchants and saints had already settled in the regions of Sind, the Punjab and a number of towns in the areas of what we today recognize as Uttar Pradesh and Bihar. The Ghurids were familiar with the fabulous wealth of western and central India too. They, therefore, first followed the southern route into India via the Gumal Pass, with an eye set on eventually getting Gujarat. It was only after suffering a severe defeat at the hands of the Chalukya army of Gujarat that they turned to the northern route through the Khyber Pass.

Unlike Mahmud of Ghazni, Muhammad of Ghur was more interested in permanently annexing northern India under a Muslim banner. He was opposed to the senseless destruction of temples and plundering of riches, being keener on organizing his newly conquered regions through a sound and enduring system of administration.

Muhammad first seized Multan from the Karmatian heretics, led by Abd Allah the Karmati, in 1175 CE, following it up by occupying the important fort of Uchh—all former Ghaznavid provinces. Muhammad eventually returned to Ghazni after stationing a strong garrison at each place of conquest. He invaded India yet again after three years, and marched against Bhimdev, the ruler of Anhilvara in Gujarat. The Indian ruler was more than a match for Muhammad, who was forced to retreat with heavy losses, in 1178 CE.

Not discouraged by his initial defeats, Muhammad once again invaded India in the following year, capturing Peshawar and Sind. He was, however, unable to capture the fort of Lahore, which was well defended by Sultan Khusro Malik, the last of the Ghaznavid dynasty; and Muhammad was forced to come to terms with the sultan. As soon as he left the scene, Sultan Malik tried to gain control of Sialkot too. Upon hearing this, Muhammad evolved a strategy to capture the sultan, which turned out to be successful. This invasion got the Ghurids a foothold in Lahore in 1185 CE, leading to the end of the Subuktagin dynasty. Muhammad had now become the master of the Punjab, which made a clash with the Rajputs inevitable. The Tomaras of Delhi, the Chauhans of Ajmer, the Rathors of Kannauj, the Baghelas of Gujarat, and the Palas and Senas of Bihar and Bengal stood in stiff opposition to Muhammad by forming a confederacy. The leader of this confederacy was Prithviraj Chauhan. The Rajput and Muslim forces met in a decisive battle at Tarain, near Thaneshwar, in which the Rajputs emerged victorious. Known as the First Battle of Tarain (1191 CE), it forced Muhammad to retreat with heavy losses.

The very next year Muhammad planned a fresh attack on India and met the Rajputs for a second time at the same battlefield. At this Second Battle of Tarain (1192 CE) Muhammad emerged victorious. Prithviraj Chauhan was captured and killed; and with his death ended the Rajput resistance. Ajmer and Delhi were occupied first, followed by the conquest of Sarsuti, Samana, Kahram and Hansi. Muhammad left his lieutenant, Qutbuddin Aibak, in charge of his Indian conquests and returned to his capital. Qutbuddin made Delhi his headquarters in 1193 CE, before embarking on a campaign of expansion.

Muhammad was clever enough to realize that his Indian dominions would not be secure until he had defeated Jayachandra, the Raja of Kannauj, who had not stood along with the other Rajputs, being a fierce opponent of Prithviraj Chauhan. Chand Bardoi in his ballad, *Prithviraja Raso,* mentions that Jayachandra's daughter, the princess Sanyogita, had eloped with Prithviraj. This was the main cause of animosity between Jayachandra and Prithviraj. But now with the death of his sworn enemy, Jayachandra nurtured fond hopes of leading the Rajputs. In 1194 CE Muhammad marched against Jayachandra with 'a huge force of 50,000 mounted men clad in armour and coats of mail' (Tripathi 1989, 329) and killed Jayachandra, forcing the Rathors to migrate to modern Jodhpur.

Muhammad's adventure in India was not yet over. After the Rajput escapade, he proceeded against Banaras, destroying temples and constructing mosques. Meanwhile, Bakhtiyar Khilji, the sagacious general of Qutubuddin Aibak, had conquered Bihar and Nadia (1202 CE), the capital of the Sena kings of Bengal, with incredible ease Within two years Bakhtiyar had embarked upon a campaign to conquer Tibet for plundering the treasures of its Buddhist monasteries. With this Tibetan campaign he also wanted to gain control over Bengal's traditional trade route, which led to Southeast Asia's gold and silver mines. The attempt, however, proved disastrous; and Bakhtiyar managed to return to Bengal with only a few hundred men, dying there in 1206 CE.

Despite Bakhtiyar Khilji's Tibetan misadventure, almost the whole of northern India was soon to be brought under Muslim hegemony. When Qutubuddin Aibak marched against the Chandela king of Bundelkhand, seizing the fortresses of Badaun, Kannauj (1198–99 CE) and Kalinjar (1202 CE), the few remaining Indian bastions came under foreign rule.

Impact of the Ghurid Invasions

Muhammad returned to Ghazni laden with rich spoils, and was crowned king on the death of his brother. In 1205 CE, however, he suffered a severe defeat at Andkhvoy (Andkhui) at the hands of the Khwarezm-Shah. As news of his defeat stirred up a rebellion among some of his followers in the Punjab, he was forced to return to India to suppress the Gakkars who had taken advantage of his absence. It was mainly because of the timely arrival

CHRONOLOGY

1001 CE	Invasion by Mahmud of Ghazni
1017 CE	Alberuni travels to India
1100 CE	Rule of the Chandelas, Cholas, Kadambas, Chalukyas and Rashtrakutas
1191 CE	First battle of Tarain between Muhammed of Ghur and Prithiviraj Chauhan
1192 CE	Second battle of Tarain between Muhammed of Ghur and Prithiviraj Chauhan
1193 CE	Qutbuddin makes Delhi his headquarters and embarks on an expansion campaign
1194 CE	Battle of Chandawar between Muhammad of Ghur and Jayachandra
1198–99 CE	Qutubuddin Aibak marches against the Chandela king of Bundelkhand, seizes the fortresses of Badaun and Kannauj
1202 CE	Bakhtiyar Khilji, the general of Qutubuddin Aibak, conquers Bihar and Bengal
1202 CE	Qutubuddin Aibak seizes Kalinjar
1205 CE	Muhammad of Ghur defeated at Andkhvoy by the Khwarezm-Shah
1206 CE	Muhammad of Ghur assasinated by the Gakkars in Lahore

of Qutbuddin's troops from Delhi that this formidable rebellion could be suppressed. While returning to Ghazni from his last Indian campaign, Muhammad was assasinated by the Gakkars in Lahore (1206 CE). The Ghurids by this time were in firm control of the major towns of the Punjab, Sind, and of much of the Gangetic Plains; but most of the rural/semi-urban areas outside of these cities remained under the control of Hindu chiefs. Even in the Doab (the land between the Ganga and the Yamuna, near Delhi), the Gahadavalas held out against the Turks. Most significantly, the chiefs of Rajasthan had not yet been permanently subdued.

Yet in spite of all these political shortcomings, Muhammad's conquests had far reaching results in India—laying down the foundations for subsequent Muslim rule in the land. He not only crushed Rajput power, but also consolidated his conquests by providing all resources necessary for the continuance of Muslim rule. He left behind him a band of trusted workers, well trained in the art of administration, who fulfilled his expectations. Muhammad's political exploits, and his slightly more enlightened religious posture, when compared with Mahmud of Ghazni, prepared the ground for the advancement of Islam into India.

One of the important factors for the quick Ghurid conquest of the major cities and forces of the northern Indian plains was the availability of a large number of Central Asian military adventurers who travelled with the successful commanders. Other important factors included better horses that facilitated swift movement during war, and also the deft handling of weapons, armour and stirrups by the Ghurids than most of their opponents. The Ghurids were well aware of organizing and planning on a centralized level, which was necessary after the end of large-scale military campaigns. They also knew the art of effective consolidation of post campaign occupation. The Rajputs considered the Ghurids as a potent force competing for power in northern India, while the Ghurids looked upon Mahmud of Ghazni's vast centralized kingdom as a model successor state to the Abbasid caliphate. A confused struggle would eventually ensue among the remaining Ghurid leaders, making it easier for the Khwarezm-Shah to take over Ghurid conquests by 1215 CE.

SUMMARY

- The eastern expansion by the Arabs and their conquest of Kabul had brought the Arabs to the very frontiers of India.
- Some Arabs ventured for trading pursuits, whereas others made repeated attempts to plunder the Indian coasts.
- Muhammad bin Qasim's conquest of Sind, although short lived, was of great political, economic and socio-cultural significance.
- Though the Arabs did not conquer India, they led the way for later Islamic invasion.
- Alaptagin established an independent kingdom with his capital at Ghazni. His successor, Sabuktagin, extended his kingdom through conquests and sound administration.
- Mahmud, the eldest son of Subuktagin, succeeded his father's throne.
- Within a short span Mahmud strengthened the Northern Frontier, completely destroyed the Samanid Empire and extended his kingdom as far as the River Oxus, thus establishing a large but short-lived rule.
- Mahmud conducted a series of almost annual raids on India till his death. This was mainly done to acquire wealth required to finance successful campaigns in Central Asia and strengthen his rule there.
- Following his 17 raids into northern India between 1001 and 1027 CE, Mahmud succeeded in establishing a firm hold over the Punjab. This established the first Muslim kingdom of Afghanistan with Ghazni as its capital.
- After the Ghaznis came the Ghurids. The early history of the latter is closely associated with the changing balance of power in Central Asia.
- Ghurid power rose to its zenith during the reign of both Ghiyasuddin and Muizuddin (popularly known as Muhammad of Ghur) between 1173 and 1202 CE.
- While Ghiyasuddin's political exploits were concentrated in Central Asia, Muhammad of Ghur and his lieutenant, Qutbuddin Aibak, established Ghurid rule over northern India—right from Multan in Sind to Gaur in Bengal.
- Muhammad of Ghur, unlike Mahmud of Ghazni, was more interested in the permanent annexation of northern India as the founding Islamic state in India. He desired to achieve this by organizing his fresh conquests through a sound and enduring system of administration.
- After crushing all the remnants of Rajput power over northern India, Muhammad consolidated his conquests by consolidating all necessary resources for a continued Islamic rule in India.
- In comparison to Mahmud of Ghazni, Muhammad's political exploits, and his more enlightened religious posture, prepared the ground for the advancement of Islam into India.

KEYWORDS

Invasion	Raid	Vandalize	Eyvan
Encounter	Mercenary	Monotheism	Consolidation
Plunder			

REVIEW QUESTIONS

1. Give an account of the Arab conquest of Sind and explain why it was short-lived.
2. Briefly describe the political exploits of the early Turks that led to an Islamic foothold in northern India.
3. What were the primary motives behind Mahmud of Ghazni's raids on India?
4. Bring out the difference between the raids of Mahmud of Ghazni and Muhammad of Ghur.
5. Establish the significance of the Second Battle of Tarain on the history of India.
6. Briefly discuss the establishment of trading routes that were established during this era, together with their global historical impact.
7. Write short notes on:
   - Jiziya
   - Jauhar
   - Impact of the Ghaznavid invasions

CHAPTER **5**

Foundation and Consolidation of the Delhi Sultanate

Review and Discussion

- Qutbuddin Aibak
- Iltutmish
- Raziyya Sultan
- Balban

The Delhi Sultanate, the foremost Muslim sultanate of northern India which existed between the thirteenth and the sixteenth centuries CE, owed much of its origin to the campaigns of Muhammad of Ghur and his lieutenant, Qutbuddin Aibak. Between 1175 and 1206 CE, the political exploits of Muhammad secured for him vast regions of northern India and led to the establishment of a power that was to last several generations. Till the rise of the Mughals in 1526 CE, the Delhi Sultanate saw a line of numerous dynasties lending their family name to their reign and going down in the annals of history as constituents of one of the most important periods of Muslim rule in India.

Qutbuddin Aibak (1206–10 CE)

The Slave Dynasty (1206–90 CE) was among the first prominent lines of the Delhi sultans that lasted for nearly a century. The dynasty obtained its family name of Muizi from Muizuddin, the popular Muhammad of Ghur. Qutbuddin Aibak, one of Muhammad's most trusted Turkish officers who had been entrusted with the task of overseeing his Indian conquests, was the founder of this dynasty. Qutbuddin—originally employed as a young slave in the household of the qazi of Nishapur, who had trained him efficiently—was later to come under the guardianship of Muhammad of Ghur. He proved to be a man of extraordinary abilities, soon distinguishing himself both as a soldier and a general. Much impressed by his slave's capabilities, Muhammad appointed Qutbuddin as his military commander. Following the Second Battle of Tarain (1192 CE), which had won the Turks a number of Indian territories, when Muhammad returned to Khurasan in 1193 CE, he left Qutbuddin in charge of consolidating his conquests in north-west India. Establishing his headquarters at Delhi, Qutbuddin occupied the Doab region between the Ganga and the Yamuna with ease. He then turned his attention to the Rajputs who continued to resist Ghurid domination, leading a series of campaigns against their strongholds from 1195–1203 CE. While Qutbuddin engaged himself with the Rajputs, his lieutenant, Bakhtiyar Khilji, conquered Bihar and Bengal.

By the time Muhammad of Ghur died in 1206 CE, it was but natural and inevitable that Qutbuddin Aibak would declare himself to be the sultan of Delhi. On becoming the ruler of Delhi, the former slave attained the status of a free individual and soon shifted his base from Delhi to Lahore. There he got involved in a conflict with another of Muhammad of Ghur's slaves, Tajuddin Yildoz of Ghazni, who also laid claim on his former master's Indian conquests. Qutbuddin dealt cleverly with the situation by marrying the daughter of Tajuddin Yildoz. Through other judiciously arranged marriages, he was to consolidate his rule further. In 1208 CE, Qutbuddin defeated Tajuddin Yildoz and captured Ghazni—but was soon to be driven out again. Thereafter, he was to content himself with being confined within his Indian territories. After his death in 1210 CE during a polo accident, the sultanate passed on to his son-in-law, Iltutmish, who was able to consolidate the independence of the Delhi Sultanate on the basis of the territorial acquisitions made by Qutbuddin Aibak.

Surviving inscriptions describe Qutbuddin as *malik* or king, the qualities of which reflected in his persona. As a ruler, Qutbuddin Aibak distinguished himself as a just and knowledgeable individual, who exerted himself to promote peace and prosperity among his subjects. He took care to eliminate the menace of rampant highway robbery and restored peace and order in his kingdom. He is generally described as a mighty soldier of Allah, and his devotion to his faith is seen displayed in the two mosques that he built at Ajmer and Delhi. It is widely believed that most Hindus were treated as equals during his reign. Qutbuddin is often praised for his generosity too, which won him the title of *Lakhbaksh* or giver of lakhs. Having made little effort towards extending his Indian conquests (Delhi's Qutb Minar still stands as a grand commemoration of his exploits in the region), he is still considered to have made a significant contribution to history by establishing the foundation of a Muslim state in India.

DELHI, THE QUTB MINAR, *late 12th–14th centuries. Originally over seventy meters high, the great minaret on the south side of the Quwwat al-Islam mosque was begun in 1199. Its first storey dates from the reign of Qutbuddin Aibak. Its form, so unlike anything in India's indigenous architectural traditions, was derived from minarets in the Ghurid homelands of Afghanistan. Towering over the plain around Delhi, it underscored Islam's ascendancy in northern India. The inscriptions of the first story are primarily Qur'anic, while those of the additional four storeys are mainly historical epigraphs dating from the reigns of Iltutmish and Firuz Shah Tughlaq.*

Iltutmish (1211–36 CE)

Qutbuddin Aibak was succeeded by his son, Aram Shah, who proved incapable of maintaining order during troubled times. As a result, he was deposed and killed after a short reign of merely one year by the more capable Iltutmish, who was requested by Delhi's nobility to take charge of the state. After killing Aram Shah, his rival claimant to the throne of Delhi, Iltutmish quickly and

Slavery

Slavery is known to have existed in many societies throughout history, such as China, Korea, India, England, Russia, the Middle East, Africa and in the circum-Caribbean world. Across history slaves held a wide range of occupations—right from being ministers in the Byzantine Empire, Merovingian France, Germany during its eleventh century Salian dynasty, medieval Muscovy and the Ottoman Empire, to becoming sultans and founding Islamic empires. While some slaves were known to have worked in government offices and in provincial administrative posts, still others worked as estate managers. A large number of slaves were also employed in agriculture, domestic households, prostitution and other occupations demanding hard physical labour. In eastern Islamic polities of this period, slavery formed a core institution from which well-trained and loyal military followers known as the *mamluks* served the ruling elite. Slaves trained in warfare and government duties were usually of Turkish descent, and were considered to be loyal to their masters. Being a slave was considered to be an honour by many as it was one of the only ways for the commoner to gain wealth and higher social status by moving closer to the ruling elite. Once slaves became efficiently trained in military activities, they could be relied upon more than others in times of military need. But sometimes talented slaves misused their authority by trying to get more powerful than their masters. All in all, slaves formed an integral part of medieval India's political system.

effectively dealt with a revolt by a section of the Delhi guards and proceeded to establish himself as the next sultan.

Shamsuddin Iltutmish, although descending from a noble Turkish family, was a slave of Qutbuddin Aibak, rising to a position of influence and authority by dint of his own merit. Known in history as 'a slave of a slave', Iltutmish was well-trained in war and state administration. Recognizing his worth, Qutbuddin had made him his son-in-law.

Iltutmish ascended the throne at a time when confusion reigned everywhere. The weak administration of Aram Shah had encouraged local governors to assert their independence, causing several internal and external problems within the system. In his political career Iltutmish had to deal with three main issues: defending his western frontiers, establishing control over the Muslim nobility in India, and subjugating several Hindu chiefs who continued to rule independently.

Iltutmish's rivals, Tajuddin Yildoz of Ghazni, Nasiruddin Qabacha of Sind and the Khilji Maliks of Bengal (led by Ali Mardan Khan who had declared himself the king of Bengal and Bihar) however, refused to acknowledge his authority as the new ruler. To strengthen his position, Iltutmish had to subjugate his rivals before firmly securing himself as the sultan. Iltutmish first chose to maintain a wait-and-watch attitude with his old rival, Tajuddin Yildoz. But when Yildoz was driven out from Ghazni into the Punjab by the Khwarezm-Shah in 1215 CE, Iltutmish siezed his opportunity by defeating Yildoz at Tarain. The rebel governor was promptly seized and put to death.

Now it was the turn of Nasiruddin Qabacha, another of Muhammad of Ghur's slaves, to maintain a loose hold over Lahore and Multan. Iltutmish forced Qabacha to submit in 1217 CE, but his submission was merely nominal. Meanwhile, Chengiz Khan had attacked the Khwarezm-Shah, leading to the infiltration of refugees—including the heir to the Khwarezm-Shahi throne—into the Punjab. Iltutmish may have faced a serious threat from the Shah himself if Chengiz Khan's attack had not been directed against the Shah. In the given situation, Iltutmish tried hard to avoid a direct confrontation with the armies of Chenghiz Khan. Cleverly, he refused to help the Khwarezm heir against the Mongols and restrained himself from countering Chengiz Khan. As luck would have it, the Mongols only sent raiding parties into the Salt Range—a development which Iltutmish could afford to ignore. Interestingly, the Mongol hoards did not venture into India, unsure of the climatic conditions, and retired after just ravaging the frontiers. Eventually the Khwarezm-Shah prince fled India after causing massive devastation within Qabacha's sphere of influence. As a result, Iltutmish was finally able to drive out Qabacha from Multan and Uchh in 1228 CE. Now that he could avoid a direct confrontation with the Mongols, Iltutmish chose to expand his frontiers to the east of the Beas. The western Punjab region became difficult to bring under control as the area was frequently raided by the hill tribes.

Turning his attention towards the Khilji Maliks in 1225 CE, Iltutmish launched a successful campaign against Ghiyasuddin Iwaz Khilji, one of Bakhtiyar Khilji's lieutenants who had occupied Lakhnauti in Bengal and was now making plans of invading Bihar. Iwaz Khilji was defeated and slain by Iltutmish in 1226 CE. Subsequently, in 1229 CE Iltutmish again invaded Bengal and slew Balka, the last of the Khilji chiefs to assert independent power. The Khilji Maliks were now forced to accept the vassalage of Iltutmish.

Now Iltutmish turned his focus on conquering the last remaining independent principalities of Hindustan. A case in point being Ranthambhor, which had asserted its independence during the confusion following the accession of Aram Shah—it was now subdued in 1226 CE. Next he took charge of Mandu in 1227 CE; and proceeded to capture Gwalior in 1232 CE, despite the desperate resistance offered by its ruler, Mangala Deva. A year later, the sultan captured and plundered Bhilsa and Ujjain in Malwa, pushing the southern boundary of the sultanate almost to the banks of the Narmada. In his stormy military career, although there were territorial gains, his generals suffered defeats at the hands of the Chauhans of Bundi, the Chalukyas of Gujarat and the Chandelas of Narwar.

Iltutmish's claim to fame lies in the establishment of the independent sultanate of Delhi, which freed the city from the shackles of being a mere subordinate to Ghazni. From being a mere frontier outpost Delhi emerged to be a centre of Islamic power and culture in India. By the time of Iltutmish's death in 1236 CE, the Delhi Sultanate had been clearly established as the largest and most powerful state in northern India.

The Khwarezm-Shahi Dynasty

The Khwarezm-Shahs were a ruling dynasty of Central Asia and Iran between 1077 and 1231 CE. From being the vassals of the Seljuqs at first, they later became independent rulers. With the defeat of the Seljuq sultan, Sanjar, in 1141 CE by the Karakitai confederation of northern China, the Khwarezm-Shahs were forced to acknowledge the sovereignty of the Karakitai. It was only after Sanjar's death (1157 CE) that the dynasty could come to power in Iran. During this period of struggle the Khwarezm-Shahs succeeded in founding a kingdom that stretched from the borders of India to those of Anatolia. But Chengiz Khan's Mongol hoards conquered Transoxania in 1220 CE; and by 1231 CE the last ruler of the line, Jalaluddin Mingburnu, was defeated by the Mongols and his territories taken over.

The progressive thoughts of Iltutmish reflected in his concept of statecraft. He was clear about the extent to which Islam and the *Shariah* could have an effect on Indian politics and culture, keeping in mind the majority of non-Muslims living in the subcontinent. Earlier on in his reign when he was advised by a group of *ulema* to deal severely with the Hindus by converting them to Islam, he had informed them about the impracticality of such an idea, adding that the Muslims in the land were few in number. This broadminded vision of Iltutmish was also replicated by his nobles in many ways. Likewise, he depended on the guidance of his advisers—especially the *wazir* Junaidi, who has been praised by his contemporaries. Iltutmish's open-mindedness may be further witnessed in his recommendation on the legal structure of the state not to be strictly based on Islamic law alone; and also in the nomination of his daughter, Raziyya, as his successor. These liberal influences gradually led to the evolution of a distinctive feature in the newly founded Turkish rule which was the hallmark of a careful balance between the *Shariah* and the needs of the time.

Using his discretion of not giving refuge to the last Khwarezm-Shah, Jalaluddin Mingburnu, who was fleeing the Mongol attack, Iltutmish made it clear that the Turkish power in Delhi was not ready to involve itself in the power politics of the Islamic East. To give legitimacy to his rule, Iltutmish first obtained a letter of investiture from the caliph; then he issued bullion currency on which the caliph's name appeared in Hindi. Such a move was to ensure that the common people might be able to understand the full import of the new regime.

Iltutmish was thus able to preserve and protect his kingdom against the ravages of the Mongol invasions that coincided with his reign. He also succeeded in building an efficient administrative machinery for his kingdom. The sultan took pains to seek out Islamic classics written in the eleventh century on the art of effective governance; and the *Adab-ul-Muluk*, the first Indo-Islamic classic on the art of government and warfare, was written for him. He constructed waterworks, mosques and various civil amenities at Delhi, making it a fitting seat of government for the first time. He also completed the beautiful monument of Qutb Minar begun by Qutbuddin Aibak, which stands to this day as a memorial of greatness of both the sultans. Iltutmish patronized the historian Minhaj us Siraj and the saint Qutbuddin of Ush. By successfully recovering and extending the kingdom left by his master; by establishing peaceful order in his state; and by organizing efficient administrative systems—Iltutmish achieved glory by dint of his own genius and exertion.

Raziyya Sultan (1236–40 CE)

After the death of Iltutmish, the state was torn by severe factional disputes for almost ten years, when four of Iltutmish's children and grandchildren were in turn raised to the throne before being deposed. Other than Raziyya, there were no successors worthy enough to rule the kingdom after Iltutmish. Largely through the efforts of the 'Corps of the Forty' or *Chihilgan*—a political faction consisting of Iltutmish's personal slaves—support was mustered for the sultan and his family members. The *Chihilgan* envisaged by Iltutmish to form a base for the kingdom actually proved to be its worst enemy. It made and unmade kings until Raziyya, the daughter of Iltutmish, was placed on the throne.

Raziyya Sultan was a woman of exemplary qualities—wise, brave, courageous and generous. With tact and diplomacy, she suppressed rebellions in the kingdom and restored much needed order. She generally wore male attire and did not hide her face behind a veil. She even hunted and led her army in war. Understandably, Muslim nobles, advisors and the *ulema,* who had formed the inner circle of the sultan, could not accept the idea of being ruled by a woman. Her appointment of an Abyssinian slave, Yaqut, to an important position was considered insulting by the Corps of the Forty, even leading to some of her nobles rising against her. Iltutmish's *wazir,* Nizam-ul-Mulk Junaidi, led a rebellion against her but was forced to flee in the end. Trying to suppress rebellions in Sirhind and Lahore, Raziyya was imprisoned at Tabarhinda; and Yaqut was killed. Though she eventually won over her captor, Altunia, and married him, she would never be able to regain control over Delhi. Raziyya would finally succumb to the designs of the powerful Shamsi nobles; and be killed by bandits while trying to flee. Her death marked the beginning of the decline of the line of Iltutmish.

Following Raziyya's death, Iltutmish's son and grandson ruled for a period of six years. But both of them being incompetent, they were soon replaced by Iltutmish's younger son, Nasiruddin Mahmud (1246–66 CE). The new sultan was more inclined towards leading a spiritual life and entrusted the administration of the kingdom to his capable minister and son-in-law, Balban. Nasiruddin passed away after a reign of 20 years, passing on the reins of the sultanate to Balban. This was a time when there were frequent Mongol raids on Indian frontiers. It was with sheer tact and strategy that Balban would save the sultanate from Mongol attacks.

Balban (1266–86 CE)

Balban was one of the most striking figures of the Delhi Sultanate. The political situation in India on the eve of Balban's ascent to the throne was strife ridden. His reign was characterized by significant factors; it was a continuous struggle to maintain Delhi's position against the revived power of the Mewatis, Jats and the Rajput chiefs. At the same time, vigilance also needed to be maintained against the marauding Mongols in the West. Even in the central regions of the state, sultanate rule was sometimes challenged by discontented Muslim nobles. To top it all, the Corps of the Forty had become very strong during the rule of Nasiruddin—even to the point of becoming extremely jealous of Balban's ascent to the throne. This necessitated Balban to curb the power of the revolting *Chihilgans* so that all internal threat to his authority could be permanently removed.

Born in 1205 CE, Ghiyasuddin Balban, son of a Turkish Khan, fell into the hands of slave dealers who brought him to India, where he was acquired by sultan Iltutmish. Starting his career as a water carrier, he was soon enrolled into the Corps of the Forty. Under Raziyya Sultan, he was promoted to the rank of the Lord of the Hunt, and obtained the fief of Rewari and the district of Hansi which he governed efficiently earning for himself the goodwill of the people in the process. His competence in dealing with the Mongols gained him the title of 'Ulugh Khan' (meaning 'powerful lord'). The sultan Nasiruddin Mahmud, made him his prime minister and gave his daughter's hand in marriage to him.

Balban had initially been a junior member in the Corps of the Forty, but by 1246 CE, in a changed political environment, he had gained enough power to attain a controlling position within the administration of sultan Nasiruddin Mahmud. The saintly sultan who was interested in the affairs of the other world had practically left all state authority in the hands of his brilliant slave commander-in-chief. Balban would serve Nasiruddin faithfully for nearly 20 years as his prime minister.

From 1246–52 CE, Balban functioned as an efficient prime minister, putting down the Khokas in the Punjab, forcing the Doab into obedience, plundering Mewar and Ranthambhor, and leading victorious campaigns against Gwalior, Chanderi and Marwar. He thus succeeded in establishing peace in the entire region. On his return to Delhi, however, he found that he had become a victim of courtly conspiracy spun by jealous nobles who had prevailed upon the sultan to expel him from the kingdom. But the disgraceful behaviour of the leader of the rebel group made people clamour for Balban's return. Balban then returned with a vengeance and eliminated all remnants of disorder and strife, before successfully repelling

Balban's Concept of Kingship

Balban believed that a king was God's representative on earth, and as such had unparalleled powers. He organized his court along the pattern of Persian courts, and was very particular of courtly discipline and decorum. He even disliked his nobles laughing loudly or passing light and humorous remarks in his presence. All kings and princes who had taken refuge in his court were also supposed to stand obediently in his presence. People attending his court were to be properly dressed, prostrating before the sultan in the prescribed manner. Except for the prime minister, no other noble could address the sultan directly. In an effort to build up a royal image and create an aura around the office of the sultan, armed and well-built soldiers marched alongside him wherever he went.

two Mongol invasions in 1259 and 1260 CE. But for his energy and vigour, the sultanate of Delhi could hardly have survived the shocks of internal revolt and external aggression. Thus, acting first in a prime minister's capacity and later as a sultan, Balban emerged as one of the most important political figures of his time.

In the first ten years of Nasiruddin Mahmud's reign, Balban was only partially successful in quelling the revolt of Rajput chiefs, but by 1266 CE, on becoming the sultan, his military strategy became more aggressive. His first focus was on tasks that he felt were the pressing needs of the hour. Elevating the authority of the sultan, which had almost disappeared during the weak rule of his predecessors, was an essential task. Simultaneously, he endeavoured to put down the Corps of the Forty—which had become a standing menace to the sultanate—while attempting to protect the state from the Mongol invasions.

Balban raised the status of the institution of the sultanate through the royal spectacle of elaborate state ceremonies and rituals, the strict administration of justice, and through the formulation of a despotic relationship between the ruler and his subjects. The most significant aspect of his reign was probably the elevated position of the sultan, which made it possible to reorganize and strengthen the army, and also to impose a tighter administrative apparatus.

Administration Under Balban

Balban systematically tried to end all disorders in his state with a firm hand. First, he dealt with the robber menace by effectively getting the forests cleared of the Mewatis, next he developed the infrastructure in the kingdom by constructing roads, building fortresses and garrisoning them with trusted soldiers. He also restored order in the Doab and Awadh, before suppressing a revolt in the Badaun and Amroha districts. Balban's thrust was more on reorganizing the internal state administration on efficient lines and establishing peace and order in his home territory, rather than embarking upon expeditions against Hindu territories.

To enforce complete control of the centre over the nobles in the *iqtas,* Iltutmish had ensured that they were periodically transferred. To intensify this check, Balban went a step further by examining the actual collection and expenditure of the *iqta* lands. For this, a new category of officials, the *khwajas*, were appointed to estimate the income of the *iqta* holders as well as the expenses they incurred in maintaining their troops. Any surplus amounts, termed as *fawazil,* were supposed to be remitted to the sultan's treasury. Through these measures, Balban could consolidate his rule over the provinces in his kingdom.

Balban's policy of consolidation was in large measure the result of suppressing the Corps of the

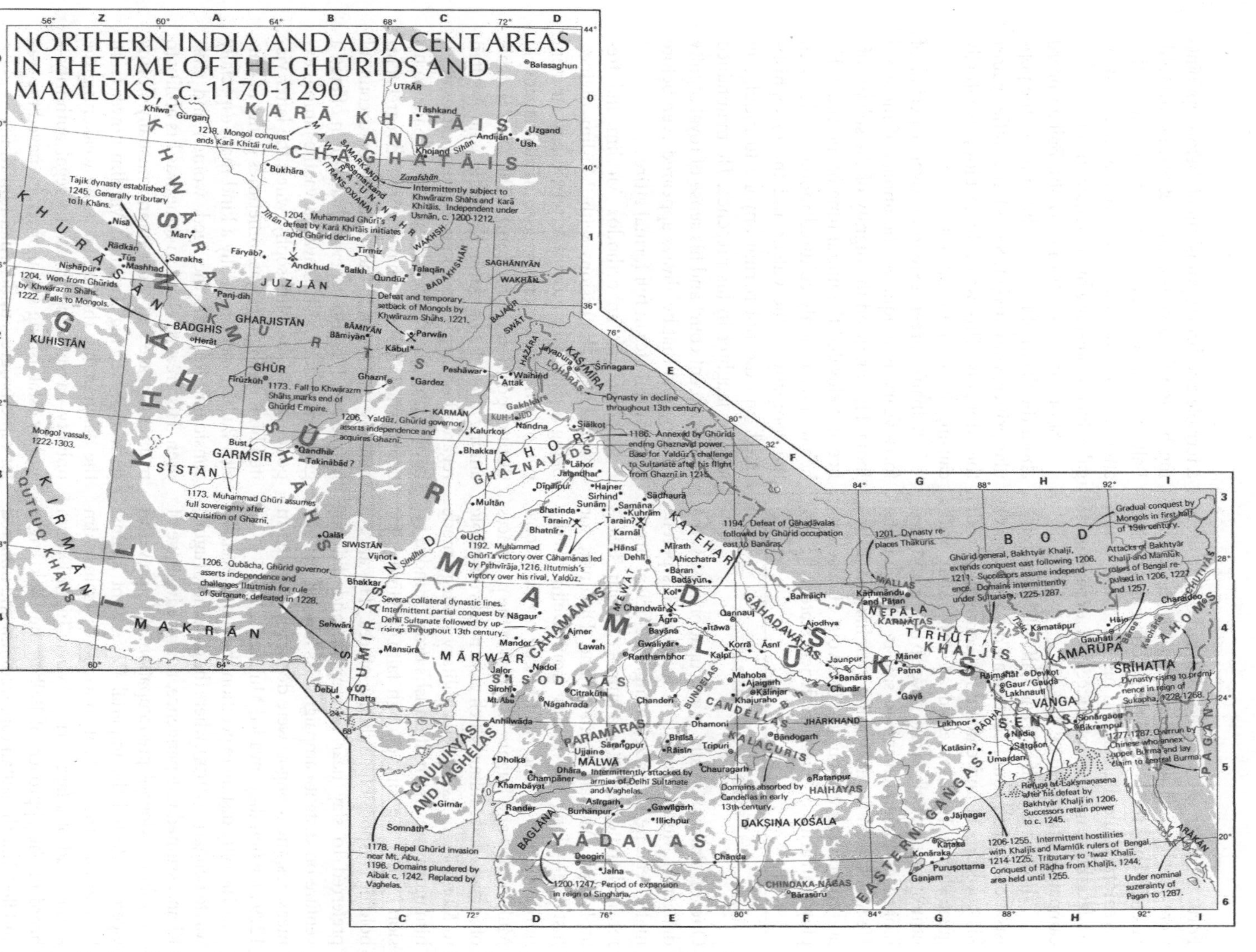

Map 5-1 *Northern India and Adjacent Areas in the Time of the Ghurids and Mamluks, 1170–1290 CE*

Forty together with the good fortune that there were hardly any rival claimants to the throne. Strengthened further by a grand court and formal ceremonial rule, Balban and his successors could undertake a number of successful expansionist campaigns after 1290 CE.

Through his half civil and half military administration Balban could control all departments of his government and enforce his commands with great vigour. He suppressed all immorality with utmost cruelty. Balban also gave up liquor and prohibited its manufacture and sale in his sultanate. He was known for dispensing even handed justice and enforcing it without fear or favour. He also employed an army of spies for efficient statecraft.

Mongol Threat

One of Balban's main preoccupations was the danger of Mongol invasion. To meet this perennial threat, he organized a highly efficient army, repaired and constructed a number of fortresses—at Lahore, Multan, Samana and Dipalpur, for instance—along the routes from Delhi to the north-western frontier, and placed his own sons, Muhammad and Bughra Khan, over the provinces of Samana and Multan which were most vulnerable to Mongol attacks. But his military strategy made him move away from Iltutmish's broad minded vision by not reposing enough faith in Hindus for holding responsible military offices. He always preferred to stay near his capital, and did not venture on distant campaigns. As a result of such measures, the Mongols were decisively defeated in 1279 CE when they invaded Multan.

The only distant expedition the sultan ever led was to Bengal (1279 CE), where the governor, Tughril Khan, assumed independence, taking advantage of the sultan's Mongol preoccupation. The powerful viceroy defeated the imperial forces sent against him, forcing the aged sultan to march against him at the head of a large army. When Tughril Khan heard of the approach of Balban, he took fright and fled. But the sultan captured him and inflicted a terrible and brutal punishment, before appointing his son as governor and returning to Delhi. Balban's vigorous and effective action against this attempt to establish an independent state in Bengal helped in keeping his sultanate intact.

Soon after his return to Delhi, Balban heard about the death of his son, Muhammad, the popular prince, who died (1285 CE) in a battle against the Mongols. This was a huge blow, eventually causing his death in 1286 CE.

Balban's career, extending over a period of forty years, is unique in the annals of medieval India. He enhanced the dignity of the sultan's office and elevated the moral tone of the court. He behaved as a highly cultured monarch, despised the company of the vulgar and the unsophisticated, and did not permit anyone to indulge in joke or laughter in his presence. He maintained a magnificent court and his sense of royal dignity was so great that he always appeared even before his subordinates in full formal attire.

Balban was an orthodox Muslim and frequently held discussions with Muslim divines. Being a patron of men of letters, many eminent personalities, historians, poets and litterateurs held distinct positions in his court. The most notable among them being Amir Khusrau, who is often regarded as the prince of poets. He is also said to have invited the famous Persian poet, Sadi, to his court, who is known to have expressed regret at his inability to respond to the invitation on account of his old age. It is also believed that Balban offered a grand reception to Madhavacharya, the famous exponent of *Dvaita* philosophy, when the latter visited him. Though he was sometimes guilty of cruelty, Balban was essentially a kind man, especially considerate towards the aged, women and children. His greatest claim to fame was his ability to maintain peace and order in an unusually stormy period; preserving an infant Muslim power from the dangers that threatened it. By weakening the nobility—a standing threat to regal authority—and by establishing social order, he paved the way for rapid progress under Alauddin Khilji.

After the death of Balban, his grandson, Kaiqubad, immediately ascended to the throne; but was unable to manage either the administration of the sultanate or the factional conflicts between the old Turkish nobility and the new forces led by the Khiljis. This resulted in a struggle between the two factions, the consequence of which was the murder of Kaiqubad and the ascension of Jalaluddin Firuz Khilji to the throne in 1290 CE. Not being a homogeneous political entity, it became easy for the Delhi Sultanate to whither away—leading to other Muslim powers to emerge in succession. Kingship was thus usurped from one family to another, with the constant change of power.

SUMMARY

- The Slave Dynasty (1206–90 CE) comprising the first line of the Delhi sultans, signifies the reign of those sultans at Delhi that lasted for nearly a century.
- Qutbuddin Aibak was among Muhammad of Ghur's most trusted Turkish officers, who was rewarded by his master with the charge of his Indian conquests.
- Establishing his headquarters at Delhi, Qutbuddin easily occupied the areas between the Ganga and the Yamuna in northern India.
- Following the death of Muhammad of Ghur in 1206 CE, Qutbuddin Aibak declared himself as the sultan of Delhi.
- After shifting from Delhi to Lahore, Qutbuddin got involved in a conflict with Tajuddin Yildoz of Ghazni, who also laid claim to his former master, Muhammad's, Indian conquests.
- After Qutbuddin's death in 1210 CE, the sultanate passed on to Iltutmish, his son-in-law, who was able to consolidate the independence of the sultanate of Delhi.
- Iltutmish ascended the throne at a time when there was confusion everywhere, but his training in war and administration helped him tackle all issues effectively.
- In his political career, Iltutmish had to deal with the defense of the western frontiers of his kingdom, control the Muslim nobles in India, and subjugate the Hindu chiefs who continued to rule independently.
- Iltutmish overpowered his rivals who refused to acknowledge his authority as the new ruler.
- Iltutmish's progressive ideas led to the creation of state laws that struck a careful balance between the *Shariah* and the contemporary socio-cultural environment.
- Largely through the efforts of the 'Corps of the Forty', a support structure was created or the protection of the sultan and his family members.
- This internal group made and unmade kings until Raziyya, the daughter of Iltutmish, was placed on the throne of Delhi.
- With tact and diplomacy, Raziyya Sultan suppressed rebellions in her kingdom and restored order., But despite her exemplary qualities, she succumbed to the designs of the powerful Shamsi nobles—marking the beginning of the decline of the line of Iltutmish.
- Nasiruddin Mahmud, the new sultan was more inclined towards a spiritual life and entrusted the administration of the kingdom to his capable minister, Balban.
- It was the tact and strategy of prime minister Balban that saved the sultanate from the frequent Mongol raids. Balban succeeded Nasiruddin as the sultan in 1266 CE.
- As a sultan, Balban had to tackle the revolt of the Jats, Rajput chiefs, discontented Muslim nobles as well as the invasions of the Mongol armies.
- Balban's policy of consolidation was in large measure the result of suppressing the Corps of the Forty and also the lack of rival claimants to the throne. Strengthened by a grand court and formal ceremonial rule in addition to all these aspects, helped him and his successors undertake a number of successful expansionist campaigns.

KEYWORDS

Sultanate	Mamluks	Ulema	Fawazil
Slavery	Shariah	Iqta	

REVIEW QUESTIONS

1. What was Qutbuddin Aibak's contribution to the foundation of the Delhi Sultanate?
2. How did Iltutmish consolidate the sultanate rule in India to make it the largest and most powerful in northern India?
3. Give an account of Balban's services as prime minister of the Delhi Sultanate.
4. How did Balban tackle the Mongol menace facing northern India?
5. Briefly discuss and compare the socio-political significance of the reigns of Iltutmish and Balban.
6. Write short notes on:
   - Raziyya Sultan
   - Slavery in South Asia
   - Balban's Concept of Kingship

CHAPTER 6

The Khiljis

Review and Discussion

- Jalaluddin Khilji
- Alauddin Khilji

As discussed in Chapter 5, Balban's immediate successors could neither handle the administration of the Sultanate nor could they resolve the intrigues between the old Turkish nobility and the new forces led by the Khiljis. This resulted in a struggle between the two factions, leading to the murder of Kaiqubad, the grandson and successor of Balban and the ascension of Jalaluddin Firuz Khilji to the throne in 1290 CE.

The origin of the Khiljis lacks clarity, with some historians believing that they belonged to the Turkish stock while others attribute their origin to the Afghans. The older nobility of the Delhi Sultanate did not recognize the Turkish origin of the Khiljis. Considering them to be low born Afghans, they even desisted from helping them come to power. Interestingly, they were helped by outsiders in their rise to power—some of whom were Indian-born Muslims, who anticipated the betterment of their own position if the Khiljis were to break the monopoly of the Corps of the Forty. To some extent then it were the changes that followed the establishment of Turkish rule in northern India together with the political developments in Central Asia and Iran that shifted the balance of power, leading to the rise of the Khiljis in Delhi.

The independent Delhi Sultanate was progressing from strength to strength in northern India through the consolidation of its territories, and due to the migration of people from regions beyond its boundaries towards the northwest. The tribes of the eastern steppes, for instance, had begun a westward shift—thus ending the threat hitherto posed by the rival Turks in Ghazni and Ghur. These migrations also forced a number of Central Asian Muslims to move into India.

Jalaluddin Khilji (1290–96 CE)

Jalaluddin Khilji, the first ruler of the Khilji dynasty, was almost seventy years of age when he ascended the throne. He ruled for a fairly short period; his age making him mild and generous, restricting the severity and vigour required of a sultan. In his second year of reign there was a rebellion from the fief holder of Kara, which Jalaluddin suppressed. The rebel was later pardoned, and Kara along with Awadh were awarded by the sultan to his nephew and son-in-law, Alauddin Khilji. Jalaluddin then proceeded to put down a rebellion by some of Balban's officers and led an unsuccessful expedition against Ranthambhor.

In the absence of any kind of dynamism, the sultan's lacklustre kingship was displayed even in

The Mongols of Central Asia

Defining Central Asia, the vast landlocked region of Asia, as a distinct region of the world, the traveller–geographer Baron Alexander von Humboldt in 1843 made people take note of its physical attributes. The gaps in the availability of indigenous written sources make it difficult to reconstruct the history of a land that was known for its nomadic barbarians and the Silk Road. Its importance can be ascertained from the fact that for the neighbouring sedentary civilizations, the region acted as a crossroad for the movement of people, goods, and ideas between Europe, the Middle East, South Asia and East Asia. Almost contemporary to the establishment of the Delhi Sultanate was the creation of the Mongol empire by Chengiz Khan in Central Asia, a development which was to have a huge impact on the destinies of both Asia and Europe. The earlier settlers of the region—the Turks, the Uighurs, and the Khitans were probably incorporated into the Mongol empire when it emerged in the early thirteenth century. This was a period of tribal wars and forceful campaigns. The aggressive policies followed by Chengiz Khan were primarily aimed against Chin China, the Naimans and the Khwarezm Shahs. In the course of these raids many prosperous cities such as Khwarezm, Khurasan, and Afghanistan had taken a beating. The intensified Mongol campaigns led to the occupation of Korea in 1231, fall of the Chin dynasty in 1234 and more importantly the establishment of the Yuan (Mongol) dynasty in China (1260–1368) by Kublai Khan (1260–94), the grandson of Chenghiz Khan. While Kublai set off to China, his brother Hulaku had the task of consolidating the Mongol hold on Iran. The way in which the Yuan rule developed in China under Kublai, the Il khanate developed in Persia under Hulaku which embraced, in addition to the Iranian plateau, a large part of Iraq, Northern Syria, and Eastern and Central Anatolia. The ripples of these campaigns were to be felt in North India too, when, with the Mongol plunder of Central Asia and eastern Iran, there was a break-up of the Turkish *mamluk* clan, resulting in groups of people belonging to the elite of these regions finding refuge in northern India. These new migrants claiming origin from Central Asia were admitted into various levels of military and administrative service by the early Delhi sultans and came to constitute an important section of the nobility in the thirteenth century CE. Many of these nobles were the slaves bought in the markets of Central Asia.

his foreign policy. Although he succeeded in driving back a substantial Mongol force commanded by Abdullah, the grandson of Hulaku from the banks of the Sind River in 1292 CE, he gave the Mongols the dangerous concession of settling down in India. Ulghu, a descendent of Chengiz Khan and a few thousand of his Mongol followers embraced islam and settled at Mughlpura near Delhi. The descendents of these Mongols came to be known as the new Mussalmans who continued to be a source of trouble and anxiety. His weak policies coupled with his kind disposition exasperated his followers and encouraged them to indulge in seditious acts. Alauddin himself joined the disgruntled nobles and treacherously murdered the sultan who had proceeded to Kara to welcome his nephew on his triumphant return from Devagiri.

By the end of his reign, Jalaluddin had sowed the seeds for two major changes that mitigated the harsher aspects of Balban's rule. The first being the Afghan descent of the Khiljis, which was used by Jalaluddin to harness the support of the Afghan nobles; and the second was giving higher offices to Indian Muslims, who had so far been ignored by Balban because of his belief that the right to govern was vested in the Turks alone. This practice would subsequently help Jalaluddin in strengthening his Sultanate.

Alauddin Khilji (1296–1316 CE)

After murdering his uncle, Jalaluddin Khilji, in a deceitful manner, Alauddin Khilji entered Delhi unopposed and proclaimed himself the sultan amidst pomp and show. He was soon to realize that he had to face a number of grave problems, including the recurring invasions of the dreaded Mongols, hostility and insubordination of powerful nobles, opposition from Hindus, and the weakness of the central authority. His main aim was therefore to repress these disruptive forces, before establishing Muslim rule more securely in India.

In order to centralize and expand his Sultanate, Alauddin realized the need for an efficient administration, a powerful army, a full treasury and dependable nobility under his personal control. He had earlier partly solved the issue of improving the kingdom's finances by conducting a rewarding raid into Bhilsa (1292 CE) in Central India. Building upon his initial success in improving his position and raising a fresh army, he raided Devagiri (early 1296 CE), the capital of the Yadavas in the Deccan, and defeated Raja Ramachandra. The phenomenal wealth procured from Devagiri helped provide for a good foundation for his future plans of building the state. Alauddin had already gained the support of many dissatisfied Turkish nobles, now he obtained the support of more nobles by luring them with money and promotions. During Alauddin's reign, therefore, the Sultanate gained colossal proportions.

The Imperial Period of the Delhi Sultanate

With Alauddin Khilji begins what may be called the imperial period of the Sultanate of Delhi. Firstly, the Mongol invasions—numbering five during the decade from 1297–1306 CE—were effectively checked by Alauddin with savage cruelty. From 1306 CE, there was a marked decline in the frequency of the Mongol raids. It is said that these fierce encounters had lead the Mongols to fear Alauddin so much that they saw the sword of the Islamic armies hanging above them even in their sleep.

Alauddin began his formal expansionist activities with the subjugation of Gujarat in 1299 CE. Next he moved against Rajasthan, before subduing Ranthambhor (1301 CE), which was ruled by Hamirdeva. Amir Khusrau, who had accompanied Alauddin Khilji on this conquest, poignantly describes the event at the close of three months of siege when all the noble Rajput women had performed *jauhar* to uphold their honour. Alauddin then turned towards Chittor (1303 CE), ruled by Ratan Singh who had annoyed him by refusing permission to his armies to march into Gujarat through Mewar. According to popular legend, another reason for subduing Chittor was that Alauddin had heard about the beauty of the queen of Chittor, Rani Padmini, and desired to acquire her for his harem. This account, however, cannot be authenticated. Chittor was subdued and assigned to Alauddin's minor son, Khizr Khan and a Muslim garrison positioned in the fort of Chittor. Alauddin also subdued Mandu (1305 CE), before adding Siwan (1308 CE) and Jalor (1312 CE). His successful campaigns in Rajasthan opened the door for further campaigns towards the South of his kingdom.

Alauddin's primary motto in these raids was to make these small principalities recognize his supremacy and to collect huge amounts of booty to finance his consolidation in the north. His adventure into southern India was an ambitious venture led by his lieutenant, Malik Kafur. Under

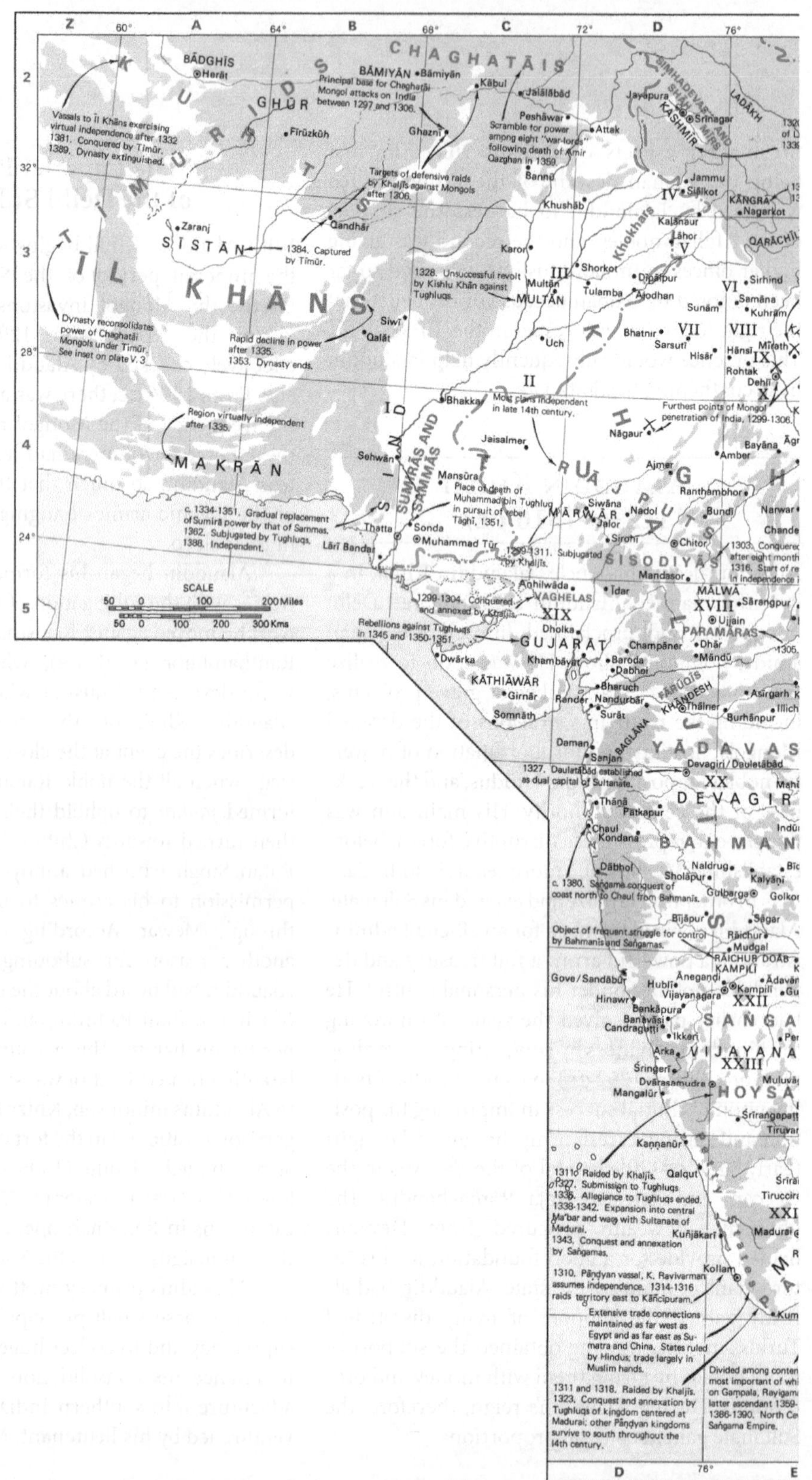

Map 6-1 *South Asia, 1290 CE Onwards in the Time of the Khiljis and Tughlaqs, 1290–1390 CE*

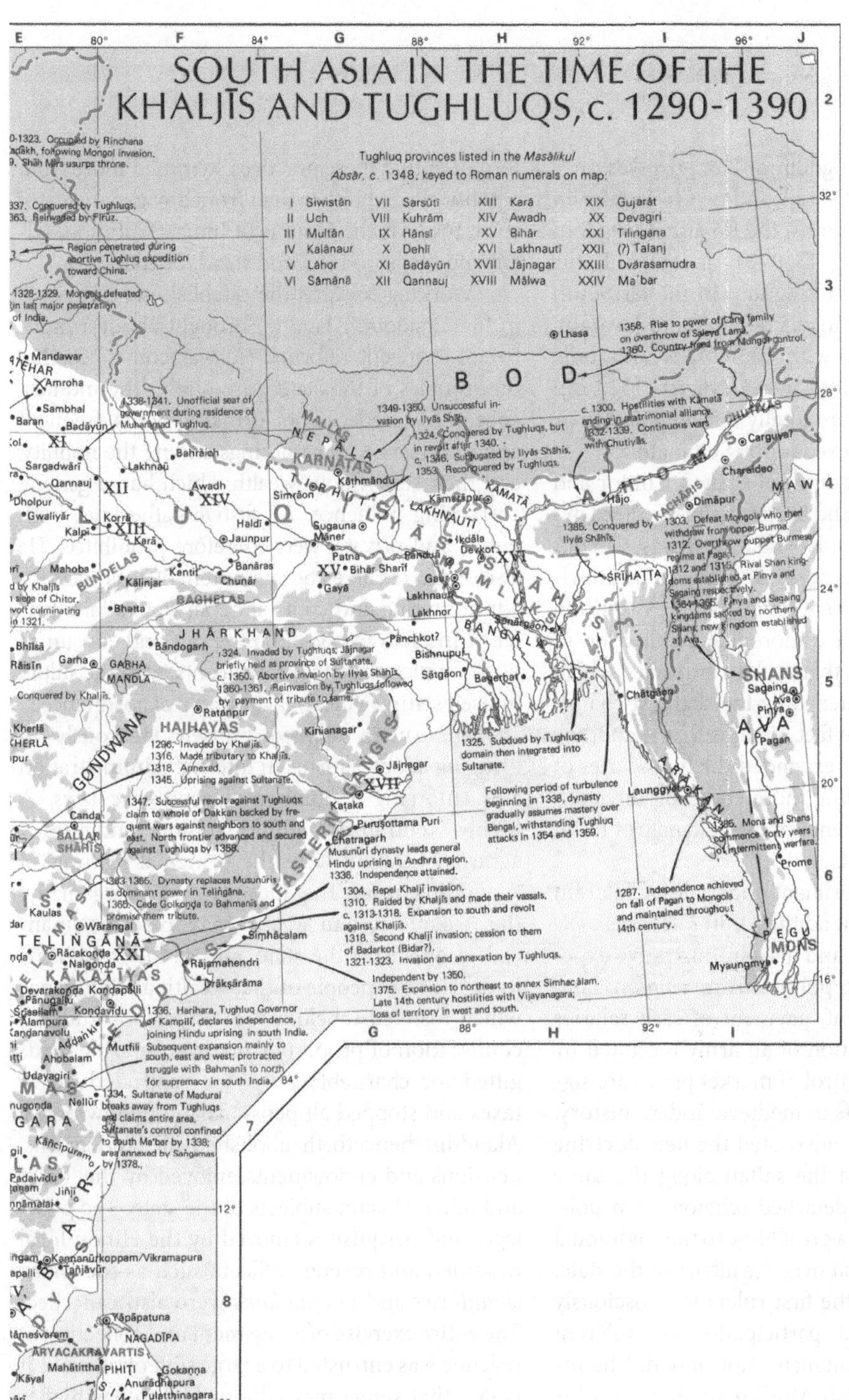

SOUTH ASIA IN THE TIME OF THE KHALJĪS AND TUGHLUQS, c. 1290-1390
Tughluq provinces listed in the Masālikul Absār, c. 1348, keyed to Roman numerals on map:
I Siwistān
II Uch
III Multān
IV Kalānaur
V Lāhor
VI Sāmānā
VII Sarsūtī
VIII Kuhrām
IX Hānsī
X Dehlī
XI Badāyūn
XII Qannauj
XIII Karā
XIV Awadh
XV Bihār
XVI Lakhnautī
XVII Jājnagar
XVIII Mālwa
XIX Gujarāt
XX Devagiri
XXI Tilingana
XXII (?) Talanj
XXIII Dvārasamudra
XXIV Ma'bar
Region penetrated during abortive Tughluq expedition toward China.
1358. Rise to power of Lang family on overthrow of Sakya Lama. 1360. Country freed from Mongol control.
Lhasa
B O D
1338-1341. Unofficial seat of government during residence of Muhammad Tughluq.
1349-1350. Unsuccessful invasion by Ilyās Shāh.
1324. Conquered by Tughluqs, but in revolt after 1340. c. 1346. Subjugated by Ilyās Shāhīs. 1353. Reconquered by Tughluqs.
c. 1300. Hostilities with Kāmatā ending in matrimonial alliance. 1332-1339. Continuous wars with Chutiyās.
1385. Conquered by Ilyās Shāhīs.
1303. Defeat Mongols who then withdraw from upper Burma. 1312. Overthrow puppet Burmese regime at Pagan. 1312 and 1315. Rival Shan kingdoms established at Pinya and Sagaing respectively. 1364-1365. Pinya and Sagaing kingdoms sacked by northern Shans, new kingdom established at Ava.
1324. Invaded by Tughluqs; Jājnagar briefly held as province of Sultanate. c. 1350. Abortive invasion by Ilyās Shāhīs. 1360-1361. Reinvasion by Tughluqs followed by payment of tribute to same.
1325. Subdued by Tughluqs; domain then integrated into Sultanate.
Following period of turbulence beginning in 1338, dynasty gradually assumes mastery over Bengal, withstanding Tughluq attacks in 1354 and 1359.
1296. Invaded by Khaljīs. 1316. Made tributary to Khaljīs. 1318. Annexed. 1345. Uprising against Sultanate.
1347. Successful revolt against Tughluqs; claim to whole of Dakkan backed by frequent wars against neighbors to south and east. North frontier advanced and secured against Tughluqs by 1358.
Musunūri dynasty leads general Hindu uprising in Andhra region. 1336. Independence attained.
1383-1385. Dynasty replaces Musunūris as dominant power in Teliṅgāna. 1365. Cede Golkonda to Bahmanīs and promise them tribute.
1304. Repel Khaljī invasion. 1310. Raided by Khaljīs and made their vassals. c. 1313-1318. Expansion to south and revolt against Khaljīs. 1318. Second Khaljī invasion; cession to them of Badarkot (Bidar?). 1321-1323. Invasion and annexation by Tughluqs.
Independent by 1350. 1375. Expansion to northeast to annex Simhacalam. Late 14th century hostilities with Vijayanagara; loss of territory in west and south.
1386. Mons and Shans commence forty years of intermittent warfare.
1287. Independence achieved on fall of Pagan to Mongols and maintained throughout 14th century.
1336. Harihara, Tughluq Governor of Kampilī, declares independence, joining Hindu uprising in south India. Subsequent expansion mainly to south, east and west; protracted struggle with Bahmanīs to north for supremacy in south India.
1334. Sultanate of Madurai breaks away from Tughluqs and claims entire area. Sultanate's control confined to south Ma'bar by 1338; area annexed by Saṅgamas by 1378.
NEPĀLA
KARNĀTAS
TIRHUT
KĀMATĀ
LAKHNAUTI
BANGĀLA
ĀHOM
CHUTIYĀS
KACHĀRIS
SHANS
AVA
ARAKAN
PEGU
MONS
JHĀRKHAND
GARHA MANDLA
HAIHAYAS
GONDWĀNA
BUNDELAS
BAGHELAS
EASTERN GAṄGAS
TELIṄGĀNĀ
KĀKATĪYAS
REḌḌIS
ĀRYACAKRAVARTIS
SIṂHALA
ROHANA
NAGADĪPA
Kāṭhmāndu
Patna
Gaur
Lakhnauti
Jājnagar
Kataka
Purusottama Puri
Chatragarh
Simhācalam
Rājamahendri
Warangal
Chātgāon
Sagaing
Ava
Pinya
Pagan
Launggyet
Prome
Myaungmya
Dimāpur
Charaideo
Hājo
Jaunpur
Banāras
Chunār
Kālinjar
Kālpī
Gwāliyār
Amroha
Sambhal
Badāyūn
Bahrāich
Lakhnaū
Awadh
Anurādhapura
Gampala
Kotta
Devanagara
Yāpāpatuna
Kannanūrkoppam/Vikramapura
Tañjāvūr

Kafur, the Yadava kingdom of Devagiri was once again suppressed (1307 CE), and two years later an attack was directed against the Kakatiya kingdom of Telingana. During 1310–11 CE Malik Kafur plundered the Pandya kingdom in the far South of the country, reaching as far as Rameshwaram. He returned to Delhi with immense wealth, only to lead yet another raid into Devagiri (1313 CE) when the Yadavas were totally defeated and their kingdom finally annexed to the Sultanate.

Thus, the royal houses of Malwa, Chittor and Gujarat in the north; and the powerful southern dynasties of the Yadavas, Hoysalas, Pandyas, Cheras, Cholas and Kakatiyas were all made to acknowledge Alauddin as their sovereign. But the vast Khilji dominions now seemed more like a collection of diverse people rather than a close knit state, which appeared to be threatened by the slightest change in leadership. Yet, the fact remains that Alauddin's energetic rule rapidly expanded the boundaries of the Sultanate, providing more enduring direction to the continued existence of the Sultanate of Delhi over any other period.

Besides being a brilliant imperialist, Alauddin Khilji was also a great administrator. He was a pioneer in many fields and his administrative experiences of separating politics from religion, land survey and settlement, payment of cash salaries to soldiers, organization of an army recruited by the state, and the control of market prices are significant achievements in medieval Indian history.

Alauddin wisely advocated the new doctrine of the sovereignty of the sultan along the same lines as Balban. He detached religion from politics, thereby striking a great blow to the traditional influence of the *ulema* over the affairs of the state. He was also one of the first rulers to consciously expand the political participation of different groups within the Sultanate. Not only did he include the non-Turkish Muslim nobility into his political gamut (some of whom were converted Hindus), but he also sent positive signals by being open to the idea of including Hindus into the administrative apparatus. Although it is not to be forgotten that these practices stemmed more from a political need rather than from any generosity of spirit towards the Hindus of India. Ambition, talent and tact stood in good stead for Alauddin.

Working towards the establishment of peace in his kingdom, Alauddin brought about a number of stringent reforms. He was convinced that the troubles of the state were due to the indifference of his predecessors, drinking bouts, frequent and intimate social gatherings among the nobility, and their superfluous wealth which had a general corrupting influence. All festive gatherings, both public and private, were therefore prohibited. He also organized an elaborate system of espionage for administering and controlling all state affairs better. A freeze was placed on the sale and consumption of liquor and other intoxicants, with the sultan himself setting a personal example of abstinence.

The sultan applied himself vigorously to bringing about reforms in internal administration and enforcing a number of repressive laws. A highly centralized administration and heavy agrarian taxation were the principal features of Alauddin's rule. The idea behind reorganizing the revenue system was to maximize the financial resources of the state, and at the same time to deprive the people of that wealth and affluence which fostered rebellion. He undertook ruthless confiscation of property—not even sparing lands gifted for charitable purposes—collected heavy taxes and stopped all pensions and endowments. Alauddin henceforth abolished all land grants, pensions and endowments enjoyed by the Turks and other Muslim subjects of the state. The privileges and perquisites enjoyed by the Hindu local headmen and revenue officers such as the *khuts*, *chaudhries* and *muqaddams* were also cancelled. The entire exercise of assessment and collection of revenue was entrusted to a large staff of officials. It is said that sometimes Hindus had to pay higher taxes than others living in the state, bringing deterioration in their overall standard of living.

Since the state had no stable economic base, it was dependent in large measure for its financial resources on the tribute paid by the petty principalities that had been subjugated, together with the wealth acquired from the sultan's campaigns of plunder and raid. To provide a fixed income to the nobles, Alauddin introduced the *Iqta* system in which a revenue district was assigned to the nobleman in lieu of a salary on a transferable basis. The incumbent nobleman was also given the right to collect taxes from that land, of which a part amount had to be paid to the state. Besides making the nobles financially solvent, this system also ensured that the state exchequer got a fixed income through the imposition of *kharaj* or land tax in the form of surplus agrarian produce.

By introducing the practice of the measurement of land as a preliminary to land settlement, Alauddin became the first ruler of the Delhi Sultanate to establish direct relations with the peasants in order to know the actual amount paid by them towards land revenue. The land tax that was imposed amounted to half the produce (in weight or value) on each individual peasant's holding, regardless of the land size. This was to be supplemented by a house and cattle tax. These revenue resources were constituted into *iqta*s, or different territorial units of land, which were distributed among the nobles. But the nobles did not have an absolute control over their *iqta*s. They had to submit periodic statements of their income and expenditure and send the balance amount to the sultan's treasury. Since the sultan already had an account of the estimated produce from each *iqta*, it was impossible to deceive him. Officers in each *iqta*, appointed directly by the sultan, ensured his control over it. The *khalisa* lands—the territory whose revenues accrued directly to the sultan's own treasury—were expanded significantly, enabling the sultan to pay a much larger number of his infantry and cavalry troops in cash. The Doab formed an important *khalisa* land, and the state directly collected taxes from it. State agents, called the *amils*, collected the revenue helped by the local chiefs—the *muqaddams* and *khuts*. Land revenue was collected in kind; and these collected food grains were transported to the towns. Ziauddin Barani speaks in exalted terms about Alauddin's revenue policy. He says that in the matter of assessment and collection of revenue, the entire kingdom was brought under one efficient administrative system. But the revenue laws were enforced so strictly that the revenue officer came to be looked upon as a curse on society. Alauddin's intention of making the state financially secure could be realized only if the share of the local chief was checked and the revenue collection machinery was sincere. Through these measures the sultan made those who had a share in his economic and political power accountable to him by keeping both his officials and local rural leaders on a tight leash.

As a true military strategist, Alauddin saw clearly that his kingdom could not be maintained without a good army. He, therefore, created a huge, well-organized and powerful standing army. His unique military reforms included the creation of a large standing army, directly recruited and paid by the state. The payment of salaries in cash to the soldiers was a new feature, which replaced the former land assignment system. He also began the practice of branding horses and preparing descriptive rolls of soldiers to prevent any fraud.

A contemporary writer states that the imperial army of the Khiljis consisted of 475,000 disciplined Muslim soldiers whose names were recorded in the imperial muster roll and whose pay and rations were entered in the records of the deputy victualler who was in charge of army supplies. Alauddin Khilji revived Balban's frontier policy by following the same strategies of strengthening the fortresses and garrisoning them with trusted soldiers. In order to enable the soldiers to live on the pay fixed by the state, he controlled and regulated the prices of food grain, sugar, horses, cattle, slaves, perfume, cloth and other daily necessities. He established three different markets in Delhi catering specifically to these commodities.

Understanding the responsibility of providing a continuous supply of cheap food grains to the towns, and the fact that the loyalty and

The Chagatai Mongols

The history of the Chagatai Mongol name goes back to the reign of Chenghiz Khan. After Chengiz Khan's death, Chagatai Khan, his second son, became the ruler of a vassal kingdom which included the territories of Kashgaria and most of Transoxania between the Amu Darya and the Syr Darya with his capital at Almarikh. When compared with the other Mongol rulers he appears to have been more benevolent ruling until his death in 1242. His line later came to be known as the Chagatai Khanate, a part of the Mongol Empire that lasted several generations over Persia and present day Afghanistan and Pakistan.

support of the town citizens was dependent upon the availability of food, Alauddin adopted a strict vigilance on the maintenance of prices. The peasants were to sell their produce only to the merchants who were bound by the state to sell their wares on fixed price only. A 'Superintendent of Markets' was appointed, who strictly enforced fixed prices with the help of a team of assistants. Punishments for breach of regulations were severe and even barbarous. A shopkeeper defrauding his customer by giving short weight had to make up for the deficiency by an equivalent amount of flesh cut off from his body. Barani tells us that prices were not allowed to be increased even by a single *dam* or paisa even during famine. Thus, a *man* of wheat cost 7½ *jitals,* barley four *jitals,* and superior quality rice five *jitals.*

Although Alauddin's main aim in controlling the market was his desire to recruit soldiers at a low salary, and to enable them to meet the higher costs of living, yet the idea to keep prices down by declaring all articles of daily need be sold at a fixed price regulated by the state was a commendable effort in itself. Through a systematized agrarian taxation policy the sultan could achieve two important objectives: ensure supplies at low prices to grain carriers and fill the state granaries with a buffer stock, which along with his price regulations helped in ensuring that his soldiers could lead an affordable life. From Barani's reports one can assume that the regulations were in force not only in the region of Delhi but in other parts of the kingdom too.

After occupying Afghanistan, when the Chagatai Mongols began to penetrate the Punjab, a comprehensive defence programme had to be formulated for the Sultanate, including the capital Delhi, which was subjected to a two-month siege in 1303 CE. Other than fortifying the capital and deputing able commanders at the frontier towns and forts, it was necessary to organize a large army. The vast expenditure was to be financed through the existing resources of the state. At such a time, Alauddin's plan to compensate his soldiers by a policy of market controlled low prices enhanced the purchasing power of the soldiers and enabled them to live comfortably. His successful control of the market was a remarkable experiment which remained unparalleled in medieval Indian history.

The market regulations of Alauddin Khilji were put to an end after his death in 1316 CE, while his agrarian measures proved to be more enduring. His land revenue policy was continued by his successors, and formed a base for the land revenue reforms of the emperors Sher Shah and Akbar too.

Alauddin's multi-faceted persona as an able statesman may be seen in many more forms. Other than being a good administrator and military strategist, he also showed interest in the development of his state. He built the city of Siri, enlarged the *Qutbi* mosque and erected a gateway known as the *Alai Darwaza*. He began the construction of a massive *minar* which was meant to outshine the Qutb Minar in its glory, but failed to finish it. Though illiterate, he was a patron of literary men and many famous scholars adorned his court. The most illustrious among them being Amir Khusrau, who was also a courtier of Sultan Balban during the earlier dynasty.

Fall of the Khilji Dynasty

In a very short time after the death of Alauddin, the Khilji dynasty waned away. Disruptive forces began to assert themselves, followed by political confusion and turmoil. For a brief period Malik Kafur emerged strong in the political arena, when most of the claimant princes were done away with. Only Qutbuddin Mubarak Shah, the third son of Alauddin, escaped a tragic fate. The atrocities of Malik Kafur caused general dissatisfaction among the people, leading to some conspirators murdering him in 1316 CE and making Qutbuddin Mubarak Shah the new sultan of Delhi.

Qutbuddin Mubarak Shah began his reign on a positive note by releasing a number of prisoners who had been unjustly detained during Kafur's reign. He also removed restrictions on agriculture and trade. He put down rebellious chiefs and suppressed revolts in Gujarat and Telingana. He led an expedition against Raja Harpal Deo of Devagiri, whom he captured and killed. But soon the sultan abandoned himself to a life of debauchery and left the state's administration in the hands of his favourite general, the Hindu convert, Nasiruddin Khusro Khan, who murdered his master and set up a reign of terror. Opposition to Khusro's rule arose immediately, led by Ghazi Malik, the Warden of the Western Marches at Deopalpur. Ghazi Malik organized a confederacy of nobles, captured Khusro and beheaded him in 1320 CE. In the absence of any surviving members of Alauddin's bloodline, Ghazi Malik started a new dynasty by assuming the title of Ghiyasuddin Tughlaq.

SUMMARY

- The changes that followed the establishment of Turkish rule in northern India and the developments in Central Asia and Iran shifted the balance of power, leading to the rise of the Khiljis in the late thirteenth century CE.
- Jalaluddin Khilji's fairly short period of reign (from 1290–96 CE), coupled with his mild disposition and advanced age, made his kingship incompetent in matters of both internal and foreign policies.
- When Alauddin Khilji came to the throne after murdering his uncle, Jalaluddin, he initiated what may be termed as the imperial period of the Sultanate of Delhi.
- Alauddin Khilji had to face the recurring invasions of the dreaded Mongols, hostility and insubordination of the powerful nobles, opposition from the Hindus, and the weakness of the central authority.
- The royal houses of Malwa, Chittor and Gujarat in the north and the powerful ruling dynasties of the south—the Yadavas, Hoysalas, Pandyas, Cheras, Cholas and Kakatiyas—were all made to acknowledge Alauddin as their sovereign.
- Alauddin's forces defeated serious Mongol onslaughts, numbering five during the decade from 1297–1306 CE with savage cruelty.
- Alauddin Khilji was a pioneer in many fields and his administrative experiences of separating politics from religion, land survey and settlement, payment of cash salaries to soldiers, organization of an army recruited by the state, and the control of market prices are very significant.
- Working towards the establishment of peace in his kingdom, Alauddin brought about a number of stringent socio-economic reforms.
- Among all his reforms, his successful control of the market was a remarkable achievement to which there is no parallel in medieval Indian history.
- Other than being a good administrator and military strategist, Alauddin Khilji also showed interest in architecture and literary activities, which led to the further development of the state.

KEYWORDS

Balance of power
Espionage
Land settlement
State endowments
Solvency
State exchequer
Kharaj
Khalisa land
Amils
Muqaddams
Khuts

REVIEW QUESTIONS

1. 'With Alauddin Khilji begins what may be called the imperial period of the Delhi Sultanate.' Justify this statement.
2. Examine the revenue policy of Alauddin Khilji, discussing its socio-economic significance in medieval India.
3. What were the measures adopted by Alauddin Khilji to check the menace of the Mongol invasions?
4. What was Alauddin Khilji's aim in implementing a policy of market control, and how did he achieve it?
5. Write a short note on the rise of the Khiljis to power.

CHAPTER 7

The Tughlaqs

Review and Discussion

- Ghiyasuddin Tughlaq
- Muhammad bin Tughlaq
- Firuz Shah Tughlaq

The Khiljis were supplanted by the Tughlaqs, who form the last significant dynasty of the Delhi Sultanate. Like the Khiljis, the origin of the Tughlaqs is also debated. It is generally believed that Ghazi Malik was the son of a slave of Balban and a Jat woman from the Punjab. He had served during Alauddin Khilji's reign as the Warden of the Western Marches and had also distinguished himself through his valuable services during the Mongol invasion. This aged and experienced warrior ascended the throne as Ghiyasuddin Tughluq at the request of the nobles, who at that point considered him capable enough to be able to restore order in a strife ridden kingdom. Ghiyasuddin reluctantly consented to shoulder the responsibility that was thrust upon him, initiating the rule of the Tughlaqs in 1320 CE.

GHIYASUDDIN TUGHLAQ (1320–25 CE)

Ghiyasuddin's reign was short but eventful. Initially he tried to return to the members of the old royal family of the Khiljis all that they had lost in the previous years by appointing them to high offices and suitably marrying off their unmarried daughters. He then set himself to justifying the confidence reposed in him by establishing a sound administration. The departments of police and justice were overhauled and reformed. The land revenue system was revamped in a manner beneficial to agriculturalists. The army was trained well and maintained in a high state of efficiency and discipline. Ghiyasuddin also made excellent postal arrangements by establishing a system of couriers consisting of both horsemen and foot runners. However, he was not generous towards the Hindus and like Alauddin Khilji, his dependence on the Hindus was merely need-based as far as the delegation of administrative tasks was concerned.

Having established order at home, he turned his attention towards Warangal, whose ruler had ceased to pay tribute. He defeated the powerful raja and annexed Warangal to the Tughlaq dominions, renaming it Sultanpur. He then laid a raid against Jajnagar and reconquered Bengal, which had been independent under its Muslim kings following the death of Balban. While returning from the Bengal campaign with a large booty, a ceremony was planned to felicitate Ghiyasuddin, for which a huge pavilion had been constructed on the banks of the Yamuna. While the royal party was busy celebrating, a wooden shelter erected especially for this purpose collapsed over Ghiyasuddin, killing him. Based on the accounts of Ibn Batuta, Ferishta and Badauni, some modern historians share the view that this mishap was not an accident but a pre-planned conspiracy led by his son, Juna Khan. On the other hand, other historians—especially Ziauddin Barani who lived in the courts of Muhammad bin Tughlaq and Firuz Shah Tughlaq—have tried to absolve Juna Khan of all responsibility of this murder. The matter, however, has remained inconclusive. After the death of Ghiyasuddin Tughlaq, Juna Khan ascended the throne as Muhammad bin Tughlaq.

Muhammad bin Tughlaq (1325–51 CE)

The reign of Muhammad bin Tughlaq marks the zenith of the Delhi Sultanate, after which began its decline. The period 1296–1335 CE was witness to a process of continuous centralization and expansion of territories within the Indian subcontinent. The sultan's authority was by and large complete, except for a few pockets where it could be challenged. After 1351 CE, however, it became difficult for Muhammad bin Tughlaq to maintain the consolidation drive. Gradually the territories acquired in southern India were lost and much of the conquests in northern India too were engulfed in rebellion. The proportions his domain had come to acquire made it grander and wider than that of his predecessors, and never would a medieval kingdom centered in Delhi ever rule over so broad a dominion till the time of the Mughal emperor, Aurangzeb. Interestingly, Aurungzeb's rule also marked the high point of the Mughals, after which the great empire began to gradually wane away.

After coming into power, Muhammad bin Tughlaq's first measure was to compile a register that would contain details about the lands and the revenue assessed on them. This was done with the intention of establishing a uniform system of taxation. To improve cultivation in the Doab, Muhammad bin Tughlaq set up a separate department called *diwan-i-amir-kohi,* which divided the Doab into development blocs headed by an official who would give loans to farmers and engage them in the cultivation of superior crops. During this time the taxes on the Doab were greatly enhanced. The scheme failed due to the dishonesty of the officers involved in the project and the eventual death of Muhammad bin Tughlaq himself. Combined with severe famine conditions and the inability to meet increased demand, ground realities drove most cultivators to abandon their lands in the region and resort to plunder. This was how one of the richest and most fertile regions of the subcontinent became the seat of war between the people and the sultan's troops.

Muhammad bin Tughlaq's grand schemes of conquest included two terribly disastrous expeditions to Khurasan and China during the earlier part of his reign. Barani and Ibn Batuta cite the Chinese expedition as being merely directed against a Himalayan chief. While embarking upon new areas of conquest, Muhammad bin Tughlaq faced serious problems, especially during his expansion into southern India. Giving up on the Khilji policy of maintaining Hindu tributary states in the South, Muhammad bin Tughlaq subdued two of the three remaining southern Hindu powers under the direct control of the Sultanate: Warangal and Dwarasamudra. While Warangal was annexed to the kingdom in 1327 CE, Dwarasamudra was destroyed. In 1326–27 CE, the Hindu kingdoms of Kampili and Madura were also added to the sultan's list of conquests. In the very second year of his reign, Muhammad bin Tughlaq was faced with a serious rebellion from Bahauddin, his cousin in the Deccan. Shortly afterwards the governor of Multan also revolted. But these rebellions were easily put down.

The unwieldy extension of his kingdom southwards, the lack of security on the highways,

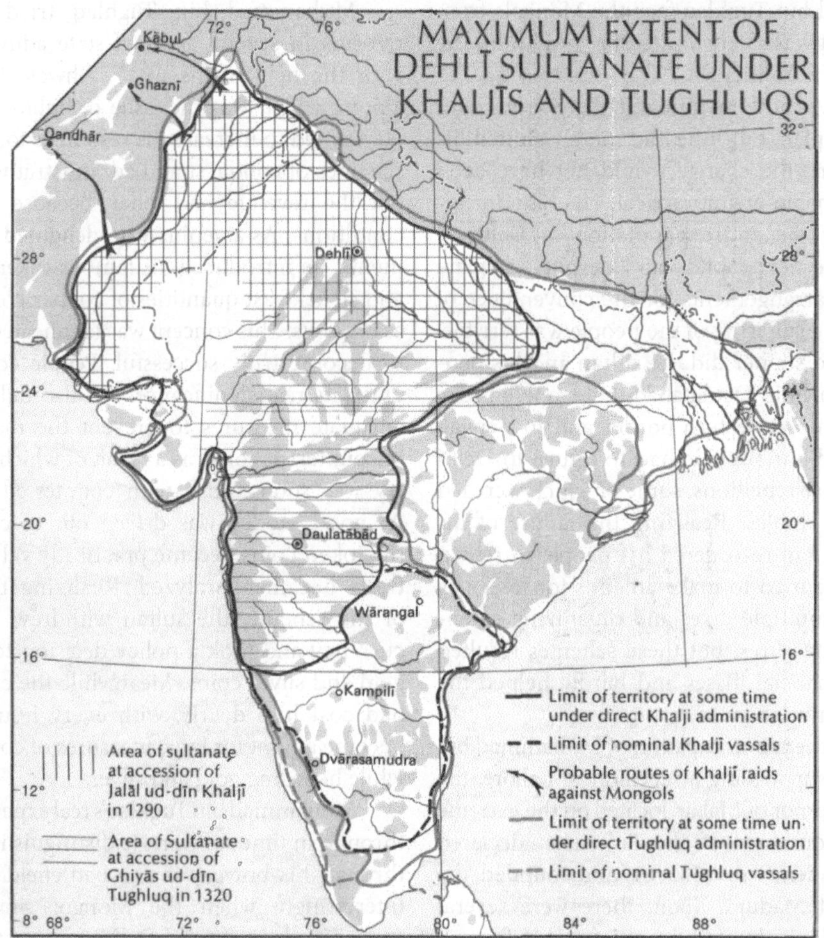

Map 7-1 *Maximum Extent of the Delhi Sultanate Under the Khiljis and the Tughlaqs*

the recurring Mongol menace, famine conditions in parts of the land, and the revolt of Bahauddin—all induced Muhammad bin Tughlaq to transfer his capital in 1327 CE to the more centrally located Devagiri, in the Deccan, which was renamed Daulatabad. Directly ruling over southern India did not necessarily signify complete control over the zone from Delhi.

The sultan had multiple motives for making Daulatabad his second capital. Firstly this move would give him a chance to establish control over the rich and fertile lands of Deccan and Gujarat, and as such provide him with access to the western and southern ports. During this time India carried on brisk overseas trade from its busy ports in Gujarat, the Coromandel Coast and Bengal. Large volumes of textiles and other trading goods (including glass and metal objects manufactured in these regions) were exported to the countries of the Middle East, Africa, and East and Southeast Asia. In return, imports came into India in the form of horses, precious metals and raw materials. The second reason for the transfer was that the location of the new capital helped

Muhammad bin Tughlaq face the Mongols from a venue that was safely located far away from the northwestern frontier.

There was nothing fundamentally wrong with the sultan's plan, but if he had merely shifted his official court, the change would not have been so unreasonable or impractical. His blunder lay in ordering the entire population of Delhi to move to the new capital, and despite adequate and liberal arrangements for the convenience of travelers, the suffering of the people was terrible. However, no sooner did the sultan and his people settle down in Daulatabad that trouble broke out on the northwestern border and in Bengal. Muhammad bin Tughlaq had to return to Delhi to crush these rebellions, some of which were led by his own nobles. Realizing the failure of his plan, the sultan re-ordered his people to return to Delhi. He tried to make amends for losses by abolishing multiple taxes and organizing extensive relief measures, but these schemes resulted in heavy financial losses and hardly helped the people, inciting them to revolt.

Seeing the pre-occupation of Muhammad bin Tughlaq in suppressing a rebellion in Lahore, the Muslim governor of Mabar, located on the extreme southern boundary of the Sultanate, declared his independence in 1335 CE and founded the Sultanate of Madura. Soon, there were several more rebellions by Hindu chiefs who formed new principalities, the most important of which was Vijayanagar. All through the next few years, while the sultan struggled to put down upheavals in almost every other province, he lost control of most of his southern Indian conquests. After successfully rebelling, Gulbarga (1339 CE), Warangal (1345–46 CE) and Daulatabad—which led to the founding of the Bahmani kingdom in 1347 CE—broke away from the Tughlaq domain. Having lost much, Muhammad bin Tughlaq then got involved in trying to repress another revolt in Gujarat towards the last few years of his reign. This did not leave him with any time to be able to recover Daulatabad till his end.

Muhammad bin Tughlaq tried to bring reforms in several areas of state administration with the help of his *wazir,* Khwaja Jahan, one among which was the issue of bullion currency. He wanted to increase his resources for his grand schemes of conquest and administrative reforms, but the revenue had fallen because of famine conditions. As a genius who delighted in experiments, he introduced his famous token currency and struck vast quantities of copper coins known as *dirhams*. This concept was far ahead of his time to become truly successful. People could never grasp its real significance. He also failed to take adequate measures to prevent the manufacture of counterfeit coins, as a result of which the country was soon awash with counterfeit currency. As good money was driven out of circulation, the token coins became practically valueless and trade became paralyzed. Realizing the failure of the scheme, the sultan withdrew all copper currency and took a policy decision to revert to gold and silver coins. Meanwhile the experiment had cost him dearly, with every house having become a mint for large measures of copper coins while hoarding gold and silver.

Muhammad bin Tughlaq's real expertise shone through in times of war. He distinguished himself through his bravery in the battlefield. However, interestingly when the Mongols invaded the Punjab and threatened Delhi, he sent them back with large offerings of gold and jewels rather than countering them with stiff resistance. This move cost him the respect that he had earned in the eyes of his people.

Muhammad bin Tughlaq tried to organize the services of the state along efficient lines. Unlike other Muslim rulers, he tried to check the power of the Muslim orthodoxy through his tolerant attitude towards Hindus and the appointment of some of them to high offices of state. Like Alauddin Khilji, Muhammad bin Tughlaq too had made attempts to keep a check and proper balance between the power of the nobility and the *ulema*. He also realized the necessity of a certain amount of mobility within the army and civil administration for non-Islamic groups to represent significant interests of the polity. Such a policy also enhanced the power of the sultan over the nobility, because it removed old nobles and provided grateful new ones.

Muhammad bin Tughlaq maintained several departments in the state of which the department of agriculture and industrial department are worthy of special note. He was especially interested in the administration of justice and meted out impartial rulings even against powerful people. Ibn Batuta records that among all the sultans, Muhammad bin Tughlaq was the most humble, and held justice and fair play in great esteem. He also imposed a ban on *sati,* condemning it as an unfair practice. He introduced many reforms to relieve the distress of the poor during his eventful reign.

Despite being a renowned figure of his time, Muhammad bin Tughlaq also displayed peculiar traits in his personality. While bringing in good reforms, he also conducted impractical exercises which made contemporary writers describe him as a freak of creation and a mixture of opposites. Being well versed in the humanities, he was a keen student of mathematics, astronomy, logic, Aristotelian philosophy and poetry. An eloquent speaker and a good debater, he was a good writer and delighted in making use of elaborate metaphors and similes. His writings were long regarded as models of style and composition, which made Barani comment that even scientists and philosophers would not have had the presumption to argue with him. His exquisite calligraphy and beautiful coinage bear witness to his artistic taste, and his love of Persian, Arabic and Sanskrit literature is proof of his catholic literary outlook. He was complete in all that high culture could offer an individual of his stature in that age, yet his whole life was spent in pursuing irrational and impractical visionary schemes.

Muhammad bin Tughlaq failed to hold his realm together, till gradually his Sultanate fell apart. The innovations of the sultan, famine conditions, heavy taxation, disloyalty of foreign *amirs* and the ruthlessness and severity of Muhammad bin Tughlaq in suppressing revolts embittered his people against him, resulting in large scale insurgencies. The sultan was usually victorious over his rebels, but he could not be everywhere at the same time; so while one rebel was crushed the other raised his head elsewhere. As a result, at the time of his death, he left behind a shattered kingdom and defiant tendencies among the people. As Badauni rightly observed, when Muhammad bin Tughlaq died in 1351 CE 'the king was freed from the people and they from the king'.

Close studies of the records left by Barani and Ibn Batuta, which are fairly honest in their opinion, reveal that Muhammad bin Tughlaq was guilty of much bloodshed and oppression despite his good intentions. He was a poor judge of human nature and failed to realize that his reforms, however optimistic and idealistic, would lead to disaster if pushed without popular approval. Hence, with the best of intentions, excellent ideas, exceptional ability, and a highly cultivated mind, he failed miserably as a king.

FIRUZ SHAH TUGHLAQ (1351–88 CE)

Muhammad bin Tughlaq did not leave behind any sons to succeed him and the nobles chose his cousin, Firuz Shah, as the next ruler. Firuz was the son of a Rajput princess of Dipalpur and had been brought up by his uncle, Ghiyasuddin Tughlaq. He had also been trained by Muhammad bin Tughlaq in the art of administration.

Gentle by nature, Firuz hated war and the few expeditions he undertook were not vigourously executed. Bengal remained independent despite Firuz twice attempting to conquer it, once during 1353–54 CE and then again in 1359 CE. Upon returning from Bengal, Firuz marched against Jajnagar in Orissa (1360 CE) where he destroyed the famous temple at Puri and forced the ruler to pay tribute. Firuz then led an army against

Nagarkot (1361 CE) and the old and venerated temple of Jwalamukhi was plundered and its ruler—who had assumed independence during the reign of Muhammad bin Tughlaq—forced to submit. The sultan also organized two expeditions against Thatta in Sind in 1362 CE and 1366–67 CE, but the region remained no more than a tribute paying state throughout his reign. Realizing that these wars did not benefit the kingdom in any way, Firuz showed no interest in recovering the southern provinces even when he was invited, in 1365 CE, by a Bahmani prince to intervene in the Deccan politics. These provinces had been allowed to become independent under Hasan Gangu, the founder of the Bahmani kingdom. In addition to this, Firuz also marched on Etawah (1377 CE) and Katehr (1380 CE).

The accession of Firuz Shah inaugurated a rule of benevolent policies; there was a marked improvement in the overall socio-cultural condition of the kingdom and its people. Being of a kind, generous and sympathetic disposition, Firuz was best suited for peaceful pursuits. He fulfilled the role of a patriarch and his efforts to address the problems of the people won him grateful appreciation. His administrative reforms too entitled him to a position of respect among the Muslim rulers of India. Ably assisted by his famous *wazir,* Khan-i-Jahan Maqbool, a converted *brahman,* the sultan strove towards improving the welfare and prosperity of his subjects. He inaugurated his reign by paying compensation to the people who had suffered under Muhammad bin Tughlaq's tyranny. Many of the taxes were abolished and the peasants were relieved from the intolerable oppression of the tax gatherers. Improved irrigation and reduction in land tax made cultivation profitable and more areas could be brought under crop growing. Firuz took care to improve the currency system, and he issued half and quarter *jitals,* which were used largely by the poor. Through all these measures, the old prosperity returned in a large measure to the Sultanate.

The only negative tendency in Firuz Shah's nature was his religious bigotry which made him intolerant towards Shias and Hindus. He penalized them, prohibited public worship of idols, and imposed the *jiziya* even on *brahmans* who had been exempted from it so far. There are reports of Hindu temples being destroyed and new mosques being constructed in their place. Firuz acted like a zealous missionary and offered perquisites to those who converted to Islam. This temperament may have been the outcome of his appeasing stance towards the *ulema* and the nobility, the two influential Muslim groups of the period. While Alauddin Khilji had made a clear demarcation between religion and religious leaders and the political policies of his kingdom, and Muhammad bin Tughlaq had not yielded to the unreasonable demands of some Sufis who were asking for state support, Firuz liberally rewarded Sufis and other religious leaders and took their opinion in matters of statecraft.

Firuz Shah had a passion for constructing magnificent buildings. Ferishta credits him with not more than 845 public works, new cities, buildings, palaces and mosques, besides the construction of schools, hospitals, public rest houses and other charitable institutions. One of the best cities founded by him was Firuzabad on the banks of the Yamuna. He relocated the two famous Ashokan pillars from Topra and Meerut and set them up in Firuzabad and near Delhi.

But the most useful and lasting of his public works was a double system of canals from the Yamuna and the Sutlej—one of which continues to service Delhi, irrigating nearly 150 miles along its course. These and other canals were meant for irrigation purposes and supplying water to newly built towns, like Hissar, Firuzah and Firuzabad. The sultan was also a great gardener and is said to have laid not less than 1,200 gardens in Delhi and adjoining areas. Besides beautification, these gardens proved to be a fruitful source of income for the state. Despite being uneducated himself, Firuz was a liberal patron of education. He created charities to aid poor Muslims, built colleges and mosques, and abolished taxes not recognized by the *Shariah.* He founded numerous schools and colleges for theological instruction and gave pensions and land grants to learned men. It was during his time that Barani and Shams-i-Siraj Afif composed their works; and when several Sanskrit texts were translated into Persian. He founded a free hospital in Delhi and created a separate fund for the comfort of foreign pilgrims, besides instituting an Employment Bureau that tried to provide work to the unemployed. The sultan even made provisions for the payment of dowries for Muslim girls. But the most important of his measures was the revision of the code of punishment by which many of the brutal forms of torture were abolished.

In organizing the military which was dependent on a feudal set-up, Firuz Shah Tughlaq put an end to a number of corrupt practices and brought in an efficient cavalry. The sultan impaired the general efficiency of the army by his excessive generosity in dealing with the soldiers and the revival of the land grant system in lieu of cash salaries that had been implemented by Alauddin Khilji. The employment of a large number of slaves imported from various parts of the country by the sultan for civil and military duties proved to be heavy burden on the state exchequer.

Though Firuz's policies gave the nobility much more autonomy, it also meant loss of authority for the sultan, especially over many of the new political circumstances that arose. Paying officers through land grants instead of cash, granting hereditary appointments, and extending the system of revenue farming were measures which reversed the earlier policies that had been followed by Firuz's predecessors. It tended to decrease his control and authority over his nobility and the state revenue system.

After the death of Firuz Shah Tughlaq in 1388 CE, the Sultanate collapsed almost immediately. He was followed in quick succession by six weak sultans whose reigns were disgraced by political murders, corruption and fights for the throne. Taking advantage of the situation, many provincial governors, who profited by the disorders at the capital, set up independent principalities.

SUMMARY

- Ghiyasuddin Tughlaq set the stage for the rule of the Tughlaq dynasty in 1320 CE by establishing a sound administration and conducting a few campaigns.
- Upon the accidental death of Ghiyasuddin Tughlaq, his son, Juna Khan, ascended the throne as Muhammad bin Tughlaq. His reign marks the climax of the Delhi Sultanate as well as the beginning of the end.
- In Muhammad bin Tughlaq's time, the proportions the Tughlaq dominions had come to acquire made it grander and wider than that of its predecessors; and never again would a kingdom based out of Delhi rule over so broad a dominion till the reign of the Mughal emperor, Aurangzeb.
- Muhammad bin Tughlaq's experiments with state administration, although well intentioned, caused undue misery to his people.
- The taxes on the Doab were greatly enhanced. Combined with severe famine conditions and the inability to meet increased demand, these measures drove most of the cultivators to abandon their lands and resort to plunder. Thus, one of the richest and most fertile regions became the seat of war between the people and royal troops.
- The transfer of capital from Delhi to Daulatabad would not have been fundamentally wrong, had merely the official court been shifted to the new city. But the entire population was relocated to Daulatabad; and despite adequate arrangements for the convenience of travelers, the suffering of people was terrible. In a few years the capital was shifted back to Delhi, causing further distress to many.
- As a genius who delighted in experiments, Muhammad bin Tughlaq introduced his famous token currency and struck vast quantities of

copper coins. He failed to take adequate measures to prevent manufacture of counterfeit coins and good money was driven out of circulation, which paralyzed trade.

- Quelling the Mongol invasions by offering them monetary compensations made Muhammad bin Tughlaq grossly unpopular with the people. Gradually the kingdom started to fall apart.
- Firuz Shah Tughlaq succeeded as the next sultan. Being a man with a gentle nature, the land saw fewer wars; and his expeditions were not vigourously executed.
- Firuz Shah inaugurated a rule of benevolent policies. He fulfilled the role of a patriarch and his efforts to address the problems of the people won him grateful appreciation.
- However, sometimes Firuz Shah acted like a zealous missionary and offered perquisites to those who converted to Islam. This may have been the outcome of his appeasing policy towards the *ulema* and the nobility.
- After the death of Firuz Shah in 1388 CE, the kingdom collapsed almost immediately.

KEYWORDS

Diwan-i-amir-kohi Dirhams Jitals Jiziya
Token currency

REVIEW QUESTIONS

1. Write a short note on how Ghiyasuddin Tughlaq established the Tughlaq dynasty in Delhi.
2. Analyze the experimental policies of Muhammad bin Tughlaq. Why did they not go well with his people?
3. What were the measures taken by Muhammad bin Tughlaq to organize the services of the state?
4. Describe the political exploits of Firuz Shah Tughlaq.
5. Examine the benevolent policies of Firuz Shah Tughlaq that led to an improvement in the overall conditions of the kingdom.

CHAPTER **8**

Decline of the Delhi Sultanate

Review and Discussion

- Timur's Invasion
- The Sayyids and Lodis
- Rise of Regional States

The fifteenth and early sixteenth centuries form the crucial period between the death of the last Tughlaq king in 1413 CE and the emergence of a new Turkish power in the subcontinent—the Mughals. There were two main processes at work in Muslim India at this point in time: the disintegration of the Delhi Sultanate and the rise of independent regional Muslim kingdoms. The centralizing authority of the Delhi Sultanate ceased to be a paramount factor in Indian political life, and its power and position were taken over by other regional kingdoms, which were more powerful than Delhi with better organized state machineries. Many of these were also centres of great artistic achievement. Though the Delhi Sultanate had fallen from its former glory during this period, it continued to be viewed as a symbol of prestige and a source of wealth for which many factions struggled and fought.

After the death of Firuz Shah Tughlaq in 1388 CE, the decline of the Delhi Sultanate became imminent. Several centrifugal tendencies raised their heads, leading to major succession disputes and palace intrigues between the sons and grandsons of Firuz who were in turn supported by various pressure groups at the court. These puppet sultans lacked statesmanship and personal prowess to run the kingdom, which was already heavily dependant for its existence on the military strength of its different provinces. This made the kingdom more vulnerable to disintegration. The unwieldy size of the Sultanate, the communication difficulties between vast regions and the ill-conceived policies of Muhammad bin Tughlaq had induced many provincial governors to rise in revolt and assert their independence. Firuz Shah Tughlaq had also failed to check the disintegration by not adopting a vigorous policy towards such mutinous behaviour; and his excessive leniency only undermined the authority of the crown further. The revival of the land grant system in lieu of salaries also led to serious social and economic discrepancies and the wide-scale employment of slaves in the kingdom only added to the general confusion. These slaves, who had converted to Islam without any personal conviction, could not be expected to remain attached to a Muslim state through strong ties of loyalty. All these factors together helped to accelerate the Sultanate's process of decline.

In the struggle that ensued for the throne, the authority of the Delhi Sultanate diminished rapidly, providing opportunities to Muslim nobles and Hindu chiefs to increase their autonomy. By 1390 CE, the governor of Gujarat proclaimed his independence, and between 1391–94 CE, the

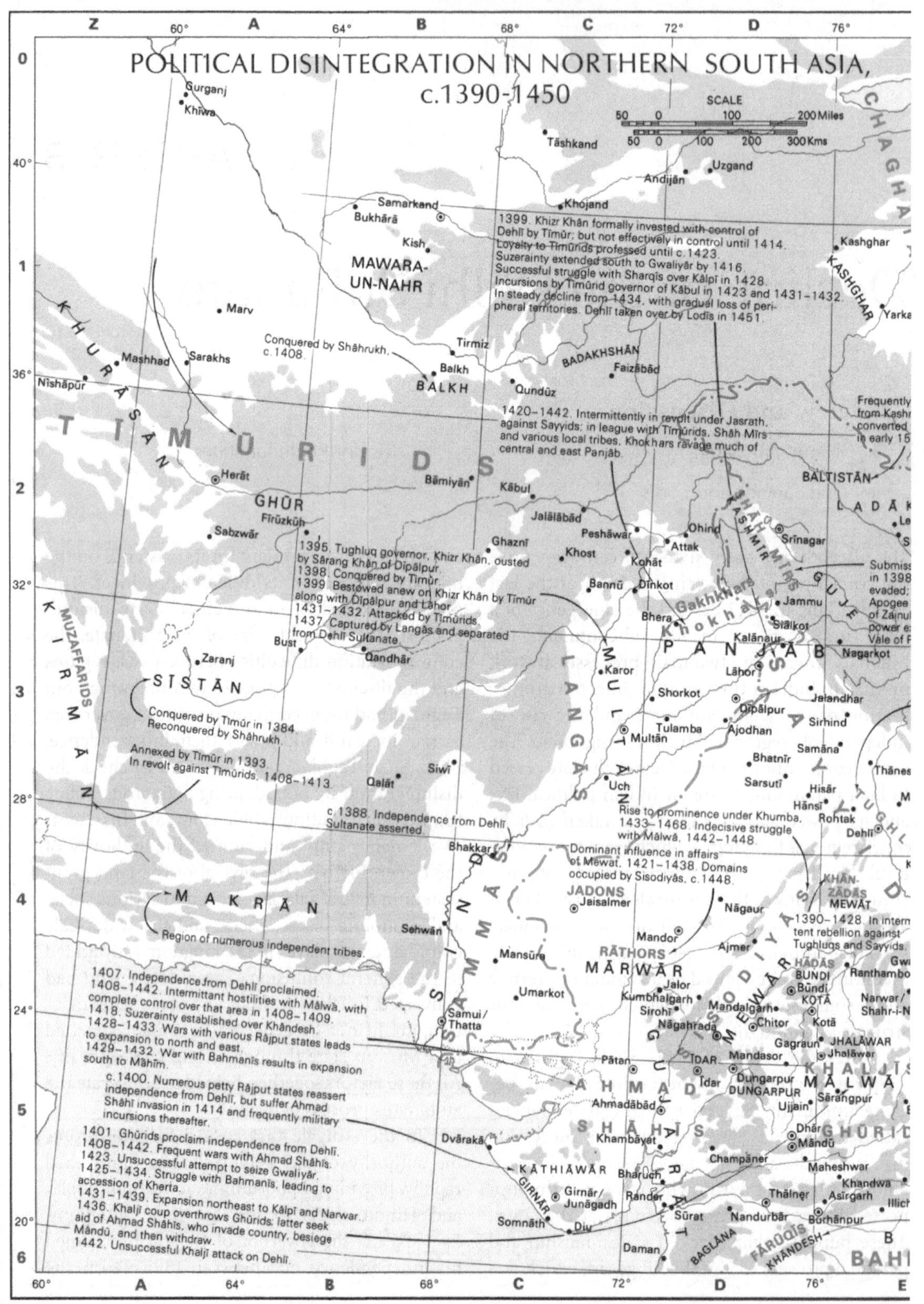

Map 8-1 *Political Disintegration in South Asia and the Major States of Northern South Asia, 1390–1450* CE

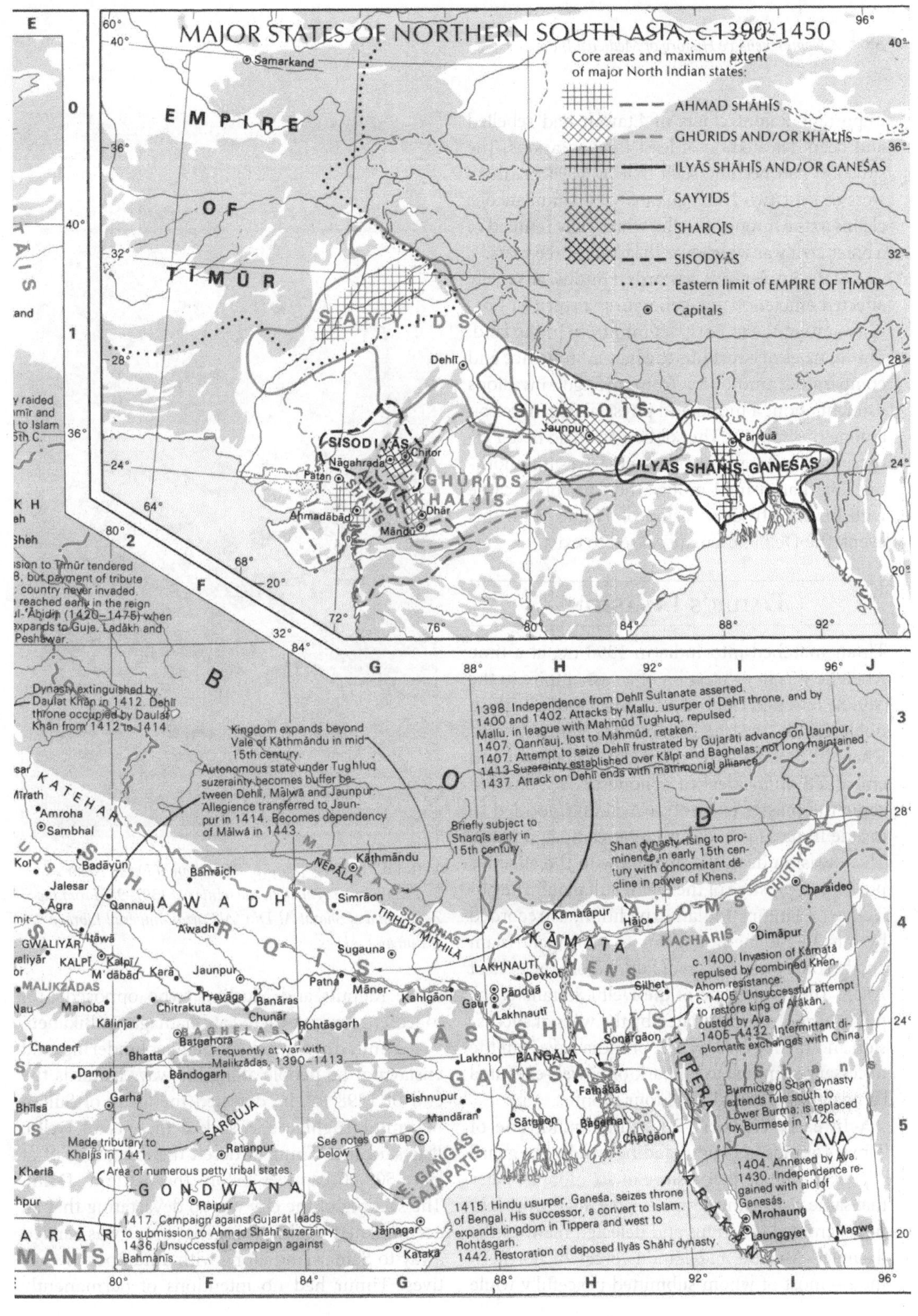

MAJOR STATES OF NORTHERN SOUTH ASIA, c.1390–1450
Core areas and maximum extent of major North Indian states:
AHMAD SHĀHĪS
GHŪRIDS AND/OR KHALJĪS
ILYĀS SHĀHĪS AND/OR GANEŚAS
SAYYIDS
SHARQĪS
SISODYĀS
Eastern limit of EMPIRE OF TĪMŪR
Capitals
EMPIRE OF TĪMŪR
Samarkand
SAYYIDS
Dehlī
SHARQĪS
Jaunpur
Pānduā
ILYĀS SHĀHĪS-GANEŚAS
SISODIYĀS
Chitor
Nāgahrada
Paṭan
AHMAD SHĀHĪS
GHŪRIDS KHALJĪS
Ahmadābād
Dhār
Māndu
Dynasty extinguished by Daulat Khān in 1412. Dehlī throne occupied by Daulat Khān from 1412 to 1414.
Kingdom expands beyond Vale of Kāthmāndu in mid-15th century.
Autonomous state under Tughluq suzerainty becomes buffer between Dehlī, Mālwa and Jaunpur. Allegience transferred to Jaunpur in 1414. Becomes dependency of Mālwā in 1443.
1398. Independence from Dehlī Sultanate asserted.
1400 and 1402. Attacks by Mallu, usurper of Dehlī throne, and by Mallu, in league with Mahmūd Tughluq, repulsed.
1407. Qannauj, lost to Mahmūd, retaken.
1407. Attempt to seize Dehlī frustrated by Gujarātī advance on Jaunpur.
1413 Suzerainty established over Kālpī and Baghelas; not long maintained.
1437. Attack on Dehlī ends with matrimonial alliance.
Briefly subject to Sharqīs early in 15th century.
Shan dynasty rising to prominence in early 15th century with concomitant decline in power of Khens.
KATEHAR
Mīrath
Amroha
Sambhal
Badāyūn
Kol
Jalesar
Āgra
Qannauj
AWADH
Bahrāich
Kāthmāndu
NEPĀLA
MALLAS
Simrāon
SUGAONAS
TIRHUT/MITHILA
Awadh
Itāwā
GWALIYĀR
Gwaliyār
KALPĪ
Kālpī
Mādābād
Karā
Jaunpur
Sugauna
Patna
Māner
Kahlgāon
LAKHNAUTĪ
Devkot
Pānduā
Gaur
Lakhnautī
Kāmatāpur
KĀMATĀ
KHENS
Hājo
AHOMS
CHUTIYĀS
Charaideo
KACHĀRIS
Dimāpur
Silhet
MALIKZĀDAS
Mahoba
Prayāga
Banāras
Chitrakuta
Chunār
Kālinjar
Rohtāsgarh
BAGHELAS
Batgahora
Chanderī
Bhatta
Frequently at war with Malikzādas, 1390–1413.
Damoh
Bāndogarh
ILYĀS SHĀHĪS
GANEŚAS
Lakhnor
BANGALA
Sonārgāon
TIPPERA
Fathābād
Bishnupur
Mandāran
Sātgāon
Bāgerhāt
Chātgāon
Bhīlsā
Garha
SARGUJA
Made tributary to Khaljīs in 1441.
Ratanpur
See notes on map below
GANGAS GAJAPATIS
Kherlā
Area of numerous petty tribal states.
GONDWĀNA
Raipur
1417. Campaign against Gujarāt leads to submission to Ahmad Shāhī suzerainty.
1436. Unsuccessful campaign against Bahmanīs.
Jājnagar
Kataka
1415. Hindu usurper, Ganeśa, seizes throne of Bengal. His successor, a convert to Islam, expands kingdom in Tippera and west to Rohtāsgarh.
1442. Restoration of deposed Ilyās Shāhī dynasty.
c.1400. Invasion of Kāmatā repulsed by combined Khen-Ahom resistance.
c.1405. Unsuccessful attempt to restore king of Arākān, ousted by Ava.
1405–1432. Intermittant diplomatic exchanges with China.
Shan
Burmicized Shan dynasty extends rule south to Lower Burma; is replaced by Burmese in 1426.
AVA
1404. Annexed by Ava.
1430. Independence regained with aid of Ganesás.
ARĀKĀN
Mrohaung
Launggyet
Magwe
BAHMANĪS

important Rajput chiefs of Etawah had rebelled and been defeated on at least four occasions. The situation had become such that by 1394 CE, there were at least two Delhi sultans with simultaneous claims to the throne of Delhi, which only resulted in a bitter civil war which was to last for three years.

State intolerance towards Hindus adversely affected efficiency too, generating a spirit of hostility among the majority community in the land. The luxuries of court life, the harem influence and comparative immunity from Mongol invasions brought about a moral and physical degeneration among the nobility. The soldiers were no better either; they had transformed themselves into nothing less than armed mobs. The final blow came with the disastrous invasion of Timur. With this event, the Delhi Sultanate ceased to exist.

Timur's Invasion

Timur marched into India in 1398 CE, at a time when he was in possession of a vast empire in the Middle East and Central Asia. Born into a Turkish noble family that had blood ties with Chengiz Khan, he ascended the throne of Samarqand and embarked on a career of conquests. He soon became the master of Central Asia and decided to invade India as part of his larger campaign plans. This invasion dealt the final blow to the effective power and prestige of the Delhi Sultanate. The objective of Timur's Indian expedition, as recorded by him in his memoirs, was to propagate Islam and become a champion of faith before the eyes of Allah. The feeble state of the Delhi Sultanate, the political confusion initiated by the wars of succession and the reputed wealth of India gave him the necessary stimulus to embark on a well-executed campaign that lasted all of four months.

In early 1398 CE, Pir Muhammad, one of Timur's grandsons, commanding an advance guard captured Multan after a siege of six months. Later that same year, Timur himself led a huge army into India, crossed the Indus and defeated many of the disunited Muslim and Hindu forces of northern India—most of whom submitted peacefully while those Rajputs and Muslims, who opposed him together, were massacred at Bhatnagar in Bikaner.

THE DEFEAT *by Timur of the Sultan of Delhi, Nasir Al-Din Mahmud Tughlaq, in the winter of 1397–98. From the Zafarnama of Sharaf Al-Din 'Ali Yazdi. Imperial Library of Emperor Akbar.*

Timur then reached Delhi, plundering and enslaving the people along his way. Towards the end of 1398 CE, he defeated the army of Sultan Mahmud Tughlaq and sacked the city of Delhi. It is said that Timur ordered the execution of at least 50,000 captives before the battle at Delhi. The sacking of the city was so devastating that all accumulated wealth over generations was carried away to Samarqand along with a number of captives. Timur had no intentions of permanently settling in India. He marched to Meerut, stormed the city and annihilated its inhabitants, before proceeding towards Haridwar and leaving India through the Himalayan foothills and the Punjab, plundering and burning villages on his way.

Timur's whirlwind march into India left behind him widespread anarchy, famine and pestilence. Of the Delhi Sultanate, hardly a trace remained and the city of Delhi could not regain its former glory till the days of the Mughal emperors. The massacre of thousands of men caused untold misery, while plunder of property brought about scarcity of gold and silver. The relatively pure silver coins that were used as standard currency of trade in almost the entire northern part of India were replaced by an alloy called billon tanga. The only exception was of Bengal, where imported silver from Myanmar (Burma) and China, still

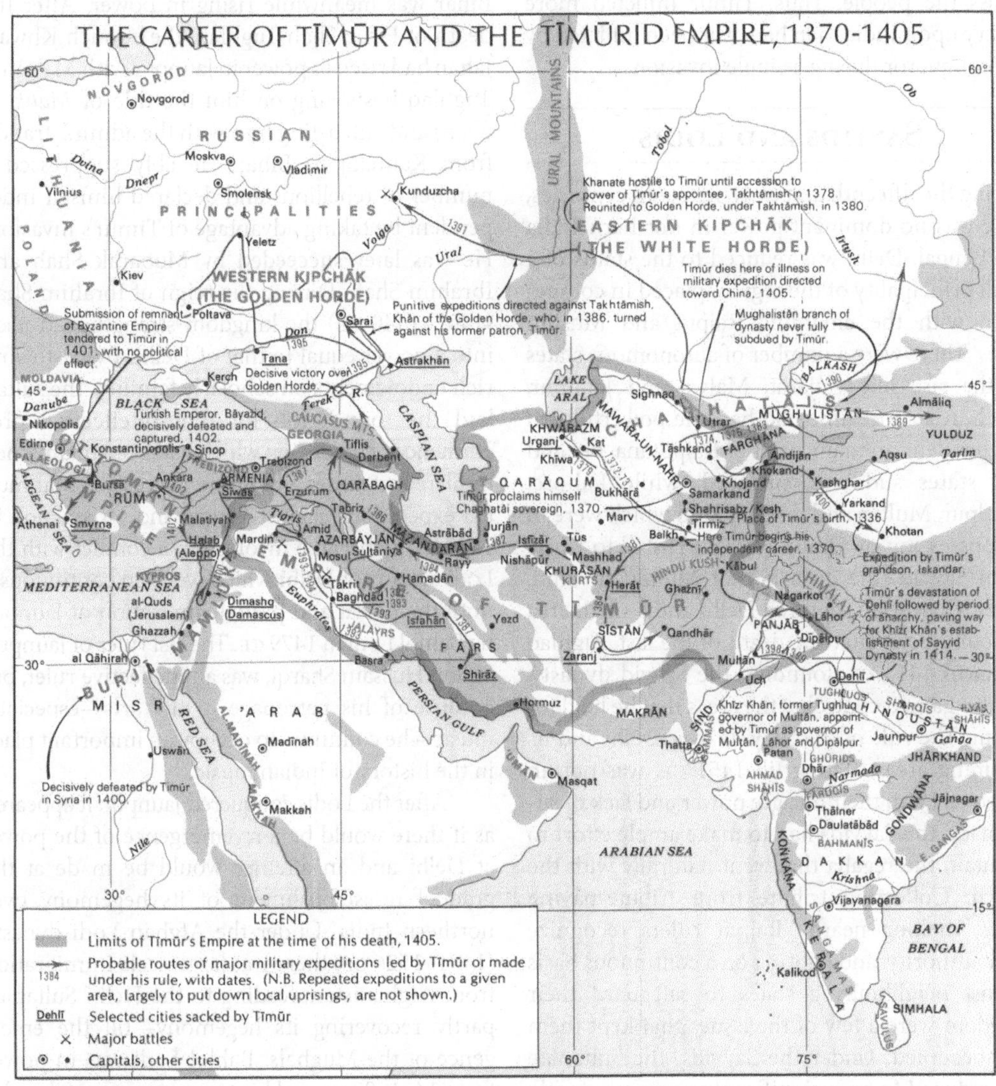

Map 8-2 *The Career of Timur and the Timurid Empire, 1370–1405* CE

continued to reach. The silver and gold coins struck in the period of the last Tughlaqs and their successors in Delhi in the fifteenth and early sixteenth centuries hardly remained. This general economic distress was further accentuated by a rude disturbance in the social fabric. The absence of any political authority capable of enforcing order, encouraged unscrupulous military adventurers to organize themselves into cliques and harass the people. Thus, Timur inflicted more misery upon India than had ever been inflicted by any conqueror during a single invasion.

Sayyids and Lodis

During the fifteenth and early sixteenth centuries, there was no dominant power in northern India and Bengal. Delhi was reduced to the status of a small principality of the region, placed in competition with the emerging Rajput and Muslim states. There were a number of autonomous states on the rise like Gujarat, Malwa and Jaunpur, which in a short time had become powerful and independent. In many parts of Rajputana, old and new states suddenly surfaced, while Lahore, Dipalpur, Multan and parts of Sind which were in the possession of Timur, were entrusted to Khizr Khan Sayyid, the governor of Multan in Sind. Khizr Khan soon captured Delhi and a small area surrounding it after the death of the last Tughlaq sultan in 1413 CE, founding the Sayyid dynasty. He also gained control of the areas that he held for Timur. The rule of the Sayyids over Delhi and its adjoining areas, lasting till 1451 CE, was not an easy one. With their meagre power and lack of supremacy, the Sayyids had to make ample effort to maintain the regalia that went naturally with the crown. Collecting tribute from tribute-paying states, making nearby Rajput rulers recognize their authority, and fighting on a continuous basis against neighbouring states to safeguard their kingdom were a few of the issues that kept them well-occupied. Under the Sayyids, the Sultanate was reduced to an insignificant power constantly competing with other petty Muslim and Hindu principalities. The last Sayyid ruler, Alauddin Alam Shah (1445–51 CE), quietly gave Delhi away to his vassal, the Afghan, Bahlol Lodi, and retired to Badaun district where he spent the rest of his life until his death in 1478 CE. Before gaining Delhi, Bahlol Lodi had cleverly expanded his territories towards the Punjab making his dominions larger than those of the Sayyid sultans.

The neighbouring kingdom of Jaunpur in Bihar was meanwhile rising in power. After the death of Firuz Shah Tughlaq, the eunuch Khwaja Jahan had risen to power in Jaunpur with Mahmud Tughlaq bestowing on him the title of *Malik us Sharq* and entrusting him with the administration from Kannauj to Bihar. He ably suppressed a number of rebellions and declared himself independent by taking advantage of Timur's invasion. He was later succeeded by Mubarak Shah and Ibrahim Shah. During the reign of Ibrahim Shah (1402–1440 CE) the kingdom strengthened itself into a power equal to that of Delhi. By bestowing rich endowments on scholarly families, the sultan laid the foundation for that intellectual preeminence of the region which had been maintained until recent times. Ibrahim's successor, Mahmud led expeditions against Bengal and Orissa, and in 1452 CE he became involved in a conflict with the Lodi sultans of Delhi which went on continuously until the defeat and partial annexation of Jaunpur by Bahlol Lodi in 1479 CE. The last ruler of Jaunpur, Sultan Hussain Sharqi, was an ineffective ruler, but because of his patronage to the arts—especially music—he continues to occupy an important place in the history of Indian music.

After the Lodis conquered Jaunpur, it appeared as if there would be a re-emergence of the power at Delhi and an attempt would be made at the gradual re-establishment of its hegemony over northern India. Under the Afghan Lodi dynasty (1451–1526 CE) there was large-scale immigration from Afghanistan, leading to the Delhi Sultanate partly recovering its hegemony—till the emergence of the Mughals. Bahlol Lodi was in power from 1451–89 CE and his two successors, Sikandar Lodi and Ibrahim Lodi followed suit by reigning from 1489–1517 CE and 1517–26 CE, respectively. The challenges before them were daunting. All of them were active expansionists and continued to expand their span of control over the surrounding territories. Bahlol subdued the Ganga-Yamuna Doab, Etawah, Chandwar and Rewari, while Sikandar turned his attention towards Jaunpur. After subduing Jaunpur in 1493 CE, Sikandar also led a campaign into Bihar, and founded the city of Agra in 1504 CE as a base for controlling Malwa and Rajasthan. When there was a severe earthquake in Agra in 1505 CE which shattered buildings and buried thousands, Sikandar constructed a grand fort on the ruins of the earthquake. Before his death in 1517 CE, he also built the *Moth ki Masjid* (Mosque of Lentil) in Delhi. Legend has it that Sikandar picked up a single lentil and gave it to his minister to be sown, which resulted in bumper crops year after year, thus financing the mosque.

When Sikandar Lodi died, although the Afghans could assert a certain amount of control over the Punjab and most of the Gangetic plains till Bihar, yet the issue of Lodi hegemony in northern India was far from settled decisively. They continued to face massive obstruction from Rana Sanga of Mewar, who not only checked their advance into central India but also resisted a Lodi attempt to invade Mewar and threatened to move towards Bayana and Agra instead. It was Rana Sanga's luck that at this time Eastern Malwa, under a Khilji sultan, and Chanderi which was under the Rajput leader, Medini Rai, came under his authority. Rana Sanga is known to have defeated the former and taken him prisoner to Chittor. These moves made Rana Sanga emerge as another formidable contender for supremacy in northern India. In the meantime, Babur, a progeny of Timur, was about to enter India.

At this given situation, Ibrahim Lodi chose to become more autocratic than his predecessor, Sikandar, as he found it difficult to control his nobility, which had grown in enormous proportions following the immigration into India of a considerable number of Afghans. They were inclined to see the Lodi sultans as powerful claimants to the throne in northern India. Ibrahim soon faced an Afghan rebellion in the east under the leadership of his brother, Jalal Khan; and while Ibrahim suppressed this and other Afghan revolts in the region, the foundation of the last blow was being laid in the West. Daulat Khan Lodi, the governor of the Punjab, and Alam Khan Lodi, Ibrahim's uncle, invited Babur, the ruler of Kabul, to help them oust the sultan. This invitation turned out to be a good opportunity for Babur who at that time was probably thinking of annexing the Punjab alone. Taking advantage of the situation, he invaded northern India. In 1524 CE Babur led an expedition to Lahore and defeated Ibrahim Lodi's army. After defeating his Afghan allies, Babur appointed his own officials in the Punjab, before finally defeating and killing Ibrahim Lodi at the famous Battle of Panipat, near Delhi, in 1526 CE.

Rise of Regional States

The disintegration of the Delhi Sultanate marks the struggle of various regions in carving out regional dynasties and establishing separate identities for themselves. It was a time when effective regional rule was either restored or developed, as in Rajasthan, Orissa, Bengal, Gujarat, Malwa, Jaunpur, and various the large and small states of North India and the Deccan. Politically, these regional states had enough vigour and strength to place checks and balances on the growth of each other's power.

The absence of any unified rule has made historians describe the period as one of political anarchy and confusion, in which people suffered because of a lack of a strong power at the helm of affairs. But this period also saw the evolution of the Muslims as a distinct socio-political group, together with the continuance of cultivation and trade as before. Agriculture and handicraft production carried on in Gujarat and Bengal along with a brisk overseas trade. Gujarati traders operated in the markets of the Middle East and Africa, while the Chittagong port in Bengal was a flourishing trading centre

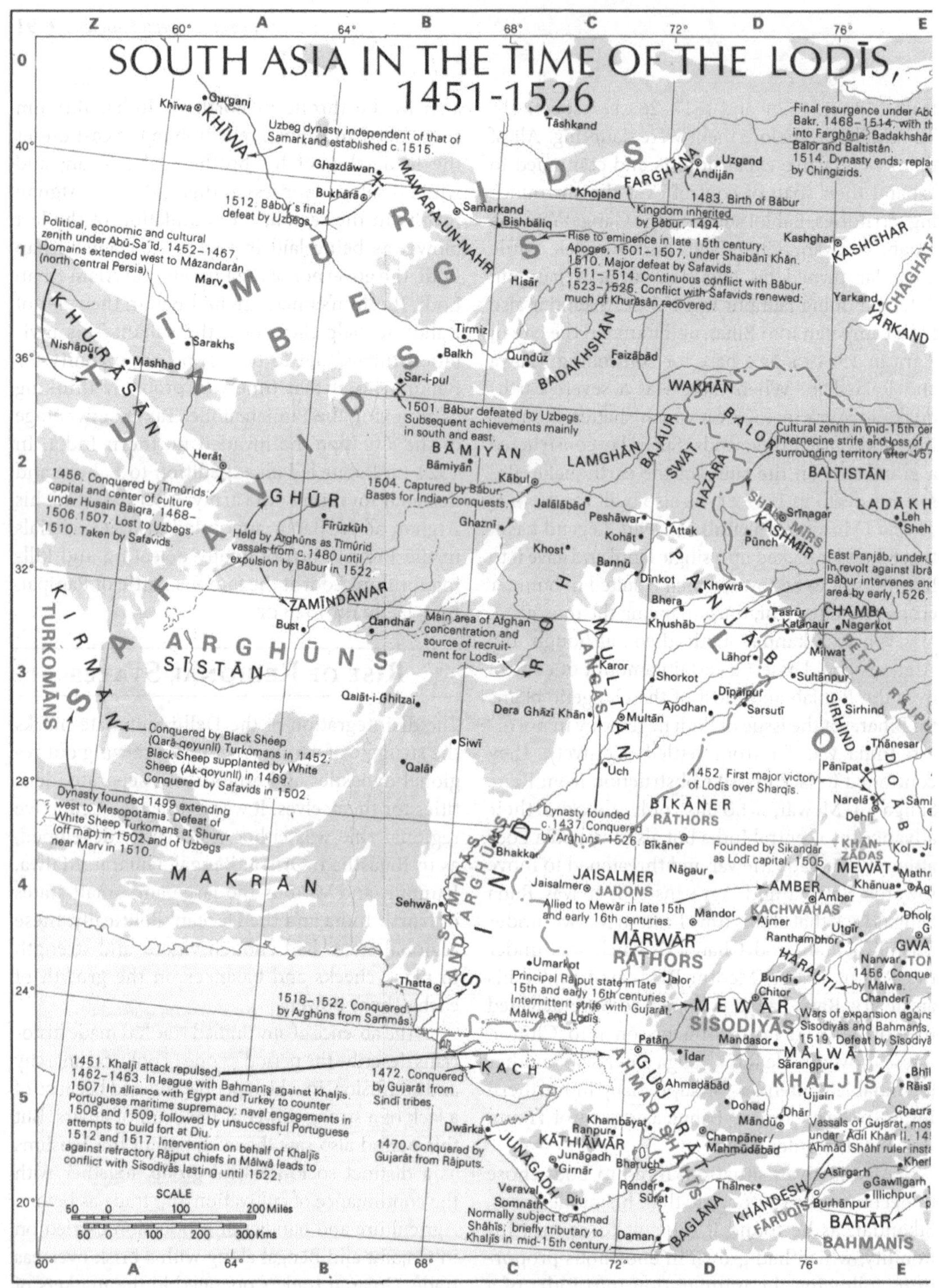

Map 8-3 *South Asia in the time of the Lodis and the Major Powers of Northern South Asia, 1451–1526* CE

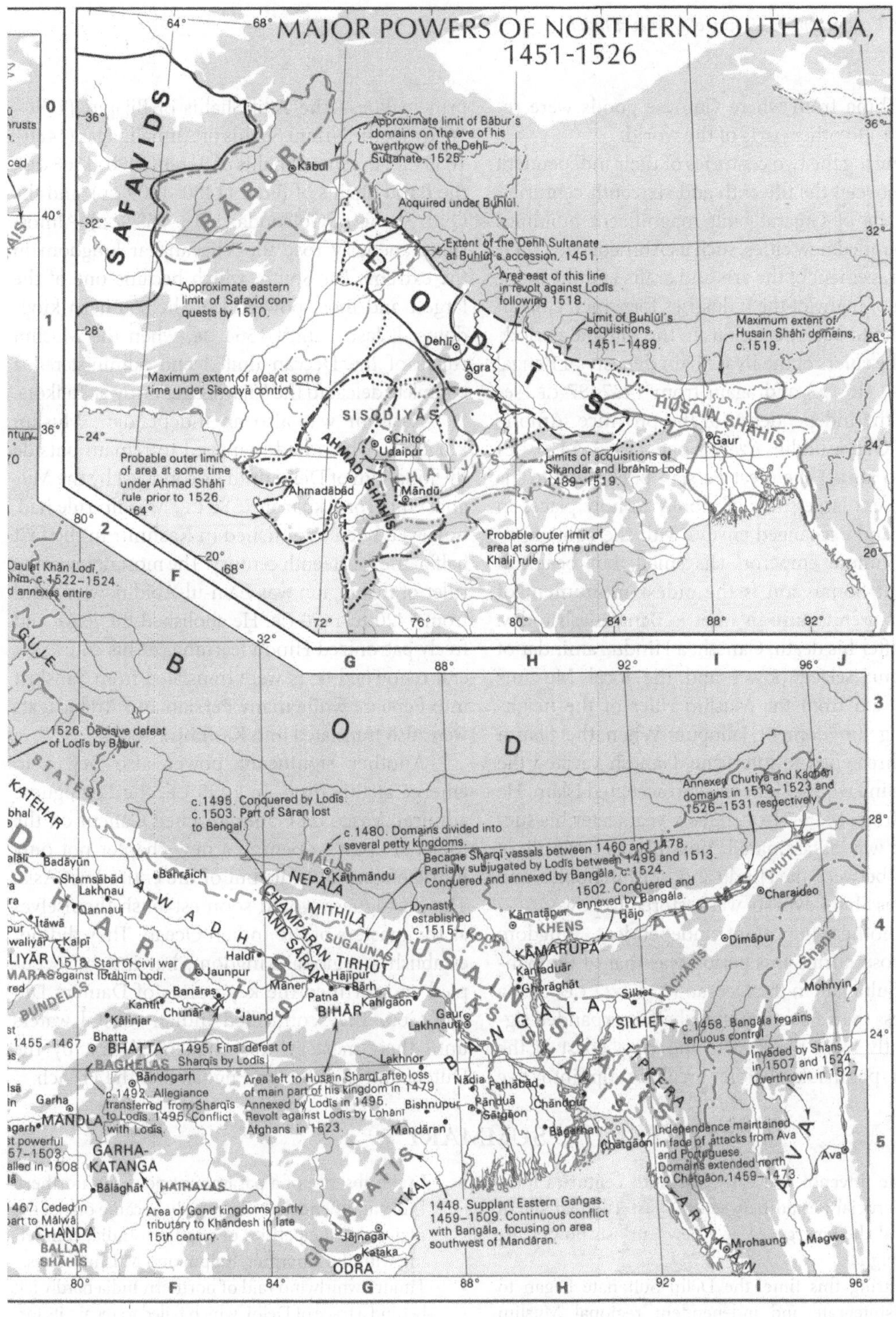

MAJOR POWERS OF NORTHERN SOUTH ASIA, 1451-1526

with China from where Chinese goods were re-exported to other parts of the world.

During the two centuries of their independent rule between the fifteenth and sixteenth centuries, the kings of Gujarat built magnificent buildings and founded new cities, such as Ahmedabad. Their encouragement of the arts and crafts laid the foundation of many of the industries for which Gujarat was later to become famous in the Mughal period.

The rulers of the Ilyas Shahi dynasty of Bengal (1338–1415 CE) and again from 1437–87 CE, secured the independence of the province. Among them, Ghiyasuddin Azam Shah (1393–1410 CE) tried to attract the great Persian poet Hafiz to his court, sent large sums of money to holy places in Hijaz, and exchanged envoys with the contemporary Chinese emperor. His small, but beautiful tomb at Sonargaon is the oldest monument of Islamic architecture in what is Bangladesh today. Soon after his death, Ganesh, a Hindu zamindar of Dinajpur, seized power and the local Muslims sought aid from the Muslim ruler of the neighbouring kingdom of Jaunpur. When the Sharqi king threatened to intervene, Ganesh vacated the throne in favour of his son, who accepted Islam. He ruled from 1415–31 CE, but six years later his successor was assassinated, possibly as a result of rivalry between the Hindu and Muslim nobles, and the Ilyas Shahi dynasty was restored to power.

Another important independent kingdom that arose during this period was that of the Bahmani Sultanate in the Deccan (1347–27 CE). For a little less than a century and a half, it expanded significantly from the East to the West coast of the Indian peninsula, before breaking up into five principalities—the Adil Shahis of Bijapur (1490–1686 CE), the Nizam Shahis of Ahmadnagar (1480–1633 CE), the Imad Shahis of Berar (1490–1568 CE), the Barid Shahis of Bidar (1480–1609 CE), and the Qutb Shahis of Golconda (1518–1687 CE). Almost simultaneously rose the Vijayanagar kingdom in the extreme Far South, which became one of the largest and most powerful of the southern kingdoms. It lasted until 1564 CE, when the Muslim rulers of the Deccan united and administered a complete defeat to the Vijayanagar army at Talikota.

Kashmir was also an independent Muslim kingdom, which had managed to remain outside the kingdom of Delhi until its conquest by the Mughal emperor Akbar in 1586 CE. Muslim rule had, however, been established in Kashmir in the first half of the fourteenth century. The most noteworthy ruler of this region was Zain-ul-Abidin, who ruled from 1420 to 1470 CE. He abolished the *jiziya* and freely patronized Hindu learning. At his court several renowned texts were translated from Sanskrit into Persian, while many Persian and Arabic texts were also translated into Kashmiri.

Another significant power also began to emerge at this time. In 1498 CE, the Portuguese admiral, Vasco da Gama, reached Calicut on the Malabar coast—opening a new chapter not only in the history of India but of the entire East Asia. The Portuguese would soon establish themselves as the masters of the Indian Ocean. They did not establish a regional kingdom, but instead occupied and fortified the key points of Daman, Diu and Goa. They controlled Indian coastal waters until their mastery was challenged first by the Dutch, and then by the English and the French.

SUMMARY

- The fifteenth and early sixteenth centuries form a crucial period between the last Tughlaq sultan and the emergence of a new Turkish power, the Mughals.
- During this time, the Delhi Sultanate began to disintegrate and independent regional Muslim kingdoms began to emerge instead.
- In the absence of a paramount power in northern India and Bengal, Delhi merely became one of the regional principalities of northern India, competing with the emerging Rajput and Muslim states.
- Timur's whirlwind raid of northern India hardly left behind a trace of Delhi, which failed to regain its former glory until the days of the Mughal emperors.

- The sack of Delhi was so devastating that all accumulated wealth of generations was carried away to Samarqand along with a number of captives.
- Though the rule of the Sayyids and Lodis was short-lived, yet it appeared as if there would be a re-emergence of the old power of Delhi, and that an attempt would be made at the gradual re-establishment of its hegemony over northern India.
- In the post Delhi Sultanate period, effective regional rule was either restored or developed in Rajasthan, Orissa, Bengal, Gujarat, Malwa, Jaunpur, and in various small and large states of Northern India and the Deccan.
- Many of these kingdoms developed as centres of great artistic achievement, some of which were better organized and more powerful than Delhi.

KEYWORDS

Anarchy
War of succession
Massacre
Billon tanga
Clique
Hegemony

REVIEW QUESTIONS

1. Examine the causes that led to the decline of the Delhi Sultanate.
2. Give an account of Timur's invasion of India by especially reflecting upon its impact.
3. Write a short note on Jaunpur as an emergent kingdom.
4. How did the Sayyids and Lodis attempt a gradual re-establishment of hegemony over northern India?
5. Describe how effective regional rule was either restored or developed in various parts of North India in the fifteenth–sixteenth centuries.

CHAPTER 9

State and Society Under the Delhi Sultans

Review and Discussion

- The Sultan
- Central Administration
- The Army
- The Judiciary
- Provincial Administration
- Local Administration
- Economic Life
- Social and Religious Conditions
- Literature, Art and Architecture

As discerned from the earlier chapters, the Delhi Sultanate was the first Muslim state to be established in India. It finds significant mention in India's medieval history not only on account of the five important dynasties that consecutively came to power, but also because of the resultant political and socio-economic changes under the rule of the Delhi sultans. When the Muslims first came to India, they did not bring with them any perfected machinery of administration and were required to evolve a practical system based on their previous experiments, their own knowledge and the new system's applicability to the Indian scenario. Thus, many elements of the Rajput political system, with or without changes, were incorporated into the Turkish administration in India. This metamorphosed system of administration continued in India for centuries to come. This new administrative structure of the Delhi Sultanate had a powerful impact on small states and principalities that were formed after its disintegration as well as on the Mughal administration that would come into existence in the sixteenth century.

Though the Delhi sultans ruled independently in India, they perceived themselves to be a part of the Islamic world that operated through the Caliphate of Baghdad. The recognition of the Turkish rulers by the Caliphate was necessary as it strengthened the position of the former. It rendered them support and gave them recognition at par with other Muslim states spread across the world. Most of the sultans included the name of the caliph in their *khutba* or Friday sermon, on the coins that they issued, and in the titles they assumed, which were all symptomatic of their humility to the caliph. There are historical records on three Delhi sultans who were known to have approached the caliph for letters of investiture known as *mansur*. The first among them being Iltutmish, who in 1229 CE obtained this sanction from the Abbasid

Caliphate; the sanction recognized him as the lieutenant of the faithful. Next, Sultan Muhammad bin Tughlaq tried to appease the *ulema* by securing an investiture from the Abbasid Caliph in Egypt, legitimizing his rule in India. On ascending the throne, Firuz Shah Tughlaq also obtained a letter of this nature from the caliph, not once but twice. A noteworthy point is that even after the Caliphate of Baghdad came to an end in 1258 CE, the sultans of Delhi continued to acknowledge its presence as the sanctioning authority of their power in India. While doing so, the sultans were clever enough to reaffirm their own status and individuality too. Balban, for instance, used to say that after the Prophet the most important office was that of the sovereign; and hence, called himself the Shadow of God on Earth. Although Balban had retained the name of the caliph in the *khutba* and on the coins, he made no other mention of the caliph anywhere else. Later, Muhammad bin Tughlaq assumed Balban's style during the early years of his reign. In fact he was the first Delhi sultan to try to remove the name of the Caliph from his coins, but when he was faced with political threats, he restored the practice; and like other sultans before him, he too obtained a letter of investiture from the descendant of the Abbasid Caliph. The only sultan who refused to acknowledge the caliph's presence was Qutbuddin Mubarak Khilji. By and large, however, none of the Delhi sultans had enough power to totally disregard the caliph's existence, whether virtually or other wise.

The Sultan

It was the omnipotent position of the sultan that really mattered in the absence of any regular law of succession. The insecurity that accompanied the throne resulted in frequent civil wars, military revolutions and large-scale massacres of royal families. In some cases, the sultan nominated his heir, or else the claimants to the throne were left to fight a war of succession. The rulers could continue to be in power as long as they were able to garner the support of the nobility and the military. As a result, the sultan's dependence on the feudal elite gradually increased. Since the sultans were expected to enforce the law of the *Shariah,* they were also obliged to take the opinion of the *ulema.* Alauddin Khilji and Muhammad bin Tughlaq tried not to let the *ulema* rise to a position superior to that of the sultan's, and in their attempt to do so they shirked the dictates of the *ulema,* introducing secular discretion in their state administration. Although most of the sultans wielded absolute power, the theoretical restrictions on the sultan's power imposed by the *Shariah,* the constant threat of revolts and revolutions, and the presence of an advisory council—all helped to limit the sultans' despotic powers in many ways.

Although the Delhi sultan as the head of the state owed only nominal allegiance to the Abbasid Caliphs, yet for all practical purposes he was an independent monarch. He was in charge of the state's administration and of the army. His primary responsibilities included protection of the state, settlement of disputes, enforcement of laws, collection of taxes, welfare of the people and the defence of Islam. Therefore, with help from all sectors—the nobility, the military and the *ulema*—the sultan carried on the state's administration. Being in charge of maintaining law and justice, the sultan appointed judges to dispense justice and also acted as a court of appeal to hear cases against the decisions taken by the judges. A direct appeal could be made to the sultan against any of his officials. Balban and Muhammad bin Tughlaq stand out as good examples of sultans who adopted a strict judiciary system.

The Delhi sultans for the most part acted in a responsible manner towards the running of the state. They took the opinion of an advisory council on all important matters dealing with the administration of the state. The advisory council was not a legally constituted body and the number of advisers varied according to the importance of the matters discussed and also according to the personal preferences of the monarch. But the advice given by this body was taken seriously by the sultans and often had a moderating influence on the decisions taken on matters of state policy.

Central Administration

For efficiently governing the state, the sultan was assisted by a team of ministers who were individually responsible for various departments, such as revenue, public works, war, local and provincial governments, etc. The number, power and functions of the ministers varied from time to time. The *wazir* or prime minister was the most important officer, next only to the sultan. By the fourteenth century, the *wazir,* whose earlier duties were confined only to the military, had now become an expert on revenue affairs too, and was made responsible for the entire fiscal administration of the realm and all matters relating to income and expenditure. He was entrusted with powers to appoint revenue officials, organize and collect taxes, and largely control the state's expenditure. The department headed by him was known as the *diwan-i-wizarat.* A separate auditor general was appointed for supervising expenditure and there was also an accountant general for inspecting the income. Both officers assisted the *wazir* in discharging his duties. The *mustauf-i-mumalik* was the auditor general whose duties involved auditing of accounts. The *musharraf-i-mumalik* was equivalent to the present day accountant general whose office used to maintain the accounts of the state.

The *sadr-us-sadar* was another important minister who was also known as *qazi-i-mumalik.* The *qazi-i-mumalik's* role was to deal with religious affairs and provide scholarships to academics and men of piety. The *diwan-i-risalat* headed by the chief *sadr* took care of religious matters while the *diwan-i-insha* under the *munshi-i-mumalik* dealt with the entire state's postal correspondence. Groups of horsemen or runners were used to carry the correspondence across the kingdom. Sultans planted spies, called *barids,* in different parts of the kingdom to obtain information on people, events and occurrences. The royal household was another important department which looked after the personal comforts of the sultan and the requirements of the harem. Firuz Shah Tughlaq had set up a separate department of slaves, many of whom were employed in royal workshops. The officer in charge of this was known as the *wakil-i-dar,* who other than being responsible for maintaining court decorum, also oversaw the seating arrangement of nobles at court.

There was also a minister appointed as a link between the provincial and central governments, and another who controlled the markets. There were a number of other departments like the public works department, the agricultural department, the audit department and the department of slaves—each under the charge of a minister.

The Army

The army was a critically important unit of the state placed under an officer known as the *ariz-i-mumalik,* whose responsibility was to provide horses and rations to the soldiers. His office maintained descriptive rolls of soldiers, assigned different tasks to each, and was also responsible for the transfers of military personnel. The sultan was the commander-in-chief of the army, but the *ariz-i-mumalik* was its captain for all practical reasons, and exercised a lot of influence on the state. Understanding the strategic importance of a well maintained army, Balban had set up a separate military department; and Alauddin Khilji had systematized it during his rule. Under the latter a regular muster of armed forces was maintained. The *dagh* or branding system of horses, *chera* or maintaining descriptive rolls of soldiers and the payment of salaries to soldiers in cash were some of the measures adopted by him.

Cavalries, forming important constituents of armies, was not new to India. Many Hindu kingdoms in the twelfth century had always maintained large standing armies that included a cavalry unit. But the difference now was that the armies of the Turks had far superior horses and horsemen. The cavalry was in fact the strength of the Sultanate armies, and a lot was spent on keeping it in good shape by procuring premium war horses that were extremely expensive. In the mid-fourteenth century an ordinary horse from Central Asia would cost about 100 silver *tangas,* while a good one would cost about five times more. Arabian or Persian racehorses cost a lot more, usually in the range of 1,000 to 4,000 silver *tangas.* Iron stirrups and heavy armour, for both horses and horsemen, also became common during this period. War amour had a significant impact on methods of warfare as well as on military organization. The First and Second Battles of Tarain, between Prithviraj Chauhan and Muhammad of Ghur, were witness to an extensive deployment of cavalrymen armed with bows and spears.

Turkish warfare tactics were decisive because of proper investment in horses and soldiers. It was only during the reign of the Tughlaqs that there was a setback in procuring the best of horses. This was because Bengal and the southern provinces had become autonomous by then, thus cutting off the supply of gold and silver to Delhi. This affected the imperial government's capacity to import horses and soldiers, in turn severely affecting the Sultanate army's cavalry unit. Hypothetically, one could assume that Muhammad bin Tughlaq's proposed expeditions to Khurasan and the Himalayas were perhaps meant to find new sources of horses and precious metals; while Firuz Shah Tughlaq's withdrawal of cash payments to the soldiers was to ensure an end to the military crisis and to build an army from among the huge group of slaves gathered from across the Sultanate. These slaves were, however, no match for the mounted archers who were imported especially from the north-western provinces.

The Judiciary

The Sultanate had an effective system of judicial administration. The sultan usually addressed an audience himself to hear complaints against officials of the state at least twice a week. From the time of Balban, court culture and ceremonial pomp was on an upward swing. A grand court was maintained and *darbars* held on a number of occasions. During these *darbars,* every one had free access to the sultan and had the right to appeal to him to intervene in certain judicial matters. The sultan would be advised on legal matters by the *qazi-i-mumalik* or the chief qazi, who was the head of the judicial department with junior *qazis* appointed to assist him. Decisions were taken according to the law of the *Shariah* for cases involving the Muslims. Cases involving non-Muslim subjects were decided according to their own particular religious laws by *panchayats* in the villages. The rulers also framed regulations related to criminal law.

Provincial Administration

The administration followed by the Delhi sultans was essentially of a military nature. The kingdoms of the various dynasties were categorized into a number of divisions called *iqtas,* each under an *iqtadar, muqti* or *wali.* Therefore, *iqtas* were territorial units allotted to nobles, performing civil and military duties, in lieu of their salary. The main functions performed by the *iqtadars* included collection of land revenue, which was payable to the central treasury, and the maintenance of law and order. Out of the total land revenue collected, a fixed share was given to the state, while the rest went towards the expenditure of governing the *iqtas* and the personal expenses of the *iqtadars.* The *iqtadars* were not the owners of the land assigned to them. They were granted the *iqtas* on a temporary basis, remaining responsible for them as long as they enjoyed the confidence of the sultan. In principle, the *iqtadars* could be transferred within the kingdom. This also proved to be helpful for peasants, especially those living under exploitative conditions of feudal elites, whose authority became restricted by the sultan's undisputed power. Strict measures often had to be adopted by sultans to check the injustices of the *iqtadars*, since the Delhi Sultanate was more like a conglomeration of nearly-independent principalities, *jagirs* and provinces, each ruled by a hereditary chief or *zamindar*, with their subjects looking more to their immediate governors who had absolute power in the provinces than to the sovereign who was far away. Hence, the assigning of land grants in some way threatened the integrity of the Sultanate itself, making some powerful governors aim directly for the throne of Delhi. Jalaluddin Khilji, Ghazi Malik and Bahlol Lodi, for example, had all served as provincial governors before becoming the sultan.

Local Administration

The Sultanate was divided into provinces and tribute paying states. The sultan never interfered in the matters of the latter as long as they were loyal to the central authority and paid their tributes on time. The provinces were again divided into *shiqs* and *parganas*. While the *shiq* was under the control of the *shiqdar*, the *parganas* were again further sub divided into a number of villages that were headed by *amils*. The village headman was known as the *muqqaddam* and the landowners as *khuts*. The village accountant or *patwari* assisted the officials in the discharge of their functions at the village level. The villages enjoyed a more-or-less autonomous status, with village republics managing their own affairs. The sultan did not usually interfere with the workings of local institutions.

Economic Life

The early Muslim rulers were more interested in conquest and plunder rather than in the material prosperity of the land and the people they had conquered. Balban was the first sultan to introduce features that were conducive to the economic growth of the Sultanate. In the annals of the history of the Delhi Sultanate, Alauddin Khilji stands out as a daring political economist who organized the revenue system and kept down the prices of commodities through his famous market regulation policies. Though the market control mechanism affected agriculturalists adversely by fixing the prices of all commodities including grain, the state as a whole benefited from the move. But there was no continuity in the enforcement of Alauddin Khilji's market regulations after his death. Muhammad bin Tughlaq was another monarch, whose administrative experiments put the people into a lot of inconvenience. There was a recovery during Firuz Shah's reign, with the general condition of the Sultanate improving over previous rules. While evolving new administrative systems, although the Delhi sultans were influenced by Islamic traditions inherited from the Ghaznavids, it was for the most part the result of building and adapting structures in accordance with local needs and practices.

The agrarian system of the times was no different either. According to Ibn Batuta, the soil was fertile and paddy was grown thrice a year. Sesame, sugarcane, pepper, ginger, indigo and cotton were other crops that constituted raw materials for many village industries, such as oil pressing, making of jaggery, weaving, etc. The state depended on agricultural produce as an important constituent of revenue earning. Three methods of land revenue assessment were usually in practice: sharing, assessment and measurement. In the first method, a simple crop division was achieved; the second entailed an assessment of the quantity of the state's demand on the value of probable crop yield on the land; and the third method involved a calculation of demand on the basis of actual measurement of land. Whatever the method adopted, the state's share was generally fixed at one third of the total produce. In fertile areas such as the Doab, Alauddin Khilji and Muhammad bin

Tughlaq imposed an enhanced tax amounting to almost half of the produce as land revenue. Other levies paid by peasants included house tax, grazing tax, tax on ponds, tax on sale of articles and professional tax.

Taxes and other forms of dues were also collected from the people in the form of cash or kind. The hard-working peasants managed a bare subsistence with difficulty. Recurring wars and famines in different regions of the Sultanate added to their difficulties. It is, however, important to note that the sultans tried to minimize the sufferings of the peasantry by following a liberal and enlightened famine policy. Still, the life of the peasantry could not rise beyond the shackles of mere existence. In comparison to the peasantry, the village officials, such as the headmen and small landlords or *chaudhries* and *khuts* enjoyed a better standard of life. The Hindu *rais* who were the autonomous rajas of small principalities continued to hold on to their previous estates and were also well-placed like their Muslim counterparts. They were given land grants which were either non-taxable or lands on which revenue was payable at modest rates. Their lives were luxurious, replete with all comforts. They enjoyed many benefits, like riding on expensive Arabian and Iraqi horses, dressing up in good clothes and indulging in numerous leisure activities.

The sultans, in general, liberally encouraged trade and industry. Silk weaving constituted an important industry and profitable items of sale included cotton, pepper, ginger, wines and indigo. From the accounts of foreign travellers it is clear that there was brisk trade, both internal and foreign, but towards the close of the fourteenth century there was an economic depression, a direct result of Timur's invasion. That was a time when centrifugal tendencies were threatening to disintegrate the Sultanate.

Under the general influence of the economic and technological developments in other parts of the world, Delhi in the thirteenth century had grown to be one of the largest cities of the Muslim world. A number of other cities had emerged as major urban centres during this period—Multan, Lahore, Anhilwara, Kara, Kambath, Sonargaon and Lakhnauti, to name a few. An impetus in textile and horse trade further sustained the economies of these towns. Bengal and Gujarat had especially developed as production centres for both coarse cloth and fine fabrics. While Kambath was reputed for textiles, and gold and silver work, Sonargaon was famous for raw silk and muslin.

Since cavalry had become the basis of the political and military system, a large number of horses were imported from the early thirteenth century onwards. The flourishing urban economy saw an equivalent increase in craft production and commerce. With the introduction of the wooden cotton-gin, the spinning wheel, the treadle loom and sericulture, the textile industry made unusual progress. As far as architecture and construction was concerned, cementing lime and vaulted roofing changed the face of urban settlements forever. The production of paper gave rise to increased record keeping in government offices, and to the widespread use of bills of exchange called *hundis*. Fortunately, the economic stability of the period was not interrupted by the repeated Mongol invasions on some cities in north-western India.

The major communities involved in trade during this period were Marwaris and Gujaratis of Jain origin who had acquired a monopoly over coastal trade, as well as on trade between ports and the northern hinterland. Muslim Bohra merchants, Multanis and Khurasanis, however, controlled long-distance overland trade. Like the small landlords in the rural countryside, wealthy merchants and skilled craftsmen too lived a comfortable life. Middlemen or brokers known as *dallals* suddenly gained prominence with increased urbanization and commercial expansion. They took part in transactions for which expert knowledge was required, such as the sale of horses, slaves and cattle. Alauddin Khilji, for instance, extended loans to the Multanis for bringing goods from other parts of India into Delhi.

Communication links improved during the period of the Delhi sultans. Major roads connecting cities were maintained in good condition. Apart from the royal road from Peshawar to Sonargaon, Muhammad bin Tughlaq also built a highway connecting Delhi to Daulatabad.

With a fast growing and lucrative economy, there was a stability of precious metals like gold and silver. This in turn helped in putting together an impressive coinage system, both in terms of quality and volume. For about a hundred years from 1250–1350 CE, there was immunity from the Mongol hoards, which made the unification of the Central Asian steppes possible, opening up a new and safe trade route from India to China and the Black Sea. North Indian merchants benefitted a great deal from this development. There also arose a string of trading stations along the Indian Ocean that contributed towards enriching the Sultanate. However, it was the plunder and tribute that came in from Gujarat, the Deccan, eastern and central India and Rajasthan, along with the inflow of taxation from the Indo-Gangetic plains, which contributed to a sound economy and facilitated the process of centralization of Delhi.

Towards the close of the Delhi Sultanate era, there emerged an important and interesting development along the countryside. This region began to see the emergence of the maximum number of Hindu autonomous rajas, as a reaction to Alauddin Khilji's stringent measures. Alauddin Khilji's land reforms and his strict policy of taxation had hampered the power of the former ruling chiefs, who paid tribute only under military pressure. It also meant heavy loss of revenue for the small landlords and village headmen who were tortured if dues were not paid. Ghiyasuddin Tughlaq brought in some changes in Alauddin Khilji's system by exempting the village headmen from paying agricultural tax, but he too like his predecessor insisted that the headmen were not to levy anymore taxes other than the existing ones on the peasantry. Muhammad bin Tughlaq's tough stance on taxation roused rebellious feelings among rural chiefs and peasants, but, interestingly, he was also the first Indian ruler who gave *takavi* or advance loans to the peasantry for restoring the fertility of their lands after a famine. He also planned out methods for improving the cropping patterns and cultivation. Firuz Shah Tughlaq for his part created the biggest network of canals known in pre-modern India, pardoned loans on the peasantry taken by them in earlier times and imposed a new taxation policy which gave a larger share of surplus to the intermediaries in comparison to the earlier one. The Tughlaqs thus handled the rural classes with care and diplomacy.

But after the demise of Firuz Shah Tughlaq, the former rural elite resurfaced as new groups among the Rajput caste who were spread over a very large part of northern India. They tried to reassert their earlier power and prestige, at least at the local level, by including small groups such as the Chauhans and the Gahadawalas as sub-castes and clans. It was during this period that the term *zamindar* began to denote superior rights over land and its produce for the first time. Much later the term came to represent the local landed gentry. This new caste structure that emerged changed the dynamics of village society by bringing a certain amount of inter-dependence between the village elite and the peasantry.

Social and Religious Conditions

Many of the traditions from the later Hindu period were continued by the Delhi sultans who seemed more interested in establishing dominance over different regions rather than exercising a total autonomy over the existing rulers of the small states in India. This was one of the reasons why there were many tribute paying states in existence and why several Hindu chiefs continued to hold petty principalities. It was only powerful sultans like Alauddin Khilji and Muhammad bin Tughlaq who succeeded in expanding the dominions of the Delhi Sultanate till the southern zone.

Medieval Indian society was a mix of different races, castes and creeds; and a heterogeneous population was the hallmark of the Delhi Sultanate. For practical and administrative reasons, the sultan had under his control people from various backgrounds—Turkish, Afghan, Khilji and Hindu. Muslim society was also divided into ethnic and racial groups, with Muslim officials generally being entrusted with military duties. Officials and local governors of Hindu origin were involved in the organizational apparatus of the state, and were delegated specific duties related to financial administration and local governance which required knowledge and understanding at the grass roots level.

With Muslim rule gaining strength in northern India, the number of Muslims in the demographic profile of the land gradually increased too. Forced conversions, immigrations from abroad and official patronage were factors that increased the Muslim mass base in India. Receiving a good amount of patronage from the sultans, the Muslims were fast evolving into a conspicuous, upwardly mobile and culturally prominent group that was able to secure special privileges and lead a life of luxury and ease. The group began to redefine the subcontinent's politics in a way little imagined earlier, clearly occupying centre-stage. The prominence and pleasure-filled life of the new elite group could not remain insulated from negative tendencies for long. Vices and moral weaknesses set in and sultans like Balban had to adopt strict measures to put down the evils of debauchery, drinking and gambling. Class distinctions arose despite the emphasis on the Muslim ideal of universal brotherhood. This was also a time when many Hindus converted to Islam to save themselves from oppressive taxes. These new converts still clung on to their social ideas and customs, forming a separate class by themselves.

The non-Islamic group, or *zimmis* as they were called, living in the Sultanate were opposed to the basic principles of the Muslim state. Religious persecution, prohibition of public worship and destruction of temples was often vigorously enforced by the early Muslim rulers. But such cruelties were neither systematic nor regular. Imposition of heavy taxes and the closure of their avenues of work also added to their misery. But Hindu talent could not be dwarfed; and this multicultural feature peculiar to medieval India remained undisturbed. The contribution of philosophers like Ramananda, Chaitanya Mahaprabhu, Sri Ramanuja and a host of others helped in promoting better understanding in a society where people of all beliefs co-existed.

The sultan and his important nobles lived a high standard of life. Their lifestyle was compared to that of the ruling classes of the Islamic world of West and Central Asia. The sultans built lofty palaces, gave expensive gifts to the nobility and others on occasions such as the sultan's birthday, *Nauroz* (the Persian New Year) and coronation ceremonies. The royal workshops (known as *karkhanas*) catered to the needs of the elite by producing a full range of rare commodities. The harems, where the queens, consorts, concubines and a large number of women resided, were maintained on a regular basis at a huge cost to the state exchequer. The nobility imitated the lifestyle of the sultan. A display of cultural extravagance was a sign of higher social and political status for the sultan, and likewise the goal of any courtier was to move into closer proximity to the sultan with ostentatious displays of wealth and status. To be appointed to the staff of the chamber of the sultan was a sign of great privilege and assured higher status. Like the imperial court, aristocratic households became not only political centres but also artistic, intellectual and cultural centres for the state. An aristocrat's power was directly reflected in the magnificence of his household. The practices of the imperial court, together with the aristocratic households it sanctioned, contributed to the making of a culture that was to become the order of the day.

Other than the ruling elite, the demographic profile of medieval India included many theologians, a large number of lesser nobles and clerks who ran the government offices, shopkeepers, artisans, beggars and many more on the margins of society. The people who were part of the administration were educated since their nature of work required them to be literate. The *ulema* were the Muslim counterparts of the *brahmans* among Hindus, and used to impart religious education. Domestic servants comprised another large group of the population in urban centres.

Slavery was an established institution in several parts of the world, including India. For the Arabs and Turks slavery formed an integral part of the political system. Prisoners of war were normally taken by the victorious armies as slaves. In India, like in West Asia, slave markets for men and women were prevalent for Turkish, Caucasian, Greek and Indian slaves at high prices. Young slaves were also imported from Samarqand, Bukhara and Tirmiz. Skilled slaves had a higher market value over unskilled ones. The institution of slavery provided the basis for well-trained and loyal martial slaves (the *mamluks*) to the sultans. The best examples of this segment were the Delhi sultans themselves, who had risen to the highest social position. One of the main aims of this form of slavery was to groom experts in warfare and government. Contrary to popular belief, slave status was considered honourable in medieval India. It was in fact the principal avenue for social mobility and the acquisition of wealth for talented individuals whose origins lay outside the ambit of the ruling elite. A slave was often considered better than a son, since the former was tried and tested on his efficiency and loyalty to his master. However, slaves with high qualifications would often defy authority, resulting in slaves or former slaves sometimes controlling their masters. Sultans, therefore, not only keenly kept track of the slave market, but also appointed slave merchants as their agents.

Owing to the high degree of social mobility that came with their status, a slave lived in an atmosphere of keen competition and if he did not meet expectations he could simply be brushed out of existence. He had to be ever vigilant, hard working and talented enough to catch the eye of his master. It was hardly surprising that some of the slaves proved to be equals of their masters. But the system was not without defects. It gave rise to a feeling of instability and a spirit of inhuman, cut-throat competition. Under such conditions of uncertainty, intrigues and struggles for succession and survival, it was impossible for the sultans to develop sustained progressive and far sighted policies.

Under the impact of the Muslim rule, a number of old social and legal customs underwent change. The influence of the *brahmans* increased, owing to the decrease in the prestige of the *kshatriyas* as the ruling class. The rigidity of the caste system was also modified and the lower classes made notable material progress and improved their status. The old social structure continued in the regions of Bihar, Bengal and southern India, which produced a large volume of digests and commentaries on Hindu law. While *brahmans* occupied an exalted social status, the *shudras* and lower classes began to face restrictions on their mobility. There were no changes as far as customs, manners and ceremonies were concerned. The position of women too remained similar to the earlier period. Early marriages, wifely duties and unquestioned devotion to the husband continued. Though incidents of *sati* were recorded, property rights for women improved under the Hindu law, which now gave a widow a share in her husband's property.

The *purdah* system became a widespread practice as it now became associated with elite culture.

Seclusion of women became more common with the coming of the Muslims to India. Intermarriages were generally not accepted among Turks, Persians, Afghans and Indian Muslims; and there was less social interaction between the Hindu and Muslim elite classes. Social mixing among the lower tiers of society was as prevalent as before, and it is this very feature that contributed to the strengthening of the land's social fabric despite the existence of inequalities.

Religious toleration towards the non-Muslims forms one of the significant aspects of the Delhi Sultanate. In the early phases of Muslim rule in India, many temples and cities were sacked, Hindu temples were converted into mosques, and Hindus subjects of Muslim regimes were not treated at par with their fellow Muslim brethren. Hindus were often subjected to persecution, higher taxation and forced conversions. Islamic conversion was generally resorted to in cases of prisoners of war and in cases of criminals in lieu of harsh punishment. Interestingly, a few Muslims converted to Hinduism under the Bengal Bhakti reformer, Chaitanya Mahaprabhu's influence. Conversions were mainly determined by personal, political and regional factors.

In the subcontinent, *jiziya* had its beginnings in the Delhi Sultanate. Though it was a tax imposed on non-Muslims for living in a Muslim state, it is often argued that these measures were inevitable to control a heterogeneous population that wanted to retain its identity. It must also be stated that the conflicts and sufferings of the common people were not due to religious factors alone, and most of them had a political background too. The expansion of the Muslim regime over northern India led to the rise of a number of small independent or semi-independent Muslim principalities; and the Delhi sultans were busy conquering these too. Again, between 1193 and 1526 CE, nearly 35 sultans ascended to the throne of Delhi with the majority of them being killed or displaced—not by Hindus, but by the Muslims themselves. Sultans could not afford to estrange the feelings of their Hindu subjects who contributed largely to the material strength and prosperity of the Sultanate. In fact, the sultans soon realized that it was impossible to carry on administration without the assistance of Hindus, therefore appointing them to posts of trust and responsibility.

During the regime of the Khiljis and Tughlaqs, the sultan's understood the concept of working through people; and adopted a generally appreciative posture towards local social and religious practices. A few Hindus and Jains even held high positions in the state under the Khiljis and Tughlaqs, rising to extremely high and responsible offices, such as those of provincial governors. It was Muhammad bin Tughlaq who should be credited for making the first sincere effort to induct Hindus into his administration. He also encouraged literary and religious debates between Indian scholars and saints. Firuz Shah Tughlaq also showed keen interest in Indian culture by encouraging the translation of Sanskrit epics and other works and placing an Ashokan pillar in his palace premises. Similarly, a few upper caste Hindus also interested themselves in Persian and Islamic literature. Inter-community understanding was further facilitated by the development and growth of a common language—Urdu, a mixture of Arabic, Persian, Turkish and Hindi. The process of reciprocal assimilation advanced to such an extent that even as early as Babur's entry into India, the Muslims could characterize their distinct mode of life as the 'Hindustani way'.

All such developments while pointing to the secular policies of the sultans, also showed the emerging relations between the rural Hindu gentry and the urban Muslim aristocracy. This sharing of power was to become a crucial source for political stability. By the fourteenth century, the Sultanate state in India had evolved as an Islamic power, but working on moderate lines it was based increasingly upon the opinion of the sultans and their advisers, rather than on any religious texts as interpreted by the *ulema*. Although the sultans enforced the *Shariah* and appointed the *ulema* to profitable offices, they also formulated their own state laws known as the *zawabit* to bring in a practicality in solving disputes involving the people.

When faced with threat from the natives, as well as from the Muslim nobles in control of the provinces, the sultans sometimes asserted their Islamic connections rather forcefully. This method adopted by the sultans was helpful in balancing both the orthodox demands and the needs of the state. Ghiyasuddin Tughlaq's victory over the last Khilji, Khusro Khan, a Hindu convert, was seen as an attempt to rejuvenate Islam in India. Although Muhammad bin Tughlaq had tried to remove the name of the Abbasid caliph from his coins, he looked for a caliph who would provide legitimacy to his rule when he was hard pressed with rebellions from all quarters. Firuz Shah Tughlaq enforced the *Shariah* stringently by not only obtaining a letter of investiture from the caliph but pleasing the *ulema* by giving them important concessions and enforcing religious policies conducive to the growth of Islam.

Thus, the state under the Delhi Sultanate was largely military and aristocratic in nature. Hindus formed the dominant rural aristocracy, while Muslims residing in urban centres had better chances of working in the state's administration. The *brahmans* and Rajputs who had formed the most privileged sections of the pre-Delhi Sultanate period were now replaced by the Turks and later the Persians, Afghans and Indian Muslims. Although, the sultans never violated the *Shariah,* they never allowed the *ulema* to entirely dictate policies of state either. The medieval Indian state was not based on the idea of equality, but on the concept of privileges.

Literature, Art and Architecture

There was a marked progress in literature during this period, and valuable contributions were made in the fields of philosophy, jurisprudence, logic, historical and vernacular literature. Mithila became famous for juristic learning, while Vikramasila and Navadvipa grew vigorously as centres for the study of logic. Vijnanesvara's famous commentary on *Mitakshara* which was the chief authority on Hindu law was written around 1200 CE; Jimutavahana, an authority on the Hindu law of inheritance lived in the first half of the twelfth century, while the jurist Neelakanta is assigned to the sixteenth century. Apart from legal texts, some good dramas were also written during this period. Gujarat evolved as a great centre of Sanskrit learning, with a great resurgence of Sanskrit under the literary activities of Hemachandra Suri and the patronage of Viradhavala and his learned minister, Vastupala. In Rajputana, the most outstanding figure was that of Kumbha, the author of *Sangitaraja,* an encyclopedic work on music. This period also witnessed a mass of Jain literature, secular as well as religious. Sanskrit attracted the attention of a few Muslims and some Sanskrit works were translated into Persian too.

Another notable feature of the times was the development of vernacular literature. In Bengal, there was an efflorescence of vernacular literature, with Vaishnav songs and verses offering a glorious example of the synthesis of Hindu and Muslim ideas. Hindi also made great progress during this period, with its earliest writers being Chand Bardoi, the author of *Prithviraj Raso;* Jagnayak who wrote *Alhakhand,* describing the chivalrous deeds of Alha and Udal; the works of Amir Khusrau and Baba Gorakhnath, apart from others. The greatest encouragement to the growth of Hindi was given by the saints of the Bhakti movement, who composed devotional songs in the vernaculars.

The Delhi sultans and other Muslim rulers were great patrons of the Persian language. Some of the capital cities in India became great centres of Persian learning rivalling Bukhara, Baghdad, Cairo and Constantinople. The greatest of the Persian poets was perhaps Amir Khusrau. Since the Muslim rulers had a fondness for historical literature, almost every powerful ruler had his own court historian. The most prominent Muslim writers of the period were Ziauddin Barani, Ferishta and the famous Hindu historian from Kashmir, Kalhana. Barani, a contemporary of Muhammad bin Tughlaq and Firuz Shah Tughlaq, wrote a number of renowned texts, such as the *Fatwa-i-Jahandari,* which elaborates on the principles to be followed by Muslim rulers to attain merit, and the *Tarikh-i-Firuz Shahi,* which narrates the history of the Delhi sultans from Balban to the sixth regnal year of Firuz Shah Tughlaq. This text is still important for the information it furnishes on the conquests of the sultans, their administrative regulations and other state measures. Barani speaks with frankness on the unpopularity of revenue officers, the miserable condition of the peasantry and the hardships of merchants. The fact that historians like Badauni and Ferishta based their texts on the *Tarikh-i-Firuz Shahi* is enough testimony to establish the reputation of Barani as a historian.

Even though the Muslims had evolved a distinct style of architecture, they could not ignore the influence of Hindu architectural ideals, resulting in the development of a distinct Indo-Islamic style of architecture. There is still some controversy about the indebtedness of Islamic architecture to Hindu art. While Havell and his followers regard it as wholly Indian in soul and spirit, some others regard it as only a variety of Islamic art.

Even before the coming of the Muslims, a heterogeneous style of architecture had evolved in India. The Muslims had brought with them only soldiers equipped for military conquest and not artists or architects. Later, to give a concrete form to their artistic needs, they needed to employ Hindu master craftsmen. Since the newcomers could not escape the artistic influence flourishing around them, Hindu influences naturally crept in. While retaining the Hindu characteristics of solidity, balance and grace, the craftsmen developed Muslim features like the use of brick and mortar, arches, domes, minarets and geometric designs.

Of the many buildings belonging to the Sultanate architectural style developed at Delhi during this period, the earliest ones were the *Qila Rai Pithora* with the *Ghazni Darwaza* on the western side of the fort. Qutbuddin Aibak also built a palace in the *Qila Rai Pithora* and named it *Qasr-i-Safed.* Today there hardly remains any sign of this palace. Among the many historical remains at Delhi, the most notable is the Qutb—a name given to the group of monuments embracing the *Quwwat ul Islam* mosque and its grand *Minar* that were built by Qutbuddin Aibak to commemorate the fall of Delhi. This landmark monument illustrates the way Islamic architecture developed in India during the early days of its conquest.

The structure of the mosque and *minar* is said to have been built out of the beautiful and elaborately carved materials collected from 27 dismantled temples. Not following a regular plan or design, it was an improvisation of a Muslim mosque with a Hindu form. Another important monument begun by Qutbuddin Aibak, and later to be finished by Iltutmish, was the *Qutb Minar.* Fergusson regards this as a perfect example of a tower. Among the monuments of Iltutmish, mention may also be made of the sultan's mausoleum at Delhi. Iltutmish died in 1236 CE, but had his tomb built a year earlier. This structure does not have a dome anymore, and apart from its archways, has a fairly plain exterior. The interior, however, displays some intricate carvings. Both geometric and traditional Hindu designs, such as wheels, lotus flowers and diamonds were used. This is the most ornate monument of early Indo-Islamic art. The tomb of Iltutmish and the surrounding *madrassa,* believed to be the tomb of Alauddin Khilji, are included in the same group of these Qutb structures. Balban constructed a palace in Delhi called the *Kushk-i-Lal* before he became king. He made the *Qila-i-Marzghan* near this palace after he became king.

The next landmark in the development of Indo-Islamic architecture was seen in the regime

DELHI, THE QUWWAT-UL-ISLAM MASJID. *With its construction commencing in 1193, this is the first mosque to be built in Delhi after the Muslim conquest and one of the finest examples of the fusion of Hindu and Islamic art. It is built on a raised and paved courtyard surrounded by pillared cloisters added by Iltutmish between 1210 and 1220 CE. The entrance to the courtyard shows an ornate mandap dome from the Jain temples built during the time of Prithviraj Chauhan. Twelfth century Hindu motifs, like tasseled ropes, bells, tendrils, cows and leaves, are to seen decorating the mosque. The very first indication of the Islamic character of the building comes from the elegant pointed arches with calligraphy of texts from the Quran in Arabic crowning them, towards the west of the mosque. Later additions and improvements were made by Iltutmish and Alauddin Khilji.*

of Alauddin Khilji. By this time, Indian workmen had mastered the art of fitting their beautiful style of embellishments to Islamic architectural forms. The fusion of the best features of these two styles is found in the *Alai Darwaza*, which has been highly praised by art critics. Described as one of the most treasured gems of Islamic architecture, this gate was built by Alauddin Khilji in 1311 CE. The gateway formed the main access through the southern wall to the enlarged *Quwwat ul Islam* mosque. It is the first building to employ Islamic principles of accurate construction and geometric ornamentation. The *darwaza* is a square, domed building with intricate carvings in red sandstone and marble. The *Jamaat Khana* mosque built by him at Delhi is also noteworthy as the earliest example in India of a mosque built entirely in accordance with Islamic ideas and materials specially dug out for the purpose.

During the Tughlaq period, the spirit and tone of Indo-Islamic architecture underwent a distinct change. Monuments were now characterized by rigid simplicity and puritanical austerity—in striking contrast to the lavish and elaborate ornamentation of the earlier period. Hence, they are dull and unimpressive with a monotonous repetition of the same features, plainness of ideas and absence of charm.

The monuments of the Sayyids and Lodis were mostly funerary. The domes were bigger in size and elevation. An important feature was the introduction of what is known as the double dome which greatly influenced later buildings. The most important among the mosques built during this period was the *Moth ki Masjid* built by the prime minister of Sikandar Lodi in the beginning of the sixteenth century. It displays freedom of imagination, a bold diversity of design, and an appreciation of contrasting light and shade. There is a sense of harmony in line and colour, which combine to make it one of the more spirited and picturesque buildings of its kind in the whole range of Islamic art in India. To the east of the *Alai Darwaza* is the tomb of the saint Imam Zamin, who carried out his duties in the *Quwwat ul Islam* mosque. During Sikandar Lodi's reign, Imam Zamin came to Delhi from Turkey. His tomb is small and attractive with a dome rising from an octagonal drum with latticed screens along the sides.

Though the state that evolved under the Delhi Sultanate was military and aristocratic in nature, its social order was an embodiment of varied hues. An inequitable society, which made some rich and others poor, paradoxically helped to establish equity where laws were concerned. The sultans were not dictated by religious laws alone; and they framed their own laws of state based on secular considerations. All these factors together led to the making of a state that constituted an important phase of Muslim rule in India. The changes that came about in the nature of polity, economy and society under the Delhi sultans transformed the complexion of Indian life, leading to the development of new systems.

SUMMARY

- The Muslims did not bring with them any perfect machinery of administration and had to evolve a practical system based on their previous experiments, knowledge and the applicability of the system to the Indian scenario.
- Though the Delhi sultans ruled independently in India, they continued to perceive themselves as part of the Islamic world that operated through the Caliphate of Baghdad.
- Recognition by the Caliphate was necessary as it strengthened the position of the sultans, giving them recognition at par with other global Muslim states.
- In reality it was the imperial position of the sultan that really mattered in the absence of any regular laws of succession. In some cases, the sultan nominated his successor, or else the claimants had to fight a war of succession.
- The uncertainty involved in competing for this position resulted in frequent civil wars, military revolutions and wholesale massacres of royal families.
- The Delhi sultan was responsible for the state's administration, and was the head of the army. His primary responsibilities included protection of the state, settlement of disputes, enforcement of laws, collection of taxes, welfare of the people and the defence of Islam.
- With help from all the social sectors—the nobility, the military and the *ulema*—the sultan administered the state.
- For effective administration of the state, the sultan was assisted by a team of ministers who were individually responsible for various subjects, such as revenue, war, local and provincial governments, and markets.
- The army was an important unit administered by the *ariz-i-mumalik,* who maintained descriptive rolls of soldiers, assigned different tasks to them and was also responsible for the transfers of military personnel.
- There was an effective system of judicial administration during the Sultanate period.
- The Sultanate was categorized into a number of divisions called *iqtas,* each under an *iqtadar. Iqtas* were allotted to nobles, performing civil and military duties, in lieu of salary. The main functions of the *iqtadars* were collection of land revenue and the maintenance of law and order in their *iqtas.*
- *Iqtas* were divided into provinces that were further sub-divided into *shiqs* and *parganas.*
- Balban was the first sultan to introduce features that were conducive to the economic growth of the Sultanate. Alauddin Khilji also stands out as a daring political economist who organized the revenue system and kept down the prices of commodities through his famous market regulations. In Muhammad bin Tughlaq's reign, the people were put to a lot of inconvenience as a result of his administrative experiments. There was a recovery during Firuz Shah Tughlaq's reign and the general condition of the Sultanate improved.
- A general policy of toleration was maintained during the Sultanate period with occasional lapses.
- The Hindus formed the dominant rural aristocracy, while the Muslims in urban centres had better chances of working in the state's administration.
- The *brahmans* and Rajputs who had formed the most privileged sections in the pre-Delhi Sultanate period were replaced by the Turks and later the Persians, Afghans and Indian Muslims.
- Although the sultans never violated the *Shariah,* they never allowed the *ulema* to entirely dictate policies of state either.

- The state that evolved under the Delhi Sultanate was military and aristocratic in nature.
- Progress in literature was not negligible, and valuable contributions were made in the fields of philosophy, jurisprudence, logic, historical and vernacular literature.
- Even though the Muslims had evolved a distinct style of architecture, they could not ignore the influence of Hindu architectural ideals; and the result was the development of a distinct style of Indo-Islamic architecture.

KEYWORDS

Khutba
Mansur
Despot/ Despotic powers
Diwan-i-wizarat /Wazir
Cavalry
Darbar
Qazi-i-mumalik /Qazi
Shiqs and parganas
Iqtadars and zamindars
Urdu
Bhakti movement
Indo-Islamic art

REVIEW QUESTIONS

1. Account for the reasons why the Delhi sultans required the recognition of the Caliphate of Baghdad.
2. Briefly describe the central administration of the Delhi Sultanate.
3. How important was the army in the administrative apparatus of the Delhi Sultanate?
4. Explain how Delhi grew in the thirteenth century into one of the largest cities of the Muslim world.
5. Examine the valuable contributions made in the fields of literature, art and architecture during the Delhi Sultanate period.

PART III–The Kingdom of Vijayanagar

"Now this King Crisnarao, when he was young and growing up in this city of Bisnaga, had an intrigue with a courtesan for whom he had much affection, and who was called Chinadevidy, and for the great love he bore her he promised many times that if ever he became King he would marry her; and though he said this in jest, it afterwards became true, so the history records. For when he was raised to the throne and taken away from the things he had done when a young man, he still did not forget the affection he felt for this woman, but used secretly to leave his palace and go to her house. And this was discovered one night by his minister Sallvatinica, who watched him until he had got into the woman's house, and he rebuked him much for it and brought him back to the palace. Then the King told him how well he loved her, and that he had promised to marry this woman and was determined to do so in any case; and the minister, seeing how he was bent on it, gave way to his wish, saying that he would accomplish it in such a way that His Highness would not be blamed for it. In order to do this he sought for him a very beautiful woman of the family of the kings of Narsymga, and after he had married him to her, at the end of the wedding ceremonies, he put this woman and the other in a house, to which he had added a tower very lofty and large, and in which he lodged her. Afterwards the King married many other wives, for these kings hold it as a very honourable thing to have many wives; and this King Crisnarao married four, and yet he loved this one better than any of the others. This King built a city in honour of this woman, for the love he bore her, and called its name Nagallapor and surrounded it with a new wall which is one of the best works that he has in his kingdom, and he made in it a street very long and large with houses all of masonry. In order to people this town he ordered all the chiefs of his kingdom to build themselves palaces therein, and so they did. This town has one principal street, of length four thousand and seven hundred paces and of breadth forty, which is certainly the most beautiful street it is possible to see; and he made and finished this town without stinting any expense on it. It now yields forty-two thousand pardaos of duties for things which enter into it, the duties in this land being very great; since nothing comes through the gates that does not pay duty, even men and women, as well as head-loads and all merchandise."

Source: Robert Sewell, Nuniz and Paes, *A Forgotten Empire: Vijayanagar,* 1900. Extract taken from Chronicle of Fernao Nuniz (1535), Chapter 19 – How the Ydallcao came against Rachol, and did not Dare to Await the King, and Fled. Text Available at Project Gutenberg.

Image: Intricate Garuda Carving on Temple in Hampi.

CHAPTER 10

A Political Profile of Vijayanagar

Review and Discussion

- Origins of Vijayanagar
- The Sangamas
- The Saluvas
- The Tuluvas
- The Aravidus
- Conclusion

Lasting for almost three centuries as the foremost power in southern India, the kingdom of Vijayanagar (founded in 1336 CE) represents the last great native phase in the annals of the history of south Indian. There were large-scale military conflicts in peninsular India after the Turko-Afghan sultans, Alauddin Khilji and Muhammad bin Tughlaq led incursions into the region, which shaped and reshaped the history and fortunes of the Deccan and the Far South. In addition to this, a significant rise in prosperity of the region made it a hub of trading activities, linking it to northern India as well as Europe and East Asia. Other factors that contributed to the major developments of the period were urbanization and modernization of the economy—in which monetization played a key role. As a result, the kingdoms of peninsular India entered into an aggressive political and military race for supremacy with one another. It was in this keenly competitive environment that Vijayanagar, a leading kingdom in the region, established its dominance over the local rulers through sheer military power. With time it also forestalled the advancing Turkish forces and emerged as the rallying mascot for the entire southern region. Several historians also hold that the kingdom of Vijayanagar became a saviour of Hinduism in the land.

The Vijayanagar kingdom may be easily categorized as the 'segmentary state', as defined by the American scholar, Burton Stein. This school of American historians in the 1970s, constituting Burton Stein and David Ludden among others, put forth the view that highly centralized bureaucratic states were not in existence in medieval southern India. What they instead opined was that the state in southern India had a 'segmentary' character with a very limited area under the actual control of the central authority, the rest owing only customary allegiance to the centre. Burton Stein's argument on state formation is interesting for the fact that other than the unitary state with a single authoritative centre, a single administrative corps, a centralized concentration of coercive means and a fixed territory, he also formulated another state model which he termed as 'segmentary' to denote a political formation that was feudal or patrimonial in structure. In his approach to a segmentary model, the entire agrarian surplus of a state does not flow from the periphery to the core and the relationship between the two remains more ritual than fiscal. But in a centre-oriented state the case is reversed, with revenue mostly flowing in from the periphery to the core. Burton Stein's model, however, does not explain the structural weakness of the medieval polity nor does it explain why it remained so salient a feature for centuries. Nevertheless, when one understands the *Nayankara* system of Vijayanagar, more clarity evolves on the state structure.

Origins of Vijayanagar

Since historians are not unanimous about the origin and early history of Vijayanagar, two different theories have been advanced. One school suggests that the city of Anegundi (a small fortified town situated about 40 miles north west of Bellary where the Tungabhadra cuts through a rocky terrain), which formed the cradle of the Vijayanagar kingdom, was established by Vira Ballala III, the Hoysala king and Harihara, who was a relative of the ruling family of the Hoysalas. Another theory states that the five sons of Sangama, of whom Harihara and Bukka were the most well-known, laid the foundations of the city of Vijayanagar on the southern bank of the Tungabhadra.

A traditional account states that Sangama and his descendents were originally feudatories of the Kakatiyas of Warangal. But the defeat of the Kakatiyas made Harihara and Bukka look towards other avenues in order to secure their position. They got a chance to become ministers in the kingdom of Kampili, which comprised Bellary, Raichur and the Dharwad districts that today form part of the state of Karnataka, India. When Kampili was occupied by Muhammad bin Tughlaq in 1327 CE, the two brothers were captured and taken to Delhi and forced to convert to Islam.

The political condition of this newly conquered southern territory was hardly stable. The people living there did not wish to submit to Turkish domination and wanted to reorganize themselves to prevent the takeover. Soon a revolt-like atmosphere spread rapidly across the southern region, which the governors of the Delhi sultans found impossible to handle. When Malik Muhammad, the governor of Kampili, informed Muhammad bin Tughlaq about the volatile state of affairs, the sultan felt that Harihara and Bukka could restore order to the troubled land. They were sent back to the Deccan in the capacity of governors of Kampili to control the local revolts and invasions by neighbouring kings. There they evolved a mechanism to placate the different rebelling groups; sometimes it took the form of an appeasing policy towards the local chieftains, many of whom had not accepted the rule of the Tughlaqs; and at other times, a process of consolidation and expansion was followed. Although their first campaign was against the neighbouring Hoysala king, Ballala III of Dwarasamudra, it was not fruitful. Meanwhile, Harihara and Bukka unexpectedly renounced their new faith, broke all relations with the sultan, and under the influence of the sage Madhava Vidyaranya and his brother Sayana (the famous Vedic commentator) they reconverted to Hinduism. The brothers proclaimed their independence from the Delhi Sultanate, regained their home base from Ballala III and established their new capital at Vijayanagar, on the southern bank of the Tungabhadra.

Harihara I (1336–56 CE) became the first king of the Sangama dynasty to rule from Vijayanagar, which came to represent the new political culture that was evolving in medieval southern India. The kingdom's expansion drive in the initial years of its formation made it the first southern Indian state to integrate multiple linguistic and cultural regions under a single power, with smaller areas and local chiefs exercising power as its representatives.

The Sangamas

As mentioned earlier, it is widely believed that the Sangama dynasty, with its roots in a feudatory family under the Kakatiyas of Warangal, laid the foundations of the city of Vijayanagar. The brothers Harihara and Bukka were the most renowned early rulers of the Sangamas of southern India.

Harihara I (1336–56 CE)

In 1336 CE, Harihara I, with the help of his brothers, began to control the region extending from Nellore on the Coromandel coast, to Badami, south of Bijapur in western Deccan. During this period, new Hindu kingdoms were enlarging their boundaries in this region—the most important among them being the Hoysala kingdom of Ballala and the Andhra confederacy led by Kapaya Nayaka. However, Dwarasamudra under Ballala, situated between the Mabar (Madurai) and Vijayanagar kingdoms, fell prey to Muhammad bin Tughlaq's southern campaigns during 1343–44 CE. It was soon conquered and annexed by Bukka, Harihara's brother, to Vijayanagar. This constituted an important achievement for Harihara, since on the basis of this, the new state formed by him could assert its sovereignty on the area extending from the Coromandel to the Malabar region. With the end of Ballala, Kumara Kampana, the son of Bukka, began to play a conspicuous role in the kingdom of Vijayanagar.

The next decade witnessed Harihara's other brothers involved in conquests of small Hindu principalities, but did not prove to be as meaningful. The foundation of the Bahmani Sultanate in 1347 CE, however, applied a brake on Harihara's expansionist drive, as it turned out to be a greater challenge to his kingdom on the northern borders. To this effect, he modelled the administration of his kingdom on the Kakatiya pattern and also reclaimed vast areas of land for agricultural purposes.

Bukka I (1356–77 CE)

Power was retained within the family when Harihara was succeeded by his brother, Bukka I. He was ably assisted by his son, Kumara Kampana, in continuing the work begun by Harihara I. Along with his efficient generals, Gopana and Saluva Mangu, Kumara Kampana first marched into the principality of the Sambuvarayas (modern North and South Arcot), and succeeded in gaining their assistance in his campaigns against the Madura Sultanate. Such was the victory that the Madura Sultanate was practically destroyed. This achievement has been described in the *Madhura Vijayam*, composed by Kumara Kampana's wife, the poetess Ganga Devi, in superlative terms. Inscriptions from the period indicate that he also conquered Kongudesa and Orissa.

The major task before Bukka I was to tackle the Bahmani sultans in numerous battles for control of strategic forts in the Krishna–Tungabhadra Doab (a fertile tract of land between the two rivers). During his first decade of kingship, he undertook this task and at the same time tried to gain a hold over the trading network of the eastern and western coasts. He failed to gain victories in his wars with Muhammad Shah I and Mujahid, and according to Ferishta's account he was even pursued by Mujahid as far as Rameshwaram. The victorious Bahmanis even forced Vijayanagar to pay a tribute in 1359 CE. The other major event of Bukka's reign was the conquest of the sultanate of Mabar (Madurai) in 1370 CE. An important feature of Bukka's administrative system was his consistent efforts to keep his kingdom centralized.

The general policy followed by Harihara was to entrust the supervision of the far-flung provinces of the growing state to his brothers, usually to the brother who had conquered that particular territory. By 1357 CE most of Bukka's nephews had succeeded their fathers as governors of these provinces, so that power remained within the larger family. In the longer run, this development could pose a serious threat of decentralizing the state as distant family members were getting more firmly fixed in their particular domains. Changing his policy Bukka removed his nephews and replaced them with his sons and favourite generals so that only his own line would succeed and power could be completely retained in his hands.

Harihara II (1377–1404 CE)

Bukka's son, Harihara II, succeeded him and ruled for nearly 28 years. It began to appear as if there would be a replay of events with rebellions spreading like wildfire. The initial period of Harihara II's reign witnessed the first revolt from the Tamil region. It is said that the rebellions were incited by the sons and officers of Bukka's deceased eldest son, Kumara Kampana. They were not ready to acknowledge Harihara II's authority, however, Harihara was able to put down the rebellion and subsequently replace his cousins with his own sons as governors of the provinces. Once again power was retained in the family through the submergence of interests of other relations other than the direct descendents of the ruler. Thus, there was a constant state of conflict between the ruler, and his relations and officers who tried to establish ruling rights over parts of the kingdom.

Following the assassination of the Bahmani sultan, Mujahid in 1378 CE, there was a temporary confusion that provided an opportunity to Harihara II to besiege Raichur, regain Goa and some other ports on the west coast and establish his authority along the Malabar coast. With the accession of Muhammad Shah II as Mujahid's successor, conflicts with the Bahmanis ceased for the time being only to be resumed later during the reign of Firuz Shah, the next Bahmani successor. During 1398–99 CE, there was a Bahmani attack on Vijayanagar in which several citizens were killed and a huge tribute had to be paid by Vijayanagar to the victor. These developments changed the complexion of the Vijayanagar–Bahmani relations and reversed the temporary truce that had been established. In later years when Vijayanagar made alliances with the sultans of Malwa and Gujarat the payment of tribute was stalled.

Harihara II was, however, more successful in his other campaigns. He attacked the Reddi kingdom of Kondavidu in the northeast and gained Kurnool, Nellore and parts of Guntur from them. His son, Prince Virupaksha, led an expedition to the south, proceeding as far as Ceylon, whose king was made to pay a tribute. Thus, Harihara II's dominions increased considerably bringing Mysore, Chingliput, Kanchipuram and Tiruchirapalli under his sway. Harihara II was fortunate to have shared a part of his reigning period with the Bahmani sultan, Muhammad Shah II, whose peace loving nature allowed Harihara II to expand his kingdom without having to face mush resistance. Thus, the end of the fourteenth century witnessed Vijayanagar emerging as the paramount power south of the rivers Tungabhadra and Krishna.

Harihara's reign was relatively successful, as he could expand the dominions of his state, maintain internal order while keeping the Bahmani sultans at bay. Vijayanagar's trade too was augmented by acquiring control of the ports on both the sea coasts, thereby leading to the increased income and prosperity.

Interim Period (1404–22 CE)

After the death of Harihara II in 1404 CE, there was a violent struggle among his three sons. In quick succession, two of them were crowned, one after another and also promptly dethroned. This cleared the path for Devaraya I (1406–22 CE), the third son of Harihara II to emerge victorious. In this period of instability that ensued, Vijayanagar and the Bahmani Sultanate supported different claimants to the throne of Kondavidu, which served to further intensify the conflict between the two powers. From time to time, rival Telugu chiefs took sides, sometimes joining Vijayanagar or sometimes the Bahmani side. One such instance saw the Sultan Firuz Shah Bahmani supporting a Reddi attack on Udayagiri, while in a related move the sultan himself laid siege to the city of Vijayanagar. Despite the stiff opposition from the Bahmanis, Vijayanagar managed to maintain its control over Panagal, Nalgonda, and other forts, besides regaining Udayagiri. It was only after Firuz Shah was defeated in 1419 CE, that Kondavidu was partitioned between Vijayanagar and the Velamas of Rajakonda. The areas that were getting involved in the protracted struggle in the Andhra–Tilangana region were on the peripheries of Orissa bringing Vijayanagar into direct contact with the kingdom of Orissa for the first time. Although an immediate confrontation was averted, this was the beginning of a rivalry that was to last for more than a century.

The short reigns of Devaraya's two sons, Ramachandra and Vijaya, were largely unsuccessful. Vijaya fought a losing war with the Bahmanis in which many temples were destroyed and he was forced to pay a huge indemnity. Next, the king of Orissa and the Velamas of Andhra together launched an offensive on Vijayanagar that resulted in a further setback for Vijayanagar, which now lost all the territories that it had gained from the partition of the Reddi kingdom of Kondavidu. Vijaya Raya's reign is said to have lasted for just about five years (1422–26 CE).

Devaraya II (1426–46 CE)

Vijaya's son and successor, Devaraya II succeeded him in due course. Taking advantage of the weak and disorganized condition of the Kondavidu region, Devaraya II once again regained the territories that had been lost to the Reddi kingdom, thereby enlarging the Vijayanagar boundaries. With these acquisitions, the Krishna River became the northeastern boundary of Vijayanagar. Devaraya II waged two wars with the Bahmanis in 1435–36 CE and 1443–44 CE for control over the forts of Raichur and Mudgal in the Krishna–Tungabhadra Doab. This ended with no gains or losses for either side. However, after these campaigns Devaraya II announced that Muslims could join his army, and assigned resident Muslim archers the task of coaching his Hindu troops. This was an upgrade for the Vijayanagar army in military know-how. Devaraya campaigned successfully in the Malabar region of the Far South, where his victories over local chieftains helped in the process of consolidation. His reign stands out for not only being able to establish centralization in the early history of Vijayanagar, but also the greatest territorial expansion as well.

Devaraya II invaded Kerala and subjugated the ruler of Quilon and other chieftains. But Zamorin of Calicut seems to have retained his independence. Abdur Razzak, the Persian ambassador who visited southern India in the fifteenth century, says that although Zamorin was not under Devaraya's authority he was mortally afraid of him. He further states that Devaraya exacted tribute from the rulers of Quilon, Ceylon, Pulicat, Pegu, etc. In achieving this, he was ably assisted by his remarkable minister Lakkana and his equally able brother, Madanna.

After Devaraya's death in 1446 CE, the state lost its power and started to weaken. A considerable amount of territory was also lost along both coasts to the Bahmani sultans and to the powerful Gajapati ruler of Orissa, who had suddenly gained prominence. The kingdom of Orissa under its famous king, Kapileshvara, and his son Hamvira, conquered the Reddi kingdom of Rajahmundry and the Vijayanagar province of Kondavidu in the 1450s and 60s. Soon Warangal and Bidar (under the Bahmanis) and Udayagiri were annexed by the Gajapatis. Encouraged by these victories, the Gajapati army tried to reach the Kaveri River, where it faced opposition from the able Vijayanagar general and governor of Chandragiri, Saluva Narasimha. This conflict with Orissa made it clear to Vijayanagar that it could face strong opposition from the Gajapatis in the east at any point in the future and also that provincial governors had to strengthen themselves to protect their territories against these onslaughts.

Later Rulers

Devaraya II's son Mallikarjuna (1446–65 CE) failed to ensure that his immediate progeny succeeds him; instead his cousin came to the throne which was an indication of the loosening of power of the Vijayanagar ruler. The new ruler, Virupaksha (1465–85 CE), who had been a provincial governor before ascending the throne did not find favour from any quarter. Neither was he supported by the other provincial governors or the direct descendants of Mallikarjuna, who quietly withdrew to the banks of the Kaveri and continued to rule a small part of the kingdom giving rise to a lateral rule of the Vijayanagar dynasty.

This was also a time when the Bahmanis were gaining territories on the Malabar Coast and northern Carnatak from Vijayanagar under their *wazir*, Mahmud Gawan. In addition, Vijayanagar also lost Goa and other ports on the same coastline which was a major deterrent as it cut off not only trade related income for the state, but also the procurement of Middle Eastern horses for the army. Around this time Kapileshvara of Orissa died in 1470 CE, relieving military pressure on Vijayanagar for the time being in the east. It was not Virupaksha, but Saluva Narasimha, an able governor, who was transferred to Penukonda, who took advantage of the situation to regain the lost territory in the Tamil region up to the river Godavari on the Coromandel coast. Hamvira asked the Bahmanis to help him in return for the surrender of all the captured forts in Tilangana, launching a full fledged war on Narasimha. Muhammad Shah and Mahmud Gawan attacked Narasimha's territories—Penukonda and the coastal region—and also plundered Kanchipuram in 1481 CE. These victories were short-lived as Ishvara Nayaka, another Vijayanagar general, recovered the loot from the returning Bahmani forces at Kandukur; subsequently Narasimha re-acquired Penukonda after turning back the Bahmani forces. Thus, it was a game of shifting fortunes for the Bahmanis and Vijayanagaras.

The Saluvas

There is not enough historical information available about the successors of Devaraya which makes it difficult to reconstruct their period. For the most part, the kings were not forceful enough resulting in a weak administrative structure, and there were widespread palace intrigues. Adding to the existent hopeless situation were the attacks by the Bahmani sultans and the Gajapati kings of Orissa that resulted in contracting the size of the Vijayanagar territory. It was at the same time that a terrible famine devastated the region. Saluva Narasimha, the governor posted at Chandragiri cleverly converted this hour of crisis into an opportune moment to seize the throne, thereby laying the foundations of the Saluva dynasty.

Saluva Narasimha was the eldest son of Saluva Gunda, the chief of Chandragiri of the Chittoor district. From relatively humble beginnings as a small chieftain (1456 CE), Saluva Narasimha had multiplied his acquisitions by leading campaigns in the south and Orissa to head a kingdom (1485 CE) that was to last until the beginning of the sixteenth century. Although he recognized Virupaksha as the Vijayanagar sovereign, he discharged more military and administrative functions than his political superior. In the meanwhile, Virupaksha was murdered by one of his own sons; this provided the ideal opportunity to Saluva Narasimha (1485–90 CE) to begin his own line of rule by displacing the successors of Virupaksha. During his reign, Saluva Narasimha effectively dealt with all his opponents except one which he could not overpower—the king of Orissa. He first turned his attention towards strengthening Vijayanagar's trading relations by opening new ports on the west coast so that the horse trade that had earlier existed with the Middle East could once again be revived. He also simultaneously made efforts to improve the army. Through these endevours coupled with the favourable internal and external political affairs, Saluva Narasimha could initiate the process of centralization once again.

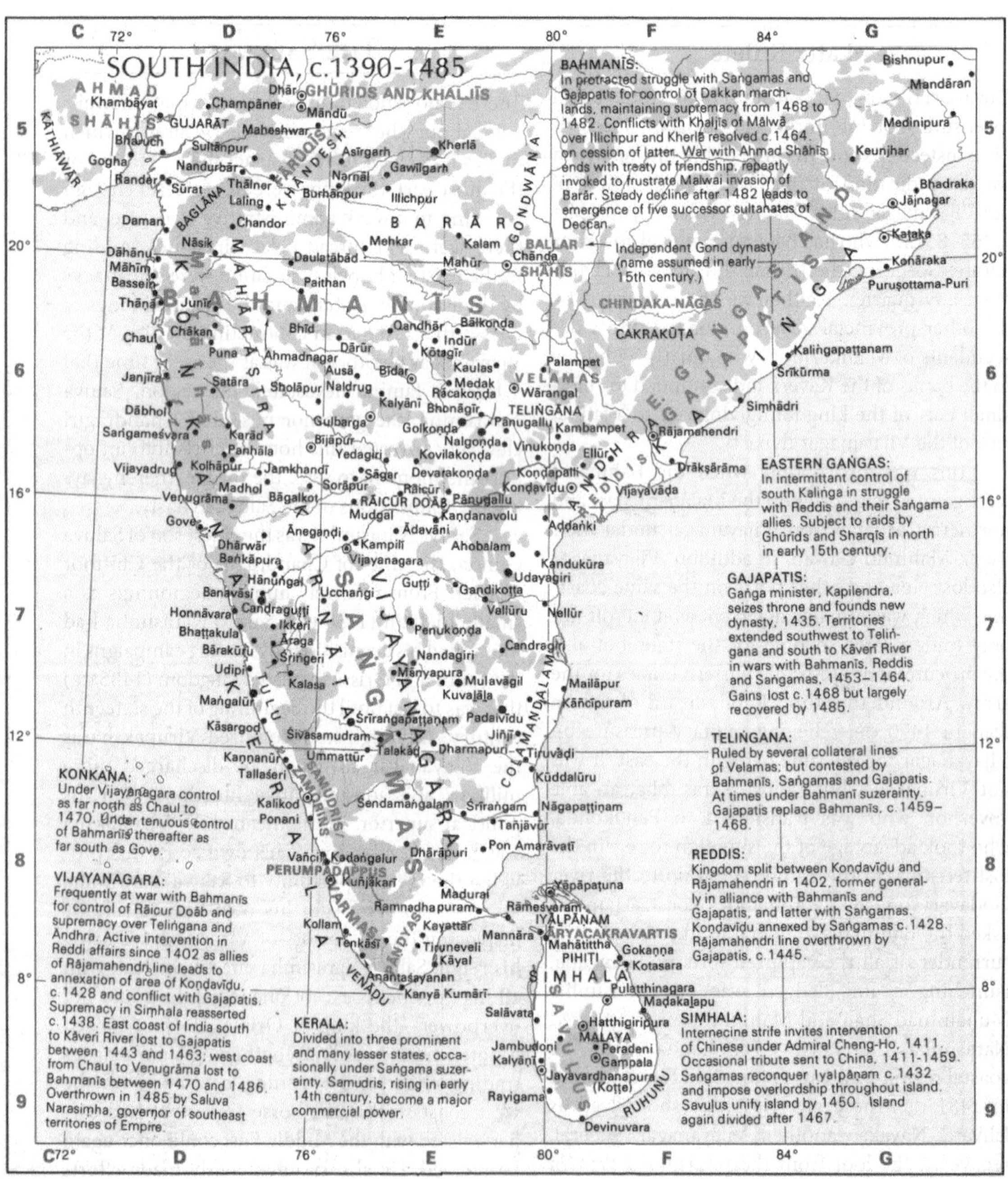

Map 10-1 *South India, 1390–1485 CE*

Saluva Narasimha sieged Udayagiri, soon after which he was imprisoned in 1490 CE by the king of Orissa and died shortly afterwards a year later. His chief minister, Narasa Nayaka, who had been appointed as regent for his two young sons held fort during this interim period. Thus, from 1490 CE until his own death in 1503 CE the administrative affairs of Vijayanagar were in the hands of Narasa Nayaka. Unfortunately, because of the factional rivalries at the court, the elder prince was murdered by one of Narasa Nayaka's rivals, and the younger prince who had been crowned as Immadi Narasimha in 1492 CE was imprisoned. Provincial governors and other chiefs were critical of the fact that Narasa Nayaka could not protect the regency of the two young princes.

During the regency years Narasa Nayaka had ample opportunities to consolidate his position further. There was a disintegrating Bahmani Sultanate which made invasion over the disputed region of the Tungabhadra–Krishna Doab in 1492–93 CE comparatively easy. Added to this, was the invitation from the Bahmani minister, Qasim Barid, who in a bid to subdue the newly independent Yusuf Adil Khan of Bijapur wanted Narasa Nayaka to invade the neighbouring territory. The occupation of the Tungabhadra–Krishna Doab by Narasa Nayaka was followed by the takeover of the strategic forts of Raichur and Mudgal but they were lost again in 1502 CE.

Vijayanagar had lost its southern territories to Orissa in 1463–64 CE. Narasa Nayaka made fresh attempts at restoring these areas back to Vijayanagar by compelling many chiefs and provincial governors to recognize his supremacy, specifically in the Tamil and Carnatak regions. Through this venture he almost succeeded in extending the boundaries of the kingdom (some eastern districts were still under Orissa) to their original size. Thus, by 1503 CE, Narasa Nayaka had accomplished the task deputed to him by Saluva Narasimha. But where the Portuguese were concerned, Vijayanagar's prestige suffered a setback because of the restrictions imposed by them on Vijayanagar's trade.

Narasa Nayaka had ensured that his own line rather than that of his old master would continue to rule. Keeping up his good name, his sons took Vijayanagar to new heights of glory. After the death of Narasa Nayaka (1505 CE), his son Vira Narasimha seized the throne, thereby bringing to an end the Saluva rule and the beginning of the Tuluva dynasty in Vijayanagar.

The Tuluvas

The Tuluva dynasty was the third dynasty to come to power in Vijayanagar. The usurpation of the throne by Vira Narasimha (1503–09 CE) again sparked off resistance, which the new king spent most of his reign attempting to crush. He was mostly successful, barring his failure to subdue the rebellious chiefs of Ummattur and Seringapatam in the south. He also failed to recover Goa from the Portuguese with whom however, he was able to establish trade relations in order to obtain a supply of better horses. By this time the Bahmanis were being assisted in their wars with Vijayanagar and in maintaining control over the Doab forts by the successor states.

Krishna Deva Raya (1509–29 CE)

Vira Narasimha was succeeded by his brother, Krishna Deva Raya (1509–29 CE), who is generally regarded as the greatest of the Vijayanagar kings. His reign took the kingdom to new heights of territorial expansion as well as internal consolidation reached a new zenith. During the first decade of his reign, Krishna Deva Raya overpowered his subordinate chieftains and governors, while simultaneously subduing assaults from the northeast.

To achieve effective political control over the conquered territories, Krishna Deva Raya appointed *brahmans* and other capable personnel as commanders, availed the services of the Portuguese and Muslim mercenary gunners in his forts, and included local forest tribals as foot soldiers.

He is known to have created a new category of small chiefs known as *Poligars* in the Vijayanagar administration. Under the Vijayanagar political hierarchy, the king was at the helm of affairs, followed in order by the *nayakas* and the *poligars* who commanded the provinces.

Krishna Deva Raya first defeated a coalition comprising the Bahmanis and the five successor states, and took over the Raichur fort. Then he restored the Bahmani sultan to his throne in 1512 CE, ending his imprisonment after a fight between Bijapur and the Bahmanis over Gulbarga and Bidar. At the same time, he successfully subdued Ganga Raja of Ummattur in the south by defeating him in battle and capturing the fortress of Sivasamudra. Krishna Deva Raya then turned towards the Gajapati ruler of Orissa, who had in his control important forts in the Andhra region and also commanded the Coromandel Coast as far as Nellore. In a series of wars during 1513–20 CE, he gained from Ganga Raja the region up to the Godavari and conquered lands as far as Kataka in Orissa. An alliance was formed with Orissa according to which the king of Orissa was to give his daughter in marriage to Krishna Deva Raya and in return regain all his territory that had been conquered up to the north of the river Krishna.

There was a substantial amount of belligerent activity on the northern frontier towards Bijapur, with the advent of the Portuguese which further disturbed the commercial relations of the kingdom with the outer world. While Krishna Deva Raya was busy campaigning in the east, Ismail Adil Shah of Bijapur had taken over the Raichur fort. Krishna Deva Raya lost no time in avenging this setback by recapturing Raichur, Mudgal and some other regions after defeating Ismail with help from the Portuguese gunners. Encouraged by his victories, in 1523 CE, he invaded Bijapur and captured more forts. He also tried to restore the Bahmani Sultanate by helping one of the sons of the reigning Bahmani sultan to the throne. In all his methodically planned conquests, Krishna Deva Raya was ably assisted by his talented and loyal minister, Saluva Timma. One important result of these campaigns, as pointed out vividly to the Muslim rulers of the region, was the serious challenge posed by Vijayanagar.

Krishna Deva Raya was clever to understand the advantages that could be gained by maintaining friendly ties with the increasingly powerful Portuguese. It was a mutually beneficial relationship in which Vijayanagar was not prevented by the Portuguese from carrying on its trade in all commodities, especially horses, with the Middle East, while the Portuguese got permission to trade within the Vijayanagar dominions. The Portuguese travellers, Domingos Paes and Duarte Barbosa certify the development of Vijayanagar as a thriving city and kingdom under Krishna Deva Raya.

Around 1524–25 CE, Krishna Deva abdicated the throne in favour of his young son, who however died shortly afterwards when he was poisoned by the former jealous chief minister. Immediately Krishna Deva Raya retaliated by imprisoning the minister and his family and proceeded to crush a rebellion three years later when one of the minister's sons tried to escape. Until his death in 1529 CE, Krishna Deva Raya led the kingdom towards the greatest military and administrative triumphs.

Krishna Deva Raya's victories of peace were not less striking either. Sewell remarks that he was not only monarch de *jure*, but he was also a *de facto* sovereign with extensive powers and strong personal influence. With the active co-operation of his famous minister, Appaji, he administered the kingdom well, maintained peace in the land, increased the prosperity of the people, earning their gratitude. The accounts of the Portuguese traveller and writer, Nuniz and Paes, respectively, testify to the imperial greatness of the city of Vijayanagar, and the wealth and luxury of the people.

Krishna Deva Raya's reign is an epoch of many sided activities. His scholarship and patronage of Telugu and Sanskrit literature have become symbols of Telugu pride and cultural traditions. Skilled in many capacities, Krishna Deva Raya's name stands out among the renowned sovereigns of the land.

Krishna Deva Raya's Successors

After the death of Krishna Deva Raya, his half brother Achyuta Deva Raya (1529–42 CE) ascended the throne as per his bother's wish under the regency of Rama Raya. Challenging a minor succession dispute Achyuta Deva Raya proclaimed himself as the king. His reign was wrought with problems as Krishna Deva Raya's death had led to renewed attacks by Bijapur, Golconda, and Orissa. The Vijayanagar minister, Saluva Viranarasimha, and the chieftains of Ummattur and Tiruvadi also opposed him. Even from the Bahmani side, there was initial opposition when Ibrahim Adil Shah tried to create a rift between Achyuta and his ministers. But the situation changed when the Bahmani sultan started to play the role of a mediator to bring Achyuta and his regent, Rama Raya, together. According to the agreement, Achyuta was to retain only nominal power while actual authority would lie with the regent.

Achyuta could not add any more territories to the Vijayanagar boundaries after the death of Krishna Deva Raya in 1529 CE. He remained preoccupied with the intrigues involving Rama Raya and the troublesome nobles and chieftains, who were challenging the central authority. Slowly, with the growth of provincial autonomy the process of decentralization was beginning to set in more deeply in which the centre was to evolve as a weak entity and the provinces would be more powerful. After Achyuta's death, Rama Raya defeated his rival in the war of succession and made his own candidate, Achyuta's nephew, Sadashiva (1542–76 CE), the next sovereign. Rama Raya cleverly elevated his position by assuming royal titles and keeping Sadashiva under cover, thus ruling the kingdom himself together with his brothers, Tirumala and Venkatadri.

Rama Raya's rule turned out to be quite successful as he was able to control the rebellious nobles in the east and the extreme south. His major achievement was limiting the expansionist activities of the Portuguese by way of an agreement in 1546 CE, so that further takeover of native settlements by them would not take place. This treaty did not last after 1558 CE, however, Rama Raya made the Portuguese pay tribute to compensate for the damages caused by them to the temples.

From Krishna Deva Raya's time, Vijayanagar and the Bahmani successor states fought on an equal footing. Sometimes the Bahmani successor states joined Vijayanagar to fight other sultanates; sometimes they opposed Vijayanagar all together. The period saw several shifting alliances between states. In 1543 CE, Rama Raya successfully repulsed a Bijapur invasion. Five years later in 1548 CE he allied himself with Burhan Nizam Shah of Ahmednagar in occupying a fort from the Barid Shahis. Then again in 1557 CE. Rama Raya helped Bijapur against Ahmednagar and Golconda. To contain the frequency of the attacks and to protect one another, a collective treaty was signed by Vijayanagar, Ahmednagar, Golconda and Bijapur, according to which if any of the four was attacked unjustly by another, it could call upon the other allies to stop the aggressor. When Hussain Nizam Shah did not honour the terms of the treaty by invading Bijapur in 1560 CE, Vijayanagar and Golconda immediately responded with an attack that resulted in Ahmednagar's loss of the fort of Kalyani to Bijapur and the defeat of the ruler of Bidar by Rama Raya. Once again the Deccani sultanates and Vijayanagar entered into a tussle with each other. Ibrahim Qutb Shah, the ruler of Golconda, allied himself with Ahmednagar against Bijapur, and Rama Raya allied Vijayanagar with Bijapur to engage in battle against the other.

Golconda and Ahmednagar had lost much at the hands of Rama Raya, hence they were eager to destroy Vijayanagar's power forever. In 1565 CE the four sultans of the Deccan came together to fight a battle against Vijayanagar at Talikota, which resulted in the disastrous defeat of the Vijayanagar forces. The Battle of Talikota, also called the Battle of Bannihatti or the Battle of Rakshasa–Tangedi, was one of the most decisive battles fought in the history of India in which the Deccani sultanates emerged victorious. Rama Raya was captured and killed, but his brother Tirumala escaped to Andhradesa with a lot of treasure.

The battle of Talikota totally crippled the kingdom of Vijayanagar, which had successfully resisted invasions from the north for more than two centuries. The battle also affected the fortunes of the Portuguese, as the Vijayanagar coast at the height of its power, was home to many foreign traders. But when Vijayanagar fell and the city became desolate, the foreign traders had no market for their goods and trade receded. Thus, it is often said that Goa rose and fell simultaneously with the rise and fall of Vijayanagar. Despite the severe setback, the kingdom of Vijayanagar continued to exist in a small way till the early part of the seventeenth century.

Battle of Talikota

The story of this terrible disaster travelled apace to the city of Vijayanagar. The inhabitants, unconscious of danger, were living in utter ignorance that any serious reverse had taken place; for their leaders had marched out with countless numbers in their train, and had been full of confidence as to the result. Suddenly, however, came the bad news. The army was defeated; the chiefs slain; the troops in retreat. But still they did not grasp the magnitude of the reverse; on all previous occasions the enemy had been either driven back, or bought off with presents from the overstocked treasury of the kings. There was little fear, therefore, for the city itself. That surely was safe! But now came the dejected soldiers hurrying back from the fight, and amongst the foremost the panic-stricken princes of the royal house. Within a few hours these craven chiefs hastily left the palace, carrying with them all the treasures on which they could lay their hands. Five hundred and fifty elephants, laden with treasure in gold, diamonds, and precious stones valued at more than a hundred millions sterling, and carrying the state insignia and the celebrated jewelled throne of the kings, left the city under convoy of bodies of soldiers who remained true to the crown. King Sadasiva was carried off by his jailor, Tirumala, now sole regent since the death of his brothers; and in long line the royal family and their followers fled southward towards the fortress of Penukonda.

Then a panic seized the city. The truth became at last apparent. This was not a defeat merely, it was a cataclysm. All hope was gone. The myriad dwellers in the city were left defenceless. No retreat, no flight was possible except to a few, for the pack-oxen and carts had almost all followed the forces to the war, and they had not returned. Nothing could be done but to bury all treasures, to arm the younger men, and to wait. Next day the place became a prey to the robber tribes and jungle people of the neighbourhood. Hordes of Brinjaris, Lambadis, Kurubas, and the like,[331] pounced down on the hapless city and looted the stores and shops, carrying off great quantities of riches. Couto states that there were six concerted attacks by these people during the day.

The third day saw the beginning of the end. The victorious Mussulmans had halted on the field of battle for rest and refreshment, but now they had reached the capital, and from that time forward for a space of five months Vijayanagar knew no rest. The enemy had come to destroy, and they carried out their object relentlessly. They slaughtered the people without mercy, broke down the temples and palaces; and wreaked such savage vengeance on the abode of the kings, that, with the exception of a few great stone-built temples and walls, nothing now remains but a heap of ruins to mark the spot where once the stately buildings stood. They demolished the statues, and

(Continued)

(Continued)

even succeeded in breaking the limbs of the huge Narasimha monolith. Nothing seemed to escape them. They broke up the pavilions standing on the huge platform from which the kings used to watch the festivals, and overthrew all the carved work. They lit huge fires in the magnificently decorated buildings forming the temple of Vitthalasvami near the river, and smashed its exquisite stone sculptures. With fire and sword, with crowbars and axes, they carried on day after day their work of destruction. Never perhaps in the history of the world has such havoc been wrought, and wrought so suddenly, on so splendid a city; teeming with a wealthy and industrious population in the full plenitude of prosperity one day, and on the next seized, pillaged, and reduced to ruins, amid scenes of savage massacre and horrors beggaring description.

Source: Robert Sewell, Nuniz and Paes, *A Forgotten Empire: Vijayanagar,* 1900. Extract taken from Chapter 15: Destruction of Vijayanagar. Text Available at Project Gutenberg.

THE ARAVIDUS

Vijayanagar's history was carried on by Rama Raya's brother Tirumala Raya, who made Penukonda in Andhradesa the new capital for the Vijayanagaras. Tirumala made an attempt at rebuilding the army through which he could suppress rebellions and banditry. Many parts of the south and southeast were already lost to the Nayakas of Madura, Tanjore (Tanjavur) and Jinji, who had gained power and made themselves independent principalities. Tirumala had no choice but to recognize the independence of these petty states. Under threat from Bijapur, Tirumala appealed to Nizam Shah of Ahmednagar for help. Both Ahmednagar and Golconda came to his rescue in a campaign against Bijapur and thus, Penukonda could be saved. After partially consolidating himself, Tirumala Raya made his three sons governors of the three linguistic regions of his kingdom—Telugu, Kannada and Tamil. Then in 1570 CE he officially inaugurated the Aravidu dynasty—the fourth and last dynasty of Vijayanagar—by crowning himself king.

Tirumala's son, Shriranga I (1572–85 CE) succeeded his father and worked on the same policy of rebuilding the state. Without support from the ruling Telugu chiefs, it had become difficult for him to consolidate his position in the midst of the powerful Deccan sultanates. Like in his father's time, he too took the help of Golconda to avert an invasion from Bijapur. later, however, Golconda itself annexed a substantial amount of Vijayanagar territory in the east. In a bid to gain security, the Vijayanagar seat of power was relocated from Penukonda to Chandragiri, yet Shriranga's difficulties did not abate. Due to the lack of support from his brothers who were busy ruling their independent principlaites and the threat posed by some of his semi-independent nobles, Shriranga found it hard to stabilize himself. Many of these nobles felt that it was more profitable to form smaller states rather than support a larger state.

Shriranga was succeeded by his younger brother Venkata II (1585–1614 CE), whose reign turned out to be more successful than his father's on account of non-interference from the Deccan sultanates. His good fortune ensured peace over the next 28 years and did not cause any more loss of territory. Rather, Venkata fought some wars between 1580 and 1589 CE., through which he could re-acquire some of the territory that had been lost to Golconda. With these acquisitions, the river Krishna once again became the northern boundary of Vijayanagar. The problem Venkata constantly faced involved the rebellions of the Nayaka chiefs in the south. The most serious threat came in 1601 CE, when the Nayakas of Madura, Tanjore and Jinji joined hands with Lingama Nayaka of Vellore to oppose him. Venkata defeated the Nayakas in the Tamil region and shifted the capital to Vellore but he could not extend his sway in

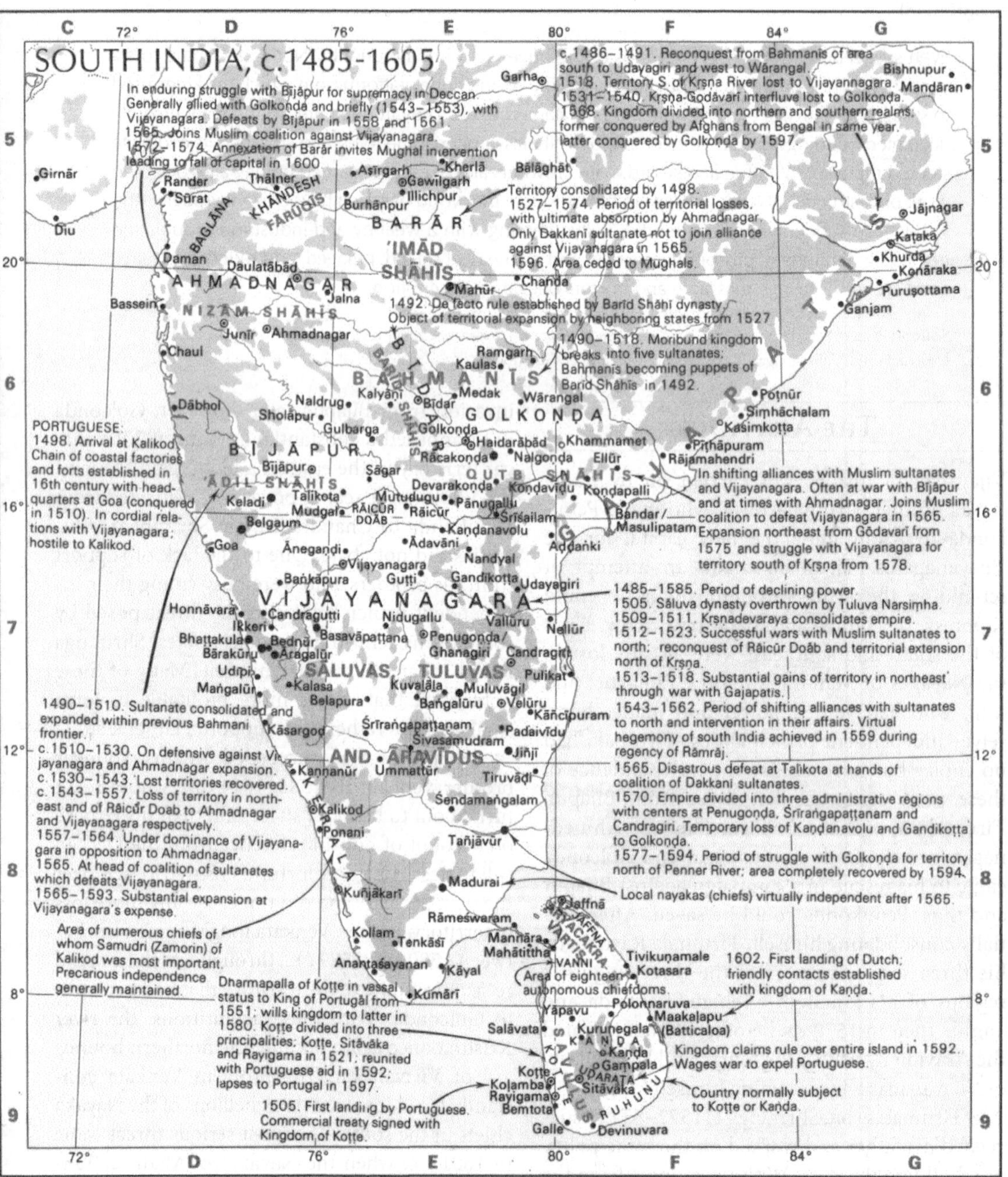

Map 10-2 *South India, 1485–1605 CE*

the Far South. The process of decentralization could only be arrested for a while, it could not be reversed. In the northern areas, Venkata tried to appease the chiefs by offering them a rebate in revenue payment. He maintained diplomatic ties with the Portuguese and the Dutch. The Portuguese established a Jesuit mission in 1607 CE; while the Dutch were allowed to build a factory at Devapattana and in a fort at Pulicat. His efforts seem to show that he had accomplished enough to revive imperial power and prosperity, but the situation was not so. At the time of his death in 1614 CE, rivalries among the nobles and chieftains were escalating leading to further decentralization of the state.

Venkata was succeeded by his nephew, Shriranga II, who was murdered within the first four months of his ascension. There followed a long civil war between several factional leaders which saw the emergence of Rama Deva Raya, one of the last members of the house of Vijayanagar; Rama Deva Raya ascended the throne in 1617 CE. By this time, the Vijayanagar kingdom had been hit on all sides by constant attacks from neighbouring states, internal rivalries and lack of strong leadership. Some loyal chieftains continued to recognize Rama Deva Raya as the sovereign and later his successor, Venkata III (1630–42 CE), during whose reign the Madraspatna fort was granted to the English as the site for a factory. Real political power rested in the hands of the Nayaka chieftains and provincial governors, who were carving out their own fiefdoms. The line of the Aravidus had thus fallen to a position of a mere provincial power.

Taking advantage of the situation, Bijapur and Golconda continued their assaults on the southern kingdom of Vijayanagar. Venkata III's situation worsened when he was betrayed by his own nephew, Shriranga, who went over to the Adil Shahi side. Then the sultan of Golconda attacked the Vijayanagar capital in 1642 CE, which resulted in the expulsion of Venkata III from Vellore. On hearing the news, Shriranga left Bijapur and crowned himself Venkata's successor. Shriranga could not gain control over the provincial Nayakas, who had become independent by then. Soon Bijapur and Golconda launched a final onslaught on Vijayanagar defeating Shriranga with their combined forces in 1645 CE. The Deccan sultanates then advanced into the Carnatak in 1652 CE, with the support of the Mughals who had incited them to partition Carnatak between themselves. By this, the Nayakas too suffered a severe setback. Shriranga retired to Mysore, where he remained in exile until he died in 1672 CE.

CONCLUSION

Beginning on a humble note, the kingdom of Vijayanagar was soon transformed into a powerful military state. The Rayas of the kingdom had to first defeat and subdue the native rulers who represented various shades of Hindu philosophy. But as the kingdom grew to become a formidable force—challenging and blocking the advances of the Persians and Turks from the north, where they had already entrenched themselves for long—it came to be described by some historians as the saviour of Hinduism in southern India. The kingdom's frequent disputes and wars with the neighbouring Golconda, Bijapur, Ahmednagar and Bidar sultanates had more to do with political domination and control of territory than with the issue of faith.

Ruled by four different dynasties—the Sangamas, the Saluvas, the Tuluvas and the Aravidus—Vijayanagar unified the region in a manner which no other kingdom had done in the past. It brought three major linguistic groups—the Tamils, the Kannadigas and the Telugus—under one banner, cemented their differences and encouraged the emergence of what was called southern Indian culture. By offering a high degree of political unity to these and other groups, the kingdom worked towards acquiring an edge in warfare against northern forces for a long time. The kingdom also ensured that no smaller kingdoms or fiefdoms could challenge its authority. It was only later that the Nayaka kingdoms arose, posing a challenge to the kingdom of Vijayanagar.

CHRONOLOGY

1327 CE	Muhammad Bin Tughlaq occupies Kampili
	Sangama Dynasty
1336–1356 CE	Harihara I (1336–56 CE)
1347 CE	Foundation of the Bahmani Sultanate
1356 CE	Bukka I (1356–77 CE)
1359 CE	Vijayanagar pays tribute to the Bahmanis
1370 CE	Madurai conquest
1377 CE	Harihara II (1377–1404 CE)
1378 CE	Bahmani sultan Mujahid assassinated
1398–99 CE	Bahmani attack on Vijayanagar
1404 CE	Death of Harihara II
1404 CE	Virupaksha Raya (1404–05 CE)
1405 CE	Bukka II (1405–06 CE)
1406 CE	Devaraya I (1406–22 CE)
1419 CE	Firuz Shah Bahmani defeated
1422 CE	Vijaya Raya (1422–1426 CE); Vijayanagar loses territories gained from the partition of the Reddi kingdom
1426 CE	Devaraya II (1426–46 CE)
1446 CE	Mallikarjuna (1446–65 CE)
1465 CE	Virupaksha II (1465–85 CE)
1470 CE	Death of Kapileshvara
1481 CE	Plunder of Kanchipuram
	Saluva Dynasty
1485 CE	Saluva Narasimha (1485–91 CE)
1491 CE	Thimma Bhupala
1492 CE	Immadi Narasimha
	Tuluva Dynasty
1491 CE	Narasa Nayaka (1491–1503 CE)
1503 CE	Vira Narasimha (1503–09 CE)
1509 CE	Krishna Deva Raya (1509–29 CE)
1512 CE	Krishna Deva Raya restores the Bahmani sultan to his throne
1523 CE	Krishna Deva Raya invades Bijapur
1529 CE	Achyuta Deva Raya (1529–42 CE)
1565 CE	Battle against Vijayanagar at Talikota
	Aravidus Dynasty
1570 CE	Tirumala Raya (1565–72 CE)
1572 CE	Shriranga Raya (1572–86 CE)
1614 CE	Venkata Raya II (1585–1614 CE)
1617 CE	Rama Deva Raya
1630 CE	Venkata III (1630–42 CE)
1645 CE	Defeat of Vijayanagar by Bijapur and Golconda

SUMMARY

- Lasting for almost three centuries as the dominant power in southern India, the kingdom of Vijayanagar, which was founded in 1336 CE, represents the last great native phase in the annals of southern Indian history.
- The Vijayanagar kingdom may be categorized as the 'segmentary state' as defined by the American scholar, Burton Stein and his school of thought to denote a political formation that was feudal or patrimonial.
- Since historians are not unanimous about the origin and early history of Vijayanagar, different theories have been advanced regarding the foundations of the city of Vijayanagar.
- Three major linguistic groups—the Tamils, the Kannadigas and the Telugus—were brought under one banner, encouraging the emergence of what was called southern Indian culture.
- By offering a high degree of political unity to these and other groups, the kingdom worked towards acquiring an edge in warfare against northern conquerors for a long time. The kingdom also ensured that no smaller kingdoms or fiefdoms could challenge its authority.
- Ruled by four different dynasties—the Sangamas, the Saluvas, the Tuluvas and the Aravidus—Vijayanagar unified the region in a manner in which no other kingdom had done in the past.
- The kingdom of Vijayanagar was a powerful military state. The Rayas of the kingdom first defeated and subdued the native rulers who represented various shades of Hindu philosophy.
- But as the kingdom grew to become a formidable force challenging and blocking the advances of the Muslims from the north, it came to be described by some historians as the saviour of Hinduism in southern India.
- The major conflicts in the region were between Vijayanagar and the Bahmanis, primarily for the fertile Krishna–Godavari delta, the Kaveri basin, the Tungabhadra Doab and the Konkan regions.
- The kingdom's frequent disputes and wars with the neighbouring Golconda, Bijapur, Ahmednagar and Bidar sultanates had more to do with political domination and control of territory than the issue of faith.
- The greatest of the Vijayanagar kings, Krishna Deva Raya, was a broadminded visionary who gave the kingdom its famed military and political prowess. He established cordial relations with the kingdom's arch rival, the Bahmanis, and made his military force superior to them.
- The allied Deccan sultans fought a battle against Vijayanagar in 1565 CE at Talikota, which resulted in the disastrous defeat of the Vijayanagar forces that initiated an end of almost three centuries of rule.

KEYWORDS

Peninsular India   Nayankara   Monetization   Segmentary state
Urbanization

REVIEW QUESTIONS

1. What do you understand by the term 'segmentary state' as applied to Vijayanagar by Burton Stein?
2. What are the different theories expressed about the origin and early history of Vijayanagar?
3. How did Harihara and Bukka establish the sway of the growing state of Vijayanagar in southern India?
4. How did Krishna Deva Raya build up the Vijayanagar kingdom as a superior military and political power?
5. Discuss the significance of the Battle of Talikota.

CHAPTER **11**

Contours of the Vijayanagar State

Review and Discussion

- Central Administration
- Provincial Administration
- Land Revenue
- The Army
- Justice
- Society and Economy
- Religion and Culture
- Art and Architecture
- Literature
- Conclusion

The establishment of the powerful state of Vijayanagar in the fourteenth century constitutes an event of great significance in the history of medieval India. It not only filled the political vacuum that existed in southern India, but also left a permanent impression in the fields of administration, culture, religion, art and literature. Conveying the depth and creativity of Hindu religious and literary expression of its times, the Vijayanagar state exuded both spiritual insights as well as tangible experiences of a rich and influential period of the country's history.

Central Administration

In the administrative apparatus that prevailed in Vijayanagar, the king was at the apex of the entire system. His authority was almost unlimited; he looked after civil administration, directed the military affairs of the kingdom and acted as the final court of justice. He was advised and assisted in all these by a number of ministers and royal officers. The administrative foundations of the Vijayanagar state were laid during Harihara I's reign.

The theory of kingship, as followed by the Vijayanagar rulers, is enunciated in contemporary literary works of the era. Krishna Deva Raya defined the prevailing concept of kingship in his *Amuktamalyada,* where the king was assisted by a council of ministers in daily administration. Other important offices were those of the Chief Treasurer and the Prefect of Police, among others.

Although the rulers of Vijayanagar tried to establish a relatively high degree of centralization in their administrative system by staying at the helm of affairs themselves, their power and influence in the kingdom's peripheries remained by and large symbolic. The kings exercised control over their kingdom through their overlords, leading to centrifugal tendencies appearing from time to time. In other words, the king was symbolically important, but he lacked coercive power. This was the segmentary state model in which Vijayanagar was categorized by Burton Stein (as discussed in Chapter 10).

During their initial period of rule, Harihara and Bukka had only five provinces—known as *rajyas*—under their control; it was only later that with the increase in territorial boundaries that newer ones were added. Within these provincial regions, there were other big and small principalities, which exercised varying degrees of power. The revenue and the military departments were under the charge of the central administration, but it was the provincial governors and their subordinates who actually collected the taxes and maintained a large body of troops. The central government maintained only a small contingent as they were provided military help from the troops stationed at the provinces. The centre had the authority to fix the value of the lands held by the provincial governors and also determine the number of troops that were to be supplied from the revenues of each province. This administrative arrangement came to be known as the *nayankara* system, in which outstanding military chieftains received land grants and privileged status as *nayakas* (local lords or governors) from the state. The *nayankara* system was modelled on that of the Kakatiyas and served as a significant foundation for the Vijayanagar state, based as it was on a distinctive form of military land tenure.

In the *nayankara* system, the military chiefs or warriors who held the positions of *nayakas* or *amaranayakas* were not given the privileged status on the basis of any fixed parameters, such as definite offices, ethnic identity, or duties or rights assigned to them. They were more like rural landed magnates who were trying to maximize their revenue returns from the lands assigned to them in order to maintain their troops. The *nayakas* did not give any fixed revenue to the state; they merely rendered military service in return for the land and privileges granted to them. There was hardly any difference between the positions of *nayakas* and *amaranayakas* except for the title. It is believed that *amaranayanka* was a designation conferred on a military officer or chief who had under his control a specified number of troops, while the territory under these military chiefs was called *amaram*.

Many historians and travellers have given their individual interpretations of the *nayankara* system. Nilakanta Sastri, a historian who has extensively studied the Vijayanagar polity has categorized the *nayakas* into two different categories—the local lords who came before 1565 CE, and those who came after 1565 CE. He says that the former were totally dependent on the rulers for their wealth and status, while the latter were semi-independent. However, later he modified his views by pointing out that the *nayakas* before 1565 CE were military leaders holding fiefs. Hence, in his opinion, the Vijayanagar state was a military confederacy consisting of many chieftains led by a powerful ruler. He emphasized that the growing threat from Islam made the Vijayanagar rulers adopt an overtly military and religious stance. By and large, although the *nayankara* system had feudal connotations, when compared with the typical European model, it is evident that features of European feudalism, such as fealty, homage and sub-infeudation were absent from it. The *nayakas* also did not pay any fixed revenue to the state, they only rendered military service. Hence, other historians like T.V. Mahalingam and D.C. Sircar have also refuted the feudal theory, and have explained the *nayankara* system in terms of landlordism, a variant of feudalism in which land was allotted to the *nayakas* in lieu of their military services for the ruler. The obligations and activities of the *nayakas* were among others, giving gifts to temples, repairing and building tanks, reclamation of wasteland and collection of dues from temples. The Tamil inscriptions, too, do not refer to any revenue given by the *nayaka* to the king or his officials. On the basis of the Mackenzie manuscripts, another historian, Krishnaswami Aiyangar, views the *nayakas* as feudal lords. He says they were commanders of the Vijayanagar army, formerly under Krishna Deva Raya, who had established independent *nayaka* kingdoms at a later date. Thus, there is a thin line of difference between all these interpretations. While Sastri explains the system in terms of a military confederacy, Sircar and Mahalingam consider the *nayakas* of Vijayanagar to be warriors holding an office known as the *kara,* bestowed on them by the central government for rendering military services, and Aiyangar views the *nayakas* as military commanders in a feudal setup.

Fernao Nuniz and Domingo Paes, who visited India during the reigns of Krishna Deva Raya and Achyuta Raya, while identifying the *nayakas* as representatives of the Vijayanagar rulers, like Aiyangar say that the *nayakas* made payments to the Rayas out of the revenue collected on the assigned lands, denoting a feudal character. By and large, the system as it evolved, feudal or otherwise, allowed the *nayakas* opportunities to build semi-independent hereditary holdings. The Vijayanagar inscriptions and the later Mackenzie manuscripts refer to the *nayakas* as landed gentry who had political ambitions, which at times came into conflict with the policies of the rulers. Therefore, on the one hand, the *nayakas* were a source of strength for the Vijayanagar state, while on the other they also became its rivals.

The process of the formation of the *nayaka* chieftaincies which had started as early as Krishna Deva Raya's reign came to a close by the end of the sixteenth century with the emergence of five powerful *nayaka* states—Ikkeri, Mysore, Senji, Tanjavur and Madurai. After the collapse of the Vijayanagar state, when the *nayakas* became completely independent in their respective principalities, they brought in new administrative measures in the socio-economic and religious fields, which lasted even after the end of the *nayakas'* rule.

Thus, the *nayankara* system, which was a political-economic-military institution, worked well in the presence of a strong central authority. Temple complexes and monastic organizations (*mathas*) representing various religious traditions emerged as major centres, where people participated in politics related to the *nayaka* chieftaincies. A fairly elaborate and specialized administrative infrastructure was required to maintain these diverse local and regional political systems. The rulers were aware of the power of the provinces and tried to counter it by appointing members of the royal family as governors of the more important military provinces. However, this was not always successful as there were a number of succession disputes between family members.

Provincial Administration

For administrative convenience, the Vijayanagar polity was divided into territorial units called provinces. Each province was placed under the charge of a governor who was like a *nayaka,* a military officer, but he was also bound to furnish a certain amount of revenue with a fixed contingent of troops. The governors generally remained in the capital city and administered their duties through their deputies. The province was a replica of the centre and provincial governors ruled as virtual sovereigns; but accountability and the uncertainty of their office tenure acted as restraints on the governors' powers. Harihara I who created an organized administrative setup patterned his system along the lines of the Kakatiyas by setting up units called *stholas, nadus* and *simas.* Officials were appointed to collect the revenues from these lands and oversee local administration. Generally, *brahmans* were preferred to men of other castes. The provinces were further sub-divided into *kottams,* which were again divided into towns and groups of villages. The self-sufficient village was the basic unit of administration, where local affairs were managed by the village assembly through hereditary officials called *ayagars.*

Like the *nayankara* system at the central level, the *ayagar* system was a distinctive administrative form, in vogue at the village level. The *ayagars* were village functionaries who constituted groups of families. They held different positions, such as those of village headmen, accountants and watchmen, and sometimes they also settled minor disputes, collected revenues and preserved law and order. They, thus, played a significant role by acting as a link between the administration and the people.

Like the *nayakas,* the *ayagars* were usually allotted portions of lands in a village. No regular tax was imposed on the agricultural income that accrued from it; only sometimes they were asked to pay a fixed rent for these lands. In special cases, the state made direct payments in kind to these village officials for services performed by them. Other members of the village community such as the washermen and the priests, for instance who provided essential services for the village community were also paid through land assignments. Other service providers, who offered ordinary goods and services, were leather workers, potters, blacksmiths, carpenters, watermen, bankers and money lenders. A distinctive characteristic of the *ayagar* system was that land was specially allocated to them and specific cash payments were also made to those holding a particular office.

With better administrative organization there was an increase in income for the state making the core more centralized. Yet, it did not result in a situation where salaried officials could directly collect revenue from the peasantry in most areas. Rather, most land remained under the control of subordinate chiefs or a hierarchy of local landholders, who paid revenue and provided troops to the king. Harihara I also encouraged cultivation in areas that had been recently reclaimed from forest lands by fixing lower taxes on them. Thus, newer institutional apparatus in the form of the *nayankara* and *ayagar* systems at the central and provincial levels of Vijayanagar administration replaced the administrative innovations that had existed under the Cholas.

Land Revenue

The Vijayanagar kings enjoyed huge income from various sources. The chief being land revenue, which was fixed after the land was measured and categorized. The old practice of payment in kind was given up and the state demanded a regular cash payment calculated on the basis of current market prices of grains.

The system of revenue farming was in operation in Vijayanagar as in other parts of medieval India. The Vijayanagar state gave the right to collect taxes to the highest bidder, who then collected the state's taxes and made payments to the state, keeping a part of the tax revenue for his own use. Other than the farming of land taxes, this system also included the farming of urban taxes. C.A. Bayly is of the view that the kind of revenue farming that existed in fifteenth and sixteenth century Vijayanagar appears to have been largely confined to the farming of customs in ports, and other levies, such as octroi. However, revenue farming had long become the established practice for the collection of land revenue in Vijayanagar.

As the *nayakas* grew to enjoy a semi-independent status, farming of land taxes seemed to suffer from several exploitative tendencies, adding to the burden on the peasantry. The insolence of tax collectors and the enhanced tax burden on the peasantry left them with the bare minimum after the forceful collection of revenues. There are records of peasants migrating to escape the oppression of local landholders. Although exact figures are unavailable, evidence suggests that the level of taxation was close to half of the produce in many areas. Much of this revenue did not even go to the state, because various layers of local landholders took their share first. Besides land tax, there were also a number of cesses that the people had to pay. It is said that there was a tax imposed on prostitutes too. Although most revenue came from agrarian taxes, commercial and artisan taxes, and tributary duties from foreign traders were levied as well.

The eminent historian, Sanjay Subrahmanyam, opines that when agricultural taxes increased tremendously, agriculture as a resource of the state began to decline in many parts of agrarian South Asia, as revenue raised from the agrarian sector began to be invested in trade. Despite such developments, historians like J. F. Richards were of the opinion that given the strong character of the peasantry, agricultural production did not halt altogether. Keeping the regional diversity of kingdoms in South Asia in mind, each with their own socio-cultural and political histories, revenue farming as a method invariably led to better administration.

The Army

It has been suggested by some historians that the Vijayanagar state was essentially a military state; however, this view is not popularly accepted as it implies a certain level of coercion with no concern for human welfare and development. Based on its military organization, it is more objective to say that the Vijayanagar state was a military confederacy of chieftains with the ruler at the helm. The king maintained his standing army, which consisted of contingents provided by provincial governors, besides the king's personal troops that were recruited and paid directly by him. The contingents of the provincial governors were mainly used in times of emergency.

Kings like Devaraya I contributed significantly to the reorganizing of the military administrative structure. Realizing how important the cavalry and well-trained archers were to an army, Persian and Arabian horses were imported, while Turkish archers as well as troopers skilled in mounted warfare were taken in too. Although it appears that Devaraya I was rarely able to defeat the Bahmanis in the battlefield, it should be noted that he had begun to narrow the strategic and technological gap between the north and south zones by building an army that would be better suited to warfare on open plains. The Vijayanagar rulers relied much more upon elephants in their military operations; care was taken in repairing old forts and keeping them in good condition. The front on which the Vijayanagar army was found to be weak was the artillery division; but as far the use of forts as military garrisons was concerned, they were the masters.

The problem of defense had compounded with the founding of the Bahmani state to the north of Vijayanagar in 1347 CE. There were frequent conflicts between the two kingdoms over the fertile Raichur Doab because of strategic importance. Keeping in view the increasing threat of external invasions, Vijayanagar had to develop sophisticated military apparatus for safeguarding its growing territory. Safety and security against external attack was given high priority and many strong forts were constructed, especially along the frontiers.

There were seven walls of fortification built around the city. It is interesting to note that there were several kinds of forts too. The *Rayavachakamu* (written by one of the governors of Krishna Deva Raya on his campaigns) mentions four kinds of forts: *giridurga* (hill fort), *sthaladurga* (land fort), *jaladurga* (water fort) and *vanadurga* (forest fort). Most of the forts were built of mud and the construction of stone walls was permitted in case of a fort being situated on the fringes of the kingdom's territorial boundaries. The forts had all the necessary commodities needed by the soldiers under the command of an officer known as *durgapati*. A well-equipped garrison sufficient enough to repel the attacks of an invader was placed under him. It is interesting to note that Krishna Deva Raya mentions his forts having *yantras* (devices) fitted to them, which might have included guns too. The forts also had deep moats to prevent the entry of the enemy. In order to hinder the progress of the enemy's cavalry, pointed stones of great height were fixed along the stone walls. Forts were sometimes erected in newly conquered regions too, or where there were rebellious tribes.

An important characteristic of fort building in the Vijayanagar period was the stone veneering technique in which neatly dressed stones were arranged on either side, with a hollow space left within the walls that was filled with earth and rubble. This construction technique gave extra strength and durability to the fort. This style is more evident in the forts of Hampi and Chandragiri.

Despite the sophisticated military apparatus of the Vijayanagar state, during Rama Raya's rule the efforts toward centralization were not entirely successful, and it was his military policies that ultimately led to disaster. There were rebellions when he replaced many members of the old nobility with relatives and close associates. Judging by the number and size of the military campaigns that Rama Raya had launched outside Vijayanagar in later years, it appears that he had complete control within his kingdom.

Rama Raya has, in fact, been criticized for allowing foreigners, such as Persians and Turks, to hold important positions within his administration. His defeat at Talikota was partly attributed to the defection of two of his Muslim generals. But most historians overlook the fact that up to the battle of Talikota, Rama Raya's policy of benefiting from the superior military and administrative abilities of the Persians and Turks worked very well in his favour. Rama Raya's early experience as an official at the court of Golconda appears to have given him ideas for improving the administration and army of Vijayanagar. As early as 1535 CE he is known to have hired 3,000 soldiers from Bijapur. Later he tried to model the Vijayanagar state apparatus along the lines of his rival sultanates. In short, he was busy building a state that would be as competitive as possible for the times. It is likely that the Deccani sultanates initially viewed Vijayanagar as just another competing state. But Rama Raya's military successes against some of them and his proven skills in diplomacy, together with his belief that Vijayanagar was stronger than any of them led to the sultanates collectively aligning against him.

Justice

There was no regular judiciary system in the Vijayanagar kingdom. The king was the supreme court of justice, and his ruling was considered final in all important cases. At the grassroots level, the village panchayat acted as a local tribunal, while big towns saw the local governor acting out multiple roles as a revenue collector, magistrate and judge. Judged by modern standards, the code of punishments for criminal offences under the Vijayanagar rulers seem to have been very severe and barbarous. Mutilation for theft, death for robbery, murder and adultery, and being trampled to death by elephants were not unusual for the times.

Society and Economy

The four-fold division of society—*brahmans, kshatriyas, vaishyas* and *shudras*—based on the *Varna* system continued to exist during the Vijayanagar period. *Brahmans* occupied a high position in society and were held in great esteem by the rulers. Nuniz describes them as, '. . . honest men, given to merchandise, very acute and of much talent, very good at accounts, lean men and well formed, but little fitted for hard work. By these and the duties they undertake the kingdom is carried on . . .' (as cited in Sewell 2004). With the Vijayanagar kings being anxious to maintain social solidarity, there were also a number of subcastes and communities in society.

The nobles led a luxurious and splendid lifestyle, and foreign visitors provide a pleasing picture of the life of the nobility. Articles of luxury like ornaments, perfumes, betel leaves and a number of other stimulants were in great demand, with foreign merchants carrying on a brisk and prosperous trade in these articles. Hunting, boxing, wrestling, gambling, cock-fighting, dice, polo, music, dance and dramas were some of the most popular amusements of the citizens of Vijayanagar.

According to Nuniz, people in Vijayanagar ate almost everything, except the flesh of oxen or cows. Animals meant for consumption were sold in the markets. Mention is also made of intoxicants comprising the usual liquors, among which a drink known as the *maireya* was very popular. Paes and

Nuniz, who visited Vijayanagar in the first and latter half of the sixteenth century, respectively, describe in glowing terms the abundance and affordability of daily provisions. Paes says of the capital city, 'This is the best-provided city in the world and is stocked with provisions, such as rice, wheat, grains, corn and a certain amount of barley and beans, moong, pulses and horse-gram, which grow in this country, and which are the food of the common people and there is a large store of these sold very cheap' (as cited in Sewell 2004). Paes was a widely travelled man, who had visited important cities of southern Europe and might have come across many cities in the course of his travels from Portugal to Vijayanagar. Therefore, his observation that the city of Vijayanagar was 'the best-provided city in the world' holds great significance. Paes is supported by Nuniz, who says, 'The markets are overflowing with abundance of fruits, grapes and oranges, limes, pomegranates, jackfruit and mangoes and all very cheap' (as cited in Sewell 2004).

The Vijayanagar kings were very liberal in granting provisions to their guests. Abdur Razzak, the Persian traveller who came to Vijayanagar during the reign of Devaraya II, received a large amount of daily provisions. In the *Matla'u-s Sa'dain wa Majma'u-l Bahrain (The Rising of the two fortunate Planets (Jupiter and Venus), and the Junction of the two Seas)*, he writes, 'The daily provisions forwarded to me comprised two sheep, four couples of fowls, five *mans* of rice, one *man* of butter, one *man* of sugar and two *varahas* in gold'. The ration that was doled out was meant for one individual for a single day.

Women enjoyed a better position in society, in comparison to their northern counterparts. They participated keenly in social, political and literary activities of the time. There were also women wrestlers, astrologers and clerks who were well-educated and experienced in state business. Yet, the Vijayanagar society was not free from the social evils of child marriage, the dowry system and the frequent practice of *sati*. Another Portuguese traveller, Barbosa, records the interesting fact that on the death of a king, even men who were his close associates were cremated along with him. Animal and human sacrifices to mark the culmination of festivals were in vogue too. Polygamy was not uncommon and even visits to brothels were considered to be fairly normal, unattached with any social stigma. Sometimes women of pleasure accompanied the army and accomplished courtesans often enjoyed special favours from the kings.

The economic prosperity of Vijayanagar is also well-documented in the accounts of Nuniz and Paes. There were certain factors that contributed to the sound economy of the Vijayanagar kingdom. The development of agriculture and the resultant agrarian surplus was a potential factor in the growth of the kingdom's wealth. Another major factor was the development of industries, such as textiles, mining, metallurgy, diamonds, perfumes, salt, etc. Vijayanagar's flourishing trade and commerce was yet another important factor contributing towards economic development. Internal trade within the kingdom was conducted by the well-organized merchant and craft guilds, while external trade was carried on by the Arab and Portuguese traders. Calicut, Cochin, Pulicat, Bhaktal and Mangalore were the chief ports of the kingdom, abuzz with trading activities. The many countries with whom Vijayanagar had commercial relations included the islands in the Indian Ocean, Malay, Burma, China, Abyssinia, South Africa and Persia. While the major export commodities were textiles, rice, iron, saltpetre, sugar and spices, the major imports included horses, elephants, coral, mercury, Chinese silk and velvet. Abdur Razzak, states that in Vijayanagar, three kinds of coins were in use—*varaha, dinara* and *fanam*. Of these the *fanam* was most popular.

While the affluent sections of society were rich and prosperous from their income from agriculture, trade and manufacture, the poor peasants lead a miserable existence sunk in poverty and squalor, over burdened as they were with taxes.

The description of Vijayanagar by Abdur Razzak bears testimony to the greatness of the kingdom, with

The Celebration of the Mahanáwí

The infidels of this country, who are endowed with power, are fond of displaying their pride, pomp, power, and glory, in holding every year a stately and magnificent festival, which they call *Mahanáwí*. The manner of it is this: The King of Bíjána-gar directed that his nobles and chiefs should assemble at the royal abode from all the provinces of his country, which extends for the distance of three or four months' journey. They brought with them a thousand elephants, tumultuous as the sea, and thundering as the clouds, arrayed in armour, and adorned with howdahs, on which jugglers and throwers of naphtha were seated; and on the foreheads, trunks, and ears of the elephants extraordinary forms and pictures were traced with cinnabar and other pigments.

Source: Elliot, H. M., Sir, *The History of India as Told by its Own Historians, Vol. IV: To the Year AD 1450*, Edited by John Dowson, London: Trubner Company, 1867–1877. Extract taken from *Matla'u-s Sa'dain*, of Abdu-r Razzák. Text available at Persian Literature in Translation: The Packard Humanities Institute.

the city of Vijayanagar symbolizing vast power and wealth. It was a royal ceremonial and administrative centre with a hub of trade routes. Foreign travellers and visitors were struck by the variety and quality of trade goods that the city offered, the grand architecture of the palace complex and temples, and by the ceremonial significance of the annual *Mahanavami* celebrations, at which the *nayakas* and other chiefs came together to pay tributes.

The grandeur of the city, the magnificence of its buildings and the general prosperity of the people are attested by a number of contemporary witnesses as well as by an archaeological survey of the ruins. Soon after being founded, the city grew speedily in importance. Ferishta admits that as early as 1378 CE the Rayas of Vijayanagar were greatly superior in power, wealth and extent of territory as compared to the Bahmani kings. His account of the marriage of Firuz Shah Bahmani to Devaraya I's daughter gives a good idea of the grandeur of the capital in 1406 CE. Nicolo Conti, who visited Vijayanagar in 1420 CE, estimated the circumference of the city to be sixty miles and was impressed by the strength of its fortifications. Abdur Razzak observes that the city of 'Beejanagaur' is such that the eye has not seen nor the ear heard of any place resembling it in the whole world. We then come to the detailed description recorded by Paes in 1522 CE when the kingdom was at the height of its glory under Krishna Deva Raya. Paes says that Krishna Deva Raya made the city as extensive as Rome with more than 1,00,000 houses inhabited by countless people belonging to every nation and people, because of the city's trading relations with the world. In Paes' opinion this was a city where people led a luxurious life on a whole.

The vast and fertile state of Vijayanagar contained 300 sea ports, was well cultivated and populous. Abdur Razzak describes the seven-walled city, its markets, houses, king's palace, throne, public buildings, festive occasions, brothels, etc. The police and army were well-organized. The king's elephants were as 'lofty as the hills and gigantic as demons'. In short, the city was unparalleled in its grandeur from its accounts by foreign travellers.

Religion and Culture

The rulers of Vijayanagar followed a policy of religious tolerance for the most part. Though the kings were ardent champions of Hinduism, in keeping with the best traditions of Hinduism, they did not persecute other religions. They respected the sentiments of the people of other faiths and gave them all opportunity to practice their beliefs. Most of the rulers—Bukka I, Harihara II and Devaraya II—had a catholic point of view. An important event of Bukka's reign was the diplomatic mission he sent to the Chinese emperor. He assumed imperial titles like *Maharajadhiraja, Rajaparameshwara* and Lord of the Eastern, Southern and Western Oceans, yet in his religious policies he exhibited liberal views. In 1368 CE, while trying to settle a dispute between the Jains and Vaishnavites, he remarked that since all religions were like one body, there could not be any quarrel between the followers of different faiths. Harihara II followed the traditional policy of tolerance towards all religions too, and as a pious Hindu, he made grants to the temples of Kalahasti, Srisailam, Ahobilam, Chidambaram, Tirupati and Srirangam. Irugappa, his general and minister was a Jain, who had authored the *Nanartharatnamala,* one of the best dictionaries in Sanskrit, and had also built a Jain temple in the capital in 1385 CE. Harihara's chief minister was the celebrated Sayanacharya, brother of Madhava and a reputed Vedic scholar.

Krishna Deva Raya, though a follower of Vaishnavism, treated Shaivites, Jains, Christians and Jews with kindness and compassion. The slaughter of cows, considered sacred by the Hindus, was permitted too. This rare spirit of tolerance attracted the attention of many foreign travellers like Barbosa (1504–14 CE) who remarked in admiration, 'The king allows such freedom that every man may come and go and live according to his own creed without suffering any annoyance and without enquiring whether he is a Christian, Jew, Moor or Heathen. Great equity and justice is observed by all.' Elaborate arrangements were made for celebrating temple festivals on a grand scale in order to forge strong emotional integration.

Art and Architecture

Art and architecture attained a certain fullness and freedom of expression during the Vijayanagar rule. The elaborate ceremonial observances strengthened the temple system of worship. The Vijayanagar rulers built magnificent cities and beautified them with temples and splendid houses, grand palaces, public offices, irrigation works, and aqueducts that bear testimony to the wealth and prosperity of the times. These buildings elicited the wonder and praise of the tourists of those days. The

HAMPI, VIRUPAKSHA TEMPLE. *It is the oldest and the principal temple in Hampi. Of the three towers, the eastern tower rises to a height of 160 feet and is nine tiered. It dates back to the first half of the fifteenth century and was renovated in the sixteenth century by Krishna Deva Raya. The presiding deity here is Lord Shiva known popularly as Virupaksheshwara. The temple complex also contains ornate shrines dedicated to Hindu goddesses Bhuvaneshwari and Pampa.*

HAMPI, BALAKRISHNA TEMPLE. *Built by the ruler Krishna Deva Raya in 1513 CE. Dedicated to Bala Krishna and it is one of the few temples where stories of Puranas were carved on the walls of the temple. There is also the murti of Bala Krishna worshipped by Madhvacharya in his Sri Krishna Matha of Udupi.*

Vijayanagar style of art and architecture was essentially opulent, ornate and exuberant.

The numerous temples built throughout the kingdom bear eloquent testimony to the general consciousness of the rulers and of the people as the custodians of Hindu religion and culture. Among the temples built within the capital city of Hampi, the Virupaksha temple also known as Pampapati was the most sacred and noted for its architectural values. The ruins of Hampi bear witness to the distinct style of Vijayanagar's architecture, the finest in the city being the Vittalaswamy and Hazara Ramaswamy temples built by Krishna Deva Raya. The Vittalaswami temple is a fine example of the magnificence in floral sculpture, patronized by the Vijayanagar court; while the Hazara Ramaswamy temple with its walls and pillars adorned with sculptures illustrates the main events from the Ramayana. The former, according to Fergusson, 'shows the extreme limit in floral magnificence to which the style advanced' and is regarded as the flower of sculptured art patronized by the Vijayanagar court. The latter is significant for the continuous panels of sculptures illustrating various legends from the Ramayan. Another important temple built by Krishna Deva Raya was the Balakrishna temple for the image of Balakrishna brought from Orissa.

Other than the temples containing numerous sculptures conceived and executed with original and imaginative art work, another aspect worth noting in these temples are the pillars that are a major architectural marvel and are remarkable for their intricacy and delicate beauty. Mention must also be made of the huge monolithic of Ganesha, Hanuman and Narasimha which are some of the most beautiful examples of this sculptural style.

The religious zeal of the kings was expressed in the construction of new temples, renovation of

GANESHA MONOLITH, *Hampi*

NARASIMHA MONOLITH, *Hampi*

old ones and additions made to a number of temples in different parts of the country. There was an elaboration of the temple complex by the addition of a number of structures of which the shrine of the chief goddess (*ammankoil*) and the *kalyanamandapam* were considered to be indispensable. Among the latter, the most distinguished were those of the Varadaraja and Ekambaranatha temples at Kanchipuram, the Jambukeswara temple near Tiruchirapalli, the Parvathi temple at Chidambaram and the Jalaganteswara temple within the Vellore fort. The last one is regarded by Percy Brown as 'the richest and the most beautiful structure of its kind'.

The Vijayanagar rulers were also famous for the construction of colossal towers (*gopurams*) that formed the entrances to temples. These several storied pyramidal structures added to the picturesque grandeur of the temple complex. The most magnificent among them being the southern *gopuram* of Ekambarantha temple built by Krishna Deva Raya. It is an imposing structure, 188 feet high and made up of 10 storeys, all of which are embellished with exquisite sculptures. The exuberance of sculptures and ornamentation breaks up the stupendous mass in a manner that imparts to it an effect of airy lightness, enhancing the impression of soaring height. Though it has served as a model for many later *gopurams*, it remains unsurpassed in its grandeur, balance and rhythm.

The city of Vijayanagar was also studded with a number of grand palaces, public offices and irrigation works. The most splendid among the secular buildings was the royal palace, which according to Paes, enclosed a greater space than all the castles of Lisbon. Another building was that of the Lotus Mahal, which Longhurst regarded as a fine specimen of Indo-Sarcenic architecture. Not far from this were the elephant stables, an extremely elegant and well designed building. Here too one finds a harmonious blend of Hindu and Islamic architectural features. The Hampi bazaar on the banks of the Tungabhadra displayed a fine example of street architecture. Krishna Deva Raya also built a huge tank for water supply and irrigation purposes as well as a small town called Nagalapuram.

LOTUS MAHAL, *Hampi*

STONE CHARIOT, *Vitthala Temple, Hampi*

A BEAUTIFULLY DESIGNED STEP WELL, *Hampi*

Vijayanagar Art

Patronage was extended to the genre of painting because of the interest taken by the kings, viceroys and nobles in this particular art form. There is textual evidence from Domingo Paes and Du Jarric that testifies to the presence of painters in the court of Krishna Deva Raya and Venkata II. Specimens of Vijayanagar paintings are found at Tirupati and Lepakshi, the Chennakesava temple at Somapalle, the Varadaraja temple at Kanchipuram and the temples at Hampi and Anegundi. Some of these have been executed with mastery, skill and imagination and are characterized by beautiful form, sure and bold lines, and artistic colour schemes. But the themes of Vijayanagar paintings are considered uninteresting, except for some charming specimens that depict the marriage of Parvati, Arjuna's penance, Rama's coronation, Krishna lying on a banyan leaf, and the representation of Shiva in various forms. Unfortunately, many of these paintings were destroyed during the battle of Talikota. Today the UNESCO World Heritage site of Hampi remains merely a vast, open air museum of monuments, as if frozen in time.

LITERATURE

The resurgence of Hinduism was abundantly reflected in the religious literature of the age. A number of religious books were written to strengthen the philosophic foundations of Hinduism. Great philosophers wrote scholarly treatises on the different schools of Hindu philosophy. The *Bhakti* cult was given a new stimulus and there was a rich harvest of devotional literature in Sanskrit, Tamil, Kannada and Telugu. These emphasized the importance of devotion, morality and austerity as a means of attaining sublimity and salvation. The *Puranas* and epics were translated into Telugu and Kannada, along with accounts of sacred sites (*sthalapuranas*).

Therefore, the period witnessed prolific literary activity under the patronage of the kings which led to the birth and growth of new forms and trends in Sanskrit and the major southern languages. Some of the finest pieces of literature in these regional languages were produced during this period. Three centuries of rule opened neo-classical and romantic vistas, especially in the realm of Telugu literature.

Sanskrit Literature

Vedantadesika, a reputed religious teacher of the period, was a great exponent of *Vishishtadvaita* philosophy. He was invited by the Vijayanagar ruler to occupy a seat in the royal court but he preferred to remain in the holy city of Srirangam in Tamil Nadu for his scholarly pursuits. His *Sankalpasuryodaya,* an allegorical drama, *Tatvamuktakalapa* and *Satadushani* were the most important works in which he established the soundness of the *Vishishtadvaita* philosophy. He also wrote a commentary on Sri Ramanuja's *Sribhashya* and *Gitabhashya,* and a *mahakavya* called *Yadavahyudayam,* describing the life of Lord Krishna. He composed a number of devotional songs too, which were collectively known as *Desikaprabandham.*

An able exponent of the *Advaita* philosophy was Madhava Vidyaranya who was closely connected with the foundation of the kingdom. His *Panchadasi* gives a classical account of this school of thought, and his *Sarvadarsana Sangraha* examines 16 systems of philosophy, ultimately establishing the superiority of the *Advaita* school of thought. Appaiya Dikshita was another exponent of *Advaita* philosophy. He is credited with a hundred books, including a fine treatise known as *Parimala.* Vyasathirtha, hailed as one of the founders of the *Dvaita* philosophy, gives an authoritative exposition of this philosophical branch in his *Bhedoj Jivana* and *Tatparya Chandrika.* His greatest work, *Nyayamrita,* is devoted to a denial of the *Advaita* philosophy.

There were also a number of secular works composed during this period, of which Ganga Devi's *Madhura Vijayam* (which describes the conquests of her husband, Kumara Kampana), Rajnatha Dandima's *Saluvabhyudaya* (a historical eulogy of his patron, Saluva Narasimha), Tirumalamba's *Varadambika Parinayam* (which describes the marriage of Achyuta Raya with Varadambika), and Krishna Deva Raya's *Jambavati Kalyanam* and *Ushaparinayam* are important texts. Lakshmidhara wrote a treatise on music called *Sangita Sarvodaya,* while Chetana Kalinatha wrote an elaborate commentary on the *Sangita Ratnakara* of Sarangadeva.

Kannada Literature

Several attempts were made to acquaint the masses with religious teachings, which consequently led to the development of various vernacular languages. Many books were written on Jainism during this time, including biographies of some Jain *Tirthankaras.* The earliest of such Jain writers were Bahubali and Madhura, each of whom wrote a biography of Dharmanatha, the fifteenth *Tirthankara.* The greatest work of this genre is the *Bharatesa Vaibhava* by Ratnakara. Texts illustrating Jain teachings and scholarly works on the doctrines of Jainism were also written during this time.

Virasaivas wrote a number of books to popularize their faith too. These consisted mainly of stories narrating the lives of the 63 Shaiva saints and Basava, commentaries on Basava's teachings and Virasaiva mythology. One of the famous Vaishnava writers was Narayanappa, also known as Kumara Vyasa. Composing his texts around the middle of the fifteenth century, he wrote a Kannada version of the *Mahabharata* which is acclaimed as one of the finest works in Kannada literature, because of his fertile imagination, vivid portrayal of characters, picturesque description of situations and high spiritual ideals.

Besides these, there were innumerable devotional lyrics popularly known as *Dasara Padagalu*. Some of them were in the form of devotional songs (*kirtanas*) and others were compositions in rhythmic prose (*suladis*). The popular masters of this art were Puranadaradasa and Kanakadasa. The former's soul stirring devotional songs are popular with devout Kannadigas to this day. Kanakadasa's *Mohana Tarangini*, narrating the life of Sri Krishna, *Haribhakti* (a moral story book for children) and *Nalacharitra* bear testimony with a simple and graceful style of narration.

Tamil Literature

Arunagirinatha was patronized by Devaraya II. His 1360 songs in praise of Lord Subramanya or Kartikeya are collectively known as *Tirruppugaz*. Considered to be exquisite pieces of Tamil poetry, these songs teach a simple philosophy of faith and devotion to Kartikeya. Haridasa, a poet protégé of Krishna Deva Raya, in his literary work, *Irusamaya Villakam*, gives a scholarly exposition of Saivism and Vaishnavism. Kalamegha, a Tamil scholar, was also well known for his powerful style and bitter sarcasm.

Telugu Literature

It is in the field of Telugu literature that this period is most distinguished. Among the poets of the fifteenth century, the greatest was Srinatha. His *Naishadakavya*, also known as *Sringara Naishada* is a translation of the Sanskrit original written by Sriharsha. He was a prolific writer and wrote a number of works on Shaivite themes. He is said to have been the author of *Sringara Dipika*, a work on poetics and *Palnati Viracharitram*, which commemorates the heroic deeds of the warriors of Palnad. He also inaugurated a new development in Telugu drama called *Vithinataka*. He was essentially a court poet who described the grandeur and sensuous aspects of the lives of princes and nobles. His extraordinary literary talents earned for him the patronage of kings and nobles, and he had the honour of being bathed in gold for his literary excellence by Devaraya II who liberally patronized literary men.

A striking contrast to Srinatha was his brother-in-law, Potana, who preferred poverty to prosperity and spent his life in devotion to God and austere literary pursuits. His masterpiece, *Bhagavata*, written in simple, artistic and melodious style, is still one of the most popular works among the Teluguites.

Vemana, another great Telugu writer, composed the *Sataka* or hundred verses that were intended to inculcate philosophical and moral ideas among the Telguites. Pillalmarri Pina Virabhadra patronized by Saluva Narasimha is yet another great scholar known for his popular works of *Jaimini Bharatam* and *Sringara Sakuntala*.

The reign of Krishna Deva Raya marked the dawn of a new era in the literary history of southern India. Rightly called *Andhra Bhoja*, Krishna Deva Raya was a great author. Apart from his important Sanskrit works, the famous *Amuktamalyada*, written in Telugu, relates the story of a great *bhakta* and provides insights into human nature and expresses elusive moods through striking phrases. A number of Sanskrit, Telugu and Kannada poets enjoyed his patronage, the chief among them being Vyasatirtha, Vallabha, Chaitanya, Kumara Sarasvathi and the *Ashtadiggajas*. This is why the period is regarded as the glorious age of Telugu literature. Krishna Deva Raya's court was adorned by eight poets popularly known as the *Ashtadiggajas*. They were: Allasani Peddana (*Manu Charita*), Mukku Timmana (*Parijatapaharana*), Dhurjati (*Kalahasthisvaramahatyam*), Ramaraja Bhushana (*Vasucharitra*), Pingali Suranna (*Raghava-Pandaviyam*), Ayyalaraju Ramabhadra (*Ramabhyudayam*), Tenali Ramakrishna (*Panduranga-Mahatyam*) and Dhoorati (*Sri Kalahasteeshwara Mahatyam and Kalahasteeshwara Satakam*).

Peddana, rightly referred to as *Andhra Kavipithamaha*, was the court poet. He was the most illustrious poet of the age and his *kavya Manucharita* set the model for later *kavya* composers. Suranna was a pioneer in Telugu *dvanda kavya,* a literary genre in which verses have double meanings. His *Raghava Pandaviyam* narrates the stories of the *Ramayana* and the *Mahabharata* with the same verses. He also wrote the *Kalapurnodaya,* which is an interesting comedy of errors. His real greatness lay in the fact that he lent dramatic interest to his works. Patronized by Ramaraja, Ramaraja Bhushana was a pupil of Peddana. His ambition was to combine the skill of his teacher in descriptive art and the ingenuity of Suranna in using words with double meaning. His *Vasucharita* has been acclaimed as an artistic gem, almost a song set to music. He also wrote the *Harishchandra Nalopakhyana Advanda Kavya* which narrates the stories of Harishchandra and Nala. Tenali Rama who lived in the court of Venkatapati Raja was known for his humour and wisdom. He was also a great poet and his *Panduranga Mahatymam* is regarded as one of the *Pancha Mahakavyas* of Telugu literature.

The Telugu *kavyas* that were written dealt with heroic themes and romantic experiences describing elusive moods of passion, suspense, anxiety, fear and suspicion. There was ample scope for a free display of individual genius, poetic skill and literary excellence.

Even while uniting the three major linguistic groups—the Tamils, the Kannadigas and the Teluguites—under one banner, the rulers of Vijayanagar welcomed and accommodated people of different faiths in their kingdom with freedom to practice their own faiths. They gave the populace a feeling that the kingdom was the protector of the Hindu *dharma.* Although they followed their own version of Hindu philosophy, the kings were liberal towards other faiths such as Christianity, Judaism and Islam.

Conclusion

Thus we can see that the development of agriculture and the resultant agrarian surplus along with the development of industry was a potential factor in the growth of wealth in Vijayanagar. This was one of the reasons why several travellers of the era describe the capital of Vijayanagar as the 'best-provided city in the world'. While trying to establish a relatively high degree of centralized administration, kingship in Vijayanagar remained by and large symbolic in the peripheral areas. The rulers promoted mining of metals and diamonds, built craft guilds and encouraged their subjects to produce the best of fabrics and perfumes. They patronized Hindu religion and made extensive developments in the field of architecture through the construction of impressive temples and monuments. In addition, they also took extensive interest in the promotion of Sanskrit, Tamil, Kannada and Telugu literature, and united the three major linguistic groups under one banner. With the Battle of Talikota in 1564 CE, the glory of Vijayanagar finally came to an end.

SUMMARY

- The establishment of the powerful state of Vijayanagar in the fourteenth century constitutes an event of great significance in the history of India. It left a permanent impression of its existence in the fields of administration, art, culture, religion and literature.
- Although the Vijayanagar rulers tried to establish a relatively high degree of centralization in the administration, kingship in peripheral parts remained by and large symbolic.
- The rulers exercised control through their overlords, leading to centrifugal tendencies appearing from time to time.
- The administrative arrangement led to the development of the *nayankara* system, in which prominent commanders received land grants and high status as *nayakas* (local lords or governors).
- For administrative convenience, the kingdom was divided into provinces under the charge of

governors who were bound to furnish a certain amount of revenue and a fixed contingent of troops.
- The *ayagar* system like the *nayankara* system was another foundational institution of the Vijayanagar state. The *ayagars* were village functionaries who helped in settling minor disputes, collecting revenues and preserving law and order.
- The Vijayanagar kings enjoyed huge income from various sources, such as land revenue, and other taxes and cesses.
- The system of revenue farming in operation in Vijayanagar had the state giving the right to collect taxes to the highest bidder, who then deposited the same with the state, keeping a part of the tax revenue for his own use. Other than the farming of land taxes, this system also included the farming of urban taxes.
- The king maintained his standing army which consisted of contingents provided by provincial governors, besides the king's personal troops, which were recruited and paid directly by him.
- There was no regular judiciary system in the Vijayanagar kingdom. The king was the supreme court of justice and punishments were severe.
- The four-fold division of society based on the *Varna* system continued to exist. The nobles led a luxurious life and women enjoyed a good status in society.
- The development of agriculture and the resultant agrarian surplus along with the development of industry was a potential factor in the growth of wealth in Vijayanagar.
- The rulers of Vijayanagar followed a policy of religious tolerance. Though the kings were ardent champions of Hinduism, in keeping with the best traditions of Hinduism, they did not persecute other religions.
- Art and architecture attained a certain fullness and freedom of expression during the Vijayanagar rule.
- The rulers patronized Hindu religion and built beautiful temples, magnificent cities, grand palaces, public offices and irrigation works that bear testimony to the wealth and prosperity of the times. They also took interest in the promotion of Sanskrit, Tamil, Kannada and Telugu literature.
- It has been suggested by some historians that Vijayanagar was essentially a military state, but it is more objective to say that the Vijayanagar state was a feudal polity based on a military organization.

KEYWORDS

Rajyas
Amaranayaka
Nayankara system
Nayakas
Octroi
Landlordism
Ayagar system
Ayagars
Varna system
Gopurams
Advaita philosophy

REVIEW QUESTIONS

1. What do you understand by the term 'nayankara' system?
2. Write a short note on the 'ayagar' system.
3. How was revenue farming practiced in Vijayanagar?
4. 'Though the Vijayanagar kings were ardent champions of Hinduism, in keeping with the best traditions of Hinduism, they did not persecute other religions.' Elaborate.
5. Justify the epithet of Andhra Bhoja generally used to describe Krishna Deva Raya.

PART IV–The Bahmani Kingdom and the Deccani Sultanates

"Chand Bibi is the favourite heroine of the Deccan, and is the subject of many legends. Her wisdom and self-reliance, her pure administration and noble deeds in critical days deserve their lasting place in the people's affection. Of remarkable beauty, she was unblessed by children, and retained her grace of figure until the day of her violent death. Always elegantly dressed, she used to ride astride on a richly caparisoned steed, whether to the field, on tour, or hunting. In deference to custom, her face used to be slightly concealed by a wisp of some fine material, but she never wore a formal veil. At Bijapur there is a portrait taken of her by a Persian artist before her husband's death. It is a profile, exquisitely painted in body colour, with none of the stiffness which usually accompanies Oriental pictures. The features are regular and very beautiful. The complexion is fair, with a faint tinge of carnation through the cheeks, the eyes blue-grey, with long dark eyelashes. The mouth is very gentle and sweet in expression, and bears a slight smile, but there is a decided tone of firmness about the full round chin and graceful throat, and the forehead has a breadth and power which must have been very remarkable.

Her education proceeded for many years after her marriage, and she became skilled in Persian, Arabic, and Turki, and spoke the dialects current in the army with fluency. She drew and painted flowers with ease and delicacy, played upon the veena with skill, and had a great many other accomplishments. With her husband, she fostered trade, literature and the arts of peace, and prosecuted those works for the defence and adornment of his capital which still remain as monuments of his enlightened liberality. The city of Bijapur at this period had a population of 1,500,000, and the kingdom was powerful and prosperous.

On her husband's death, her independent political life began as regent for the minor king. In those times, it was a rare thing to find nobles, ministers, and generals of a native kingdom true to their allegiance for long and serious dissensions occurred between powerful factions and encouraged the invasion of the kingdom by the kings of Berar, Beedu and Golconda, and the close investment of the city. The queen, accompanied by her nephew the king, used to go from post to post at night, cheering, encouraging and directing all. The weather was the severest of the rainy season and after days of drenching rain and bombardment by the enemy, a portion of the city wall gave way. Notwithstanding the torrential downpour the queen guarded the breach in person, collected the masons of the city, and personally superintended the work of repair, leaving the spot neither by day nor night till it was safe against attack by storm. Her devotion and spirited personal valour inspired confidence in all, which now amounted to positive enthusiasm. The leaders of the various factions went to her in a body, and submitted themselves to her authority. In less than a month many thousands of the followers of the different nobles were collected under proper command within and outside the city, and the besieging armies thought it advisable to raise the siege. It had lasted a year. By her personality Chand Bibi maintained perfect order till Ibrahim Adil Shah, the young king, came of age and her regency terminated."

Source: Cowley, Captain Cecil, *Tales of Ahmednagar*, Bombay: Thacker and Company Limited, 1919. Extract taken from Chapter XIII – Chand Bibi.

Image: Chand Bibi, Playing Polo, Golconda, 1750 CE.

CHAPTER 12

Political Developments in the Bahmani Kingdom

Review and Discussion

- Establishment of the Kingdom
- Political Lineage of the Bahmanis
- Conclusion

The Bahmani kingdom was the first Muslim kingdom to be established in the Deccan in the mid-fourteenth century, with its origins in the region itself. Prior to the establishment of the Bahmani kingdom, the Khiljis followed by the Tughlaqs had extended their sway into the Deccan only after establishing themselves in northern India. The fact that the rule of the Bahmani dynasty corresponds to the period of a unified Deccan makes this period significant in the history of medieval India. With the fall of the Bahmanis, till the establishment of the Asaf Jahi rule, there was complete disunion in the region. When the Bahmanis began their rule there was large-scale instability in the Deccan, with many petty principalities emerging as a result of polarization of the larger states. The greatest contribution of the Bahmanis in this situation was the uniting of the different political groups of the Deccan. Remaining politically active for nearly two centuries to come, the Bahmanis ruled from both Gulbarga and Bidar. For the sake of convenience their political history is generally divided into the Gulbarga period and the Bidar period.

Establishment of the Kingdom

The *Tarikh-i-Ferishta* and the *Burhan-i-Maasir* provide details about the origins of the Bahmani dynasty. The rebellions that occurred in retaliation to the measures of Muhammad bin Tughlaq had nowhere been more successful than in the South where the nobles had setup an independent kingdom with an Afghan noble, Ismail Mukh, as the king. But Ismail was least interested in kingship and wisely abdicated in favour of Hasan Gangu, a brave soldier who had distinguished himself during the rebellions. Hasan Gangu, the nephew of Zafar Khan Alai who was connected to the royal family of Isfahan and Hamadan, was proclaimed as the sultan on Friday, the third of August, 1347 CE. Upholding the religious sanctity of Friday for Muslims, he ascended the throne on the same day at Daulatabad as Abul Muzaffar Alauddin Hasan Bahman Shah—also known as Alauddin I. Founded by Alauddin I, the Bahmani Sultanate played a conspicuous role in the politics of the Deccan for nearly two centuries to come.

Alauddin I (1347–58 CE)

Hailing from Persia, Alauddin I's family had taken their name from the legendary hero, Bahman, of the Persian epic, the *Shah Namah*. Thereafter the new line of rulers came to be known as the Bahmanis. One of the first things the new ruler of Deccan did was to give the title of his predecessor, Zafar Khan, to his son, Prince Muhammad. This is significant for there was now going to begin an era where imperial ideology in the Deccan would be projected with extended motifs from the Persian world. Alauddin I's entire reign was spent in consolidating the Bahmani kingdom in the Deccan and establishing his control over those Muslim nobles who chose to remain there instead of joining Muhammad bin Tughlaq in Delhi.

The Bahmani, Vijayanagar, and other subregional kingdoms that had emerged at this time heralded the onset of newer technological developments in the political and military history of the Deccan. Just after the fall of the Tughlaqs, small fortified strongholds had surfaced under both Muslim and Hindu local chiefs. These petty principalities were eager to upgrade themselves militarily; and in the process they acquired advanced military techniques that had been introduced into Indian artillery and heavy cavalry. Learning quickly from their neighbours and eager to keep abreast of military innovations, the Bahmanis did not remain far behind. They too felt the need to gain control over fortifications and technology that was essential to establish military supremacy in an area that was already wrought by major and minor divisions. Thus, with the aid of technology, the Bahmanis chose to primarily consolidate their position in the Deccan over expanding their frontiers beyond the region. This in itself was a colossal task where so many small local rulers existed.

After establishing his capital at Daulatabad, Alauddin I ruled for 11 years till his death in 1358 CE. During the greater part of his reign, he was busy putting down rebellious chiefs and strengthening the state. He first turned his attention towards Warangal, a Hindu state that had emerged from the break-up of the southern tip of the Tughlaq Sultanate. He was successful in enforcing an annual tribute payment on Warangal; and likewise other neighbouring states were also made to pay tribute. Often, however, such states defaulted on payments which lead to wars between the Bahmanis and its neighbours—Malwa and Gujarat in the north, Orissa and the Reddi kingdoms of Rajahmundry and Kondavidu in the east, and Vijayanagar in the south.

Alauddin I gave to the Bahmani kingdom an effective administrative set-up which was based on the same structure established by Muhammad bin Tughlaq. There were four territorial divisions known as *tarafs* or provinces, each under the control of a provincial governor to administer the newly formed state. He also undertook frequent tours of inspection and maintained a firm control over his subordinate officers. Not only was his administration modelled along the lines of the Tughlaqs, but he also established departments and appointed officials similar to those of the Delhi sultans. Thereafter, for administrative convenience, Daulatabad was divided into smaller fiefs under the command of the *amiran-i-sadah* and the vast amounts of treasure that had accumulated in the province were distributed among the troops. The capital initially established at Daulatabad was soon moved to Gulbarga which was found to be more centrally located in the Deccan plateau. Alauddin I's ceaseless activity impaired his health and he succumbed to an attack of malaria in 1358 CE. At the time of his death, the Bahmani kingdom stretched from Waiganga in the north to the Krishna in the south and from Daulatabad in the west to Bhongir in the east.

Muhammad Shah I (1358–75 CE)

With the accession of Muhammad Shah I, the eldest son and successor of Alauddin I, begins the Gulbarga period of Bahmani rule. During his reign, there began a severe struggle with Vijayanagar which had as its prime agenda the acquisition and control of the Tungabhadra–Krishna Doab that in course of time became more and more complicated—extending well into the seventeenth century. The fertility of the Doab had always been a contentious issue even before the foundation of either the Bahmani or Vijayanagar kingdoms, but it had now become a major score to settle. In his wars against Vijayanagar and also Tilangana, Muhammad Shah I was assisted by his father's able minister, Saifuddin Ghur, who continued in service until the accession of the sixth Bahmani sultan.

Muhammad Shah I made use of the freshly organized artillery to defeat armies much larger than his own and was facilitated in his military endeavours by the newly introduced gunpowder, which led to massive fortifications. His two wars with Vijayanagar did not yield much, but his attack on Tilangana in 1363 CE was lucrative bringing in a huge war indemnity, the coveted turquoise throne and the region of Golconda. But in 1365 CE, the rebellion that brought Muhammad Shah I into immediate political focus was his effective suppression of the governor of Daulatabad and some Maratha and other chieftains of Berar and Baglana, who had risen in opposition.

Being a hard-working and disciplined administrator, Muhammad Shah I devoted the latter part of his reign to the re-organization of his government which resulted in sound administration of the kingdom. Thus, under the sultan, a solid foundation of the Bahmani kingdom could be laid. To elevate the status of Gulbarga as a capital city, Muhammad Shah I ordered the construction of the Jami Masjid within the precincts of the Gulbarga fort. In addition to improving the military organization, he brought reforms in both central and provincial administration and introduced his famous council of eight ministers—which was later to be emulated by Shivaji, the founder of the Maratha state. After ruling for 17 years, Muhammad Shah died in 1375 CE.

Mujahid and Dawud

After Muhammad Shah I's death, there followed a period of instability during the reigns of his immediate successors, Mujahid and Dawud. His son and successor, Mujahid ruled briefly from 1375–78 CE, when he was assassinated by his cousin Dawud while returning from a campaign in Vijayanagar. Dawud too barely held the position of sultan for a few months before being murdered by Alauddin I's supporters, who then placed Dawud's brother, Muhammad Shah II, on the throne.

Muhammad Shah II (1378–97 CE)

Muhammad Shah II was the fifth ruler of the Bahmani dynasty. He was essentially a peace loving man and more than political affairs, he showed deep inclination towards furthering the cultural traditions in his kingdom. During his reign, Goa and its adjoining territories along the western coast were lost to Vijayanagar in protracted warfare; and towards the end of his reign there was a rebellion at Sagar. Apart from these incidents, Muhammad Shah II's reign remained by and large serene. He showed leanings towards promoting the general welfare of his subjects. A good example of this was seen when famine broke out in his kingdom, and he tried to minimize the sufferings of the people by procuring corn from Gujarat and Malwa. He tried to promote education of his Muslim subjects by establishing schools where students were given free lodging facilities. Always thinking in favour of his subjects, Muhammad Shah II regarded himself as the trustee of the resources of his kingdom and discouraged all excessive expenditure.

The sultan's interest in philosophy and poetry was seen in his patronage of Shiraz, the famous Persian poet. Muhammad Shah II spent much of his time building his court as a cultural centre of excellence and learning. He did for Bahmani culture what Muhammad Shah I had done for administration, attracting numerous Persian and

Arab poets and theologians, individuals with expertise in cultural and military affairs, architects and literary men. He was responsible for including within the state structure certain elements of Hindu culture that were already present in local society. The edifice of the Bahmani and its successor states were thus shaped in this manner so as to embody a multi-faceted ideology and political culture that was all-inclusive.

Upon his death in 1397 CE, he was succeeded by his eldest son, Ghiasuddin who was also known as Dawud II. But there were several palace intrigues that took place during his brief reign of two months adding to the already existing confusion.

An important development accompanying the formation of the Bahmani Sultanate was the immigration of a large number of Arabs, Turks, and particularly Persians into the Deccan. Many of them had been specially invited by the sultan Muhammad I. These new settlers from Persia, known as *Afaqis,* had begun to assert considerable influence in the Sultanate—a fact which became fairly evident in the formation of a distinct culture in the later years. The *Afaqis* also began vying for important positions within the political hierarchy which was not approved by the *Dakhnis* or the old nobility of the Deccan, on the basis of which they began to oppose the newcomers. Thus, the distribution of high offices among the *Afaqis* by Dawud II in 1397 CE was seen as a threat by the older nobles and Turks, and was also probably the reason behind his assassination. What complicated the situation further was the addition of Hindu converts and Hindus to the existing nobility. It was this division between the *Dakhnis* and *Afaqi*s that gained gigantic proportions and finally contributed to the disintegration of the Bahmani state at a later date.

Tajuddin Firuz Shah (1397–1422 CE)

Muhammad II's cousin, Tajuddin Firuz Shah, finally gained control and succeeded as Firuz Shah Bahmani. According to Ferishta he was the greatest ruler of the dynasty, during whose reign the kingdom reached a high degree of prosperity. Firuz was a great soldier and after securing his position, he first put down an invasion in the north by the Gond raja of Kherla in Madhya Pradesh before renewing the Bahmani wars with Vijayanagar and Tilangana. In the war against Vijayanagar, Firuz Shah emerged victorious and the ruler of Vijayanagar, Devaraya I, was forced to accept a humiliating treaty. As part of the tributary conditions imposed, Devaraya I had to give one of his daughters in marriage to the sultan. In addition, Firuz Shah received Bankapur and other districts as part of dowry from Vijayanagar. Interestingly, inter-caste marriages for political purposes were practiced in the Deccan much before the Mughal emperor, Akbar, began the practice in the sixteenth century. A noteworthy point is that even though the Bahmani–Vijayanagar matrimonial alliance was imposed after a defeat, it led to the establishment of an amicable relationship between the two rulers for a brief while. From 1417–20 CE, however, the united forces of Vijayanagar and the Velama faction of the Reddi ruling group in Andhra—who were apparently Firuz Shah's former allies—led a coalition against Firuz Shah that ended in a disastrous defeat of the latter. Firuz was helped in this tussle only by the Vemas of Kondavidu.

Firuz Shah was considered to be a generous and accomplished prince, a great general, a patron of the arts and a pious Muslim. His reign was a period of notable cultural activity in the history of the Bahmani Sultanate. Like his predecessor, Muhammad Shah II, he wanted to make the Deccan the cultural centre of India. He took interest in adorning the capital and its surroundings with a number of beautiful constructions, the most remarkable being the great mosque of Gulbarga built within the precincts of the fort. Noted for his intelligence and learning, Firuz Shah even read the *Old Testament* and the *New Testament.* He established on the Bhima river the new city of Firuzabad which developed as a great centre of Islamic culture in India at a time when the Delhi Sultanate was in a state of dissolution. Utilizing the visits of foreign travellers from Turkey, Europe and West Asia into the Deccan constructively, Firuz Shah encouraged the import of many products from Europe. He focussed his attention not only on the physical growth and development of the kingdom, but also in its administration. He initiated steps to bring about social harmony in a society that was experiencing a metamorphosis by incorporating and accepting different groups that had infiltrated into the region and had come to constitute the population of the Deccan. Perhaps in an effort to balance the high number of influential foreigners (Persians and Iraqis) and to strengthen his own position as a ruler who was all powerful, Firuz gave a number of high offices to the Hindus, many of who were *brahmans*.

Alauddin Ahmad Shah I (1422–36 CE)

The immediate successor of Firuz Shah was Ahmad Shah I whose reign lasted for 14 years. During his reign the capital of the kingdom was shifted from Gulbarga to Bidar, which begins the Bidar period of the Bahmani history. The centrality and the fertility of land in the new capital augmented the sultan's plans of expanding further. In 1425 CE he completely crushed the power of the Velama ruler of Warangal and finally annexed most of Tilangana, almost reaching the edge of Orissa on the eastern side. Ahmad Shah I's reign marks the right of primogeniture becoming firmly established in the Deccan. His reign was also characterized by a few wars with Vijayanagar, domestic troubles and the beginnings of quarrels between the *Afaqis* and the *Dakhnis*.

Alauddin Ahmad Shah II (1436–58 CE)

By virtue of being the eldest son of Ahmad Shah I, Alauddin Ahmad Shah II, succeeded him as the new sultan. There were many futile campaigns against Vijayanagar, Malwa and Gujarat. By now the conflicts between the *Afaqis* and *Dakhnis* intensified further and became more frequent. His own son-in-law, supported by the sultan of Malwa, revolted in Tilangana. It was at this time that Mahmud Gawan, a newly arrived noble from Persia, entered Bahmani politics by trying to bring the situation under control through his tact and diplomacy.

Alauddin Humayun Shah (1458–61 CE)

Alauddin Humayun Shah was the tenth ruler in the Bahmani line of kings. He displayed dictatorial tendencies which antagonized many, especially the *Afaqis* who were devising several ways of deposing him. It was under Humayun that Mahmud Gawan began to get further involved in the affairs of the Bahmani state. He distinguished himself by his victories in war and peace and soon won the confidence of the sultan.

Ahmad Shah III (1461–63 CE)

Humayun was succeeded by Ahmad Shah III, who like his predecessor also ruled for just two years. But his rule was inconsequential and there were no noteworthy occurrences. Ahmad Shah III recognized Gawan's striking abilities and continued him in service. During the minority of Nizam Shah he was an important member of the Council of Regency and it was because of his courage and energy that invasions from the rulers of Orissa, Tilangana and Malwa could be repelled.

Muhammad Shah III (1463–82 CE)

The next ruler was Muhammad Shah III who reigned for nearly 20 years. He regained many lost territories through his extensive conquests, the most famous being his raid on Kanchipuram. He came to be known as *Ghazi*—the killer of infidels. Acting solely on the intelligent advice given by Mahmud Gawan, the sultan could bring some advantages for the Bahmani kingdom. Likewise, Mahmud Gawan's political career progressed rapidly during the reign of Muhammad III as he was appointed prime minister and was given full responsibility for the Bahmani state's affairs. He restored the authority and reputation of the Bahmanis through sound administrative reforms and extensive conquests. He was responsible for compelling the chief of Konkan to surrender the fortress of Kalna, exacting tributes from the raja of Orissa, recapturing Goa from the Vijayanagar king and seizing territory from the raja of Belgaum, who had revolted at the instigation of the raja of Vijayanagar. The Bahmani kingdom expanded to an extent as never witnessed before because of these military achievements under Muhammad Shah III.

Besides helping Muhammad Shah III in his military achievements, Mahmud Gawan also saw increasing the efficiency of administration as his chief aim. Mahmud Gawan's most significant measure was his policy of giving equal number of appointments to both *Dakhnis* and *Afaqis* so that disputes among the nobility could be reduced, helping him build up a benevolent image of himself as *wazir*. This balancing act won him accolades from the locals, while making people realize that being an *Afaqi* himself he was promoting the cause of the Shias.

Mahmud Gawan's sound administrative system included centralizing the state, and revising land measurement and revenue assessment. His reforms embraced a wide field and no department escaped his attention. The phenomenal growth of the Bahmani Sultanate had extended the area of the provinces, and had greatly increased the resources and powers of the provincial governors, who began to defy the orders of the centre. Gawan's reforms in administration were effective in curtailing the power of the provincial governors, who threatened by the new measures, had begun to conspire against him.

The administrative reforms of Mahmud Gawan and the irrigation works executed by the Bahmani sultans conferred lasting benefits upon the people. The observations of the Russian merchant, Athanasius Nikitin, who visited the Bahmani kingdom and stayed there from 1469–74 CE under the Muslim name Khwaja Yusuf Khurasani, testifies in glorious terms that 'the Bahmanis rule the country and serve in war'. He also speaks about the general prosperity of the kingdom. Islamic education was not neglected, while architecture too made progress. Being well-versed in mathematics, medicine and literature, Gawan understood the importance of education. His remarkable contribution is seen in the theological college he built at Bidar, which was named after him and called Mahmud Gawan's *madrassa*. The construction of this grand *madrassa* was also a sign of asserting the supremacy of Shiism at the Bahmani court, as it conformed to the influence of Persian architectural and religious traditions in the Deccan.

Further intensification of the factions at court proved to be unfortunate for Mahmud Gawan and the Bahmani dynasty. A group of *Dakhni* nobles hatched a plot against him on the grudge that he was an *Afaqi* and that he was making efforts to establish a centralized regime. A letter of treason falsely attributed to him was placed in the hands of the sultan, who without finding out the actual facts ordered the execution of the aged and faithful Gawan—now 78 years old and having served the dynasty for over 35 years. The Bahmani kingdom thus lost its ablest counsellor in 1481 CE. The execution was widely disapproved by the *Afaqi* groups and even by some of the *Dakhnis*. Grief-stricken and shattered with the event, most of the *Afaqis* returned to their provinces and refused to come to the capital, and the sultan was left only with the support of the conspirators. Muhammad Shah III himself heart broken over his miscalculated judgment died in 1482 CE. It was then that the leader of the conspirators, Malik Naib, made himself regent for Muhammad Shah III's minor son, Shihab-uddin Mahmud.

Undoubtedly, the kingdom had reached its zenith under the guidance of Mahmud Gawan, but his death saw the unsettlement of the political equilibrium that had been created. As the power of the Bahmani sultanate waned, its provincial governors increasingly took over control and became the actual rulers of their respective provinces.

Shihab-uddin Mahmud (1482–1518 CE)

The next ruler Shihab-uddin Mahmud ruled for a considerably long period. This was a time when the process of disintegration of the Bahmani kingdom had begun. There was confusion, and courtly intrigues and political murders caused the dynasty to practically come to an end. This was also a time when the most important military commanders established themselves with greater authority in their provincial headquarters—Nizam-ul-Mulk at Ahmednagar, Imad-ul-Mulk at Achalpur, Yusuf Adil Khan at Bijapur and Sultan Quli Qutb-ul-Mulk at Golconda. Qasim Barid, a *kotwal* from Bidar challenged the sultan's authority and forced Mahmud to appoint him as his prime minister in 1488 CE. This move encouraged other provincial governors to get ready to declare their autonomy too. Meanwhile, the threat from Vijayanagar continued, especially under Narasimha Saluva. Yusuf Adil Khan, the governor of Bijapur, who was leading the Bahmani forces, met Narasimha Saluva on several occasions in ensuing wars. With the arrival

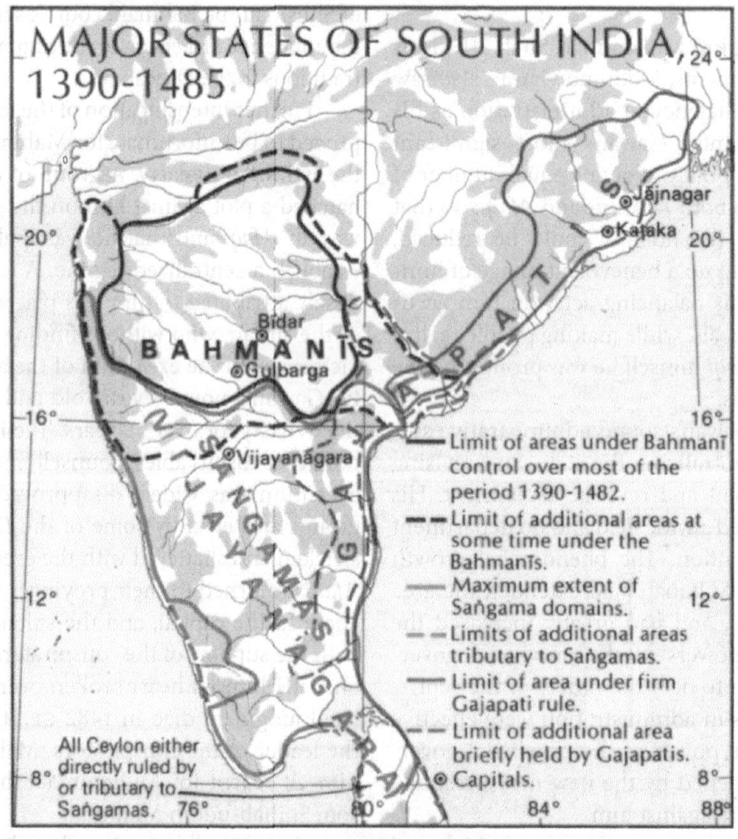

Map 12-1 *The Bahmani Kingdom Before Disintegration, 1390–1485 CE*

of the Portuguese, the Bahmanis were hit harder even on the western coastal front where they suffered losses in Goa and other places.

Conclusion

Ahmad Shah IV (1518–20 CE), Waliullah Shah (1520–26 CE) and Kalamullah Shah (1526–38 CE) were the last of the three Bahmani rulers to sit on the throne before the 170-year-rule of the Bahmanis came to a close. Without any dynastic changes, the Bahmani rule provided the necessary conditions under which people felt secure, and there was all round development. Persian Shias, native Muslims and Hindus, together influenced the cultural edifice of the Bahmanis. The phase between the death of Muhammad I and the accession of Firuz Shah was a period of struggle for the integration of different cultures into one mould. Attempts were made to achieve a synthesis of Hindu cultural elements, the foreign influences represented by the *Afaqis* from Persia and the indigenous tradition represented by the *Dakhnis*.

The continuous influx of Persians into the Deccan had a direct influence on the court life and

CHRONOLOGY	
1347–58 CE	Alauddin I
1358 CE	Bahmani kingdom extends from Waiganga in the north to the Krishna in the south, and from Daulatabad in the west to Bhongir in the east
1358–75 CE	Muhammad Shah I, Gulbarga period of rule begins
1363 CE	Muhammad Shah I attacks Tilangana and gets huge war indemnity
1375–78 CE	Mujahid; Assassinated by cousin Dawud
1378–97 CE	Muhammad Shah II
1397–1422 CE	Tajuddin Firuz Shah
1417–20 CE	Vijayanagar and the Velama faction of the Reddi ruling group in Andhra lead a coalition against Firuz Shah which ends in the defeat of Firuz
1422–36 CE	Alauddin Ahmad Shah I; Capital shifts from Gulbarga to Bidar
1425 CE	Velama crushed; most of Tilangana annexed
1436–58 CE	Alauddin Ahmad Shah II
1458–61 CE	Alauddin Humayun Shah; Mahmud Gawan gains importance in Bahmani politics
1461–63 CE	Ahmad Shah III
1463–82 CE	Muhammad Shah III; Mahmud Gawan appointed prime minister
1481 CE	Execution of the aged and faithful Mahmud Gawan
1482–1518 CE	Shihab-uddin Mahmud
1488 CE	Qasim Barid challenges the sultan's authority and forces Mahmud to appoint him as his prime minister
1518–20 CE	Ahmad Shah IV
1520–26 CE	Waliullah Shah
1526–38 CE	Kalamullah Shah

politics of the kingdom. Many of the Persians had begun to occupy good administrative positions, with some even becoming powerful provincial governors. This bred separatist tendencies among the nobles, whose reactionary activities were in a way facilitating the spread of Shia ideas in Bijapur and elsewhere.

The opening decades of the sixteenth century witnessed the fragmentation of the Bahmani kingdom into smaller sultanates, each governed by an independent dynasty—the Nizam Shahis of Ahmednagar, the Imad Shahis of Berar, the Adil Shahis of Bijapur and the Qutb Shahis of Golconda. The Bahmani kingdom was ultimately restricted to a small area only around the capital of Bidar. Reduced in status, its vestiges continued to linger on during the period of the fifth Deccani sultanate—that of the Barid Shahis at Bidar. Of the smaller sultanates, the three most important dynasties were those of the Nizam Shahis of Ahmednagar, the Adil Shahis of Bijapur and the Qutb Shahis of Golconda.

SUMMARY

- Bahmani history forms a significant component of the history of medieval India, as it corresponds to the period of a unified Deccan.
- The Bahmanis started to rule at a time when there was large-scale instability in the Deccan. In such a situation their greatest contribution was seen in the uniting of different groups that constituted the population in the Deccan.
- The Bahmanis ruled from both Gulbarga and Bidar; their political history for the sake of convenience is divided into the Gulbarga period and the Bidar period.
- The Bahmani kingdom was established in the Deccan in 1347 CE by a brave soldier named Hasan Gangu who took the title of Abul Muzaffar Alauddin Hasan Bahman Shah and ascended the throne at Daulatabad. He was also known as Alauddin I.
- During the greater part of his reign Alauddin I was busy putting down rebellious chiefs and trying to consolidate his dominions. He entered into conflicts with Warangal, Malwa Gujarat, Orissa, the Reddi kingdoms of Rajahmundry and Kondavidu, and Vijayanagar.
- Alauddin I gave to the Bahmani kingdom an effective administrative setup based on the same structure as established by Muhammad bin Tughlaq. The capital initially established at Daulatabad was moved to Gulbarga, which was found to be more centrally located.
- With the ascension of Muhammad Shah I, there began a severe struggle with Vijayanagar which had as its prime agenda the acquisition and control of the Tungabhadra–Krishna Doab.
- Muhammad Shah I reorganized his government and improved the military organization; thus, under him a solid foundation of the Bahmani kingdom was laid.
- The ruler next in importance was Muhammad Shah II, who was essentially a peace loving man and showed immense interest in developing his court as a centre of artistic excellence.
- During Muhammad Shah II's reign, numerous Persian and Arab poets, theologians, and individuals with expertise in cultural and military affairs came to the Deccan.
- According to Ferishta, Tajuddin Firuz Shah was the greatest ruler of the dynasty, during whose reign the kingdom reached a high degree of prosperity. His military exercises were directed towards Vijayanagar and Tilangana.
- Like Muhammad Shah II, Firuz too wanted to make the Deccan the cultural centre of India. He took interest in adorning the capital and its surroundings with a number of beautiful constructions.
- Firuz Shah focussed his attention not only on the physical growth and development of the kingdom, but also initiated steps to bring about social harmony in the pluralistic Bahmani society.
- The next significant Bahmani ruler was Muhammad Shah III, who retrieved the fortunes of the dynasty through extensive conquests. Added to this was the help he received from Mahmud Gawan, a great general and an able administrator.
- Mahmud Gawan became the sole adviser to the king and served the state with ability and success. He restored the authority and reputation of the

Bahmanis through major conquests and sound administrative reforms.

- Mahmud Gawan's most significant measures included his policy of giving equal number of appointments to both *Dakhnis* and *Afaqis,* and reforms in the fields of education and land revenue.
- The long reign of Shihab-uddin Mahmud coincides with the disintegration of the Bahmani kingdom, a process hastened by courtly intrigues because of which the dynasty practically came to an end.
- Seeing a weak sultan at the helm of affairs, most military commanders established themselves with greater authority in their provincial headquarters.
- The opening decades of the sixteenth century witnessed the fragmentation of the Bahmani kingdom into smaller sultanates each governed by an independent dynasty—the Nizam Shahis of Ahmednagar, the Imad Shahis of Berar, the Adil Shahis of Bijapur, the Qutb Shahis of Golconda and the Barid Shahis of Bidar.

KEYWORDS

Tarafs　Amiran-i-sadah　Afaqis　Dakhnis

REVIEW QUESTIONS

1. How was the Bahmani kingdom established?
2. Examine the contribution of Muhammad Shah I in establishing a sound system of administration.
3. 'Muhammad Shah II spent much of his time building his court as a cultural centre of excellence and learning'. Comment.
4. Evaluate the role of Tajuddin Firuz Shah in making the kingdom attain a high degree of prosperity.
5. Discuss the role of Mahmud Gawan in assuming complete responsibility of the Bahmani state's affairs.

CHAPTER **13**

Administrative, Socio-Economic and Religious Conditions of the Bahmani State

Review and Discussion

- Administration
- The Army
- The Economy
- Religion and Culture
- Art and Architecture

From the fourteenth century onwards, with the arrival of the Persians, a new Indo-Islamic synthesis began to emerge in the Deccan, which became especially significant in the context of the Indo-Persian cultural sphere. Growing further, this metamorphosis in the fifteenth and sixteenth centuries drew the entire Deccan into the orbit of Persian culture with the augmentation of peninsular India's commercial and cultural interaction with the Persian plateau. The open-mindedness of the Persian ruling classes, coupled with the desire to make the Deccan their homeland, inspired and championed new traits in art, architecture, literature and religion. Persian culture which was considered to be prestigious and cosmopolitan, and was being imported to faraway lands. Over the centuries this evolved into a unique amalgam peculiar only to the Deccan, and came to be known as the *Dakhni* culture.

Administration

To govern an area as vast as the Deccan, an effective administrative setup was necessary. The administrative apparatus of the Bahmanis—patterned on the model of the Delhi Sultanate—was well-developed and played a major role in legitimizing their rule in the Deccan. The sultan was the embodiment of supreme power in the state, in him were vested the powers of a ruler, judge, administrator and military leader; and his duties were as all embracing as his authority. The ruler was considered to be the shadow of god on earth, but only Mujahid Shah Bahmani, who ruled from 1375–78 CE, seems to have claimed this distinction.

Though the Bahmani sultan's authority was unlimited, he also depended on the advice of his ministers in deciding questions concerning state policy. The chief duty of the ministers was to be implicitly obedient to the ruler and fulfil all his wishes. They were responsible to him for the smallest of matters and continued in office as long as they enjoyed his support and pleasure.

In the Bahmani Sultanate, the prime minister was known as *wazir* or *vakil-us-sultanate*. All orders issued by the ruler were executed through him and were marked with his seal. The minister responsible for the finances of the kingdom was known as the *amir-i-jumla,* while the *wazir-i-ashraf* was the minister responsible for external affairs. There were two other ministers known as the *wazir-i-kull* and the *peshwa* who held authority, but did not have any clearly defined duties. The *sadr-i-jahan* was the chief judicial authority and was in charge of religious matters and endowments. There were various other subordinate ministers to assist in the discharge of civil and military functions. The *nazir* and the *kotwal* assisted in civil administration, while the *qur beg-i-maisarah* (commander of the left wing) and the *qur beg-i-maimanah* (commander of the right wing) assisted in military administration.

Alauddin I was responsible for giving to the Bahmani kingdom its provincial administration. He divided the kingdom into four divisions called *tarafs* each entrusted under the command of an officer called *tarafdar*. The provincial governors were supreme in their respective territories. During the reign of Alauddin I's son, Muhammad Shah I, the *tarafdars* were deputed to collect revenue, command the army and make civil and military appointments in their provinces. Naturally, in course of time they became very powerful. The early Bahmani rulers could keep them in check by virtue of the strong personality of the ruler himself, who every year spent some time in touring the various divisions and personally supervising the administration of the officers. To ensure that *tarafdars* do not develop local roots they were routinely transferred from one province to another. The later rulers did not have the same hold over the provincial governors, which was one of the main reasons for the disintegration of the Bahmani kingdom. The *tarafs* were divided into *sarkars,* which in turn were further divided into *parganas*. A *pargana* consisted of a certain number of villages, and the village remained the smallest unit of administration.

Muhammad Shah I was a diligent and methodical administrator, who devoted the early part of his reign to the reorganization of the government. He could effectively put down rebellions because of the improved military technology, especially the newly organized artillery. Of note is the role his minister, Saifuddin Ghur, played in planning the course of action during battles. Saifuddin Ghur also assisted him in bringing about reforms in the central and provincial administration in a similar way.

Mahmud Gawan was appointed as the *vakil-us-sultanate* under Humayun Shah, as well as the *tarafdar* of the Bijapur division. He also served in the dual capacity of both *amir-i-jumla* and *wazir-i-kull* of the province. Similarly, during the succeeding reign, Khwaja Jahan, who was *vakil* to Nizam Shah Bahmani, was also the governor of Tilangana. Each of the *tarafdars* was a military officer who held the rank of a commander with 2,000 horses under him. During the reign of Muhammad Shah III, the Bahmani kingdom grew in extent and reached its furthest limits. As *wazir,* Mahmud Gawan's chief aim was to increase the efficiency of the administrative machinery, bring reforms and root out corruption.

Mahmud Gawan attempted to enhance the central authority through a series of administrative reforms and political exercises. Till the 1470s the kingdom was divided into the four provinces of Gulbarga (with Raichur and Mudgal), Daulatabad (with Bir, Junnar and Chaul), Berar (with Mahur), and the Bahmani Tilangana province (with Indur and Kaulas). The governors of the four provinces had within their control almost all aspects of civil and military administration of their territories. Administration was thus in a way decentralized right from the beginning. But the power of the provincial governors had grown with the increase in size of the four provinces. To keep a check on the power of the governors, Mahmud Gawan divided each of the unwieldy provinces into two, under separate governors. Hence, the old four provinces were divided into eight portions known as *sarlashkarships*. He also strictly enforced the regular transfer of the provincial governors. Besides halving the old provinces, portions of each province were placed directly under the central administration too, and their revenue reserved for the state. With smaller provinces and lesser power, the authority of the *tarafdars* was doubly curtailed. Gawan's administrative reforms, thus, weakened the power of the provincial governors.

The *tarafdari* system worked well as long as it had behind it the energy of a strong personality—either of the ruler himself or of an able minister. Later, it became apparent that the power of the sultan was much less than that of several of his nobles put together. The emergence of separatist tendencies led to a depletion of imperial power and provincial governors became unwilling to help the sultan when he faced refractory forces.

The Army

Mahmud Gawan transformed the whole system of military administration for the Bahmanis to bring in efficiency and good organization. He reduced the military control of the governors by bringing all forts but one in each province directly under the control of the sultan. He also made the centre totally responsible for controlling the employment and payment of troops within the provinces. This meant that the provincial governors were allowed personal control over only one fort in their territory; the remaining forts in their territory were surrendered to the commanders appointed by the central government. The military commanders were paid partly in cash and partly through *jagir* assignments. Those military commanders who had received *jagirs* were directly accountable to the sultan for revenue collection and the payment of salaries to their soldiers. The soldiers' salary was increased and according to Meadows Taylor, an Anglo-Indian administrator and novelist, the Bahmani army in 1470 CE was better paid than the English native army in 1830 CE.

One of the goals of Mahmud Gawan was to root out corruption in all areas so that order could prevail throughout and the administration could be strengthened. Earlier, each commander was given a certain *jagir* without taking into consideration whether he was capable or loyal enough, which resulted in corruption and mismanagement. Although the amount to be given to the *jagirdar* had originally been fixed in proportion to the troops at his command, in practice land grants were made without paying attention to the number of troops maintained. To bring reforms in the system, Gawan decreed that every *jagirdar* should be paid at the rate of one lakh huns annually for every 500 armed soldiers; and if *jagirs* were granted in lieu of cash payments, provision was made whereby the *jagirdar* was to be compensated to the extent of losses incurred in the collection of rent. If the *jagirdar* failed to maintain the stipulated number of soldiers, he had to refund the proportionate amount to the royal treasury. With the implementation of these measures, Mahmud Gawan brought in major reforms in the military system.

The Economy

The accounts of contemporary Muslim writers are replete with information about the military campaigns of the Bahmani rulers, but other than giving passing references these works do not give any such information about the economic conditions or trade and commerce. We get a glimpse of the conditions of the common people from certain observations made by the Russian traveller, Althanasius Nikitin, who travelled in the Bahmani kingdom from 1470–74 CE, during the reign of Muhammad Shah III. He writes that the country was populous, the lands well cultivated, the roads safe from robbers, and that the capital of the kingdom was a magnificent city. While the nobles had an affluent lifestyle, the life of the people in the countryside was miserable. Though he has not mentioned of any specific trade as such in his text, it can nevertheless be surmised that inland trade was carried on extensively as roads were safe. The means of transport used for trading purposes were similar to those used in Vijayanagar.

Mahmud Gawan was the first Muslim administrator to have introduced a system of measurement and valuation of agricultural land, creating a large block of crown land within each province. He ordered a systematic land survey, fixed the boundaries of villages and towns, and organized an enquiry about the assessment of revenue. Revenue records were reorganized too. In terms of tax collection and administration, the Bahmanis more or less employed the policies devised by the Delhi sultans. To quote Prof. H. K. Sherwani, 'On the one hand, Gawan made it easy to determine the income of the state, and to furnish record of rights, forestalling Todar Mal's reforms by a century, and on the other hand, he tried to curb the power of the nobles and thereby raise the status of the central government.' (Sherwani and Joshi 1973) It was his far reaching measures that curtailed the power of the governors.

With Mahmud Gawan's reforms and a sound irrigation policy adopted by the sultans, the people benefitted to a great extent. The observations of Althanasius Nikitin too testify to the general prosperity of the Bahmani kingdom during this period.

Religion and Culture

Islam existed in all forms together with Hinduism in Bahmani society. The atmosphere created was such that it led to the evolution of a liberal and open-minded approach based on sharing and adoption of mutual traditions and customs. In such a liberal atmosphere, the rigorous and efficient administration did not allow inter-religious conflicts to escalate. The activities of the sultans were in accordance with the spirit of the times when Persian culture was being transported into the Deccan transforming the identity of the region; but this does not mean that there were no religious, ethnic or regional conflicts. There were struggles between the *Afaqis* and the *Dakhnis* to gain an upper hand over each other and acquire good positions at the court. There were also rulers of one faith sitting in the seats of power and getting a hold over a whole range of areas of public life. But in spite of all this, the one overriding factor was that Deccani society in Bahmani and post-Bahmani times sustained beyond the Hindu–Muslim, northern India–Deccan and Shia–Sunni divides leading to the integration and acceptance of the native Hindus, northern Indian Muslims and *Afaqis* into the plural society of the Deccan.

The Bahmani kingdom was officially a Sunni state, but Shiism and Sufism were practiced abundantly. Firuz Shah and Ahmad Shah I showed inclination towards Shiism, and Mahmud Gawan being a Persian was himself a Shia. The reaction that set in after Gawan's murder fanned the progress of Shiism in the Deccan at the hands of Yusuf Adil Shah (the governor of Bijapur who was almost like the adopted son of Mahmud Gawan). Yusuf Adil Shah declared Shiism as his faith in the June of 1503 CE. Even Shihab-uddin Mahmud is said to have cried out for help to none other than Hazrat Ali, the fourth Caliph, when he was overwhelmed by defeat and hopelessness.

As already mentioned in Chapter 12, during Firuz Shah Bahmani's time, a number of high offices were given to the Hindus, many of whom were *brahmans*. It was Firuz's piety that had made Hazrat Gesu Daraz settle in the Bahmani capital. Sufism as a movement had taken root by now in many parts of India. Some Sufi saints had even settled in the Deccan long before the first Khilji incursion. The beginning of the fourteenth century witnessed the popularity of a large number of such saints and holy men who were mystics of various Sufi orders. Their *dargahs* had become religious centres attracting large followings. The tomb of Sirajuddin Junaidi who had died at Gulbarga in 1379 CE had become a centre of *urs* soon after his death. Similarly, the *dargah* of Makhdoom Shaikh Alauddin Ansari at Aland near Gulbarga had grown into a sacred shrine soon after the Shaikh's death and the annual *urs* held around it attracted large number of devotees.

The most important and widely venerated Sufi saint of the Deccan was, however, Hazrat Syed Muhammad Gesu Daraz—popularly known as Banda Nawaz. His mausoleum at Gulbarga, erected by Ahmad Shah I, became a centre of pilgrimage. The arrival of Gesu Daraz (1321–1422 CE) to Gulbarga gave a boost to *Dakhni* language and literature. Later known as *Dakhni* Urdu, it took shape as an independent and important spoken language. It was a mixture of northern Indian Hindi, Persian, Gujarati and Marathi—languages spoken by soldiers who came from different regions, and by wandering mendicants and Sufi *fakirs*. Though Gesu Daraz knew Persian well and wrote in this language, he adopted *Dakhni* as his medium of instruction and preaching. Most of his earlier works were written in *Dakhni,* while his later works were written in Persian. Persian continued to be the court language of the Bahmanis, but through *Dakhni,* Gesu Daraz reached across to the masses, who were drawn towards his teachings. He was

GULBARGA, TOMB OF GESU DARAZ. *The Dargah of Gesu Daraz is one of the holiest Muslim shrines in South India. Every year people assemble to celebrate urs (death anniversary) which takes place on the 15th, 16th and 17th day of Zul-Qa`dah of Muslim calendar.*

the foremost disciple of the famous Chiraghi, who along with Nizamuddin Auliya, was the most respected Sufi scholar of his time. Gesu Daraz also had a good number of non-Muslim followers. The *urs* or annual pilgrimage at his *dargah* in Gulbarga attracts people of all sects even today.

There was a problem between Firuz Shah and his brother Ahmad Shah I in the former's later years, which was aggravated by Gesu Daraz's support for the latter. The rift widened when Hasan Khan, the son of Firuz Shah, was appointed crown prince. After the ceremonies were over and the nobles had paid homage to the new crown prince, Firuz Shah sent his son to the saint for blessings. The saint gave a sharp rejoinder by saying that seeking blessings after the emblems of royalty had already been bestowed on the prince was futile. When further pressed by the royal emissaries, he said that God had already appointed Ahmad Shah I as Firuz Shah's successor and it was no use now to offer any prayers for Hasan Khan. This annoyed Firuz and he sent a message to the saint saying that since the saint's *khanqah* was located too near the palace and since it attracted a lot of people, he should move outside the city because the sultan's peace of mind was being disturbed. On hearing this, the saint moved to a place where his mausoleum now stands and lived there till his end.

Firuz Shah was forced to abdicate in favour of his brother Ahmad Shah who ascended the throne with the support of the Bahmani army under the crown name of Ahmad Shah I. Ahmad Shah I's new capital at Bidar other than being more centrally located with a higher percentage of fertile land, also marks a perceptible change in the course of Bahmani history, which thereafter witnessed increasing contacts with Persia and Central Asia. As a result, the *Afaqis* became more dominant at the Bahmani court. Another manifestation of the increased contacts with Persia and Central Asia were the links that Ahmad Shah I established with saints such as Shah Khalilullah, son of the revered Shah Nimatullah of Kirman, who arrived at Bidar in 1431 CE.

Art and Architecture

Different religious groups in the Bahmani kingdom allowed each other's influences to take root, making the life of commoners practically devoid of religious strife. This also helped in the emergence of a fusion culture and can be attributed to the influence of the neighbouring Hindu kingdom of Vijayanagar and the predominant Persian culture that had been brought into the Deccan. Although relations between the Bahmanis and the Vijayanagaras remained perpetually in conflict, their co-existence influenced the cultural environment of the day.

In the realm of architecture, mixed cultural influences led to the evolution of a style that was a harmonious blend of both Hindu and Islamic. The Bahmani architecture in the Deccan is marked by its distinct originality and independence of style, deriving its elements from the architectural styles of the Delhi Sultanate and that of distant Persia. With the transfer of capital from Gulbarga to Bidar, the purely Tughlaq influence in architecture seemed to have waned and the influx of Persian and Arab cultural forms from overseas, together with Hindu traditions, seemed to have developed. These aspects were best illustrated in the tomb architecture of the Deccan. The earliest specimen was the tomb of Alauddin I built in the fourteenth century in an imitation of the Tughlaq style of the Delhi Sultanate, while the tombs built by the Bahmani rulers in the fifteenth century at Ashtur in Bidar depict distinct Persian elements deftly combined with those of the northern Indian style. Tomb architecture further developed during the time of the Adil Shahis and Qutb Shahis in the sixteenth and seventeenth centuries, whose fully developed spherical domes indicate their complete evolution by the amalgamation of various differing styles. The earliest period of architectural

JUMMA MASJID, *also known as the Jami Masjid, inside the Gulbarga Fort*

INSIDE ARCHES, *Jumma Masjid*

development began in 1347 CE, when Alauddin I constructed the Gulbarga Fort. Next, in the reign of Muhammad Shah I the famous Jumma Masjid known as the Great Mosque was constructed and completed in 1367 CE by Rafi an architect hailing from Persia. Said to resemble the famous Cordova mosque in Spain, it has neither a courtyard nor a *hauz* found in traditional mosques. Supported on 140 pillars it has 250 arches and five large domes; the mosque could accommodate 5000 worshippers. Firuz Shah also laid out a new city near Gulbarga, which he named Firuzabad. His tomb consisting of twin domes is situated very close to the Gulbarga fort.

The second phase of Bahmani architecture is represented by the Bidar group of monuments constructed under the patronage of Ahmad Shah I and his successors, which include the Bidar Fort, Mahmud Gawan's Madrassa and Ali Barid's Tomb. The fort at Bidar built by the earlier Hindu rajas was either demolished or new fortifications added to the existing one by Ahmad Shah I in 1428 CE. According to Ferishta, Muhammad Shah III and Shihab-uddin Mahmud developed the fort on scientific lines. The Bidar fort boasts of a dominating presence over the surrounding landscape. Nestled inside this moated fort was the royal town now dotted with crumbling ruins of the bastions and gates, royal baths and kitchens, audience halls and pleasure pavilions, such as the Gagan Mahal, the Diwan-e-Aam where the fabulous turquoise throne once rested, the Takht Mahal, the Royal Pavilion and the Naubat Khana.

BIDAR FORT

MAHMUD GAWAN'S MADRASSA

ALI BARID'S TOMB

BAHMANI TOMBS, *Ashtur, Bidar*

The Solah Khamba Mosque is a prominent structure inside the fort. One of the largest mosques in India, it presents an imposing picture with its massive circular columns. Interestingly, the dome is held up by small arches built across the interior angle of two walls to support spires fashioned as elephant trunks. This is an incredible feature for Islamic art forbids the use of any animal or human figurines—even on one's robes while prayers are being offered. To have animal figurines displayed within a mosque, therefore, reveals the cosmopolitan character of Deccani art. Like the Jumma Masjid at Gulbarga, the Bahmanis employed architects and craftsmen from Persia to build the Chand Minar at Daulatabad and the Madrassa of Mahmud Gawan at Bidar.

The forts built by the Bahmanis were perhaps the greatest and indestructible monuments, far exceeding any of the same period in Europe. In addition to the forts at Gulbarga and Bidar, the mountain fortresses of Gavilgad and Narnala are considered as choice specimens of grandeur. Ferishta records that Ahmad Shah I while constructing the Gavilgad fort carried out repairs to the existing fort at Narnala. Similarly, the existing

SOLAH KHAMBA MOSQUE

ELEPHANT SUPPORTED ARCHES, *inside the Solah Khamba Mosque*

forts at Panhala and Parenda were used by the Bahmanis as outposts. Thus, the military architecture of the Bahmanis was influenced by European ideas, while other constructions reveal Hindu and Persian influence.

The Bahmani court in the Deccan manifested a distinct Indianized Islamic culture that was different from that of northern India. It reflected the composite character of the Indians, some of whom had converted to Islam while retaining several elements from their previous traditions in terms of social customs, language, literature, music, art and architecture. It paved a way in which a consistency Bahmani cultural tradition continued in the successor states. The cultural trends in the Bahmani kingdom and its five successor states led to an enriching synthesis and fusion that was already present in Indian society.

SUMMARY

- From the fourteenth century with the arrival of the Persians, a new Indo-Islamic synthesis began to emerge in the Deccan, which became especially significant in the context of the Indo-Persian cultural sphere.
- The metamorphosis, in the fifteenth and sixteenth centuries, drew the entire Deccan into the orbit of Persian culture with the augmentation of peninsular India's commercial and cultural interaction with Persia.
- The administrative apparatus of the Bahmanis was well-developed and played a major role in legitimizing their rule in the Deccan. It was modelled on that of the Delhi Sultanate.
- Mahmud Gawan as *wazir* of the Bahmanis increased efficiency in central and provincial administration and rooted out corruption.
- Mahmud Gawan transformed the whole system of military administration by bringing in reforms to ensure efficiency and good organization.
- The Bahmani kingdom was economically prosperous with well-cultivated lands and safe roads. But, while the nobles lived an affluent life, the life of the rural folk was miserable.
- Islam existed in all forms together with Hinduism in Bahmani society, creating an atmosphere that led to the evolution of a liberal and open-minded approach based on sharing and adoption of mutual traditions and customs.
- The integration and acceptance of the native Hindus, northern Indian Muslims and *Afaqis* into the plural society of the Deccan is a noteworthy fact.
- The Bahmani kingdom was officially a Sunni state, but Shiism and Sufism were practiced abundantly.

Firuz Shah and Ahmad Shah I showed inclination towards Shiism, and Mahmud Gawan being a Persian was a Shia himself.

- During Firuz Shah Bahmani's reign, the famous Sufi saint, Gesu Daraz, settled in the Bahmani capital.
- The Bahmani architecture in the Deccan is marked by its distinct originality and independence of style. It derived its elements from the architectural styles of the Delhi Sultanate and that of distant Persia.
- The Bahmani court in the Deccan manifested an Indianized Islamic culture that was different from that of northern India. It reflected the composite character of the Indians.
- The cultural trends in the Bahmani kingdom and its five successor states led to enriching the synthesis and fusion that was already present in Indian society.

KEYWORDS

Vakil-us-sultanate	Wazir-i-kull	Nazir	Qur beg-i-maimanah
Amir-i-jumla	Peshwa	Kotwal	Taraf/tarafdar
Wazir-i-ashraf	Sadr-i-jahan	Qur beg-i-maisarah	Sarlashkarship

REVIEW QUESTIONS

1. Critically examine the tarafdari system of the Bahmanis.
2. How was the Bahmani army revamped by Mahmud Gawan to bring in efficiency and good organization?
3. Write a brief note on the economic conditions of the Bahmani kingdom.
4. How did Sufism receive official patronage from the Bahmani sultans?
5. In what way did Bahmani architecture reflect the composite character of the Indians?

CHAPTER 14

The Bahmani Successor States

Review and Discussion

- The Nizam Shahis of Ahmednagar
- The Imad Shahis of Berar
- The Adil Shahis of Bijapur
- The Qutb Shahis of Golconda
- The Barid Shahis of Bidar

The late fifteenth century was a time when there was a surge in conflicts between various groups in the Deccan—the former provincial governors, important nobles and Qasim Barid, originally a *kotwal*, who had made himself all-powerful under the Bahmani sultan, Shihab-uddin Mahmud. They were all involved in interplay of rivalries with one another. As a result, a number of temporary alliances were being formed between these groups to win positions of strength. Many smaller nobles were either defeated or won over, and their territories added to the already existent dominions of the provincial governors or continued to remain under the weak rule of the Bahmani sultan at Bidar. Such a state of affairs led to the formation of the five successor states, which came about with the break-up of the Bahmani Sultanate. The successor states were Ahmednagar, Berar, Bijapur, Golconda and Bidar.

It is interesting to note that the rivalries and antagonism between the *Afaqis* and *Dakhnis* that had played a major role in destroying the unity of the Bahmani Sultanate had become almost inconsequential after 1492 CE. It was now replaced by a major rivalry that ensued between Qasim Barid and Yusuf Adil Khan, both provincial governors of the Deccani provinces. Qasim Barid, however, had the support of the *Dakhnis* of Bidar when he was being opposed by another *Dakhni*, Malik Ahmad of Ahmednagar. The older parties of nobles had now given way to the formation of semi-independent states whose rulers were trying to consolidate their position within their particular dominion. The provincial governors and more important nobles, thus, no longer represented separate blocs against the sultan, but were themselves the emerging rulers of independent states. Many of the provincial governors in a bid to establish their own independent state even did not mind allying with their old enemy of Vijayanagar, particularly in the conflicts with larger states. Or occasionally, some of the Bahmani successor states came together to contest against Vijayanagar from where they felt they could gain some territory.

The formidable rivalry between the *Afaqis* and the *Dakhnis* did not allow the groups to come together, which resulted in them retaining their separate identities. The Bahmani sultans were Sunni in faith, while under the growing influence of the *Afaqis* the five successor states mostly followed Shiism. This may appear paradoxical but relations between Deccan India and

Map 14-1 *The Deccani Sultanates, 1485–1605 CE*

Persia led to the formation of new local elites and minority groups in the Deccan. Mercantile and diplomatic exchanges enhanced the bonds between the Safavids of Persia and the people of the Deccan. Persian travelers, such as adventurers, artisans, scholars and mystics had come to the Deccani courts in various capacities, some on a permanent basis and some in transit. Thus, important judicial and religious personnel from Persia began to form the new intelligentsia in the newly formed successor states. Under this influence, Shiism became the state religion of the successor kingdoms, probably to establish an affinity with Persia; likewise the nobles in the respective kingdoms chose to follow Shiism in order to come closer to the rulers. The role that Shiism was to play in local society was crucial—it was a religious phenomenon as well as an important factor affecting the political and social environment of the region.

The Nizam Shahis of Ahmednagar

The Nizam Shahi kingdom which lay in the northwestern part of Deccan, between the states of Gujarat and Bijapur, was the first sultanate to gain independence among the Bahmani successor states. The Nizam Shahis claimed to have descended from Malik Hasan Bahri, originally a Hindu, who had created a good name for himself by aiding Mahmud Gawan in the wars of the Bahmani Sultanate. This goodwill made it easy for the successive rulers to don the role of the sultans of the Nizam Shahi dynasty. When Malik Hasan Bahri was murdered in 1486 CE, his son, Ahmed Nizam ul Mulk fought against the forces of Qasim Barid of Bidar and Yusuf Adil Khan of Bijapur, establishing his headquarters in Junnar in western Deccan by declaring independence under the name of Ahmed Bahri Nizam Shah. He ruled from 1486–1510 CE. This was a time when shifting political alliances were being formed and broken.

Taking advantage of his close proximity with the Marathas, Ahmed Bahri Nizam Shah tried to strengthen his position by taking over the territories of Daulatabad and Panhala in 1499 CE. To further increase the territorial boundaries of his kingdom, he also tried to add Khandesh to his list of acquisitions. He is credited with founding the capital city of Ahmednagar in the latter part of his reign. Known as Bhinar in early Yadava times, the new capital of the Nizam Shahis was named after its founder sultan. Ahmed Bahri Nizam Shah was an illustrious ruler with a great amount of talent and character. Although an absolute despot, he was modest, brave and forgiving of his subordinates. As the sultan of Ahmednagar he had the good fortune, like Shivaji, of being served well by his officers.

Ahmed Bahri Nizam Shah was succeeded by his young son, Burhan Nizam Shah I, who saw a long eventful reign of almost 40 odd years. Reigning from 1510–53 CE, Burhan I as he was popularly known was helped by his able commanders to protect the kingdom against the Imad Shahis of Berar and the Adil Shahis of Bijapur—the bone of contention being Sholapur. Burhan I made a pact with Sadasiva Raya of Vijayanagar, occupied Bijapur, Sholapur and the neighbouring districts. In the almost continuous struggle with Bijapur, Burhan I always looked to Vijayanagar and Golconda for support. Apart from this, Burhan I could not avoid entering into clashes with Gujarat and Khandesh over territorial issues.

Shah Tahir Ismaili, a migrant Shia scholar from Persia visited the Deccan in the sixteenth century and seeing the political advantages he could gain, settled down in the domains of Burhan I. He soon became a minister in the sultan's government and started to influence religious policies of the state. Under his influence, Burhan I became a Twelver Shia and Shiism was adopted as the state religion. This in turn facilitated in establishing good relations of the Nizam Shahis with Persia. Shiism remained influential in elite culture for several generations thereafter in Ahmednagar. Even though the Nizam Shahis lost their independence when the Mughal emperor Akbar made them pay tribute, and Shah Jahan formally absorbed the area into the Mughal empire in 1633 CE, their tryst with Shiism saw the development of several new trends in the region.

Burhan I's son and successor, Hussain Nizam Shah I, ruled from 1553–65 CE. While trying to consolidate his territories he was defeated by a coalition of rulers of Vijayanagar, Bijapur and Golconda. Since it was a time of shifting political alliances, Hussain Nizam Shah I later joined hands with the sultanates of Bijapur, Bidar and Golconda, taking part in the battle of Talikota in which Rama Raya was defeated. Hussain Nizam Shah I saw Ahmednagar's interests in establishing cordial relations with the Portuguese.

Hussain Nizam Shah I was succeeded by his son, Murtuza I, who ruled from 1565–88 CE. During his reign, the alliance with Bijapur and Golconda was broken while Berar was annexed to Ahmednagar in 1574 CE. Murtuza I now turned his attention towards Khandesh, where he had to fight against the Mughal army—which had from 1586 CE started to pose a new threat in the Deccan. Becoming a victim of his own son's politics, Murtuza I was imprisoned in 1588 CE, leading to a period of uncertainty till Burhan II came to the throne in 1591 CE. Barely ruling for four years, Burhan II was succeeded by short-lived sultans, who spent their time participating in court politics.

The Adil Shahis invaded Ahmednagar in 1595 CE and occupied the throne for a few months when its ruler died. At this time, Chand Bibi, the daughter of Hussain Nizam Shah I, who was married to Ali Adil Shah I of Bijapur, took over the reigns of power in her parental kingdom of Ahmednagar to stand in opposition against the Mughals. When the Mughal commander, Abul Fazl, invaded Ahmednagar in 1600 CE, the task of organizing resistance devolved on Chand Bibi. In spite of her heroic efforts to stem the tide of Mughal aggression, she was forced to purchase peace by ceding Berar to the Mughals. This was interpreted as treachery by the nobles and an infuriated mob killed her. Beautiful and widowed at an early age, she is considered one of the most remarkable women in Deccan history to have gallantly resisted the Mughals. But Ahmednagar fell after the queen's death in 1600 CE, and came under the control of emperor Akbar who made his son, Murad, the governor of the province.

Despite Mughal occupation, a part of the state of Ahmednagar had remained and was revived by Malik Ambar, an Abyssinian slave, who assumed full power as the de facto ruler under Murtuza II. He took advantage of Akbar's return to northern India in 1601 CE and consolidated his position in the southern part of Ahmednagar. After installing Burhan III on the throne in 1610 CE, Malik Ambar continued his attacks on Bijapur and Golconda. But he submitted to prince Khurram in 1617 CE; and in 1621 CE he gave back the territories conquered from the Mughals. He then raided Bidar and besieged Bijapur. In 1624 CE, he scored a victory over the Mughals and Bijapur at Bhatvada. This was followed by the unsuccessful siege of Burhanpur in alliance with the Mughal rebel prince, Shah Jahan. He died at the age of 80. His chief military achievement was his success in checking the imperialist designs of the Mughals against Ahmednagar. Along with being a master in the art of guerrilla warfare, he was also an enlightened administrator who understood Todar Mal's revenue system and modelled his revenue system on the same pattern as the Mughals. Mutamad Khan, a historian critical of Ambar writes, 'In warfare, in command, in judgement and in administration he had no rival. He maintained his exalted position till the end of his life. History records no other instance of an Abyssinian slave reaching such eminence. In the death of Malik Ambar, Ahmednagar lost its best protector against Mughal aggression.'

In subsequent years, Ahmednagar was attacked by the Mughals with Adil Shahi help. In 1633 CE Shahji, a Maratha nobleman helped Ahmednagar regain some territory at Pune and Junnar. However, the Mughals, under their viceroy Aurangzeb, attacked the existing Ahmednagar state in 1636 CE and took Murtuza III prisoner. Shortly after this the remaining portion of the sultanate was absorbed into the Mughal empire.

THE IMAD SHAHIS OF BERAR

Berar was one of the original four provinces of the Bahmani kingdom. The founder of the Imad Shahi dynasty, Fathullah Imad Shah, was originally a *brahman* who had converted to Islam under the Bahmani sultan, Muhammad Shah III, and had been made a military officer. Like Malik Hasan Bahri, he too had assisted Mahmud Gawan in his campaigns in 1472–73 CE, in return for which he was made the governor of the province of Berar. The forts of Gavilgad and Narnala were strengthened under his orders. Dismayed at the state of affairs at the Bahmani capital after the execution of Mahmud Gawan, Fathullah declared his independence in 1490 CE and ruled for 20 years. He was succeeded by his son, Alauddin Imad Shah, who ruled for another 20 years from 1510–30 CE. From the time of the inception of the Sultanate, Berar had quarrels with Ahmednagar. Burhan Nizam Shah of Ahmednagar claimed Pathri, a place lying within the borders of Berar, as his patrimony. This sparked off a war between the two sultans in which Pathri fell into the hands of

Burhan Nizam Shah in 1518 CE. In this endeavour, Alauddin Imad Shah sought the assistance of Bahadur Shah of Gujarat. This was not a well thought out action for it provided an opportunity to the ambitious ruler of Gujarat to gain foothold on the Deccan.

During the reign of the next ruler, Darya (1530–62 CE), the hatred continued between Berar and Ahmednagar. Darya tried to forge an alliance with Bijapur on order to counter Ahmednagar. Burhan Imad Shah, the next sultan who ruled from 1562–74 CE remained aloof even after joining the confederacy against Vijayanagar with the other Deccani sultanates, causing great dissatisfaction among them. Meanwhile, a revolution took place in Berar which resulted in the deposing of Burhan Imad Shah and the seizure of power by his minister, Tufal Khan. Taking advantage of the confusion, Murtuza Nizam Shah of Ahmednagar invaded Berar in 1572 CE, with the objective of restoring Burhan Imad Shah to the throne, but in reality it was a move to annex Berar to his kingdom. Tufal Khan was defeated and the minister, his son and the sultan were imprisoned in a fortress where they all died shortly afterwards. Thus, the conquest of Berar was completed. But Murtuza Nizam Shah could not retain his ill-gotten territory for long. Ahmednagar was attacked by the Mughals and Akbar appointed his son, Murad, as its governor. The Mughals finally got a firm hold on Berar during the reign of Jahangir.

The Adil Shahis of Bijapur

The Adil Shahis along with the Qutb Shahis formed the two principal successor states of the Bahmani Sultanate in the Deccan. The Adil Shahis remained in power from 1489–1686 CE.

Yusuf Adil Khan of Turkish descent was the son of king Agha Murad of Turkey. He came to the Deccan and joined the office of Mahmud Gawan in the court of the Bahmani sultan at Bidar. His bravery and personality raised him rapidly in the sultan's favour, resulting in his appointment as the governor of Bijapur. He declared independence in 1489 CE to establish the Adil Shahi sultanate and ruled till 1510 CE under the name of Yusuf Adil Shah. Being highly cultured and an ardent follower of the Shia faith, his tolerance towards other religions was evident. Other than constructing several beautiful buildings, inviting poets and artisans from Persia, Turkey and Rome to his court, he displayed great faith in Sufi saints like Chanda Hussaini. The highlight of his career was his marriage to Punji, the sister of a Maratha warrior, Mukhandrao. The successor of Yusuf, Ismail Adil Shah was her son. Later renamed as Bubuji Khanum, Punji's marriage to Yusuf Adil Shah displays the secular credentials that the Deccan was becoming famous for. He treated Hindus with consideration and admitted them to high offices in the kingdom's administration. Among his first tasks was the fortification of Bijapur.

The birth of the Bijapur Sultanate was, however, followed by incessant warfare. No sooner had Yusuf Adil Shah become the sultan of Bijapur that Saluva Narasimha conquered the fertile doab comprising the districts of Mudgal and Raichur in 1490 CE. This region had been the reason of bitter and constant warfare between the Bahmanis and the Vijayanagar kings for long. Threatened by the situation, Yusuf Adil Shah came to terms with the Vijayanagar ruler by agreeing to the latter's retention of the doab. But he tried to strengthen his own position by diplomatically arranging important marriage alliances of his daughters with the princes of other sultanates. One of his daughters was married to Burhan I of Ahmednagar and another to Alauddin Imad Shah of Berar, while a third to Prince Ahmed Bahmani.

When Amir Barid, Qasim Barid's son, with the support of Ahmednagar and Golconda declared war on Bijapur, Yusuf Adil Shah, unable to withstand the attack, sought refuge in Berar. He then prevailed upon Ahmednagar and Golconda to secede from the confederacy, defeated Amir Barid and returned to Bijapur in 1505 CE. Thereafter he regained Goa from the Portuguese by allying himself with the Egyptian and Gujarat fleets. But the Portuguese regained control of Goa from 1510 CE onwards on a permanent basis.

Ruling with ability and skill, Yusuf Adil Shah was one of the best generals and sultans of the Deccani sultanates. At the time of his death, Bijapur's territories extended from the river Bhima in the north to the Tungabhadra in the south.

Bijapur became exposed to Persian influence in the sixteenth century when Persian merchants used to ply the horse trade from the Persian Gulf to Bijapur. The proclamation of Shiism as the state religion by Yusuf Adil Shah encouraged even more Persians to immigrate to the Deccan, where they were employed as administrators or army personnel. As early as 1506 CE, Yusuf Adil Shah ordered the Shiite *khutba* to be read from the pulpit of the Great Mosque at Bijapur. His public declaration of Shiism was considered heretical and the Bahmani sultan, Shihab-uddin Mahmud, was instigated by his nobles to take action against Yusuf Adil Shah. At the instance of Amir Barid the sultan is said to have sent summons to the generals Qutb-ul-Mulk, Imad-ul-Mulk, Khudawand Khan and others, to present themselves at the court where a *farman* was read out to Yusuf Adil Shah, ordering him to put an end to the propagation of Shiism in his kingdom. Although Yusuf Adil Shah's propagation of Shiism was very moderate and tolerant, yet the objection raised by the Bahmani sultan was significant in itself.

His son, Ismail Adil Shah, succeeded him in 1510 CE and ruled till 1535 CE. Since he was a young boy of 13, a regent called Kamal Khan was appointed for him. Kamal Khan made peace with the Portuguese who had captured Goa in 1510 CE; in the following year Krishna Deva Raya annexed the Raichur doab. When Kamal Khan restored Sunni faith in the kingdom, the *Afaqis* rose against him and stabbed him to death in 1512 CE. Then began a period of confusion in which Amir Barid, helped by Krishna Deva Raya, tried to invade parts of the Adil Shahi territory. When the Gujarat army came to the rescue of Bijapur, they were able to recover at least some of the lost territories.

The sixteenth century was a period of proselytizing activity for the Shiite Muslims, and under the guidance of Shah Ismail Safavi of Persia, the propagation of Shiism was gaining momentum. Ismail Adil Shah restored Shiism in Bijapur, establishing close connections with Persia. In 1514 CE, Shah Ismail Safavi sent an ambassador to the Bijapur court with expensive gifts. The sultan received him well. The same ambassador was also sent to the courts of Bahadur Shah of Gujarat and Krishna Deva Raya of Vijayanagar who also received him cordially. But to spite Ismail Adil Shah and partly to defend his own Sunni faith, Amir Barid who was looking after a disintegrating Bahmani kingdom at Bidar, took a different view of things and detained the ambassador for two years. It was only after Ismail Adil Shah wrote to Amir Barid that the envoy was allowed to proceed to Bijapur. Upon hearing this, Shah Ismail Safavi was greatly pleased at the conduct of the ruler of Bijapur and sent him lavish presents and even addressed him as Shah; this raised the prestige of Bijapur before the other Deccani kingdoms.

Ismail Adil Shah in recognition of his alliance with Persia ordered his soldiers to wear a twelve-peaked cap (standing for the Twelver Shia sect) as part of their uniform; and to include the name of the Safavid ruler in the Friday *khutba*. The sultan was so captivated by Persian culture and manners that he also vowed to admit only *Afaqi* officers to his army and court. His reign was on the whole successful. He was a man of exemplary character, proficient in painting, music and poetry, and was a patron of learned men.

Ibrahim Adil Shah, the next ruler in power from 1535–58 CE, appointed Asad Khan as his prime minister. In contrast to Ismail Adil Shah, Ibrahim showed leanings towards Sunni Islam and adopted a pro *Dakhni* stand by giving military and court appointments to *Dakhnis*. During his reign there were victories won against Vijayanagar and Ahmednagar. When the Portuguese attacked the western borders of Bijapur, Ibrahim had to sue for peace. Inscriptions of the period show that Ibrahim Adil Shah continued to be a Sunni, although the state religion was Shiism. One of the inscriptions in the fort of Bijapur, interestingly, has the Shia *kalima* dated 1539 CE, while on the other hand it is significant that on his mausoleum there is an inscription that has recorded the names of Allah, Muhammad and the four caliphs in order of their succession, as well as all other companions (of the Prophet). This could have been permitted only by a person who was a devout Sunni. It shows that whatever his pretensions may have been with the Shah of Persia, Ibrahim died a Sunni.

Ali Adil Shah I, who ruled from 1558–80 CE, reverted to Shiism—favouring the *Afaqis*. He entered into an alliance with Vijayanagar to besiege Ahmednagar in 1559 CE; but later joined the other Muslim states of Ahmednagar, Bidar and Golconda against Vijayanagar in the battle of Talikota in 1565 CE.

The long reign of Ibrahim Adil Shah II, also known as Ibrahim II, stretched from 1580–1627 CE. Becoming the ruler at the young age of nine, he was put under the charge of two regents—Kamal Khan and a *Habashi,* Ikhlas Khan. Upon growing older, he fought bravely with the help of his regents against Ahmednagar and other opposing forces. Wars with the neighbouring states, which were a common feature of this period, continued unabated. He sent an embassy to Emperor Akbar's court in 1603 CE, and it was believed that a secret treaty was made by virtue of which Bijapur was to be protected in return for giving a free hand to the Mughals to attack Ahmednagar. Bijapur was left in peace by Akbar for some time. After the fall of Ahmednagar, Ibrahim II sent a message of goodwill to Akbar and gave his daughter in marriage to Akbar's son, Prince Daniyal. Ibrahim II annexed Bidar in 1619 CE, arousing the wrath of Malik Ambar who marched against the new city of Nauraspur that was being built by Ibrahim II. By and large, Ibrahim II was victorious in his ventures except for the loss of Janjira to the *Habashi* naval generals in 1619 CE.

Ibrahim II greatly improved the land revenue system and settlement patterns in Bijapur by implementing, with necessary modifications, the revenue organization of Raja Todar Mal. He constructed aqueducts for the supply of water to all parts of the city; and also built the spacious audience hall of Gagan Mahal. Though a Sunni he was tolerant towards all faiths and employed *brahmans* and Marathas in his service on a large scale. He maintained friendly relations with the Portuguese of Goa and protected the Christian missionaries. He beautified his capital city with fine architecture too. It was at his command that Ferishta wrote his famous history, *Gulshan-i-Ibrahimi* also known as *Tarikh-i-Ferishta.* After his death the kingdom began to decline.

Known in Indian history as the 'Jagadguru Badshah', Ibrahim II tried to bring about cultural harmony between the Shias and the Sunnis, and between Hindus and Muslims. He was a great exponent of music; he played many musical instruments, and even sang and composed verses in praise of Hindu deities like Saraswati and Ganapati. He wrote the book *Kitab-e-Navras* (Book of Nine Rasas) in *Dakhni.* As a legacy of the past, in Karnataka, there are many shrines which signify the religious amity between Hindus and Muslims even today. Shirahatti's Fakiraswamy and Bababudan Giri shrines are among the many that attract devotees of both communities in good numbers. The *jathras* (fairs) of Hampi, Kottur, Keragodu, Koppal, Gulbarga, and the *Muharram* event of Mudgal and other places also witnesses the participation of people from various communities.

After the death of Ibrahim II, Muhammad Adil Shah, his second son, was promoted to the throne by the *Dakhnis* as the sultan under the regency of Khawas Khan. During his reign, the Emperor Shah Jahan sent the Mughal army to attack Bijapur in 1631 CE under the command of his father-in-law, Asaf Khan. Although this attack was repulsed with help from Ahmednagar, the Mughals sent a better organized campaign five years later, when Muhammad had to sign a 'Deed of Submission'.

This held the Mughal threat at bay for a while, and Bijapur could occupy Vellore and Ginjee after opposing the Nayakas of Thanjavur during this time. Meanwhile, Muhammad tried to gain the friendship of the Dutch in order to counter the maritime supremacy of the Portuguese.

Seeing Muhammad Adil Shah pre-occupied with adding territories to his kingdom on the southern side, Shivaji who had become the governor of Poona, occupied Torna in 1646 CE, and Purandhar and Rairi in 1650 CE. By the time Ali Adil Shah II assumed power in 1656 CE, in addition to the Mughals, Shivaji too had become a potent threat for Bijapur. Ali Adil Shah II died in 1672 CE, and was succeeded by the infant king Sikandar Adil Shah. Frequent Mughal attacks, Shivaji's rising power and internal civil strife continually weakened the kingdom until it was ultimately annexed by Emperor Aurangzeb. Aurangzeb captured Bijapur in 1686 CE after a long siege of 18 months, in which the bribe offered to any soldier for throwing a bucket of mud into the moat was a rupee to a gold coin. Corpses of men and even animals were added to the bucket of earth before the moat was filled and the wall could be stormed. The assault failed, but a week later the garrison surrendered. On 12 September 1686 CE, Aurangzeb entered the city, and rejoicing at his victory he scattered gold coins. He had an inscription carved on the great Bijapur gun, the *Malik-i-Maidan,* to celebrate this achievement, and mounted the throne in Sikandar Adil Shah's palace.

The Adil Shahis were great patrons of the arts and architecture. Their patronage was responsible for the development of an independent provincial style of architecture, which excelled other artistic Islamic styles in the Deccan. The buildings constructed by them can be categorized into three kinds on the basis of their nature—mosques, tombs and palaces that are noted for their rich pageantry and imperial splendour. The most important are the Bijapur fort, the Ibrahim Rouza, the Gol Gumbaz, the Gagan Mahal and the Mihtar Mahal. The fort and the citadel within it were built by Yusuf Adil Shah and are studded with palaces, mosques, tombs and gardens built by the Adil Shahis. The Ibrahim Rauza built in 1627 CE contains the tomb of Ibrahim Adil Shah II and his queen Taj Sultana. The Gagan Mahal or Heavenly Palace was built by Ali Adil Shah I in 1561 CE as a royal palace with a darbar hall. The Gol Gumbaz is the mausoleum of Muhammad Adil Shah, which shows the Bijapur style of architecture in its most grandiose form. One of the largest domes in the world, with an area of 18,000 square feet, the Gol Gumbaz shows the skill and mastery of Bahmani architecture. The Mihtar Mahal, which is an ornamental gateway to the courtyard of a mosque, is also a notable building.

The Qutb Shahis of Golconda

The Qutb Shahis ruled the kingdom of Golconda from 1518–1687 CE. In the Bahmani kingdom, Sultan Quli Hamadani had risen in position and was rechristened Khawas Khan and conferred the title of Qutb-ul Mulk. In 1493 CE, he was also appointed the *tarafdar* or fief-holder of the province of Tilangana under the Bahmani sultan, Shihab-uddin Mahmud. With the weakening of the position of the Bahmani sultan, the loyalty and respect that fief holders had for royal authority began to diminish and most of them assumed royal titles and declared themselves independent. The same was the case with Sultan Quli Qutb-ul-Mulk, who established the Qutb Shahi lineage in 1518 CE, with Golconda as its capital. His ancestors hailed from the Turkman tribe of *Qara Quyunlu* of Persia, which had the black sheep as their emblem. He enjoyed a long and prosperous reign lasting for 35 years from 1518–43 CE.

Sultan Quli Qutb-ul-Mulk strengthened the already existing fortress of Golconda situated on a hillock on the northern bank of the river Musi, about seven miles from Hyderabad. It was surrounded by strong walls within which the city of

Golconda was located. He led expeditions against Vijayanagar, Bijapur and Bidar, and tried to recover Warangal from Shitab Khan. But Warangal would be annexed to the Golconda dominions only much later during the reign of Ibrahim Qutb Shah. His campaigns gained for him an extended kingdom till the river Godavari in the north. His son, Jamshid, got him murdered in 1543 CE who then placed himself on the throne and remained in power from 1543–50 CE. Although Jamshid did not proclaim himself as the sultan, local chiefs were forced to accept his authority. He succeeded in taking several forts from the Barid Shahis. For some time he also established an alliance with Ahmednagar and Berar. Jamshid was succeeded very briefly by his son Subhan, whose rule was devoid of any major event.

With the succession of Ibrahim Qutb Shah, the son of Sultan Quli Qutb-ul Mulk in 1550 CE, the Qutb Shahis began to steadily expand their dominions by taking advantage of the political divisions between the Telugu kings and the Nayakas. They also posed to be a potent threat to the Vijayanagar rulers and the Gajapatis of Orissa. Ibrahim Qutb Shah with the other Deccani sultans formed a coalition against Vijayanagar, which led to the battle of Talikota in 1565 CE. As a result of this victory, Ibrahim Qutb Shah took over the hill forts of Adoni and Udayagiri. He then attacked the fortress of Penukonda, where the last remnants of the Vijayanagar court had shifted. For a long period of his reign, Ibrahim Qutb Shah fought battles with the Nizam Shahis. He was the first sultan of Golconda to assume the title of sultan and to issue coins in his own name. Finding the warrior Nayaka groups beneficial for the sultanate, he extended a hand of friendship towards them which would help in bringing many Telugu warrior groups into Golconda's military service.

Ibrahim Qutb Shah's son and successor, Muhammad Quli ruled from 1580–1612 CE. Other than increasing the fortification of the Golonda fort, he improved irrigation, encouraged trade, built the city of Haidarabad as his residential capital and called it Bhagyanagar. Muhammad Quli frequently entered into conflicts with Bijapur and was also threatened by the Mughal army. He did not heed Chand Bibi's appeal to join hands with the Ahmednagar army to fight together against Akbar. He put down a rebellion at Kondavidu in eastern Deccan and occupied the Vijayanagar stronghold of Gandikota.

Muhammad Quli Qutb Shah was succeeded by Muhammad Qutb Shah who ruled from 1612–26 CE. The Mughals had grown very powerful in the Deccan by this time, and receiving Shah Jahan's envoy at Golconda in 1616 CE, Muhammad Qutb Shah agreed to further the Mughal cause by withdrawing all support to Malik Ambar. During his reign, Golconda evolved into a large and prosperous trading centre, famous for its trade in diamonds, fabrics and steel, which attracted merchants from all over the world.

Abdullah Qutb Shah, the sixth ruler enjoyed a long reign of 46 years from 1626–72 CE. He made further additions to the Golconda fort, making it impregnable. But he did not take the Mughal advancement into the Deccan with much seriousness. Hence in 1636 CE, he was forced to accept Mughal suzerainty by signing the 'Deed of Submission', according to which Qutb Shahi territories came directly under Shah Jahan's supervision reducing Golconda to the status of a mere Mughal protectorate. Shiism as the state religion was to be replaced by Sunni Islam, and the Mughal emperor's name was to be added in the Friday *khutba*.

The Mughals were not satisfied by merely making Golconda accept their protection. They found a reason to invade Golconda when Abdullah's relations with his powerful minister, Mir Jumla, became strained. The latter appealed against his master in 1655 CE to Aurangzeb, who was the Mughal viceroy in the Deccan. This gave Aurangzeb the much awaited opportunity to invade Golconda, in which Golconda–Haidarabad was ravaged. Abdullah was compelled to make peace by clearing all arrears of tribute and giving away his daughter in marriage to Prince Muhammad Sultan, the eldest son of Aurangzeb. As a result of this matrimonial alliance, Golconda remained free from Mughal attacks for the next 30 years.

When Abdullah Qutb Shah died without a male heir in 1672 CE, the nobles proposed that Abul Hasan, his nephew, come to the throne. Abul Hasan was a man of ease, who entrusted the administration of his kingdom to his two capable ministers, Akkanna and Madanna, and buried himself in the pleasures of harem life. He was given the epithet of Tana Shah as he was considered to be of dictatorial nature. Since he was not interested in the matters of state, he spent most of his time in the pursuit of music, fine arts and sensuality. It was during his reign that Gopanna, also known as Ramdas swami, constructed the famous Bhadrachalam temple.

When Prince Azam and Prince Muazzam—Aurangzeb's sons—marched on Bijapur, Aurangzeb ordered them to invade Golconda with the intention of annexing the state. The primary motive ascribed to this invasion by Aurangzeb was that Golconda was a Shia state. There were, however, other more important reasons as we will see. Abul Hasan took Shivaji's help against the Mughals, which made the Maratha leader spend considerable time in Golconda–Haidarabad in 1677 CE. The armed struggle between Golconda–Haidarabad and the mighty Mughal empire was hopelessly unequal.

In the previous battles between the Mughals and the Qutb Shahis, treaties were signed, the terms of which had been more favourable to the Mughals. However, each time a consensus had been drawn. This time it turned out to be different. Abdullah Qutb Shah had no choice but to make peace with the Mughals on terms set by them. A settlement was reached according to which the Golconda Sultanate agreed to pay one crore and twenty lakh as war indemnity in addition to the usual annual tribute of two lakh huns. In addition, the territories of Malkhed and Seram were to be ceded to the Mughal empire. And, Abdullah re-affirmed his subordination to the Mughals and agreed to dismiss his two *brahman* ministers, Akkanna and Madanna, from service. Through these terms, the Qutb Shahis could continue for the time being without any fresh Mughal threat, but even this truce seems to have been short-lived.

After a few years, the Mughals attacked Golconda and its neighbouring city of Haidarabad, which was seized and sacked by Prince Muazzam in 1685 CE; but the sultan once again withdrew to his impregnable fortress of Golconda. It was this vast and big fortress that Aurangzeb began to besiege, but living up to its reputation, the fortress could not be invaded. For eight months Aurangzeb's army, suffering greatly through the monsoons made no headway. Finally, in September 1687 CE, not relying on his military strength alone, Aurangzeb bribed an Afghan official, Mir Muhammad Ibrahim, the commander in chief of Abul Hasan, who joined hands with the Mughals. Through bribery the gate to the fort was opened and the Mughal troops were admitted. The sultan surrendered without a fight; it was only Abdur Razzak Lari, the commander of the Golconda forces who fought the Mughals at the risk of his life. Golconda was annexed to the Mughal empire, and Abul Hasan was sent as prisoner to the Daulatabad fort. All the assets of the Qutb Shahis, including crores of rupees in cash, heaps of jewellery, gold and silver ornaments, and other commodities of great value, were acquired by Aurangzeb. The kingdom of Golconda, with its strategic location, its high level of economic prosperity because of the fertile plains of the Tilang–Andhra region, its advanced trading activity at the ports of Masulipatam, Nizamapatnam and Narsapur, and the reserves found in its diamond mines, had for long been a great temptation for the Mughals to possess.

The political legacy of the Qutb Shahis was supported by a sound system of administration. The state adopted a system by which a proportion of fiscal rights were given out in assignment to an aristocracy. The revenue farmers, who acted as a middle or contact zone between the state and civil society, represented this aristocracy. Revenue farming was advantageous, since in a way it guaranteed the state with a steady flow of income by ensuring a fixed amount of revenue. On the other hand, assigning of fiscal rights to an aristocracy also led to instability within the state, as the revenue farmers sometimes acquired long term fiscal rights, developing local roots. The delegation of administrative and fiscal rights seems to be justified by the increasing inability of the Qutb Shahis to centrally control and administer large peripheral areas with the help of salaried ministers and officers. Provincial units such as *tarafs* and *parganas* were granted in the form of *jagirs* to the *amirs* and *wazirs* of the royal court. Every minister had a *jagir,* but this was hardly ever in the proximity of the capital. The *jagirdar* was like an absentee landlord who stayed in the capital, and his nominees known as *hawaldars* and *thanedars,* transacted the daily administration with the help of hereditary officials and landholders.

Like the Adil Shahis, the Qutb Shahis patronized Shiism. They supported Shia *ulema*, built mosques and *ashurkhanas* for the commemoration of Imam Hussain's martyrdom, seminaries, and Shia burial grounds. They had the Friday prayer sermons read in the name of the Twelve Imams and of the Safavids. Twelver *ulema* of the Usuli School predominated in Golconda. As a consequence, Shiism became the religion of the ruling elite, popularized with royal support. Despite this, Sunnism that had been followed by the Tughlaqs and Bahmanis in the Deccan, seemed to predominate.

Tavernier, the French traveller, who had visited Golconda, surmises in his travels, 'As for the kingdom of Golconda, Qutb Shah maintains with great zeal the law of the Shias, and as most nobles of his court are Persians, they observe customs of the sect of the Shias with the same strictness and the same freedom from restraint as in Persia.'

The Mughals, who were Sunni Muslims, had over the centuries watched the Shia rule of the Deccan with considerable dismay. They had tried in vain to conquer the Deccan on many occasions. Rather than going over to the Mughals, the Qutb Shahis felt inextricably linked with the local Hindu population. It was only in 1636 CE, that the Mughal emperor Shah Jahan forced the Qutb Shahis to cease the Shia form of worship in the Friday congregational prayer sermons, including the mention of the Safavids. After 1648 CE, the Mughals became more rigid towards the Deccan states, gradually culminating in the invasion of Golconda and Bijapur in 1656 CE and 1657 CE, respectively.

Shiism, Sunnism and Sufism existed together with Hinduism in the Qutb Shahi society. For maintaining religious harmony in society, the Qutb Shahis supported and aided many religious institutions—temples, *mathas, agraharas,* mosques, *dargahs, khanqas* and *ashurkhanas* became the focus of propagation and preservation of their respective faiths. One of the main aims of these religious institutions was to promote spiritual welfare in society. Apart from being great religious and spiritual centres, these institutions channelized the sentiments of the masses and had a profound influence on the political, social, economic and cultural life of the people. While promoting multiculturalism where all people could co-exist in peace and harmony, the Qutb Shahis succeeded in giving indications that they were not in favour of projecting an orthodox face of Islam. They incorporated various native traditions and bestowed on local aristocracy the royal touch. This was done with a view to evolving a new secular political system that would derive popular consent to their rule and make governance smoother. This is the unique paradigm of the *Dakhni* culture so typical to the region that was continued by successive states.

The spirit of the *Dakhni* culture was even seen in the Qutb Shahi architecture, which was the most powerful expression of Indo-Persian architecture in the Deccan. It had distinct components of Hindu,

MINARET OF HAYAT BAKSHI BEGUM'S MASJID, *1667 CE. The mosque attached to the tomb of Hayat Bakshi Begum (daughter of Sultan Muhammad Quli Qutb Shah, the fifth ruler and wife of Muhammad Qutb Shah, the sixth ruler), lies inside the Ibrahim Bagh. The mosque is a grand structure built by her son Sultan Abdullah Qutb Shah in 1667 along with her mausoleum. The inscriptions in the masjid are unique examples of calligraphic art. The roof of the masjid is flanked by two tall minarets, each crowned by a pot resting on lotus leaves and adorned with two false balconies.*

Persian, Moorish and Mughal styles, culminating in its own unique identity. The buildings and monuments comprised large, spacious halls and compartments with lofty arches rising to two or three storeys that even today give an idea of their original grandeur, glory and magnificence.

Qutb Shahi architecture can be categorized into five broad types—residential architecture (including royal palaces), military architecture (such as forts), religious architecture (mosques and *ashurkhanas*), funerary architecture (tombs and *dargahs*) and civil architecture (such as bridges, roads, bazaars, hospitals, *hammams* and tanks). The monuments constructed by the Qutb Shahis which deserve special mention are the Golconda Fort, Qutb Shahi Tombs, Jami Masjid, Purana Pul, Badshahi Ashurkhana, Darush Shifa, Charminar and Charkaman, Mecca Masjid and Toli Mosque.

It was Ibrahim Qutb Shah who ordered the present fort of Golconda to be built in stone and lime. The original fort was built in mud and brick by the Kakatiya Rajas of Warangal in the thirteenth century, who ceded it to the Bahmanis in 1364 CE. Apart from its fort walls, gateways, bastions and the citadel on top of the hill, there is a magnificent group of *zenana* palaces, which are associated with the names of romantic personalities such as Bhagmati, Taramati, Pemamati, Hayat Bakshi Begum and others. The citadel on top of the fort, known as the *Bala Hissar*, was the residence of the Qutb Shahi kings. The other places of interest inside the fort include the offices of Akkanna and Madanna, *Darbar-e-Am* (general assembly), *Darbar-e-Khas* (special assembly) and the *Diwan-e-Am* (official and administrative purpose). In addition to this, there are guardrooms, ammunition storehouses, armoury, mosques, temples, wells, reservoirs and gardens in the fort area.

About three furlongs northwest of the Golconda fort, surrounded by the garden of Ibrahim Bagh, grand tombs of the Qutb Shahi kings and their relatives were built. The most imposing tombs are those of Muhammad Quli Qutb Shah and Abdullah Qutb Shah. On the entrance of every tomb was inscribed the name of the king, his period of reign and the date of his death. The major tombs belong to Quli Qutb-ul Mulk, Jamshid, Subhan, Ibrahim Qutb Shah, Muhammad Quli, Muhammad Qutb Shah, Abdullah Qutb Shah, Abul Hasan Tane Shah, Hayat Bakshi Begum, Pemamati and Taramati. There are nine other minor tombs belonging to the relatives of the sultans.

BALA HISSAR, GOLCONDA FORT. *This is the highest point in the fort and served as the inner palace area. The eastern gateway, one of the biggest gates in the entire fort, is the only entrance to the Bala Hissar. The Bala Hissar gate has crafted figures of peacocks with ornate tails and the granite block lintel below has sculpted yalis, a perfect blend of Hindu and Muslim architecture.*

QUTB SHAHI TOMB, *located close to the Golconda Fort. The tombs are domed structures built on a square base surrounded by pointed arches. They display a distinctive style of architecture—a mixture of Persian and Hindu forms.*

The Barid Shahis of Bidar

Although Bahmani power lingered on without much ado till 1538 CE, direct control at Bidar was in the hands of Qasim Barid's son, Amir Barid, who upon his father's death formed the sultanate of the Barid Shahis at Bidar. The Barid Shahi rulers of the small state of Bidar, now in Karnataka, ruled from about 1531 CE until 1619 CE. They were ministers under the Bahmani sultans at their new capital of Bidar. When the Bahmani kingdom disintegrated, the sultans retained a small principality around Bidar.

Qasim Barid had taken over complete control at Bidar from the time of Shihab-uddin Mahmud by getting appointed as the Bahmani prime minister. Though he declared his independence in 1487 CE, he had to fight hard for his existence against Bijapur. He joined the other Muslim states against Bijapur and even sought the assistance of Vijayanagar whenever it suited his purpose. Despite Qasim Barid's attempts, Bidar did not become a fully independent sultanate of the Barid Shahis before 1531 CE. Real power had by then passed into the hands of Amir Barid, the son of Qasim Barid, and his grandson, Ali Barid, who assumed the royal title of Shah in 1542 CE. Like his grand father Ali Barid followed a hostile policy against Bijapur, but Bijapur always gained an upper hand. Ruling till 1579 CE, Ali Barid Shah was followed by short-lived rulers. In 1619 CE, Ibrahim Adil Shah II of Bijapur invaded Bidar and took captive its ruler, Ali Barid II, and annexed Bidar to his kingdom. However, Bidar was taken under Mughal sway by its viceroy, Aurangzeb, in 1657 CE, and formally annexed to the Mughal empire in 1686 CE. After the breakup of the Mughal empire, Bidar fell into the kitty of the Nizam of Hyderabad in 1724 CE. Later when the state of Hyderabad was partitioned in 1956 CE, the city of Bidar and the district were transferred to the Mysore state.

Thus, evolving from the disintegration of the Bahmani kingdom, the five sultanates of Ahmednagar, Berar, Bijapur, Golconda and Bidar—of which, Ahmednagar, Bijapur and Golconda were the largest and the most powerful—were merged in systems where there was a community of religion and common interests, yet the pursuit of short-sighted and selfish goals prevented them from presenting a united front to their common enemies like the Vijayanagar rulers or the Mughals. This ultimately led to their annexation to the Mughal empire. Conflicts between the *Dakhnis* and Afaqis or frontier disputes between Bijapur and Ahmednagar for controlling Sholapur, and even between Ahmednagar and Berar were not uncommon. During this period of mutual conflicts, Golconda tried to maintain a balance of power as the extinction of belligerent states would endanger its own existence. It always tried to retain a diplomatic stand. But the one over-riding factor was that the five sultanates together represented a Deccan, which is viewed as quintessential and multicultural.

SUMMARY

- The late fifteenth century was a time when there was a surge in conflicts between the former provincial governors, important nobles and Qasim Barid in the Deccan.
- A number of temporary alliances were formed between various groups to win positions of strength. Many smaller nobles were either defeated or won over, and their territories added to the already existent dominions of the provincial governors or retained at Bidar under a weak Bahmani ruler.
- This situation yielded to the formation of the five successor states—Ahmednagar, Berar, Bijapur, Golconda and Bidar—that came about with the break-up of the Bahmani Sultanate.
- The Nizam Shahi kingdom that lay in the north-western part of Deccan, between the states of Gujarat and Bijapur, was the first sultanate among the Bahmani successor states to gain independence in 1486 CE, with its capital at Ahmednagar.
- Berar was one of the original four provinces of the Bahmani kingdom and became the seat of power of the Imad Shahi dynasty in 1490 CE.
- The founder of the Adil Shahi sultanate was Yusuf Adil Shah, who made himself independent from Bidar and began ruling from Bijapur in 1489 CE.
- The Qutb Shahi kingdom, founded by Quli Qutb-ul Mulk, ruled over Golconda from 1518–1687 CE. It formed one of the principal successor states of the Bahmani kingdom.
- Although Bahmani power lingered on without much ado till 1538 CE, direct control at Bidar was in the hands of Qasim Barid's son, Amir Barid, who upon his father's death formed the sultanate of the Barid Shahis at Bidar in 1531 CE.

- The pursuit of short-sighted and selfish interests prevented the Deccani sultanates from presenting a united front to the Vijayanagar rulers or the Mughals, which ultimately allowed the Mughals to invade and conquer.
- The one overriding factor that the five sultanates together represented was a Deccan which is viewed as quintessential and multicultural—the hallmark of the unique *Dakhni* culture.

KEYWORDS

Shiism	Mathas	Dargahs	Ashurkhanas
Sunnism	Agraharas	Khanqas	Dakhni culture
Twelver Shia			

REVIEW QUESTIONS

1. What were the factors that led to the formation of the Bahmani successor states?
2. Assess the role played by Ahmed Bahri Nizam Shah in consolidating the position of the Nizam Shahis.
3. Write a short note on the Imad Shahis of Berar.
4. How did the Barid Shahis break away from the lingering Bahmani rule?
5. Briefly examine Qutb Shahi architecture as a powerful expression of Indo-Persian architecture in the Deccan.

PART V–Religious Thought in Medieval India

On this subject the ancient Greeks held nearly the same view as the Hindus, at all events in those times before philosophy rose high among them under the care of the seven so-called pillars of wisdom, viz. Solon of Athens, Bias of Priene, Periander of Corinth, Thales of Miletus, Chilon of Lacedasmon, Pittacus of Lesbos, and Cleobulus of Lindos, and their successors. Some of them thought that all things are one, and this one thing is according to some τό λανθάνειν, according to others ή δύναμις; that e.g. man has only this prerogative before a stone and the inanimate world, that he is by one degree nearer than they to the First Cause. But this he would not be anything better than they.

Others think that only the First Cause has real existence, because it alone is self-sufficing, whilst everything else absolutely requires it; that a thing which for its existence stands in need of something else has only a dream-life, no real life, and that reality is only that one and first being (the First Cause).

This is also the theory of the Súfis, i.e. the sages, for súf means in Greek wisdom. Therefore a philosopher is called paildsopd, i.e. loving wisdom. When in Islam persons adopted something like the doctrines of these philosophers, they also adopted their name; but some people did not understand the meaning of the word, and erroneously combined it with the Arabic word súffa, as if the Súfi were identical with the so-called 'Ahl-assúffa among the companions of Muhammad. In later times the word was corrupted by misspelling, so that finally it was taken for a derivation from súf, i.e., the wool of goats. Abu-alfath Albusti made a laudable effort to avoid this mistake when he said, "From olden times people have differed as to the meaning of the word súfi, and have thought it a derivative from súf, i.e. wool. I, for my part, understand by the word a youth who is safi, i.e. pure. This safi has become súfi, and in this form the name of a class of thinkers, the Súfi."

Further, the same Greeks think that the existing world is only one thing; that the First Cause appears in it under various shapes; that the power of the First Cause is inherent in the parts of the world under different circumstances, which cause a certain difference of the things of the world notwithstanding their original unity.

Others thought that he who turns with his whole being towards the First Cause, striving to become as much as possible similar to it, will become united with it after having passed the intermediate stages, and stripped of all appendages and impediments. Similar views are also held by the Súfi, because of the similarity of the dogma.

Source: Alberuni, Muhammad ibn Ahmad, *Alberuni's India,* Vol I, London: Kegan Paul, Trench, Trübner and Co., 1910. Extract taken from CHAPTER III: On the Hindu belief as to Created Things, Both "Intelligibilia" And "Sensibilia", pp. 33–34.

Image: Jalauddin Rumi, Founder of the Order of the Whirling Dervishes, Showing His Love for His Young Disciple Hussam al-Din Chelebi.

CHAPTER 15

Bhakti Ideology

Review and Discussion

- The Bhakti Cult
- Shaivism
- Vaishnavism
- The Genesis of Bhakti Philosophy
- Bhakti Saints
- Impact of the Bhakti Ideology

History has shown an all-encompassing influence of religion on human life. In the hinterlands of philosophy, religion and mysticism, tracing the historical origin and development of religious communities provides an understanding of the evolution of the human mind. But beyond the boundaries of history, lies the daunting task of looking at the religious, or rather spiritual experience, from a holistic perspective.

An analysis of Indian history explains that in its many phases, religious thought and activity have been closely linked with political, socio-economic and cultural factors. With the arrival of the Muslims in India, came new social and religious ideas. Before Islam, people of numerous other faiths and philosophies had arrived in India, with most of them having merged into the local population. Instances of such assimilation include the Greeks, Sakas, Kushans, Huns and many others who had initially come as conquerors, but were eventually absorbed into the folds of Indian tradition, culture and even religious philosophies. The experience was, however, different with the Muslims, since the basic social and religious tenets of Islam differed considerably from those of Hinduism. Though the new Muslim settlers retained their distinct socio-religious identity, it did not prevent them from getting absorbed within the general Indian social milieu.

Conquest automatically constituted legitimization to own and rule the conquered territory in ancient and medieval India. The victor settled down in his new domain and became part of it. The conquest of India by Persians, Central Asians, Turks and Afghans gave rise to distinctly fresh trends that symbolized more of mutual assimilation than cultural conflict. Therefore, these Muslim conquerors are considered by historians to be part of the heterogeneous Indian population representing a pan-Indian culture. In due course of time, the crossbreeding of the Muslims in the Indian subcontinent lead to the emergence of a society based on integration and inclusion.

Except for a few pockets here and there, India remained under Muslim domination for almost 800 years—from the end of the tenth century to the mid-nineteenth century. During this period, India's interaction with the Muslims was intense. When the natives came into contact with the new conquerors and immigrants, a substantial number of them embraced Islam for various reasons. In Sind, Punjab and Bengal, the Muslims grew in greater numbers, and the interaction between the communities took place at every level. From military and administrative to religious and cultural, new ideas were taking birth at every level. The common man was more excited and involved at this fusion. It is a historical fact that whenever two clashing civilizations have come into contact with each other, both have been mutually influenced. Medieval India was no exception to this historical rule when Hinduism and Islam came face to face with each other.

The ideas of brotherhood of man, social equality, belief in and complete surrender to one god—which are the basic tenets of Islam—made a deep impression on the minds of Indian social thinkers and reformers. Simultaneously, the Hindu theory of *karma* or the belief that good or bad actions carry their own reward or punishment, the accommodation of multiple belief systems and a deep devotion to matters of spirituality among the Hindus also influenced the Islamic mind. This prolonged intercourse and amalgamation of such spiritual concepts was partly responsible for the growth of the Bhakti movement among the Hindus and of Sufi thought among the Muslims.

The Bhakti Cult

The origins of the Bhakti cult, which became popular in twelfth century India, can be located in antiquity. Its philosophical base has been part of India's ancient religious denominations. The discoveries at Mohenjodaro and Harappa suggest that the people of the Chalcolithic Age were not entirely unfamiliar with some of these philosophical concepts. A number of hymns in the *Vedas* and *Upanishads* emphasize an intimate relationship between the deity and the devotee. Founded before the rise of Buddhism, the *Bhagavata* religion (based on monotheism) emphasized that salvation may also be attained through the love of god. This concept of the *bhakti marga* or the path of love and devotion finds an in-depth exposition in the *Bhagavad Gita* as well as in the *Shvetashvatara Upanishad.*

The Meaning of Bhakti

The term *bhakti* denotes devotion to god; and the *bhakti marga* or the path of devotion represents a way of worship or salvation, which establishes a clean and pure relationship between god and his devotee. In this state of being, the devotee becomes oblivious of his own sense of self, and struggles to merge into that of the Supreme Being through pure love and devotion in thought and action. Such humility and modesty helps the *bhakt* or devotee in eliminating his ego, thereby freeing and leading his soul to salvation.

Though the genesis of the *bhakti marga* lies in ancient India, the spread of Buddhism and Jainism in southern India led to the revival of the Bhakti cult from the sixth century onwards, reaching its culmination in the seventh and eighth centuries. The early medieval period saw the growth of new devotional religious movements that were centred on saints who preached in the popular languages/regional dialects of the time. While the rationalistic interpretations of Hinduism were strengthened through various systems of philosophy, the concept of *bhakti* provided the devotee with an emotional appeal by assuring immortality through faith, devotion and prayer.

Despite its central focus on devotion to one's personal god, the Bhakti movement did not evolve into a homogeneous form, and the movement kept to the fringes of the dominant socio-religious structure. The cult manifested itself in two main forms—Shaivism and Vaishnavism. And these became the most popular Hindu sects of the time. These new movements probably began with the appearance of hymns in Tamil, associated with two main groups of poets—the *Nayanars,* worshippers of Shiva, and the *Alvars,* devotees of Vishnu. The aim of the *Nayanars* and *Alvars* was to save Hinduism from being eclipsed by Buddhism and Jainism, bridging the gulf between the Shaivas and the Vaishnavas. These saints and mendicants travelled from place to place, singing songs in praise of their patron gods and holding discussions with Buddhist and Jain monks.

Shaivism

Shaivism initially became a popular faith in southern India, with the *Nayanar* saints playing an important role in popularizing it. The Tamil region was to soon emerge as a centre propagating Shaivism that was based on the devotional poetic compositions of the saints and the Tamil *Purana* called *Periya Puranam.* Moving away from the traditional concept of Brahmanism where the priest was held in great esteem, the new philosophy of the Shaiva saints appealed to popular sentiments by teaching the masses selfless devotion as a way to salvation. The Shaiva saints challenged the social order of the time by taking within their folds people belonging to the lowest castes. Later on, within Shaivism three major schools of thought developed—Shaiva Siddhanta, Kashmir Shaivism and Vira Shaivism.

The Shaiva Siddhanta school identifies three *padarthas* or divisions—god (*pati*), soul (*pashu*) and earthly bonds (*pasha*)—that are generally believed to be inseparable from one another. Siddhanta philosophy lays emphasis on the plurality of souls, and on understanding the real nature of the individual soul and its relationship with god. The Shaivite philosophical traditions that developed in Kashmir between the ninth and the eleventh centuries had a distinct doctrine of their own, very different from the model of Shaivism prevalent in southern India. While the Shaivism practiced in Kashmir was totally monotheistic with Lord Shiva being the only supreme entity, the southern model was more pluralist. This particular element made Kashmir Shaivism an idealist philosophy.

The third branch of Shaivism that developed in Karnataka in the mid-twelfth century came to be known as Virashaivism. The founder of this philosophical school was Basava. The main ideology of this branch stresses on the three aspects of the Guru (the preceptor), *Jangama* (the realized soul) and the *Linga* (Lord Shiva). It was the worship of Shiva in the form of the *Shivlingam* that earned the Virashaivas the name of *Lingayatas*—a major community in Karnataka to this day. The Virashaiva school is known for its religious militancy, which along with the other features distinguished it from the other Shaivite schools. All the three philosophical schools believed in the worship of Shiva as the core of devotion, but each of them had different ways of realizing the Ultimate Truth.

In medieval times new devotional forms, like the *Nath Panthis* and Shaktism, developed within the Hindu philosophical traditions. The *Nath Panthis* claimed a divine origin and according to belief, *Adinatha* or Shiva was the first *Natha.* They stressed upon the value of yogic *sadhana* in attaining immortality and discarded the belief that knowledge of Sanskrit was important to the understanding of spirituality or the absolute truth. This was the reason they began to preach abstract religious philosophy in the regional languages. Naturally, it appealed to the masses. The text, *Gorakhbodh,* suggests that the believer of the *Natha* order can attain Shivahood not only in a monastery but even in a marketplace or under a tree. In Bengal, the *Nath Panthis* were strongly influenced by Shaivism; and much later an esoteric offshoot of their basic beliefs was manifest in the Baul sect.

Worshipping goddesses had always been practiced in India since ancient times. This trend continued taking on newer forms in medieval India with Shaktism evolving as a devotional practice within Hinduism. In its new avatar, the worship of the primordial female power personified as a goddess in the various forms of Uma, Durga, Kali and Chandi gained popularity. The worshippers of Shakti or the universal female energy were called the *Shaktas.* In the *Shakta* scheme of cosmological evolution, the Great Mother had created Brahma, Vishnu and Shiva; and in both Shaivism and Vaishnavism, Shiva and Vishnu along with their consorts form an integral part of the *Shakta* tradition. The movement gained momentum when the *Shakta Puranas* popularized the legend of the *Pithas* or pilgrimages where the goddess was believed to reside. Many Shakti temples, thus, came up all over India—a tradition that is alive to this day.

Vaishnavism

Vaishnavism refers to the form of worship associated with Vishnu (also called *Bhagavata, Narayana, Hari,* etc.) as the main deity. From the later Vedic period, Vishnu's position in the Hindu pantheology became prominent with each passing age. This is documented in the *Aitereya Brahmana*, which has accorded him the highest place. Later on, in the *Bhagavad Gita,* Lord Krishna was recognized as an incarnation of Vishnu. Vaishnavism believes in the doctrine of incarnation or *avatarvad,* which implies that whenever there is a desperate need for Vishnu's intervention in earthly matters, he incarnates himself in various forms in order to help his devotees achieve spiritual evolution. Vishnu is believed to have manifested himself through ten avatars (*dasavataram*), with his last avatar, Kalki, yet to appear on earth.

Vaishnavism believed that salvation could be attained through *bhakti* or devotion to one's personal god. By discarding the rigid and sacrifice-ridden Brahmanical order, Vaishnavism was successful in cutting across social barriers and appealing to a wider section of society. In medieval India Vaishnavism developed into a full-fledged religious movement. The *Vaishnava acharyas* of southern India added a new dimension to it by explaining the concept of *bhakti* in terms of the relationship between *brahman,* or the soul, and the world. They advocated the path of complete devotion and surrender to god as the final aim of all human beings. Thus, a revolutionary change was brought about in Hindu philosophy through emphasis on faith and devotional love over the performance of rites and ceremonies of self mortification and pilgrimages.

In continuation to what had already evolved, Bhakti thought and ideology advanced to greater popularity and mass appeal in the twelfth century. Religion, which merely satisfies the intellect without any emotional appeal, is generally uninspiring; and therefore, it was the devotional aspect of the Bhakti cult that appealed to the masses. Bhakti philosophy focused on simplicity by avoiding theoretical discussions, severe asceticism and the worship of an impersonal god—which were all beyond the understanding of ordinary human beings. Preaching a religion based on faith and devotion to a single god made monotheism the main theme of the system. The Bhakti reformers brought with them new hope and a simple way of worship, which could be followed even by the humble and the poor. It was a religion of the masses and not just of the spiritual elite.

The works of the *Alvars* formed one of the sources of the Visishtadvaita exponent, Sri Ramanuja's teachings; and thus, played a vital role in the history of *Vaishnavism.* Swami Shankaracharya, an advocate of Advaitin philosophy, is said to have been the first and principal exponent of this reform movement. The Bhakti reformers were cosmopolitan in their outlook and preached spiritual equality for all. They laid emphasis on the fundamental equality of all religions, and held that the dignity of man depended on his actions and not on his birth. They protested against the formalities of religion and the domination of ritualistic practices. They emphasized on simple devotion to god and believed in reposing full faith in Him as a sure means of salvation for one and all. They rendered immense service to the masses by preaching and writing in the language of the common man, making it easier for all to understand the essence of Hinduism. In short, the *bhaktas* gave a new sense and vigour to Hinduism.

The main principles of Bhakti philosophy had a generality that pervaded across time. But the early sources of Bhakti thought, the *Upanishads,* the *Puranas* and the *Bhagavad Gita,* represented devotion that was restrained and unemotional. On the other hand, this new form, associated with singing in the languages of the common people, was highly charged with emotion, emphasizing the personal relationship of the devotee with his god—often equated with that of the lover and the beloved. This devotional poetry had a mystical fervour not found in the *Upanishads* and the *Bhagavad Gita*. The Tamil saints, however, felt an intense love towards their god, experiencing great joy in His presence and deep sorrow when He did not reveal himself to his devotee. Their poetic compositions often reflect spiritual bliss and have an ethical content based on the virtues of love, humility and brotherhood. These ideas spread northward and probably formed the origin of Bhakti thought in northern India around the same time.

The Genesis of Bhakti Philosophy

The first challenge faced by orthodox Hinduism came from the simple teachings of the Jain and Buddhist philosophies; and with the advent of Islam, Hinduism had to brace itself up against a new set of ideas once again. In this entire process, the growth of the Bhakti ideology became the most important factor that facilitated better understanding between Hindus and Muslims. The complexities that had set into Hinduism were a result of dogmatic teachings that had led to spiritual stagnation, causing it to lose its simplicity and appeal. So when Hinduism came into contact with the simple teachings of Islam with its emphasis on monotheism, the former was naturally stirred, and a religious revival followed.

On the eve of the establishment of the sultanate rule in northern India, Hinduism was the dominant ideology, but its vitality was to be seen more in the southern areas. Right through the centuries, the system of class and caste had become ever more rigid, with each region being dominated by a complex hierarchy of castes that were strictly forbidden to interact with each other. Their actions were controlled and regulated by rulers who acted on the advice of court *brahmans*. Although the large-scale Vedic sacrifices had practically vanished, simple domestic Vedic sacrifices continued, and new forms of animal sacrifice emerged, especially in connection to the cult of the Mother Goddess.

By this time, the main deities of later Hinduism had begun to be worshipped in India. The cult of Rama, the hero of the epic *Ramayana*, and the eighth *avatar* of Vishnu, grew steadily—although it was yet to reach the prominence of later ages. Rama's monkey aide, Hanuman, had also become one of the most popular divinities in India, while Krishna was worshiped along with his divine consort, Radha. Many more deities had appeared by this time, such as Harihara, a combination of Vishnu and Shiva, and Ardhanarishvara, a combination of Shiva and his companion, Parvati or Durga.

The Hindu social structure too was suffering from the burden of various rigid practices, which were incompatible with the doctrine of the brotherhood of man. Society had degenerated into a caste-ridden community, which patronized segregation, untouchability, polytheism and idolatry as common practices. As a result, Islam which was based on the philosophy of a single god and equality among all humans was able to win over followers from the Hindu fold, especially those belonging to the lower castes. Hinduism as a popular religion was caught in a tight spot, since economic factors too were leading to the embedding of the once flexible caste system with the development of the feudal system in India.

Early medieval India's economic structure was different from that of ancient India. Medieval India, like much of the world, was characterized by feudal elites and the country was governed by a fragmented hierarchy of feudal chiefs, lords, and kings—one owing allegiance to the next in order. While some amount of coastal trade continued along the eastern and western coasts of India, the heartland—divided as it was by chiefdoms and kingdoms—became inward looking and had little economic or cultural contact with the outside world. This somewhat forced self-sufficiency of the villages led to a decline in trade, while promoting caste-based occupations. The hoarding of gold, the barter system and the practice of granting land in lieu of cash salaries—all quickened the deceleration of the economy that ultimately led to economic stagnation and political fragmentation. Although there were pockets of courtly prosperity, the country as a whole had become politically and economically fragile by this point in time, making it vulnerable to external powers and influences—such as that of Islam.

Sufism had attained popularity in Persia by this time, and Sufi saints had begun to propagate the doctrine of equality among men. Sufi philosophy with its emphasis on social equality and brotherhood, influenced medieval Indian society at large. Its basic principles of tolerance, liberality and universal brotherhood were very similar, if not identical, to those of the Bhakti reformers in India. These Bhakti reformers tried to bring about a rapprochement by preaching a doctrine that aimed at eliminating most of the ills prevailing in Hindu society. Bhakti saints protested against the exclusive spirit of caste domination and asserted the dignity of the human soul as being independent of one's birth and social rank. They also advised their followers to respect all religions and live in peace and harmony with their fellow human beings. The Bhakti movement, therefore, served Indian society in two ways—by bridging the

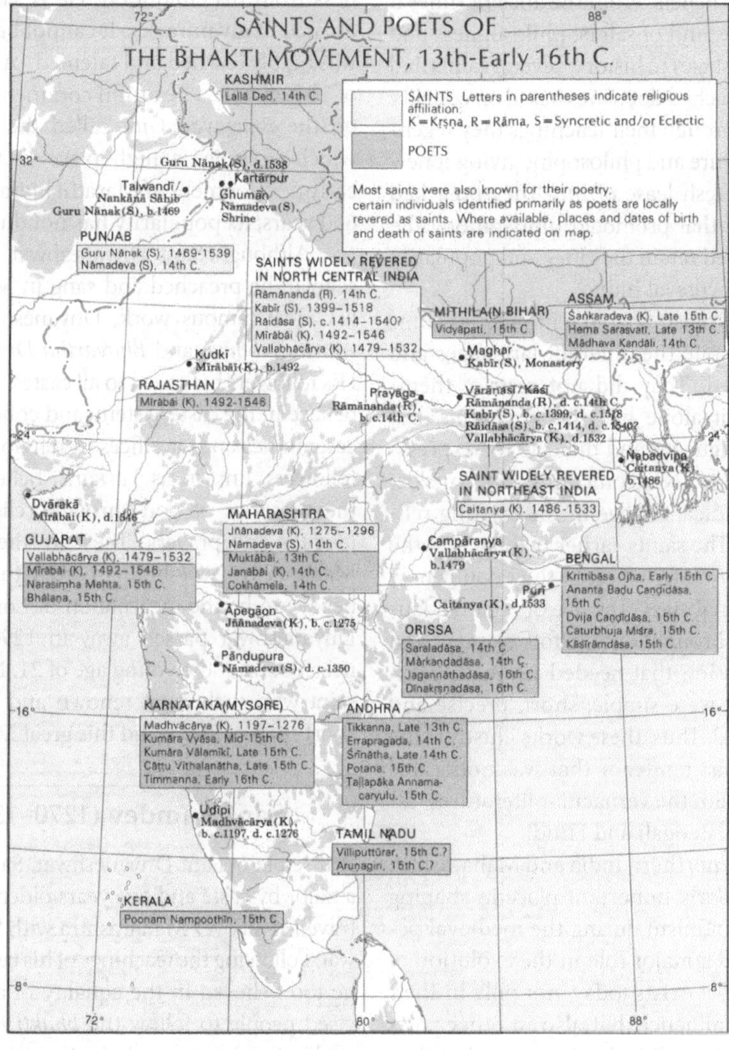

Map 15-1 *Saints and Poets of the Bhakti Movement, 13th–Early 16th Century*

gulf between Hinduism and Islam and by rescuing Hinduism from the challenges of its own complexities. Kabir, Chaitanya, Ramdas, Namdev, Mira Bai, Tukaram, Eknath, Dnyaneshwar, Vallabhacharya and Guru Nanak were all among the most prominent exponents of the Bhakti cult in medieval India.

Bhakti Saints

India had always been rich in terms of heritage, culture and religious beliefs. From the ancient times it was known as the land of saints, philosophers and sages. At various stages in history, several saints had practiced and preached doctrines based on equality and simplicity. Through their teachings they regenerated Hindu culture and philosophy, giving it new direction and a fresh lease of life. They preached a religion of love that promoted unity among the Hindus, and helped retain the glory and popularity of Hinduism in medieval India.

The Bhakti lyricists shared a number of common features despite the different languages and dialects they used. They did not restrict themselves to Sanskrit alone like the *brahmans*, but used regional languages and dialects for expressing their thoughts. Nonconformity to Sanskrit also implied a radical change in the existing religious hierarchy. The saints earlier belonged to the priestly *brahman* caste, whereas they could now belong to any social class. The use of regional languages in poetry brought out the folk element and an earthy expression that needed no further explanation. Lyrics were simple, short, precise and intensely personal. Thus, these works illustrate the local and reformist tendency that was noticeable throughout India in the vernacular literatures, especially in Tamil, Bengali and Hindi.

The saints of northern India and Maharashtra occupy a particularly important place in shaping the destiny of Hinduism during the medieval period. They played a major role in the evolution of Hindu society, as it exists today, not only in their own regions of influence, but also in other parts of the country. The political awakening that they aroused among the Hindus and the contribution made by them to native cultural heritage has made Indians indebted to them in many ways.

Sant Dnyaneshwar (1275–96 CE)

Sant Dnyaneshwar is considered to be one of the greatest saints of Maharashtra. He was born in 1275 CE to a *brahman* family at Apegaon near Paithan, on the banks of the Godavari. He was blessed with divine knowledge and showed signs of greatness from his childhood. He is said to have performed many miracles. It cannot be denied that he was highly learned and talented. At the tender age of 15 he wrote a beautiful commentary in Marathi on the *Bhagavad Gita* called the *Dnyaneshwari,* which occupies a high place in the origin and early development of Marathi literature. Even after 600 years, its popularity has not diminished.

Although Sant Dnyaneshwar was a Sanskrit scholar, he preached and sang in Marathi. Besides his most famous work, Dnyaneshwar also wrote *Amritanubhava* and *Bhavartha Dipika* in Marathi. His followers belonged to all castes, since he did not believe in the caste system, and condemned rituals, ceremonies and sacrifices in religious worship. His followers, known as *Varkaris,* believe in attaining the presence of god through religious songs or *bhajans* and prayers. They are the Vaishnavas of Maharashtra, worshiping Lord Vithoba whom they believe to be the incarnation of Lord Vishnu. Sant Dnyaneshwar passed away in 1296 CE at Alandi near Poona at the young age of 21. No other Indian saint won such great renown and fame in such a short span of life, as did this great Maratha saint.

Sant Namdev (1270–1350 CE)

A disciple of Sant Dnyaneshwar, Sant Namdev was a tailor by caste and five years older to his *guru.* He travelled all over Maharashtra with Sant Dnyaneshwar. Following the teachings of his celebrated master, he too believed in the equality of all men. He advised people to follow the *bhakti marga,* and created in them a strong desire to protect their religion and develop a deep love for their motherland. Like

Kabir, he condemned idol worship. Namdev carried on the work of Sant Dnyaneshwar after the latter's death in 1296 CE. He composed songs not only in Marathi but also in Hindi and spread the message of equality, travelling all over India. Some of his devotional songs are found in the *Granth Sahib* and other religious books of the Sikhs of Punjab too. His songs are still sung with great love and devotion.

Ramananda (1400–70 CE)

Ramananda, the fifth in apostolic succession to Sri Ramanuja, was the connecting link between the Bhakti movements of the South and the North. He was born in a *brahman* family of Allahabad, and probably lived during the last quarter of the fourteenth and the first half of the fifteenth centuries. Initially an *Advaitin,* he became a Vaishnavite under the influence of Raghavananda. He was a bold and uncompromising reformer who introduced radical changes in Vaishnavism by founding a new school based on the doctrine of love and devotion. He ignored caste distinctions and introduced the cult of Rama and Sita in place of Krishna and Radha. His followers were called Ramanandis, some of whom became founders of different schools, spreading the message of *bhakti* widely throughout northern and central India. Ramananda occupies a unique place in the history of religion in medieval India for successfully ushering in a new epoch in medieval mysticism.

Kabir (1425–1518 CE)

Unfortunately nothing very definite is known about the early life of Kabir, who lived either towards the close of the fourteenth century or in the beginning of the fifteenth century. Kabir made earnest efforts to create a spirit of harmony between the Hindus and the Muslims.

It is said that he was born to a Hindu widow, who abandoned him by a tank in Banaras. He was eventually found and brought up by Niru, a Muslim weaver. When he grew up, he became a disciple of Ramananda, the famous saint of Banaras. Kabir's teachings are contained in his *dohas* or couplets, which are sung with devotion throughout India to this day. He did not believe in caste distinctions, neither in the supremacy of the *brahmans* nor in idol worship. He did not attach any importance to the performance of rituals and ceremonies or to pilgrimages to holy places. Temples and other places of worship were not considered important by him. Above all, he denounced insincerity and hypocrisy. To him, Hindus and Muslims were pots of the same clay. Ram and Rahim were different names that he gave to the same Supreme Being. According to Kabir, salvation could be attained by performing good deeds and by means of *bhakti* or sincere devotion to god.

Guru Nanak (1469–1539 CE)

Born in Talwindi in 1469 CE, Guru Nanak was another great preacher of the *bhakti* message. He spent

TANJORE STYLE PAINTING, *from the late 19th century depicting the ten Sikh Gurus with Guru Nanak in the centre.*

his entire life preaching universal brotherhood, religious tolerance and unity of the godhead. Like Kabir, he too condemned caste distinctions, idol worship, rituals and ceremonies. According to him, good deeds alone would be counted in god's court of judgement. He advised his followers to achieve a state of mind where there would neither be pain nor happiness; and preached that this state could be attained by constant recitation of the *Sat Nam* or the sacred name of god. As a result of his simple teachings, Guru Nanak won a large number of followers and founded Sikhism, the fifth largest organized religion in the world. He died in 1539 CE at a ripe age.

Vallabhacharya (1479–1531 CE)

Vallabhacharya was the most distinguished preacher of the Krishna cult, hailing from Andhradesa. From his early boyhood, he showed signs of intellect and distinguished himself as a great scholar. He undertook pilgrimages to Mathura, Vrindavan and other sacred places, before finally settling down at Banaras. He is said to have visited the court of Krishna Deva Raya where he defeated some Shaiva scholars in debate. He wrote a commentary on the *Brahmasutras* and the *Bhagavad Gita* and his philosophy is called *Suddhadvaita* or pure non-duality or pure monism. He preached that man should develop a spirit of detachment from worldly affairs and dedicate everything to Lord Krishna. But some of his followers misunderstood the spirit of his teachings and interpreted them in a material sense by indulging in objectionable practices.

Chaitanya Mahaprabhu (1485–1534 CE)

Chaitanya was perhaps the greatest and most popular among the Vaishnava saints of India. He was born in 1485 CE into a learned *brahman* family of Nadia in Bengal. He left home at the age of 24 and spent the rest of his life preaching the message of love and devotion. He became so popular that his followers came to regard him as an *avatar* or incarnation of Lord Vishnu. He was popularly known as Mahaprabhu. Like other preachers of the Bhakti cult, he did not believe in caste distinctions and rituals. He preached belief in Vishnu and taught that through love and devotion, song and dance, a state of bliss could be attained in which the personal presence of god could be realized. His teachings were meant for all and his followers included low caste Hindus as well as Muslims. He had mass followers in Bengal, Orissa and other parts of eastern India.

GOVARDHAN, VALLABHACHARYA, *shown meeting and honouring the image of Sri Nathji on the mountain-side of Vrindavan. 19th century Rajasthani painting, British Museum.*

SRI CHAITANYA MAHAPRABHU, *shown performing a 'kirtan', a devotional song, in the streets of Nabadwip, Bengal. 19th Century painting (Calcutta Art Studio).*

Mira Bai (1500–50 CE)

Mira Bai belonged to a royal family of Rajasthan, yet she is known more for her devotional pursuits than her royal status. There are many stories about her life that make it difficult to separate facts from legend. She was born around 1500 CE and was married at the age of 13 to a prince. From an early age she showed more interest in religious devotions than towards her worldly responsibilities. It is said that she neglected her marital responsibilities and when queried about it, she said that it was impossible for her to be married to the king when she was already married to Lord Krishna.

A major change in her life occurred at the death of her husband. It was customary in those days for a wife to commit *sati*, but when she refused to comply, her in-laws began harassing her. She then left the palace and began wandering throughout Rajasthan, singing her *bhajans*, preaching the *bhakti marga* and gaining followers. She dedicated her entire life to god and endured all the difficulties of life. Awake or asleep, she thought only of Krishna. Mira is known for the many *bhajans* that she had composed in praise of Lord Krishna. They are still held in great esteem for their high literary value. She is believed to have died around 1550 CE. Mira Bai continues to live in the hearts of Indians as the very embodiment of *bhakti* or devotion to god.

Sant Eknath (1533–99 CE)

Born in 1538 CE to a *brahman* family at Paithan on the banks of the Godavari, Sant Eknath displayed an inclination towards spiritualilty at a very early age. He became a disciple of Janardhan Swami, a deeply religious man who was then in charge of the fort of Daulatabad. Eknath was permitted by his Guru to lead the life of a householder, and his wife, Girijabai, proved to be an ideal companion who assisted him in his mission of social reformation. He was opposed in his reformist activities by high caste Hindus. Sant Eknath's beliefs and teachings were similar to those of the great Maratha saints, Dnyaneshwar and Namdev. He advocated social equality and preached the abolition of distinctions based on class, caste and creed. He thus carried on the work of his predecessors by preaching that one could devote oneself to god by leading a normal householder's life. He did not believe in rituals, ceremonies and other orthodox ways of worship. He preferred the use of Marathi in his religious discourses and composed songs in the same language of the common people.

His numerous religious songs were called *abhangas, owees* and *bharuds,* which are still very popular in Maharahtra. He was a friend and advisor to the poor and down trodden, teaching them true devotion to god. He advised his followers to love all creatures and practiced what he preached. Besides devotional songs, Eknath also wrote a commentary in Marathi on the *Bhagavad Purana*, known as *Eknathi Bhagwat*. He also wrote the *Rukmini Swayamwar*. Though he was unable to complete the last of his works, the *Bhawartha Ramayan*, it was completed by one of his brilliant disciples after his death in 1599 CE.

Sant Tukaram (1608–51 CE)

Sant Tukaram was a contemporary of Chattrapati Shivaji, and though the two never met in their lifetime, Shivaji was greatly influenced by his teachings. Sant Tukaram was born to a Vaishya family in 1608 CE, in a village near Poona. He was deeply religious even in his childhood and spent his time singing devotional songs in praise of his favourite deity, Lord Vithoba of Pandharpur. Like Dnyaneshwar, Namdev, Eknath and other Maratha saints before him, he too believed in the *bhakti marga*. He often sang songs in praise of Lord Vithoba, visiting the temple of Lord Vithoba at Pandharpur twice a year in the months of *Ashad* (June–July) and *Kartik* (October–November).

Sant Tukaram sang self-composed devotional songs called *abhangas,* and performed *keertans* at devotional gatherings. As he preached the virtues of piety, forgiveness and peace of mind, thousands

POET-SAINT TUKARAM, *being taken up into Vishnu's heaven, Vaikunth. Ravi Varma Press, 1910.*

of devotees flocked to listen to him. He also spread the message of equality and brotherly feeling towards one another. Even today people all over Maharashtra sing songs composed by him, accepting them as their common heritage. The actual credit for uniting the various communities of Maharashtra goes to Sant Tukaram. The temple of his favourite deity, Lord Vithoba, serves as the meeting place for all communities of Maharashtra to this day. According to a popular legend, when Sant Tukaram died in 1651 CE, Lord Vithoba is believed to have sent a vehicle to escort him to heaven.

Samarth Guru Ramdas (1608–81 CE)

Guru Ramdas was also a contemporary of Chattrapati Shivaji. He was Shivaji's chosen friend, philosopher and guide. Shivaji was as strongly influenced by the ideas of Guru Ramdas as of Sant Tukaram. The former advised Shivaji even on his duties as a king and exerted more influence on him than Sant Tukaram did. Guru Ramdas was born on Ramnavami day (the day of Rama's birthday) in 1608 CE at Jamb, on the banks of the Godavari. His real name was Narayan, but he preferred to call himself Ramdas—meaning the servant of Rama. He was deeply spiritual from his childhood and had decided to devote himself to the worship of Lord Rama at an early age. He carried out a great amount of penance (*tapasya*) at Panchavati (Nasik), a place associated with Lord Rama's life in exile. Ramdas became a great admirer of Hanuman and looked upon him as the god of strength and an apostle of Bhramacharya.

Guru Ramdas lived during the period when the Deccan was fast emerging as a melting pot of cultures, but where instances of religious persecution by Muslim sultans took place occasionally. In response to this, he advised his followers to be strong enough to protect their faith. Laying immense importance on Lord Rama and Hanuman, he built a number of temples in honour of the latter in Maharashtra. Like the other Maharashtrian saints, he did not believe in the distinctions of caste, or creed. He inspired Shivaji to gather all Marathas together for accomplishing their aims. Through his great book, *Dasbodh,* he taught people the ways of a good life. His work brought about a great awakening among the people of Maharashtra, who united under Shivaji and fought against injustice.

Impact of the Bhakti Ideology

The missionary activities of the saints introduced important changes in the social and religious lives of the people of medieval India. Their undivided and all absorbing devotion to a personal god, whether worshipped in the form of Rama or Krishna or Shiva, emphasized that all these representations of god were only symbols of the one eternal Supreme Being, thus helping the revival of monotheism.

The Bhakti reformers purified and elevated religion by purging it of formal rituals and ceremonies through their emphasis on sanity of thought, purity of life, selfless sacrifice and devotion above all else. The virtues taught by them, of service, equality, brotherhood and love for one's god and one's motherland promoted peaceful co-existence between the Hindus and Muslims to a large extent.

Namdev taught that vows, fasts and austerities were neither necessary, nor important for one to go on a pilgrimage. Kabir too expressed the same ideas. Some of the saints like Namdev condemned idol worship, believing instead that stone images did not speak, and that being omnipresent, god was not to be found within a restricted space alone. Emphasizing on the fact that the kingdom of god was within every individual, Kabir too chanted that god was neither in temples nor in mosques, neither in the Kaaba (Mecca) nor in Kashi (Banaras), neither in rites and ceremonies nor in yoga and renunciation, but was omnipresent, omniscient and omnipotent.

The Bhakti reformers' message reiterated that selfless devotion and love of god alone would lead to salvation. As a saying of Kabir goes, 'The man who is kind and practices righteousness, remains passive amidst the affairs of the world, considers all creatures of the world as his own self—he alone attains an immortal being, for god is ever with him'.

A significant point to note is that although some of the saints were born into *brahman* families, they felt unbound compassion for humanity and were opposed to caste distinctions. They stridently emphasized the concept of equality among all human beings. This fact is best illustrated by the social identity of the prominent disciples of Ramananda—Ravidas was a cobbler, Kabir was born in a Hindu family, but raised by a Muslim, Dharna was a Jat, and Sena a barber. Namdev himself belonged to a class of calico printers and even had a few Muslim converts to Hinduism among his disciples, besides people of the lower social order like the Mahars, Kunbis, tailors, gardeners, potters, goldsmiths, repentant prostitutes and slave girls.

Above all, the reformers emphasized respect for all religions and paved the way for Hindu–Muslim unity. Kabir called himself the child of Allah and Ram, pointing out that Hindus and Muslims had the same goal before them and were like two pots of the same clay. Kabir also equated Mecca with Kashi and Ram with Rahim. He also condemned distinctions of caste and believed that the right to approach god was not restricted by dominant social sanction, but was granted to all who were characterized by sincerity of heart. The overall effect of the activities of the saints was immense on the local populace. From lessening the rigidity of the caste system, checking the tyranny of priests, discouraging polytheism and encouraging toleration, stressing upon charity and devotion, the moral and spiritual tone of society was uplifted.

The core of Bhakti thought is essentially selfless love for god. The path of devotion or the *bhakti marga* represents a way of worship, which establishes a relationship between god and his devotee through a pure emotional attachment. The element of *bhakti* enables a worshipper to become completely oblivious of his or her ego by setting the soul afloat.

The concept of pure love of god is universal and is to be found in all major world religions. India is a land of spirituality, where the concept of *bhakti* in its various forms has been present for at least 3,000 years. Its traces have been found in the ruins of Harappa and Mohenjodaro. Some of the hymns in the *Vedas* and *Upanishads* emphasize an intimate relationship between the deity and devotee. But it was not until the confluence of Indian philosophy, an amalgamation of various streams of religious thought, and Islamic precepts in medieval times that the Bhakti cult of took birth. Bhakti became a mass movement that broke through caste, creed and class barriers. Great Bhakti saints like Kabir, Chaitanya, Ramdas, Namdev, Mira Bai, Tukaram, Eknath, Dnyaneshwar, Vallabhacharya and Guru Nanak used popular languages like Hindi, Marathi and Bengali instead of Sanskrit to convey their messages of love and peace. The common man comprehended their simple but profound concepts and followed them in hordes, and Bhakti became a way of life for the people of this land.

SUMMARY

- An analysis of Indian history explains that in its many phases, religious thought and activity have been closely linked with political, socio-economic and cultural factors.
- With the arrival of the Muslims in India, came new social and religious ideas. The prolonged mixing of such ideas gave impetus to the Bhakti movement among the Hindus and Sufi thought among the Muslims.
- The origins of the Bhakti cult, which became popular in twelfth century India, can be located in antiquity.
- The word *bhakti* means devotion to god and the *bhakti marga* or the path of devotion represents a way of worship, which establishes a clean and pure relationship between god and his devotee.
- The early medieval period saw the growth of new devotional religious movements that were centred around saints, who taught in the popular languages of the time.
- While the rationalistic interpretations of Hinduism were strengthened through various systems of philosophy, the concept of *bhakti* provided the emotional appeal by assuring immortality through faith, devotion and prayer.
- The Bhakti movement did not evolve as a homogeneous movement. Devotional forms such as Shaivism, Vaishnavism, *Nath Panthis* and Shaktism were developed within Hinduism in the medieval times.
- Many complexities had set into Hinduism as a result of dogmatic teachings, making it lose its simplicity and appeal. Hindu society was also suffering from the ills of caste system, untouchability and idolatry.
- Kabir, Chaitanya, Ramdas, Namdev, Mira Bai, Tukaram, Eknath, Dnyaneshwar, Vallabhacharya and Guru Nanak—the most prominent exponents of the Bhakti cult—tried to transform the socio-religious fabric of medieval India.
- From lessening the rigidity in caste system, checking the tyranny of priests and encouraging toleration, the Bhakti saints stressed upon charity and devotion, and lifted up the moral and spiritual tone of society.
- The Bhakti movement served Indian society in two ways—it tried to bridge the gulf between Hinduism and Islam, while rescuing Hinduism from the ills of its own complexities.

KEYWORDS

Karma/karmic action	Shaktism	Idolatry	Abhangas, Owees and Bharuds
Bhakti marga	Monotheism	Bhajans	
Nath Panthis	Polytheism	Keertans	Sati

REVIEW QUESTIONS

1. Write a short note on the meaning of 'bhakti'.
2. Analyze the development of Vaishnavism into a great religious movement in medieval India.
3. 'In Indian religious thought, the Nath Panthis and Shaktism were new devotional forms that developed within Hinduism in the medieval times.' Discuss.
4. Examine the contribution of the Bhakti saints in serving Indian society.
5. What was the impact of Bhakti ideology on religious thought in medieval India?

CHAPTER **16**

Sufi Thought

Review and Discussion

- Origins of Sufism
- Practices of Sufi Philosophy
- Sufi Traditions in India
- Sufi Orders in India
- Impact of Sufism

Very similar to the basic tenets of the Bhakti movement (discussed in Chapter 15) in India, Sufism may also be described as Islamic mysticism, in which the devout seeks divine love and spiritual realization through direct communion with the Supreme Being or Allah. Variously described as *tasawwuf*, literally meaning 'to dress in wool' in Arabic, Islamic mysticism acquired the term Sufism in the early nineteenth century. An abstract concept, Sufism originates from the Arabic term for a mystic, *sufi*, which in turn is derived from *suf* or wool, probably as a reference to the woollen clothing used by early Muslim ascetics. The Sufis are also variously known as *fuqara* (meaning 'poor' in Arabic) and *dervish* (meaning 'disciple' in Persian).

Though its origin may be traced to Prophet Muhammad, Sufi philosophy surfaced almost 150 years after his demise. This philosophy is primarily based on the concept of *tawhid* or unity with god, advocating a yearning for a personal union with him. Sufism is also laced with the Judaic and Christian traditions of total faith in the Supreme Being and abstinence from worldly pleasures. Every Sufi aspires to be a *wali*, literally meaning friend or patron; in Sufi terminology referring to a saint. This necessitated the evolution of a methodology or path (*tariqah*) to reach the goal of ultimate reality (*haqiqah*). The Sufis believed that the fulfilment of god's will was to be realized out of love, rather than from a sense of duty.

Origins of Sufism

Islamic mysticism evolved through several stages of growth, which included the initial appearance of early asceticism, followed by the development of a classical mysticism based on divine love, and lastly the creation of various mystical orders. Despite these broad stages, Islamic mysticism evolved more out of a history of individual mystic experiences.

The first stage of mystic concepts appeared among devout Islamic circles as a reaction to the worldliness of the early Umayyad period (661–749 CE). Thereafter, a spiritual way of life was adopted by individual Sufis in the ninth and tenth centuries, which came to be known as the *tariqah*. After the twelfth century, a large number of followers gathered around the *shaikhs* also known as *pirs* or *murshids* who were the Sufi masters. The *shaikh's* entire belief system or *tariqah* would be disseminated among the community members of the mystic order. The mystics led a life of constant meditation, entirely involved in fulfilling the injunctions of the *Quran* and other Islamic traditions. They carried out many acts of piety and laid special emphasis on nightly prayers.

When Sufism developed into dervish orders around the twelfth century, it was an excellent means of bringing together the spiritually interested members of the community. The teachings of the Sufi masters emphasized the emotional quotient and attainment of an ecstatic state of mind in order to experience ultimate union with god. The masters of these orders organized celebrations, such as the *urs* (death anniversaries of founders of mystic orders) at their hospices where the followers engaged themselves, thereby getting a chance to express their emotions and to purge negative feelings and attain a state of sublimity. Thus, in this manner the orders adapted to every social level; and various local customs and non-Islamic folkloristic practices, such as the veneration of saints, crept in too. It was a general belief of the times for each mystic order to claim spiritual descent (*silsilah*) from Prophet Muhammad. The orders established procedures for the initiation of members into the community and set rules of conduct that had to be followed. These principles were known as *adab al Sufia,* which stressed upon Sufi etiquette, while trying to establish that Sufism was not a total departure from the *Shariah* or traditional Islamic law. *Dervish* orders frequently established monasteries or *khanaqas* in which the members as well as common men were invited to stay. In order to live in the *khanaqa*, the disciples had to serve their Sufi masters and establish a good rapport with them.

Practices of Sufi Philosophy

Among the important rituals practiced by the Sufis was the *zikr,* which involved the repeated recitation of a devotional formula in praise of Allah as a means of attaining bliss. *Zikr* first began as a simple recitation of the *Quran* and later evolved into an elaborate ritual practiced in a congregation. A popular form of *zikr* which had a powerful influence on the Sufis was the *sama*, literally meaning 'to listen'. It was a kind of gathering where musical instruments were played and mystic verses were chanted. Both singers and listeners attained a sublime state of mind, experiencing divine ecstasy. Among some Sufi orders, ecstatic dancing was a common phenomenon at these gatherings and sometimes the level of ecstasy reached such a crescendo that the Sufis in a state of trance even removed their clothing. Keeping these features in mind, there arose a debate about the admissibility of the *sama* in Sufi traditions since these ritual sometimes lead to excesses in the form of hypnotic states of mind and ecstatic trances through divine recitations and physical exertions, such as whirling and dancing. Though all orders did not follow these excesses, the search for spiritual ecstasy sometimes led to practices that earned for some the names of 'whirling (even howling or dancing) dervishes'.

The doctrine of *fanaa* or annihilation of the self was considered by all Sufis to be the ultimate step in achieving divine communion with god. The Sufis—either in their lifetime—or their tombs—after their death—became a symbol of supernatural powers with metaphysical features ascribed to them under the guidelines of the *Quran* and the *Sunnah.* The usage of the term *sunnah* in Islam refers to the sayings and living habits of Prophet Muhammad as recorded in the *hadith*.

During the late twelfth and early thirteenth centuries, Ibn al-Arabi, the great Andalusian Sufi, spoke about the doctrine of *wahdat al-wujud* or unity of being, that had a profound influence on Sufi thought worldwide. In simple terms it refers to the profound concept of the entire universe being nothing but a manifestation of god's own attributes. It emphasized that in reality nothing existed but god, and that a union with god resulted from an intuitive contact with him that led to detachment from the world. Medieval India, which was already home to a strong pre-Islamic heritage of mysticism, was influenced by the concept of *wahdat al-wujud*, which is even reflected in the formulation of Akbar's policy of *Sulh-i-kul* or peace with all.

The importance of Sufism in Islamic history is incalculable. Through intellectual and educational activities, Sufism deepened the spiritual concerns of the Muslims and played a dynamic role in the formation of the Muslim society. In the development of specific language vocabularies of Persian, Turkish, Urdu, Sindhi, Pashto and Punjabi, Sufi literature has contributed substantially. The poetry composed in these languages had a special appeal through which mystical ideas could be spread widely among the Muslims. The high point of Sufi literature, especially mystical love poetry, represents the Golden Age of Arabic, Persian, Turkish and Urdu literature. Some of the orders, such as the Chishtiyah contributed much to the genre of classical Indo-Islamic musical traditions.

As mentioned earlier, the followers of Sufism aspired for divine communion with god (*muqarrab*) and accordingly devised activities to please god. As a result, the main role of the Sufis became their large-scale missionary activity, which continues to this day. When the diverse Sufi orders proliferated in India from the early thirteenth century onwards, they attracted thousands of non-Muslim devotees through their philosophy of love for god and for one's brethren, as well as through the belief in the equality of all men before god. Missionary activity was sometimes coupled with political activity—as in sixteenth, seventeenth and eighteenth century India, Central Asia and North Africa. As Eaton says, 'In the Perso-Islamic literary and cultural world, it was the spiritually powerful Sufi saints, not sultans who were understood to be the actual valid sovereigns of the world. It was they who leased out political sovereignty to kings, entrusting to them the worldly business of administration, warfare, taxation, etc.' (Eaton 2002). Hence, close links began to develop between the spiritual and political traditions of the age.

As Sufism spread to different regions of the Islamic world, its various dervish orders—the Chishtiyah of Mughal India, Naqshbandiyah of Central Asia, Tijaniyah of North Africa, Qadiriyah of Baghdad, and the Rifa'iyah of Egypt, Syria and Turkey— started gaining popularity. By the mid-twentieth century, there were millions of Sufis worldwide, but the greatest expansion of Sufi *tariqahs* was to take place in West Africa, Eastern Europe, India, and in Central and Far Eastern Asia, where they played a vital role in the religious life of the Muslim community.

Whirling Dervishes

The great Sufi mystic and poet, Jalauddin Rumi founded the Order of the Whirling Dervishes in the thirteenth century. Born in Afghanistan in 1207 CE, Rumi came to Turkey when his homeland was invaded by the Mongols and settled in the city of Koyna with his family. A firm believer that the love of god is both transcendent and unifying, Rumi turned to poetry, dance and song as a means of expressing his desire to be subsumed in a mystical union with god. Rumi's disciples called him 'Mevlana' (our leader) from where the Mevlevi Whirling Dervishes took their name. Today, the world famous Whirling Dervishes use dance as worship, reaching ecstatic trance-like states to commune with god. As the spectacular performance begins, dancers are clad in long white robes, tall conical hats and black cloaks. During the performance, the cloaks are shed, representing the symbolic casting off of all worldly attachments and ego. There are commemoration ceremonies held in Koyna every December to celebrate Rumi's death (Seb-i-Aruz). His followers consider this Rumi's wedding night as he was finally united with the Divine Beloved.

Sufi Traditions in India

Historically, the long encounter between the Islamic and the Indic civilizations stirred and inspired the people of the subcontinent to such an extent that this land became a vital, global centre of a new Indo-Islamic culture.

The Sufis made every effort to deepen and intensify spiritual experience in India by preaching their message across diverse intellectual levels of society. In this way, their thoughts found expression in literary, ritualistic and institutional forms, with Sufi literature forming an important component of propagating Sufi philosophy. It was either written in the form of prose or verse by the Sufi himself; or was presented in the form of a collection of sayings of the Sufi master called *Malfuzat*, recorded in writing by a disciple. The *malfuzat* literature forms interesting reading, and like the collections of letters of the *shaikhs* gives an insight into the political and social situation of the Muslim community. Since the laymen had more access to the *malfuzat* literature than to the prose compositions, it became a dominant literary form for transmission of Sufi teaching in India. Sufi literature also abounds in hagiographies (biographies of well-known saints) and poetry, the latter being the greatest contribution of Sufism to Islamic literature.

Like the Bhakti saints, the Sufi masters too explained profound Islamic concepts in a simple and lucid style, which was vastly different from the obtuse teachings of professional *mullahs* who were educated in religious seminaries. While preaching their philosophy to the people, the Sufi masters added their own personal insights and experiences to the existing corpus of knowledge shared by their audiences, making it easier for the common people to comprehend. This process of transmitting spiritual truth was simple and appealing, but it often led to slightly disturbed listeners, since it usually led to an assessment of the self.

The Sufi masters asked their devotees to be attentive towards god at all times and during all daily activities instead of merely attending to their religious obligations at specified prayer times. By drawing parallels and metaphors from daily life the Sufi masters disseminated deep thoughts and effectively demonstrated how Islamic rituals and literature could be adapted to the needs of indigenous Indian traditions.

The establishment of Sufi *khanaqas* (hospices) and *dargahs* (shrines) also had their impact on society at large. The *khanaqa* was a place where the Sufi master stayed during his lifetime while the *dargah* was the place where he was interred after his death. Life at the *khanaqa* carried on with a new *shaikh* taking the place of the older master who had died. Thus, the *khanaqa* and the *dargah* evolved as two important institutions in the history of Sufism. The Sufis did not accept financial help from the state administration to run their establishments, which were maintained by the Sufis themselves with the support of their disciples. But in some cases, the Sufi saints received the state's patronage in the form of financial and land grants and actively participated in court intrigues and politics.

As far as institutional activities were concerned, the *khanaqas* were well-disciplined and well-maintained. The Sufis seldom liked to remain away from their hospices, except for daily prayers, which preferably were to be performed in a congregation at the mosque situated close. Other than this they would either be attending a funeral or an *urs* or visit a fellow Sufi. They would also teach their disciples and other lay followers through short discourses during the intervals between prayer times. At the *khanaqa*, *murids* were initiated into the order in a traditional procedure that was meaningful. *Murid* is an Arabic term meaning 'committed one' referring to a person who is committed to a teacher in the spiritual path of Sufism. The ceremony took place in the presence of the *murid* and close devotees took the oath to adhere to the *Shariah*, to repent for sins, to give up material pleasures, and to submit to and obey the orders of the *pir*.

Like the *khanaqas*, the *dargahs* of the saints, which have survived from the thirteenth and fourteenth centuries to the present times, also played a major role in the propagation of Sufi concepts and practices. The lives of Muslims in India have been marked by customs and festivals relating to saints and their tombs. Both Muslim and non-Muslim pilgrims of the subcontinent have always been drawn to the *dargah* of a particular saint for specific purposes—their aspirations, faith, and their general socio-religious outlook. Ritualistic practices performed by the followers on a regular basis—more so during the annual *urs* ceremonies at the *dargahs*—were an embodiment of various cultural traditions. Crossing religious boundaries, the *urs* was attended as much by Muslims as by non-Muslim participants—the Hindus, Jains and tribals—demonstrating the universal appeal of Sufism. Consequently these *urs* and other such ceremonies developed into significant cultural institutions that were eagerly awaited by the poor and the rich alike. Within the religious life of Indian Muslims, therefore, the *dargah* played a central role in shaping the cultural practices of the region.

There are interesting examples to illustrate the visits of patrons to Sufi shrines in northern India that far outnumber their visits to mosques. For the Mughal emperor Bahadur Shah Zafar visiting a shrine was almost a weekly ritual; the same being the case with many other rulers. Rulers with Sufi leanings also generously bestowed charity to the shrine keepers whenever they presented themselves at court. Sufism was not confined to the masses alone; it held the interest of the royalty and nobility too. It is sufficient to visit the shrines to become aware of the degree to which Sufism is still alive in the land, which has been witness to some of the greatest *pirs* and *murshids* over centuries.

Sufi Orders in India

In the early thirteenth century with the establishment of Turkish rule in northern India there was a heavy influx of Sufis from Persia, Afghanistan and Central Asia which led to a proliferation of numerous Sufi orders in India. According to Abul Fazl, three centuries later, there were close to 14 different orders. A point to be noted is that none of the Sufi orders were native to India and of all only four—the Chishti, the Suhrawardi, the Qadiri, and the Naqshbandi—had any sizeable impact on the life and thought of medieval India. Apart from these orders, there were other sects, such as the Madari, Firdausi and Tayfuri, which were active in India. Soon, these orders organized themselves by having their own spiritual territories called *wilayats* and formed an infrastructure consisting of their *khanaqas* where several disciples and attendants lived with the Sufi saint.

The Chishtis

In terms of the popularity and spiritual influence of Sufi orders, the Chishtis were unparalleled in India. The first Sufi to settle in India was Sultan Sakhi Sarwar, who did not live long enough to leave his mark. It was left to another Sufi immigrant of the Chishti order, Khwaja Moinuddin Chishti, to establish the order in a well entrenched manner. But there is no substantial evidence to establish accurate facts about his life and activities in India. The two major Chishti texts of the fourteenth century, *Fawaid al Fu'ad* and *Khair al Majalis*, do not refer to him at all; while the *Siyar al Aulia*, another Sufi text, gives some brief details only. Therefore, information about the Sufi saint is available only in a Suhrawardi text, *Siyar al Arifin* compiled almost 300 years after his death.

The text of *Siyar al Arifin* gives details with regard to the ancestry of Moinuddin, who is supposed to have been a native of Sijistan in Central Asia. While still a young boy, he had met a Sufi, Ibrahim Qanduzi, who had had a profound influence on his life. Displaying a spirit of generosity by distributing alms to the poor and needy from the sale of his ancestral property, Moinuddin travelled to Bukhara and Samarqand in the pursuit of knowledge. When Moinuddin came in contact with Shaikh Usman Harwani during a trip to Persia, he was inducted into the Chishti order. He was almost 52 years old when he was chosen as the *khalifa* or successor by his spiritual master. He embarked upon a tour of Persia and Central Asia before coming to India, where he is said to have settled down at Ajmer. Once again, there is no contemporary record to substantiate his missionary activities, except for the information available in the Sufi hagiographies and a few medieval chronicles. Moinuddin is said to have led the simple life of a Sufi, concentrating his efforts on fashioning his disciples into good human beings and on working for the moral upliftment of the people.

In 1236 CE, Moinuddin passed away at Ajmer at the ripe age of 95. He was buried without any special ceremonies in the same land where he had lived; and it was only later, in the fifteenth century, that Khwaja Hussain Nagauri, a descendent of the Sufi saint, Hamiduddin Nagauri (who had established a *khanaqa* at Nagaur), constructed a mausoleum over his grave. Even to this day, the annual *urs* at Ajmer continues to be celebrated with undaunted spiritual fervour by all communities.

We get a fair idea about Moinuddin's thought from the writings of the medieval Indian hagiographers. He instructed his followers to observe religious rituals and restrict themselves from indulging in the forbidden. He considered prayer or *namaz* and generosity of spirit to be of prime importance for a Muslim. He lived a life of high ideals and was committed to the welfare of humanity.

Moinuddin's leading disciple was Qutbuddin Bakhtiar Kaki. Born in Aush in Farghana, Qutbuddin joined Moinuddin's mystic circle when the latter visited Aush. In 1221 CE, Qutbuddin came to Delhi where he was warmly welcomed and extended patronage by Iltutmish, who was the ruling sultan at the time. Qutbuddin led a simple householder's life in Delhi; and upon his death his son became the *sajjada nashin,* his spiritual successor. Qutbuddin led a life of piety and self-denial, and remained uninspired to participate in the political affairs of the Delhi Sultanate. He is said to have turned down Iltutmish when the latter offered him a rewarding office of *shaikh ul Islam* (advisor on religious affairs). He acquired the nickname, Kaki (man of bread), for the very reason that he and his family led a life of abject poverty and did not even have the means to feed themselves. But his faith in god ensured that his household miraculously received bread whenever the need arose. Qutbuddin died in 1235 CE and was buried in Mehrauli in Delhi, at the site which he had himself chosen and purchased. His son, Shaikh Ahmed, became the *mutawalli* or the custodian of his shrine, but the honour of becoming the saint's spiritual successor went to Fariduddin Masud, his disciple from Punjab.

Popularly known as Baba Farid Ganj-i Shakar (fortune of sweets), Fariduddin Masud was a native of Khatwal, a village in Multan, Punjab. While studying in Multan, he came across Qutbuddin and was so impressed by him that he became a disciple. As desired by his master, Fariduddin completed his formal education in a span of five years before joining the former in Delhi. Farid led a simple life of devotion and soon became famous for his divinity, which resulted in a number of devotees coming to seek his blessings. His fame became a cause of unnecessary disturbance as he was unable to find peace and quiet within this continuous

TOMB OF QUTBUDDIN BAKHTIAR KAKI, *Mehrauli*

flow of visitors. As a result, he decided to move to Hansi in Haryana, visiting Delhi periodically to meet his master. At the death of Qutbuddin, however, he was forced to assume the leadership of the Chishti order. But he later moved back to Hansi, and from there to Khatwal, before he finally settled down in the small town of Ajodhan in Punjab. In Ajodhan, he established a *khanaqa* close to the main mosque of the town.

Farid set standards of penance for himself—wearing ordinary clothes, sleeping on a plain wooden cot, and eating berries and millet bread for sustenance. It is said that only when he grew old did he change his diet, once adding butter to his simple meal of millet bread. He was offered large tracts of land as grants, but he was not interested in material gains and advised his followers to keep away from kings and courts. His *khanaqa* was home to the common man from all communities—mendicants, monks, yogis and ascetics were all welcome. He took a personal interest in their lives and was always willing to help. When Farid died in 1271 CE, he was buried in his *khanaqa*.

Shaikh Farid was succeeded by a young disciple from Delhi, Shaikh Nizamuddin, whose family originally came from Bukhara before settling down in Badaun (in today's Uttar Pradesh) in the early thirteenth century. The date of his birth is not known for certain, but he himself fixed it somewhere in 1248 CE. In 1264 CE, Nizamuddin shifted to Delhi along with his family, where he met Baba Farid's younger brother, Najibuddin Mutwakkil. Nizamuddin was keen to meet Shaikh Farid and travelled to Ajodhan to meet the saint. It is said that the very first meeting inspired him to such an extent that on same day he became a member of the Chishti order.

Nizamuddin was accepted as a spiritual guide by all the disciples in the *khanaqa* within a short period. After becoming the head of the order, he decided to establish his own *khanaqa* at Delhi. Sustaining himself and his fellow inmates on *futuh* (voluntary gifts) alone, life seemed tough and on many occasions his brethren had to go without food. After many years of misery, he was officially acknowledged by the Khilji ruler, Jalaluddin Khilji (1290–96 CE), who offered him a steady income from a particular village to meet the expenses of his *khanaqa*. The residents of the *khanaqa* were keen that the *shaikh* should accept the offer, but the latter did not relent and continued his life of mendicancy and piety.

A characteristic feature of the *khanaqa* of Nizamuddin was the frequent *sama* gatherings. Six such *sama mehfils* were supposed to have been held in which the *shaikh* participated. Nizamuddin's concept of *sama* was simple in that he felt that it was not against the *Shariah*, and quoted prophetic traditions in support of his views. He fixed a particular procedure to convene these gatherings, where the singer had to be a mature adult male, and the lyrics of his song were forbidden from being lewd. The audience too had to be absolutely devoted to god, while the accompanying instruments had to be the harp, lute or violin.

One of the most outstanding traits of Nizamuddin was his ability to take informed decisions on the basis of what seemed best suited for the time and place, instead of following a single doctrine. Belief in the unity of god was the foundation of his basic philosophy, because of which people from all walks of life came together in his *khanaqa*. He had great respect for the customs and traditions of all religions, disbelieving in forced conversions to Islam. In fact, in the entire Sufi text of *Fawaid al Fu'ad*, there is only one reference to conversion. Nizamuddin died in 1325 CE, to be succeeded by his nephew's son, Khwaja Rafiuddin Harun, as the *sajjada nashin*. In accordance with his last wishes his grave lay in a forested area,which was later converted into a shrine with a mosque by Sultan Muhammad bin Tughlaq.

Nizamuddin's spiritual successor was Nasiruddin Mahmud, popularly known as *Chiragh-i-Delhi*. He was born in Awadh, and by the time he reached the age of 25 Nasiruddin had become a practicing Sufi. Even after taking over as the head of the Chishti order in Delhi, he continued to lead a life of austerity; and like his master had to struggle to survive. There remained, however, certain areas where Nasiruddin differed from his master. While Nizamuddin preached strict obedience to the *pir* or spiritual master, Nasiruddin believed that one need not blindly obey authority, even encouraging his followers to question practices—something that went against the *Shariah*. In Islam, for instance, prostration was to be done only before god, but earlier Sufi saints, although reluctantly, had allowed their disciples to prostrate before them. Nasiruddin did not allow this practice, but neither did he object to his disciples joining government services to eke out a living.

Upon his death in 1356 CE, Nasiruddin was buried in his own house, as per his wishes. This area came to be known as *Chiragh-i-Delhi*. Many years later, Firuz Tughlaq built a shrine over his grave, the administration of which was entrusted to the saint's nephew, Maulana Zainuddin Ali. In Bengal, the Chishti order was introduced by Sirajuddin Akhi Siraj who lived in Gaur and died in 1357 CE. His successor, Nur Qutb-i Alam, established a *khanaqa* at Pandua.

Nasiruddin had chosen some of his disciples as his spiritual successors, the criterion for which was the possession of knowledge. Syed Muhammad Gesu Daraz, born in a Sufi family in Delhi in 1321 CE, was the most accomplished disciple of Nasiruddin. His early education was at Daulatabad, since Sultan Muhammad bin Tughlaq had shifted his capital there and had ordered the entire city of Delhi to relocate to the place—among which was Gesu Daraz's family. When the capital was shifted back to Delhi, Gesu Daraz returned to northern India. Soon, he joined the Chishti order of Nasiruddin, and 20 years later Nasiruddin proclaimed him as his spiritual successor. Not much is known about Gesu Daraz after 1356 CE. With Timur's invasion of Delhi in 1398 CE, Gesu Daraz with many others migrated to the Deccan once again. By this time he had reached an advanced age. Travelling through Malwa and Gujarat, he arrived in the Bahmani capital of Gulbarga in 1399 CE.

The arrival of Gesu Daraz (1321–1422 CE) to Gulbarga gave a boost to the *Dakhni* (or Deccani) language and literature. Later known as *Dakhni* Urdu, the dialect took shape as an independent and important spoken language. It was a mixture of north Indian Hindi, Persian, Gujarati and Marathi—languages spoken by soldiers, who came from different regions, and by wandering mendicants and Sufi *fakirs*. Although Gesu Daraz knew Persian well and wrote in this language, he adopted *Dakhni* as his medium of instruction. Most of his early works were written in *Dakhni*. Though Persian continued to be the court language of the Bahmanis, Gesu Daraz could reach the masses—of which a good number were his non-Muslim followers—only through *Dakhni* The *urs* or annual pilgrimage at his *dargah* in Gulbarga attracts people of all religions even to this day.

During the reign of Firuz Shah Bahmani, Gesu Daraz had a rift with the sultan, which caused the sultan to order him to leave the palace premises and go into exile. Firuz had never been on good terms with the saint, and neither was he in agreement with Ahmad Shah, his brother, who supported the saint. The rift widened when Hasan Khan, the son of Firuz Shah, was appointed as the crown prince. The saint refused to bless the crown prince as he believed that god had already appointed Ahmad Shah as Firuz's successor and it was now no use to offer any prayers for Hasan Khan. This annoyed Firuz immensely and he sent a message to the saint stating that as the *khanaqa* was located too near the palace premises it attracted daily visitors in large numbers, which disturbed the sultan's peace of mind. The sultan, therefore, wished the saint to relocate his *khanaqa* outside the city walls. On hearing this royal reproof, the saint moved to a new location (where his mausoleum, built by Ahmad Shah, stands to this day) till his end in 1422 CE.

But after the death of Firuz, his brother, Ahmad Shah Bahmani (1422–36 CE), realized the spiritual and moral influence which Gesu Daraz had come to exercise on the people of the Deccan and utilized it to his advantage. Apart from the kindness he bestowed on the saint's immediate retainers and followers, he often visited the saint's *khanaqa* during his séances. The sultan also gave generous land grants to the saint's descendents, which in all likelihood they accepted.

The Chishti order took firm root in the Deccan because of Gesu Daraz's presence in Gulbarga. Following in his footsteps, his grandson and spiritual successor, Sayyid Yadullah, and disciple, Shaikh Piyara, continued to live in Gulbarga. Chishti influence continued to grow in the area at the hands of Jamaluddin Maghribi, his disciple, and his successor, Kamaluddin Biyabani. Kamaluddin's disciple, Miranji Shams al Ushshaq, popularized the order in Bijapur too. Fasihuddin Baba Sanjal Khaksar and Burhanuddin Janam were other saints of this line who promoted the order in the Deccan.

The Chishti Sufis were referred to as the *ulema-i-akhirat* in northern India and as the *ulema-i-duniya* in the Deccan. The end of the fourteenth century saw a decline of the Chishti order in northern India, primarily because there were no enterprising disciples left to take the lead in Delhi after the migration of Gesu Daraz to the Deccan. Malwa, Gujarat, Bengal and the Deccan had emerged as new Chishti centres and had taken the focus away from Delhi by this time. Further, the political instability in northern India following the decline of the Tughlaqs, coupled with court intrigues and strife among the political elites of Delhi, contributed to the decay of spirituality. The principles of Chishti traditions were no longer followed and Sufis participated in political affairs of state, while their progeny laid claims to hereditary succession.

As an interim relief to the Chishti order in sixteenth century northern India, there was a brief revival of the order by Makhdum Alauddin Ali Sabir, a close relative of Baba Farid. This is known as the Sabiri branch and information about them may be found in the *Iqtibas al anwar*, a seventeenth century Chishti text. The text gives an account of Sabir being held in esteem by Baba Farid. One of the most well known saints of this line was Abdul Quddus Gangohi, who along with other Sufis revived the old glory of the Chishtis in the North. Abdul Quddus wrote extensively on Sufism and out of his 18 known works, only 10 have survived. The saint was deeply interested in yoga and is reported to have taught it to his disciple, Sulaiman Mandavi, in return for lessons in Quranic recitation. The *Rushd Nama* also informs about his fascination for yogic philosophy.

Muhibbullah Allahabadi, another great Sufi of this line received the title of *Shaikh-i-Kabir* (the great Shaikh) because of his learning and mastery over metaphysics. He advocated the concept of *wahdat ul wujud* and wrote commentaries on it in Arabic and Persian. Seeing his philosophy, many *ulema* accused him of heresy and issued a *fatwa* for his execution, which was revoked with great effort.

A name that most people are familiar with to this day is that of Salim Chishti, who lived during Emperor Akbar's reign. Brought up in Sikri, where his family had migrated from Punjab, he was a descendent of Baba Farid. He became part of the mystic circle of the Pakpattan shrine; and thereafter undertook several journeys to the Middle East and performed the *Hajj* many a time. In 1538 CE, he returned to Sikri and established a *khanaqa* there. He was patronized by the rulers of the Sur dynasty and after their fall Salim once again embarked on a religious journey to foreign lands.

As historical records state, the Mughal prince Salim, later known as Jahangir, was born as a special blessing received by Akbar from the saint. In gratitude, Akbar built a magnificent city in Sikri and shifted his capital there. Decorating the new city with a huge *khanaqa* and a mosque made of mother of pearls, Akbar raised the *shaikh* to an exalted status. When the *shaikh* died, he was buried in a corner of the mosque on which a mausoleum was built.

In the eighteenth century, among the Chishti saints, the name of Shah Kalimullah stands tall. He received his educational training with Shaikh

Abu Riza, the famous Naqshbandi saint and Maulana Burhanuddin. Thereafter, under the guardianship of *shaikh* Yahya Madani he gained spiritual knowledge. The saint taught him the science of the *Hadis* and initiated him into the Chishti order. Kalimullah started a *madrassa* and a *khanaqa* in the heart of Delhi, which was the beginning of his long spiritual career. He asked his disciples to follow a code of conduct that stood for the welfare of the people, irrespective of their faiths. He also propagated social and religious harmony and led a simple and unostentatious life. After his death in 1729 CE, his *khanaqa* was run by his son Hafiz Sayeed. His prominent disciple was Shah Nizamuddin Aurangabadi, while his son, Maulana Fakhruddin, succeeded him and is considered to be the last great Chishti saint of the eighteenth century. By this time, other Sufi orders like the Suhrawardis and Qadiris had also established themselves and the successors of Maulana Fakhruddin could no longer hold on to the spiritual prowess of the order.

The Suhrawardis

Shaikh Abu Najib Suhrawardi of Suhraward, Persia, was responsible for the birth of this order. It was brought by the *khalifas* of his nephew and successor, Shaikh Shahabuddin Suhrawardi in India. The first Sufi of the Suhrawardi order to preach in India was, however, Bahauddin Zakariya from Multan. The Suhrawardis chose the North West frontier province, as their base for missionary activities for the very reason that it had been tattered by Mongol invasions. Multan and Sind, thus, became the core centres of the order's activities.

The *shaikh* showed immense interest in political affairs and was not hospitable to everyone who visited his *khanaqa*, showing more affiliation towards the elites who visited him. He died in 1262 CE at the age of 81, and was buried in Multan where a tomb was built over his grave (which was later enlarged in the seventeenth century by the Mughal noble Qulij Khan Turani). Bahauddin was succeeded by his son, Sadruddin Arif, who was very different from his father; and like a true Sufi he did not crave for wealth, giving away whatever he had. Ahmad Mashuq, a renowned disciple of Sadruddin, was known for his ability to maintain an ecstatic state of mind for long periods of time. Sadruddin was succeeded by his son, Ruknuddin Multani, who following in the footsteps of his grandfather, once again aligned the *khanaqa* with the political elite. He visited Delhi often to meet the ruling sultans as well as Shaikh Nizamuddin Chishti.

Gradually through the efforts of Ruknuddin's disciples, the order spread to many other places in India. One of the famous disciples of Ruknuddin was Hussaini Sadat, whose poems on Sufi metaphysics show the spirit of toleration and accommodation towards all. Another disciple of Ruknuddin was Sadruddin Zafarabadi, better known as *Hajji Chiragh-i Hind* who established the order in Jaunpur. After Ruknuddin's death, the Suhrawardi order seemed to lose its verve in Multan. Shaikh Jalaluddin Tabrezi, another saint of the Suhrawardi order, established a *khanaqa* and a *langar* at Lakhnauti, to be followed by another at Devatalla in Bengal.

New spirit was infused into the order by Sayyid Jalaluddin Makhdum Jahaniyan Jahangasht at Uchh in modern-day Sind, where a Suhrawardi *khanaqa* had been established. The saint was widely travelled and saw no harm in maintaining cordial relations with the state. Muhammad bin Tughlaq appointed him as *Shaikh al Islam* and granted him a *jagir* of 40 villages in Sehwan (Sind). The *shaikh* was held in high esteem by Firuz Tughlaq too. It is said that on the saint's recommendation, the sultan had abolished many taxes not sanctioned by Islam. The saint's contribution to Sufi literature is also noteworthy for he wrote commentaries on several Sufi texts and translated Qutbuddin Damishqi's *Al Risalat al Makkiyah* into Persian.

Hamid bin Fazullah, more popular as Jamali Kanboh, was another important Sufi of the Suhrawardi order. His extensive travels to many Islamic lands gave him wide exposure; and upon his return to India in the last decade of the fifteenth century, he started his missionary activities. Jamali maintained cordial relations with Sikandar Lodi, Babur and Humayun. He wrote a *qasidah* in praise of Babur and went along with Humayun on his Gujarat campaign, during which he passed away. Jamali's poetic genius is apparent in his *masnavi Mihr o mah*, but his literary skills rest on his book *Siyar al arifin*, which is a biographical account of 13 Chishti and Suhrawardi saints. Jamali's eldest son, Shaikh Gadai, played an influential role in Akbar's time and held the important position of *Sadr* in his Department of Religious Affairs.

The Suhrawardi Sufis of Uchh were patronized to a large extent by the sultans of Gujarat. The *Mirat-i-Sikandari* gives details about Zafar Khan, the founder of the Muslim kingdom of Gujarat, who came to the throne with the blessings of Makhdum Jahaniyah. Sultan Ahmad became part of the mystic circle of the Makhdum's grandson, Nur Qutb i Alam, whose spiritual successor was Shah Manjhan. Like many Suhrawardi saints, he took a keen interest in the political affairs of his time and helped the sultans of Gujarat fight against Malwa. His tomb lies in Ahmedabad, which still attracts numerous devotees.

By the sixteenth century, the Suhrawardi order declined and remained confined only to Kashmir and Punjab. The only Suhrawardi saint in India at this time was Hajji Abdul Wahhab Bukhari, who lived during Sikandar Lodi's regime in Delhi.

The Suhrawardi order was popularized in Kashmir by Makhdum Hamzah Kashmiri. He was not in favour of the Shia influence in Kashmir and made constant efforts to weaken it. After his death, his disciples continued in their master's footsteps; Baba Dawud Khaki Suhrawardi being Hamzah's most eminent disciple. Credited with the composition of the famous text *Wird al Muridin*, a biography of Makhdum Hamzah in verse, Dawud too like his master was opposed to Shia influence in Kashmir, and often spoke of the persecution of the Sunnis. His successor was Mir Nazuk, who opposed the concept of *sama* and discouraged Sufis from involving themselves in it.

Another prominent Sufi of the Suhrawardi order was Shaikh Hasan, who lived in sixteenth-seventeenth century Lahore, in the Punjab. Before joining the Suhrawardi order he lived in the company of Gorakhnath, a famous yogi. Reputed nobles, like Abdur Rahim Khan-i Khanan and Nawab Murtuza Khan were his followers. His tomb lies in Lahore and has today become a pilgrimage site.

Evolving out of the Suhrawardi branch, the Firdausia Sufis were confined to Bihar. The order was popularized by Shaikh Harfuddin Yahya, a disciple of Nizamuddin Firdausi, who tried to bring about moderation between Islamic law and the concept of *wahdat-ul wujud*. He laid great emphasis on service to humanity, which formed the core of his philosophy.

The Qadiris

Established by Shaikh Abdul Qadir Jilani in the mid-fifteenth century, the Qadiris were orthodox Sufis who zealously followed the *Shariah*. The early Qadiris formed their hospices in the Deccan, under the patronage of the Bahmani sultan, Ahmad Shah, who was a great patron of Persian and Arab cultural traditions. As part of this policy, Ahmad Shah invited many Sufis from Persia to his new capital of Bidar in the Deccan. It was said that the sultan wanted the Deccan to benefit from the spiritual knowledge of other parts of the Islamic world. Ferishta quotes that the sultan persuaded the famous Qadiri saint of Persia, Shah Nimatullah Wali, to send his grandson, Shah Nurullah, to his court. Ahmad Shah not only married his daughter to Nurullah but also built a new town of Nimatabad in honour of the saint's grandfather. Later Nurullah's entire immediate family migrated to Bidar. His brothers, Habibullah and Muhibullah, established a Qadiri *khanaqa* at Bidar, which in due course emerged as an important Qadiri centre in India. Other famous Qadiris of Bidar were Shaikh Ibrahim Multani and his son and successor, Ibrahim Makhdumji.

Another branch of the Qadiris was established in the Punjab in the mid fifteenth century. It was founded by Sayyid Muhammad Halabi Uchhi, a descendent of Shaikh Abdul Qadir Jilani. The Sayyid had visited India while he was still young, lived for a while in Lahore and Nagore, subsequently returning to his hometown in Halab (Aleppo). When he visited India again in 1482 CE, he settled in Uchh, where Sultan Hussain Mirza became his disciple. Abdul Qadir II, the son of Sayyid Muhammad, succeeded him. Initially, Abdul Qadir was a supporter of the *sama*, and was also fond of material pleasures, leading a lavish life. But after becoming the head of the Qadiri *khanaqa* in Uchh, there was a marked change. He became an ascetic, gave up his official position along with all the grants and stipends associated with the *khanaqa*. The saint's piety and spiritual attainments have been recorded by Abdul Haqq Muhaddis Delhavi in the form of numerous miracles performed by him.

Extensive missionary activity of the Qadiris was also seen in Agra and Delhi in the sixteenth century. A resident of Mecca, Abul Fath bin Jamaluddin Makki, on the invitation of Sikandar Lodi, introduced the Qadiri order in Agra. The saint is also said to have accompanied Ibrahim Lodi to Panipat, where Ibrahim Lodi was engaged in his historic battle with Babur. Other outstanding Qadiri saints of Delhi were Amanullah Panipati and Mir Sayyid Abdul Awwal. The latter was a great scholar who wrote the commentary on Ibn Al Arabi's *Futuhat al Makkiyah*.

Srinagar was another prominent Qadiri centre in the sixteenth century. When Shaikh Ahmad Qadiri was invited to Kashmir by Baba Dawud Khaki, he settled down in the land, where the sultan of Kashmir became his disciple. He also enrolled into the order a number of believers, including his friend Dawud Khaki. Dawud was succeeded by Mir Nazuk and his grandson, Mir Muhammad Ali, who popularized the Qadiri traditions in Srinagar.

Mir Muhammad Miyan Mir, who became a disciple in the order under the guidance of Khazir Sivistani, stands out as a prominent Qadiri of the seventeenth century. After completing his education, he devoted his time to learning difficult ascetic exercises, gradually becoming famous (according to some hagiographers he would even converse with the flora and fauna). He firmly believed in the concepts of *wahdat ul wujud* and *sama*, and insisted on complete observance to the *Shariah*, believing that this was a medium of attaining *fanaa*. Miyan Mir was held in high esteem by the Mughal emperors, Jahangir and Shahjahan. Shahjahan and his son, Dara Shukoh, were regular visitors to his *khanaqa* and received spiritual training from him. Miyan Mir's biography, *Sakinat al awliya* was, in fact, written by Prince Dara Shukoh.

The most prominent disciple of Miyan Mir was Mulla Shah Badakhshi. After completing his education, he joined Miyan Mir's spiritual circle as a disciple at Lahore, before establishing his *khanaqa* at Kashmir. His activities soon won the hearts of the poor and needy, as the mulla was an ardent exponent of *wahdat al wujud*. During a visit to Kashmir, Shahjahan learnt a number of elements concerning Sufi philosophy from Miyan Mir. The emperor's children, Dara Shukoh and Jahan Ara, became disciples of the saint. Altogether Prince Dara Shukoh was enamoured by Sufi thought; it was only in the Qadiri order that he was initiated as a Sufi. Dara's contribution to Sufi literature is worth mentioning; the *Majma al Bahrayn*, a comparative analysis of Islam and Hinduism, the *Sirr-i Akbar*, a translation of Upanishads, *Safinat al aulia, Risala i Haqnuma, Hasnat al arifin* are his notable works.

Many immigrant saints from the Middle East propagated the Qadiri order in the Deccan too. Sayyid Abdul Qadir Yusuf, Badruddin Habibullah and Shah Abdul Hasan Qadiri were some of the significant Qadiri saints of Bidar and Bijapur. Shah Abdul Hasan Qadiri was close to the sultan of Bijapur, Ibrahim Adil Shah II, whom he taught the intricacies of Sufism. He was not in favour of the Sufis who remained in a state of intoxication. He wrote *Sukh Anjam*, the well known mystical work in the Dakhni language. Another Deccani Sufi who became popular was Shah Abdul Latif Lawoobali, who had emigrated to the Deccan from Baghdad, settling in a village near Kurnool.

The maximum influence of the Qadiri order was seen in the Punjab and the Deccan alone, since unlike the Chishtis, the Qadiris did not evolve a network of disciples based on devotion and allegiance all over the subcontinent. The Qadiris did not even appreciate the missionary activities of the other orders, considering them to be their rivals.

JAHANGIR PREFERRING A SUFI SHEIKH TO KINGS, *Miniature painting by Mughal artist Bichitr, 1620 CE. Opaque watercolour and gold on paper.*

The Naqshbandis

The Naqshbandiyyah order, originally established in Central Asia by Bahauddin Naqshband, became popular in India in the sixteenth century. Although the order was instituted in Kashmir in the fifteenth century, it was only during Akbar's reign that its activities gained momentum. The Naqshbandis were patronized by the Mughal family to a large extent; and Emperor Babur's father, Umar Shaikh Mirza, was also a disciple of the Naqshbandi saint, Khwaja Nasiruddin Ubaidullah Ahrar. Babur himself was very close to the saint's sons. Later during Akbar's reign, when the saint's progeny visited India, the emperor granted him the pargana Jamari or Chamiari in sarkar Bari Doab in Lahore to meet his expenses. He developed a large following during his stay of 16 years before returning to Samarqand.

It was, however, Khwaja Baqi Billah, a native of Kabul, who popularized the Naqshbandi order in India. At the advice of his *pir*, Khwajgi Amkingi, the saint had come to India, settling in Delhi and leading a short but spiritually active life. The Khwaja absolutely believed in the doctrine of *wahdat al wujud* and composed several verses in praise of the doctrine too. He was of the view that mystics could attain spiritual solace through *sama*, and keenly propagated the observance of Islam in the Mughal dominions, writing regularly to the Mughal nobles to be pious in their activities.

Khwaja Baqi was succeeded by Shaikh Ahmad Sirhindi. After being appointed as the *khalifa*, the *shaikh* was allowed to return to Sirhind from where he sent his disciples to different parts of the subcontinent—becoming instrumental in creating a large following in all parts of India. He was against religious innovations in Islam and made sincere efforts to reform Indian Islam. In recognition of this, he came to be known as *Mujaddad Alf i Sani.* He did not favour the doctrine of *wahdat ul wujud*, which he considered too difficult and complex to understand. By and large the *shaikh* stood for the restoration of orthodox Islam; and was critical of the religious beliefs and political appointments of the Hindus, to the extent of wanting the *jiziya* re-imposed. He was equally critical of Shia beliefs and condemned the Shias for their denunciation of the first three *khalifas* of Islam. In some respect the *shaikh* evoked sharp criticism, especially with regard to his claim to prophethood, succeeding Prophet Muhammad. For this strange claim he was imprisoned in the Gwalior fort by Emperor Jahangir, later to be released and returned to Sirhind, where he eventually died. But he had active disciples like Adam Bannori and Shah Abdur Rahim, who worked for the propagation of the order in different parts of the Mughal Empire.

Shaikh Ahmad was succeeded by his son Muhammad Masum who insisted on the strict recitation of the *Quran* and trained a large number of disciples like his father. The saint avoided the company of the elite and although he corresponded with emperor Aurangzeb, the latter was denied the benefit of his company. His son, Saifuddin, was deputed instead for the emperor's spiritual training. Khwaja Masum had left behind six sons and a number of disciples—all of whom were outstanding Sufis through whom the Naqshbandi teachings were propagated all over the Indian subcontinent. Hujatullah Muhammad Naqshband succeeded his father as the head of the *khanaqa* in Sirhind. Hujatullah's son and successor, Muhammad Zubayr, was likewise known for his spiritual and intellectual attainments. Khwaja Muhammad Nasir, was one of the well known *khalifas* to succeed Khwaja Zubayr.

Among the Indian Naqshbandis, Khwaja Khawand Mahmud was one who was not associated with the Mujaddadi line. He had settled in Kashmir, and the Mughal emperors Akbar, Jahangir and Shahjahan as well as the ladies of the Mughal harem are reported to have sought his blessings. But his

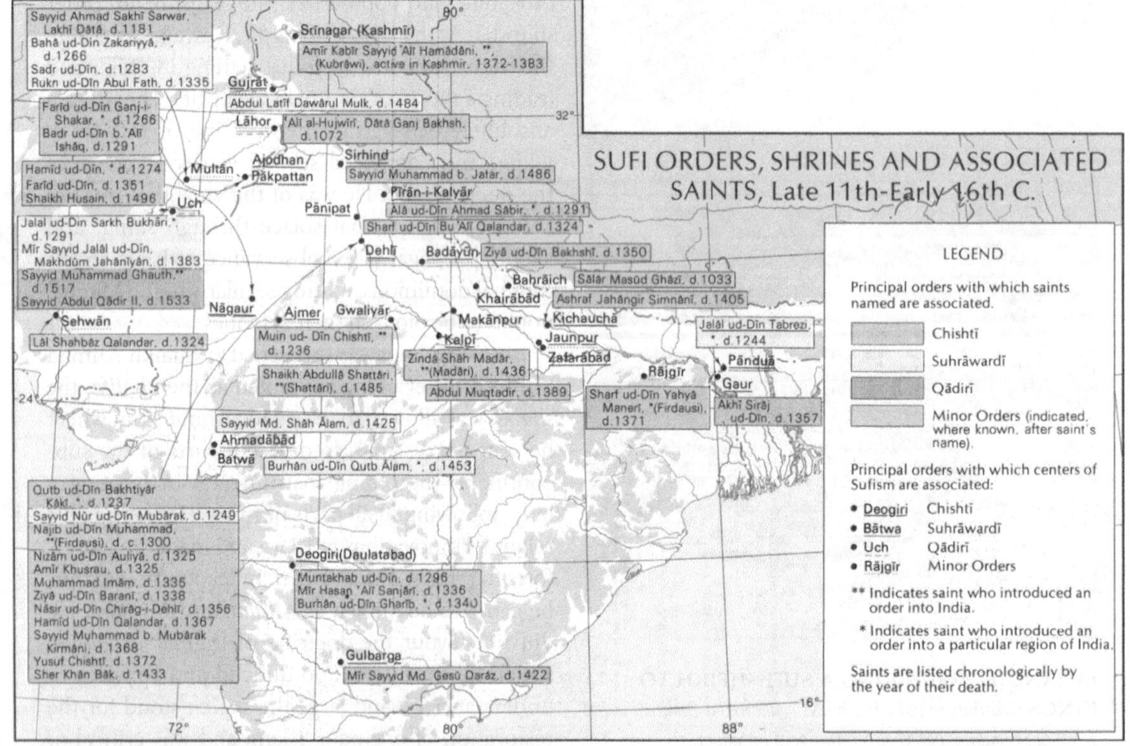

Map 16-1 *Sufi Orders, Shrines and Associated Saints, Late 11th–Early 16th Century*

anti Shia campaign in Kashmir led to his eventual banishment to Lahore, where he died and remains buried. The Naqshbandi line was later continued by his sons, Khawand Ahmad and Muinuddin.

The Shattaris

The Shattari order was introduced in India during the Lodi regime. Muhammad Ghauth of Gwalior was the most famous Sufi saint of the order. He authored two well-known texts, *Jawahir-i-Khamsah* and *Khalid-i-Makhazin*, which deal with Sufi doctrines and practices. Emperor Humayun and Miyan Tansen, the renowned Hindustani musician, seem to have been attracted to this order. The Shattari saints tried to find a number of similarities in the thoughts and practices of both Hindus and Muslims. The members of this order led a spiritual life, while living in comfortable worldly surroundings.

Impact of Sufism

As discussed, Sufism had its own history before its arrival in India. Martin Lings in his book, *What is Sufism,* describes mysticism as, 'From time to time a Revelation "flows" like a great tidal wave from the Ocean of Infinitude to the shores of our finite world; and Sufism is the vocation and the discipline and the science of plunging into the ebb of one of these waves and being drawn back with it to its Eternal and Infinite Source' (1999).

It was through their simple philosophy, uncomplicated practices, and spirit of tolerance and accommodation that the Sufis won the hearts of the masses, who thronged the *khanaqas.* Among the Sufis, most of the Chishti saints became popular on account of their ability to perform miracle and for their lack of interest in matters related to the state. They avoided the company of state officials, discouraged their disciples from holding lucrative posts in the government and turned their back on all association with the state. On the contrary, the Suhrawardi Sufis received political favour, lucrative appointments and material comforts. They also preferred to associate with the political elites of the land.

Many Chishtis adopted local languages as a medium of their expression. Not only was Sufi poetry an expression of the mystic love seeking an intuitive understanding of god, it was also an avenue for the outlet of emotions and spiritual feelings that would otherwise never have been expressed in the midst of the fury of the orthodox, social inhibitions and political repression of the times. The *khanaqas* offered peace and comfort to thousands of people, while the *urs* and other ceremonies performed in the *khanaqas* and *dargahs* developed into significant cultural institutions that were eagerly awaited by both poor and rich alike.

The message of peace, harmony, universal brotherhood and peaceful co-existence of the Sufis along with the efforts of their Bhakti counterparts helped create a society free of religious, sectarian and communal tensions. The caste-ridden Indian society required the healing Bhakti–Sufi touch to bring about a fusion of Hindu and Islamic thoughts and practices worthy of emulation. Medieval mysticism, whether in the form of Bhakti or Sufi ideology, had a tremendous impact on Indian socio-religious thought. Its effects were such that it predisposed people to accept the powerful teachings of the reform movements, evolving a synthesis of Hinduism and Islam. By speaking about the universal love in quest of the Almighty, Sufi philosophy thus heightened the atmosphere of religious tolerance, echoing the spirituality and cultural refinement inherent in Islam.

SUMMARY

- Sufism was the mystical interpretation that developed within Islam. By speaking about the universal love in quest of the Almighty, Sufi philosophy heightened the atmosphere of religious tolerance and echoed spirituality and cultural refinement in Islam.
- Islamic mysticism saw several stages of growth—the appearance of early asceticism, the consequent development of a classical mysticism of divine love, and lastly the rise and proliferation of mystical orders.

- Among the main rituals practiced by the Sufis was the *zikr*, which involved the repeated recitation of a devotional formula in praise of Allah as a means of attaining bliss. A popular form of *zikr* that had a powerful influence on the Sufis was the *sama*, a gathering where both singers and listeners reached a sublime state of mind and experienced divine ecstasy. The doctrine of *fanaa* or annihilation of the self was considered by all Sufis to be the means of achieving divine communion.
- During the late twelfth and early thirteenth centuries, Ibn al-Arabi, the great Andalusian Sufi, spoke about the doctrine of *wahdat al-wujud* or unity of being that had a profound influence on Sufi thought worldwide.
- As Sufism developed in each region, the dervish orders gained global popularity, such as the Chishtiyah of Mughal India, Naqshbandiyah of Central Asia, Tijaniyah of North Africa, Qadiriyah of Baghdad and the Rifa'iyah of Egypt, Syria and Turkey, to name a few.
- Sufis made every effort to deepen and intensify the spirituality of Indian society by preaching their message across diverse intellectual levels and disseminating Sufi thought within Indian culture. This penetration of thought was usually achieved through literary, ritualistic and institutional forms.
- There was a proliferation of numerous Sufi orders in India, although none were native to India; only four—the Chishtiyah, the Suhrawardiyah, the Qadiriyah, and the Naqshbandiyah—had a sizeable impact on the life and thought of medieval India.
- These orders organized themselves by having their own spiritual territories called *wilayats* and formed an infrastructure consisting of their hospices called *khanaqas* where several disciples and attenders lived with the Sufi saint.

KEYWORDS

Tasawwuf	Muqarrab	Khanaqa	Ulema-i-akhirat
Fuqara	Tariqah	Zikr	Ulema-i-duniya
Dervish	Haqiqah	Dargah	Mehfil
Tawhid	Shaikhs, Pirs and Murshids	Fanaa	Hadith
Mutawalli		Wahdat al-wujud	Sunnah
Wali	Urs	Murid	

REVIEW QUESTIONS

1. Write a short note on the meaning of Sufism.
2. How did Sufi teachings penetrate through all levels of Indian culture?
3. How did the Sufis create a society free of religious, sectarian and communal tensions?
4. Briefly explain the activities of the Chistis.
5. How did the khanaqa and dargah emerge as cultural institutions in India?

PART VI–The Mughal Empire

"On the 22nd of March 1617 the scouts brought in news of a tiger. Mounting immediately, I went against the tiger and with three shots I delivered the people from his wickedness, and himself from the wickedness of his vile nature. Masihu zaman produced before me a cat, and represented that it was a hermaphrodite, and that in his house it had young ones, and that when it had connection with another cat, young were born to the latter.

On the 25th the contingent of Itimadud daulah passed before me in review on the plain under the jharoka. There were 2,000 cavalry well horsed, most of whom were Moghuls, 500 foot armed with bows and guns, and fourteen elephants. The bakhshis reckoned them up and reported that this force was fully equipped and according to rule. On the 26th a tigress was killed. On Thursday, the 1st Urdibihisht, a diamond that Muqarrab Khan had sent by runners was laid before me; it weighed 23 aurkh, and the jewellers valued it at 30,000 rupees. It was a diamond of the first water, and was much approved. I ordered them to make a ring of it. On the 3rd the mansab of Yusuf Khan was, at the request of Baba Khurram, fixed at 1,000 with 1,500 horses, and in the same way the mansabs of several of the amirs and mansabdars were increased at his suggestion. On the 7th, as the huntsmen had marked down four tigers, when two watches and three gharis had passed I went out to hunt them with my ladies. When the tigers came in sight Nur Jahan Begum submitted that if I would order her she herself would kill the tigers with her gun. I said, "Let it be so." She shot two tigers with one shot each and knocked over the two others with four shots. In the twinkling of an eye she deprived of life the bodies of these four tigers. Until now such shooting was never seen, that from the top of an elephant and inside of a howdah (amdri) six shots should be made and not one miss, so that the four beasts found no opportunity to spring or move. As a reward for this good shooting I gave her a pair of bracelets 2 (pahunchi) of diamonds worth 100,000 rupees and scattered 1,000 ashrafis (over her)."

They say that a poet recited this impromptu couplet —

"Though Nur Jahan be in form a woman, in the ranks of men she's a tiger-slayer." The point of this couplet is that before Nur Jahan entered Jahangir's harem she was the wife of Sher Afghan, the tiger-slayer. The line may also read "In battle she is a man-smiter and a tiger- slayer."

Source: Extract taken from Jahangir's *Tuzuk-i-Jahangiri* or Memoirs of Jahangir: Nur Jahan Shoots Four Tigers, Translated into English by Rodgers and Beveridge, London: Royal Asiatic Society, 1909, p. 375. Available at Persian Literature in Translation: The Packard Humanities Institute.

Image: Idealized Portrait of Empress Nur Jahan (1577–1645)?, Rajasthan, Kishangarh, India, 1725–50 CE.

CHAPTER **17**

Establishment of Mughal Rule in India

Review and Discussion

- India on the Eve of Babur's Ascent
- Babur's Central Asian Connection
- The Consolidation of Babur's Kingdom in Hindustan

At the height of its glory, the Mughal Empire—an essentially Turkish imperial power which ruled from the early sixteenth to the mid-nineteenth centuries—controlled most of the Indian subcontinent and parts of what is now Afghanistan. Although Babur, a Chaghatai Turkish leader, laid the foundation of the Mughals in 1526 CE, the empire's classic period began with the accession of Akbar in 1556 CE, ending with the death of Aurangzeb in 1707 CE. During this period of the Great Mughals, the empire was marked by vast acquisitions of territory, a highly centralized administrative system that efficiently connected these different regions, innovations in economy and religion, and significant architectural activity—for many Mughal monuments, their most visible legacy, date back to this period.

India on the Eve of Babur's Ascent

After the disintegration of the Tughlaq dynasty in the early fifteenth century, northern India faced political instability as both the Sayyids and the Lodis failed to cope with disruptive forces. The insecurity of the Northwestern borders and the frequent rebellions of the nobles added to the general political chaos and weakened the center further. While the Punjab in the north was under the hold of Daulat Khan Lodi—who was opposed to Ibrahim Lodi's domination—Sind and Multan, to the west of Delhi, had transformed into independent principalities since the Tughlaq rule. The south too was dominated by the powerful kingdoms of Vijayanagar and Bahmani, with the latter having broken up into the five independent sultanates of Ahmednagar, Berar, Bijapur, Golconda and Bidar. Meanwhile in all this political turmoil, the three Central Indian kingdoms of Gujarat, Malwa and Mewar were vying to retain their supremacy.

Gujarat was ruled by Muzaffar Shah II, while the power of Sultan Mahmud Khilji II of Malwa was on the decline. During this period, under the leadership of the Sisodia ruler Rana Sanga, Mewar was the most powerful kingdom. Malwa's fertile soil and prime location as the key trade route to the seaports of Gujarat made it a coveted place for Mewar and Gujarat, as well as for the Lodis. Besides, Malwa had other advantages—it was a place to procure good elephants and served as a buffer zone against the Lodis for both Mewar and Gujarat. The incompetence of the sultan of Malwa, however, made the kingdom prone to internal strife; and not even the intervention of its able prime minister, Medini Rai, could improve the situation. Thus, conditions were ripe for Rana Sanga to successfully extend his influence over Malwa and Gujarat, establishing his sway almost completely over Rajputana with the occupation of Ranthambhor and Chanderi.

It was the same story towards the east, where Nusrat Shah of the Hussaini dynasty was ruling in Bengal. The Afghan chieftains, Nasir Khan Lohani and Maruf Farmuli among others, had succeeded in helping Sultan Muhammad Shah form the kingdom of Jaunpur. In addition to these kingdoms, there were other small Afghan chieftaincies around Agra, operating more or less independently—such as that of Hasan Khan in Mewat, Nizam Khan in Bayana, Muhammad Zaitun in Dholpur, Tatar Khan Sarang Khani in Gwalior, Hussain Khan Lohani in Rapri, Qutub Khan in Etawa, Alam Khan in Kalpi and Qasim Sambhali in Sambhal.

The political situation in the Indian subcontinent on the eve of Babur's ascent was thus complex to say the least. Analyzing these political complexities, the British historian, Rushbrooke Williams proposed an interesting line of thought. Awarding the power of the Rajput confederacy with utmost importance, he proposes that had Babur not entered India when he did, the Rajputs—led by their illustrious leader Rana Sanga—would have captured power in northern India. Basing his assumption on the *Baburnama* (Babur's account of India), which refers to the 'five Musalman rulers'—the Lodis, Gujarat, Malwa, Bahmani and Bengal—and the two 'pagans' (Rana Sanga and Vijayanagar), he argues that the regional states were aligned with each other on the basis of religion and the Rajput confederacy meant to establish a Hindu empire by overthrowing the Islamic rule in India. Such observations, however, are questionable as there is no evidence to prove that these powers were hostile to each other on religious grounds. Babur, in fact, admits in his memoirs that many Rajput chieftains were submissive to Muslim rulers. Further, many Muslim chieftains, such as Hasan Khan Mewati and Mahmud Lodi were part of the Rajput confederacy formed by Rana Sanga against Babur. It may also be noted that Babur was more wary of the Afghans than of Rana Sanga and it was Mahmud Lodi not Rana Sanga, who proclaimed himself as the sultan of Delhi. In this context, therefore, the theory of Rushbrooke Williams becomes unacceptable when the historical situation is analyzed objectively.

Babur's Central Asian Connection

It is commonly believed that the Mughals were descendents of the Mongols, who had settled in central and western Asia between the thirteenth and the fifteenth centuries. In course of time, the Mongols embraced Islam and joined the Turks of western Asia, adopting the Turkish language, customs and manners. Timur, who had invaded India in 1398 CE, also belonged to this same stock. Zahiruddin Muhammad Babur, the founder of the Mughals in India, was a descendent of Timur from his father's side, and related to Chengiz Khan on his mother's. Hence, according to the Turko-Mongol theory of kingship, as enunciated by R. P. Tripathi, the Mughals were descendents of both Chengiz Khan and Timur, but were better known as Turks than as Mongols.

On the one hand, by the end of the fifteenth century, the power of the Central Asian Timurids had waned considerably, but on the other hand, the Uzbeks had succeeded in establishing themselves in Transoxiana and Khurasan under their ruler, Shaibani Khan. This was also a time when the Safavid dynasty had risen to prominence under Shah Ismail in Persia; and on the western side the Ottoman Turks had become more dominant.

After his initial victories, Shaibani Khan was defeated by Shah Ismail of Persia in 1510 CE; but within two years Shah Ismail was defeated by the Ottoman sultan. This development once again opened up new avenues for the Uzbeks to gain control over Transoxiana. Meanwhile upon his father's death in 1494 CE at the tender age of twelve, Babur ascended the throne at Farghana (a small principality of Transoxiana). His succession was replete with problems, since various interested parties had their own stake in the kingdom. Contesting the throne were both the Mongols as well as the Timurid princes, among whom was Sultan Ahmad Mirza of Samarqand, an uncle of Babur.

Babur cherished the desire of occupying Samarqand, the capital of his celebrated ancestor Timur. His two attempts to take possession of this coveted city in 1497 CE and again in 1500 CE were temporarily successful, but he could hardly hold on to it for very long. To add to his misfortunes, he was deprived of his own kingdom of Farghana and had to remain homeless for a year. Babur also realized that after Shaibani Khan had established himself at Khurasan—a major Timurid bastion of power in Central Asia—he was hardly left with any option other than Kabul, where conditions seemed to be more favourable for him. The ruler, Ulugh Beg, died in 1501 CE, making it easier for Babur to conquer Kabul in 1504 CE. But nurturing the desire of ruling over all of Central Asia, Babur made another attempt to establish control over Samarqand in 1511 CE with the help of Shah Ismail Safavi. However, the Shah was defeated in 1512 CE by the Uzbeks, who had not left Babur with any alternatives but to consolidate himself at Kabul.

There were, thus, several reasons for Babur to turn his attention towards Hindustan; and taking advantage of the right opportunities, he led several expeditions to India from 1512–25 CE. Firstly, the complex political situation in Central Asia forced Babur to abandon his hopes of ever creating an empire there, while the rich resources of India seemed more enticing in comparison to the poor economic condition of Afghanistan. The unstable political situation of northern India that followed

FIRST BATTLE OF PANIPAT, *miniature painting from the Baburnama, (National Museum, New Delhi, India)*

Sikandar Lodi's death, coupled with the discontentment and disorder in the Lodi regime, was another reason that kindled Babur's ambitions of invading India. After the siege of Bhira in 1519 CE, Babur asked Ibrahim Lodi to return western Punjab, which belonged to his uncle Mirza Ulugh Beg. He then occupied Sialkot in 1520 CE and Lahore in 1524 CE, before finally meeting Ibrahim Lodi at the historic battlefield of Panipat in 1526 CE.

The Consolidation of Babur's Kingdom in Hindustan

It was from 1525–26 CE that Babur made most of his opportunity to advance into the heart of Hindustan, with the Delhi Sultanate on the point of disruption under its haughty ruler, Ibrahim Lodi. The Delhi nobility were dissatisfied with the arrogant and weak willed Lodi sultan, which led to the rise of centrifugal forces. The Delhi Sultanate had by then dwindled much in size, and its territories now extended only across the regions of modern Punjab, Haryana, Delhi, Uttar Pradesh and Bihar—reducing its status to that of a mere regional kingdom. Armed with their self-serving motives, Ibrahim's uncle, Alam Khan, and Daulat Khan Lodi, the governor of Punjab, invited Babur to invade India. Babur responded with readiness, marching into the Punjab and occupying Lahore (1525 CE). By the time Daulat Khan Lodi realized that Babur wished to conquer India for himself, and turned against him, it was too late. Babur returned to Kabul, only to come back a few months later with a larger force, with which he defeated Daulat Khan's troops and invaded Lahore. Then marching towards Delhi with an army of Mongols, Turks, Persians and Pashtun warriors, he met Ibrahim Lodi on the battlefield of Panipat in 1526 CE. A seasoned military commander with a well-trained, veteran army of 12,000 horsemen—which was much leaner and swifter—Babur inflicted a heavy defeat on the sultan's unwieldy and disunited force of approximately 1,00,000 soldiers and 1,000 war elephants.

Babur's success in this First Battle of Panipat is mainly attributed to his army's cohesion and mobility, his horse-mounted archers and superior artillery. Employing firearms, gun carts, moveable artillery, superior cavalry tactics and the highly regarded Mughal composite bow—a weapon even more powerful than the English longbow of the same period—Babur achieved a resounding victory. Ibrahim Lodi died on the battlefield, while Babur became the master of Delhi and Agra. The First Battle of Panipat, therefore, catapulted Babur to the position of the first Mughal emperor of India.

Babur now had to fight two of his other formidable enemies—Rana Sanga of Mewar and the Afghan nobles of Bihar and Bengal. Babur had, in fact, expected Rana Sanga to help him in his battle against Ibrahim Lodi, but the Rana had kept away, expecting Babur to return to Kabul and leaving him free to establish his domination over Rajputana. But the Rana's ambitious plans were foiled when Babur decided to remain in India. It was an equally anxious situation for Babur, who too was aware that it would be impossible to consolidate his position in India without shattering the Rana's powers. To check Babur's rising influence, Rana Sanga formed a confederacy with the states of Mewar, Amber, Marwar, Ajmer, Bundi, Sikri, Chanderi and Gwalior, with help from the Afghan nobility. Hasan Khan Mewati not only joined the Rana but also played a crucial role in forming the confederacy. Hasan Khan of Bari and Hussain Khan Gurgandaz also joined the Rana. But despite all their efforts, Babur defeated the Rajput confederacy led by Rana Sanga at the Battle of Khanwa in 1527 CE. Babur's disciplined army, his cavalry and artillery units yet again played a decisive role in the battle in which the Rajputs suffered huge losses. The victory facilitated Babur's task of establishing the rule of the Mughals in India.

Though the Mewar Rajputs received a considerable setback at Khanwa, Medini Rai at Malwa was still a power to reckon with. Rana Sanga had bestowed Malwa on Medini Rai in 1520 CE, but when Babur marched to the great bastion of Chanderi—the stronghold of the Rajputs—and stormed the fort in 1528 CE, Medini Rai was overcome. With his defeat, the Rajput resistance against Babur was completely eliminated. The victories gained over the dominant warrior coalitions, which were themselves struggling for control over Hindustan, provided Babur with the base to consolidate his rule in northern India.

Babur now had to deal with the Afghans, who had surrendered Delhi, but were still powerful in Bihar and parts of Jaunpur, where the Nuhani Afghans led by Sultan Muhammad Nuhani were dominant. The Afghans of Chunar, Jaunpur and Awadh were, however, not ready to co-operate with the Nuhanis in opposing the Mughals. The Afghans, including the non-Nuhanis, accepted the leadership of Ibrahim Lodi's brother, Mahmud

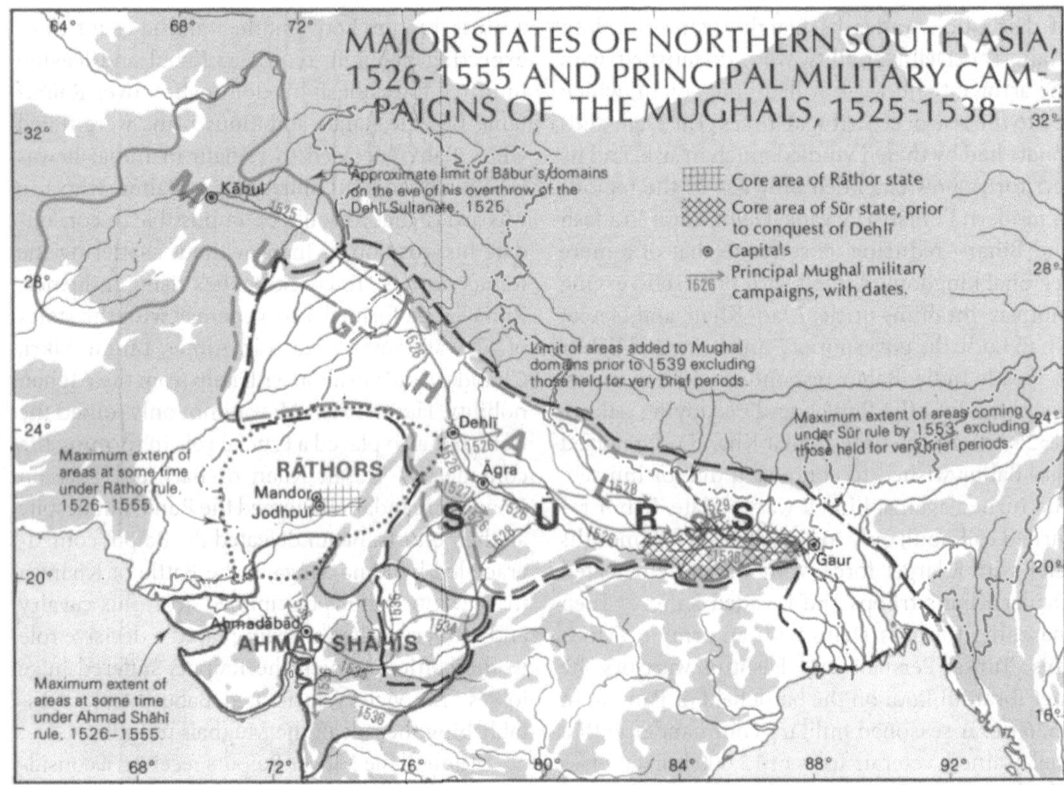

Map 17-1 *Major States of South Asia, 1526–1555 CE and the Principal Military Campaigns of the Mughals, 1525–1538 CE*

Lodi, who had escaped to the east and had formed a coalition. Babur met them on the banks of the river Ghagra, near Patna, and inflicted a crushing defeat in 1529 CE by routing the joint forces of the Afghans and the sultan of Bengal. Having won three decisive battles within the very first few years of his Indian invasion, Babur gained for himself a kingdom that stretched across almost the whole of northern India. He made Agra his capital, but could not enjoy the fruits of his hard won victories for long, as he died shortly after in 1530 CE, aged merely 47.

During his short five-year reign, Babur took considerable interest in erecting buildings, though few have survived to this day. But most importantly, he left behind as his chief legacy a set of descendants, who were to fulfil his dream of establishing one of the greatest Turkish empires in the Indian subcontinent. To quote Percival Spear, 'Babur is one of the most attractive characters in Indian or any other history. He was not only a soldier-statesman of a familiar type, but a poet and man of letters, of sensibility and taste and humour as well. Wherever he went he laid out Persian gardens and his memoirs are dotted with references to natural beauties. It was the absence of the hills and streams of his homeland that he felt so keenly in India . . .'

Babur's *Memoirs*, written in Turkish, recounts his adventures from his early youth in the valley of Farghana to his conquest of India. An assessment of Babur's personality, as penned down by his cousin, Mirza Haider Dughlat, in his text, *Tarikh-i-Rashidi*, seems to be most appropriate

Reflections on the Conquest of Hindustan

On Thursday, the 28th of Rajeb, about the hour of afternoon prayers, I entered Agra, and took up my residence at Sultan Ibrahim's palace. From the time when I conquered the country of Kabul, which was in the year 910, till the [1504] present time, I had always been bent on subduing Hindustan. Sometimes, however, from the misconduct of my Amirs and their dislike of the plan, sometimes from the cabals and opposition of my brothers, I was prevented from prosecuting any expedition into that country, and its provinces escaped being overrun. At length these obstacles were removed. There was now no one left, great or small, noble or private man, who could dare to utter a word in opposition to the enterprise. In the year 925 I collected an army, and having taken the fort of Bajour by storm in two or three gharis, put all the garrison to the sword. I next advanced into Behreh, where I prevented all marauding and plunder, imposed a contribution on the inhabitants, and having levied it to the amount of four hundred thousand shahrokhis in money and goods, divided the proceeds among the troops who were in my service, and returned back to Kabul. From that time till the year 932, I attached myself in a peculiar degree to the affairs of Hindustan, and in the space of these seven or eight years entered it five times at the head of an army. The fifth time, the Most High God, of his grace and mercy, cast down and defeated an enemy so mighty as Sultan Ibrahim, and made me the master and conqueror of the powerful empire of Hindustan. From the time of the blessed Prophet (on whom and on his family be peace and salvation!) down to the present time, three foreign kings had subdued the country, and acquired the sovereignty of Hindustan. One of these was Sultan Mahmud Ghazi, whose family long continued to fill the throne of that country. The second was Sultan Shahabeddin Ghuri, and for many years his slaves and dependants swayed the sceptre of these realms. I am the third. But my achievement is not to be put on the same level with theirs; for Sultan Mahmud, at the time when he conquered Hindustan, occupied the throne of Khorasan, and had absolute power and dominion over the Sultans of Khwarizm and the surrounding chiefs. The King of Samarkand, too, was subject to him. If his army did not amount to two hundred thousand, yet grant that it was only one hundred thousand, and it is plain that the comparison between the two conquests must cease. Moreover, his enemies were Rajas. All Hindustan was not at that period subject to a single Emperor: every Raja set up for a monarch on his own account, in his own petty territories. Again, though Sultan Shahabeddin Ghuri did not himself enjoy the sovereignty of Khorasan, yet his elder brother, Sultan Ghiaseddin Ghuri, held it. In the Tabakat-e-Nāsiri it is said, that on one occasion he marched into Hindustan with one hundred and twenty thousand cataphract horse. His enemies, too, were Rais and Rajas; a single monarch did not govern the whole of Hindustan. When I marched into Behreh, we might amount to one thousand five hundred, or two thousand men at the utmost. When I invaded the country for the fifth time, overthrew Sultan Ibrahim, and subdued the empire of Hindustan, I had a larger army than I had ever before brought into it. My servants, the merchants and their servants, and the followers of all descriptions that were in the camp along with me, were numbered, and amounted to twelve thousand men. The kingdoms that depended on me were Badakhshan, Kunduz,

(Continued)

(Continued)

Kabul, and Kandahar; but these countries did not furnish me with assistance equal to their resources; and, indeed, some of them, from their vicinity to the enemy, were so circumstanced, that, far from affording me assistance, I was obliged to send them extensive supplies from my other territories. Besides this, all Maweralnaher was occupied by the Khans and Sultans of the Uzbeks, whose armies were calculated to amount to about a hundred thousand men, and who were my ancient foes. Finally, the whole empire of Hindustan, from Behreh to Behar, was in the hands of the Afghans. Their prince, Sultan Ibrahim, from the resources of his kingdom, could bring into the field an army of five hundred thousand men. At that time some of the Amirs to the east were in a state of rebellion. His army on foot was computed to be a hundred thousand strong; his own elephants, with those of his Amirs, were reckoned at nearly a thousand. Yet, under such circumstances, and in spite of this power, placing my trust in God, and leaving behind me my old and inveterate enemy the Uzbeks, who had an army of a hundred thousand men, I advanced to meet so powerful a prince as Sultan Ibrahim, the lord of numerous armies, and emperor of extensive territories. In consideration of my confidence in Divine aid, the Most High God did not suffer the distress and hardships that I had undergone to be thrown away, but defeated my formidable enemy, and made me the conqueror of the noble country of Hindustan. This success I do not ascribe to my own strength, nor did this good fortune flow from my own efforts, but from the fountain of the favour and mercy of God.

Source: *Memoirs of Zehīr-ed-Dīn Muhammed Bābur Emperor of Hindustan,* Vol II (A.H. 912–937), Written by himself, in the Chaghatāi Tūrki, Translated by John Leyden, Esq., M.D. and William Erskine, Esq., Annotated and Revised by Sir Lucas King, C.S.I., LL.D., F.S.A. Professor of Arabic and Persian, and Lecturer in Indian History in the University of Dublin; Late of the Indian Civil Service, London: Oxford University Press, 1921. Available at Persian Literature in Translation: The Packard Humanities Institute.

CHRONOLOGY

1494 CE	Babur ascends the throne at Farghana
1504 CE	Babur conquers Kabul
1510 CE	Shaibani Khan defeated by Shah Ismail of Persia
1512 CE	Shah Ismail was defeated by the Ottoman sultan
1512–25 CE	Babur leads several expeditions to India
1519 CE	Babur's siege of Bhira
1520 CE	Babur occupies Sialkot
1524 CE	Babur occupies Lahore
1526 CE	First Battle of Panipat
1527 CE	Battle of Khanwa
1528 CE	Babur storms the fort of Chanderi and overcomes Medini Rai
1529 CE	Babur defeats the Afghans led by Mahmud Lodi at Ghagra
1530 CE	Death of Babur at Agra

at this juncture. The author observes that Babur was endowed with all the fine traits of a soldier and military general. He was a born leader of men, and because of his outstanding qualities of the head and heart, he enjoyed the love and confidence of his soldiers. From his expertise in Central Asian horsemanship and battle tactics, and his command over the Turkish language (as seen in his *Memoirs*) to a cultural style derived from Timur's patronage at Samarqand and refined at the courts of his successors in Central Asia, Babur's legacy had it all. Through his efforts he established the Mughal imperial organization and political culture, which was to become distinct in the days to come. He is credited with introducing certain central Asian administrative institutions, besides establishing harmonious relations with prominent local chiefs. He is also said to have established new mints in Lahore and Jaunpur, and of trying to ensure a safe and secure route from Agra to Kabul. He advised his son and successor, Humayun, to adopt a tolerant religious policy towards his subjects. He abided by Sunni Islam and had familial connections with the Central Asian Naqshbandi Sufi order. It is more as a conqueror, therefore, and not as an administrator that Babur may be considered to have laid the foundations of the Mughal Empire in India.

SUMMARY

- After the disintegration of the Tughlaq dynasty, there was political instability in the early fifteenth century, as both the Sayyids and the Lodis failed to cope with disruptive forces.
- Intermittently rebelling nobles and the political chaos that had ensued in the Northwestern provinces weakened the centre further.
- Several independent kingdoms and principalities were spread across the Indian subcontinent, making the Delhi Sultanate almost a non-existent entity in their midst.
- According to the Turko-Mongol theory of kingship, as enunciated by R. P. Tripathi, the Mughals were descendents of both Chengiz Khan and Timur—but were better known as Turks than as Mongols.
- The foundation of the Mughal rule in India was laid in 1526 CE by Babur, a Chaghatai Turkish ruler.
- Babur ascended the throne at Farghana (a small principality in Transoxiana) in 1494 CE, at the tender age of twelve on the death of his father. His succession was, however, replete with problems.
- Babur cherished the desire of occupying Samarqand, the capital of his celebrated ancestor Timur. His two attempts to take possession of this much coveted city in 1497 CE and later in 1500 CE were temporarily successful.
- The resurgence of the Uzbeks left Babur with no alternatives but to consolidate himself at Kabul.
- There were several reasons that made Babur turn his attention towards the rich plains of Hindustan, foremost among them being the unstable political situation in northern India.
- It was in 1525–26 CE that Babur got an opportunity to advance into the heart of Hindustan, when the Delhi Sultanate was on the point of disruption under its haughty ruler, Ibrahim Lodi.
- The Delhi Sultanate had dwindled in size with its territories extending merely over the modern Punjab, Haryana, Delhi, Uttar Pradesh and Bihar, thus, reducing its status to that of a regional kingdom.
- Babur met Ibrahim Lodi on the historic battlefield of Panipat in 1526 CE, defeated him and became the master of Delhi and Agra.
- The First Battle of Panipat catapulted Babur to the position of the first Mughal emperor of India.
- Babur had to now fight against two other formidable enemies, Rana Sanga of Mewar and the Afghan nobles of Bihar and Bengal, who he defeated successfully in the battles of Khanwa and Ghagra.
- Babur was endowed with all the fine traits of a soldier and military general. He left behind as his chief legacy a set of descendants who fulfilled his dream of establishing a Turkish empire in the Indian subcontinent.
- It is as a conqueror and not as an administrator that Babur is considered to have laid the foundation of the Mughal Empire in India.

KEYWORDS

Chieftaincy
Memoir
Archers
Cavalry
Moveable artillery
Firearms
Gun carts
Mughal composite bow
Warrior coalitions

REVIEW QUESTIONS

1. Examine the political condition of India on the eve of Babur's ascent.
2. Explain the significance of the First Battle of Panipat.
3. Write a short note on the Turko-Mongol theory of kingship.
4. Discuss Babur's conflict with Rana Sanga of Mewar.

CHAPTER **18**

Humayun and the Sur Interlude

Review and Discussion

- Humayun
- Sher Shah Sur
- Sher Shah's Administration
- The Successors of Sher Shah
- The Return of Humayun

Babur had established a fairly vast empire in India, but did not live long enough to consolidate it. Upon his death in 1530 CE, he was succeeded by his eldest son, Humayun, who was only 23 years old when he ascended the throne of the newly established Mughal Empire in India. Ironically named as Nasiruddin Muhammad Humayun—meaning the fortunate—his fate was, however, far from displaying the luck that went with his name. Brought up in an atmosphere of harmony and abundance befitting a prince, Humayun received his first important assignment when he was appointed the governor of Badakhshan at the tender age of 12.

Humayun (1530–40 CE)

At the time of Humayun's accession to the throne, the political conditions in the Indian subcontinent were such that the newly founded Mughal state was threatened by numerous internal as well as external enemies. Bahadur Shah, an ambitious ruler of Gujarat had posted a significant victory over the Rajputs and was now making plans to invade Agra. Quite a few powerful Afghan nobles from the Mughal dominions of Bihar and Bengal, who had not been subdued, in their quest to regain their lost power and prestige, had found a new leader in Sher Khan. Most of the Indian feudal chieftains, powerful Mughal nobles and even the blood relations of Humayun did not extend him any cooperation. Humayun's three brothers—Kamran, Hindal and Askari, whom he had appointed as governors of the provinces of Kabul, Mewat and Sambhal, respectively—were not too faithful to him either. Kamran, already in possession of Kabul and Qandahar, behaved almost as an independent ruler and forcibly took control of the province of the Punjab as well. It was, therefore, not an easy crown that Humayun had inherited from his father. The fact that he was neither a gifted general nor a wise statesman simply added to his difficulty in establishing complete control over his kingdom. Humayun was incapable of prompt decisions and quick actions, and he lacked the perseverance to pursue his plans with determination.

In the early years of his reign, Humayun tried to face the difficulties that came his way with fortitude. He first invaded the Hindu principality of Kalinjar in Bundelkhand, which ended in a failure. His next attempts were made against Sher Khan of Bengal and Bahadur Shah of Gujarat.

Getting entwined in a serious quarrel with Sher Khan—which was to last for many years—Humayun tried to besiege the fortress of Chunar in 1532 CE, which was yet another failure. Thereafter he conquered Malwa and Gujarat, but failed to establish complete control over them. Without completing the conquest of the fortress of Chunar, Humayun rushed towards Bengal to assist Sultan Mahmud Shah against Sher Khan. Meanwhile, having kept away from his capital for a fairly long period of time, he also lost touch with the situation in Delhi and Agra. Making the most of this opportunity, his brother, Hindal, began to openly act as the independent ruler of Agra. This forced Humayun to leave Gaur, the capital of Bengal, and return to his own capital.

Of all his political adversaries, Sher Khan proved to be the most formidable. While Humayun remained occupied with his campaign against Bahadur Shah, Sher Khan utilized the opportunity to mobilize his forces in Bengal and Bihar to defeat Humayun in 1539 CE at Chausa, situated a few miles southwest of Baksar and at a short distance from the Karamnasa river of modern day Uttar Pradesh and Bihar. Sher Khan was to engage Humayun in battle once again at Kannauj in 1540 CE, when the latter became too weak to defend Agra and retreated to Bilgram near Kannauj. It was there that Humayun fought his last unsuccessful battle with Sher Khan, who had by now become a popular leader under the title of Sher Shah.

Humayun's Failure

Humayun was forced to move away to Lahore after his defeat at Kannauj and for years he wandered in search of political shelter. From Lahore he fled to Sind, from Sind to Rajputana, and from Rajputana back to Sind until he finally left India for Persia. It was during his wanderings that his son, Akbar, was born in 1542 CE at Amarkot in Sind. Humayun finally sought refuge from Shah Tahmasp I of Persia. The Shah agreed to assist him with an army on condition that Humayun becomes a Shia Muslim and acquires Qandahar, an important frontier town and commercial centre, for Persia.

The primary reason behind Humayun's failure to keep his empire intact was the lack of strength in his personality and also because of the defects in the early Mughal political organization, where the nobles owed their allegiance first to the chief of their clan and then to the ruler. In such circumstances, the threat from various chieftains asserting themselves always remained, leading to the emergence of new centres of power. Taking advantage of Humayun's forced exile from India, Sher Shah now established the Sur hegemony with his political tact and military skills. He ably held on to his empire, even successfully checking the advance of the sultan of Gujarat to the south of his kingdom.

Sher Shah Sur (1540–45 CE)

Sher Shah is considered to be one of the greatest rulers of the Indian subcontinent. Born in 1472 CE, he belonged to an Afghan family, which claimed descent from an Afghan adventurer recruited by Sultan Bahlol Lodi of Delhi during his long contest with the Sharqi sultans of Jaunpur. Named Farid Khan, he was one of the eight sons of Hasan Khan, the *jagirdar* of Sasaram in Bihar. When Farid grew up, he rebelled against his father's ill-treatment of his stepmother and left home at the age of 22 to enlist as a soldier in the service of Jamal Khan, the governor of Jaunpur. In those days Jaunpur was a great seat of Islamic learning. Farid devoted himself to study, very soon becoming proficient in Arabic and Persian literature. His exceptional talents caught the attention of Jamal Khan, who brought about a reconciliation between Farid Khan and his father, and as a result, Farid went back to Sasaram to help manage his father's family estate for the next 21 years. He managed his *jagir* so well that he

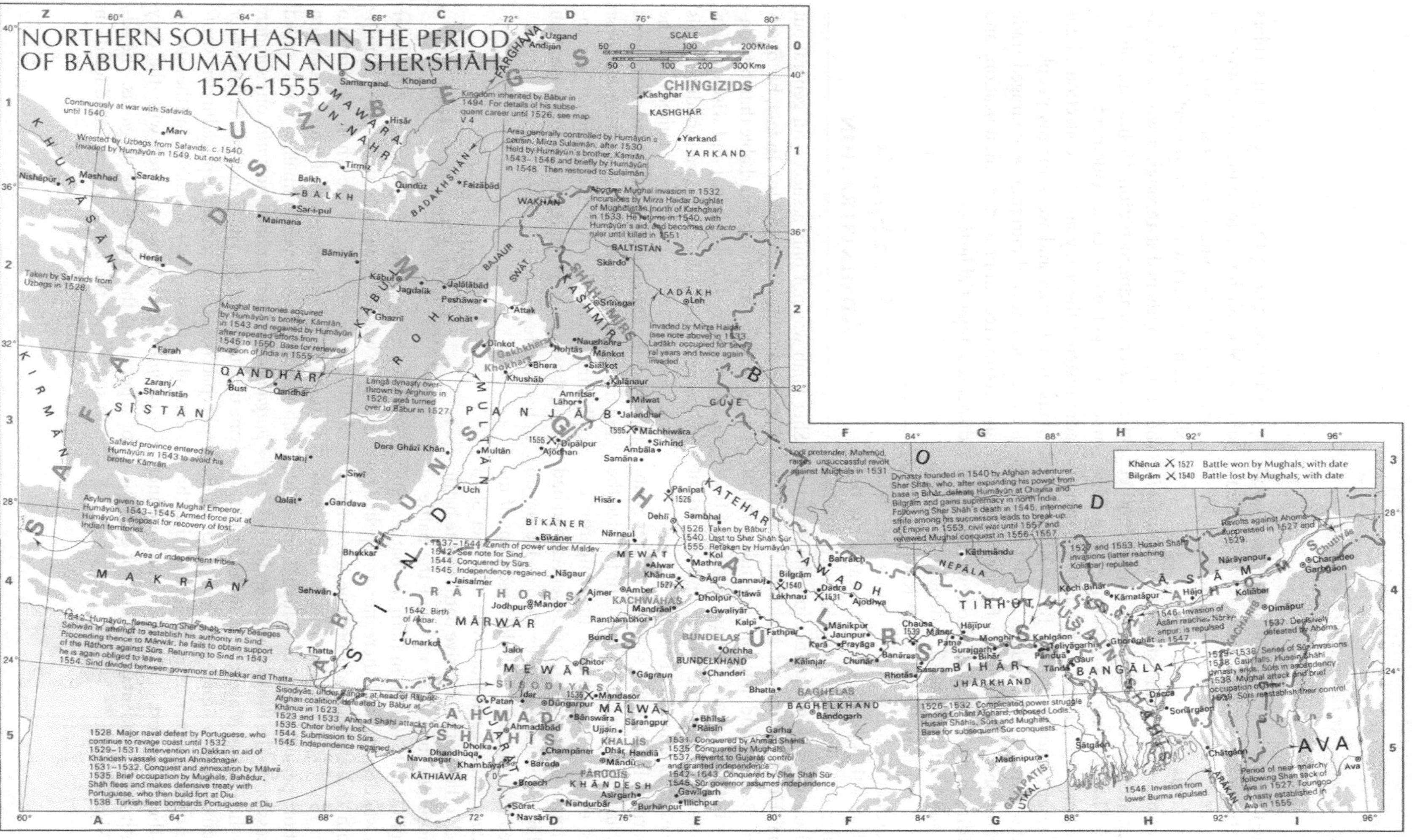

Map 18-1 *Northern South Asia in the Period of Babur, Humayun and Sher Shah, 1526–1555 CE*

won the reputation of being an honest and good administrator. This experience was to stand him in good stead later when he became the ruler of northern India.

The successful administration of their *jagir*, however, aroused the jealousy of his stepmother and Farid had to leave Sasaram once again. This time he took up service with Bahar Khan Lohani, the governor of Bihar. Bahar Khan, impressed with his service and devotion, conferred the title of Sher Khan on him for single-handedly killing a tiger. He was also rewarded with his appointment as the *vakil* or deputy governor. After Bahar Khan's death, Sher Khan became the guardian of Bahar Khan's minor son, Jalal Khan; but within a few years he became the virtual ruler of Bihar, asserting his independence in 1531 CE when Humayun became the emperor of India. He even defeated Mahmud Shah, the ruler of Bengal, and became an independent ruler of both Bihar and Bengal. By early 1539 CE, he had occupied the strong and important fortresses of Chunar and Rohtas.

Alarmed by the rising strength of Sher Shah, Humayun had marched against him to seize the fortress of Chunar. Finding the emperor too strong for an open contest, the clever Afghan had offered his submission, but as soon as Humayun returned to Agra, Sher Shah declared himself independent once again. Humayun and Sher Shah met each other in two decisive battles—the battle of Chausa (26 June 1539 CE) and the battle of Kannauj (May 1540 CE). In both the battles Humayun was defeated and, thereafter, compelled to flee from India. Sher Shah became the ruler of India in 1540 CE, reviving the rule of the Afghans for a short period within the Mughal era. After his accession to the throne, he extended his empire to the Punjab, Malwa, Multan, and a part of Rajputana. He also suppressed the Baluch chiefs on the northwestern frontier in Sind. He then besieged the strong fort of Kalinjar, where he met his death in an accidental explosion of gunpowder in May 1545 CE.

Counted among the greatest Muslim rulers of India, Sher Shah rose from the rank of an ordinary *jagirdar* to become an emperor. Not only did Sher Shah establish a vast and powerful empire, he also strengthened it through a wise and efficient system of administration. He implemented a new and equitable revenue settlement, efficiently administered the army and tax collections, built roads, rest houses and wells for his people, reformed the imperial currency, encouraged trade and commerce, improved communication, and dispensed impartial justice.

Sher Shah's Administration

Sher Shah was not only a successful general but was also an able administrator. In fact, his qualities as a ruler were more remarkable than his conquests. He introduced original and wise changes in every branch of administration during his brief reign of five years. On his father's *jagir* he had fixed the amount of tax to be paid on the land and had sternly warned the tax collectors against collecting more than the fixed amount. He applied these same principles in the administration of his empire.

Central and Provincial Administration

Power was concentrated in the hands of the ruler and there was a bureaucratic structure to administer the state. He divided the whole empire into 47 units called *sarkars*, each of which was again sub-divided into several smaller units called *parganas*. Each *sarkar* had one *amin*, one *shiqdar*, one treasurer, and one Hindi and one Persian writer to keep accounts. Every *sarkar* was placed under two officers called the *shiqdar-i-shiqdaran* and the *munsif-i-munsifan*. They were entrusted with the duty of supervising the work of the *parganas*. The administration of the *parganas* was conducted on the same lines as the *sarkars*. Each *pargana* comprised several villages and in each village there was a *muqaddam*, a *chaudhuri* and a *patwari*. The panchayats also played an important part in village administration. Sher Shah devised the system of transferring government officers every two or three years to prevent them from acquiring undue influence over one place. Sher Shah's practical approach to state administration was subsequently adopted by subsequent Mughal rulers and eventually by British colonial administration.

Land Revenue

Sher Shah introduced a number of reforms in the land revenue system. He had the entire land surveyed; and fixed one fourths to one thirds of the produce to be paid as land revenue, which could be paid out to the state either in cash or in kind. For the collection of revenue, a large number of officials were utilized, like the *amins, muqaddams, shiqdars, quanungos* and *patwaris*. He urged his officers to be lenient to the peasants during the land revenue assessments. The rights and obligations of the peasantry were clearly stated in the *qabuliyat* (deed of agreement), which the state kept in its records and gave the *patta* (title deed) to the peasants in return. Land was classified into three categories, and the land survey measurement was standardized. Sher Shah made it a point to see that no hardship was caused to his peasants. In times of drought, or any other unforeseen calamity, advances were liberally made to the farmers. Sher Shah's land revenue system was so efficient that it was later adopted by Akbar and continued throughout the Mughal period, one of the reasons why Sher Shah is often known as the forerunner of Emperor Akbar.

The Judiciary

In order to establish peace and order in the country, Sher Shah paid special attention to the administration of justice. He tried to mete out even-handed justice to all, irrespective of rank. The guilty could never escape punishment. He even punished his near relatives and high officials if they tried to break the law or attempted to harass his people. The chief *qazi* was the head of the judicial department, while there was an *amin* in every *pargana* and a *qazi* in every district to decide judicial cases. The king heard direct appeals against subordinate courts on every Wednesday in his own court. As was prevalent throughout most of the medieval world, criminals were sentenced with very severe punishments—the main objective of which was not to reform, but to set an example. The *muqaddam* or the village headman was responsible for crimes within his jurisdiction, and if he failed to trace an offender he had to compensate for the losses incurred. A network of spies was also appointed to keep the king abreast of all occurrences in his empire. As a result of such strict and efficient measures, life and property remained secure under Sher Shah's rule.

The Army

Sher Shah knew the importance of a strong and efficient army, taking great care to re-organize it. He maintained a large standing army of 1, 50, 000 cavalry, 25, 000 infantry, 300 war elephants and an efficient artillery. In order to establish a direct relationship with his soldiers, he recruited them himself and fixed their salaries according to their qualities. He introduced the system of branding horses and maintaining descriptive rolls of soldiers to avoid malpractices in the army. He treated his soldiers very kindly, but never let his benevolence interfere with the maintenance of discipline and efficiency within the army. He built many new forts, while repairing and strengthening the old, existing ones. He kept a *fauj* or garrison under the command of a *faujdar* at each of these forts. Though most of Sher Shah's soldiers were Afghans or Pathans, Hindus were also given high positions in the army.

THE FIRST RUPEE, *a* Rupiya *silver coin, issued by Sher Shah, 1540–45* CE

The Economy

Sher Shah introduced reforms in currency and tariff (custom duties) in order to improve the general economic condition of the empire. When he became the ruler, coins issued by previous kings were still in circulation which caused a great deal of confusion, since the exact rates between the various coins were not clearly specified. Sher Shah abolished the use of old coins, issued a large number of gold, silver and copper coins, and fixed their rates relative to each other. Most of the coins issued by Sher Shah, especially the silver rupee, continued to form the basis of Indian currency for a long time. For the promotion of trade and commerce, customs duties levied at various places were abolished. Merchants now had to pay customs duties only at two places—at the frontiers of the kingdom and at the place where the goods were to be sold. This basic principle of levying customs duties is followed even to this day.

Transport and Communication

Sher Shah also brought about various reforms in the means of transport and communication. A number of important roads were built, along which avenues of trees were planted. Wells were dug and *sarais* (rest houses or inns) were provided for the convenience of travellers. The most famous road that he constructed was the Grand Trunk Road, extending from Sonargaon in Bengal to Peshawar in the north-western frontier (now Pakistan). The present Grand Trunk Road (or National Highway 2) is built on the same roadway. Sher Shah also introduced a regular postage system; and the *sarais* built along the roads also served as the *dak chaukis* of the postal department. At every *sarai* or *dak chauki*, two horsemen were always kept ready to receive the *dak* or mail from the previous *chauki* and carry it to the next one. This was how news from all corners of the empire was efficiently communicated to the imperial capital within a short span of time.

The Successors of Sher Shah

The Afghan kingdom established by Sher Shah in northern India remained in power from 1540–56 CE. After the untimely death of Sher Shah (1545 CE), the kingdom remained in power for about a decade. Sher Shah was succeeded by his son, Jalal Khan, who took the title of Islam Shah, commonly known as Salim Shah. He was a capable ruler who managed the kingdom in his father's tradition. Following his death in 1554 CE his minor son, Firuz Khan, was murdered, and anarchy and confusion descended on the empire. The throne was usurped by Islam Shah's brother-in-law who proclaimed himself emperor and took the title of Adil Shah.

Adil Shah was an indolent ruler, who left the affairs of state in the hands of Hemu, his Hindu chief minister, who was a capable administrator, but more interested in seizing the throne for himself. There were revolts in various corners, which ultimately led to the decline and disintegration of the Afghan kingdom. While Sher Shah's nephew, Sikandar Sur, declared himself independent in the Punjab, Humayun (who had recovered Kabul in the meantime) took advantage of the anarchy to return to India in 1555 CE. Humayun now defeated Sikandar Sur and occupied Lahore, before marching into Delhi. In 1555 CE Humayun, thus, re-established the Mughal empire in India bringing the rule of the Sur dynasty to an end.

The Return of Humayun (1555–56 CE)

After returning to Kabul from Persia, Humayun kept a keen eye on the political situation in India, preparing to recover his kingdom. Affairs took a favourable turn when Sher Shah passed away, and the resultant chaos and confusion, induced Humayun to win back his lost kingdom. Capturing Qandahar and Kabul from his brothers, Humayun re-asserted his position and consolidated the nobles who remained loyal to him. By 1554 CE he had become the master of almost the whole of Afghanistan; and armed with 14, 000 men he was ready to charge into India and reclaim the throne of Agra. In December 1554 CE, he crossed the Indus and marched into Lahore, which he took possession of without much opposition. Thereafter, he went on to occupy Sirhind, before capturing Delhi and Agra in July 1555 CE, thus regaining his throne after an interval of nearly 12 years. He proceeded to appoint his son, Akbar, as governor of the Punjab, leaving his gallant general, Bairam Khan, to assist the young prince. Humayun, however, did not live long to enjoy this Mughal recovery. He died in early 1556 CE from a fatal fall from the staircase of his library in Delhi.

SUMMARY

- Babur was succeeded by his eldest son, Humayun, who was only 23 years old when he became the ruler of the newly established Mughal Empire in India.
- When Humayun ascended the throne, the political conditions in the Indian subcontinent were such that the newly founded Mughal state was threatened by numerous internal as well as external enemies.
- Humayun had to tackle Bahadur Shah of Gujarat as well as the Afghan nobles of Bihar and Bengal, while his three brothers—Kamran, Hindal and Askari, whom he had appointed governors of the provinces of Kabul, Mewat and Sambhal respectively—were not very faithful to him.
- Humayun first invaded the Hindu principality of Kalinjar in Bundelkhand, which he failed to subdue. Next he fought wars against Sher Khan of Bengal and Bahadur Shah of Gujarat.
- While Humayun was busy in his campaign against Bahadur Shah, Sher Khan got adequate time to mobilize his forces in Bengal and Bihar, defeating Humayun at Chausa in 1539 CE. Sher Khan was to defeat Humayun yet again in 1540 CE at Kannauj.
- Humayun had no option but to flee India, taking refuge under Shah Tahmasp I, the Shah of Persia.
- Taking advantage of Humayun's exile from India, Sher Shah established the Sur hegemony with his political tact and military skills.

- Sher Shah, originally known as Farid Khan, was the son of Hasan Khan, the *jagirdar* of Sasaram in Bihar.
- Farid left Sasaram to enlist as a soldier in the service of Jamal Khan, the governor of Jaunpur. He later returned to Sasaram and efficiently managed his father's family estate for 21 years.
- Farid left Sasaram once again. This time he went to Bahar Khan Lohani, the governor of Bihar and took up service with him.
- After Bahar Khan's death, Sher Khan became the guardian of his minor son, Jalal Khan. Within a few years, he became the virtual ruler of Bihar and asserted his independence in 1531 CE.
- He even defeated Mahmud Shah, the ruler of Bengal, and became an independent ruler of both Bihar and Bengal. In the meantime he occupied the strong fortresses of Chunar and Rohtas by early 1539 CE.
- Counted among the great Muslim rulers of India, Sher Shah rose from the rank of an ordinary *jagirdar* to become an emperor. Not only did Sher Shah establish a vast and powerful empire, he also strengthened it with a wise system of administration.
- Sher Shah implemented a new and equitable revenue settlement, efficiently administered the army and tax collections, built roads, rest houses and wells for his people, reformed the currency, encouraged trade and commerce, improved communication, and administered impartial justice. The reforms established by him were incorporated by the subsequent Mughal as well as British colonial administration.
- The Afghan kingdom established by Sher Shah in northern India remained in power from 1540–56 CE. After the untimely death of Sher Shah in 1545 CE, it lingered on for a decade until Humayun re-established Mughal rule in India in 1555 CE.

KEYWORDS

Political shelter/refuge	Shiqdar-i-shiqdaran	Quanungo	Patta
Exile	Munsif-i-munsifan	Patwari	Sarai and dak chauki
Sarkars and parganas	Muqaddam	Fauj and Faujdar	
Amin and Shiqdar	Chaudhuri	Qabuliyat	

REVIEW QUESTIONS

1. Examine the political condition of India when Humayun ascended the throne.
2. Give a detailed account of Sher Shah's administration.
3. How did Sher Khan become an independent ruler of Bihar and Bengal?
4. Why is Sher Shah known as the forerunner of Akbar?
5. Explain how Humayun lost and regained his empire in India.

CHAPTER **19**

Akbar the Great

Review and Discussion

- Bairam Khan's Regency
- Political Conquests of Akbar
- Akbar's Rajput Policy
- Akbar's Religious Policy

Jalaluddin Muhammad Akbar—the illustrious son of Humayun and his Persian wife, Hamida Banu Begum—was destined to be one of the most celebrated monarchs of medieval India. At Humayun's sudden death, a 14-year-old Akbar was immediately declared emperor (1556 CE) by his guardian, Bairam Khan. At that point the young prince was busy hounding Sikandar Sur at Kalanaur in the Gurdaspur district of Punjab, with his guardian. Owing to Akbar's young age, Bairam Khan, a dominant member of Humayun's nobility, naturally assumed the role of regent for the young emperor.

Needless to say, it was not an easy throne that Akbar inherited from his father, surrounded as he was by adversaries on all quarters. In the northwest, Mirza Muhammad Hakim, Akbar's half-brother, governed Kabul almost independently. The Surs still occupied a large portion of Sher Shah's dominions. Sikandar Sur was still very strong and threatening to recover Punjab, while Adil Shah Sur was trying to re-establish his authority over northern India. His ambitious minister, Hemu, had occupied Agra and Delhi, declaring himself independent under the title of Vikramaditya.

The Rajput princes had also asserted their independence in Rajputana, Orissa, Malwa and Gujarat. Likewise, Kashmir was being ruled by an independent Muslim king, while Rani Durgavati was ruling Gondwana on behalf of her minor son. In the Deccan, meanwhile, the Bahmani kingdom had broken up into five independent sultanates and the Vijayanagar kingdom in the extreme south continued to enjoy an autonomous existence. The Portuguese too had become powerful in the Arabian Sea and the Persian Gulf, establishing their settlements along the western coast of India at Goa, Daman and Diu.

Akbar, however, faced all these adversities boldly with the help of his capable regent, Bairam Khan, and succeeded in establishing a vast and long-lasting empire in India.

Bairam Khan's Regency

Within a few months of Akbar's enthronement, he had to face Hemu, the ambitious chief minister of Adil Shah Sur, who marched with a huge army to attack Delhi. A much smaller Mughal army, brought together by Bairam Khan with Akbar at his side, met Hemu's forces at the historic battlefield of Panipat in 1556 CE. The battle saw Hemu being defeated, captured and beheaded by

Bairam Khan, while Delhi and Agra were occupied for Akbar. This Second Battle of Panipat is significant in the history of India because it led to the re-establishment of Mughal rule in India.

In the next six months the Mughals won another major battle against Sikandar Sur, forcing him to flee east to Bengal. Under Bairam Khan's direction, Mughal armies occupied Lahore and seized Multan in the Punjab. In 1558 CE, Bairam Khan conquered north India's vital cities and strongholds of Ajmer, Gwalior, Jaunpur, Nagaur and Jaitaran for Akbar and brought them under Mughal control. When Akbar turned 18, however, he decided to take up the reins of state in his own hands, compelling Bairam Khan to proceed to Mecca. Enroute his journey Bairam Khan met his end in 1560 CE at the hands of an enemy at Patan in Gujarat.

Political Conquests of Akbar

After the death of Bairam Khan, Akbar became greatly influenced by Maham Anaga, his foster-mother who dominated both the personal life and the political decisions of the young emperor. This continued for a year, which came to be known as the period of the 'Petticoat government'. In 1561 CE, Maham Anaga's son, Adham Khan, was sent to subdue Baz Bahadur, an Afghan who had captured Malwa. When he failed in his mission, a disappointed Akbar led an army to Malwa himself, conquering it and appointing Pir Muhammad as the governor. Baz Bahadur, however, took advantage of the weak government of Pir Muhammad and re-conquered Malwa.

In November 1561 CE, Akbar appointed Shamsuddin Muhammad Atgah Khan as his prime minister. That same year he also took possession of the Afghan stronghold of Chunar, which had always maintained a defiant stand towards Humayun.

In 1562 CE, Akbar married the daughter of the Rajput Raja Bharmal of Amber, which heralded the beginning of a long and firm relationship between the Mughals and the Rajputs. In the middle of 1562 CE, Atgah Khan was murdered by Maham Anaga's clique, which angered Akbar to such as extent that he found it a valid reason to extricate himself completely from the influence of Maham Anaga, her son Adham Khan, and various ambitious courtiers of that same clique. Atgah Khan was succeeded by Munim Khan as the next prime minister.

PUNISHMENT OF ADHAM KHAN, *from the Akbarnama, 1590-95. A series of images in a single painting—Akbar first emerging from his private quarters with a sword in his hand, Adham Khan being thrown down at two different places from the walls of Akbar's palace within Agra Fort, Agra. People shown running away after the incident.*

Akbar now devoted himself entirely to the task of expanding his empire; and the state policies shaped by him were implemented by his ministers under his instructions. After assuming independent power, Akbar first inflicted a crushing defeat on Baz Bahadur and occupied Malwa in early 1564 CE. In this venture, he was assisted by Abdullah Khan Uzbek, one of his trusted officers.

Abdullah Khan Uzbek along with other Uzbek nobles, however, revolted against Akbar (July 1564 CE), but they were soon forced to retire to Gujarat when Akbar waged a war against them. From Gujarat Abdullah Khan went on to Jaunpur, where he was joined by another Uzbek chief, Khan Zaman or Ali Quli Khan who had served in the Second Battle of Panipat. Thereafter, many Uzbeks joined the movement against Akbar, feeling that the emperor was partial towards Persians. The Mughal forces sent against Khan Zaman were defeated in 1565 CE; and thereupon Akbar himself led the battle in which Khan Zaman was killed and Bahadur Khan, his brother, was taken prisoner and executed.

Akbar then went on to subdue Gondwana, before beginning his campaign against the Rajput princes. Rajputana occupied a prominent place in Akbar's consolidation scheme, for he realized that without establishing his suzerainty over it, he could not lay claim to his sovereignty over northern India. Another factor that made Rajputana covetable was its proximity to neighbouring Gujarat, which enjoyed active commercial relations with kingdoms of western Asia and Europe. Almost all the Rajput princes accepted Akbar's suzerainty, except for Mewar. In 1567 CE, Akbar invaded Chittor, the capital of Mewar and by early 1568 CE, the Chittor fort was captured by him. Though Chittor was made a district within the Mughal domains by appointing Asaf Khan as its governor, the western half of Mewar remained in the possession of Rana Udai Singh.

After the death of Rana Udai Singh, his son, Rana Pratap, ascended the throne. Rana Pratap valiantly continued to fight the Mughals from taking over Chittor for the rest of his life, never accepting Akbar as the ruler of India. Akbar, for his part, tried in vain to win over the Rana with diplomacy. Rana Pratap maintained that he had no intention to fight Akbar, but could not bow down and accept him as the sovereign either. Eventually Akbar went on to defeat Rana Pratap in the famous Battle of Haldighatti in 1576 CE, conquering a large part of the kingdom of Mewar, yet the Rana did not submit and continued his struggle for the liberation of his homeland until his death in 1597 CE. In contrast, the other Rajput rulers of Bikaner, Jaisalmer, Kalinjar, Ranthambhor and Amber not only submitted before the Mughal emperor, but also gave their daughters in marriage to him. Thus, almost all of Rajputana was brought under Akbar's suzerainty either through war or through diplomacy. During this period Akbar also abolished the pilgrimage tax (1563 CE) and the *jiziya* (1564 CE) imposed on non-Muslims, gaining the faith and respect of his Hindu subjects.

After subduing the Rajput rulers, Akbar's next mission was the conquest of Gujarat and Bengal—regions that connected the subcontinent with the trading world of Asia, Africa and Europe. Apart from being an important centre of trade, Gujarat had also become a refuge for rebelling Mughal nobles. After conquering Gujarat in his second attempt in 1573 CE, Akbar celebrated his victory by constructing the *Buland Darwaza*, a lofty victory gate, at his new capital of Fatehpur Sikri. Having conquered Gujarat, the Mughal Empire's frontiers now stretched to the western coast of India. In Bengal and Bihar, however, the Afghans under Daud Karrani still posed a serious threat, but by 1576 CE, Akbar occupied Bihar and Bengal, adding the eastern coast to his empire too.

After consolidating the coastal areas, the northern frontiers of Kashmir, Sind and Qandahar were also annexed to the Mughal Empire. Kabul, Qandahar and Ghazni constituted strategically important regions, since they linked India through overland trade with central and west Asia, from where horses could be secured for the Mughal cavalry. After Mirza Hakim's death, Akbar brought Kabul under his direct control, which also helped avert an Uzbek threat simmering in the region. To make a public spectacle of his military strength, Akbar paraded his mighty Mughal army through Kashmir, Baluchistan, Sind and the tribal districts of the northwestern frontier. The last center to be

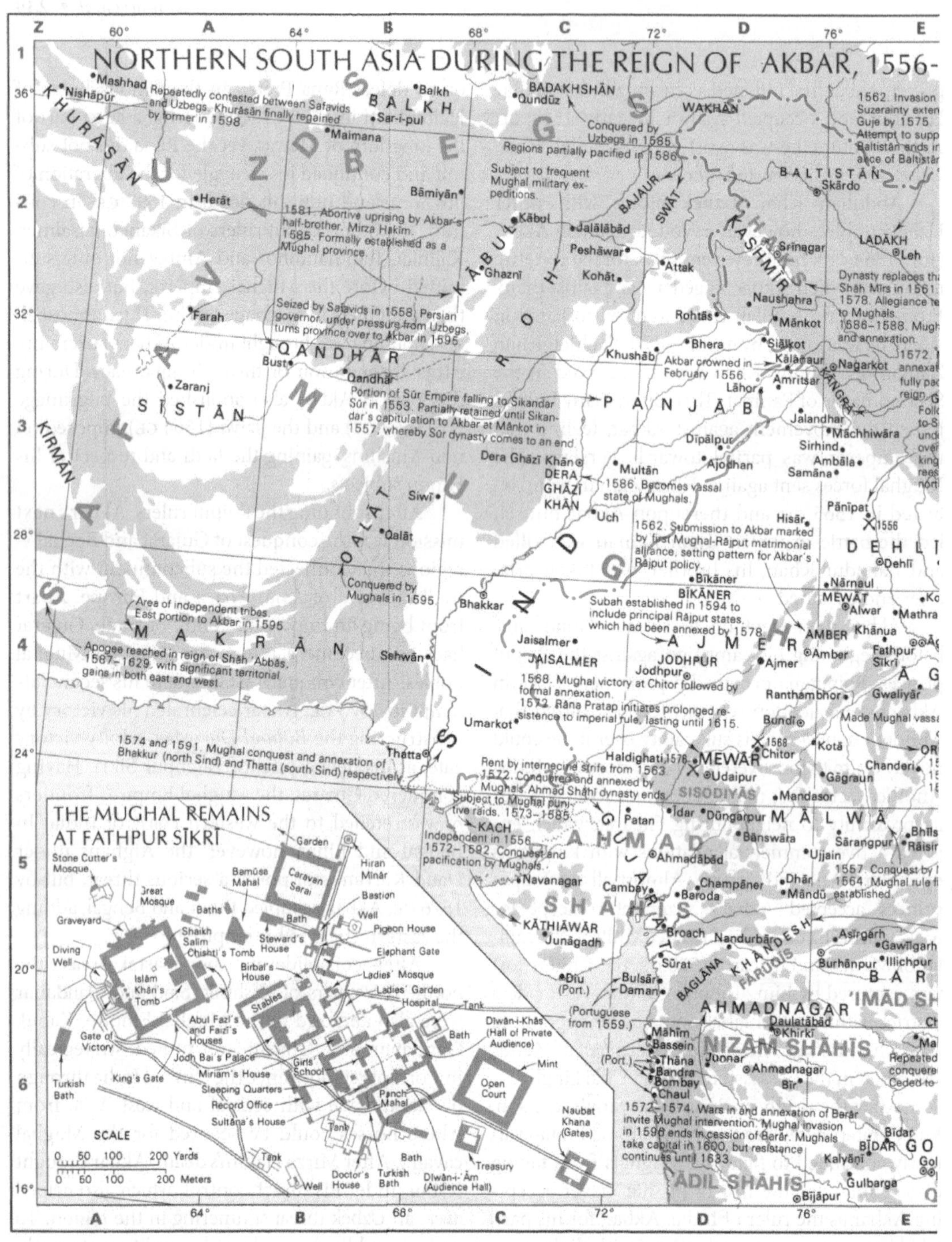

Map 19-1 *Northern South Asia During the Reign of Akbar, 1556–1605 CE; Mughal Expansion Under Akbar, 1556–1605 CE*
Inset: *The Mughal Remains at Fatehpur Sikri*

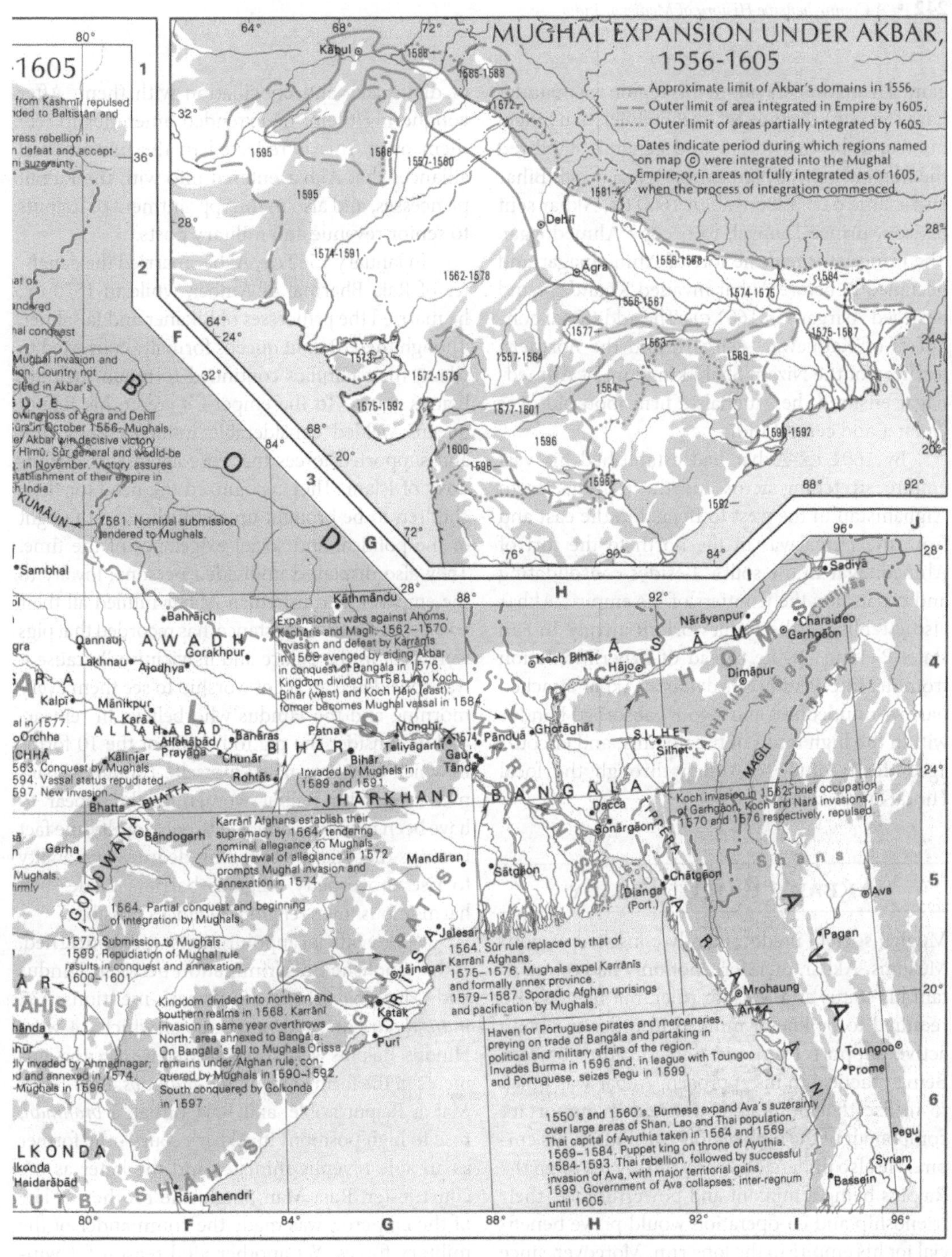

MUGHAL EXPANSION UNDER AKBAR, 1556-1605
Approximate limit of Akbar's domains in 1556.
Outer limit of area integrated in Empire by 1605.
Outer limit of areas partially integrated by 1605.
Dates indicate period during which regions named on map © were integrated into the Mughal Empire, or, in areas not fully integrated as of 1605, when the process of integration commenced.
Kābul
Dehlī
Āgra
-1605
from Kashmīr repulsed
nded to Baltistān and
press rebellion in
n defeat and accept-
ni suzerainty
Mughal invasion and
ion. Country not
cised in Akbar's
owing loss of Āgra and Dehlī
ūrs in October 1556, Mughals,
er Akbar win decisive victory
r Hīmū, Sūr general and would-be
, in November. Victory assures
stablishment of their empire in
th India.
KUMĀUN
1561. Nominal submission tendered to Mughals.
Sambhal
Kāthmāndu
Bahrāich
AWADH
Qannauj
Lakhnau
Gorakhpur
Ajodhya
Kalpi
Mānikpur
Karā
ALLAHĀBĀD
Allahābād/Prayāga
Banāras
Chunār
Orchha
Kālinjar
1563. Conquest by Mughals.
1594. Vassal status repudiated.
1597. New invasion.
Rohtās
Patna
BIHĀR
Bihār
Monghir
Teliyāgarhi
Invaded by Mughals in 1589 and 1591
JHĀRKHAND
Bhatta
BHATTA
Bāndogarh
GONDWĀNA
Garha
Karrānī Afghans establish their supremacy by 1564, tendering nominal allegiance to Mughals. Withdrawal of allegiance in 1572 prompts Mughal invasion and annexation in 1574.
1564. Partial conquest and beginning of integration by Mughals.
1577. Submission to Mughals.
1599. Repudiation of Mughal rule results in conquest and annexation.
1600-1601.
Kingdom divided into northern and southern realms in 1568. Karrānī invasion in same year overthrows North; area annexed to Bangāla. On Bangāla's fall to Mughals Orissa remains under Afghan rule; conquered by Mughals in 1590-1592. South conquered by Golkonda in 1597.
dly invaded by Ahmadnagar;
d and annexed in 1574.
Mughals in 1596.
Mandāran
Jalesar
Jājnagar
Katak
Purī
ORISSA
GAJAPATIS
Rājamahendri
Haidarābād
Expansionist wars against Ahoms, Kachāris and Magli, 1562-1570. Invasion and defeat by Karrānīs in 1568 avenged by aiding Akbar in conquest of Bangāla in 1576. Kingdom divided in 1581 into Koch Bihār (west) and Koch Hājo (east); former becomes Mughal vassal in 1584.
Koch Bihār
Hājo
Ghorāghāt
Pānduā
Gaur
Tāndā
BANGĀLA
KARRĀNĪS
SILHET
Silhet
Dacca
Sonārgāon
Sātgāon
TIPPERA
Chātgāon
Dianga (Port.)
Nārāyanpur
Sadiyā
Charaideo
Garhgāon
Dimāpur
ĀSĀM
AHOMS
KACHĀRIS
Nāgas
NARAS
MAGLI
Chutiyās
Koch invasion in 1562; brief occupation of Garhgāon. Koch and Nara invasions, in 1570 and 1576 respectively, repulsed
Shans
Ava
Pagan
1564. Sūr rule replaced by that of Karrānī Afghans.
1575-1576. Mughals expel Karrānīs and formally annex province.
1579-1587. Sporadic Afghan uprisings and pacification by Mughals.
Haven for Portuguese pirates and mercenaries, preying on trade of Bangāla and partaking in political and military affairs of the region. Invades Burma in 1596 and, in league with Toungoo and Portuguese, seizes Pegu in 1599.
Mrohaung
Arakan
ARAKAN
AVA
Toungoo
Prome
1550's and 1560's. Burmese expand Ava's suzerainty over large areas of Shan, Lao and Thai population. Thai capital of Ayuthia taken in 1564 and 1569. 1569-1584. Puppet king on throne of Ayuthia. 1584-1593. Thai rebellion, followed by successful invasion of Ava, with major territorial gains. 1599. Government of Ava collapses: inter-regnum until 1605.
Pegu
Syriam
Bassein

gained from the Safavids in this region was Qandahar (1595 CE). To the east, meanwhile, Man Singh, his Rajput brother-in-law and general, stabilized the Mughal gains by annexing Orissa, Koch Bihar and a large part of Bengal. In 1600 CE, Akbar sent his son, prince Daniyal, to occupy Ahmednagar. The prince stormed the fort of Ahmednagar and occupied it, before Akbar invaded Khandesh and besieged Asirgarh in 1601 CE. The additional conquests of Kathiawar, Asirgarh and the northern territory of the Nizam Shahi kingdom of Ahmednagar ensured the Mughals a firm foothold over Gujarat and central India.

By 1601 CE Akbar had established his vast empire stretching across northern India, from Afghanistan in the west to Bengal in the east and from the Himalayas in the north to the fort of Ahmednagar in the south. Besides consolidating and expanding the frontiers of his empire, Akbar also established the framework of a truly Indian state. Picking up the thread of experimentation from the intervening Sur dynasty, Akbar attacked narrow-mindedness and bigotry, absorbed Hindus within the high ranks of the nobility, and encouraged the tradition of ruling through the local Hindu landed elites.

Akbar's Rajput Policy

Mughal society predominantly consisted of non-Muslims. Akbar, therefore, not only had to maintain his status as a Muslim ruler, but he was also required to be liberal-minded in order to obtain active support from his non-Muslim subjects. Being practical in his approach, Akbar was quick to realize that the Rajputs formed an important component of the bulk of non-Muslims in his empire. He also understood early during his reign the Rajputs being a militant and powerful race, their friendship and co-operation would prove beneficial for his empire in the long run. Moreover, since the Rajputs were not dependent on Mughal privileges, Akbar opted to follow a far-sighted policy of diplomacy and conciliation with them. After conquering them, he extended amenities to win them over. This is reflected in the matrimonial alliances that Akbar entered into with the Rajput princesses, and also in the appointment of Rajputs to senior revenue and military posts.

In January 1562 CE, Akbar married the daughter of Raja Bharmal of Amber, while in 1570 CE, he married the princesses of Bikaner and Jaisalmer. Though these Rajput queens formally converted to Islam, their families continued to retain their religious status. To the emperor's credit, his Rajput queens welded considerable influence over him and supported forces that rose against the orthodoxy of Islam. They recognized the need for their children to be brought up as Muslims in the light of the political and social exigencies of the time. They also displayed undivided personal loyalty to the emperor, and in return Akbar fulfiled all their wishes. Badauni, for instance, has recorded that pigs were kept in the palace and its vicinity, 'because it was considered an act of worship to see them every morning and the Hindus who believe in reincarnation consider the pig to be one of the 10 forms in which God incarnated himself'. Though Akbar's marriages with Rajput women might appear to have been merely conducted to gain loyalty, the fact remains that Akbar's broadmindedness and ability to rise above petty religious barriers made such harmonious inter-religious alliances possible.

Where official appointments were concerned, Akbar abolished discrimination between Hindus and Muslims. The *Ain-i-Akbari* mentions 137 *mansabdars* of 1000 rank, out of which 14 were Hindus. Rajputs were also bestowed with key assignments in the form of *jagirs* and *mansabs*. Raja Todar Mal, a Rajput noble, and Raja Birbal, a *brahman,* rose to high positions in Akbar's court—the former as an able revenue minister and the latter as the court jester. Raja Man Singh, the brother-in-law of the emperor, was made the commander of the military forces. Yet another vital reason for winning over the Rajputs was to exploit their militant nature to combat the Afghans.

Akbar's close association with the Rajputs and the loyal involvement of the Rajputs with the Mughal court not only stirred Akbar's imperial ambitions but also further broadened his vision and liberal outlook. A friendly Rajputana was indispensable for the creation and consolidation of an empire with a pan-Indian presence, because the major routes to Gujarat, Malwa, Sind and the Deccan passed through Rajputana and any Rajput hostility would have hampered the Mughals from conquering and controlling the rest of the subcontinent too. He therefore initiated a policy to integrate the Rajput *ranas* or chieftains and their territories in such a way that they accepted Mughal suzerainty, while retaining their individuality within their territories which became autonomous states within the Mughal empire.

Akbar's Religious Policy

The liberal and humanitarian principles propagated by the Sufis and preachers of the Bhakti cult had their impact on the religious views of Akbar. Being liberal by nature, he became an enlightened ruler who granted religious freedom to all communities and never discriminated among his subjects on the basis of religion. He realized that it was the Hindus who formed the bulk of the population in India, and that he could never establish a united and strong empire without their cooperation. In order to win the goodwill of the Hindus he abolished the pilgrimage tax in 1563 CE, which the Hindus had to pay to visit Hindu pilgrimage sites. Next year, he put an end to the much hated *jiziya* which all the non-Muslims living in the empire had to pay. This was a very wise step enforced by the emperor to bring unity in his empire, especially for the feeling of inclusiveness that it brought to the Hindus. The *jiziya* had always been looked upon as an insult and had been resented bitterly; its abolition helped Akbar considerably in gaining the support and loyalty of his non-Islamic subjects, especially the Rajputs who had fought consistently against the sultans of the Delhi Sultanate for more than 350 years. They now became staunch supporters of the Mughal Empire.

LORD KRISHNA IN THE GOLDEN CITY, *from the* Harivamsha *(Geneology of Vishnu, a section appended to the* Razmnama*). Akbar had translations made of major Hindu texts, including the Sanskrit epic the* Mahabharata, *known in its Persian translation as* Razmnama. *The mythical city of Dwarka is shown where Krishna is enthroned on a golden palace. (Smithsonian Institute, Freer Sackler Gallery)*

The liberal views of Akbar resulted in the formulation of a new religious policy. Although Akbar was born and brought up as a Sunni Muslim, his mother, Hamida Banu, was a Shia as was his guardian, Bairam Khan. His early tutor, Abdul Latif, too was a man of very liberal views. It was under his influence that Akbar developed the ideas of universal love and toleration. Being unorthodox in his religious approach, Akbar accorded permission to build several temples and churches in his empire. While new temples were built at Brindavan and Banaras, Jain temples at Satrujaya and Ujjain, old temples were also reconstructed at Kangra, Thaneswar and Batala. The Christians too built churches at Agra, Lahore, Kambath and Thatta. A translation bureau was also established for translating Hindu religious texts into Persian. In 1562 CE, Akbar issued a *farman* abolishing the custom of enslaving prisoners of war, who were converted to Islam. People were given the freedom to follow the religion of their choice. Persecution of Hindus and conversions to Islam became less frequent. And a close association was established between Akbar and the Rajputs.

Sheikh Mubarak and his two sons, Abul Fazl and Faizi who were the emperor's chief advisers, also held liberal views; and under their influence many new regulations were enforced in Akbar's empire. Vincent Smith is of the view that it is not possible to ascertain the chronological order of all the minor regulations that were issued since most were not even recorded; but he does give us a list of the regulations that were issued—such as no child was to be named Muhammad and if he had already been named thus, it had to be changed. New mosques were not to be built and neither old ones repaired. Cow slaughter was prohibited and abstinence from meat for a hundred days in a year was to be followed; preparations were made for the appearance of a *Mahdi* or Saviour; beards were to be shaved; and certain food items like garlic, onions and beef were prohibited. *Sijdah* or prostration due only to God was now to be performed before the king; people were allowed to dress flashily while offering prayers; *namaz, roza* and *hajj* were no longer compulsory. Arabic language suffered a setback. A *farman* was issued forbidding *sati*. The emperor initiated the practice of *Jharokadarshan* according to which the emperor appeared before a public audience every morning for a brief while. This practice was in keeping with the norms of Hinduism. The ceremonies of honouring the emperor by bowing (*Kurnish* and *Taslim*) were also introduced. Although due to opposition from the orthodox section this was stopped in the open court, it continued in private chambers. The Hindu practice of *Tuladan* or weighing the emperor against gold and silver was also adopted by Akbar, the contents of which were distributed equally among his subjects.

Through these new regulations, Akbar secularized the existing system by according due importance to different faiths. At the same time, he succeeded in undermining the role of the *ulema* which was essential for the establishment of a centralized state.

Akbar's intensely inquisitive mind desired to attain the truth behind all religions. In January 1575 CE, the *Ibadath Khana*, the famous 'House of Worship' was constructed at Fatehpur Sikri with the purpose of bringing together men of learning, mystics and nobles from various religions—Hinduism, Jainism, Buddhism, Islam, Zoroastrianism, and Christianity—to explain their core beliefs. These learned men assembled in the *Ibadath Khana* every Thursday evening to discuss the tenets of their religions. Although constructed mainly for religious discussions, the *Ibadath Khana* was more of a platform where Akbar felt he could psychologically defeat the *ulema* by exposing them to the deliberations of other religions, thereby making them realize that their intellect or power was not the only one.

The discussions in the *Ibadath Khana* brought to light the positive aspects of every religion, including the belief that a common religion could be founded on the basis of all these positives. A comparative study of religions convinced Akbar that there was truth in all of them, but that none of them possessed the absolute truth. In order to promulgate a new religion, Akbar played a masterstroke by enacting the *Mahzar* or Infallibility Decree, which accorded him a semi-divine status. By declaring himself as the chief religious arbitrator he assumed powers that hitherto did not exist within his position. It also made him superior

The Arrival of H.M.* at the Capital and Building of a House of Worship

H.M. had in the course of seven months done the work of many years in conquering new countries, administering the old, in favouring the sincere and serviceable, and overthrowing the ungrateful, in extending justice, in general benevolence, and in advancing the science of worship. On the day of Ardibihisht (18 January 1575) 3 Bahman, Divine month, he illuminated Fatehpur by his presence.

Quatrain.

What ray is it that fortune sheds upon the earth?
What commotion is it that dominion casts into the sky?
Is it the dust of the cortège or the breeze of success
Which sends a fragrance of peace and repose to the nostrils of my soul?

The degrees of sovereignty and the stages of world conquest, which are based upon increase of wisdom, and on perception, went on augmenting, and that which is apt to become in mortals, whether in former or in present times, a source of insouciance, only increased his circumspection. Although Almighty God raised the pure-dispositioned one to lofty heights, *viz.*, to increased territory, abundance of devotees, the overthrow of enemies, the gaining possession of the wonders of the world, and the opening of the doors of knowledge, and lofty perception, yet this suppliant of Deity increased his supplications, and the thirst for inquiry augmented.

At this time when the capital (Fatehpur Sikri) was illuminated by his glorious advent, H.M. ordered that a house of worship ('Ibadatkhana) should be built in order to the adornment of the spiritual kingdom, and that it should have four verandahs (aiwan). Though the Divine bounty always has an open door and searches for the fit person, and the inquirer, yet as the lord of the universe, from his general benevolence, conducts his measures according to the rules of the superficial, he chose the eve of Friday, which bears on its face the colouring (*ghaza*) of the announcement of auspiciousness, for the out-pouring (*ifazat*). A general proclamation was issued that, on that night of illumination, all orders and sects of mankind—those who searched after spiritual and physical truth, and those of the common public who sought for an awakening, and the inquirers of every sect—should assemble in the precincts of the holy edifice, and bring forward their spiritual experiences, and their degrees of knowledge of the truth in various and contradictory forms in the bridal chamber of manifestation.

Wisdom and deeds would be tested, and the essence of manhood would be exhibited. Those who were founded on truth entered the hall of acceptance, while those who were only veneered with gold went hastily to the pit of base metal. There was a feast of theology and worship. The vogue of creature-worship was reduced. The dust-stained ones of the pit of contempt became adorners of dominion, and the smooth-tongued, empty-headed rhetoricians lost their rank. To the delightful precincts of that mansion founded upon Truth, thousands upon thousands of inquirers from the seven climes came with heartfelt respect and waited for the advent of the Shahinshah. The world's lord would, with open brow, a cheerful countenance, a capacious heart

*His Majesty

(Continued)

(Continued)

and an understanding soul, pour the limpid waters of graciousness on those thirsty-lipped ones of expectation's desert, and act as a refiner. He put them into currency, sect by sect, and tested them company by company. He got hold of every one of the miserable and dust-stained ones, and made them successful in their desires,—to say nothing of the be-cloaked and the be-turbaned. From that general assemblage H.M. selected by his far-reaching eye a chosen hand from each class, and established a feast of truth. Occasionally he, in order to instruct the courtiers, sent perspicuous servants who could discriminate among men, and these reflective and keen-sighted men brought every description of person to perform the *kornish*. Then that cambist and tester of worth examined them anew and invited some of them. There were always four noble sections in that spiritual and temporal assemblage. In the eastern chamber of worship (*'Ibadat-kada*) were the great leaders and high officers who were conspicuous, in the courts of society, for enlightenment. In the southern compartment the keen-sighted investigators, both those who gathered the light of day (*i.e.* the Illuminati) and those who chose the repose of the night-halls of contemplation, sate in the school of instruction. In the western compartment those of lofty lineage practiced auspicious arts. In the northern compartment were the Ṣufis of clear heart who were absorbed in beatific visions. A few of felicitous and wide comprehensiveness which they had attained to by the bliss of H.M.'s holy instructions lighted the torch of knowledge in all four compartments. Lofty points and subtle words passed from the holy lips, and physical and Divine truths trickled from that soothsayer of the court of variety, so that the leaders of the arena of manifestation, and the swift coursers on the mountains of contemplation burned with shame.

Source: Collection of Oriental Works, New Series No. 910, *The Akbarnama* of Abul Fazl, Chapter XXI, Translated from The Persian by H. Beveridge, I.C.S., Retired, Asiatic Society: 57, Park Street, Calcutta (1897–1939). Available at Persian Literature in Translation: The Packard Humanities Institute.

to the *ulema* who were already waning with the number of limitations imposed upon them.

In 1579 CE, Sheikh Mubarak was given the task of drawing up the *Mahzar*, which while being in conformity with Islamic legal thinking did not give unlimited authority to Akbar, did proclaim him as the *Badshah-i-Islam* and gave him the right to arbitrate on any controversial religious matter related to Islam. Abul Fazl was aware of the narrow role that the *Mahzar* had originally defined for Akbar and the role that he was later to assume. For this reason alone Abul Fazl is said to have omitted the draft of the *Mahzar* from the *Akbarnama*, although his own father had prepared it. He only gave a summary of it and purposely left out the word *Badshah* or King of Islam, thus claiming a wider role for the emperor over all religions and creeds. Though the *Mahzar* did not make Akbar infallible, it did give that power to Akbar, which had hitherto been the special privilege of the *ulema*. The emperor had by then also undertaken a number of severe measures to reform the administration of religious grants, which were now available to learned and pious men of all religions, not just Islam.

The logical outcome of the *Mahzar* was the promulgation of a new religious philosophy called the *Din-i-Illahi* (1582 CE). Akbar's *Din-i-Illahi* or the divine faith brought followers of different religious creeds under one banner. He freely borrowed from Hinduism, Islam, Jainism, Christianity and other religions for the formulation of this new religion, which was a combination of mysticism, philosophy and nature-worship. It upheld no dogma, and recognized neither creeds nor prophets. The essential points of the *Din-i-Illahi* were faith in one God and the recognition of the emperor as his representative on earth. He asked the followers of this new order to sacrifice property, life, honour and religion in the service of the emperor. The member of the Divine Faith greeted each other with the words *Allah ho Akbar* and *Jalla-Jallalhu*. They were asked to abstain from meat on certain days, and worship was regulated by the sun, while fire and light were used as symbols of divine power.

Akbar's *Din-i-Illahi* was an intellectualized philosophy understood only by his close associates and himself, and was beyond the grasp of the common man. Though the word *Din* means religion, *Din-i-Illahi* was not a religion, nor was it intended to be one. It had no scriptures, no priests, no temples, no ceremonies and no prescribed form of prayers and no place for offering it—although its members had to pray thrice a day at sunrise, noon and sunset. The one and only religious belief for them was the belief in the unity of God. 'Of the nearly 500 courtiers of the front rank, only 18 chose to enter what Faizi calls "the new *Kaaba* built by Akbar with stones from *Sinai* and other holy places".' They were Abul Fazl, Faizi, Sheikh Mubarak, Jafar Beg, Asaf Khan, Qasim-i-Kali (a poet), Abul Samad (a poet and painter) Aziz Khan Koka, Mulla Shah Muhammad (a historian), Sufi Ahmed Qadr Jahan (a lawyer) and his two sons, Mir Sharif of Amul, Sultan Khwajah, Mirza Jani Taqi of Shustar (a poet), Sheikh Zada Gosalah of Banaras and Raja Birbal.

When the new faith was to be spread, Akbar did not act as a missionary, always refraining from using force or compulsion for conversions. Neither did he offer temptations of honour or reward to induce men to give up their faith and embrace the *Din-i-Illahi*. There were not very many followers of the *Din-i-Illahi*, among whom Birbal was the only Hindu. The *Din-i-Illahi* was merely a political experiment for achieving unity and bringing about stability in the empire. The new faith, therefore, did not become popular among the masses and slowly died with the death of Akbar.

Akbar's liberalism and unorthodoxy, even led some to try and influence him into accepting religions other than Islam. The Jesuit fathers, for example, tried to convert him to Christianity. Some ambitious nobles also tried to gain support by praising him as not only a great monarch, but also a spiritual leader with mystic attainments, religious insight and superior wisdom.

EMPEROR AKBAR HOLDS A RELIGIOUS ASSEMBLY IN THE *IBADAT KHANA* IN FATEHPUR SIKRI.
The two men dressed in black are the Jesuit missionaries Rodolfo Acquaviva and Francisco Henriques. Illustration in the Akbarnama, miniature painting by Nar Singh, 1605 CE.

The main consequence of Akbar's religious policy was the ideal of *Sulh-i-kul* or peace with all. He had learnt this philosophy in his childhood from his tutor and it had impressed his heart. Therefore, later as an emperor, he wanted to establish unity and peace, which he felt would be easier, if everyone followed the same religion. The concept of *Sulh-i-kul* was hence Akbar's religious motto. To achieve this, Akbar systematically initiated various experiments in the form of the construction of the *Ibadath Khana,* drafting the *Mahzar,* promulgating the *Din-i-Illahi* and so on. Through all these tasks he delegated to himself the powers to interpret various Islamic norms, which had been too frequently used by the *ulema* to scuttle the processes of Indianization of state institutions. Although the *ulema* did express their hostility towards these measures, the significant achievement of these efforts points to a Mughal state that succeeded in establishing a vast centralized empire in India with regional participation.

SUMMARY

- Akbar is ranked among the greatest rulers in Indian history.
- After Humayun's death, Akbar was proclaimed king by Bairam Khan, a dominant member of Humayun's nobility, who also assumed the role of regent for the young prince.
- Akbar occupied the Mughal throne under adverse circumstances, which he faced boldly with the help of Bairam Khan, and succeeded in establishing a vast and long-lasting empire in India.
- Within a few months of Akbar's enthronement, he faced Hemu in the Second Battle of Panipat (1556 CE), which resulted in the re-establishment of Mughal rule in India.
- Mughal armies occupied Lahore, Multan, Ajmer, Gwalior and Jaunpur for Akbar.
- After the death of Bairam Khan, Akbar came under the influence of Maham Anaga, his foster-mother who dominated both his personal life and political decisions for a year. After which, he extricated himself from the influence of Maham Anaga and devoted himself to the task of expanding his empire.
- Akbar first inflicted a crushing defeat on Baz Bahadur and occupied Malwa, he then suppressed the Uzbek nobles and Gondwana, before beginning his campaign against the Rajput princes.
- Rajputana occupied a prominent place in Akbar's scheme of conquest; without establishing his suzerainty over that region, he could not claim to be the sovereign of northern India.
- Almost all the Rajput princes accepted Akbar's suzerainty, except for Mewar. Rana Pratap never accepted Akbar as the ruler of India, and fought him all his life. Akbar defeated Rana Pratap in the famous Battle of Haldighatti (1576 CE), and conquered a large part of the kingdom of Mewar, yet the Rana never submitted to the emperor and continued his struggle for the liberation of his homeland until his death.
- Akbar annexed Gujarat, Bengal, Bihar, Kashmir, Sind, Qandahar, Ahmednagar, Khandesh and Asirgarh—thereby establishing a vast empire.
- Akbar was quick to realize that the Rajputs were a militant and powerful race, whose friendship and co-operation would be useful for ruling his empire with greater strength.
- He entered into matrimonial alliances with the Rajput princesses and appointed Rajputs to senior revenue and military posts. He married the princesses of Amber, Bikaner and Jaisalmer. Raja Todar Mal, Raja Birbal and Raja Man Singh rose to high positions under him.
- Being liberal by nature, he adopted an open-minded attitude towards all religions. He gave religious freedom to all communities and did not accept any discrimination of his subjects on the basis of religion.
- Sheikh Mubarak and his two sons, Abul Fazl and Faizi who were the emperor's chief advisers, held liberal views too; and under their influence many new regulations were imposed by Akbar in the empire.
- Through these new regulations, Akbar secularized the existing system by giving due importance to different faiths. At the same time, he also succeeded in undermining the role of the *ulema* which was essential for the establishment of a centralized empire.
- The *Ibadath Khana* was constructed by Akbar at Fatehpur Sikri with the purpose of bringing together men of learning, mystics and nobles from various religions.

- The discussions in the *Ibadath Khana* brought to light the positive aspects of every religion and the realization that a common religion could be founded on the basis of all these positive aspects.
- In order to promulgate a new religion, Akbar played a masterstroke by enacting the *Mahzar* or Infallibility Decree which accorded him a semi-divine status. By declaring himself as the chief arbitrator of religion he assumed powers that hitherto did not exist with him.
- The logical outcome of the *Mahzar* was the promulgation of a new religion called the *Din-i-Illahi* in 1582 CE, which brought followers of different faiths and religious creeds under one banner.
- The main consequence of Akbar's religious policy was the ideal of *Sulh-i-kul* or peace with all, which was also his religious motto.

KEYWORDS

Clique
Farman
Jharokadarshan
Tuladan
Kurnish and Taslim
Sulh-i-kul
Ibadath Khana
Mahzar
Din-i-Illahi

REVIEW QUESTIONS

1. What were the difficulties faced by Akbar on his accession to the throne?
2. What is the significance of the Second Battle of Panipat in Indian history?
3. Explain the conflict between Akbar and the kingdom of Mewar.
4. Examine the policy adopted by Akbar towards the Rajputs.
5. What were the essential features of Akbar's Din-i-Illahi?

CHAPTER 20

Jahangir and Shah Jahan

Review and Discussion

- Jahangir
- Shah Jahan
- The War of Succession

Even after the death of Akbar, the Mughal Empire's journey of conquests and territorial expansion continued as a result of the administrative policies initiated during Akbar's reign. In additon to this was the striking increase in the number of Mughal nobles and *mansabdars*, whose resources and responsibilities amplified likewise. This gradually began to forge a critical relationship between the rulers and the nobility. In the light of these developments the Mughal state needed to tighten its control over the local socio-economic environment. To regularize and institutionalize the state's structure, the imperial authorities adopted centralizing measures that imposed increasing demands upon both the Mughal officials and the local chiefs, resulting in tensions, which were through various forms of resistance. Hence, in the seventeenth century, the reigns of Jahangir and Shah Jahan, comprise a period when attempts were being made to consolidate and continue with the gains and achievements of Akbar's reign. The period became noteworthy for political stability, brisk economic activity and artistic excellence.

The widespread political unification and establishment of law and order facilitated the growth of large centers of commerce, and arts and crafts in various parts of the empire. Extensive foreign trade and flamboyant elitist lifestyles had heightened the demand for luxury products. Commercial enterprise had put cities, such as Lahore, Delhi, Agra and Ahmedabad on the world map. The streamlining of the taxation system had expanded both the cash nexus and commodity production, which, in turn, promoted a network of grain markets (*mandis*), bazaars and small, peripheral townships (*qasbahs*). The period witnessed an increasing use of bills of exchange (*hundis*), direct participation of Mughal nobles in trade, huge shipping fleets owned by the emperor, and funds being advanced by governors to merchants from state treasuries. This patronage of commerce owed a good deal to the growing Persian influence in the Mughal court, especially with the Persians coming from a long tradition of the state supporting trade and commercial activities.

JAHANGIR (1605–27 CE)

Following Akbar's death in 1605 CE, his son, Salim, ascended the throne under the title of Nuruddin Jahangir. Prince Salim was born in 1569 CE to

Akbar's Rajput queen, the daughter of Raja Bharmal of Amber. Salim received his early education in all the popular literary languages of the times—Persian, Turkish, Arabic and Hindi. From a young age he exhibited an aptitude for arithmetic, history, geography and the general sciences. Prince Salim was also fond of music and the fine arts; he is said to have composed verses in Persian and songs in Hindi. The young prince took a keen interest in horse riding, hunting and swordsmanship, later growing up to be a fine warrior worthy of his stature. Although fond of the pleasures of courtly life, Jahangir was not devoid of the fine qualities which his great father possessed. He too harboured considerable regard for the sentiments of his Hindu subjects. Though he did not modify the policies further (perhaps wisely), Jahangir maintained his illustrious father's system of administration. His reign of about 22 years was, therefore, one of continuity and stability, with hardly any change of policy since Akbar's rule.

Prince Khusrau's Revolt

Within barely five months of Jahangir's accession to the throne, his eldest son, Prince Khusrau, revolted against him. The prince was backed by many influential supporters, but Jahangir's army marched against Khusrau, defeated his forces at Lahore and captured him along with his chief followers, including the Sikh guru, Arjun Dev. When Khusrau was brought before the emperor in chains, he was promptly imprisoned and his followers cruelly put to death. For his complicity in the revolt, even Guru Arjun Dev was not spared—he was asked to pay a heavy fine of two lakh rupees. Upon his refusal to meet the terms set by royal decree, he was tortured to death. It was the Guru's execution that was to permanently estrange the Sikhs from the Mughals. Following Prince Khusrau's rebellion, there arose a few more uprisings that were easily suppressed.

The Loss of Qandahar

Taking advantage of the unrest in the Mughal capital, Shah Abbas I of Persia besieged the fort of Qandahar in 1606 CE, but was forced to quickly abandon his attack when Jahangir sent an army against him. Sixteen years later when Shah Abbas attacked Qandahar once again in 1622 CE,

JAHANGIR'S DREAM, 1618-22 CE. *Painting by Abul Hassan. Jahangir, on the right, hugs Shah Abbas, the Safavid ruler of the Persian Empire. They are shown standing on the top of the world, on the backs of a lion and a lamb representing peace and harmony. The suggestion is that that the two rulers are at peace with one another. The submissive posture of Shah Abbas also suggests that Jahangir is in charge—which was not the case. (Freer Gallery of Art, Smithsonian Institution).*

the emperor's third son, Prince Khurram, was deputed to tackle the situation. Being in a rebellious mood against his father himself, the prince did not take the campaign seriously, eventually leading to the siege of the fortress. When Shah Abbas justified his Qandahar win as a rightful claim over what belonged to Persia, Jahangir accused him of treachery and sent forces to recover the fortress, but even this was to end in failure. The loss of the Qandahar fortress was a grievous blow to the prestige of the Mughal Empire. The only saving grace was Jahangir's clever strategy of insulating Kabul by inducting the Afghans under Khan Jahan Lodi into the Mughal nobility. This act appealed to the tribesmen in the north western frontiers, whose loyalty Jahangir had successfully gained.

The Conquest of Mewar

During his lifetime, Akbar had been unable to conquer the whole of Mewar because of the stiff resistance from Rana Pratap. Jahangir was, therefore, naturally anxious to conquer the Rajput kingdom for the Mughal empire. To this end he sent numerous expeditions to Mewar, but nothing definite could be achieved. At last, in 1614 CE, Prince Khurram defeated Rana Pratap's son and successor, Rana Amar Singh. Thereafter the Rana and Jahangir entered into negotiations that led the Rana to accept the suzerainty of the Mughal emperor; upon which all territories—including Chittor, which had been seized from the valiant Rana Pratap—were restored to him. The lone clause for the Rana was that Chittor could not be fortified. Apart from this, neither was Rana Amar Singh forced to attend the imperial court (his son was to represent him), nor did he have to enter into any matrimonial alliance with the Mughal royal family. The Rajput rulers of Kangra, Kistwar (in Kashmir), Navanagar and Kutch also accepted the supremacy of the Mughals. As a result of his generous treatment, Jahangir won Rana Amar Singh's friendship and no Rajput prince remained hostile to the Mughal empire in his reign.

Soon after the conquest of Mewar, Jahangir also subjugated the last Afghan domains in eastern Bengal in 1612 CE and Orissa in 1617 CE.

Events in the Deccan

Right from Akbar's reign, attempts were being made to gain Berar and Balaghat in the Deccan for the Mughal Empire. By 1596 CE, Berar was finally conquered, while Ahmednagar accepted Mughal suzerainty. The issue of clearly defined frontiers, however, could not be resolved, and the Mughal attacks continued under Jahangir. When Malik Ambar of Ahmednagar allied with the Adil Shahis of Bijapur, the Mughals were forced to retreat. The Marathas, meanwhile, also emerged as a potent force in the Deccan. Realizing their importance, Jahangir encouraged them to come over to his side in 1615 CE. Thereafter the Mughals gained victories in the Deccan in 1618 and 1620 CE.

Jahangir's Marriage to Nur Jahan

Jahangir's marriage to his Persian wife, Nur Jahan, was one of the most important events of his reign. Originally named Mehrunissa, she was the daughter of Mirza Ghiyas Beg, a Persian adventurer, who had come to India during Akbar's reign in search of employment. After joining the imperial service, he soon rose to a high position. As a young girl, Mehrunissa used to visit the royal palace along with her mother. Prince Salim is said to have fallen in love with her, attracted by her beauty and uncommon grace. Since Akbar was against the alliance, he hastily married her off to the Persian officer, Ali Quli Beg, better known as Sher Afghan. A *jagir* was granted to Sher Afghan in Burdwan (Bengal), and Mehrunissa was shipped right across the country, at a safe distance from the young impressionable prince. After ascending the throne, Jahangir got Sher Afghan murdered in 1607 CE and Mehrunissa was brought back to Agra with her daughter, Ladli Begum. When the emperor proposed to marry her, she initially resisted his offer, till four years later when she consented to the marriage. Jahangir made her his empress, and gave her the title of Nur Mahal or 'light of the palace', which was later modified to Nur Jahan meaning 'light of the world'.

Nur Jahan was a woman of extraordinary talents, and she soon acquired complete control over the emperor. While Jahangir busied himself with a life of luxury and pleasure, Nur Jahan became the real ruler of the country. She began to participate actively in the state's affairs, working hard to master the details of administration. She was ably assisted in all her tasks by her kinsmen, who received rapid promotions to key positions in the administrative hierarchy. Her father, Mirza Ghiyas Beg, and her brothers, Asaf Khan and Itemad Khan, were given high ranks; while the empress and her kith and kin, including Prince Khurram, came to constitute the *Nur Jahan junta*, acquiring the power of the state in their own hands. Prince Khurram (later to become the Emperor Shah Jahan) was the most prominent member of Nur Jahan's coterie who nurtured aspirations to the throne. Her influence on Jahangir and her emergence as the power behind the throne proved to be generally beneficent for the empire, although, in the long run, it did produced some negative results too. Other than utilizing the opportunity to advance the interests of her family, Nur Jahan's name appeared on coins along with that of the emperor, and she began to issue royal *farmans* in her own name. She exercised great influence not only over state policies, but also on the personae of Jahangir. She looked after the emperor with great care and devotion; and it was due to her influence that Jahangir greatly reduced his habits of excessive drinking.

The rising influence of Nur Jahan roused the jealousy of not only the royal family, but also the nobles and generals. After she married her daughter Ladli Begum to Prince Shahriyar, the youngest son of Jahangir, Nur Jahan tried to persuade the emperor to name him as his heir apparent. This drove Prince Khurram to revolt against Jahangir in 1622 CE. After failing to take over Fatehpur Sikri in 1623 CE, Khurram retreated to the Deccan, from there to Bengal, and from Bengal he returned to the Deccan again. The talented Mughal commander, Mahabat Khan, had been deployed against him. After Khurram's plans failed, he submitted to his father in 1626 CE. He was forgiven and appointed governor of Balaghat. Meanwhile, the prince's three-year-long rebellion had caused a considerable loss of men and resources for the Mughals.

Interestingly, the very next year Mahabat Khan revolted too. Nur Jahan had decided to chastise Mahabat Khan for his refusal to take orders from anyone but Jahangir; and to this end she ordered him to go to Bengal, framing charges of disloyalty and disobedience against him. Mahabat Khan proceeded to the Punjab instead, where Jahangir was camping. When Jahangir refused to grant him audience, Mahabat Khan tried to take both the emperor and his empress in custody out of sheer anger; but the emperor deftly dealt with the coup, and Mahabat Khan was overpowered. But these revolts shattered the influence and prestige of the royal couple.

After Jahangir's death in 1627 CE, Nur Jahan tried to secure the throne for her son-in-law, Shahriyar, but her own brother, Asaf Khan, turned against her. Asaf Khan instead supported the cause of Prince Khurram, to whom he had married his daughter, Mumtaz Mahal. He, understandably, raised his own son-in-law to the throne.

Visit of the British Missions

During the reign of Jahangir, representatives of the English East India Company visited the Mughal court and gained valuable privileges. Captain William Hawkins and Sir Thomas Roe, who visited the court of Jahangir, were permitted to establish their own trading stations in India. Hawkins visited in 1608 CE and carried with him a letter from James I for the Mughal emperor. He was well received by Jahangir; and lived at the Mughal court from 1608–11 CE, enjoying the royal hospitality. Hawkins, in his accounts, gives immense details of the royal court and of Jahangir himself. Later, Sir Thomas Roe was also sent by James I to India in 1615 CE. After reaching Surat, he proceeded to Ajmer where Jahangir had encamped. He remained at the Mughal court from 1615–18 CE, and succeeded in obtaining a *farman* from Jahangir, allowing the English to trade at Surat. The journal of Sir Thomas Roe and the diary of the clergyman, Edward Perry, form valuable sources for the reign of Jahangir.

Shah Jahan (1627–58 CE)

Prince Khurram assumed the title of Shah Jahan upon ascending the throne in 1627 CE after his father's death. He was the third son of Jahangir, whose two elder sons, Khusrau and Parvez, had died during his lifetime. Shah Jahan secured the throne by murdering his younger brother, Shahriyar, and had Asaf Khan, his father-in-law kill all other royal contenders to the throne too. Asaf Khan was later appointed as his prime minister, while Nur Jahan was sidelined with an adequate pension.

Internal Problems

During Shah Jahan's reign, the Mughal governor of the Deccan, Khan Jahan Lodi, was sent to recover Balaghat from Ahmednagar. On failing to do so, he was recalled to the Mughal court; but rose in rebellion and fled back to the Deccan. Shah Jahan recognized the gravity of the danger involved in Khan Jahan Lodi winning over all the rulers of the Deccan and the resulting faction threatening to break off from the Mughal Empire with their combined troops. In the interest of retaining the empire's southern provinces, Shah Jahan himself led a campaign to the Deccan in 1629 CE, with his Mughal general, Azim Khan. Khan Jahan was ultimately defeated, and he temporarily sought shelter with the ruler of Bijapur. The allies of Khan Jahan—Shahji Bhonsle and Kaluji Bhonsle—voluntarily surrendered before the Mughal armies, whereupon they were confined to their *jagirs*. When Khan Jahan failed to get any help from Bijapur, he proceeded towards Bundelkhand to instigate its chiefs to revolt. But once again luck did not favour him, and the chiefs opposed him. He was finally driven to the north, and killed by Shah Jahan at Shihonda in January 1631 CE.

It was now the turn of the Hindu Orchha chief, Jujhar Singh, of Bundelkhand—who had commanded the crucial passage to the Deccan—to revolt against Shah Jahan. Jujhar was compelled to submit when the Mughals cleverly won over his kinsman, Bharat Singh. Though Jujhar was later killed in 1634 CE, unrest in the region continued to simmer.

Famine and Plague

During Khan Jahan Lodi's revolt, the provinces of Gujarat, Khandesh and many parts of the Deccan faced a terrible drought and famine situation (1630–32 CE), which took a heavy toll on human life. Foodstuff became scarce, prices soared, and homes were deserted as people left with their cattle in search of water, food and fodder. To make matters worse, the famine was accompanied by the outbreak of plague. Peter Mundy, who was in the Deccan in November 1630 CE, describes the horrifying conditions witnessed by him. On Shah Jahan's orders, officials established *langars* at Burhanpur, Ahmedabad and other places to feed the poor and destitute. The royal treasuries were also thrown open for helping the poor. Nearly fifty thousand rupees were given out in charity at Ahmedabad and one lakh at Burhanpur over a period of four or five months. To deal with the emergency, the relief measures adopted by Shah Jahan and his officers, though inadequate, were highly commendable.

Conflict with the Portuguese

Shah Jahan had to face a serious threat from the Portuguese in 1631 CE. The town of Hughli in

Bengal had risen to prominence on account of the establishment of Portuguese factories along the river. These Portuguese settlers were often known to capture orphan Hindu and Muslim children, and forcibly convert them to Christianity. These forceful acts were resented by the Mughal authorities. But things came to a head when Mumtaz Mahal's slaves were captured and the Portuguese refused to release them in spite of her requests. It was then that Shah Jahan decided to crush their power; and appointed Kasim Khan as the Governor of Bengal in 1631 CE, ordering him to exterminate the Portuguese. Large forces were then sent in to capture Hughli, which lasted for more than three months. After a stiff resistance, the Portuguese surrendered.

The Deccan Conquest

The Deccan frequently proved to be a hotbed of rebellion for Shah Jahan. He tried to solve the problem permanently by entering into a military alliance with Bijapur in 1636 CE, with the objective of partitioning Ahmednagar. Through this accord Ahmednagar was wiped out and Bijapur received one-third of its southern territories. The other Deccan states too accepted the substantial presence of the Mughals in the Deccan. Bijapur too decided not to interfere with Golconda, which had also became an ally of the Mughals. The treaty limited any further Mughal advances into the Deccan, and gave Bijapur and Golconda an opportunity to conquer the regions beyond the Krishna, stretching up to Thanjavur, including Karnataka. The Mughals, on the other hand, concentrated on the north, and regained Qandahar in 1638 CE, while consolidating their presence along the Bengal and Assam borders in 1639 CE.

In an effort to consolidate his control over the northwest provinces of the empire, Shah Jahan moved his capital from Agra to Delhi in 1648 CE. Having strengthened his position in northern India, Shah Jahan once again turned to the south. The inability of the Mughals in managing the financial affairs of the Deccan changed their benevolent stand towards the Deccani states after 1648 CE, culminating in the invasion of Golconda in 1656 CE and Bijapur in 1657 CE. As a result, Bijapur had to surrender Ahmednagar, which it had received according to the treaty of 1636 CE; and Golconda was to cede a part of the *jagir* of Mir Jumla (the Golconda *wazir*), which comprised a rich and fertile tract along the Coromandel Coast, to the Mughals. Another factor influencing Shah Jahan's new policy in the Deccan was the growing importance the Coromandel Coast had acquired as a centre for the export of textiles and indigo.

Central Asian Policy

Shah Jahan, like his ancestors, always hoped to conquer Samarqand, the original homeland of the Mughals. His first opportunity arrived when the brother of the ruler of Samarqand invaded Kabul in 1639 CE and captured Bamian. Shah Jahan would once again be given the opportunity to interfere in Central Asian politics in 1646 CE. Balkh and Badakhshan constituted a part of the dominions of Nazar Muhammad Khan, the Uzbek ruler of Bukhara. In 1646 CE, Abdul Aziz, the son of Nazar Muhammad Khan, revolted against his father, demanding for a partition of the empire. When Nazar Muhammad was defeated by his son and took shelter in Balkh, he turned to Shah Jahan for help. The latter sent a big contingent under the leadership of Prince Murad and Ali Mardan to Balkh. But on seeing the approaching Mughal army, Nazar Muhammad realized his folly of having incited the greed of the Mughals, and quickly made peace with his son by accepting to partition his empire. Thereafter Samarqand and Bukhara were handed over to his son, while Balkh and Badakhshan were left with him.

In spite of the reconciliation between father and son, the Mughals overran Balkh and Badakhshan in July 1646 CE, seizing a lot of booty. Without informing Shah Jahan, however, Prince Murad left his charge to Ali Mardan and went away to

Kabul; whereupon Shah Jahan immediately sent reinforcements to Balkh under his other son, Aurangzeb, in 1647 CE. The Central Asian tribes felt that the Mughals were intruding into their homeland and took up arms against them en masse. With the onset of winter, Aurangzeb handed over the charge of Balkh to Nazar Muhammad and returned to Kabul with the entire Mughal force. The Central Asian policy of Shah Jahan, hence, turned out to be a dismal failure. It proved to be a serious setback to Mughal prestige in Central Asia, ruining the fortunes of the Mughal Empire in the long run.

The loss of Qandahar to the Persians was the direct outcome of the failure of the Central Asian policy of Shah Jahan. Upon hearing of the humiliation of the Mughals in Balkh, Shah Abbas of Persia made up his mind to recover Qandahar by force. He shifted his camp to Herat, and under his personal supervision, launched an attack on Qandahar in the winter of 1648 CE. The Persians laid siege to the stronghold till the Mughal governor, Daulat Khan, failed in his efforts to resist them. After 11 years, Qandahar once again went back into the hands of the Persians. Shah Jahan made frantic efforts by sending three full-fledged expeditions to recover Qandahar in 1649 CE and again in 1655 CE, but his efforts went in vain. The failure of the expeditions to Qandahar exposed the weakness of the Mughal army throughout the Muslim world, shattering the belief in the invincibility of the imperial Mughal army.

SHAH JAHAN WITH ANGEL MUSICIANS, *riding upon his royal horse on the rugged banks of the river Yamuna. Taj Mahal is not built, yet. Following the Christian tradition introduced to the Mughal court by the Jesuit missionaries at the time of Akbar, the Emperor appears like a saint with a halo around his head. Four angels are shown descending from the heavenly clouds. Painting by Amal Khurram, mid-17th century.*

The War of Succession

The developments in the last part of Shah Jahan's reign did not bode well for the future of the empire. Out of his four sons, Shah Jahan had named his eldest, Dara Shukoh, as his heir apparent. All his other sons—Shah Shuja, Aurangzeb and Murad Baksh, who were governors of various Mughal provinces—decided to contest Dara's claim. A war of succession (end-1657 CE) broke out among his sons during Shah Jahan's lifetime. His third son, Aurangzeb, emerged victorious by murdering his three brothers, and imprisoning Shah Jahan in the Agra fort. Shah Jahan was kept in close custody as a prisoner until his death on 1 February 1666 CE at the age of 74.

Shah Jahan was a tolerant and enlightened ruler, who patronized scholars and poets of Persian, Sanskrit as well as Hindi. With both his mother and grandmother being Rajput princesses, Shah Jahan was more Indian than Mughal. He showed great tolerance towards all faiths; and in some respects, especially in his treatment of Hindus, he was as great as his celebrated grandfather, Emperor Akbar. During his reign Hindus were appointed to the highest posts in the government and the army. Though as the emperor he had to wage a few wars, largely there was peace and prosperity in the country. The subcontinent also achieved excellence in artistic and architectural pursuits during Shah Jahan's reign for which it may be rightly called the Golden Age of the Mughals. Shah Jahan is particularly famous for the splendid architecture commissioned by him—such as the World Heritage monument of the Taj Mahal, the Red Fort, the Jama Masjid and the Peacock Throne. Also, trade and commerce flourished between India and West Asia; and his rule marked the beginning of exports to European nations.

SUMMARY

- Akbar died in 1605 CE, and was succeeded by his son, Salim, who assumed the title of Nuruddin Jahangir.
- Even after the death of Akbar, the Mughal Empire's journey of conquests and territorial expansion continued as a result of a continuation of his policies.
- To regularize and institutionalize the state's structure, the imperial authorities adopted centralizing measures.
- The rule of Jahangir and Shah Jahan comprise a period when attempts were being made to consolidate and expand the gains and achievements of Akbar's reign. The period became noteworthy for political stability, brisk economic activity, and excellence in the arts and architecture.
- When Jahangir's eldest son, Khusrau, revolted against him, the emperor defeated his forces and captured him along with his chief followers. Even the Sikh Guru, Arjun Dev, who had supported Khusrau, was tortured to death.
- Shah Abbas I of Persia besieged the fort of Qandahar in 1606 CE; but abandoned the attack when Jahangir sent an army against him. The Shah once again attacked Qandahar in 1622 CE and succeeded in acquiring it.
- After Rana Pratap's son and successor, Rana Amar Singh was defeated by Jahangir, the Rana accepted the suzerainty of Jahangir, and was restored all territories, including Chittor.
- Jahangir's marriage to his Persian wife, Nur Jahan, was one of the most important events of Jahangir's reign. Jahangir made her the empress and gave her the title of Nur Mahal or 'light of the palace', which was later changed to 'Nur Jahan' meaning 'light of the world'.
- Nur Jahan was a woman of extraordinary talents, who soon became the real ruler of the country. She participated actively in the state's affairs and worked hard in mastering the details of administration.
- She was ably assisted in the discharge of her tasks by her kinsmen, who received rapid promotions to key positions in the administrative hierarchy.
- During the reign of Jahangir, Captain William Hawkins and Sir Thomas Roe, representatives of the English East India Company, visited the Mughal court and gained valuable trading privileges.
- Prince Khurram assumed the title of Shah Jahan and ascended the throne in 1627 CE after the death of his father.
- During Shah Jahan's reign, the Mughal governor of the Deccan, Khan Jahan Lodi, rebelled. Ultimately he was killed by Shah Jahan at Shihonda in 1631 CE.
- Gujarat, Khandesh and many parts of the Deccan witnessed terrible drought and famine during 1630–32 CE. On Shah Jahan's orders, relief measures were undertaken to help the poor and destitute.
- The Deccan frequently proved to be a hotbed of rebellion for Shah Jahan. He tried to solve the problem permanently by entering into a military alliance with Bijapur in 1636 CE, with the objective of partitioning Ahmednagar.
- The inability of the Mughals to manage the financial affairs of the Deccan changed their benevolent stand towards the Deccani states after 1648 CE, culminating in the invasion of Golconda and Bijapur in 1656 CE and 1657 CE, respectively.
- Shah Jahan interfered in the politics of Central Asia in 1646 CE. The Central Asian tribes felt that

the Mughals were intruding into their homeland and took up arms against them en masse.

- When the Central Asian policy of Shah Jahan failed, and it proved to be a serious setback for Mughal prestige in Central Asia. The loss of Qandahar to the Persians was the direct outcome of the failure of the Central Asian policy of Shah Jahan.
- A war of succession broke out among Shah Jahan's sons in his lifetime. His third son, Aurangzeb, came out victorious and ascended the throne.

KEYWORDS

Mandis
Hundis
Nur Jahan junta
Farman
Qasbahs

REVIEW QUESTIONS

1. Briefly describe the political and economic conditions in the Indian subcontinent in the beginning of the seventeenth century.
2. Write a short note on Jahangir's conquest of Mewar.
3. Explain the role of Nur Jahan as the power behind the Mughal throne.
4. Examine the conquest of the Deccan by Shah Jahan.
5. How was Shah Jahan's Central Asian policy a serious setback to Mughal prestige?

CHAPTER 21

Aurangzeb

Review and Discussion

- Aurangzeb's Policies
- Aurangzeb's Military Campaigns

When Aurangzeb ascended the throne in 1658 CE, the state was about to enter the colonial era, there was an emergent agrarian crisis and the *ulema* were staging a massive comeback. At the same time, the beginning of the seventeenth century India witnessed a serious intellectual and socio-political crisis of confidence among many communities, since it heralded the gradual decline of Muslim power and the emergence of European colonial rule in India. Ethnicity began to play a dominant role instead of the hitherto existing dynastic, religious or caste factors. This is seen in the period's Maratha and Sikh uprisings against Mughal domination. Alongside was the threat posed by European trading companies, who had acquired bases for conducting their commercial activities.

Muhiuddin Muhammad Aurangzeb, who took the soubriquet of Alamgir, was the last of the great Mughals of India. He was the third son of Shah Jahan and his famous queen, Mumtaz Mahal. According to Jadunath Sarkar, the history of Aurangzeb is practically the history of India, because the sixty years of his reign (1658–1707 CE) cover the second half of the seventeenth century, marking a crucial period in the annals of Indian history. Under him the Mughal Empire was to achieve territorial dimensions covering almost the whole of India—from Ghazni to Chittagong, and from Kashmir to Karnataka.

Prior to becoming emperor, Aurangzeb was the governor of Gujarat for two years from 1645 CE to 1647 CE, when he was given charge of leading the Balkh expedition, which established his reputation as a military general. Upon returning from Balkh in 1648 CE, he was made the governor of Multan and Sind, an assignment that he held from 1648 CE to 1652 CE. During this period, he led two expeditions to Qandahar—one in 1649 CE and the second in 1652 CE. Towards the close of 1652 CE, he was sent to the Deccan as its viceroy for the second time. Making the Deccan his base, Aurangzeb successfully fought the war of succession (1657–58 CE) against his brothers, and usurped the throne. Soon after ascending the throne, Aurangzeb had the *khutba* recited in his name, which is a permitted practice in Islam in the case of a worthy son succeeding to the sultanate. The process through which he had it done made it clear to him that he must have the *ulema* to support him at all times. As the *ulema* had been a deprived lot since Akbar's implementation of an unorthodox religious policy, Aurangzeb felt that extending patronage towards them would help him immensely in his task of administration.

Aurangzeb's Policies

Contrary to the popular opinions regarding Aurangzeb, there were many remarkable aspects of administrative excellence implemented by him in the larger interests of the public. With the objective of providing some tax relief to his subjects, he abolished the *rahdari,* a tax which was collected on every highway frontier or ferry. He also abolished the *pandari,* which was a ground tax or house tax. On the whole, about seventy kinds of taxes collected from Hindus and Muslims were all abolished during his reign. Khafi Khan, the official historian of Aurangzeb's reign, mentions only 14 of these. In spite of this, the zamindars did continue to levy taxes on the people. However, through these reforms the state reduced its unproductive expenditure by augmenting its finances to a large extent.

But the good reforms brought into effect by Aurangzeb were offset by his religious policy, which was strictly in consonance with Islamic law. Aurangzeb was an orthodox Sunni Muslim and ruled according to the precepts of the *Shariah.* He lived a pious and virtuous life and had learnt to follow religion in every walk of life. Religious considerations were, therefore, uppermost on his mind while dealing with either his people or his state affairs. From his early life he had been under the influence of the *ulema*, who not only helped him come to power, but also acted as his principal guides all through his life. His accession to the throne, therefore, led to the revival of Muslim orthodoxy in state politics. He regarded the Mughal Empire to be an Islamic state and did his best to act as an ideal Muslim ruler.

In 1659 CE, he issued an order forbidding the construction of new temples by the Hindus, while a few years later he even prohibited the repair of old ones. Soon an attempt was made to dismiss all the Hindu *quanungos* and *patwaris* occupying official positions in the lower rungs of the revenue administration. In 1664 CE, he also forbade the practice of *Sati.* Gradually Aurangzeb's religious strictness grew, till he took steps to ban music at his court (1668 CE), stop festivities on the emperor's birthday, and put an end to the practices of *Tuladan* and *Jharokadarshan* which the preceding Mughal emperors—Akbar, Jahangir and Shah Jahan—had followed before him.

Aurangzeb prohibited the use of the *kalima* on the coins so that they could not be defiled by the non-Muslims. He ended the practice of celebrating *Nauroz* or the Persian New Year, which was a borrowed institution from Persia. He appointed *muhtasibs* or censors of public morals to look after the good conduct of people and to see that they acted according to the *Shariah.* People were not to indulge in alcohol, intoxicating drugs and other consumables forbidden in Islam. Aurangzeb ordered the repair of mosques and *khanaqas;* and *imams* and *muezzins* were to be paid regularly by the state. The solar *Illahi* year was withdrawn for counting the regnal years. It was retained only for administrative purposes and to keep track of the emperor's solar calendar birthday. The cultivation of *bhang* was prohibited throughout the empire.

The *ulema* were pleased with all these measures and the encouragement shown by the emperor towards the maintenance of mosques and religious charity. In 1679 CE Aurangzeb's played his masterstroke in his attempt to win the support of the *ulema* by trying to resume the land grants held by Hindus. Although this was not fully enforced, by 1690 CE according to the new policy the *ulema* were allotted more number of land grants, which also became hereditary in nature.

In 1679 CE, Aurangzeb also re-imposed the *jiziya* on the Hindus which had been abolished by Akbar and had not been re-imposed even by Jahangir or Shah Jahan before him. Certain discriminatory orders were issued against the Hindus, such as the imposition of higher customs duties—five per cent on the goods of the Hindus as against two per cent on those of the Muslims. He granted stipends and gifts to converts from Hinduism and offered them posts in public service. He also persecuted Shiites and Sufis. Thus, Aurangzeb's religious policy marked the beginning of an intolerant treatment towards the Hindus, who formed the bulk of India's population. As a result, the Jats of the Mathura region, the Bundelas of Bundelkhand, the Satnamis and the Sikhs rose in revolt against the Mughal emperor.

Nevertheless, it may be mentioned here that the temple destruction order passed by Aurangzeb is mentioned only in one contemporary historical source, i.e., the *Maasir-i-Alamgiri*. To look at Aurangzeb more objectively, a mention must also be made of the temples that were constructed under his patronage. The Gopinath temple with a tank was built at Gopamau in Hardoi district by Naunidhi Rai in 1669 CE; and some temples in Bishalpur were built in 1681 CE and 1690 CE. Certain *farmans* are known to have been issued by Aurangzeb granting *inam* lands free of taxes to even non-Muslims. For example, the Jogis of Jakhbar, and the Jains at Banaras, Ujjain, Guwahati, Khandesh and Multan were given a number of concessions by Aurangzeb. As a result, Jain sources speak very highly of Aurangzeb. Lal Vijaya, a Jain monk, met Aurangzeb at Agra and was granted permission to build a huge monastery (*poshala*) for the *Tapagachcha* sect of Jains. In 1679 CE, Bhim Vijaya Suri, another Jain saint, met Aurangzeb at Ajmer and was granted relief of certain kinds for the Jain monasteries at Ajmer, Merta, Sojat and Jodhpur.

Hence, what one finds during Aurangzeb's rule is his tendency to fluctuate between pleasing the *ulema* and realizing that fact that the sentiments of his non-Muslim subjects could not be completely overlooked either. But it was the former policy that more often than not took precedence and let loose forces that were ultimately to bring about the decline of the great Mughal Empire in India.

Aurangzeb's Military Campaigns

Aurangzeb was able to extend the boundaries of his empire to the extreme south of the Deccan as a result of his military campaigns. Almost the whole of India had come under the direct control of the Mughals under Aurangzeb.

Eastern Borders (1661–66 CE)

Mir Jumla, the *wazir* of Golconda who had joined the Mughal service, had been sent by Aurangzeb in pursuit of his brother, Shah Shuja. He chased him from Dhaka in Bengal to the Arakan frontier in 1663 CE. Impressed with Mir Jumla, Aurangzeb appointed him as the governor of Bengal and encouraged him to venture into Koch Bihar and Assam. However, sudden floods made him retreat and he died soon after. Shaista Khan, another Mughal general, was then transferred, as governor, from the Deccan to Bengal.

The new governor found that the Portuguese and Burmese pirates had become bold enough to carry their attacks right into the sub-divisions of Dhaka. Shah Jahan had earlier initiated some stern measures to suppress the problem of Portuguese pirates in Bengal, but the Mughals had failed to recognize the need for building a strong naval force to safeguard their coasts. As a result, the Portuguese had become active in Bengal once again, resorting to piracy with a vengeance. They plundered merchant boats, raided villages and abducted people for the slave trade.

Mir Jumla had occupied Chittagong before his death, but the Portuguese re-occupied the port town thereafter. Shaista Khan dealt with the situation by strengthening the Bengal fleet and then storming Chittagong through both land and sea routes. After some initial resistance, the Portuguese laid down their arms in 1666 CE and Shaista Khan could get the Bengali villagers—who had been held as slaves—released. The town was renamed Islamabad; and the small island of Sandwip, which was used by pirates for their base operations, was also acquired by the Mughals and converted into a military post.

Northwest Frontier Policy

Being the shrewd politician that he was, Aurangzeb handled all his military exploits with tact. With regard to the northwest frontier, he followed a forward policy, taking into consideration the political and economic concerns of the region. The Muslim tribes living there had always been a source of danger and trouble for the Mughals; and Aurangzeb occasionally tried to put them down through oppression as well as bribery. In 1667 CE, however, when the Yusufzais revolted under their leader, Bhagu, they were suppressed within months. In 1672 CE, the Afridis revolted under Akmal Khan, who also enlisted the Pathans to join in against the Mughals, who were defeated at the Ali Masjid. When the Afridis were joined by the Khattaks under their leader, Khush Hal Khan, Aurangzeb realized the gravity of the situation and took over the matter personally. He was able to control the situation in 1674 CE by using a combination of diplomacy and force of arms. Many Afghans were won over through gifts, *jagirs*, pensions and offices. Amir Khan, the Mughal governor of Afghanistan, followed a conciliatory policy, which helped reinstate the Mughals in the Northwestern frontier.

Revolt of the Jats of Mathura

The first revolt against Aurangzeb's religious policy occurred in the district of Mathura in 1669 CE, where the sturdy Jats rose in revolt under their gallant leader, Gokul, by murdering the oppressive *faujdar* of Mathura, Abdul Nabi. Though the Mughals put down the revolt with a heavy hand, and Gokul was killed, the anger of the Jats could not be suppressed. They continued to harass Aurangzeb throughout his reign, only becoming stronger after his death, and proving to be an important cause of the decline of the great Mughal Empire.

Revolt of the Satnamis

The Satnamis were a sect of simple-minded Hindus who lived near Delhi, in the districts of Narnaul and Mewat (in modern Haryana). They were basically agriculturists and traders. In 1672 CE, they revolted when a tax collector insulted a Satnami farmer. They were initially successful and even managed to occupy some Mughal territory, but were defeated when a large Mughal force was sent against them. Under Aurangzeb's order almost all of them were ultimately put to death.

Rise of the Sikhs

The execution of Guru Arjun Dev by Jahangir in 1606 CE had turned the Sikhs against the Mughal Empire. When the ninth Sikh guru, Tegh Bahadur, protested against the anti-Hindu policy of Aurangzeb, he was arrested in 1675 CE and brought to Delhi with threats of conversion to Islam. Upon his refusal, he was tortured to death. His son, Gobind Singh, the tenth and the last of the Sikh gurus, resolved to avenge the death of his father; and began to train the Sikhs in warfare, before rising in revolt against Aurangzeb. He fought against the Mughals throughout his life, while his followers continued to harass the Mughal emperors even after his death. The rise of the Sikhs in the Punjab ultimately wiped out the influence of the Mughals in the northwest.

Wars with the Rajputs

The Rajputs had worked closely with Akbar, Jahangir and Shah Jahan, but the bigoted policies of Aurangzeb antagonized them and turned them into his enemies. In order to weaken Rajputana, Aurangzeb decided to destroy Marwar, the most powerful Hindu state at the time. The ruler,

Raja Jaswant Singh, was a vassal of the Mughal emperor, posted in Jamrud in the Northwestern Frontier Province. His untimely death in 1678 CE, prompted Aurangzeb to occupy Marwar. Despite the initial success of the Mughals, the Rajputs soon rose in revolt under their gallant leader Durgadas Rathor. The Rana of Udaipur also joined them and the situation became critical for Aurangzeb.

When Aurangzeb sent his son, Prince Akbar, to suppress the revolt, he too was won over by the Rajputs. Soon Akbar proclaimed himself as the emperor of India and advanced against his own father, who was camped at Ajmer. On becoming aware of his son's plans, Aurangzeb adopted a clever strategy by writing Akbar a letter congratulating him for successfully deceiving the Rajputs and then cunningly letting the Rajputs discover the correspondence. Aurangzeb's strategy worked and the Rajputs deserted the prince, who was left with no choice but to flee to Persia. Although in the end, in 1681 CE, the Rana of Mewar concluded peace with the Mughals, the Rajputs of Marwar continued their struggle until the death of Aurangzeb.

The Deccan Conquest

Aurangzeb spent the last 25 years of his rule (1682–1707 CE) in the Deccan. His attitude towards the Shia states of Bijapur and Golconda had always been aggressive—partly influenced by his imperialist ambitions and partly by religious bigotry. To add insult to injury, both the Shia rulers of Golconda and Bijapur had established friendly relations with the Marathas, uniting as allies against the Mughals. Aurangzeb, perhaps rightly, felt that the alliance was more advantageous for the Marathas than the two Deccan states because of the administrative experience and stronger financial position of the Deccan states. Calculating that the Maratha power would weaken if these states were annexed to the Mughal Empire, Aurangzeb proceeded to conquer them.

Conquest of Bijapur (1686 CE)

Sikandar Adil Shah was the young ruler of Bijapur. In 1682 CE Aurangzeb had sent an expedition against him under Prince Azam, but it failed and the prince was called back. For the next two years Aurangzeb was busy fighting the Marathas and Prince Akbar. This interim period was utilized by Sikandar to re-organize his army with the help of his minister, Sharza Khan. When Aurangzeb demanded the dismissal of Sharza Khan, his order was not complied with, forcing the emperor to proceed against Bijapur and besieging it in April 1685 CE. A breach was made in the fortifications of the city through which the Mughal army is said to have invaded Bijapur. Even the help of the Marathas could not save Bijapur from the Mughals; and Sikandar Adil Shah was captured and his kingdom annexed in 1686 CE. He was later to be inducted into Mughal service.

Conquest of Golconda (1687 CE)

Abul Hasan, the ruler of Golconda was not on good terms with Aurangzeb either. Aurangzeb's grievance was not only that he was a Shia, but also that he employed Hindus in his kingdom. During the Mughal invasions of Bijapur under Jai Singh (1665–66 CE), under Dilir Khan (1679 CE) and under Prince Muhammad Azam (1685 CE), the sultan of Golconda had always sent his troops to assist the Bijapur sultan. Moreover, the sultan of Golconda had helped Shivaji during his visit to Haidarabad in 1677 CE, behaving like a humble vassal of the Maratha by promising him an annual subsidy of one lakh huns for the defense of his territory. He had also taken into service, Akkanna and Madanna, two *brahman* brothers as his ministers. All these reasons combined to set Aurangzeb against Abul Hasan. The war between Golconda and the Mughals, however, dragged on for a while. Ultimately, Aurangzeb himself arrived at Golconda in January 1687 CE and tried to lay siege to the fort. Despite heavy assaults, the fort could not be breached, until Aurangzeb resorted to treachery by bribing one of the officers of the garrison who opened a gate of the outer bastions of the fort. Abul Hasan was captured and the kingdom of Golconda was annexed in September 1687 CE to the Mughal Empire.

Aurangzeb and the British

Seeing the chaotic condition prevailing in the Deccan, the English had fortified their possessions in many places. In 1685 CE, Shaista Khan, the governor of Bengal, imposed local duties upon the English. The Company resisted these demands with force, giving rise to a sort of a semi-official war between the English and the Mughals. James II, the King of England, was persuaded to send warships to capture Chittagong, which further infuriated Aurangzeb. The latter ordered the capture of the English factories at Surat, Masulipatnam and on the Hughli; and the English factory workers were forced to leave the premises in 1688 CE. This defeat was a setback for the English, but subsequently peace was restored between the parties. The new governor of Bengal invited Charnock, the chief of the English factory at Hughli, to return to his settlement in 1690 CE. Charnock received the royal *farman* and was allowed to start a small trading station, which later grew into the city of Calcutta (Kolkata).

Aurangzeb and the Marathas

The relationship between the Mughals and the Marathas marks a vital phase of medieval Indian history exhibiting all the diplomatic, military, political plots and treacheries typical of the times. Aurangzeb sent Shaista Khan to suppress Shivaji in 1663 CE, but the latter failed in his attempt and saved his own life with great difficulty. Later on, Prince Muazzam and Raja Jai Singh were sent on a similar mission, where Jai Singh forced Shivaji to sign the Treaty of Purandhar in 1665 CE. According to one of the clauses of the treaty, Shivaji had to attend the Mughal court at Agra in 1666 CE. Although placed under detention, Shivaji managed to escape to his headquarters in the Deccan. After the death of Shivaji in 1680 CE, Aurangzeb carried on the struggle against his son, Sambhaji who was defeated by Aurangzeb in 1689 CE and tortured to death. Sambhaji's son, Shahu, was imprisoned till 1708 CE. Sambhaji's step brother, Raja Ram, now became the ruler of Maharashtra and continued the struggle against the Mughals. After his death the same struggle was continued by his widow, Tara Bai; and the Marathas once again became the dominant power in the Deccan. Despite his best efforts, Aurangzeb failed to crush the Maratha resistance, which ultimately ruined the the Mughals in general and Aurangzeb in particular. In 1706 CE, Aurangzeb at last gave up the struggle and ordered the return of the imperial camp back to northern India.

By then, Aurangzeb had become an old man of 89, breathing his last in 1707 CE. He was buried at Khuldabad, four miles west of Daulatabad, where his simple tomb stands. During his last days, he was frustrated with the wars of succession between his two sons, Azam and Kam Baksh.

Aurangzeb was the most powerful of the Mughal emperors of India when he ascended the throne in 1658 CE. He was naturally endowed and had industriously cultivated self-learning and discipline. He was extremely hard-working, methodical, and disciplined and his private life was virtuous. The empire under Aurangzeb experienced phenomenal growth by reaching its maximum territorial dimensions in 1686–87 CE, with the conquest and annexation of Bijapur and Golconda. But the empire also started to manifest signs of weakness; and the vastness of the empire, coupled with the excessive centralization of authority in the hands of an autocratic emperor, prompted its disintegration. In addition, Aurangzeb's religious bigotry and the loss of Rajput support also paved the way for a gradual decline. He failed miserably at holding together the sprawling Mughal political edifice. His bigotry strengthened the hands of those who opposed him for political or other reasons. Added to this, was his prolonged absence

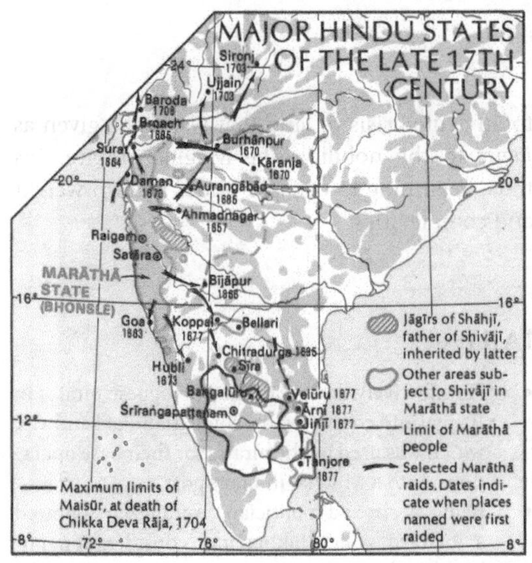

Map 21-1 *Major Hindu States of the Late 17th Century*

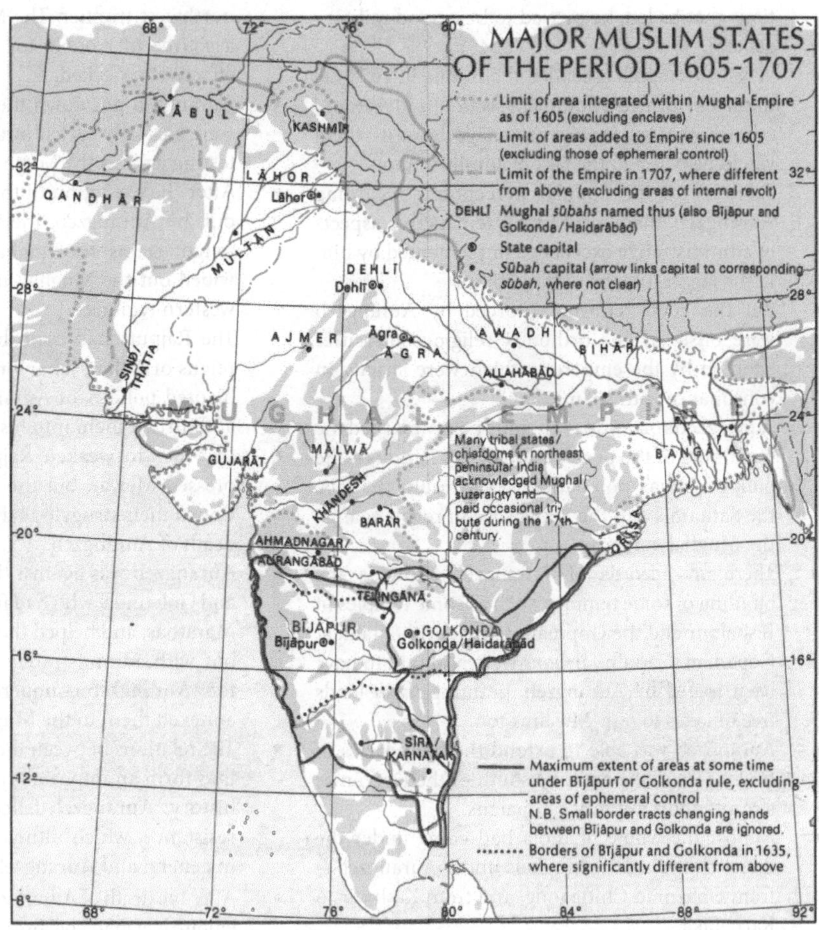

Map 21-2 *Major Muslim States of the Period, 1605–1707 CE.*

from the capital. In many economically prosperous regions, the local gentry and their followers were becoming assertive. The appointment of a large number of *mansabdars* was leading to an acute crisis of land that was to be given as *jagirs* to the nobility. The Mughal empire was thus, beginning to collapse under its own weight and complexities.

SUMMARY

- The reign of Aurangzeb (1658–1707 CE) covers the second half of the seventeenth century; and marks an important period in the annals of Indian history.
- Before becoming the Mughal emperor, Aurangzeb was appointed as the governor of Gujarat and then of Multan and Sind. In the several expeditions that he led, he proved to be a good military general.
- When Aurangzeb ascended the throne in 1658 CE, the *ulema* formed a dominant section; and Aurangzeb felt that extending patronage towards them would help him in the task of administration.
- Contrary to the popular perceptions regarding Aurangzeb, there were many remarkable aspects of administrative excellence implemented by him in the larger interest of his subjects.
- But the good reforms enforced by Aurangzeb were offset by the orthodox religious measures adopted by the emperor, which were strictly in consonance with Islamic law.
- Aurangzeb's orthodox religious policy marked the beginning of the persecution of the Hindus—the bulk of India's population. As a result, the Jats, the Satnamis and the Sikhs rose in revolt against the Mughal emperor.
- There are records of Aurangzeb allowing the building of some temples, such as some temples in Bishalpur and the Gopinath temple with a tank at Gopamau. Certain *farmans* were also said to have been issued by Aurangzeb, granting *inam* lands free of taxes to non-Muslims too.
- Aurangzeb was able to extend the boundaries of his empire to the extreme south of the Deccan as a result of his military campaigns.
- Almost the whole of India had come under the direct control of the Mughals under Aurangzeb—from Ghazni to Chittagong, and from Kashmir to Karnataka.
- He effectively dealt with the Portuguese pirates in Bengal and converted the small island of Sandwip, which was used by the pirates for their base operations, into a Mughal military post.
- Being a shrewd politician, Aurangzeb followed a forward policy taking into consideration political and economic concerns with regard to the northwest frontier. The Muslim tribes, who were a source of trouble for the Mughals, were also effectively checked.
- Aurangzeb put down the Jats and Satnamis, who were basically agricultural groups frequently protesting against the Mughals.
- After the execution of the Sikh guru, Tegh Bahadur, by Aurangzeb, the Sikhs rose in revolt and fought against the Mughals consistently until they wiped out the Mughal influence from the northwestern regions.
- The Rajputs had contributed greatly during the reigns of Akbar, Jahangir and Shah Jahan, but the bigoted policies of Aurangzeb antagonized them and turned them into his worst enemies.
- In order to weaken Rajputana, Aurangzeb suppressed Mewar; but the Rajputs of Marwar continued their struggle against the Mughals until the death of Aurangzeb.
- Aurangzeb was against the Shia rulers of Bijapur and Golconda, who had friendly relations with the Marathas; and helped the latter not only militarily but with administrative experience and finances too. Aurangzeb conquered both these states and annexed them to the Mughal Empire.
- The relations between the Mughals and the Marathas form an important phase of medieval Indian history. Aurangzeb failed to crush the Maratha resistance, which ultimately ruined the Mughals in general and Aurangzeb in particular.
- After the death of Aurangzeb in 1707 CE, the Mughal empire began to collapse.

KEYWORDS

Colonial

Soubriquet

Slavery

REVIEW QUESTIONS

1. What were the measures adopted by Aurangzeb to please the ulema?
2. Discuss the relations between Aurangzeb and the Rajputs.
3. Account for the reasons why Aurangzeb undertook the conquest of the Deccan.
4. Why did the Jats revolt frequently against Aurangzeb?
5. Write a brief note on Aurangzeb's personality.

CHAPTER 22

Mughal Administration

Review and Discussion

- Central Administration
- Provincial Administration
- Local Administration
- Land Revenue
- The Army
- The Judiciary

Mughal administration was essentially the result of Akbar's genius. Babur and Humayun were more involved in consolidating their gains in northern India and did not rule long enough to implement a system of civil government. In establishing the administrative machinery, Akbar had before him Sher Shah's example and the need to accommodate a large number of nobility in official, civil and military positions, which made it essential to implement a proper system of administration. Akbar was not only a great conqueror, but also a capable administrator, who introduced useful reforms and established an excellent administrative system in his conquered territories. As a result of his efficient administration, Akbar was able to establish a long-lasting empire in India.

The Mughal state was a combination of Indian and foreign elements. To be more accurate, it was a 'Perso-Arabic system in an Indian setting', which was also military in nature and every officer had to be enrolled in the army. Not being able to ignore the existing system of administration, Akbar tried to affect a compromise with the older native system and the new principles of government, rules of taxation, departmental arrangements and titles of officials imported from outside India. What came up was an arrangement that was a highly centralized autocracy, with the emperor as the head of the state with unlimited powers. Interestingly, the Mughal emperors of India did not pay homage to any Caliph as some of their Turkish and Afghan predecessors had done. Most of the Mughals believed that the position of the monarch would be strengthened only in a secularized state. Hence for all practical purposes, the Mughal emperors kept religion separate from the state, except during the reign of Aurangzeb.

Central Administration

While gifted with political and administrative genius of a high order, Akbar was indebted in many respects to Sher Shah's organizational skills. The Mughal government established by Akbar was a centralized despotism, with the emperor at the pivot of the administrative edifice, enjoying absolute power. By virtue of being the head of the state, the Mughal emperor was also the supreme commander of the army, and the chief executive of the civil administration. He was the source of all honours, administrative power, and the supreme dispenser of justice.

The Mughal emperor was assisted in the daily task of administration by a number of ministers through whom the policies of state were dispensed. The ministers were, therefore, mere implementers of the emperor's decisions and in no way acted as a check on the authority of the emperor. Thus, as Ibn Hasan observes, 'They were pillars of the empire, but pillars of the Mughal Taj, which do not support the structure, but add to the dignity, majesty and beauty'.

The Mughal emperor also had a council of ministers, and other officers and nobles who met to discuss administrative, political and military policies. The office of the *wakil,* who was the representative of the emperor, came into prominence when Bairam Khan was appointed as Akbar's regent and had to act on his behalf. After the death of Bairam Khan, this office lost its importance. Only theoretically, the position continued to exist, but none were appointed to it. Naturally, losing its significance, the position completely disappeared during the reign of Shah Jahan.

After the emperor, the position of the *wazir* or *diwan,* who was the Prime Minister, was most important. In his capacity as *diwan,* the *wazir* sometimes headed the revenue department too. However, all *diwans* were not *wazirs;* and in the absence of a *wakil,* the *wazir* performed his duties as well. In the course of time, the *wazirs* became more empowered and started exercising control over other departments too, such as the army. The *wazir's* office received revenue papers and despatches from the provinces and the armies in the field. All orders of payment had to be signed by him and passed through his department alone. After consulting the emperor, he passed orders and settled queries concerning revenue. Assisted by two junior officers—the *diwan-i-am,* who was in charge of salaries, and the *diwan-i-khas,* who was in charge of crown-lands—he supervised the income and expenditure of the provinces, distributed income from the central treasury among various departments and also kept an overall account of the entire income and expenditure of the empire.

Under the *diwan* was the *mir bakshi* or the chief military adviser and the Inspector General of the contingents. His duties included maintaining a complete record of all *mansabdars* serving in various capacities within the empire, dealing with the matters associated with the ranks and salaries of the *mansabdars,* and holding annual reviews of troops and troopers.

The *khan-i-saman* or High Steward headed the emperor's department of manufacturers, stores and supply, taking care of military and domestic household requirements. He often travelled with the emperor on his journeys and campaigns, being in charge of the daily expenditure, food, stores, tents, imperial servants and state-owned factories and industries.

The *muhtasib* was appointed by the emperor to inspect public morals. He used to perform both religious and secular duties, supervising the shop-keepers and traders for the right market prices, and maintaining and inspecting markets. With the help of soldiers, he demolished liquor shops, distilleries and gambling dens.

The *sadr-us-sadur* was the chief *sadr* of the empire, also known as the *sadr-i-kul* and *sadr-i-jahan.* Being the guardian of Islamic law and the spokesman of the *ulema,* only men of exemplary character were appointed to this rank. It was the duty of the *sadr* to look into and decide cases relating to grants and distribution of money for charitable purposes. According to Ibn Hasan, the function of the chief *sadr* seems to have been limited to the awarding of stipends and *jagirs* by the state to the *ulema* and the needy. Every *sadr* was directly under the command of the chief *sadr.* While recruiting *sadrs* to the provinces, the chief *sadr* acquainted them with all the details pertaining to those who held rent-free lands.

Other important officials who assisted in the central administration were the *darogha-i-dak chauki* (Superintendent of Intelligence and Posts), *mir bahri* (Revenue Secretary), *mir barr* (Superintendent of Forests), *qur begi* (Lord Standard Bearer), *akht begi* (Superintendent of the Royal Stud), *mushrif* (Chief Admiral and Officer of Harbours), *nazir-i-buyutad* (Superintendent of Imperial Workshops), *mustaufi* (Auditor-General), *awarjah nawis* (Superintendent of Daily Court Expenditure), *khwan salar* (Superintendent of the Royal Kitchen), and *mir arz* (Officer for Petitions to the Emperor). Apart from these officials, there were also the Superintendent of Artillery and the imperial news-writers, among many others.

Provincial Administration

Akbar divided the Mughal Empire for administrative convenience into 15 provinces called the *subas*. Provincial administration was mostly modelled on the pattern of the central government. The number of provinces in the empire frequently varied; while Akbar's empire (before 1602 CE) consisted of 12 *subas,* with the conquest of the Deccan provinces, the number rose to 15. During Jahangir's reign there were 17 provinces, which further increased to 22 in the time of Shah Jahan's rule. By the time of Aurangzeb's reign the number of provinces stood at 21.

Every *suba* was governed by a *sipah salar* who was also known as the *subedar*. He was assisted by other officials, such as the *diwan, bakshi, faujdar, kotwal, qazi, sadr, amil, bitikchi, potdar, waqi-i-navis, quanungo* and *patwari*. The *subas* were divided into *sarkars* or districts and the *sarkars* were sub-divided into *parganas*. The *subedar* wielded both civil and military powers, and was the representative of the emperor in the province. He was authorized to hold a court and hear appeals on the decisions of the *qazis* and *mir adils*. But without the approval of the emperor he could not declare war, make peace or even inflict capital punishment. As he was in charge of the provincial forces, it was his duty to maintain order, help in the collection of revenue and execute royal decrees and regulations sent to him. The *subedars* were transferred every two to three years for fear that they might abuse the power delegated to them or become independent chiefs. A *faujdar* was appointed to help the *subedar,* who was the commander of the provincial troops and was responsible for maintaining law and order in the province.

Every province had a *diwan,* who was as powerful as the *subedar*. In fact these two officers helped to keep a system of checks and balances on the power of the two offices. Selected by the imperial *diwan,* the provincial *diwan* looked after the finances of the province; and the duties delegated to him included the collection of land revenue and maintenance of records, remissions and arrears of land revenue from various parts of the province. The *diwan* was required to cooperate with the *subedar* in the administration of the province; and in case of a difference of opinion between the two, the emperor's word would be final.

In the provinces, the third important official was the *bakshi*. Appointed by the imperial *bakshi* on the advice of the emperor He was entrusted the duties of looking after recruitment, discipline, training and supplies of the provincial army. Sometimes, duties of the *waqi-i-navis* were also handed over to him in which case he sent news from the province to the centre.

There was a *sadr* in every province, appointed by the central government, whose main duty was to supervise the *sayurghuls* or rent-free lands granted for religious and charitable purposes. The *qazis* and *mir adils* worked under him.

The *amil* was primarily the revenue collector in the province, but often he was required to multi-task. It was his duty to see that the quality of land improved, waste land was brought under cultivation, land measurement was done correctly, and the registers of the *karkuns, muqaddams* and *patwaris* were updated. He was also required to submit monthly reports concerning the condition of the people. The *bitikchi* acted as a check on the *amil* and enjoyed the same status as that of the latter. He prepared abstracts of revenue every season and sent an annual report to the central government. He also supervised the work of the *quanungos*. The *potdar's* duty was to receive money from the cultivators for the treasury. He also issued receipts and kept accounts of all payments to be made. He could

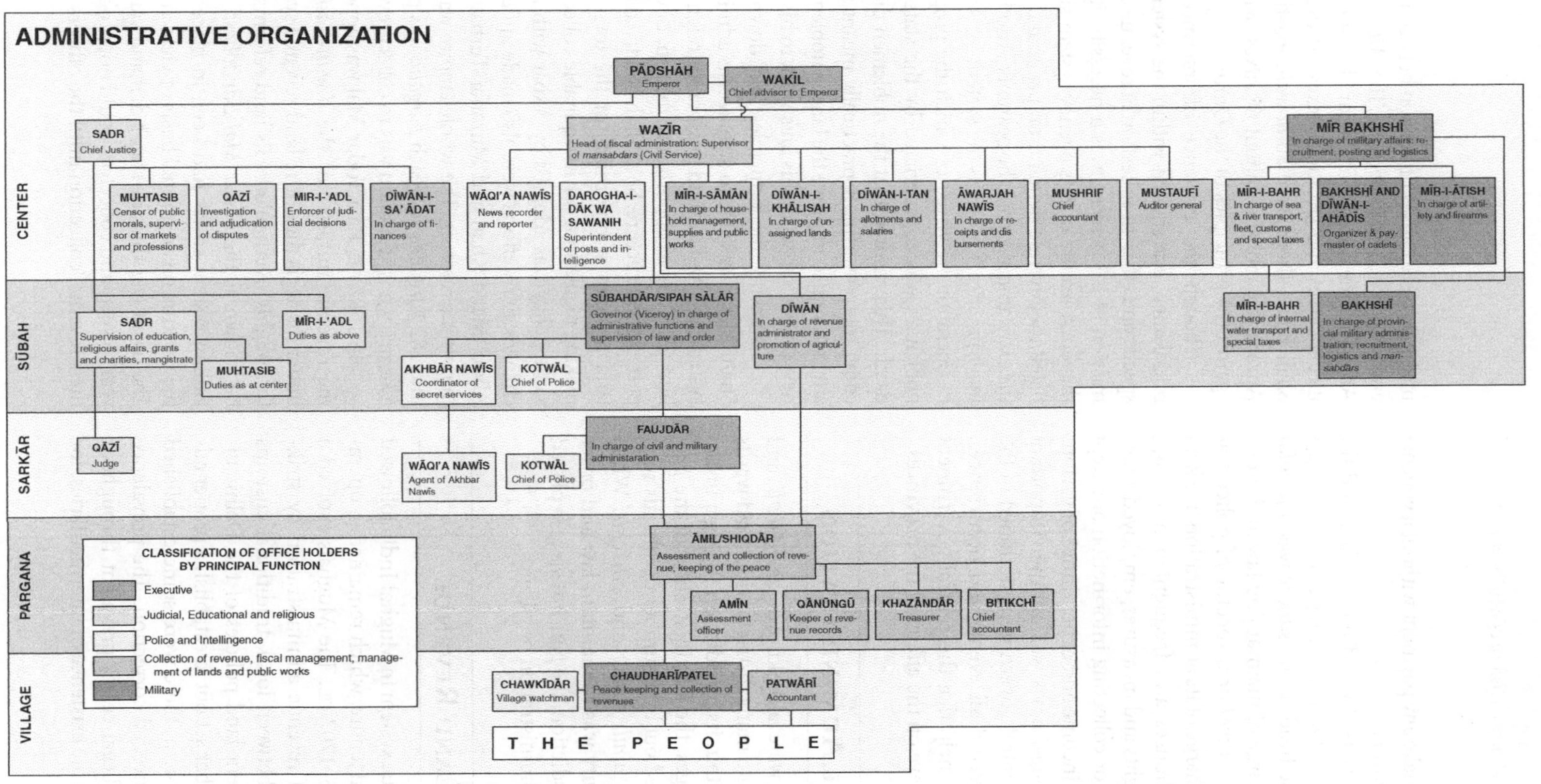

Administrative Organization, Mughal Empire, 1605 CE

not, however, make any payment without a voucher signed by the *diwan*.

The *subas* were divided into *sarkars* and the *sarkars* into *parganas* consisting of many villages and towns. The head of the *sarkar* was a *faujdar* who was in charge of maintaining law and order. In a town, the *kotwal* or inspector of police was given overall charge of its administration. He kept a register of houses and frequented buildings, examined weights and measures, employed a network of spies for collecting information and kept a check on the income and expenditure of various classes. The *waqi-i-navis* was another important officer of the central government stationed in the provinces to record all events and occurrences. It was with his help that the central government could keep an eye on the affairs of the provinces.

Local Administration

The *parganas* were also known as *mahals* and were divided into many districts which had wards or *mohallas* within its jurisdiction. Being a union of several villages, the administration of the *pargana* was carried out by a number of officials such as the *shiqdar, amil, potdar* and *bitikchis*. While the *shiqdar's* duty was to maintain law and order within his jurisdiction, the *panchayats* also played a role in the administration of villages.

Land Revenue

The land revenue system in Mughal India followed a system of land tenure, which remained in operation from 1526–1707 CE. The Mughals evolved a unique type of revenue administration by striking a balance between local, traditional customs and the prevalent land policies of the Delhi sultans. When Akbar set out to establish a proper administrative system, there were some established practices that needed correction. The prevalence of *abwabs* or illegal cesses prevalent throughout the empire and the existence of intermediaries, for instance, were causes of tension between the peasantry and the tax collectors. The *Ain-i-Akbari* of Abul Fazl mentions that Akbar abolished 29 such illegal cesses and vexatious taxes. At the death of Shah Jahan there were 50 *abwabs* existing, while Aurangzeb abolished about 68 taxes, which were against the principles of the *Quran*.

Though the existence of intermediaries or middlemen, entrenched within the system for the speedy and efficient collection of revenue on a commission of 2.5 percent, was a necessity, it was also the worst feature of this agency system since it inflated the revenue demand on paper and extracted the extra amount from the peasants. Another prominent practice, known as the system of escheat, was in operation by virtue of which the property of a nobleman was appropriated by the state after his death. This ensured that the noblemen did not become too powerful. It practically meant that even after striving to improve the land, a nobleman could never hope to pass on his life's work to his progeny.

Following the principles laid down by Sher Shah, Akbar was able to stabilize his administrative system, and his long and prosperous reign provided him with ample opportunity to plan, develop and perfect the structure. Sher Shah had fixed the state's land revenue at one-thirds of the total produce, making regulations for its equitable collection. The same policy was adopted by Akbar with necessary changes. Early efforts were also made under Khwaja Abdul Majid Khan and Muzaffar Turbati to bring in revenue reforms. The whole empire was divided into 182 *parganas* and each *pargana* was put under a *karori*, whose function was to collect revenue.

In 1582 CE, Raja Todar Mal was appointed as the revenue minister or the *diwan-i-ashraf*; and under his aegis the entire land revenue system was thoroughly overhauled. His land reforms came to be known as the *Todar Mal Bandobast*. The prevailing system so far had been in place to assess the revenue on an annual basis of yield and prices. The result was that the state's demand varied from year to year; and collectors could not proceed with their revenue collection until the officers fixed the rates to be charged. Todar Mal brought a change in this existing system by taking out an average rate of collection for the last 10 years (1570–80 CE); and one-thirds of this amount was fixed as the tax payable to the state. The procedure of surveying land was known as *paimaish,* which formerly involved the use of hempen-ropes; but this practice often resulted in faulty measurements, since the ropes contracted and expanded arbitrarily. Todar Mal introduced a new measuring instrument called the *jarib,* which was made of bamboo and was joined together with iron rings. This now gave a more correct measurement of land than the earlier method.

Land was primarily divided into four categories according to its level of fertility; and the share of the state was fixed accordingly—*polaj, parauti, chachar* and *banjar*. *Polaj* land was regularly cultivated and yielded revenue every year, while *parauti* land was occasionally left uncultivated to let it regain its productivity. On the other hand, *chachar* land was left uncultivated for three to four years, while *banjar* land was almost uncultivable and would be left for five or more years. *Polaj* and *parauti* lands were again subcategorized into three grades—good, middling and bad. The average of the three was taken as the basis of land assessment and one-thirds of the produce was fixed as the share of the state. In the case of *banjar* and *chachar* lands, however, the share was not fixed at one-thirds, but was increased gradually.

Land revenue could be paid either in cash or kind. And during famines, droughts and other unforeseen calamities, remission of land revenue was often granted. Sometimes loans were advanced to farmers for the purchase of seeds and livestock. Remissions of revenue were also allowed in a bad season. A record of all the holdings and liabilities of every cultivator was maintained and collectors were required to send reports of monthly returns to the royal treasury. Voluntary payments by cultivators were encouraged; and the state employed force only as a last resort. This was known as the *zabti* system, which was prevalent in Bihar, Allahabad, Lahore, Multan, Delhi, Agra, Awadh, Malwa, and parts of Gujarat. There were other systems of assessment prevalent in other parts of the Mughal Empire, such as the old Indian system of *galla baksh,* which assessed land on the basis of the division of crops. This prevailed in Thatta, and in parts of Kabul and Kashmir. Another system known as the *nasaq* did not involve any intermediary between the farmer and the state.

As a result of the land reforms introduced by Akbar, the farmers were better off than before and the land became prosperous. As the share of the state was fixed, the chances of fraud on the part of government servants too were considerably lessened. Peasants enjoyed the security of a fixed tenure and were freed from various miscellaneous exactions. Agriculture improved and the necessities of daily life became more affordable. Akbar's land revenue system continued to exist during the time of his successors, with minor alterations.

Closely linked with land revenue administration was the *jagirdari* system followed by the Mughals. The Mughal *mansabdars* were assigned *jagirs* in lieu of cash salaries; and the revenue from such *jagirs* usually maintained the *mansabdars* and their establishments. These *jagir* assignments initiated by Akbar, however, gave the *mansabdars* only the right to collect revenues; and they had no other responsibilities, including the maintenance of law and order in their *jagirs*. They were strictly prohibited from interfering in the traditional proprietary rights of the cultivators of the particular *jagirs*. Hence, this arrangement was purely fiscal giving only to the Rajput *mansabdars* more extensive rights of residence within their homeland of Rajputana. Rajput *mansabdars* generally received patrimonial (*watan*) lands as a part of the *jagirs* assigned to them; but in the course of time most *mansabdars* assumed the role of *jagirdars,* as they were vested with judicial powers (both civil and criminal in their regions).

The conditions for granting *jagirs* were clearly specified. On many occasions, one and the same person was asked to perform both civil and military duties, yet there was a clear distinction between

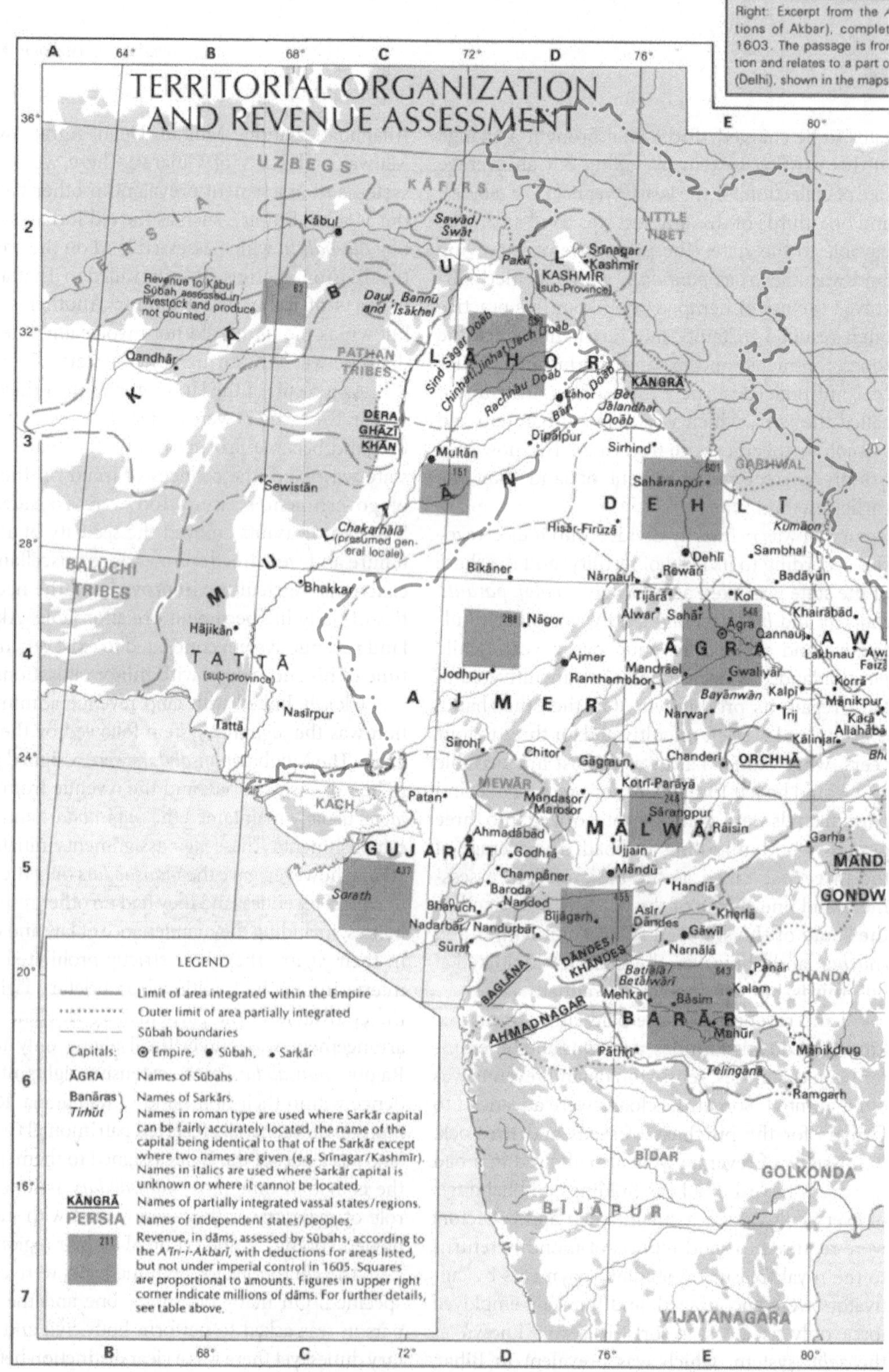

Map 22-1 *Territorial Organization and Revenue Assessment, Mughal Empire, 1605 CE*

ari (Institu-
ul Fazl in
etteer sec-
ār of Dehlī

SARKĀR OF DELHI

Contains 48 *Mahals*, 7,126,107 *Bighas*, 17 *Biswas*.
Revenue 123,012,590 *Dāms*. *Suyūrghāl* 10,990,260 *Dāms*.
Castes various. Cavalry, 4,000. Infantry, 23,980.

Parganās/Mahals[1]	Bighas Biswas[2]	Revenue Dāms[3]	Suyur-ghāl[4]	Cav-alry	Infan-try	Castes
Islāmābād Pākal, has a stone fort on a hill	97,067-19	1,779,407	31,462	50	1000	Rājpūt, Sānd
Adhah	14,912-8	513,081	45,420	20	200	Ahir
Pānipat, has a brick fort	568,444	10,756,647	3,540,632	100	2000	Afghān, Gujar, Ranghar
Pālam	245,240	5,726,787	1,231,880	70	1000	Jāt
Baran, has a brick fort on the Kālī Nadī	171,160	3,907,928	153,190	20	300	—
Bāghpat, on the Jamnā, between two streams	200,515	3,582,368	180,156	20	200	Brahman, Chauhān
Palwal, has a brick fort & it stands on a mound	234,783	1,769,493	218,225	25	500	Rājpūt, Gujar
Barnāwah	145,000	1,379,125	50,759	25	200	Shaikhzādah
Pāth, has a brick fort	48,191	621,749	7,243	60	600	Tonwār (Tuar)
Beri Dobaldhan	119,002-19	—		40	800	Jāt

Notes: 1) *Parganās/mahals* are territorial units on which revenue assessments were imposed. 2) *Bighas* and *biswas* are measures of land area, Akbar's standard *bigha* being 5/8 of an acre in size and a *biswa* 1/20 of a *bigha*. 3) Revenue was ordinarily assessed in *dāms*, at forty to the rupee. 4) *Suyurghāl* payments are assignments of revenue for charitable purposes.

Source: Abul Fazl-i-'Allāmi, *Ā'in-i-Akbarī*, tr. by Col. H. S. Jarrett, 2nd Ed., corrected and further annotated by Sir Jadu-Nath Sarkar, Calcutta: Royal Asiatic Society of Bengal, 1949, Vol. II, p. 291, with slight modifications.

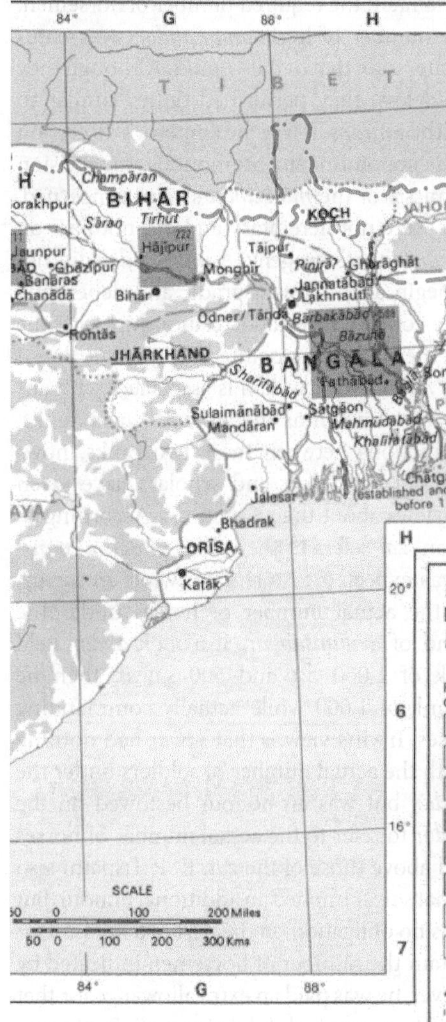

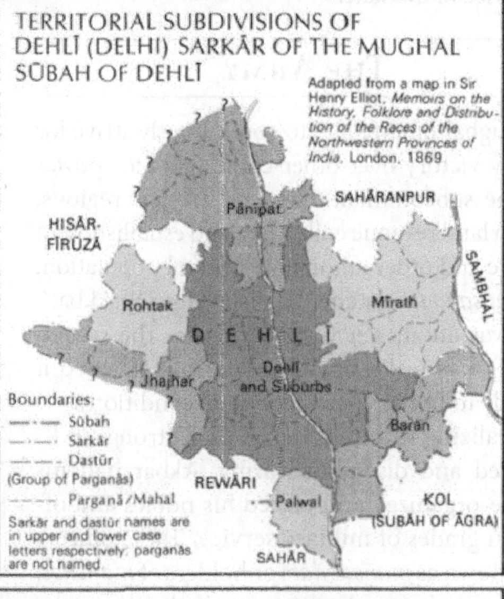

TERRITORIAL SUBDIVISIONS OF DEHLĪ (DELHI) SARKĀR OF THE MUGHAL SŪBAH OF DEHLĪ

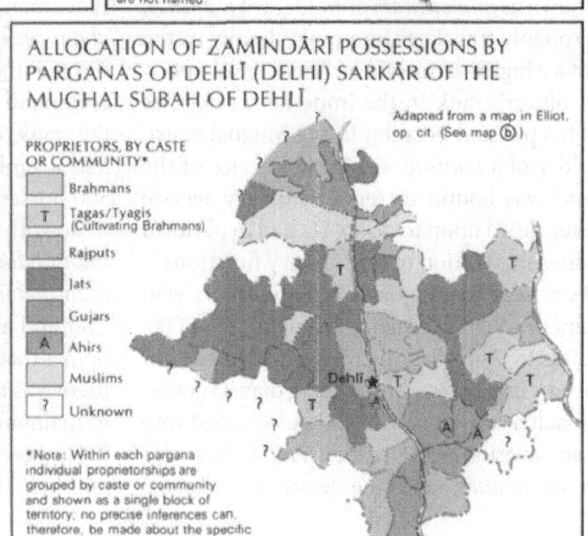

ALLOCATION OF ZAMĪNDĀRĪ POSSESSIONS BY PARGANAS OF DEHLĪ (DELHI) SARKĀR OF THE MUGHAL SŪBAH OF DEHLĪ

civil and military officers. In the case of a military *jagirdar*, for instance, the kind of personal service to be rendered and the maintenance of a specified number of horsemen were distinctly mentioned. There were also instances of a single *jagir* having been granted to more than one person, with each one's individual shares fixed. The most important element of the *jagir* assignments was that they were transferable and non-permanent. The success of the *jagirdari* system depended on the ability of the *jagirdar* to procure sufficient resources for his livelihood, and maintain a sufficient quota of troops for the service of the state.

The Army

The Mughal Empire had to continuously strive for military victory over other contestants for power over the subcontinent, conquest of new regions, smooth land revenue collection, and establishment of peace and order among the general population. The *mansabdari* system established during Akbar's reign was an answer to these needs. The system had its roots in Persia, but Akbar had adapted it uniquely to India's socio-economic conditions.

Realizing the importance of a strong, well-equipped and disciplined army, Akbar had his army re-organized and placed his nobles and officers in grades of military service. These officers were known as *mansabdars* or holders of *mansabs*, which roughly translates into rank, dignity or the office of a Mughal army officer. The *mansab* specified an officer's rank in the imperial services, as well as his pay and position in the Mughal court. The holder of a *mansab* was in the service of the state and was bound to render military service whenever called upon to do so. He had to perform civil duties in addition to his military functions.

There were many grades of *mansabdars* who maintained soldiers ranging from 10 to 5,000. According to Abul Fazl there were 66 grades of *mansabdars* in all; however, not more than 33 grades were in actual existence. They were classified into two main divisions—the higher *mansabdars*, also known as *umrahs*, and the lesser *mansabdars*. Those *mansabdars* who held the rank of one *hazari* or two *hazari* or any higher rank were known as the *umrahs*. Those who held a rank lower than that of 1,000, but not below 10, were called *mansabdars*. There were two methods of making payments to the *mansabdars*. The lesser *mansabdars* drew their pay directly from the imperial treasury and had to present their horsemen and horses for periodical inspections. In order to prevent fraud, these horses were branded and muster rolls of horsemen were maintained. The higher *mansabdars*, however, were granted *jagirs* out of the revenue from which they had to maintain the required number of horsemen.

The number of lesser *mansabdars* was naturally greater than that of the *umrahs*. Although they were paid less, they performed duties similar to those of the *umrahs*. It was the emperor's discretion where the appointments, promotions, supervision and dismissal of the *mansabdars* were concerned. *Mansabs* were not hereditary and did not pass on to the *mansabdar's* progeny. A *mansabdar* did not always begin at the lowest grade; and depending upon his competencies and relationship with the emperor, he could be appointed to any rank.

The *mansabdari* system is associated with another feature known as the *zat* and *sawar* ranks. The distinctions between these two ranks, however, are not very clear and scholars have given various views about their functions. According to Blochman, *zat* refers to the troops which a *mansabdar* was expected to maintain, while *sawar* indicated the actual number of horses under the command of a *mansabdar*. If a *mansabdar* held the rank of 1,000 *zat* and 500 *sawar*, then he had a rank of 1,000 while actually commanding 500 horses. Irwin's view is that *sawar* had nothing to do with the actual number of soldiers under the *mansabdar*, but was an honour bestowed on the *mansabdar* to refer to the actual number of horses over and above those of the *zat*. R. P. Tripathi also opines that *sawar* implied an additional honour, but there was no obligation on the part of a *mansabdar* to maintain the number of horsemen indicated by it. However, he was paid an extra allowance for that number. The view of Abdul Aziz and S. R. Sharma is that *zat* imposed an obligation on a *mansabdar* to maintain a fixed number of elephants, horses, beasts of burden and carts, but no horsemen or cavalry. However, the *sawar* represented the actual number of cavalry under a *mansabdar*.

Based on the *zat* and *sawar* ranks, there were three categories of *mansabdars*. A *mansabdar* was fixed in the first category if his *zat* and *sawar* ranks were equal. He belonged to the second category if the *sawar* was half of his *zat*, and in the last if the *sawar* was less than half the *zat* or if there was no *sawar* at all.

The *mansabdar*i system worked efficiently during the time of Akbar as the number of *mansabdars* was limited. However, with the passage of time, the number of *mansabdars* increased under Akbar's successors, resulting in frequent quarrels among the nobility for higher *mansabs*. Higher *mansabs* were, therefore, created partly as a matter of requirement and partly to appease the defiant nobles and princes; but by the end of Aurangzeb's reign the system totally collapsed.

The Judiciary

In their administration of justice, the Mughals followed the pattern established by the Delhi sultans. No written code of laws existed in the Mughal era; and the only notable exceptions were the 12 ordinances of Jahangir and the *Fatwa-i-Alamgiri* of Aurangzeb. In dispensing justice, the judges chiefly followed the Quranic injunctions, the *fatwas* or previous interpretations of the *Shariah* by eminent jurists and the *qanuns* or ordinances of the emperors. The judicial department was headed by a chief legal officer known as the *qazi-ul-quzat* at the central level and *qazis* at the provincial level. The position of the *qazi-ul-quzat* in legal matters was next only to the emperor, and he was responsible for the proper and efficient administration of justice. *Qazis* were appointed by him in every province, district and city. The duty of the chief *qazi* was to hear appeals from their courts and supervise their conduct. Every city and even large villages had their local *qazi,* assisted by the *mufti* and the *mir adil.* The *muftis* explained Islamic law, and the *mir adils* drew up and pronounced judgments. When there was a difference of opinion among the provincial judicial officials, the decision of the central authorities was taken to be final.

The Mughal emperors were great lovers of justice and tried to be as just as possible. The judicial system even placed senior officers within the purview of law, and perhaps the only person above the law was the emperor himself. The legal procedures were, in fact, much simpler and quicker than today. Babur and Humayun were known to have held an open court once a week, while Akbar devoted time on a daily basis to hear the complaints of his people and to settle their disputes. In addition to this, Akbar set aside every Thursday exclusively for holding an open court for the administration of justice. This was a formal procedure and was attended by high judicial officials, such as the chief *qazi, muftis* and other important legal dignitaries. Acting as the highest court of appeal in the land, the emperor a certained facts about every case personally before pronouncing judgments. Jahangir followed in the footsteps of his father and is popular for his legendary chain of justice; and Shah Jahan, too, besides listening to complaints each morning, held a court for deciding cases every Wednesday. For some time Aurangzeb also followed this ancestral practice of administering justice; but in his later years, he left it to the provincial governors. Capital punishment was given only in extreme cases and that too by the emperor himself. There were no primary courts below the *qazis,* and the village *panchayats* decided minor cases. Fines were generally imposed as punishment, but sometimes criminals were also imprisoned and whipped. There were no separate prisons or jails as they exist today, and prisoners were kept in dark dingy cells within the dungeons of forts.

The administrative system of the Mughal Empire was largely the handiwork of Akbar during whose time the system worked like a well-oiled machine. It continued to exist during Jahangir's and Shah Jahan's reigns; but began to gradually deteriorate during Aurangzeb's rule.

SUMMARY

- The administrative system of the Mughal empire was largely the handiwork of Akbar, whose task was simplified by Sher Shah's system of organization, which Akbar incorporated to a large extent.
- During Akbar's time the system worked very well, but it began to deteriorate from the time of Aurangzeb.
- The emperor was at the helm of affairs, with unlimited freedom in making laws. He had a council of ministers to assist him in implementing his policies.
- The Mughal administrative structure was highly centralized. This centralization was manifested in the efficient working of the land revenue system, *mansab* and *jagir* systems, as well as in the judicial system.
- The empire was administered by a number of departments with officers assigned to each of them.
- For administrative convenience and revenue collection, the Mughal Empire was divided into a hierarchical system of areas—*subas, sarkars* and *parganas*—with officers working in various capacities.
- Raja Todar Mal was appointed as the revenue minister by Akbar and under his aegis the whole land revenue system was thoroughly overhauled. His land revenue reforms came to be known as the *Todar Mal Bandobast*. Surveying land, division of land into four classes according to its fertility for fixing the share of the state, and granting relief in times of unforeseen calamities, were some of the features of the system.
- Realizing the importance of a strong, well-equipped and disciplined army, Akbar re-organized his army and placed his nobles and officers in grades of military service. In the *mansabdari* system instituted by Akbar, every officer was assigned a rank which denoted his social rank and the contingent he had to maintain. Every *mansabdar* had to perform civil duties in addition to his military functions.
- With regard to law and justice, the emperor was the final authority. Though there was no written code of laws, disputes were speedily settled, often on the basis of equity and natural justice. The aim of the judicial system was primarily to settle individual complaints and disputes rather than to enforce a legal code.

KEYWORDS

Wakil
Wazir
Diwan
Diwan-i-am
Diwan-i-khas
Mir bakshi
Sadr
Suba
Todar Mal Bandobast
Paimaish
Mansabdari system
Zat and sawar
Qazi, mufti and mir adil

REVIEW QUESTIONS

1. Enumerate the main features of provincial administration as instituted by the Mughals.
2. What were the reforms brought in by Raja Todar Mal in land revenue administration?
3. Explain in detail the judicial administration of the Mughals.
4. Examine the role played by the mansabdars in Mughal administration.
5. What are the different views of historians on the concepts of 'zat' and 'sawar'?

CHAPTER **23**

Socio-Economic and Religious Conditions in Mughal India

Review and Discussion

- Social Conditions
- Economic Conditions
- Religious Conditions

There is no doubt that the study of territorial conquests and administrative policies of the Mughals offers a broad insight into the period, however, it is only through an analysis of the socio-economic institutions and religious innovations of that era that we gain a complete understanding of the conditions prevailing in the Indian subcontinent. The Mughals bequeathed to the Indian subcontinent a rich legacy of Indo-Islamic civilization and culture. While implementing long-lasting administrative and economic reforms, they made invaluable contributions to the growth and development of a society that was a culmination of both indigenous and foreign elements in the land.

Social Conditions

The Indian society during the medieval period was largely organized on the basis of a feudal structure that continued even in the time of the Mughal rule. Society was stratified primarily into three sections—upper, middle and lower. While the king and his nobility formed the upper section, the court poets, physicians, traders, artisans and farmers comprised the middle, and the masses constituted the lower section. The emperor, who was the final authority heading this social hierarchy was held in high regard by his subjects. Under him were the nobility, some of whom were given high offices in the state. Raja Todar Mal, Raja Man Singh, Asaf Khan, Murshid Quli Khan, Mir Jumla, Abdur Rahim and Mahabat Khan were some of the distinguished generals and administrators who occupied important ranks in the military and administrative setup of the Mughals. The nobility played an active role in assisting the ruler in implementing the policies of state, especially during the reigns of Akbar, Jahangir and Shah Jahan. But in course of time, the nobility lost its power and strength of character, which was one of the reasons that led to the decline of the Mughal Empire.

The Nobility

The life of the nobles who lived during the Mughal period was opulent and luxurious and they comprised the affluent section of society. The *mansabdars* and *jagirdars* who formed a large part of this section maintained landed estates, used luxury products lavishly and indulged in a life of debauchery and extravagance. Frequent drunken soirées and harems with a large number of women were common features of the times. Sports like hunting and gambling amusements were other favoured pastimes. The incomes of the upper crust was spent as quickly as it was acquired.

The Mughal aristocracy was a status symbol of the Mughal court and symbolized a culture that was magnificent and opulent. A display of cultural extravagance was a sign of higher social and political status for the nobles, who constantly desired proximity to the emperor. To be appointed as a staff of the royal chamber was a sign of great privilege and assured higher social status. Mughal courtly culture was reflected in various forms—in the architecture of personal homes, in fashionable dressing, and in one's conduct, manner and speech. Over a period of time, this courtly culture filtered down even to popular literature, art and architecture. Like the imperial court, aristocratic households too became not only political centres but also artistic, intellectual, and cultural centres. Without the extravagant lifestyle of the nobles, Mughal life and art would have been devoid of much of its richness. The nobles patronized art and culture by indulging in artistic pursuits, encouraging artists, poets and craftsmen as a part of cultural enterprise. These courtly ideals of arts and manners were, therefore, easily diffused even among the middle classes, affecting their customs, ideas, aspirations, tastes and pleasures.

Others in the Social Hierarchy

Contrary to the nobility, the middle segment of society and the poorer masses below them did not lead a luxurious life, and neither did they have the financial means to indulge in the vices of the nobility. The middle class was a heterogeneous group of well-off merchants, professionals and petty *mansabdars*. It is said that the merchants usually did not reveal their sound financial status, as there was always the danger of their wealth being forcibly taken away by the local governor or *faujdar*. The petty *mansabdars* did not play any significant role in society and instead tried to replicate extravagant lifestyles of their higher counterparts. In order to maintain such aspirational lifestyles, they needed extra incomes, which they tried to garner through corrupt practices

Cultivators, artisans, small traders, shopkeepers, household servants and slaves comprised the lower classes of Mughal society. Most of them worked hard for their livelihood and lived a life of bare sustenance. Their lives were simple and their possessions limited. Financially, the petty shopkeepers were better off than the artisans, who had to wander in search of work as there was never enough work in a single village. In general, the masses had no economic liberty, no right to justice or personal freedom, and were by and large an oppressed lot.

Besides the local Hindus and the Muslims, there were foreign visitors who came as temporary residents from Europe, Arabia, Persia, China, Japan and many other nations. The Parsis, though a relatively small group, were a very influential section, particularly during the time of Akbar, who was attracted to some of their religious practices. The increase in foreign trade invited an increasing number of Portuguese, Dutch, Danish, English, and French traders and adventurers who were eager to establish a base in Mughal India.

The Position of Women

In Mughal society, women generally occupied a subordinate position. This was a result of social practices, such as the *purdah,* polygamy, female infanticide and *sati*, which relegated women to the background. *Purdah* or veiling of women was a common practice among the Muslims, and it was also adopted by Hindu women after the advent of the Muslims. This system was particularly prevalent among affluent families of both communities, as it came to be associated as an elitist practice. Polygamy was common among the Muslims while

Hindus mostly practiced monogamy; but Hindu rulers were an exception to this rule. Girls were married off at an early age in both the communities; and while divorce and widow remarriage was permitted among the Muslims, they were non-existent customs among the Hindus. The practice of *sati* and female infanticide were also widely prevalent among Hindus. Akbar is, in fact, said to have taken steps to curb the evil practice of *sati*. The position of Muslim women in Mughal India was economically better than their Hindu sisters, since they were entitled to a fixed share in the family inheritance according to the *Shariah*, whereas Hindu women could not claim any.

Yet, there were quite a few talented women who made noteworthy contributions in different social spheres. Some of the remarkable women worth mentioning are Gulbadan Banu Begum, the sister of Humayun; Jahan Ara and Roshan Ara, the daughters of Shah Jahan; Zebun Nisa, the daughter of Aurangzeb; Chand Bibi and Rani Durgavati, the heroic defenders of Ahmednagar and Gondwana; Nur Jahan, the queen of Jahangir; Jija Bai, the mother of Shivaji and Tara Bai, who continued the war of Maratha independence against Aurangzeb.

Economic Conditions

As a result of their grand schemes of conquest and territorial expansion, the Mughal emperors became masters of enormous resources in their empire. From Akbar's annexation of Malwa in 1561 CE to the fall of Golconda in 1687 CE, every victory yielded large amounts of wealth from the defeated kingdoms. In addition to this loot, revenue was collected through taxes on agricultural production and trade.

Agricultural Production

Agriculture was the chief occupation of the people and the main source of income for the state. The methods of cultivation and agricultural crops were almost the same as those that are grown today. Raja Todar Mal's revenue administration during Akbar's reign gave an impetus to agriculture, thereby making consumables considerably cheap. The chief crops grown were rice, wheat, barley, cotton, sugarcane, millet, pulses, indigo, etc. Tobacco was introduced by the Portuguese, and was cultivated from the beginning of the seventeenth century. From the ordinances of Jahangir and Manucci's *Storio do Mogor*, it becomes clear that the use of tobacco was prevalent. Peasants in Bengal quickly learned techniques of mulberry cultivation and sericulture, turning the region into a major silk-producer of the world. Later, with the cultivation of cotton, opium and sugar as cash crops, there was a marked increase in export trade.

In nearly every region within the Mughal Empire, sedentary agricultural activity encompassed large areas of land, pushing pastoralists and shifting cultivators to further areas as was the case in the north-east along the foothills of the Himalayas, as well as in eastern Bengal and Assam.

Akbar took special care to look after the interests of farmers, as a result of which they lived comfortably during his reign, but their condition deteriorated under his successors. Inadequate artificial irrigational facilities, frequent famines and heavy demands of the state were some of the aspects that added to their misery and suffering.

Non-Agricultural Production

The chief items that came within the purview of non-agricultural production were fisheries, minerals, salt, sugar, opium, indigo and liquor. Copper was produced in the mines of central India and Rajputana; iron was produced in many parts of India; salt was prepared from the Sambar Lake and refined sugar was made in Bengal. Opium was produced in Malwa and Bihar while indigo was produced at Biana and other places. The most noteworthy feature of non-agricultural production during the reigns of Akbar's successors was the enhanced demand for saltpetre, the production of which gave employment to a considerable number of workers.

Silk weaving flourished at Lahore, Agra and Gujarat. The famous Indian muslin was produced at Sonargaon in the Dhaka district of Bengal. Woollen shawls and carpets, jewels, decorative swords and jade bowls were also produced. Agra, Fatehpur Sikri and Lahore evolved to be notable trading centres.

The Jagir System

An important feature of the Mughal agricultural economy was the prevalence of *jagirs*, which came up as the successor to the earlier *iqta* system of the Delhi Sultanate.The new institution of the *jagir* was unique in many respects. The *jagirdars* were officers of the emperor who were assigned *jagirs* or land grants in lieu of salary. The *jagirdar* was periodically transferred so that he did not develop local roots. After the death of the *jagirdars*, the *jagirs* were taken back by the state, leading the *jagirdars* to try and make long term gains in a short time. Hence, these procedures led to a system of excessive exploitation of the peasantry, who were left with hardly any option but to rebel against the established structure. There were frequent peasant uprisings of the Jats, Sikhs and Satnamis, who were the major agricultural communities facing hardships as a result of the general economic impoverishment.

The peasantry formed an important component of the Mughal agrarian economy. They were the agrarian classes right at the bottom of the feudal pyramid. The topmost level consisted of the traditional ruling class of *zamindars* and below them was the class consisting of the *chaudhuries, thakurs, rais, rawats* and people in the posts of *quanungos, muqaddams* and *patwaris*. The *zamindars*, irrespective of whether they cultivated the land received 1/10th of the produce of the cultivators' own lands. The next level of officials (*patwaris, muqaddams, quanungos*, etc.) also received a percentage of the total revenue collected from the rural areas.

Among the class of peasantry, the *khud-kasht* cultivators were those who had well-assigned hereditary rights and duties. The Jats and Ahirs in northwestern India and the Marathas in western India were examples in this category. Local officials like *muqaddams, kulkarnis* and *patels* as well as intermediary *zamindars* belonged to the *khud-kasht* group. There was a mutually dependent relationship between the state, the *zamindars* and the cultivators, wherein the *khud-kasht* predominated. This was a major contibutor to Mughal economic stability.

Among all segments of Mughal society, the worst off were the landless rural labourers who often belonged to the lower castes like *chamars* or *begaris*. Although it appears that the peasants were better off than the landless labourers, historical evidence shows that the peasantry were in an equally deplorable condition. Apart from the tax burden, there were other factors that made the life of peasants miserable. Arrears were regularly collected and the peasants who could not fulfil the revenue demands were imprisoned. Sometimes, the peasants did not get the right market price for their produce either, since low prices were maintained by the state. To top it all, they were frequently exploited by the *jagirdars* who were granted *jagirs* for short durations. During the later Mughal period, the increase in the number of *jagirdars* was so phenomenal that there was an acute shortage of lands that could be assigned as *jagirs*. This agrarian crisis worsened in the later years of Aurangzeb's reign, when peasants started migrating from region to region and frequent conflicts erupted between the peasantry and the *jagirdars* and *zamindars*.

Industrial and Craft Production

The accounts of foreign travellers and other contemporary texts reveal that trade and commerce was in a flourishing condition and Indian goods were highly prized abroad. The Mughal emperors encouraged production in the state *karkhanas* or factories, where high quality goods were produced. The most important industry in India at that time was the cotton cloth industry; the main centres of which were Patan in Gujarat, Burhanpur in Khandesh, Jaunpur, Banaras, Malwa, Deccan and Dhaka. Cotton cloth was either dyed or printed with fast colours. Fine muslin was produced at Sonargaon, in the Dhaka district of Bengal. Silk was also manufactured in Bengal; and its production was particularly patronized by the Mughal emperors. Miscellaneous goods, such as cotton carpets, rugs and ropes were woven everywhere.

Besides supplying its domestic markets, India also supplied cotton cloth to the east coast of Africa, Arabia, Egypt, Burma, Malacca, the Straits, and certain minor Asian markets. The industry, which was well established in Akbar's time, continued to flourish under Jahangir and Shah Jahan, and received further impetus when the Dutch and English traders brought India into direct contact with the western markets. Though silk weaving was in practice, its demand was confined to the upper classes, who primarily wore it; therefore, the products of Indian looms faced competition from silk goods imported from the Far East, Central Asia and Persia. Akbar's patronage and interest in this industry was directly responsible for the expansion of silk-weaving in Lahore, Agra, Fatehpur Sikri and Gujarat. Akbar's influence was likewise felt in the shawl and carpet-weaving industries too. While shawls were woven at Lahore, carpets were manufactured in both Lahore and Agra.

Apart from these major industries, handicrafts, such as jewellery, metal work, ornamental discs, ivory articles and many other goods were also manufactured in large quantities in Mughal India. Gold and silver articles were in great demand among the royalty, nobility, temples and monasteries. Similarly, luxury goods of pearls, ivory, coral and sandalwood were also in great demand among different classes. These articles were famous for their delicate workmanship, artistic designs and excellent finish. Among the principal crafts of the Mughal age, carpentry was important. The manufacture of wooden bedsteads, chests, stools, boxes, leather goods, paper and pottery articles were all encouraged. Since earthenware was used by the vast majority, potters worked in almost every village to meet the requirements of their locality.

Iron goods were in equal demand, right from the peasant to the emperor. Ironsmiths produced both civilian articles as well as military equipment. Delhi with its adjoining areas and Bengal were also known for the manufacture of high quality copperware. Banaras specialized in brassware, while Bengal produced fine domestic utensils of a variety of bronze alloys.

As a result of the growth of industry and trade, some of the chief cities and ports of India—Agra, Fatehpur, Multan, Lahore, Ahmedabad, Banaras, Patna, Dhaka, Chattagram, Kambath, Bharuch, Surat and Hughli—became very prosperous.

Trade and Commerce

The organized internal administration and the general peace and prosperity in Akbar's empire paved the way for the progress of trade and commerce. India always had substantial internal and external trade relations with the rest of the world, such as Ceylon, Burma, China, Japan, the East Indies, Nepal, Persia, Central Asia, the Red Sea ports and East Africa. India's flourishing overseas trade caused many European nations to vie with one another for a share in the lucrative trade with Mughal India. During Akbar's reign, the main trading ports were Kambath, Surat, Bharuch, Lahri, Bassein, Goa, Calicut, Kochi, Nagapatnam, Masulipatnam and Satgaon. The trade routes via land operated from Lahore to Kabul and beyond, and from Multan to Qandahar and beyond. The chief markets of foreign trade were Lahore, Multan, Lahri, Kambath, Ahmedabad, Surat, Satgaon, Patna and Agra.

The exports from India consisted of textile fabrics, indigo, pepper and other spices, opium and other herbal narcotics. These goods were exported to Africa, Arabia, Egypt, Burma, Malacca, the Straits and several other countries of Asia. Though India did not depend on any country for manufactured goods, yet its imports included gold, silver, copper, zinc, lead, horses, raw silk, ivory, coral, amber, precious stones, textiles—silk, velvet, brocade, broad cloth—and perfumes. European wines, African slaves and Chinese porcelain were much appreciated by Akbar and his nobles.

During the reigns of Jahangir, Shah Jahan and Aurangzeb, the Dutch and English were the chief overseas traders who established their presence in all major markets from Sind to Bengal. They established important trading bases that offered unlimited opportunities for the expansion of direct trade between India and the foreign markets. Indigo and Indian calicoes formed important commodities of trade from 1625 CE; and the port of Surat emerged as a major centre for European imports and exports on the west coast. The four items of India's trade with Europe during Aurangzeb's reign included calicoes of Madras, and saltpetre, silk and sugar of Bengal.

Foreign traders had to pay low customs duties. At Surat, for example, the customs duties were 3.5 percent on all imports and exports of goods and two percent on either gold or silver money. Domestic traders on the other hand also had to pay taxes and ferry tolls for the use of roads and rivers.

Coinage and Exchange

Since Muhammad bin Tughlaq's reign, several kinds of currency had prevailed leading to confusion in the market. Babur and Humayun did not get enough time during their reigns to bring in financial reforms, but Sher Shah had attempted to correct the irregularities by introducing a rupee of 175–178 grains and the copper *dam*. It was largely left to Akbar to reform the currency.

Khwaja Abdul Samad of Miraz who was appointed as the master of the imperial mint at Delhi in 1577 CE, as part of his financial reforms issued new gold, silver and copper coins; and also put the provincial mints under important officials. Various kinds of gold coins were issued, around 26 in number. The gold coin, known as *ilahi*, was worth Rs. 10 while the chief silver coin was the square silver rupee, known as *jalali*, made of 172 ½ grains. The chief copper coin was the *dam*, more popularly called *paisa*, which was used by the rich and poor alike.

Religious Conditions

The Mughal Empire was a purely Indian historical experience. Mughal culture blended Perso-Islamic and regional Indian elements into a distinct whole. Babur and Humayun had struggled against heavy odds to create the Mughal domain, while Akbar—apart from consolidating and expanding its frontiers—had provided the theoretical framework for a truly Indian state. Akbar attacked narrow-mindedness and bigotry through his policy of toleration and understanding, which was enforced keeping in view the vast majority of non-Muslims in Hindustan. This tradition continued until the end of Shah Jahan's reign; but thereafter Aurangzeb gave in to opposing forces—but this too was done for a certain larger cause.

Babur, the first Mughal ruler, was not strict in his religious observances and practices. He did not allow Islamic principles to interfere with his political ambitions of consolidating the most powerful state. He loved the company of learned men from every faith and was himself a gifted writer. With such an outlook, Babur did not persecute any sect or creed. His successor, Humayun, also followed the footsteps of his father; and his principal adviser, Bairam Khan, was a Shia. While living in exile in Persia, Humayun closely associated himself with Shiism, while remaining tolerant towards other religions.

Humayun's son and successor, Akbar, was born to queen Hamida Banu Begum, the daughter of a cultured Shia family. By personal conviction, however, Akbar was a Sunni. He was brought up in a cosmopolitan atmosphere and was broad minded by nature. He, therefore, displayed the spirit of toleration and harmony in all his actions and decisions. When Akbar assumed power, he found that the participation of the regional political elite in running the affairs of the state was not only essential to overcome certain hurdles, but also important for the healthy existence of the state. Therefore, Akbar had to choose between the Islamic orthodoxy and the more fruitful Indianization of his political regime.

Under the influence of his regent, tutors and friends, Akbar's religious views underwent a great change with the passage of time. He was inquisitive by nature and wanted to learn the true essence behind every religion; he never condemned any religion by word or by deed. In 1562 CE, Akbar married the daughter of Raja Bharmal of Amber—a matrimonial alliance which marked the beginning of his new religious policy aimed at appeasing the Rajputs and other non-Muslim groups. The marriage helped to end the age-old friction between the Rajputs and the Muslims in India. In 1563 CE, Akbar abolished the pilgrimage tax which was levied on Hindus during their pilgrimages; and the very next year (1564 CE) he abolished the *jiziya*, or the poll tax, which was levied on all non-Muslims. He also removed the restrictions imposed on the construction of places of worship by non-Muslims. As a result, new temples and churches came up in various parts of the empire.

Akbar also established a Translation Department, which was given the task of translating Hindu religious scriptures, such as the *Atharvaveda*, the *Mahabharata*, *Harivamsa* and the *Ramayana* into Persian. Akbar opened the gates of government service to people from all religions, castes and creeds. He appointed Hindus to important posts in the state (both in civil and military administration), while Raja Todar Mal appointed Hindus with knowledge of the Persian language in the revenue department. The result was that most Hindus learnt Persian, bringing the two communities closer to each other. There were no forcible conversions during Akbar's reign and the construction of the *Ibadat Khana* at Fatehpur Sikri in 1575 CE is testimony to the fact that Akbar wanted to engage in a meaningful dialogue with all religions and faiths.

Akbar systematically initiated various experiments like the *Sulh-i-Kul, Din-i-Illahi*; and above all the promulgation of the *Mahzar*, through which he delegated to himself the powers to interpret various Islamic norms, which had so far been the *ulema*'s

THE *RAZMNAMA* OR BOOK OF WARS, *the Persian translation of the Mahabharata. Naqib Khan was commissioned by Akbar to produce the translation for circulation among the Amirs in furtherance of Akbar's desire to promote understanding between Muslims and Hindus. In this painting the patriarch Bhishma is shown dying pierced by arrows under an immense ficus tree. He is being watched over by Krishna and the five Pandava brothers. The Pandavas are all dressed in Islamic armour and robes.*

domain. Although the *ulema* expressed their hostility, the significant achievement of these efforts was that the Mughal state succeeded in undermining the role of Islam in the interplay of politics by establishing a kind of common citizenship.

Jahangir, the successor of Akbar, was as liberal and enlightened as his father. He closely interacted with *brahmans*, Jain scholars and Christian missionaries. He respected the teachings of Islam, but participated in the celebrations of Hindu festivals too. As in Akbar's time, the Hindus continued to occupy high offices under him. However, certain excesses committed by Jahangir brought him disfavour. Jahangir is criticized for having destroyed the Jwalamukhi temple after the conquest of Kangra; and the Varah temple at Pushkar, near Ajmer. He suspected the Jains of having sided with Prince Khusrau and on that ground banished them from the empire. On the same charge of helping Prince Khusrau, Jahangir tortured and put to death Guru Arjun Dev.

Jahangir's son and successor, Shah Jahan, when compared with his father and grandfather was more attached to the tenets of Islam. Although he practiced Islam, there was no systematic policy of discrimination against the Hindus during his reign either. He did not revive the *jiziya*; and although he intended to revive the pilgrimage tax, he never did so. He did not deprive the Hindus of the high offices held by them; and by and large kept the sentiments of his Hindu subjects in mind.

Under Aurangzeb, however, the trend gradually reversed. The religious policy adopted by Aurangzeb was very different from that of his

His Majesty as the Spiritual Guide of the People

Men of all nations, young and old, friends and strangers, the far and the near, look upon offering a vow to His Majesty as the means of solving all their difficulties, and bend down in worship on obtaining their desire. Others again, from the distance of their homes, or to avoid the crowds gathering at Court, offer their vows in secret, and pass their lives in grateful praises. But when His Majesty leaves Court, in order to settle the affairs of a province, to conquer a kingdom, or to enjoy the pleasures of the chase, there is not a hamlet, a town, or a city, that does not send forth crowds of men and women with vow-offerings in their hands, and prayers on their lips, touching the ground with their foreheads, praising the efficacy of their vows, or proclaiming the accounts of the spiritual assistance received. Other multitudes ask for lasting bliss, for an upright heart, for advice how best to act, for strength of the body, for enlightenment, for the birth of a son, the reunion of friends, a long life, increase of wealth, elevation in rank, and many other things. His Majesty, who knows what is really good, gives satisfactory answers to every one, and applies remedies to their religious perplexities. Not a day passes but people bring cups of water to him, beseeching him to breathe upon it. He who reads the letters of the divine orders in the book of fate, on seeing the tidings of hope, takes the water with his blessed hands, places it in the rays of the world-illuminating sun, and fulfils the desire of the suppliant. Many sick people of broken hopes, whose diseases the most eminent physicians pronounced incurable, have been restored to health by this divine means.

A more remarkable case is the following. A simple-minded recluse had cut off his tongue, and throwing it towards the threshold of the palace, said, "If that certain blissful thought *(his thought was this: If Akbar is a prophet, he must, from his supernatural*

(Continued)

(Continued)

wisdom, find out in what condition I am lying here), which I just now have, has been put into my heart by God, my tongue will get well; for the sincerity of my belief must lead to a happy issue." The day was not ended before he obtained his wish.

Those who are acquainted with the religious knowledge and the piety of His Majesty will not attach any importance to some of his customs, remarkable as they may appear at first; and those who know His Majesty's charity and love of justice do not even see any thing remarkable in them. In the magnanimity of his heart, he never thinks of his perfection, though he is the ornament of the world. Hence he even keeps back many who declare themselves willing to become his disciples. He often says, "Why should I claim to guide men, before I myself am guided?" But when a novice bears on his forehead the sign of earnestness of purpose, and he be daily enquiring more and more, His Majesty accepts him, and admits him on a Sunday, when the world-illuminating sun is in its highest splendour. Notwithstanding every strictness and reluctance shown by His Majesty in admitting novices, there are many thousands, men of all classes, who have cast over their shoulders the mantel of belief, and look upon their conversion to the New Faith as the means of obtaining every blessing.

At the above-mentioned time of everlasting auspiciousness, the novice with his turban in his hands puts his head on the feet of His Majesty. This is symbolical, and expresses that the novice, guided by good fortune and the assistance of his good star, has cast aside conceit and selfishness, the root of so many evils, offers his heart in worship, and now comes to enquire as to the means of obtaining everlasting life. His Majesty, the chosen one of God, then stretches out the hand of favour, raises up the suppliant, and replaces the turban on his head, meaning by these symbolical actions that he has raised up a man of pure intentions, who from seeming existence has now entered into real life. His Majesty then gives the novice the *Shaçt* (means 'aim'; secondly 'anything round' like a ring, the way it seems to have been used here), upon which is engraved 'the Great Name,'* and His Majesty's symbolical motto, *'Allahu Akbar.'* This teaches the novice the truth that:

"The pure Shaçt and the pure sight never err."

Seeing the wonderful habits of His Majesty, his sincere attendants are guided, as circumstances require it; and from the wise counsels they receive, they soon state their wishes openly. They learn to satisfy their thirst in the spring of divine favour, and gain for their wisdom and motives renewed light. Others, according to their capacities are taught wisdom in excellent advices.

But it is impossible while speaking of other matters besides, to give a full account of the manner in which His Majesty teaches wisdom, heals dangerous diseases, and applies remedies for the severest sufferings. Should my occupations allow sufficient leisure, and should another term of life be granted me, it is my intention to lay before the world a separate volume on this subject.

Source: *The Ain-i-Akbari* by Abul Fazl, Vol. I, Ain 77. Available at Persian Literature in Translation: The Packard Humanities Institute.

predecessors. He was a staunch puritanical Muslim; and moreover, since he had come to power with the support of a group of *ulema* who stood for the restoration of orthodox Islam, he felt compelled to appease them and consistently gain their support. He, therefore, abandoned the policy of separation of religion and the state, turning away from the policy of religious toleration followed by Akbar, Jahangir and Shah Jahan. The execution of the Sikh guru, Tegh Bahadur in 1675 CE by Aurangzeb instigated the Sikhs to rebellion—permanently severing all relations between the Sikhs and the Mughals. In 1679 CE, he re-introduced the *jiziya* that had been abolished by Akbar a century earlier. The result was a revolt of the Hindu Rajputs, supported by Aurangzeb's third son, Prince Akbar, in 1680–81 CE. In the Deccan, Aurangzeb's primary grudge against the sultanates of Bijapur and Golconda was on account of their affiliation with Shia Islam which ended with their conquest in 1686 CE and 1687 CE, respectively; while the Maratha kingdom was broken up and its ruler Sambhaji executed in 1689 CE. This too initiated a long and unending campaign by the Marathas against the Mughals.

The strong Islamic presence under Aurangzeb contributed to the dissolution of most of the liberal structures of Mughal society. By this time, the economy of the Mughal Empire, which was largely dependent on agrarian returns, could not correspond to the colossal expansion of the institutional apparatus—leading to internal strife and conflict. Soon a crisis developed, in which the economic and political systems landed in jeopardy because of the state's inability to cope with the threats to its existence from various social groups like the Jats, Satnamis, Sikhs, Marathas and Afghans. The Hindu uprisings of Aurangzeb's reign seem to have had no wide religious appeal, and were soon suppressed with the help of Hindu leaders. Aurangzeb's religious policy aimed at strengthening an empire that had already stretched beyond the boundaries established during Shah Jahan's time. In such a situation of crisis, the Mughal state discovered that it was left with no other option than the one granted to it by orthodox Islam.

SUMMARY

- The Mughal rulers were not only considered as great conquerors, who politically unified the country, but as initiators of reform in economic administration and socio-religious systems.
- Mughal society was primarily stratified into three sections—the upper, middle and lower. The king and the nobility formed the upper section, while court poets, physicians, merchants, artisans and farmers formed the middle section, with the masses bringing up the rear end.
- The ruler was the ultimate authority at the head of the social hierarchy and was held in great esteem by the subject population. Below him were various categories of nobles, some among whom were given high offices in the state.
- The *mansabdars* and *jagirdars* who formed a large part of the nobility maintained landed estates and indulged in a life of extravagant pleasures.
- The middle classes and the poor masses worked hard for their livelihood and lived a life of bare sustenance. They did not have the financial means to indulge in the vices of the nobility.
- Women had a subordinate position in society. Their participation in public life was minimal.
- The economy of the period was mainly agrarian. New crops like tobacco were also introduced into India during this time. The crops and the methods of cultivation were almost the same as today. The improved system of revenue administration introduced by Akbar gave an impetus to agriculture; and food was extraordinarily affordable during his reign.
- There was a great increase in foreign trade during this period. Overseas trade was centred around Asia and Europe, Ceylon, Burma, China, Japan, the East Indies, etc; while overland trade followed the routes from Lahore to Kabul and from Multan to Qandahar.
- The most prominent feature of the Mughal agricultural economy was the prevalence of the *jagir*

system. The *jagirdars* were assigned *jagirs* or lands in lieu of salary; and were periodically transferred so that they did not develop local roots.

- The agrarian classes were typically feudal in nature. The topmost level consisted of the traditional ruling class of *zamindars* and below them was the class of revenue officials. Among the cultivating classes, the dominant segment was known as the *khud-kasht* in the Persian revenue departments.
- The Mughal emperors encouraged production in the state *karkhanas* or factories where high quality goods were produced. The most important industries were the manufacture of cotton, muslin and silk textiles, jewellery, metal work, ivory, pearls, coral, sandalwood products, carpentry, leather, brass and iron goods.
- Akbar issued new gold, silver and copper coins; and also put the provincial mints under important officials.
- Akbar attacked narrow-mindedness and bigotry through his policy of toleration and understanding, which was enforced keeping in view the vast majority of non-Muslims living in Hindustan. This tradition continued under his successors till the coming of Aurangzeb.
- Under Aurangzeb the resurgence of a strong Islamic presence contributed to the dissolution of most of the liberal structures of Mughal society.

KEYWORDS

Purdah Karkhana Monogamy Polygamy
Muslin

REVIEW QUESTIONS

1. Discuss the position of the nobility in Mughal society.
2. What was the status of women during the Mughal period?
3. Examine the agrarian conditions prevalent in Mughal India.
4. Give an account of the religious policy of Akbar.
5. 'The peace and prosperity which prevailed in the vast empire built by Akbar paved the way for the progress of trade and commerce.' Elaborate.

CHAPTER 24

Literature, Architecture and the Allied Arts Under the Mughals

Review and Discussion

- Literature
- Architecture
- Painting
- Music

The Mughals introduced numerous artistic and cultural forms to India. They brought with them their own rich languages—Arabic, Turkish and Persian—along with their art and architecture. During this period Indian literature, especially in Sanskrit, Hindi, Bengali and Tamil, was also flourishing, as were the artistic traditions of the Hindus. As a result of the encounter and continuous inter-mingling of Islamic and Hindu cultures, Indian literature, art and architecture underwent a distinct metamorphosis. The long period of Mughal rule in India, thus, witnessed enormous progress in the fields of literature, architecture, painting and music.

LITERATURE

During the Mughal era there was complete indigenization and adaptation of Islam into the Indian literary tradition. In general, the literary works that were composed in the medieval era were distinctly different from the older classical traditions of India. Being the language of the *Quran*, Arabic was primarily employed by Muslim writers to compose religious texts, while Persian became the court language of the medieval sultans. Since the early eleventh century Ghaznavid occupation of Lahore, Persian had been the official language of the sultanate states and the literary language of the elite; but with the advent of the Mughals the language entered a new phase of development. Persian had hitherto travelled to India mainly from Afghanistan, Turkey and Khurasan; but with the establishment of closer relations between India and Persia after Humayun's period in exile, and the arrival of a large number of illustrious Persians during the reign of Jahangir and later Mughal rulers, the linguistic and literary output of Persian witnessed tremendous growth in India. Many prominent Persian poets, including Urfi, Naziri, Talib and Kalim migrated to India to seek the patronage of the Mughal emperors.

Considerable literature in Persian was produced during the Mughal period, such as poetry, histories and biographies. Among biographical works, Babur's autobiography, *Baburnama*, was originally written in Turkish, and later translated into Persian by Abdul Rahim Khan-i-Khanan. In

KHUSRAU SHAH SWEARING FEALTY TO BABUR, *from the Baburnama.*

Akbar's court, many Sanskrit and other regional language texts were translated into Persian. The Persian translation of the *Mahabharata*, for instance, was renamed as *Razmnama*. The *Ramayana* was also translated into Persian in the same period. Abul Fazl and Faizi were the most prominent scholars of Akbar's court. Abul Fazl wrote the *Akbarnama* and the *Ain-i-Akbari*, two voluminous texts that are of immense value to historians as they give a complete account of Akbar's reign, administration and much statistical data relating to revenue collection. Badauni, Ferishta, and Khafi Khan wrote important historical accounts too. Jahangir wrote his own biography in Persian, the

THE COURT OF AKBAR, *from the Akbarnama.*
Although Akbar is merely 13 years of age, he is portrayed in a powerful central position exercising his first imperial act: the arrest of an unruly courtier, a favourite of Akbar's father.

Tuzuk-i-Jahangiri, which forms a very important source of the events in his life.

There were, however, other biographical works, including the comprehensive *Maasir ul-umara* dealing with the Mughal nobility, and numerous biographies of saints, poets and statesmen. A very interesting historical work written during Aurangzeb's reign was the *Dabistan-i-Mazahib* or *History of Religions*, which has been translated into English. The author, who belonged to Prince Dara

Shukoh's close group of thinkers, gives considerable first-hand information about non-Islamic sects of the period.

Hindi as a language of the people living in northern India had taken shape in the medieval period. The wandering saints of the Bhakti period, poets like Chand Bardoi, Amir Khusrau and Gopal Naik had popularized the language through their poetry, riddles and songs. Interestingly, the earliest manuscripts of their poems were written in Persian script. Hindi had, thus, become the common language of northern India when the Mughals came to India. The first Hindi scholar of the Mughal period was Malik Muhammad Jayasi—a contemporary of Humayun and Sher Shah—who composed the famous epic, *Padmawat*, in Hindi. This epic describes the legend of Rani Padmini, the queen of Mewar.

The golden period of Hindi flowered during the reign of Akbar. The practice of having a Hindi *kavi rai* (poet-laureate) along with a Persian *malik-ul-shuara* began from Akbar's time. Already Muslim poets such as Jayasi and Kabir had enriched the Hindi language, along with Tulasidas, Surdas, Abdur Rahim Khan-i-Khanan, Ras Khan and Birbal, who belong to Akbar's reign. Though Raja Birbal was the *kavi rai* of Akbar's court, the works of the famous general, Abdul Rahim Khan-i-Khanan, have been better preserved. A skilful writer in Hindi, Abdul Rahim furthered the development of the language by extending his patronage to a number of other poets too. Tulasidas is admittedly the greatest of Hindi poets; and his Hindi version of the *Ramayana*, popularly known as the *Ram Charit Manas*, is regarded as a master piece.

The title of *kavi rai* continued to be conferred even during the reigns of Jahangir, Shah Jahan and Aurangzeb. Aurangzeb's sons, Azam and Muazzam, were also known to be patrons of Hindi literature. It is interesting to observe that during the later Mughal period, many Hindi poets followed the ornate style which was popular with contemporary Persian poets—indicating the popular influence of Islamic literary genres even in regional languages.

The most significant literary development of the medieval period was the birth of the new common language of Urdu. Under the Delhi sultans and the Mughal emperors, Persian became the court language, while Hindi remained the common language of the people living in Delhi and its neighbouring territories. With the continuous inter-mingling of these two languages a new, hybrid language emerged, which was originally called *zaban-i-Hindawi* or the language of the Indians. For about five hundred years from 1300–1700 CE, Urdu and Hindi remained almost identical languages, which is apparent from the compositions of poets like Amir Khusrau. The only difference lay in the script; and later on the Persian script was used to write Urdu. Though the grammatical structure of Urdu remained Indian, Muslim scholars used Persian and Arabic words in their works. The Mughals did not patronize Urdu, with the result that it came down to dwell in the south, flourishing under the patronage of the Bijapur and Golconda sultanates. Urdu poetry, however, really began with Wali Dakhni who came in contact with the spoken Urdu of the Mughal camp during the long campaigns of Aurangzeb in the Deccan. He blended the Deccani and Gujarati phrases with the more sophisticated language of the north, and following the traditions of standard Persian literature, he produced poetry which was to set a new literary trend in India.

Muhammad Shah (1719–48 CE) was the first Mughal ruler to recognize Urdu officially; and thereafter a number of Urdu scholars began to write in Urdu on a variety of subjects. Abru, Hatim, Mazmum, Ghalib and Hali were the most prominent Urdu poets of the eighteenth and nineteenth centuries. Once Urdu was adopted as the medium of literary expression in Delhi, its development began rapidly, soon replacing Persian as the court language and principal literary language of Muslim India.

The encouragement which the growth of regional languages and literatures received in the regional Muslim kingdoms was also immense. Muslim rulers freely patronized Bengali, Kashmiri, Hindi, Dakhni, and other regional languages. Though Persian continued to be the court or official language of these kingdoms, local languages were also patronized, till they too became accepted as respectable means of literary expression.

Architecture

The Muslims brought with them new artistic traditions and methods of architectural construction to India. They introduced arches, spherical domes, minarets, window screens and imposing façades. The Muslim rulers, however, had to employ Indian craftsmen and architects, which resulted in the fusion of traditional Hindu and Islamic styles of artistic expression known as the Indo-Islamic style. This amalgamation of both styles was further made possible by the need of the early Muslim rulers to build their palaces, tombs and mosques out of the materials available in India.

As is evident from much of our medieval architectural heritage, the Mughals were passionate builders. Their love for perfection, splendour and magnificence is reflected in their architecture. As in literature, art and religion, in architecture too, the Mughal period was a continuation and culmination of the processes that had their beginnings in the later Turko-Afghan period. It was Babur who introduced the Persian style of architecture to India by building many structures at Agra, Biana, Dholpur, Gwalior and Kiul (Aligarh), but only a few of them exist today. Only a mosque in the Kabulibagh at Panipat and a *Jama Masjid* at Sanbhat in Rohilkhand have survived to this day. Humayun, though equally fond of architecture, did not leave behind any prominent architectural monuments. His palace in Delhi, the *Din-i-Panah*, was probably destroyed by Sher Shah Sur who built the *Purana Qila* in its place. Sher Shah also built a magnificent mosque known as *Qila-i-Kuhna Masjid* inside the *Purana Qila*. The most prominent monument of Sher Shah's reign, however, was his mausoleum built at Sasaram in Bihar.

Akbar's reign witnessed great development in Indo-Islamic architecture—his two large palace fortresses at Agra and Lahore, and the excellent forts in Ajmer and Allahabad bear testimony to this fact. The best examples of monuments built during his time are to be found at Fatehpur Sikri, which

SHER SHAH'S TOMB,
Sasaram, Bihar

DIWAN-I-KHAS, *Fatehpur Sikri*

ENTRANCE TO JAMA MASJID, *Fatehpur Sikri*

PANCH MAHAL, *Fatehpur Sikri*

HUMAYUN'S TOMB, *Nizamuddin East, Delhi*

include Rani Jodha Bai's palace, the *Diwan-i-Am*, the *Diwan-i-Khas*, the marble tomb of Salim Chishti, the *Jama Masjid*, the famous *Bulund Darwaza* and the pyramidal structure known as the *Panch Mahal*. The palace and fort complex of Fatehpur Sikri was huge and included Akbar's office of the *Diwan-i-Am* built in the Hindu style. The *Diwan-i-Khas* which was intended for private audience was remarkable for its Indian plan of construction. The *Jama Masjid* in Fatehpur Sikri, which served as a learning centre, is one of the largest mosques surrounded by pillared, covered passages crowned by three domes. Fergusson, the art historian, describes it as a romance in stone.

The *Bulund Darwaza* built to mark Akbar's conquest over Gujarat is also a magnificent piece of work, 40 metres high. It constitutes perhaps the most remarkable evidence of Akbar's genius. The five storied building in the *Panch Mahal* is considered another remarkable building of Akbar's period. After Humayun's death, Akbar built the Humayun's Tomb at Delhi, under the

AKBAR'S TOMB,
Sikandra

instructions of queen Haji Begum. The tomb is a mixture of the Hindu and Muslim styles and has a large enclosed garden. The centre of the monument stands on a platform of red sand stone, 6.5 metres high, with arches on its sides that open into small rooms. The dome expands slightly at the centre; and the main materials used are red sand stone and white marble. Other monuments like the *Akbari Mahal* and the Allahabad fort were also specimens of wonderful architecture. Even in the Rajput states, Mughal influence is clearly seen in constructions like the palaces built during the reign of Akbar at Amber, Bikaner, Jodhpur, Drehha and Datia.

The Indo-Islamic style continued into the reign of Jahangir, who built Akbar's mausoleum at Sikandra and the tomb of Itimad-ud-Daula, his father-in-law, at Agra. The tomb of Itimad-ud-Daula was, in fact, the first Mughal monument to have been built entirely of marble. Empress Nur Jahan, the daughter of Itimad-ud-Daula, was instrumental in building her father's tomb, whose inlay work in marble, known as *pietra-dura*, is remarkable and outstanding.

But Shah Jahan was undoubtedly the greatest architect among the great Mughals. Because of his interest in planning and architecture, he is often called the engineer king and the prince of builders. He made liberal use of marble in his buildings, constructing palaces, forts, gardens and mosques in many cities. The Taj Mahal at Agra is the most splendid monument of Shah Jahan's reign. One of the Seven Wonders of the World, its design is more Persian than Indian. As is popular knowledge, the Taj was built in pure white marble on the banks of the Yamuna by Shah Jahan in memory of his beloved wife, Mumtaz Mahal. The entire monument stands on a structure 6.5 metres high with an interior arrangement in the manner of Humayun's Tomb. There are round minarets at each corner of the building, with the central dome resembling an inverted lotus. The tomb, decorated with fine trellis and marble inlay work, is said to have taken 20,000 men over 22 years to build at a total cost of about three crore rupees. In view of its exquisite beauty, it has been described as a dream in marble, designed by fairies and finished by jewellers.

TAJ MAHAL, *Agra*

Other famous buildings of Shah Jahan's reign are the *Moti Masjid* or Pearl Mosque at Agra, the Red Fort and *Jama Masjid* at Delhi and many other edifices at Ajmer, Ahmedabad and Lahore. But the most perfect architectural legacy of Shah Jahan's reign is the *Moti Masjid* which is an example of purity and elegance at its zenith. Jahangir's beautiful mausoleum at Shahadara Bagh near Lahore was also built during the reign of Shah Jahan. The *Diwan-i-Am* and *Diwan-i-Khas* complexes in the Red Fort in Delhi also speak of the glory of Shah Jahan's reign. It is said that Shah Jahan had a huge collection of precious stones which he used to design the Peacock Throne, considered to be the most expensive throne in the world.

After Shah Jahan, the splendour of Mughal architecture gradually declined and the few structures that were constructed under Aurangzeb displayed no special beauty of design or execution. During Aurangzeb's reign, architecture did not receive much patronage; and the emperor hardly built anything as grand as his predecessors. During his period, the hitherto flourishing Indo-Islamic architecture was marked by a steady decline. The Alamgiri Gate (1673 CE) at the main entrance to the Lahore Fort and the Badshahi Mosque adjacent to this gate are the few examples of architecture of his times. The Bibi ka Maqbara in Aurangabad, a mausoleum built by his son, prince Azam Shah, as a loving tribute to his mother, Dilras Bano Begum, in the late seventeenth century, is worth mentioning.

The Mughals were also known to have constructed beautiful gardens adjoining the monuments built by them. Other than this, they also had exclusive garden complexes. Some examples include the Shalimar Gardens at Lahore, the Lalbagh Fort at Dhaka and the Shalimar Gardens of Jammu and Kashmir.

Painting

The art of painting in India became known through two principal developments—Buddhist frescos, and the paintings of Mughal and Rajput schools. Painting was not encouraged by the Delhi sultans as the *Quran* prohibits the representation of living beings. The Mughals, however, encouraged this art; and Humayun was the first Mughal emperor to show an interest in painting. He brought two famous painters, Mir Sayyid Ali and Khwaja Abdus Samad with him from Persia, They were entrusted with the task of illustrating the famous 12-volume text, *Dastaan-i-Amir Hamzah*. This task was finally completed in Akbar's time, who also took special interest in the development of the art of illustration. He employed many Indian painters to study and work under the guidance of Abdus Samad. The constructive genius of Akbar laid the real foundation of Mughal painting, which was elevated to greater heights by Jahangir.

The paintings of Akbar's time were mostly confined to book illustrations and portraits. Like architecture, paintings during this period also represented a happy inter-mingling of Indian and Islamic elements, known as the Mughal School of painting. Mir Sayyid Ali of Herat and Khwaja Abdus Samad formed the nucleus of this school of art; while Daswant, another important painter of Akbar's reign, produced many illustrations for the *Razmnama*. The well-known painting of the arrival of Tansen, the legendary singer at the court of Akbar, shows the fusion of this Persian and Hindu styles of art. Other well-known artists of Akbar's reign were Keshava Lal, Mukund, Mishkin, Farrah and Madhu.

Mughal paintings reached a high degree of perfection under Jahangir and Shah Jahan, with Jahangir taking more interest in this form of art than his father. Being an art critic, Jahangir paid generously for exquisite paintings. The two most eminent painters of his reign were Abul Hasan and Ustad Mansur. Abul Hasan painted the darbar scene during Jahangir's accession to the throne. Other famous artists of the period were Bishan Das, Manohar and Govardhan. This era is known for displaying realism in paintings. Most of the subjects, including natural themes and objects like flowers, trees, hills, birds, beasts and clouds were drawn from real life. Many of the Mughal paintings were also fine exhibits of individual portraits.

ARCHERY COMPETITION, *Mughal period, 1600 CE*

ABUL HASAN AND MANOHAR WITH JAHANGIR IN DARBAR, *from the Tuzuk-e-Jahangiri, also known as Jahangirnama*

Shah Jahan took as much interest in painting as he took in architecture. The most popular court painters of his reign were Faqirullah, Mir Hashim, Anup and Chitra. He reduced the number of court painters, keeping only the very best and forcing others to seek the patronage of other princes and nobles; yet this art did not suffer. His eldest son, Dara Shukoh, was also a patron of painting. The art of painting like that of music and architecture received a setback during the time of Aurangzeb, who had imposed a ban on many such artistic activities. Some of the paintings in the palaces of Bijapur and Golconda were even defaced when Aurangzeb conquered these kingdoms. The excellence of Mughal paintings depended not only on the taste of individual emperors, but also on their prosperity; and with the disintegration of the Mughal empire, many artists migrated from the capital to other centres of power, such as Lucknow, Hyderabad, Mysore and Bengal. The Mughal style of painting, thus, continued to flourish in these provincial courts.

Music

In the field of music, a perfect harmony of tastes and sentiments between the Hindus and the Muslims had developed during the Mughal period. Persian and Indian tunes were combined to enrich Indian music even further. The art of music received patronage from three of the most prominent Mughal emperors—Akbar, Jahangir and Shah Jahan. Akbar was a great patron of music and Abul Fazl says that there were more than 30 singers in his court, Tansen being the most famous of them all. Another great musician of the time was Baz Bahadur, the ruler of Malwa, who is said to have been a most learned musician. With the ascension of Aurangzeb, a ban was imposed on music and musicians, like other artists, had to look for patronage elsewhere.

A survey of the cultural and artistic nuances of the Mughal period gives us an insight into the emergence of a composite Indian culture in the form of an Indo-Islamic style of art, literature, architecture, painting and music. In much of these artistic works, the basic element remained Indian, while the finished form was displayed in a Persian style. The Mughal courts were instrumental in perfectly blending these two different cultures in India. Under the fostering care of the Mughal emperors, therefore, Hindu and Islamic elements were coalesced to form new cultural genres and trends.

SUMMARY

- With the coming of the Muslims to India there was an introduction of many new artistic and cultural forms and styles in varied genres.
- As a result of the interaction and continuous intermingling of Muslim and Hindu cultures, Indian literature, art and architecture underwent a distinct change.
- The long period of Mughal rule in India witnessed enormous progress in the fields of literature, architecture, painting and music.
- The patronage extended to fine arts and the vigorous building activity undertaken by emperors like Akbar, Jahangir and Shah Jahan have established beyond doubt the magnificent classical image of the Mughals in India.
- Considerable literature in Persian was produced during the medieval period. Poetry, histories and biographies were extensively written.
- Hindi as a language of the people of northern India was extensively used when the Mughals came to India.
- The most significant literary development of the medieval period in India was the birth of the new common language of Urdu. A number of scholars came forward to write in Urdu on a variety of subjects.
- Once Urdu was adopted as the medium of literary expression in Delhi, its development was rapid, and it soon replaced Persian as the court language and principal literary language of Muslim India.
- The Mughals were great architects. Their architecture was characteristic of the Indo-Islamic style. Akbar's period witnessed remarkable progress in architecture, but it was during the reign of Shah Jahan that Mughal architecture attained its supreme beauty.
- The Mughals equally extended their patronage to painting and music. Mughal paintings reached a high degree of perfection under Jahangir and Shah Jahan.
- In the field of music, a perfect harmony of tastes and sentiments between the Hindus and the Muslims had developed during the Mughal period. Persian and Indian tunes were combined to enrich Indian music like never before. The art of music received patronage from Akbar, Jahangir and Shah Jahan.
- A survey of the cultural and artistic nuances of the Mughal period gives us an insight into the emergence of a composite Indian culture in terms of Indo-Islamic elements in the fields of art, literature, architecture, painting and music.
- The assimilation between the Hindu and Islamic cultures during the Mughal era led to the birth of new styles in art, architecture, music and painting in which the basic element remained Hindu, while the finished form was displayed in a Persian style.

KEYWORDS

Kavi rai | Zaban-i-Hindawi | Indo-Islamic style | Pietra-dura
Malik-ul-shuara

REVIEW QUESTIONS

1. Examine the development of Hindi and Urdu as popular languages in medieval India.
2. Elaborate on the architectural style of the Mughals.
3. Write a short note on the Taj Mahal.
4. How did painting as an art form develop during the Mughal period?
5. What was the effect of Persian elements on Indian music?

CHAPTER 25

Decline of the Mughal Empire

Review and Discussion

- Non-Native Origin
- Weak Successors
- External Coercion
- Fragmentation of the Empire
- Factions at Court
- Rise of the British in Bengal
- The Jagirdari Crisis
- Aurangzeb's Responsibility
- Decay of Moral Standards
- Economic Impoverishment
- Influence of Religious Reformers
- Successors of Aurangzeb

From its position as the major power centre in the Indian subcontinent, the Mughal Empire began to decline rapidly since the reign of its last great ruler, Aurangzeb. The signs of degeneration were unmistakably visible in the institutions and systems intrinsic to its cultural character and administrative policies. The general rot that had begun to set in during the reign of Aurangzeb could not be curtailed by his weak successors, and the recurrent wars of succession only worsened the situation further. The Mughal army too was weakened by a dearth of able commanders; there was no further introduction of military reforms or new technologies as had been done by Akbar. The political situation in northern India clearly indicated the waning of the glorious days of the Mughal Empire.

There are several reasons identified by historians for the decline and disintegration of the mighty Mughal Empire. In this chapter we discuss some of the crucial factors.

Non-Native Origin

The Mughals essentially came from Central Asia and were not natives of India. Although over the years they adapted themselves so well to the Indian environment that they came to be regarded by the general populace as Indians and not as a foreign dynasty ruling through conquests and acquisitions. It is important to remember that in medieval India, conquest was a sign of legitimizing power; and yet, the non-native origin of the Mughals was a reason for not inspiring feelings of loyalty and patriotism among the Indians. Clans, like the Marathas and the Rajputs began to struggle to preserve the glory of their respective kingdoms. Thus, the Mughals had to work that much harder to garner popular support through their appeasement policies. Deriving the strength to rule over India also depended upon the character of the king and upon his military abilities. Gradually, with the weakening of the administrative machinery and military strength in Mughal India, there was anarchy in the country.

Weak Successors

After the death of Aurangzeb in 1707 CE, there was a bitter war of succession among his three sons for the throne—a common feature of the times. Muazzam, the eldest, was the ruler of Kabul and the Punjab; Muhammad Azam, the second son, was the ruler of Malwa and Gujarat; and Kam Baksh, the third son, was the ruler of the Deccan. Prince Muazzam emerged victorious and ascended the throne under the title of Bahadur Shah I after defeating his brothers.

As proven by the popular examples of Akbar and his immediate successors, the Mughal state functioned smoothly with a strong ruler at the helm of affairs, but a weak emperor signified deterioration in every field of administration. Unfortunately all the Mughal emperors after Aurangzeb were weak and incapable of meeting the challenges that confronted the empire. Being greatly advanced in age at the time of his ascension to the throne, Bahadur Shah I (1707–12 CE) naturally lacked the initiative and capability to maintain the empire's former glory. He wanted to appease all sections by simply granting titles and rewards. Jahandar Shah (1712–13 CE), the next in succession, was a totally incapable ruler, while Farrukh Siyar (1713–19 CE) did not have the stature to rule such a massive empire either. Muhammad Shah's reign (1719–48 CE) was considerably long, but he was addicted to the pleasures of the harem; and it was unfortunate enough for him that Nadir Shah attacked Delhi during his reign. Ahmad Shah (1748–54 CE) too was unable to cope with the forces of disintegration that had grown to alarming proportions. By now, the empire had been sadly reduced to a small district around Delhi, and the emperor was deposed and blinded in 1754 CE by his *wazir*. The next successors in line were Alamgir II and Shah Alam, who sought British and Maratha protection for their survival. Such weak emperors could hardly maintain the dignity of the once grand empire, and act as guardians of the great legacy left to them.

External Coercion

In Persia, the Safavids were displaced by the Afghans, who had earlier freed Qandahar, before conquering Herat, Khurasan, and later the capital city of Isfahan in 1722 CE. The Russians too showed considerable interest in Persia; but it was the soldier, Nadir Quli, who took up the cause of the Safavids and drove out the Afghans and the Russians from Persia. After ascending the throne as Nadir Shah in 1736 CE, he appealed to the Mughal emperor, Muhammad Shah, for assistance in recovering Qandahar from the Afghans. He wanted the Mughals to seal off the borders of Kabul, so that fugitives from Qandahar could be effectively trapped into an encounter with him. When Muhammad Shah did not oblige, Nadir Shah began to make preparations to invade the Mughal territory himself. He first defeated the Afghans at Qandahar, before capturing Ghazni and Kabul in June 1738 CE. He then proceeded to occupy Peshawar and Lahore in 1739 CE and threatened Muhammad Shah with an attack on Delhi. Both armies met at Karnal, where the Mughal army was defeated.

The battle in 1739 CE was followed by the sack of Delhi, which ended in a terrible massacre of the citizens. It is generally estimated that within a single day, almost thirty thousand were slaughtered. In addition to the seizure of Shah Jahan's Peacock Throne and hoards of jewellery from the imperial treasury, levies were imposed on the nobles, while the wealthy citizenry was plundered. Nadir Shah allowed Muhammad Shah to remain on the throne of Delhi, but annexed all territories west of the Indus, including Kabul. He also demanded that a sum of twenty lakhs—out of the revenue of the four districts of Gujarat, Sialkot, Pasrur and

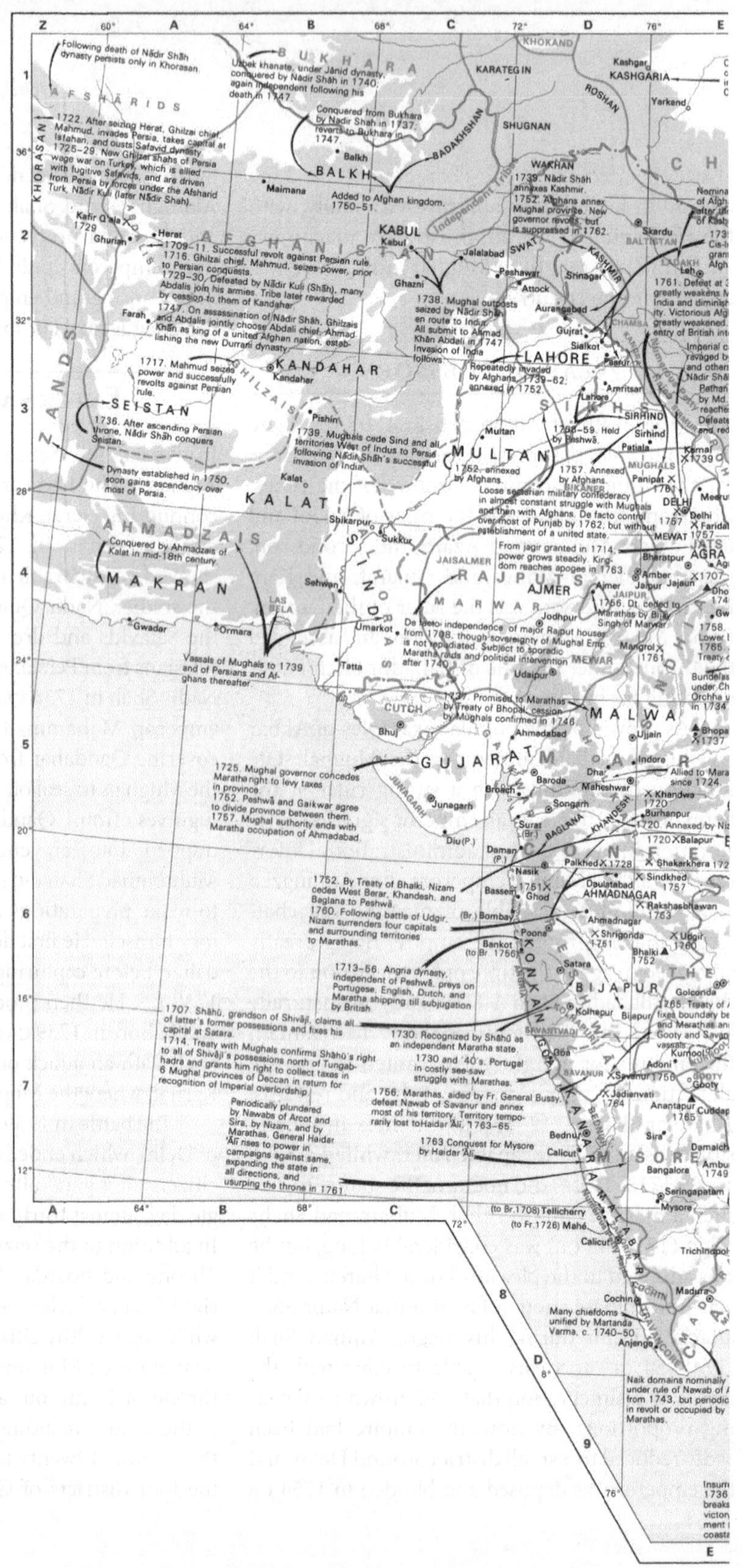

Map 25-1 *Mughal Disintegration and Rise of the Regional Powers, 1707–1766* CE

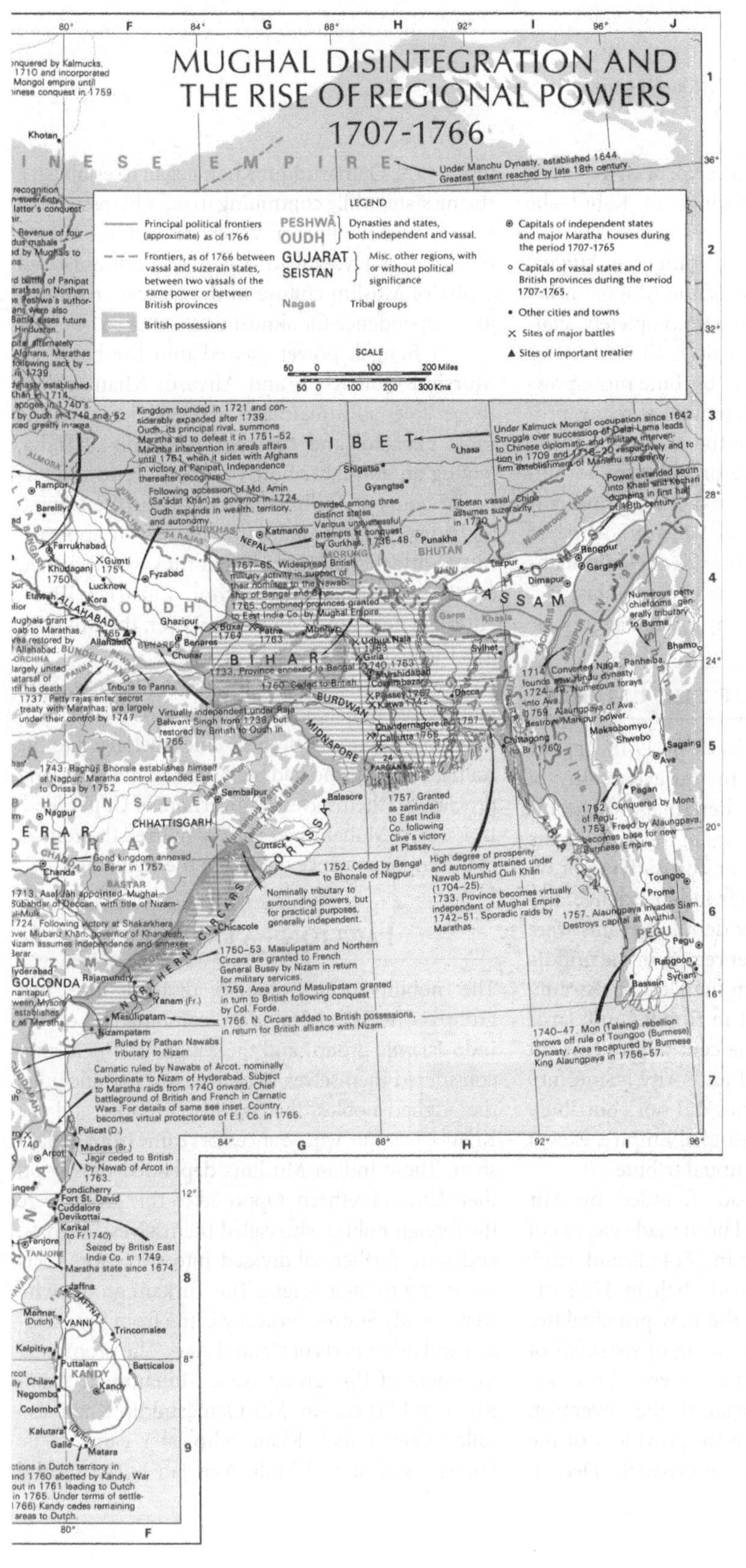

MUGHAL DISINTEGRATION AND THE RISE OF REGIONAL POWERS 1707-1766
LEGEND
Principal political frontiers (approximate) as of 1766
Frontiers, as of 1766 between vassal and suzerain states, between two vassals of the same power or between British provinces
British possessions
PESHWĀ OUDH Dynasties and states, both independent and vassal.
GUJARAT SEISTAN Misc. other regions, with or without political significance
Nagas Tribal groups
Capitals of independent states and major Maratha houses during the period 1707-1765
Capitals of vassal states and of British provinces during the period 1707-1765.
Other cities and towns
Sites of major battles
Sites of important treaties
SCALE
Under Manchu Dynasty, established 1644. Greatest extent reached by late 18th century.
Kingdom founded in 1721 and considerably expanded after 1739. Oudh, its principal rival, summons Maratha aid to defeat it in 1751–52. Maratha intervention in areas affairs until 1761 when it sides with Afghans in victory at Panipat. Independence thereafter recognized.
Following accession of Md. Amin (Sa'ādat Khān) as governor in 1724, Oudh expands in wealth, territory, and autonomy.
Divided among three distinct states. Various unsuccessful attempts at conquest by Gurkhas, 1746–46.
Under Kalmuck Mongol occupation since 1642. Struggle over succession of Dalai-Lama leads to Chinese diplomatic and military intervention in 1709 and 1718–20 respectively and to firm establishment of Manchu suzerainty.
Tibetan vassal. China assumes suzerainty in 1730.
Power extended south into Khasi and Kechari domains in first half of 18th century.
1757–65. Widespread British military activity in support of their nominees to the Nawabship of Bengal and Bihar. 1765. Combined provinces granted to East India Co. by Mughal Empire.
1733. Province annexed to Bengal.
1760. Ceded to British.
Tribute to Panna.
1737. Petty rajas enter secret treaty with Marathas; are largely under their control by 1747.
Virtually independent under Raja Balwant Singh from 1738, but restored by British to Oudh in 1765.
1743. Raghuji Bhonsle establishes himself at Nagpur. Maratha control extended East to Orissa by 1752.
Gond kingdom annexed to Berar in 1757.
1757. Granted as zamindari to East India Co. following Clive's victory at Plassey.
1752. Ceded by Bengal to Bhonsle of Nagpur.
Nominally tributary to surrounding powers, but for practical purposes, generally independent.
High degree of prosperity and autonomy attained under Nawab Murshid Quli Khān (1704–25). 1733. Province becomes virtually independent of Mughal Empire. 1742–51. Sporadic raids by Marathas.
1714. Converted Naga, Panheiba, founds new Hindu dynasty. 1724–49. Numerous forays into Ava. 1759. Alaungpaya of Ava destroys Manipur power.
Numerous petty chiefdoms generally tributary to Burma.
1752. Conquered by Mons of Pegu. 1753. Freed by Alaungpaya, becomes base for new Burmese Empire.
1757. Alaungpaya invades Siam. Destroys capital at Ayuthia.
1740–47. Mon (Talaing) rebellion throws off rule of Toungoo (Burmese) Dynasty. Area recaptured by Burmese King Alaungpaya in 1756–57.
1750–53. Masulipatam and Northern Circars are granted to French General Bussy by Nizam in return for military services. 1759. Area around Masulipatam granted in turn to British following conquest by Col. Forde. 1766. N. Circars added to British possessions, in return for British alliance with Nizam.
Ruled by Pathan Nawabs tributary to Nizam
Carnatic ruled by Nawabs of Arcot, nominally subordinate to Nizam of Hyderabad. Subject to Maratha raids from 1740 onward. Chief battleground of British and French in Carnatic Wars. For details of same see inset. Country becomes virtual protectorate of E.I. Co. in 1765.
Jagir ceded to British by Nawab of Arcot in 1763.
Seized by British East India Co. in 1749. Maratha state since 1674.
1713. Asaf Jāh appointed Mughal Subahdar of Deccan, with title of Nizam-ul-Mulk. 1724. Following victory at Shakarkhera over Mubariz Khān, governor of Khandesh, Nizam assumes independence and annexes Berar.
TIBET
NEPAL
BHUTAN
ASSAM
OUDH
BIHAR
BURDWAN
MIDNAPORE
ORISSA
CHHATTISGARH
NORTHERN CIRCARS
GOLCONDA
AVA
PEGU
KANDY
Lhasa
Shigatse
Gyangtse
Katmandu
Punakha
Rangpur
Gargaon
Dimapur
Rampur
Bareilly
Farrukhabad
Gumti 1751
Khudaganj 1750
Fyzabad
Lucknow
Kora
Ghazipur
Buxar 1764
Patna 1763
Benares
Chunar
Allahabad
Monghyr
Udhua Nala 1763
Giria 1740 1763
Murshidabad
Cossimbazar
Plassey 1757
Katwa 1742
Dacca
Sylhet
Chandernagore (Fr.) 1757
Calcutta 1756
Chittagong (to Br. 1760)
Balasore
Cuttack
Sambalpur
Nagpur
Chanda
Chicacole
Rajamundry
Yanam (Fr.)
Masulipatam
Nizampatam
Pulicat (D.)
Arcot
Madras (Br.)
Pondicherry
Fort St. David
Cuddalore
Devikottai
Karikal (to Fr 1740)
Tanjore
Jaffna
Mannar (Dutch)
Trincomalee
Kalpitiya
Puttalam
Batticaloa
Kandy
Chilaw
Negombo
Colombo
Kalutara
Galle
Matara
Bhamo
Sagaing
Ava
Pagan
Maksobomyo/Shwebo
Toungoo
Prome
Pegu
Rangoon
Syriam
Bassein
Khotan

Aurangabad, which had hitherto been reserved for administrating the province of Kabul—be paid directly into the Persian treasury.

Other than financially ruining the Mughal Empire, Nadir Shah's defeat of the Mughal army and the massacre of the capital completely shattered the prestige of the Mughals. It set a precedent for the Sikhs and Marathas to become more powerful, besides instigating defiance in many provincial governors. Following the disastrous event, Muhammad Shah tried to re-organize his administration and was successful in defeating the army of Ahmad Shah Abdali (March 1748 CE), who had succeeded to the eastern territories of Nadir Shah's empire, near Sirhind. This was to be the last victory of the Mughals against any foreign aggressor.

Fragmentation of the Empire

After Muhammad Shah's death in 1748 CE, the imperial power weakened in the eventuality of the establishment of several hereditary kingdoms in the major provinces of Mughal India. With the growing fragility of the center, the outlying provinces began to proclaim their independence. Except for the Punjab, independent kingdoms were formed in almost every other region in the middle of the eighteenth century. In the Deccan, Awadh, Bengal, and to some extent in Rohilkhand, large principalities over which the central government of Delhi had only nominal authority, came into existence. These principalities did not contribute any revenues to the dying Mughal Empire, except for the continuation of an annual tribute.

The state of Hyderabad, founded by Mir Qamaruddin Khan, who had been made viceroy of the Deccan by Farrukh Siyar in 1714 CE, and *wazir* of the empire by Muhammad Shah in 1722 CE, was the most important of the new principalities that had emerged. It was made up of six *subas* of the Deccan, which at this time generated revenue worth sixteen crores, as against the seventeen crores from all the other twelve provinces of the empire put together. Upon his return to the Deccan in 1724 CE, Qamaruddin Khan began to establish a strong state, while continuing to offer his assistance to the Mughal emperor. When he died in 1748 CE, the state of Hyderabad was a well-administered centre of Muslim culture in the Deccan, retaining its independence for almost two centuries.

In Bengal, power passed into the hands of Murshid Quli Khan and Alivardi Khan. Under these able administrators, Bengal became the most peaceful and prosperous region of India, paying an annual tribute of one crore to the imperial court at Delhi. Meanwhile, in the Punjab Sikhs used Nadir Shah's invasion as an opportunity to attack the Mughals, but they were crushed by the able Mughal governor, Zakariya Khan. After his death in 1745 CE, however, the Mughals lost the province.

Even in the days of the great Mughals, Sind had always remained in the hands of local chiefs. The most important of these chiefs belonged to the Kalhara family, who had built up land holdings, and proclaimed themselves as governors of Upper Sind. In 1736 CE, Muhammad Shah conferred the control of the entire province of Sind to the Kalharas.

Factions at Court

The nobility were broadly divided into two groups—the Hindustanis (a combination of the Indo-Islamic group) and the Mughals. The former considered themselves to be Indians, and included the Afghan nobles, the Sayyids of Barha and the Khan-i-Dauran, whose ancestors came from Badakshan. These Indian Muslims depended mostly on their Hindu brethren. Opposed to this group were the foreign nobles who called themselves Mughals, and were further subdivided into two more sects according to their origin. The Turkani group, who were mostly Sunnis, basically came from Transoxiana and other parts of Central Asia. The prominent members of this group were Muhammad Amin Khan and his cousin, Mir Qamaruddin Khan also called Chin Qilich Khan, who later came to be known as Nizam-ul-Mulk Asaf Jah I. The second sect comprised Persian Shias, the most important among them being Asad Khan and Zulfiqar Khan.

There were various factions among these main groups too, each vying to eliminate the other and win the emperor over to their side. These factions were frequently engaged in battles, upsetting the peace of the land and throwing the administration out of gear.

Rise of the British in Bengal

There were far-reaching developments outside the capital which resulted in the establishment of a strong British presence in Bengal. After the death of the governor of Bengal, Alivardi Khan, in 1756 CE, his grandson Siraj-ud-daula succeeded. Siraj-ud-daula's commander-in-chief, Mir Jafar, plotted against him and betrayed the Bengal army in the historic Battle of Plassey in 1757 CE by secretly forming an alliance with the British. This marked the first significant event in the British colonial history of the land, giving the East India Company their first political advantage in India. Thereafter, Mir Jafar was naturally made the *nawab* of Bengal, but when he opposed the British he was replaced by Mir Qasim, his son-in-law.

There was a clash between Mir Qasim and the British when the former tried to collect internal revenue from the English traders. So far the English East India Company was exempted from paying any duty to the *nawab* of Bengal which resulted in many Company servants indulging in private trade. Since the province's revenues were fast depleting Mir Qasim abolished all internal duties, thus removing the advantage given to the British over Indian traders. The British opposed Mir Qasim on this issue. In retaliation, Mir Qasim supported by Shah Alam, the Mughal emperor, and Shuja-ud-daula, the *nawab* of Awadh, met the British at Buxar in 1764 CE where the British were victorious once again. The British concluded the Treaty of Allahabad in 1765 CE, according to which Awadh became a protectorate of the English East India Company and Emperor Shah Alam was forced to give them the *diwani* rights of Bengal, Bihar and Orissa in return for the districts of Allahabad and Kara.

From now on, the British started to strengthen their position in Bengal by not keeping the activities of the East India Company there merely commercial, but also tried to make it a political centre.

The Jagirdari Crisis

The Mughal Empire was a highly centralized–bureaucratized structure with the emperor at the top, his vitality depending upon the strength of the military aristocracy, who were placed just below him. With the introduction of the *mansabdari* system in civil and military organization in the late sixteenth century, Akbar had accommodated the aristocracy within this structure. Those *mansabdars* who were not paid in cash were awarded a *jagir* or landed estate in lieu of salary. They were the *jagirdars*, who were required to collect the revenue from the particular *jagir* of which one part would go to the state and the other two parts would cover his personal expenses and the maintenance allowances for his soldiers and horses. This relationship between the emperor and the nobility formed the crux of the entire imperial edifice. This was the reason why the Mughals needed to be constantly involved in territorial expansion of their dominions. During the last years of Aurangzeb's reign, however, the number of *jagirdars* appointed had risen to such a great number that there was a serious shortage of *paibaqi* land (land earmarked to be given as *jagirs*). This decrease in the resources of the empire ruptured the functional relationship between the emperor and the aristocracy—indicating the beginning of inefficiency within the imperial Mughal administrative system.

As a result of this economic crisis in the eighteenth century, the various ethno-religious groups within the aristocracy began competing with each other. About four-fifths of the land revenue of the Mughal Empire was under the control of the *mansabdars* and *jagirdars*; but this income was unevenly distributed among them, creating jealousies within the aristocracy—particularly at the time when the resources of the empire were diminishing. This economic situation—known as the '*jagirdari* crisis' of the eighteenth century—has been defined by Satish Chandra in the following words, 'The available social surplus was insufficient to defray the cost of administration, pay for wars of one type or another and to give the ruling class a standard of life in keeping with its expectations'(Chandra 1982). In this situation, the actual revenue collection was much lesser than what had been estimated, thereby diminishing the expected income of the *jagirdars*. Adding to the crisis, there was a continuously rising rate of inflation since the late seventeenth century, as luxury goods produced in India were being sold in the European markets, making them unavailable to the Mughal nobility. With too many *mansabdars* now angling for a handful of *jagirs*, many of them had to remain without *jagirs* for years; and even when a *jagir* was given, the *jagirdars* faced the insecurity of getting transferred within a short period.

The crisis increased during the last years of Aurangzeb's reign, mainly because of the Deccan wars. Since a greater number of *mansabdars* was required, the ensuing political turmoil made the collection of revenue a more difficult task. J. F. Richards is of the view that the crisis could have been averted if Aurangzeb wanted to. He goes on to say that Aurangzeb was more interested in constantly expanding the size of the royal land or *khalisa*. After the conquest of Bijapur and Golconda, there was a 23 per cent revenue increase, which was again used to finance the Deccan campaign instead of being distributed among the *mansabdars*. An opportunity to solve the *jagirdari* crisis right at the onset was thus lost; and, therefore, historians like Richards are of the opinion that this crisis was artificially created and not due to any real scarcity of resources in the empire. He has shown, however, that revenue collections in the Deccan were gradually depleting, while Satish Chandra argues that the Deccan always was a deficit area. So, it is difficult to definitely establish whether the conquests of Bijapur and Golconda would have really solved the *jagirdari* problem.

The *jagirdari* crisis led to an unhealthy competition among the nobles to gain control over the fertile *jagirs*. This added to the already existing factionalism at court. After the death of Bahadur Shah in 1712 CE the problem intensified, as low-ranking officials now found it difficult to maintain their lifestyles with the meagre amount they got from their *jagirs*. The problem worsened further during the reigns of Jahandar Shah, Farrukh Siyar and Muhammad Shah, when more and more *mansabdars* continued to be appointed, leading to further augmentation in the number of nobles. To meet this growing demand, portions of *khalisa* land were converted into *jagir* lands. Instead of solving the problems of the *mansabdars*, this measure impoverished the emperor further. Mir Qamaruddin Khan, after becoming the *wazir* tried to tackle the problem by redistributing the land; but he was opposed by other courtiers because of which he could never implement the reform.

Frequent peasant revolts in the late seventeenth and the early eighteenth centuries are also believed to have been one of the major causes behind the decline of the Mughal Empire. Excessive centralization was perhaps not fully accepted by India's rural society; but a fear of the Mughal army prevented the peasants from revolting vociferously. However, as the weakness of the center became apparent and the Mughal army faced successive defeats, resistance to imperial authority also became more resolute and widespread. In most cases, these rebellions were led by the disaffected local *zamindars*, who were ably supported by the oppressed peasantry. The *jagirdars* were given more lands so that revenue collection through the *zamindars* would become easy for the imperial core; but the economic pressure put on the *zamindars* and the peasants as a result of the *jagirdari* crisis proved detrimental to them—eventually leading to the combined pressure of the *zamindars* and peasants, which the Mughal authorities found hard to bear.

Aurangzeb's Responsibility

During Aurangzeb's reign, the political boundaries of the Mughal Empire expanded to phenomenal proportions. With the conquest of Bijapur and Golconda, the empire grew to such an extent that it became difficult to control the far flung regions from the imperial centre. The size of the empire, therefore, contributed to its decline.

Aurangzeb's prejudiced religious policy was another reason that had caused a general discontentment among many sections of the population, such as the Sikhs, the Jats, the Satnamis, the Rajputs, and above all the Marathas. The re-imposition of the *jiziya* and the pilgrimage tax showed Aurangzeb's intolerance towards non-Muslims and offended the sentiments of the Hindus and Sikhs alike, making him unpopular. Even the annexation of the Deccan states on the grounds that they were Shia, did not go down well with many.

Aurangzeb's prolonged stay in the Deccan for his Bijapur and Golconda campaigns, followed by the Maratha wars, not only exhausted the Mughal army and made the soldiers homesick, but also drained the empire's resources. The emperor's long absence from northern India led to many provincial governors becoming independent, with some regions even turning turbulent. The long Deccan wars of Aurangzeb, thus, contributed to the decline of the Mughal Empire.

Decay of Moral Standards

The lack of moral standards among the ruling elite also contributed to the downfall of the Mughal Empire. This was partly due to the affluent lifestyles maintained by monarchs like of Shah Jahan and queens like Nur Jahan. People had got so accustomed to luxury that Aurangzeb's attempts to impose a puritanical lifestyle went in vain. Perhaps Aurangzeb's extreme frugality only intensified the reaction of the nobility, who displayed a lack of discipline and even treacherous conduct. It also led to corruption and the enrichment of the officers at the expense of the state and the people.

Economic Impoverishment

The Deccan wars had ruined the cultivable fields of the region, with the animals of the armies devouring all the standing crops and greenery. Whatever little was left was destroyed by the Marathas. The farmers were so disillusioned that they gave up agriculture altogether, taking to a life of plunder and highway robbery. There was also dislocation of trade and industry. The financial condition of the empire further deteriorated under the later Mughals, as the outlying provinces began asserting their independence and ceasing payment of revenue to the centre.

Influence of Religious Reformers

The teachings of the religious reformers emphasized the ideals of self respect and sovereignty. In the south, Guru Ramdas stressed the importance of the 'Maharashtra Dharma' and advocated that it was the duty of the state to protect religion. Encouraged by these words, Shivaji rose up in rebellion for his autonomy. The spirit of revolt and desire for independence were encouraged by the Satnamis, the Roshaniyas and many others. In the Punjab too, the Sikh Gurus emphasized the need to attain military and political power for the protection of their religion. All these ideas together precipitated the collapse of the Mughal Empire.

A result of several diverse, yet inter-related factors, led to the fragmentation of the Mughal Empire with dramatic suddenness within a few decades following the death of Aurangzeb. The period of the great Mughals, which constitutes a glorious era in medieval Indian history ended in this manner, yielding way to the establishment of many independent regional kingdoms in its wake.

Successors of Aurangzeb

After the death of Aurangzeb, there ensued a bitter struggle among his successors in which his son, Muazzam, emerged victorious and ascended the throne as Bahadur Shah I. Bahadur Shah I, who ruled from 1707–12 CE, was sixty three years old when he was crowned emperor near Lahore. On 12 June 1707 CE, Bahadur Shah I arrived at Agra and took possession of the fort. Azam Shah, the emperor's brother, met him in a battle near Samugarh on 18 June 1707 CE and was killed. Kam Baksh, his youngest brother, made preparations for contesting his right to the throne, but he too was defeated in a battle near Hyderabad on 13 January 1709 CE. Bahadur Shah I, thus, emerged as the undisputed master of the empire.

Bahadur Shah I defeated Ajit Singh of Jodhpur, who had declared his independence and threatened to invade Ajmer. Later, Ajit Singh was pardoned and conferred the rank of 3,500 with the title of Maharaja. The Sikhs rose under Banda Bahadur and raided Mughal territories in the Punjab and modern Uttar Pradesh. They succeeded in establishing control between Delhi and Lahore and prevented movement between the two cities. To punish the Sikhs, Bahadur Shah I led a Mughal army against them and defeated Banda Bahadur, but the death of Bahadur Shah I (27 February 1712 CE) ended the campaign against the Sikhs. Being mild and generous, Bahadur Shah I proved to be a weak ruler. He followed his father's policy of intolerance, retained the *jiziya* and did not appoint any Hindus to high posts.

Bahadur Shah I was succeeded by Jahandar Shah, who ruled from 1712–13 CE. In his ascension to the throne he was helped by Zulfiqar Khan, who was appointed as the prime minister. The emperor was interested in pleasures of the harem and neglected the administration of the empire.

Jahandar Shah was succeeded by Farrukh Siyar (1713–19 CE), who was also a weak ruler, helped by the Sayyid brothers to come to power. When he tried to free himself from the influence of the Sayyid brothers, he was promptly put to death in 1719 CE—proving the ineffectual authority of a Mughal emperor in his own court. In spite of his weakness, the empire remained intact during Farrukh Siyar's reign. After his tragic death, however, the Sayyid brothers raised another puppet, Rafi-ud-Darajat, to the throne, but the brothers soon deposed him and placed yet another prince, Roshan Akbar, the grandson of Bahadur Shah I, on the throne. After becoming emperor, Roshan Akbar assumed the title of Muhammad Shah.

Muhammad Shah ruled from 1719–48 CE; but he was controlled by the Sayyid brothers. Many of the nobles did not like the supremacy of the Sayyid brothers and soon another faction appeared, headed by Mir Qamaruddin Khan—also known as Chin Qilich Khan, who had established himself as the governor of the Deccan in opposition to the Sayyids. Muhammad Shah ruled for 28 years which gave him time to get rid of the Sayyid brothers with the help of his supporters. His supporters, however, soon declared their own independence—Alivardi Khan in Bengal, Ali Khan in Awadh, and Mir Qamaruddin Khan in the Deccan.

After the death of Muhammad Shah, his son, Ahmad Shah (1748–54 CE), was put on the throne. During his reign, the state fell into the hands of eunuchs and women, headed by the Queen Mother, Udham Bai. She promoted a corrupt culture wherein worthless men were raised to high offices by taking large monetary gifts in exchange for every appointment. The court became rife with intrigues, which ultimately led to the dethronement of Ahmad Shah, who was blinded and imprisoned.

Ahmad Shah was succeeded by Alamgir II (1754–59 CE), the second son of Jahandar Shah. He was a puppet in the hands of his *wazir*, Imad-ul-Mulk, who tried to form an anti-Maratha coalition to drive out the Marathas from northern India, which ended in failure. Eventually, Imad-ul-Mulk got Alamgir II assassinated in November 1759 CE.

Ali Gauhar, the son of Alamgir II, succeeded his father and took the title of Shah Alam II

CHRONOLOGY			
1526–1530 CE	Babur	1713–1719 CE	Farrukh Siyar
1530–40 CE; 1555–56 CE	Humayun	1719 CE	Rafi-ud-Darajat
1540–45 CE	Sher Shah Sur	1719–1748 CE	Muhammad Shah
1556–1605 CE	Akbar	1748–1754 CE	Ahmad Shah
1605–1627 CE	Jahangir	1754–1759 CE	Alamgir II
1627–1658 CE	Shah Jahan	1759–1806 CE	Shah Alam
1658–1707 CE	Aurangzeb	1806–1837 CE	Akbar II
1707–1712 CE	Bahadur Shah I	1837–1857 CE	Bahadur Shah II
1712–1713 CE	Jahandar Shah		

(1759–1806 CE). When his father died, he was in Bihar; and although he was declared the Mughal emperor, he did not go to Delhi for 12 years. During this period, he tried to conquer Bihar and Bengal, but failed. He was defeated in the Battle of Buxar in 1764 CE, and imprisoned along with the Nawab of Awadh. In 1765 CE, he had to relinquish the *diwani* of Bengal, Bihar and Orissa to the English East India Company. In 1803 CE the English captured Delhi and Shah Alam II became a pensioner of the East India Company, finally dying three years later in 1806 CE.

Shah Alam II was succeeded by his son, Akbar II (1806–37 CE), who remained a mere figurehead till his death in 1837 CE. Bahadur Shah II was the last Mughal ruler, who retained the emperor's title till 1857 CE—after which the British crown formally took over their Indian colony from the hands of the East India Company. The last Mughal emperor joined the Revolt of 1857 CE, for which he was arrested and deported to Rangoon, where he remained in his last days till his death in 1862 CE. After his death, the great Mughal Empire faded into oblivion.

SUMMARY

- The period of the great Mughals constitutes a glorious era in medieval Indian history; but the empire collapsed with dramatic suddenness, within a few decades of Aurangzeb's death in 1707 CE.
- Aurangzeb's successors were weak; and increasingly became mere tools in the hands of various factions of the nobility. Taking advantage of this situation, the Rajputs, the Sikhs and the Afghans openly defied the authority of Mughal emperor.
- Even more disturbing was the fact that the assertion of independence had spread to other parts of the empire too; and the governors of Hyderabad, Bengal and Awadh soon established independent kingdoms as well.
- The establishment of the Maratha kingdom by Shivaji, and its consolidation under the Peshwas advanced the destabilization of the Mughal Empire, removing any chances of its continuity. The Marathas gradually extended their control towards northern India.
- The invasions of Nadir Shah and Ahmad Shah Abdali further weakened the empire. The once glorious Mughal Empire was now reduced to a small area around Delhi.
- Economic impoverishment, degeneration of moral values and internal squabbles among the Mughal nobility, together with the demoralization of the army further contributed to the decline.
- The emergence of the British as a territorial power, with an ambition to conquer and rule over India, finally contributed to the absolute decline and disintegration of the Mughal Empire.

KEYWORDS

Factions
Jagirdari crisis
Diwani
Reformer
Maharashtra dharma
Colony

REVIEW QUESTIONS

1. What was the jagirdari crisis and how was it responsible for the decline of Mughal Empire?
2. Examine Aurangzeb's responsibility for the downfall of the Mughal Empire.
3. Give an account of Nadir Shah's invasion and its impact on India.
4. Explain the rise of regional kingdoms that paved the way for the disintegration of the Mughal Empire.
5. Write a short note on the rule of Bahadur Shah I.

PART VII–Rise of the Regional Powers

"Sundry forts which had belonged to the Kutb-Shahi kings had passed into the hands of the Adil-Shahis. Sivaji had a great reputation for skill in the reduction of forts, and he swore to Abdu-lla Shah, that if he would supply him with forces and the means for conducting sieges, he would in a short time wrest these forts from the Bijapuris, and hand them over to the officers appointed to accompany him; he would not even accept some forts which had belonged to himself, and were in the possession of the officers of Aurangzeb, if he recovered them by the means supplied him. He vowed also that for the remainder of his life he would remain the devoted servant and adherent of Abdu-lla Shah. The ultimate objects of the arch deceiver never entered into the consideration of Abdu-llah Shah. He provided a sufficient force and a suitable siege train, and he appointed to it several officers acquainted with siege operations, whom he enjoined to serve heartily in obedience to and in accord with Sivaji.

Sivaji, with the force placed under his command, marched on his enterprise. By fraud and stratagem, and by his marvellous skill in the conduct of sieges, every fort that he approached fell into his hands after a few days' investment. He cajoled the officers who had been sent with him to take charge of the captured forts, with plausible statements, with promises of giving them the command of more important places, and by using the money and property he had obtained from the captured strongholds. So he carried them with him to other forts, and in a short time he reduced Sattara, Parnala, and ten or twelve other renowned forts belonging to Bijapúr, which it would have taken years and lacs of expense to conquer. He then marched against Rajgarh, and other forts which had been captured by Raja Jai Singh, Diler Khan, and other Imperial generals, the keys of which he himself had surrendered. Having mastered them all, he placed one or two of them in charge of the officers of Abdu-llah Shah.

According to common report, and the oral statements of men of Haidarabad, Sivaji came to that city in the first or second year of the reign of Abu-l Hasan, and succeeded in wheedling and satisfying that sovereign. When he had finished his fortress-taking, according to his wont, he took up his abode at Rajgarh, and there again raised the standard of rebellion. In the days when the fortifications of the port of Surat were not yet completed, he attacked and took the place. There he obtained an immense booty in gold and silver, coined and uncoined, and in the stuffs of Kashmir, Ahmadabad, and other places. He also made prisoners of some thousand Hindu men and women of name and station, and Musulmans of honourable position. Krors in money and goods thus came into the hands of that evil infidel.

Aurangzeb, on being informed of the capture and plunder of Surat, ordered that the fortifications of that port should be completed; and he placed Diler Khan and Khan-Jahan in command of an army to punish Sivaji. It is said that Sivaji got together some ten or twelve thousand Kachh and Arab horses, so that when he sent out an army most of the horsemen were bargirs, i.e., they rode horses belonging to him. He rebuilt the forts which had formerly stood on the sea-shore, and he constructed also vessels of war, which were kept under the guns of the fortress. With these vessels he attacked and plundered ships which were proceeding to Europe and to Mecca."

Source: Elliot, H. M., Sir, *The History of India as Told by its Own Historians, Vol. VII: From Shah Jahan to the Early Years of the Reign of Muhammad Shah*, Edited by John Dowson, London: Trubner Company, 1867–1877. Extract taken from *Conquests of Sivaji*, in *Ruka'at-i 'Álamgiri*, of the Emperor Aurangzeb. Text Available at Persian Literature in Translation: The Packard Humanities Institute.

Image: The *Darwaja*, Fort Raigad, Maharashtra.

CHAPTER **26**

Ascent of the Marathas Under Shivaji

Review and Discussion

- Shivaji's Formative Years
- Shivaji's Conquests
- Confrontation with Bijapur
- Countering the Mughals
- Chattrapati Shivaji
- Maratha Administration
- An Assessment of Shivaji and the Maratha State

The eighteenth century was a time when new ideas about the construction of empire as a political concept were being redeployed and redefined along India's frontiers. With the decline of the Mughal Empire in the first half of the millennium, not only did the political boundaries of the empire shrink, but the period also saw a collapse of the administrative structure so painstakingly built by emperors Akbar, Jahangir, Shah Jahan and Aurangzeb. Responding to this crisis of imperial stability, a number of independent principalities—Hyderabad, Awadh, Bengal, Marathwada, Punjab, Rajasthan, Mysore and Thiruvitamkur (Travancore)—emerged across various parts of the subcontinent. The most prominent among these was perhaps that of the Marathas.

Credited with setting up an independent Maratha state in the seventeenth century, the Marathas under Shivaji form the historical legacy for the modern Indian state of Maharashtra. The family from which Shivaji claimed descent had two branches—that of Babaji and the Ghorpades. And Shivaji belonged to the former line of Babaji, who was in charge of the villages of Hingani Beradi and Devalgaon in the Poona district. By virtue of being the *patel* or headman of these villages, Babaji's position was fairly influential, with the result that his two sons, Maloji and Vithoji, found occupation in the army of the Jadhavs of Sindkhed in the Daulatabad district. His elder son, Maloji, soon became a trusted aide of Malik Ambar, the *Habashi* military commander of the Ahmednagar army. Pleased with Maloji's work, Malik Ambar also went on to reward Maloji in 1622 CE by granting the *parganas* of Sholapur and Poona to his son, Shahji Bhonsle. Later in 1630 CE, when Shahji received a better deal from the Mughal emperor, Shah Jahan (that of a *Punj Hazari* with a *mansab* of 5,000 *zat*, 5,000 *sawar* as well as Poona as *jagir*), he left the army of Ahmednagar to join the Mughals.

The time when the line of Babaji had settled down in Ahmednagar and the other collateral branch of the Ghorpades had settled down in the kingdom of Bijapur, there began an era during which many Marathas were employed into the civil and military services of the Bahmani successor states. The Nimbalkars of Phaltan, Ghatges of Malwadi, Savants of Savantvadi, Mores of Javali, Mohites of Supa, Dafles of Jath, Ghorpades of Mudhol and Jadhavs of Sindkhed, among many others, had found employment under the Mughal emperors and sultans of Bijapur and Golconda in civil and military capacities. Jadhavrao, for instance, had become a *mansabdar* of 5,000 under Shah Jahan. Udaji Ram, Parsoji Bhonsle, Mankoji Nimbalkar, Rawat Rai and Dattaji were all commanders of 3,000 horses (or *sawar*), while Patji, Arirai and Badoji commanded 2,000 horses, and Bhojraj 1,000 horses. As a result of the military activities, which they conducted for the Mughals and the Deccani sultanates, numerous small hill forts were also coming into the hands of the small Maratha *jagirdars* during this time. Taking advantage of the Mughal conquest of the Deccan states, many Maratha *jagirdars* tried to further their gains; but they failed to get anything more substantial than acquiring good positions under the Mughals.

Unlike the other Maratha *jagirdars*, Shahji Bhonsle was not content with merely being a loyal supporter of the Mughals. Being the political opportunist that he was, he aspired to make himself indispensable to the political power play involving the Mughals and the Deccan sultanates. He assumed the role of a king-maker with very concrete plans of establishing complete control over the Deccan. Not belonging to a higher caste like other rulers, Shahji harboured a desire to subvert the *brahmanical* order and rise above his *shudra* status, which he felt could be achieved by manipulating his relationships with the Mughals and Deccan sultanates—as and when it was advantageous for him to do so. He took the first opportunity to break his alliance with the Mughals when Shah Jahan left the Deccan. Deprived of his *jagir* he defected to the Bijapur army in 1632 CE. By leaving Ahmednagar for the Mughals, and then eventually leaving them for Bijapur, Shahji made his intentions very clear by supporting the power which benefitted him the most.

With the support of the sultan of Bijapur, he put forward a puppet claimant to the throne of the Nizam Shahis in Ahmednagar, which brought many Nizam Shahi nobles (who had gained independent charge of forts and territories in the Nizam Shahi dominions) under his direct command. In addition, a group of disbanded Nizam Shahi soldiers also joined Shahji, thus swelling the numbers under his banner. With the support of a comparatively large force of soldiers and Nizam Shahi nobles, he thus took control over a large portion of Ahmednagar's territories from the Mughals.

Responding to Shahji's challenge, Shah Jahan despatched a large force to tame the former and his ally, the Adil Shahi sultan. Under a mounting attack from the Mughals, the Adil Shahis pressed for peace; and consequently Shahji could not hold out against the Mughals without the Adil Shahi support. His possessions were reduced and he was besieged at the fort of Mahuli. The Portuguese navy too did not help him for fear of the Mughals. Shahji and Bijapur eventually had no choice but to negotiate with the Mughals in 1636 CE on the issue of Ahmednagar. By mutual consent, the Mughals and Bijapur agreed to divide Ahmednagar's territories between themselves.

The sultan of Bijapur then went on to persuade Shahji to disown the puppet claimant forwarded by him, in return for which, Shahji was to be employed by the Bijapur sultan, and have the districts of Poona and Supa restored to him. In 1638 CE, a large Bijapur army—led by the Bijapur general, Ranadulla Khan, and accompanied by Shahji—defeated Kempe Gowda III in the Karnataka, resulting in Bangalore being given to Shahji as *jagir*. Ranadulla Khan was eventually recalled and Shahji succeeded him as the supreme commander. He proved to be one of the best generals of the Bijapur army, which overran Kolar, Dood, Balapur and Sira under his command. These districts were soon conferred on Shahji as military fiefs. His success lay in adopting the Mughal policy of pardoning the conquered rajas instead of punishing or executing them—this helped the development of healthy relations and military support.

Shivaji's Formative Years

It was under such complex political circumstances that Shivaji was born in April 1627 CE to Shahji Bhonsle and his wife, Jijabai, the daughter of Lakhoji Jadhavrao who claimed descent from the ancient Yadava kings of Devagiri. During his childhood, Shivaji hardly got any opportunities to interact with his father who remained busy with his political career. As a result he grew up closer to his mother, who with her pious disposition had a positive influence upon him. Shivaji grew up listening to legends from the *Ramayana*, the *Mahabharata* and the brave feats of Hindu warriors, while Dadaji Kondadev, Shivaji's tutor and guardian, trained him in the art of horse riding, warfare and state administration. The Bhakti preachers, Ramdas and Tukaram, also had considerable influence on the life of Shivaji, who regarded Ramdas as his spiritual guru.

The history of the Marathas was largely conditioned by the economic geography and the prevalent socio-cultural make up of the people. The mountainous topography provided a sanctuary from external threats, making it difficult for invaders to negotiate their way into the kingdom. It also contributed towards making the Marathas physically strong and a self-reliant lot, capable of dealing with hardships. The rocky and precipitous terrain also proved advantageous for guerrilla warfare, providing readymade and easily defensible rock forts. As a result of the rocky terrain, cultivable land in the region was too less, leaving a large number of people to eke out difficult lives on a meagre subsistence level. Although only a handful of Marathas could be counted among the rich and affluent, the economic disparity did not cause any major divisions among the economically divergent groups. There were several other unifying factors that brought the people together and infused in them a sense of self respect and feeling of oneness. Their difficult lifestyles prevented them from falling prey to a life of indulgence and luxury.

The spread of Bhakti ideals also helped in promoting a feeling of unity among the Marathas, especially in terms of the social equality preached by the saints Tukaram, Ramdas, Vaman Pandit and Eknath, among others. Emphasizing the concept of *bhakti* or devotion to god, and believing in the equality of all men, the Bhakti preachers spoke up against the supremacy of the *brahmans*, the rigidity of rituals and the caste system. They sowed the seeds of self-awakening, which ultimately contributed to political awakening and feelings of nationalism. The Marathi language and literature also served to foster a sense of unity among the people, with hymns composed by the Bhakti saints being sung by all castes and classes.

Feelings of a common creed, a democratic temperament and solidarity were thus awakened among the Marathas. The only element lacking in the creation of a separate nation at this stage was perhaps political power and independence—both of which were provided by Shivaji in the second-half of the seventeenth century.

Shivaji's Conquests

Leaving the administration of Poona in the custody of Dadaji Kondadev, Shahji sent away his second son, Shivaji, with Jijabai to Poona; while his eldest son, Sambhaji, remained with him. Another of his sons, Vankoji, was kept at Bangalore. Like him, his sons, Shivaji and Sambhaji, soon emerged as accomplished generals.

When Shivaji began his political career, he was still very young and wanted to first acquire a base from where he could conquer adjoining territories. As Kincaid and Parasnis say, 'Shivaji had to create an army from half-savage hillmen of the Western Ghats who were ignorant of war and Marathas of the plains broken by three centuries of servitude'. He believed in regional supremacy as against Mughal imperialism and to put this belief into practice, Shivaji followed in his father's footsteps by deploying a strategy of playing the Bijapur sultans against the Mughals. In fact, he completed the unfinished tasks of his father by being more ambitious, cunning and ruthless. Thus Shivaji began to lead campaigns parallely with Shahji.

Shivaji first captured the Sinhagad (Kondana) fort in 1645 CE, and appointed his trusted men there. This was easy for him since the Adil Shahi sultan had given the *subedari* of Kondana to Dadaji Kondadev in 1639 CE. Now, however, the infuriated sultan held Dadaji Kondadev responsible for this act; and Shahji was so busy with his own conquests that he paid little attention to Dadaji Kondadev's concerns about keeping Shivaji in check. Shivaji then took over the fort of Torna in 1646 CE, followed by the fort of Raigarh, which was rebuilt after its conquest. He also took over Supa from his uncle, Sambhaji Mohite. With the death of Dadaji Kondadev in 1647 CE, Shivaji became his own master and the control of his father's *jagir* passed on to him. Mavali foot soldiers, the non-Arab Muslims with whom he had developed good relations, later became a strong component of his army. With their help, he strengthened his position by acquiring an additional series of hill forts near Poona. He also brought the forts of Baramati and Indapura under his direct control and captured Purandhar in 1647 CE. This sudden spurt in Shivaji's military activities angered the Bijapur sultan, but the matter was dropped and no action was taken against Shivaji for the time being.

Shivaji now turned towards the Konkan, and the Marathas, under General Abaji Sondar, took possession of the important town of Kalyan before proceeding southwards to the Colaba district. The sultan of Bijapur, alarmed at Shahji and the rising ambitions of his sons, captured Shahji and had him thrown into prison in 1648 CE. This automatically checked Shivaji's progress, and he gave up his raids for the time being. Simultaneously, however, Shivaji established contact with Prince Murad, the Mughal Viceroy of the Deccan, with the help of a few Muslim nobles from the Bijapur court. The move brought about its desired result, and the Bijapur state ordered the release of Shahji in 1649 CE on the condition that Shivaji refrain from furthering his raiding exercises. Since the release was conditional, the forts and territories of Bangalore, Kondana and Kondarfil were surrendered to Bijapur. Thereafter for six years (1649–55 CE) Shivaji maintained a low profile and utilized his time by consolidating his political position and strengthening his administration. Shahji soon withdrew from active life and died from a fall while on a hunt.

With the death of his father Shivaji resumed his raids and conquered Javali in 1656 CE from the Maratha chief, Chandra Rao More. The kingdom of Javali together with the treasure amassed by the Mores was significant enough to make him the undisputed master of the Mavala area on the highlands. The conquest also cleared the way for Shivaji to reach Satara and coastal Konkan.

Confrontation with Bijapur

When Muhammad Adil Shah of Bijapur died in November 1656 CE, Aurangzeb, who was then the governor of the Deccan, took advantage of the situation by conquering Bidar, Kalyani and Parinda in 1657 CE with the help of Mir Jumla, an able Mughal commander. Bijapur made peace with Aurangzeb by surrendering certain districts and agreeing to pay a huge war indemnity. Feeding on the political tension between the Mughals and the Bijapur sultanate, Shivaji sought to improve his own fortunes by proposing to help the Mughals on condition that they help him in conquering other territories.

As soon as Aurangzeb left the Deccan in 1658 CE, Bijapur decided to act against Shivaji. A huge army was collected and Afzal Khan, a reputed commander, was entrusted with the task of dealing with the Maratha leader. Afzal Khan began his campaign with the desecration of the temples of goddess Bhavani in Tuljapur and Pandharpur, with the motive of disturbing Shivaji and smoking him out into an open battlefield. Instead, Shivaji sent a letter to Afzal Khan saying that he was not eager for war and sought some sort of an informal settlement with him. After carefully weighing his options, Shivaji strategically decided to confront and surprise Afzal Khan through diplomatic negotiations. Consequently a meeting was arranged between the two at the foothills of fort Pratapgarh, but just before it was to take place Shivaji learnt that Afzal Khan planned to have him slayed during the meeting.

Arming himself secretly (with the *wagh nakh* or tiger claw and *chilkhat* or armour), Shivaji met Afzal Khan who tried to stab him in the back with a dagger as they embraced. Shivaji remained unharmed due to the armour he had worn under his clothes, and countered the attack by assaulting Afzal Khan with the *wagh nakh*, injuring him. Thereafter, Afzal Khan's deputy, Krishnaji Bhaskar Kulkarni, and his bodyguard, Sayyed Banda, immediately came to the rescue of their commander by attacking Shivaji with swords, but Jiva Mahala, Shivaji's personal bodyguard, fatally struck them down with a *dandpatta*, another weapon used during the medieval times. Before Afzal Khan could get any help he was killed by Shivaji's associate, Sambhaji Kavji.

In the ensuing battle of Pratapgarh in 1659 CE, Shivaji's armies attacked Afzal Khan's forces in the dense forests. Shivaji is said to have entered the fort with his lieutenants, ordering the firing of cannons—a signal to his infantry, strategically placed under cover of the densely covered valley, to immediately attack the enemy. The Maratha troops commanded by Shivaji's captain, Kanhoji Jedhe, swept down on Afzal Khan's 1,500 soldiers who were completely taken by surprise, routing the Bijapur army at the foothills of the fort. Then in a rapid march, a section of the Adil Shahi forces commanded by Musa Khan, Afzal Khan's lieutenant, was attacked. Musa Khan was wounded in the skirmish, and fled the battle field.

Meanwhile, the Maratha infantry descended upon Afzal Khan's artillery at close quarters, making them ineffective in providing protection to their troops. As a result, the rest of their troops rapidly succumbed to an all-out Maratha attack. Ragho Atre, Shivaji's cavalry commander, simultaneously attacked the large but unprepared Adil Shahi cavalry even before they could gear up for battle; and succeeded in completely routing them in a short time. A Maratha cavalry unit under Netaji Palkar, meanwhile, pursued the retreating Adil Shahi troops, who were to join their reserve forces at the nearby village of Wai. They were defeated in battle even before they could reach Wai and re-group.

Shivaji's victory over Afzal Khan was so absolute that he became a great hero of Maratha folklore, the incident transforming him into a legend among his people. The large quantities of captured weapons, horses, armour and other loot helped to strengthen the emerging Maratha army in times to come.

The sultan of Bijapur later sent an elite Pashtun army of Afghan mercenaries to subdue and defeat Shivaji. But the Marathas, riding high on the wings of recent victory, defeated Bijapur's Pashtun forces in the battle of Panhalgarh. The intense and bloody battle ended in the unconditional surrender of the Bijapur forces to Shivaji.

Watching these developments in the Deccan with an eagle eye, Emperor Aurangzeb could now identify Shivaji as a major threat to the mighty Mughal Empire.

Countering the Mughals

When Shivaji began to eventually attack parts of the Mughal domain, Aurangzeb could hardly remain a silent spectator. In 1660 CE, he appointed Shaista Khan as the governor of the Deccan and instructed him to keep Shivaji in check. Shaista

Khan was able to defeat the Marathas at some places, even capturing a few forts belonging to Shivaji. The Marathas, however, had become a scourge for the Mughals, forcing Shaista Khan to stay back in Poona. In fact, he took up residence at the very house that Shivaji had spent his childhood in. Being well acquainted with every nook and cranny of the neighbourhood, Shivaji devised a bold plan in April 1663 CE to deal with the Mughal governor. He is said to have entered the city of Poona one night with 400 followers—his group disguised as a marriage party—and attacked the residence of Shaista Khan. In the ensuing encounter, Shaista Khan's son was killed by the Marathas. The attack was a complete success, immensely adding to the prestige of the Marathas, especially of Shivaji. Shaista Khan was eventually recalled from the Deccan by Aurangzeb in December 1663 CE and transferred to Bengal as governor.

Flush with confidence after his success with Shaista Khan, in 1664 CE Shivaji attacked Surat—which had always been an important maritime centre on west coast—with an army of 4,000 soldiers. Victory came easily to the Marathas as the Mughal governor of Surat left the city without any resistance and the city was plundered by the Marathas who carried away almost one crore rupees as spoils of war. The English and the Dutch factories in the area were able to defend themselves with difficulty. Soon after this, Shivaji also conquered Mudhol and Savantvadi.

The very next year (1665 CE) Aurangzeb deputed Raja Jai Singh, one of the ablest Mughal commanders and diplomats, to deal with Shivaji. It was felt that as a natural outcome to this decision, the kingdoms of Bijapur and Golconda might form a formidable alliance with Shivaji to counter the entry of a large Mughal force into the Deccan. However, nothing of the sort happened. Instead Jai Singh cleverly manipulated the situation by causing a rift between Bijapur and Shivaji. He even attempted to buy off the Maratha chieftains with money and *jagirs,* writing letters to European traders and the Siddis of Janjira to support the Mughals. Making sure that all of Shivaji's help lines were cut off, Jai Singh prepared for an attack by encircling the Maratha army. Even Raigarh, Shivaji's seat of government was threatened, and many Maratha villages destroyed by the Mughals. Finding himself defenceless and debilitated, Shivaji decided to come to terms with Jai Singh. Thus, the Treaty of Purandhar was signed in June 1665 CE, which required the Marathas to surrender 23 of their forts (retaining only 12). In addition, Shivaji's son, Sambhaji, was to be made a *Punj Hazari mansabdar* along with a *jagir*. Though it was agreed that it would not be mandatory for Shivaji to attend the Mughal court, he, however, promised to lend military aid to Aurangzeb in the Deccan.

Jai Singh believed that Shivaji could be of immense help to the Mughals against Bijapur and Golconda. To this end, unlike previous Mughal generals, Jai Singh's policy towards Shivaji was to conciliate him, not to crush him. Jai Singh convinced Shivaji to join him in an offensive against Bijapur, which would be beneficial for both parties. A Mughal army of 40,000 soldiers marched against Bijapur in December 1665 CE, to which Shivaji added another 2,000 cavalry and 7,000 infantry soldiers. Jai Singh's clever move was a major political victory for the Mughals, where the Marathas and the Deccani sultanates were first kept disassociated from each other, while Shivaji was roped into joining the Mughals. Jai Singh's action was adequately rewarded with rich gifts and higher ranks for both his sons, Ram Singh and Kirat Singh.

Jai Singh also persuaded Shivaji to visit the Mughal court. Sensing the risk involved, Shivaji set up a council of regency to govern his *jagir* under the formal presidency of his mother, Jijabai. Shivaji and his son, Sambhaji, reached Agra in May 1666 CE, but were disappointed by the absence of a suitable welcome. Sensing a trap, Shivaji secretly planned his escape from Agra along with his son. When he managed to reach Marathwada, he was welcomed by his Maratha brethren amidst joyous celebrations. Aurangzeb suspected Jai Singh for Shivaji's escape and recalled him to the capital, but Jai Singh died on his way in July 1667 CE.

Once Shivaji regained his freedom, he used the much needed opportunity to rebuild his forts and consolidate his army and administration. Meanwhile the Mughals too remained busy with the Afghan risings in the northwest and shifted their concentration from Shivaji for the time being. Later in 1667 CE, the Mughal emperor ordered a fresh campaign against the Marathas. By then Prince Muazzam had replaced Jai Singh as the governor of the Deccan, assisted by Maharaja Jaswant Singh of Marwar.

Jaswant Singh adopted a benevolent attitude towards Shivaji, and through his influence Aurangzeb returned the fort of Chakan—out of the 23 annexed under the Treaty of Purandhar. In addition, Sambhaji was posted to Aurangabad, the Mughal viceroy's Deccan capital, as the commander of a 5,000 cavalry unit. A *jagir* in Berar was also assigned to him for the maintenance of his establishment. An inevitable rupture between the two sides, however, took place in January 1670 CE when Shivaji began recovering his forts at Kondana, Purandhar, Kalian-Bhimri, and finally Mahuli by the end of the year.

Meanwhile, relations between Prince Muazzam and his general, Dilir Khan, had soured in the Deccan, with the prince and Jaswant Singh writing to Aurangzeb and accusing Dilir Khan of rebellion. Dilir Khan in turn also accused the prince and Jaswant Singh of secretly allying with Shivaji and aiding his recent successes in order to take the throne from Aurangzeb. In the resultant confusion Dilir Khan escaped to northern India with his force; and Aurangzeb sent Mahabat Khan to cover the military operations in the Deccan, while keeping Jaswant Singh and Muazzam away from each other.

Between 1670–78 CE, Shivaji was successful in continuously looting and plundering ordinary villagers and businessmen, while conquering Mughal forts to expand his dominions. Many of the disbanded soldiers from the Mughal army also joined Shivaji. In 1670 CE Shivaji's officers even acquired written promises from the local authorities of certain districts in Khandesh stating that they would pay *chauth* to Shivaji. That same year Shivaji plundered Surat for the second time, securing spoils amounting to 66 lakh rupees. But the real loss of Surat was not in the loss of its treasures, but in the destruction of its trade as the richest port in India at the time.

The Mughals suspected that Jaswant Singh did not resist Shivaji strongly enough; and consequently, General Mahabat Khan was sent to the Deccan, where Jaswant Singh and Daud Khan, the governor of Khandesh, were in open clash over raising money for Muazzam. Mahabat Khan took away Jaswant Singh from Burhanpur, the capital of Khandesh, easing the tension somewhat. Mahabat Khan later joined Daud Khan near the Chandor Range, and the two laid siege to Ahivant in January 1671 CE, which Shivaji had taken over. Soon, however, differences arose between Daud Khan and Mahabat Khan, and the former was recalled to the Mughal court while Mahabat Khan was left to while away his time on pleasures of the harem. This inactivity lead Aurangzeb to send Bahadur Khan as a replacement for the general. Dilir Khan too was meanwhile recalled to the Deccan to support the new commander.

Bahadur Khan and Dilir Khan were now entrusted the task of pursuing Shivaji; and the two generals invaded the Maratha kingdom in December 1671 CE, capturing Poona. Another army under Ikhlas Khan had also advanced to Salhir, where Shivaji himself fought a tough battle, ending in the destruction of the Mughal army and the captivity of its generals. Shivaji's childhood friend, Surya Rao Kakre, was the only chief killed on the Maratha side. This triumph freed the Maratha army and forced the Mughals to withdraw from Poona. Encouraged by this succession of triumphs, the Marathas continued their war, conquering Jawhar and Ramnagar during June–July 1671 CE from the Koli Raja. But the Maratha raid into Berar and Khandesh during October–December 1671 CE was thwarted by the Mughals.

Chattrapati Shivaji

Having consolidated his position back home, Shivaji sent his emissaries to meet the English and began his operations against Bijapur. After the death of Ali Adil Shah II in November 1672 CE, his Bijapur sultanate collapsed—a result of the internal disputes among various factions of the nobility. Taking advantage of the political confusion, Shivaji sent Pratap Rao into Bijapur to loot Hubli and other towns in June 1673 CE. Later Shivaji himself, at the command of a 25,000-strong force, marched against Bijapur and sacked many towns during October–December 1673 CE. In Maharashtra, he gained other forts—Panhala and Satara—by bribing their Mughal commandants. A similar attempt on Shivner, his birthplace, however, ended in failure.

The Bijapur forces retaliated by attacking the Maratha territory of Panhala. Dilir Khan too attempted to invade the fertile Konkan belt at about the same time in January 1674 CE. But Shivaji, fighting a defensive campaign, destroyed all roads and hill paths, blocking every mountain pass with stones. While attempting to storm one such pass, Dilir Khan was defeated with the loss of 1,000 soldiers.

By April 1674 CE, the rising of the frontier Pathans had become such a serious threat that Aurangzeb had to leave Delhi and take command of the operations. The best generals and men were called upon for the emperor's support, including Jaswant Singh and Mahabat Khan. Dilir Khan too was called with his force—leaving only Bahadur Khan in the Deccan. By then Shivaji had reached the zenith of his power, and found this an opportune time to proclaim himself an independent ruler. Shivaji crowned himself as the 'Chattrapati' in June 1674 CE at the fort of Raigarh, which was to become his capital. This was possible largely because of the defeat of Dilir Khan in the Konkan and the Afghan rebellion in the northwest, which had compelled Aurangzeb to shift base and recall Dilir Khan.

As part of the coronation ceremonies, despite being a *shudra*, Shivaji underwent the *yajnopavita* or thread ceremony and married his spouse according to Vedic rites. Pandit Gaga Bhatt, a renowned *brahman* from Varanasi, officially presided over the ceremony, declaring Shivaji as a *kshatriya*. As part of the elaborate purification ceremonies, Shivaji was weighed against iron, tin, lead, zinc, copper, silver and gold. This coronation ceremony marked a distinct stage in the career of Shivaji as it conferred on him the status of an independent ruler. His coronation was attended by the English ambassador, Qxiden, and almost 10,000 to 12,000 *brahmans* were not deterred by their own status from serving him. Shivaji's coronation procedures elevated his position and established his superiority in the social strata, in a way upholding the caste-based status quo of Hindu society. This may also be viewed in terms of Shivaji's desire to underline regional supremacy over Mughal imperialism. By reinforcing social distinctions, therefore, Shivaji utilized it to his advantage.

In 1675 CE, Shivaji, supported by the mediation of Bahadur Khan, at first accepted the suzerainty of Aurangzeb. However, he then defied the truce and attacked the fort of Fonda. This characterized a typical trait of Shivaji's military campaigns—his breach of trust and alliance—a ploy that helped him win against equally treacherous generals, governors and emperors. Shivaji continued to remain hostile to the Mughals and Bijapur. At the beginning of 1677 CE, he entered into an alliance with Golconda for the conquest of Bijapur. He marched to Golconda with an army of 70,000 infantry and cavalry soldiers; and with the help of the artillery provided by the sultan of Golconda, he conquered the forts at Jinji, Tiruvannamalai, Vellore, Thanjavur and the adjoining district in Karnataka in a single year (1677 CE). He also brought the Mysore plateau under his control.

Shivaji had promised to share all this loot with the Qutb Shahi sultan, but soon turned his back on him. Sometimes using treachery against Golconda and sometimes by bribing the Bijapur generals, his campaigns in Golconda, Bijapur and Karnataka were mainly prompted by avarice. Shivaji had no particular sympathy for any religious group; and made alliances that supported his grand aspirations, irrespective of religious affiliations. 'He plundered mercilessly the Hindu population' of Karnataka as Satish Chandra says, as he plundered the popular saint Syed Jaan Muhammad's seminary too in November 1679 CE. In fact in terms of military conduct, there was little to choose between Shivaji looting and plundering villages and towns, and the mercenary army of the Mughals.

Exhausted by long-drawn wars and exertions he died in 1680 CE at just 53 years of age. At the time of his death, Shivaji's kingdom or *swarajya* comprised the Western Ghats and the Konkan strip between Kalyan and Goa, with some districts to the east of the mountains. The southern provinces comprised Western Karnataka, extending from Belgaum to the banks of the Tungabhadra.

Maratha Administration

Besides being a daring soldier and a successful military conqueror, Shivaji tried to provide his kingdom with a good system of administration. Borrowing certain administrative practices from the Deccan sultanates, he evolved for the Marathas a system of governance in which his central administration was known as the *ashtapradhan* system. His kingdom consisted of territories known as the *swarajya* and

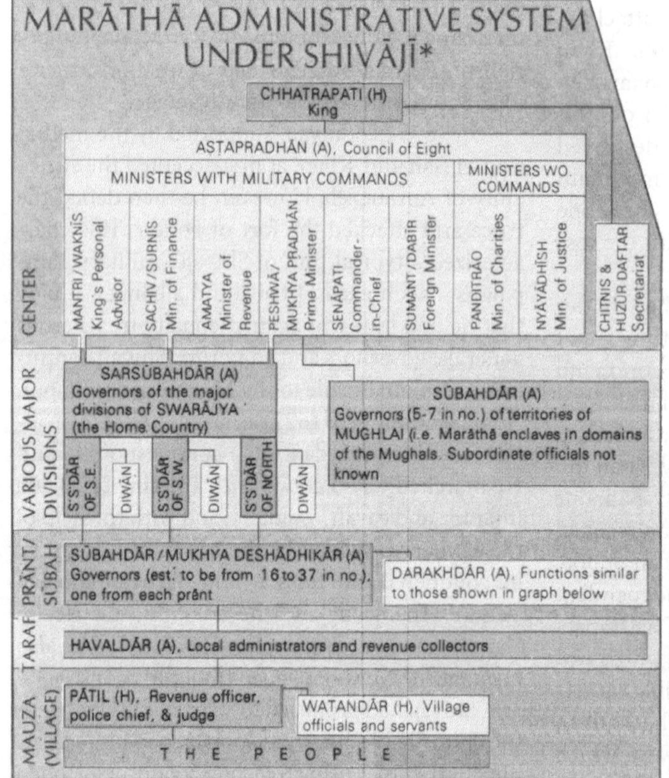

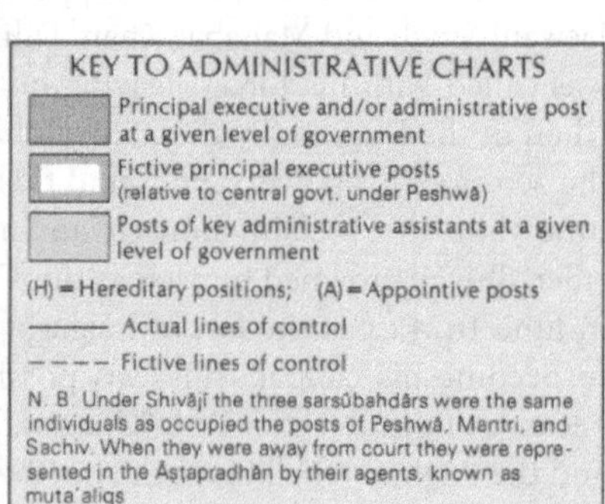

Maratha Administrative System Under Shivaji

the *mughalai*. *Swarajya* referred to the areas where his system of administration was implemented, while the *mughalai* territory fell outside the *swarajya* and was subject to Maratha and other external raids from time to time. To protect people living in the *mughalai* areas against any external invasions, a contribution was taken in the form of the *chauth*; and to safeguard them against Maratha attacks the *sardeshmukhi* was imposed. The levying of these taxes was very similar to the imposition of the *jiziya*, since all these taxes were punitive in nature and offered protection in return for revenue.

Central Government

Shivaji was the supreme head of his government, with all powers—executive, legislative, military, as well as judicial—concentrated in his hands. A council of eight ministers assisted him in the Maratha central administration—the *ashtapradhan* system. The ministers received new Sanskritized titles and their functions were purely advisory. These eight ministers included:

- **The Peshwa** or the Prime Minister, whose duty was to look after the general welfare and interests of the state.
- **The Amatya** or Finance Minister, who was in charge of checking and countersigning all public accounts of the kingdom and other areas under its purview.
- **The Mantri** or State Chronicler, who maintained a daily account of the king and his court. He was also known as the Wakia-Navis.
- **The Sumant** or **Dabir** was the Foreign Secretary, whose duty was to advise the king on external affairs, war and peace, and of affairs in other states.
- **The Sachiv** or **Surnis** or Home Secretary, whose duty was to look after the correspondence of the king. He also checked the account of the parganas.
- **The Pandit Rao** or **Danadhyaksha** was the Ecclesiastical Head, whose duty was to fix dates for religious ceremonies, punish heresy and distribute alms and charity among the *brahmans*. He was the judge of canon law and censor of public morals.
- **The Nyayadhish** or **Chief Justice** was responsible for dispensing civil and military justice.
- **The Senapati** or **Sari Naubat** was the Commander-in-Chief in charge of recruitment, organization and discipline in the army. He was also responsible for arranging and deploying troops in the battlefield.

With the exception of the Nyayadhish and Pandit Rao, all other ministers were required to command armies and lead expeditions whenever required. Each department also had a number of junior officers to assist the minister in charge. Chief among them were the *diwan, majumdar, phadnis, sabnis, karkhanis, chitnis, jamadar* and *potnis*. Every minister was in charge of more than one department; all acting as a secretary to the king and carrying out his orders.

Local Government

For the purpose of administrative convenience, Shivaji divided his kingdom into four provinces and each was placed under a viceroy. To assist the provincial governor there was a council of ministers based on the central model. The provinces were divided into a number of regions called *prants*. Each *prant* was subdivided into *parganas* and *tarafs*. The village was the lowest unit of administration, run by the village headman known as the *patel*. The *patel* carried on his duties with the help of the *gram panchayat*, whose members were elected by the villagers. Over a group of villages, there were officers known as *deshmukhs* and *deshpandes* who supervised the village functioning. Shivaji abolished the system of granting *jagirs* and started the system of paying officers in cash. When the collection of revenue of any region was assigned to an official, his main concern was only to collect the revenue and not establish control over the people residing there. None of the officers enjoyed a hereditary status.

The Army

Shivaji was a military genius and organized his army efficiently. He introduced the system of maintaining a regular standing army in place of fighting forces which spent half the year in cultivation and the other half in active military service, or whenever the need arose. The strength of Shivaji's standing army at the time of his death amounted to 45,000 *paga* and 60,000 *silahdar* cavalry, and one lakh infantry. Other than horses, there were elephants and camels in his army. There is no accurate information regarding the number of elephants he maintained in the army, while the camels comprised a very small number. He seemed to have also purchased cannons—a major technological innovation in the military record of those times.

Since his regular army consisted mostly of cavalry, every soldier had a spare horse. His army lived in the area where it operated, but his soldiers were given strict instructions not to indulge in plunder on their own account, which was the king's privilege to decide.

The soldiers were enrolled on regular salaries for the whole year; and there was a proper gradation of officers. In case of the cavalry, 25 troopers formed one unit headed by a *havaldar*, while over every five *havaldars* there was a *jumladar*, and over 10 *jumladars* was placed a *hazari*. Other higher ranks were those of the *punj hazari* and the *sari naubat* in the cavalry or supreme commander of the forces. For every 25 troopers, there was a water carrier. The cavalry was divided into two—the *bargirs* and the *shiledars*, while the *bargirs* were supplied with horses and arms by the state, the *shiledars* had to find their own equipment.

The infantry was divided into regiments, brigades and divisions. Nine soldiers, who were under a *naik*, formed the smallest unit. A *havaldar* was placed over five *naiks* and two or three were placed under a *jumladar*, while a *hazari* was placed over 10 *jumladars*, and a *sari naubat* had control over seven *hazaris*. Both Hindus and Muslims were recruited in the army without any distinction. Soldiers were paid in cash and those who displayed bravery were also rewarded.

Forts formed an important part of the security system of the Maratha military organization. Garrisons were carefully selected and great care was taken to keep the troops disciplined. There were a total of 240 forts under the command of the Marathas; and three officers of equal status—*havaldar, sabnis* and the *sari naubat*—were in charge of every fort.

Shivaji had developed his own navy and used it to good purpose. The fleet was stationed at Colaba. With the conquest of the Konkan coast, the Maratha borders stretched upto the Portuguese limits and it had become essential to safeguard Maratha coastal territory from the invasions of the Siddis of Janjira. According to a particular account, Shivaji had 400 different kinds of ships in his navy—gun ships with 60 to 100 guns (*ghurab, shibars* and *manchwas*). He also had a well-organized merchant navy. Though the achievements of the Maratha navy under Shivaji were not remarkable, nevertheless, the Maratha fleet provided a considerable challenge to the Portuguese, the Dutch and the English. Shivaji was mainly concerned about the growing dominance of the English naval forces in Indian waters and needed a navy to tackle this issue. To this end he employed Muslim-Malabar pirates in his navy.

Shivaji laid great stress upon the maintenance of discipline in his army. He issued a set of regulations for the conduct of soldiers—baggage was limited to the minimum, women, female slaves and dancing girls were prohibited from travelling with the army, and cows and *brahmans* were to be protected during battles.

Economic Reforms

As in other parts of India, a feudal way of life was in operation in Marathwada too. Under this system, the *jagirdar* or *watandar* not only collected the revenue from his *jagir* or *watan*, but also administered the region under his jurisdiction like an absolute king, maintaining his own army. But since the ascent of Shivaji, a strong military state was established where the fiefdoms were in fear of the central administration. He imposed the payment of *sardeshmukhi* whereby the *deshmukhs* or existent feudal and clan leaders paid him a tax amounting to 10 per cent of revenue. Not encouraging the granting of *jagirs* to officials, he in a way restricted the feudal way of operations. But at the same time, it is found that Shivaji also gave away *mokasa mahal* or fiefs on different occasions. He even granted them to a goddess, which was in a way providing for the priests and maintaining the superstructure of caste.

For the purpose of tax collection, the *prant* was subdivided into *parganas* and *tarafs*. The procedure entailed a careful survey of the land after which the share of the state was fixed at 30 per cent of the produce. Later when other taxes were abolished, the state's share was increased to 40 per cent. The cultivator was at liberty to pay either in cash or kind, according to his own convenience and will. The amount of money to be paid to the state was fixed, which meant that there was not much scope for tax collectors to oppress the peasantry. The state's policy was such that it promoted and encouraged agricultural activities by helping peasants through the advancement of money or grain. Shivaji was strict in the collection of land revenue and adequate steps were taken to ensure that no favouritism or oppression took place.

Shivaji's revenue system was beneficent and based on humane considerations. Loans, or the *takavi*, were advanced to agriculturists by the state for the purchase of cattle and seeds. They were repayable in easy instalments. Extension of cultivation was encouraged by greatly reducing the tax upon lands newly brought under cultivation. The concessional assessment was known as *istava*. Tax was raised in gradual stages in such a way that the maximum amount was reached over a period of eight years.

Shivaji levied the taxes of *chauth* and *sardeshmukhi* on the neighbouring tracts of land, the Mughal provinces and some districts of Bijapur—all of which were outside his kingdom. There are different opinions about the nature of these taxes. One view is that the *chauth* was a payment in lieu of protection against the invasion of a third power. The other view is that the payment of *chauth* merely saved a region from the Maratha raid, but did not impose any corresponding obligation on Shivaji to guard it from any foreign invasion or any internal disorder. Therefore, the lands subjected to the *chauth* did not come under the 'spheres of influence' that were constituted later. Still another view is that the *chauth* was a tribute realized from hostile or rival territories. Such a system was not unfamiliar in western India even before the advent of Shivaji. In theory, the *chauth* amounted to one-fourths of the revenue paid by a district to the Marathas for protection against external invasions. The *sardeshmukhi* was a tax amounting to one-tenths of the standard revenue levied on the territories which paid *chauth* to secure themselves against Maratha attacks.

The Judiciary

Despite the implementation of a proper administrative apparatus, the administration of justice in the kingdom was of a primitive nature. There were no regular courts, neither was there any regular procedure of imparting justice. The *panchayats* settled disputes in the villages and a common form of punishment was the trial by ordeal. Criminal cases were tried by the village headman or *patel*. At the imperial level, the *nyayadhish* heard appeals in both civil and criminal cases while the *hazir majlis* constituted the final court of appeal.

An Assessment of Shivaji and the Maratha State

For centuries after his death, Shivaji has caught the attention of historians, poets and politicians alike. Several plays, films, books have been created on the warrior who ruled the Maratha kingdom till 1680 CE. Credited with setting up a Maratha monarchy in Maharashtra, Shivaji espoused the ideology of independence from the Mughals. Selective portrayal by some intellectuals and politicians of his battles with the regional sultanates project him as a Hindu icon and a brave war hero who mastered the art of guerrilla warfare against his opponents. There is no doubt that he was able to harass and at times defeat the superior Mughal army owing to his military genius. At the same time, he did not hesitate to use his gifted military abilities to crush the Maratha chieftains who tried to oppose his rise. He understood and took advantage of the rivalry among the sultans of the Deccan, and the collective danger they faced from the Mughals. This scenario suited him the best as he sided with whoever afforded him the best advantage at any particular time. He showed no qualms in signing treaties and breaching them to suit his goals.

The Maratha state was basically a military organization. The conditions in Maratha society were such that everyone clung to his *watan* or hereditary land and any disturbance in the system produced disappointment among the people. Those land holders whose term was not renewed allied themselves with Shivaji's enemies, such as the sultans of Bijapur, Ahmednagar and Golconda or the Mughals, to regain their lands. Shivaji, therefore, had to not only fight his enemies, but also his own people throughout his life. The number of castes prevalent in Maharashtra in the seventeenth century also created dissension among the Marathas and stood in the way of their solidarity. The *brahmans* hated the non-*brahmans* and were themselves subdivided into *Desh brahmans, Konkan brahmans* and *Chitpavan brahmans* who frequently quarrelled among themselves.

Shivaji, as had been mentioned earlier, was influenced by the epics of the *Ramayana* and *Mahabharata* that were narrated to him by his spiritually inclined mother. He was also influenced by the *Bhakti* movement of the time that taught him the need for equality. Upon his return from Agra he visited numerous Hindu shrines and tried to understand the intricacies of his own religious background. Coupled with this, the caste divisions within the Maratha society and his own low caste forced Shivaji to come up with a plan that hardly had any precedence in history. He was aware that the higher castes would never accept him as an undisputed leader, however powerful he might become. He was also aware that he did not have the wherewithal to bring about even notional equality among the rigidly divided castes. Against this backdrop, he decided to rise in the caste-hierarchy by 'persuading' the *brahmans* to make him a *kshatriya*, the warrior caste, through prolonged rituals and rites. He also gave assurance to the *brahmans* that he would protect them and the cows they considered holy. This political master stroke worked wonders for him and to a large extent for his successors too.

His record with his Muslim subjects indicates that he did not discriminate against them. He maintained good relations with the sultans, as and when it suited him. He appeared to have taken special care in developing good ties with the nobles and military generals of the sultans and the Mughals, who at times helped him in many ways. He employed Muslims in his army and navy, and even gave grants to his Muslim subjects and to the *dargahs* of Muslim saints.

When Shivaji died in 1680 CE, he ruled over the larger part of modern Maharashtra, except for the old central provinces, Belgaum and North Dharwar, parts of Karnataka, Andhra and Madras. Shivaji fought to win and, therefore, he was not averse to guerrilla techniques when odds weighed heavily against him. He elevated the position of the Marathas on the political map of India, which remained strong even after his death. The Maratha state outlived Aurangzeb's long wars in the Deccan. After Aurangzeb's death, the Maratha wars compelled his successors to acknowledge the Marathas as partners of the Mughal empire in Central India and the Deccan.

SUMMARY

- Among the various provincial states that emerged during the seventeenth century in India, the most prominent was the state of the Marathas.
- The hilly terrain of the Marathwada region made the Marathas physically strong and warlike people.
- The spread of *Bhakti* ideals promoted a feeling of unity among the Marathas in terms of infusing in them a sense of social equality, in turn encouraged by the preaching of the Maratha saints.
- The establishment and consolidation of the Maratha kingdom by Shivaji forms an important aspect of medieval Indian history, for it advanced the destabilization of the Mughal Empire.
- Shivaji started his career of conquests at an early age. He fought against the kingdom of Bijapur and won many victories.
- In the course of the expansion of his dominions, he came into conflict with the Mughals. The war between Shivaji and the Mughals continued intermittently.
- Between 1670–74 CE, the Marathas were successful everywhere, almost crippling the Mughal power in the Deccan.
- In 1674 CE, Shivaji was coronated at Raigarh, making him the sovereign ruler of the Maratha state.
- Although he did not live long, he brought unity among the Marathas, established a Maratha state and gave to it a system of administration.
- The Maratha state was basically a military organization with a well-organized central and provincial administration. A regular army was maintained and fortifications were given much importance. Economic reforms were implemented by reorganizing the revenue system.
- The *ashtapradhan* system in central administration and the introduction of the *chauth* and *sardeshmukhi* as punitive taxes were adopted.
- Shivaji elevated the position of the Marathas on the political map of India that even his death failed to weaken what he had achieved.
- After Aurangzeb's death, his successors had to acknowledge the Marathas as partners of the Mughal Empire in Central India and the Deccan without losing their independence.

KEYWORDS

Patel	Swarajya	Peshwa	Havaldars, jumladar and hazari
Punj Hazari	Ashtapradhan system	Nyayadhish	Bargirs and shiledars
Guerrilla warfare	Chauth and sardeshmukhi	Pandit Rao	
Chattrapati			

REVIEW QUESTIONS

1. Explain how Bhakti ideals, and Marathi language and literature helped Shivaji to foster a sense of unity among the Marathas.
2. Give an account of Shivaji's career of conquests with reference to the Mughals.
3. Elucidate Shivaji's confrontation with Bijapur.
4. Write a brief note on the ashtapradhan system in Shivaji's administration.
5. What were the economic reforms introduced by Shivaji?

CHAPTER 27

Rise of the Peshwas

Review and Discussion

- The Rule of the Peshwas
- Leading Maratha Chiefs
- Invasions of Nadir Shah and Ahmad Shah Abdali
- Decline of the Marathas

Shivaji was able to build a strong Maratha state during his short lived rule, but it was now up to his successors to strengthen and consolidate it. In addition, his successors also had to continue their campaigns against the Mughals. Perhaps the most formidable challenge the Mughals had to face both in the Deccan and the north was from the Marathas.

Shivaji was succeeded by his eldest son, Sambhaji, who ruled from 1680–89 CE. He lacked the dynamism and strength of character his father had displayed, and spent more time in wasteful pleasures leaving the administration of the Maratha state unattended. Not losing an opportunity to suppress the Marathas, Aurangzeb, soon after occupying Bijapur and Golconda, decided to deal with them with a firm hand. As part of this plan, many of the Maratha forts were taken over and the Mughal general, Muqarrab Khan, in a sudden attack, took Sambhaji, his minister, Kavi Kulesh, and their wives and daughters as captives. The Marathas were brought as prisoners to the imperial camp where Sambhaji and his followers were tortured to death in March 1689 CE and his son, Sahu, was imprisoned and sent to the Mughal court. However, Sambhaji's death infused a new spirit in the Marathas who were now united into a single camp with the motive of carrying on a relentless struggle against the Mughals.

Raja Ram, the stepbrother of Sambhaji now became the leader of the Marathas, ruling from 1689–1700 CE. Sambhaji had kept him in imprisonment after the death of their father, Shivaji. Raja Ram continued the struggle against the Mughals with the help of his two great warriors, Shantaji and Dhanaji, who executed his plans with precision. By 1695 CE, the two Mughal generals, Qasim Khan and Himmat Khan, were defeated and captured; but the struggle between the Marathas and the Mughals continued to drag on. The period from 1695–99 CE was a difficult one for the Mughals as they were vigourously opposed by the Marathas—Shantaji and Dhanaji—to such an extent that they were completely demoralized. Seeing the onslaught, by October 1699 CE Aurangzeb decided to jump into the arena himself and lead the campaign against the Marathas. In December 1699 CE, Satara was besieged, but could be taken into control by the Mughals only after Raja Ram's death in 1700 CE.

After the death of Raja Ram, his widow Tara Bai, became regent (1700–07 CE) for her minor son, Shivaji II. She took a keen interest in the affairs of the state and proved to be a capable administrator with a sound knowledge of civil and military affairs, assisted in her work by Paras Ram Trimbak, Dhanaji Jadav and Shankerji Narayan. She travelled relentlessly within the kingdom to guide the Maratha operations against the Mughals. Her indomitable spirit was responsible for the success of the Marathas against the Mughals. In spite of his best efforts, Aurangzeb failed to crush the Marathas, who had once again become a dominant power in the Deccan. In 1703 CE, the Marathas attacked Berar; and in 1706 CE, they invaded Gujarat and sacked Baroda. That same year the Marathas threatened the camp of Aurangzeb at Ahmednagar.

Soon after the death of Aurangzeb in 1707 CE, Sahu was released from the Mughal court. He first claimed the Maratha kingdom from Tara Bai, resulting in a civil war between the two Maratha groups. Tara Bai was defeated in a battle fought at Khed in November 1707 CE, and retired to Kolhapur with her son Shivaji II. When Shivaji II died, his stepbrother was placed on the throne of Kolhapur. Sahu had defeated Tara Bai with the help of an ambitious Maratha chief, Balaji Vishwanath, and become the ruler of the Marathas from Satara (1707–49 CE). He found Balaji Vishwanath to be an able administrator, and made him the *peshwa* or prime minister of the Maratha state. Balaji Vishwanath soon reorganized the government of the Maratha kingdom efficiently. Sahu had practically entrusted the entire administration to him; and Balaji soon became the virtual ruler of the Marathas, while Sahu was reduced to a titular head. Balaji Vishwanath transferred the capital from Satara to Poona, but Sahu continued to live in Satara. Poona now became the seat of the Maratha government.

The real power, where the safety and integrity of the state was concerned, was in the hands of the *peshwa*; and while the king's position gradually became nominal, the *peshwa* rose in power and importance. With this political change began the second period of Maratha history—the period of *peshwa* domination, in which the Maratha state was transformed into an imperial entity in the subcontinent. After Sahu's death, his successors—Ramraja (1749–77 CE), Sahu II (1777–1808 CE), Pratap Sinh (1808–39 CE) and Shahji (1839–48 CE) did not leave behind any significant achievements.

The Rule of the Peshwas

The stiff opposition from the Marathas under Raja Ram and Tara Bai to uphold Maratha nationalism and counter Aurangzeb's armies only exposed the weakness of the Mughal Empire. And with the appointment of Balaji Vishwanath as the *peshwa* in 1713 CE, the Marathas began their journey of spreading their domination in the whole of India.

Taking full advantage of the internal conflicts between the Mughal officials, Balaji Vishwanath concluded a treaty with the Sayyid brothers, Abdullah Khan and Hussain Ali Khan in 1715 CE. According to the treaty, the Mughal court recognized Sahu as the king of all those Maratha territories, which had earlier been occupied by the Mughals. The Mughals also surrendered Khandesh, Gondwana, Berar, and the districts of Hyderabad and Karnataka. The Marathas were given the right to levy the taxes of *chauth* and *sardeshmukhi* in the six *subas* of the Mughal Deccan. In return for all these favours, the *peshwa* promised to maintain 15,000 horses for the Mughal army, pay an annual tribute of 10 lakh, and maintain peace and order in the Deccan.

Acknowledging the Mughal presence in Delhi was a clear shift from Shivaji's policy of pursuing absolute independence for the Marathas, but Balaji Vishwanath had no other option left to him at the moment. Thus, Tara Bai was neutralized and friendship with the Mughals was established. Balaji Vishwanth had adopted a two-pronged approach: one, he led a Maratha contingent to Delhi in 1719 CE, and helped the Sayyid brothers depose Farrukh Siyar; second, as part of his primary duty he also helped Sahu win over other important Maratha leaders like Kanhaoji Angre to his side.

Not only did Balaji Vishwanath work on expanding the political boundaries of the Marathas, but he also developed networks of trade, banking, and finance. As a result, there was a substantial rise in banking houses based out of Poona, with branches extending into Gujarat, the Ganges valley, and the southern regions. At the same time, expansion of the agricultural sector and maritime affairs were not neglected either.

Balaji Vishwanath died in 1720 CE and was succeeded by his son, Baji Rao I, as the *peshwa.* Like his father before him, he too was a good soldier and a statesman. Though he was only 22 years of age when he became *peshwa*, he possessed all the qualities of an able ruler. He followed a policy of expansion and extended the rule of the Marathas to the north, beyond the river Narmada.

The ambitious *peshwa* soon expanded his span of control over different regions. Baji Rao I initially extended his influence into the regions of Malwa and Gujarat. This roused the jealousy of other Maratha rivals, particularly Trimbak Rao, who was later defeated and killed in a battle. Seeing his strength, even Nizam-ul-Mulk Asaf Jah I of the state of Hyderabad compromised with the *peshwa.* Baji Rao I then shrewdly turned his attention towards the Rajputs, securing the friendship of the chiefs of Amber and Bundela. In 1737 CE, though he came close to the city of Delhi, he did not enter it. Sensing the danger, the Mughal emperor urged the Nizam to oppose Baji Rao I. But the latter defeated the Nizam in the battle of Bhopal, and forced him to pay arrears of *chauth* and *sardeshmukhi.* Not content with these raids, Baji Rao I soon attacked Delhi and defeated the Mughal forces. The Mughal emperor, Muhammad Shah, was compelled to sign the Treaty of Sironj, according to which the Marathas obtained complete sovereignty over the whole of Malwa, and the entire territory between the rivers Narmada and Chambal. Then in 1739 CE, Baji Rao I defeated the Portuguese and occupied the important ports of Salsette and Bassein.

The greatest achievement of Baji Rao I lay in his arrangement to put an end to the jealousy of different Maratha chiefs. The revival of the *jagir* system from the time of Raja Ram had encouraged feudal tendencies and as a result many Maratha chiefs had become as good as independent rulers. He partitioned the former Mughal provinces as 'spheres of influence' under the Maratha military generals. The leading Maratha chiefs at that time were Raghoji Bhonsle of Nagpur, Pillaji Gaekwad of Baroda, Malhar Rao Holkar of Indore and Ramaji Scindia of Gwalior. He granted them maximum autonomy within their own spheres of influence. They were free to levy taxes in the territories under them, but they had to pay a fixed amount to the *peshwa.* They were to work under the *peshwa* and participate in the military campaigns under the *peshwa's* leadership against common enemies. This union of the Maratha chiefs with the *peshwa* as their head came to be known as the Maratha Confederacy.

When Nadir Shah invaded India, Baji Rao I made efforts to put up a united front, but he died prematurely in 1740 CE at the age of 42. Within a short period of 20 years he had transformed the character of the Maratha state—from a mere hill kingdom the Maratha state had grown into an imperial power expanding into northern India.

After Baji Rao I's death, his 18-year-old son, Balaji Baji Rao, became the *peshwa.* Under him the Maratha power reached the zenith of its glory. When Sahu was on his death bed in 1748 CE, Balaji Baji Rao had obtained from him a written order which authorized him and his successors to manage the government of the Maratha state independently. With this permission, the *peshwas* became the real holders of Maratha power.

Balaji Baji Rao consolidated his control over Malwa, Gujarat and Bundelkhand; and marched against Bengal in 1751 CE, forcing the Nawab to cede Orissa to the Marathas. In the southern provinces, the state of Mysore and other smaller principalities were forced to pay tribute. After defeating him at Udgir 1760 CE, the Marathas also compelled the Nizam of Hyderabad to cede vast territories.

Almost at the same time, the Mughal emperor, Muhammad Shah, died, and there was further confusion in the Mughal Empire. Taking advantage of this, the Marathas increased their influence at the Mughal court. The successive Mughal emperors, Ahmed Shah, Alamgir II and Shah Alam II were weak, and sought the help of the *peshwas* against their powerful nobles and foreign invaders. It was during the reign of Shah Alam II that Ahmad Shah Abdali and the Marathas confronted each other in the Third Battle of Panipat in 1761 CE.

The Marathas had meanwhile plundered the Doab and Rajputana in northern India, bringing the Punjab under their successful control. This brought them into direct conflict with Ahmad Shah Abdali, the ambitious ruler of Afghanistan, who marched into India to plunder its wealth. The Marathas fought bravely against Ahmad Shah Abdali in the Third Battle of Panipat in 1761 CE, but they faced a crushing defeat with many Maratha leaders and soldiers losing their lives in battle. Balaji Baji Rao also died upon hearing the news of their defeat. Thereafter, the power of the Maratha Confederacy gradually weakened due to internal conflicts that arose among the various Maratha chiefs.

Leading Maratha Chiefs

While the *peshwas* had emerged as the virtual rulers of the Maratha state, the Maratha chiefs had consolidated their independent positions in a far larger domain of activity away from the original heartland of the Marathas. Gradually they established their own line of rulers from the place where they were based.

Bhonsles of Satara, Thanjavur, Nagpur and Kohlapur

The Bhonsles were a well-known Maratha clan who established their rule in several states in India. The founder of the Maratha state, Shivaji, himself belonged to this clan. His later successors

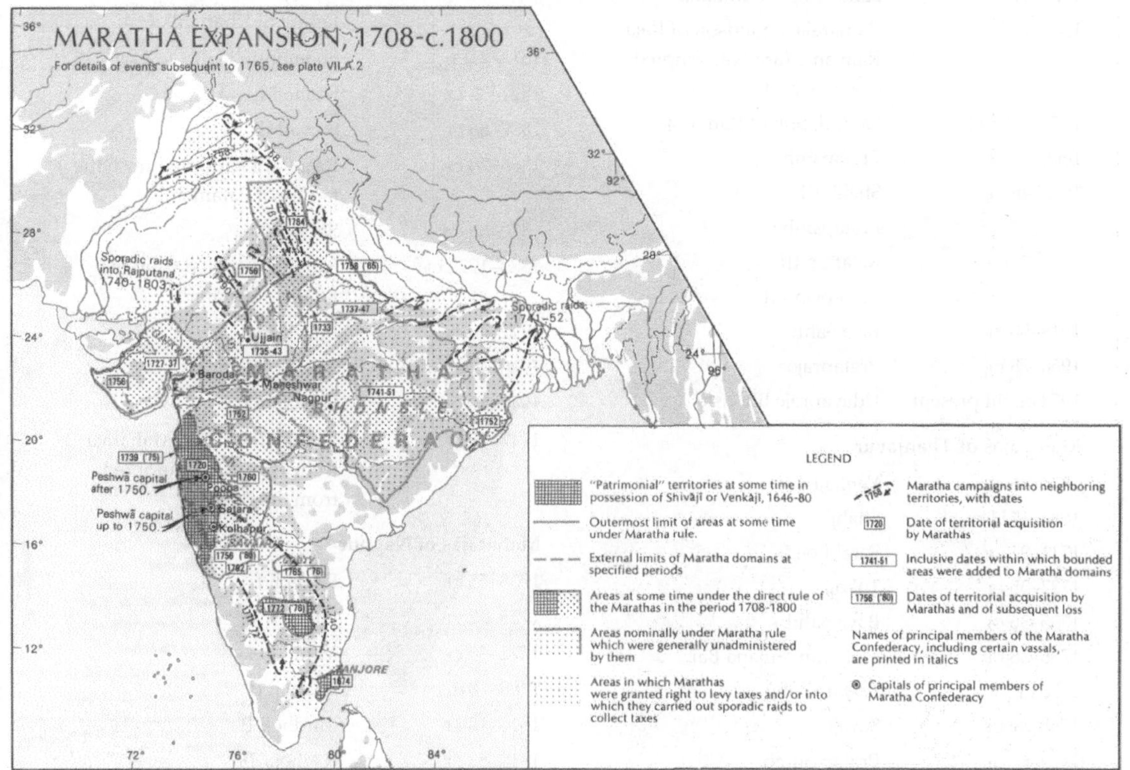

Map 27-1 *Maratha Expansion, 1708–1800 CE*

ruled as maharajas from their capital at Satara, although the *peshwas* remained the de facto rulers.

In addition to the Bhonsle rulers of Satara, members of the Bhonsle clan also established themselves at Thanjavur in Tamil Nadu in the seventeenth century, and at Nagpur and Kolhapur in present day Maharashtra in the eighteenth century. The Bhonsles of Thanjavur were descendants of Shivaji's half-brother, Venkaji, while the Bhonsles of Satara and Kolhapur descended from Shivaji's sons, Sambhaji and Raja Ram.

After the defeat of the Marathas by the British in the Third Anglo-Maratha War in 1818 CE, they had no choice but to accept British sovereignty. The

CHRONOLOGY

Maharajas of Satara

1655–80 CE	Shivaji, Leader from 1655 CE; Maharaja from 1674–80 CE
1680–89 CE	Sambhaji I, Eldest son of Shivaji
1689–1700 CE	Raja Ram, Younger son of Shivaji
1700–08 CE	Tara Bai, Wife of Raja Ram
1708–49 CE	Sahu, Son of Sambhaji I
1749–77 CE	Ramaraja, Grandson of Raja Ram and Tara Bai; adopted son of Sahu I
1777–1808 CE	Sahu II, Son of Ramaraja
1808–39 CE	Pratapsinh
1839–48 CE	Shahji III
	Pratapsinh I
	Rajaram III
	Pratapsinh II
1918–50 CE	Raja Sahu
1950–78 CE	Pratapraje
1978 CE till present	Udayanraje Bhonsle

Maharajas of Thanjavur

1674–86 CE	Venkaji
1686–1711 CE	Shahji
1711–27 CE	Sarabhoji I
1727–35 CE	Tukoji
1735–36 CE	Bava Sahib
1736–38 CE	Maharani Sujana Bai
1738 CE	Sawai Shahji
1738–39 CE	Sayaji
1739–63 CE	Pratap Singh
1763–87 CE	Tusalji
1787–98 CE	Amar Singh
1798–1824 CE	Sarabhoji II
1824–55 CE	Shivaji

Maharajas of Kolhapur

1700–12 CE	Shivaji I
1712–60 CE	Shambhoji
1760–1812 CE	Shivaji II adopted from the family of Khanwilkar
1812–21CE	Shambhu
1821–37 CE	Shahoji I
1837–66 CE	Shivaji III
1866–70 CE	Raja Ram I adopted from the family of Patankar
1870–83 CE	Shivaji IV
1883–1922 CE	Sahu IV adopted from the family of Ghatge
1922–40 CE	Raja Ram II
1940–42 CE	British rule
1942–47 CE	Shivaji V
1947–49 CE	Shahoji II, Titular Maharaja from 1949–83 CE; adopted from the Pawars

Maharajas of Nagpur

1738–55 CE	Raghoji I
1755–72 CE	Janoji
1772–88 CE	Mudhoji I
1788–1816 CE	Raghoji II
1816–18 CE	Mudhoji II
1818–53 CE	Raghoji III

four branches of the Bhonsles at Satara, Thanjavur, Nagpur and Kolhapur continued as rulers of their princely states, acknowledging the British while retaining local autonomy. All the four branches came under direct British rule by the mid-nineteenth century, when their rulers died without male heirs. Kolhapur, however, continued as a princely state until India's independence in 1947 CE, when the rulers acceded to the Indian union.

Gaekwads of Baroda

The Gaekwads were another Maratha royal family that ruled as maharajas of Baroda (Vadodara) from the mid-eighteenth century to 1947 CE. The ruling prince was known as the Maharaja Gaekwad of Baroda, or more popularly as the Gaekwad.

The rule of the Gaekwads began at Baroda when the Maratha general, Pillaji Gaekwad, conquered the city from the Mughal emperor in 1721 CE. The Gaekwads received the city as a fief from the *peshwa*. After the Third Battle of Panipat, the Gaekwads—along with several other powerful Maratha clans—established themselves as virtually independent rulers at the respective regions where they were based. They retained power by recognizing the nominal authority of the *peshwas* and the Bhonsle maharaja of Satara.

The Gaekwads, together with the other Maratha maharajas, fought the British in the First Anglo-Maratha War. In 1802 CE, the British cleverly intervened to defend a Gaekwad maharaja who had recently inherited the throne from rival claimants. Feeling obliged, the Gaekwads concluded a treaty with the British according to which they were recognized by the latter to be independent of the Maratha *peshwa*. And in return for recognizing British sovereignty the maharajas of Baroda could retain their local autonomy.

Maharaja Sayajirao III, who occupied the throne in 1875 CE, contributed immensely towards the modernization of Baroda, establishing compulsory primary education, a library system, a university, and model textile and tile factories. The status that Baroda has acquired today in terms of being a textile producing town surely goes back to the days of Sayajirao III. When India achieved it's independence in 1947 CE, the last ruling maharaja of Baroda acceded to the Indian union. Baroda was added to the Bombay state, the dominions of which were then divided into the present states of Gujarat and Maharashtra in 1960 CE.

Holkars of Indore

The leading Maratha chiefs based at Indore were commonly known as the Holkars after the founder of the dynasty—Malhar Rao Holkar. Originally a sheep farmer, Malhar Rao helped the *peshwa* Baji Rao I in his battles and in gratitude, the *peshwa* granted him a small contingent along with the estate of Indore in 1728 CE.

Malhar Rao Holkar took part in many battles, but during the Third Battle of Panipat, he

CHRONOLOGY

Maharajas of Baroda

1721–32 CE	Pillaji Rao	1818–47 CE	Sayaji Rao II
1732–68 CE	Damaji Rao	1847–56 CE	Ganpat Rao
1768–71 CE	Govind Rao	1856–70 CE	Khande Rao
1771–89 CE	Sayaji Rao I	1870–75 CE	Malhar Rao
1789–93 CE	Manaji Rao	1875–1939 CE	Sayaji Rao III
1793–1800 CE	Govind Rao (restored)	1939–48 CE	Pratap Singh
1800–18 CE	Anand Rao		

CHRONOLOGY

Maharajas of Indore

1728–64 CE	Maharaja Malhar Rao Holkar	1834–43 CE	Maharaja Hari Rao
1764–66 CE	Maharaja Malle Rao	1843–44 CE	Maharaja Khande Rao
1765–95 CE	Rajmata Ahalya Bai	1844–86 CE	Maharaja Tukoji Rao II
1795–98 CE	Maharaja Tukoji Holkar	1886–1903 CE	Maharaja Shivaji Rao
1798–1811 CE	Maharaja Jaswant Rao Holkar	1903–26 CE	Maharaja Sir Tukoji Rao III Holkar
1811–34 CE	Maharaja Malhar Rao II	1926–61 CE	Maharaja Sir Yeshwant Rao II Holkar
1834 CE	Maharaja Martand Rao		

was wounded whilst fighting against Ahmad Shah Abdali's forces and subsequently died from his injuries. He was succeeded by his son's widow, Ahalya Bai, who ruled the state with great skill and wisdom. Indore managed to maintain peace in such violent times because of Ahalya Bai's wise and just rule. Tukoji Holkar, a distant relative whom she had appointed as commander of her forces, succeeded her two years later; and on his death in 1797 CE his illegitimate son, Jaswant Rao, seized power. Jaswant Rao Holkar ranks second only to the great Malhar Rao in his achievements as a Maratha leader. He fought and defeated the British in several battles, but traitors within his own forces conspired against him, leading to his downfall. Jaswant Rao Holkar took refuge in the Punjab from where he drew up a pact with the British for his personal protection which enabled him to return to the family estate in Indore.

Scindias of Gwalior

Ranuji Scindia was one of the commanders of the *peshwa* Baji Rao I. He was responsible for establishing the Scindia rule at Gwalior, where an estate was given to him and his family surrounding the town. They were also in command of the great Gwalior fort. After Ranuji Scindia died, many of his sons continued to be the maharajas; but unfortunately in the Third Battle of Panipat only one of his sons survived—Mahadaji Scindia. He was rescued from the battlefield of Panipat by a Pathan water carrier named Rane Khan. Even though Mahadaji was badly injured, with the help of Rane Khan his life was saved. Mahadaji Scindia thereafter treated Rane Khan as his brother.

Mahadaji reorganized his forces along European lines by employing a large number of European mercenaries in the 1780s. He is known to have used effective and innovative military methods that went beyond the usual Maratha dependence on light cavalry. Mahadaji displayed a strong patriotic stance at that time. He had even helped the Mughal Emperor, Shah Alam II, ascend the throne of Delhi, for which he was made the *naib wakil-i mutlaq* (deputy regent) of Mughal affairs. The Mughals also gave him the title of *amir al-umara* (head of the *amirs*). Interestingly, it is rare to find Indian maharajas in the eighteenth century who had thrown off all pretence of allegiance to the Mughals. In fact, the Mughal system of honours and titles, as well as their administrative terminology and fiscal practices continued to remain in use despite the deterioration of their imperial power.

Mahadaji Scindia died in 1794 CE at Poona, and his adopted son, Daulat Rao Scindia, succeeded him. Daulat Rao Scindia was an inexperienced leader, unable to continue along the same dynamic lines of his predecessor. He was defeated by the British when the French general Perron resorted to treachery. The British promptly tried to capture the holdings of the Scindias; and thereafter the family continued to remain only as a princely state.

CHRONOLOGY

Maharajas of Gwalior

1726–45 CE	Ranuji Scindia	1827–43 CE	Maharaja Jankoji Rao Scindia
1745–55 CE	Jayappa Scindia	1843–86 CE	Maharaja Jayavi Rao
1755–61 CE	Jankoji I Scindia	1886–1925 CE	Maharaja Sir Madhav Rao Scindia
1761–94 CE	Mahadaji Scindia	1925–61 CE	Maharaja Sir George Jiwaji Rao Scindia Alijah Bahadur
1794–1827 CE	Maharaja Daulat Rao Scindia		

Invasions of Nadir Shah and Ahmad Shah Abdali

The incursions of the conquerors, Nadir Shah and Ahmad Shah Abdali, in the eighteenth century, shook the foundations of the Mughal Empire. Nadir Shah, a Persian adventurer invaded Qandahar in 1738 CE, the last outpost of the Ghilzai Afghans, before turning to Mughal India, which was already falling apart. Taking Peshawar, Nadir Shah crossed the Indus at Attock and marched into the Punjab. When Zakaria Khan, the governor of the Punjab, was defeated near Lahore, the Mughal emperor, Muhammad Shah, awoke to the danger to which his empire had been exposed. Nadir Shah met the imperial army at Karnal in February 1739 CE, where the battle lasted barely three hours. Nearly 8,000 Indians lost their lives in this battle. Negotiations between the Mughal emperor and Nadir Shah ended with the payment of several million rupees to the invader. Nadir Shah entered Delhi in March 1739 CE, and ordered a mass massacre that resulted in the killing of not less than 30,000 innocents. Delhi was ransacked in a short period of time and imperial treasures—including pearls, diamonds, precious jewels, the famous Peacock throne and the Kohinoor diamond—were carried away to Afghanistan. When Nadir Shah left Delhi on 16 May 1739 CE the spoils of his terrible raid amounted to 30 crore rupees in cash, besides jewels, gold, silver and other valuables. He also deprived the empire of the province of Kabul, which he annexed to Persia. The magnitude of the plunder is indicated by the fact that when Nadir Shah reached his kingdom, he ordered a remission of taxes throughout Persia for a period of three years!

Nadir Shah's invasion was a severe jolt to Emperor Muhammad Shah and his courtiers, for it disgraced the power and prestige of the country. The emperor, however, failed to learn any lessons from it; and the invasion only hastened the decline and fall of the already decadent Mughal Empire.

The next invader who came to attack the land in quick succession was Ahmad Shah Abdali, the founder of the Durrani empire in Afghanistan. He commanded a cavalry of Abdali tribesmen under Nadir Shah, who considered Abdali to be his successor. When Nadir Shah was assassinated in 1747 CE, Ahmad Shah assumed kingship and invaded India for the first time, seizing Lahore in 1748 CE. This time the Mughal army under Prince Ahmad Shah defeated him near Sirhind; however, he invaded India for the second time and defeated the governor of the Punjab. In his third invasion in 1752 CE he conquered Kashmir and the Mughal emperor was forced to cede territories as far as Sirhind. During 1756–57 CE, Abdali invaded India for the fourth time, entering Lahore and marching straight towards Delhi. Although the Mughal nobility surrendered to him, he carried on looting on an enormous scale and took away spoils valued as high as twelve crore.

The helpless Mughal emperor, Alamgir II, was forced to formally cede the provinces of the

Punjab, Kashmir and Sind. Abdali left his eldest son, Timur Shah, at Lahore as his viceroy, but the Marathas under Raghunath Rao expelled him from Lahore within a year, causing an inevitable war between the Marathas and Ahmad Shah Abdali. Abdali began his fifth campaign in 1759 CE and reconquered the Punjab. The Marathas, however, were not prepared to give up the Punjab, and a war broke out between the Afghans and the Marathas in 1761 CE at Panipat—which came to be known in history as the Third Battle of Panipat. The Marathas fought under the *peshwa* Balaji Baji Rao's cousin, Sadashiv Rao Bhau, and his own son, Vishwas Rao. Although the Maratha army was initially successful, as the battle progressed they were completely routed. Both Sadashiv Rao Bhau and Vishwas Rao fell fighting, and the news of the disastrous defeat sounded a death knell for the *peshwa*.

In 1762 CE, Ahmad Shah Abdali retired from India, imposing upon the Mughal emperor an annual tribute of forty lakh rupees. Abdali did not gain anything politically out of the battle, besides gathering enormous booty. He retreated immediately to Afghanistan—leaving Najib-ud-Daulah as his representative in Delhi—and began negotiations with the Marathas in the Punjab. In 1763 CE peace was concluded with *peshwa* Madhava Rao I, who recognized the Punjab as Afghan territory.

Ahmad Shah Abdali failed to realize his ambition of bringing northern India under his control, but his invasions had several immediate effects. His repeated invasions served as a warning to the powers in India of the vulnerability of the northwest frontier, but nothing was done to protect it. His raids completely plundered the Mughal Empire robbing it of its immense wealth and ultimately leading to its decline. It also resulted in the defeat of the Marathas and consolidation of British rule in India.

The defeat of the Marathas at Panipat was disastrous, but it did not eliminate the Marathas completely from Indian politics. The Third Battle of Panipat also significantly influenced the future course of history in the Indian subcontinent.

Decline of the Marathas

The Marathas remained a formidable power in India for almost a hundred and fifty years. The main reason for the failure of the Marathas was the lack of allies when they had to counter the growing power of the British. Abandoning the guerrilla techniques in warfare and basing the Maratha infantry along a European-style contingent, they failed to gain any allies in northern India. In the three Anglo-Maratha wars the Marathas suffered severe setbacks at the hands of the British. The descendant of Shivaji remained a pensioner of the British at Satara, the office of the *peshwa* was abolished, and all the Maratha chiefs were reduced to being dependent allies of the British. There was no unity or effective leadership in the Maratha state by the end of the eighteenth century—most of the able chiefs had died by then. In contrast, the British had remarkable leaders like Lord Wellesley, Lord Hastings, Arthur Wellesley, General Lake, and civil officers like Elphinstone and Marcome. This was one of the factors that contributed to the failure of the Marathas against the British, who were leagues ahead of them in the game of diplomacy. The disunity among the Maratha chiefs to a great extent simplified the task of the British in their expansionist plans.

The Marathas did not care to increase the economic resources of the state as they were always dependent on a system of organized plunder. This factor, to some extent, alienated the people from the Marathas. Their political ambitions, which led them to loot and plunder, had antagonized all other powers too. They had also interfered in the internal affairs of the Rajputana and levied heavy taxes and fines on them, besides having made huge territorial and monetary claims upon Awadh and Punjab. Except for the weak support of Imad-ul-Mulk of Berar, they hardly garnered support in their time of need, and had to fight their enemies single-handedly. Moreover, the incumbent Maratha chiefs had constant disputes among themselves. Each one of them had ambitions of carving out their independent states and had no interest in fighting against a common enemy. The lack of a progressive outlook among the Maratha leadership furthered their fall.

Among the different states that had emerged during the seventeenth–eighteenth centuries, the most important had been the Maratha state. It had developed as a formidable power when the Mughal Empire was on its decline. The Marathas were brave soldiers, and by their efforts they could create a strong state that expanded throughout the length and breadth of India. Thus, their emergence, as also their end, is a subject of absorbing interest as an edifice—reared by the genius of Shivaji and laboriously fostered by the early *peshwas*—that should have crumbled in a little more than a century.

SUMMARY

- Shivaji was able to build a strong Maratha state even in his short-lived rule; but it was now the turn of his successors to strengthen and consolidate it.
- Succeeding Shivaji, his eldest son, Sambhaji, turned out to be a man of weak character and ignored the administration of the state.
- Raja Ram succeeded his brother Sambhaji. After the death of Raja Ram, his widow, Tara Bai, became regent for her minor son, Shivaji II. Taking a keen interest in political affairs, she administered the state wisely.
- Soon after the death of Aurangzeb, Sambhaji's son, Sahu, was released by the Mughals. He first claimed the Maratha kingdom from Tara Bai, resulting in a civil war between the two Marathas groups.
- Sahu managed to defeat Tara Bai with the help of an ambitious Maratha chief, Balaji Vishwanath, and became the ruler of the Marathas from Satara.
- Sahu made Balaji Vishwanath his *peshwa*, who proved to be a capable administrator and reorganized the Maratha state efficiently.
- Sahu had practically entrusted the entire state administration to his *peshwa*, reducing himself to the position of a titular head.
- The capital was transferred from Satara to Poona, but Sahu continued to live in Satara. Poona now became the seat of the Maratha government.
- Balaji Vishwanath was succeeded by his son, Baji Rao I, as the *peshwa*. Like his father before him, he was both a soldier and a statesman. To realize his ambition, Baji Rao I expanded his control over different regions.
- The greatest achievement of Baji Rao I was the arrangement he made in order to put an end to the jealousy of different Maratha chiefs. He partitioned the former Mughal provinces under the Maratha military generals as their 'spheres of influence'.
- The leading Maratha chiefs of the time were Raghoji Bhonsle of Nagpur, Pillaji Gaekwad of Baroda, Malhar Rao Holkar of Indore and Ramaji Scindia of Gwalior.
- After Baji Rao I's death, his son, Balaji Baji Rao, became the next *peshwa*. Under him the Maratha power reached the zenith of its glory.
- At the death of Sahu, Balaji Baji Rao had obtained from him a written order which authorized him and his successors to manage the government of the Maratha Empire independently. With this permission, the *peshwas* became the real rulers of the Maratha kingdom.
- The intrusions of the conquerors, Nadir Shah and Ahmad Shah Abdali, in the eighteenth century, shook the foundations of the Mughal Empire.
- Nadir Shah, a Persian adventurer, invaded Mughal India, which was already falling apart. When he ransacked Delhi, vast imperial treasures—including pearls, diamonds, jewels and the famous Peacock throne and the Kohinoor diamond—were carried away to Afghanistan.
- When Nadir Shah was assassinated, Ahmad Shah Abdali assumed kingship and invaded India a number of times.
- A direct confrontation between the Afghans and the Marathas took place in 1761 CE at Panipat, which came to be known as the Third Battle of Panipat. The Marathas fought valiantly in the beginning, but as the battle progressed they were completely routed.

- The Marathas failed for lack of allies; and the advent of the British who they had to encounter. They did not increase the economic resources of the state as they were always dependent on a system of organized plunder. The Maratha chiefs had ambitions of carving out their independent states and had no interest in fighting against a common enemy. The lack of a progressive outlook among the Maratha leadership furthered their fall.

KEYWORDS

Maratha confederacy
Diplomacy
Chauth
Sardeshmukhi
Naib wakil-i mutlaq
Amir al-umara

REVIEW QUESTIONS

1. Elaborate upon the achievements of Balaji Vishwanath in expanding Maratha power.
2. Write a short note on the Holkars of Indore.
3. Give an account of Nadir Shah's invasion and the consequences it had on India.
4. Explain the consequences of the Third Battle of Panipat.
5. What were the causes of the decline of the Maratha state?

CHAPTER **28**

Emerging Regional States

Review and Discussion

- Punjab
- The Jats
- The Rajputs
- Awadh
- Bengal, Bihar and Orissa
- Rohilkhand
- Hyderabad
- Karnataka
- Mysore
- Thiruvitamkur

Reconstructing the history of the emerging regional states in seventeenth–eighteenth century India is necessary to understand the processes involved in state formation. The states that arose in different regions in India from 1700–1850 CE were different from each other in terms of nature, existence and wealth. Along with events such as the disintegration and fall of the Mughal Empire and the establishment of the British Raj, the rise and fall of the regional states determined the historical image of the Indian subcontinent during its transition from the medieval to the modern. Some of the states that emerged—Awadh (Ayodhya) in the north or Hyderabad in the south—were located in areas that had already undergone regional state formation in the immediate pre-Mughal period; and as such it was easy for them to revive an older tradition of state formation. On the other hand, there were other regional states that had a more original character, having been created from specific processes that had taken place in the late sixteenth and seventeenth centuries. Many states that came up in post-Mughal India were based on ethnicity of people like the Marathas, the Jats, and the Sikhs. Whatever the processes involved in the formation of such states, it is important to note that most of the regional states that were formed brought about a transformation in Indian polity. Marathwada and Bengal emerged as major centres of national awakening and liberation struggle at a later date, while the Deccan as a whole was a serious contender to the Mughals in initiating new systems that survived through centuries.

PUNJAB

The Punjab grew at the hands of the Sikhs who were a religious group, initially formed as a sect within the larger Hindu community in the fifteenth century. The founder, Guru Nanak (1469–1539 CE), belonged to the *Khatri* community of scribes and traders and lived during the days of Babur's reign in India. Working as a scribe for an important noble of the Lodi dynasty, Nanak became a wandering preacher before settling down at Kartarpur in the Punjab. When Nanak died, he left behind a huge number of followers in his area of operation. He was succeeded by a lineage of gurus, the first among whom was Guru Angad, who had been chosen by Nanak himself. Incidentally, all the Sikh Gurus belonged to various subcastes of the *Khatri* community.

Guru Nanak's teachings, collected in the *Adi Granth,* the Holy Scripture of the Sikhs, represents components from the *Bhakti* movement within Hinduism and the Sufi branch of Islam, to which many independent beliefs and practices were also added. Although the *Adi Granth* did not have a political agenda, it is noticed that religious movements of the period generally assumed political overtones by creating bonds of solidarity among their believers, who felt that they could then legitimately challenge the authority of the state.

It was in the early seventeenth century, when the fifth guru, Guru Arjun, was tortured and killed by Jahangir in 1606 CE because of his sympathies for the rebel prince Khusrau that the first signs of a major conflict between the Mughal authorities and the Sikhs appeared. The hitherto peace-loving sect now took up arms to fight the Mughals. Guru Arjun's successor, Hargobind, began to militarize the community so that they would be able to resist any oppression. He was a man of warlike disposition and adventurous spirit, who had gathered a small army around him. He took upon himself the dual role of a military leader as well as a spiritual guide, assuming the title of *Sacha Badshah* or the true ruler of men. The Guru also fortified Amritsar and constructed the new fort of Lohgarh. The Mughal emperor, Jahangir, was irked by the conversion of the Sikhs into a militant force and arrested him. He had to undergo 12 years of imprisonment at the Gwalior fort before he was set free towards the end of Jahangir's reign. The next Mughal emperor, Shahjahan, then began his reactionary policy against the Guru; and Hargobind had to fight many battles against the Mughals to preserve the Sikh faith. His period of leadership was in fact a long struggle against the Mughals.

CHRONOLOGY

Ten Sikh Gurus

First Guru	Guru Nanak
Second Guru	Guru Angad
Third Guru	Guru Amar Das
Fourth Guru	Guru Ram Das
Fifth Guru	Guru Arjun Dev
Sixth Guru	Guru Har Gobind
Seventh Guru	Guru Har Rai
Eighth Guru	Guru Har Krishan
Ninth Guru	Guru Tegh Bahadur
Tenth Guru	Guru Gobind Singh

He died in 1645 CE; and was succeeded by his grandson, Har Rai, who was followed by Guru Har Kishan and then by Guru Tegh Bahadur.

Under Guru Tegh Bahadur, conflicts with the Mughals once again increased—partly as a result of his success as a preacher and partly because of the orthodox line of Sunni Islam adopted by Aurangzeb. In 1675 CE, Tegh Bahadur was captured and killed by Aurangzeb when he refused to accept Islam, paving the path for increased militancy under the last of the gurus, Gobind Singh (1675–1708 CE).

It was the success of the Sikh Gurus in attracting followers and acquiring military power that prompted an antagonistic response from the Mughals. Guru Gobind Singh clashed against the Mughal forces on more than one occasion, and founded a new centre at Anandpur (1689 CE), where he began to impart military training. The creation of the *khalsa* in 1699 CE was a great achievement of Guru Gobind Singh. This was especially created with the intention of defending the faith of Sikhism. Having become well prepared, Gobind Singh staged a religious war against the Mughals, but had to face heavy odds as the Mughal forces outnumbered the Sikhs. He did not however lose courage; and in the ensuing battle of Anandpur (1704 CE) the Guru parted with his sons, Zorawar Singh and Fateh Singh, who were bricked up alive in a wall near Sirhind. In the battle of Chamkaur, two of his other sons, Ajit Singh and Jujhar Singh, were also killed. Meanwhile Aurangzeb died in 1707 CE; and his successor, Bahadur Shah, established peace and amity with the Guru.

Guru Gobind Singh was not only a military genius but also a great scholar of Persian, Hindi and *Gurmukhi*. He wrote the famous *Zafar Namah*, containing his letters to Aurangzeb in Persian, where he strongly condemned the emperor's policy of religious persecution and justified the war against Mughal oppression. He encouraged men of letters and gathered around him many scholars, who helped him in giving the final shape to the *Adi Granth*, which was renamed as the *Granth Sahib*. As he had lost all his four sons, he asked his followers to recognize the *Granth Sahib* as their spiritual guide or Guru.

In the absence of the gurus, however, military leaders emerged from the Sikh community to provide guidance to the people. Ironically, with Gobind Singh's death, the Sikh threat to Mughal domination increased. The first military leader of the Sikhs to follow the gurus was Banda Singh Bahadur, a Maratha, who had come under Guru Gobind Singh's influence during the latter's last days at Nanded in Maharashtra. Between 1709 CE and late 1710 CE, the Sikhs led by Banda Bahadur won many victories at Sirhind, Hissar and Saharanpur—all of which were situated in close proximity to Delhi. Spurred by these victories, Banda Bahadur made Mukhlispur his capital, issued coins in the names of the gurus, and began to use a royal seal on his orders like the Mughals. In an encounter with the Mughals in late 1710 CE and 1711 CE, Banda Bahadur and his forces were defeated and expelled from Sirhind. He then shifted his operations to the surrounding areas of Lahore; but being unsuccessful there too, he moved along with his forces to the fort of Gurdas Nangal. The Mughals laid siege to the fort which led ultimately to the Sikhs' surrender and Banda Bahadur's execution in 1716 CE at Delhi.

There were two major factors that edified Banda Bahadur's role in history. Firstly, under his leadership a full-scale Sikh rebellion against Mughal authority broke out for the first time which was very different from the sporadic militant activity seen under Hargobind and later under Gobind Singh. Secondly, Banda Bahadur's fearless attitude is evident in his letters, which speak in strong terms about the orthodoxy in Islam which was to be countered by the Sikhs. The Sikhs by this time were no longer acting as mere mediators between popular Hinduism and Islam; they had formed into a separate religious sect with a following of their own. The close ties that were seen to have emerged at this time between the Marathas and Sikhs would again resurface in later coalitions that would counter Ahmad Shah Abdali's attacks on the Punjab.

When Ahmad Shah Abdali raided northern India on numerous occasions in the 1750s and 60s, the principal opposition he had to face was from the Sikhs, other than the Mughal and Maratha forces. The Sikhs lost a great number of lives in these encounters. By the mid-1760s, Sikh authority over Lahore had been established, while the Afghans had been unable to consolidate their early gains. Under Ahmad Shah Abdali's successor, Timur Shah (1772–93 CE), some more territories were regained by the Sikhs—such as Multan—despite the efforts of the descendants of the Afghan invader. By the 1770s, there was a confederation of about 60 Sikh chieftains, some of whom had founded what were to remain princely states under the British—such as Nabha and Patiala. Though the confederate structure did not imply a unity between these chiefdoms, they at least came together to face their major adversary, Ahmad Shah Abdali.

Taking advantage of the confusion prevailing in the country after the downfall of the Mughal Empire, the Sikhs carved out several small independent districts of their own in the Punjab. These states were called *Misls* and were 12 in number. The ruler of one of these *misls*, Maharaja Ranjit

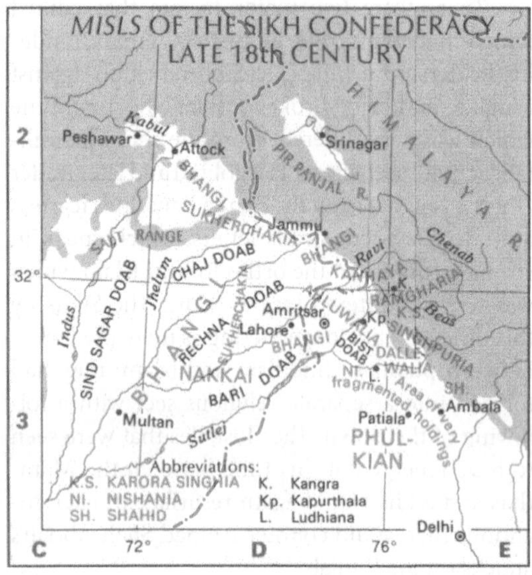

Map 28-1 *Misls of the Sikh Confederacy, Late 18th Century*

Singh (1799–1839 CE) united these states under a single banner to form a powerful Sikh kingdom in the Punjab during the first half of the nineteenth century. Known as *maharaja,* Ranjit Singh's rise to power was based on superior military force, partly serviced by European mercenaries and partly by the strategic location of the territories he had inherited. His significance comes to light when within 10 years of his death, the British managed to annex the Punjab. In the *misls*, Mughal administrative practices, the granting of *jagirs* to subordinates and the adherence to Persian culture in court practices, were continued.

Unlike the Sikh Gurus who came from *Khatri* stock, the bulk of the Sikh chieftains were of Jat origin, a caste primarily involved in agricultural operations. Thus, it can be said that besides setting up states in other regions, such as Bharatpur, the Jats also dominated state building in the Punjab.

Ranjit Singh's kingdom, on the one hand, was a culmination of nearly a century of Sikh rebellions against Mughal rule; while on the other, it adopted the newer strategies that had been learnt from the Afghans on statecraft through encounters with them. This is indicated by the fact that he made Lahore his capital, a well-established trading city captured by him in 1799 CE following the attacks by Shah Zaman, the successor of Timur Shah. Having gained control of important trade routes, he imposed monopolies on salt, grain and textiles from Kashmir to enhance his revenues, which he utilized to build up an army of 40,000 cavalry and infantry. By 1809 CE he made himself the undisputed master of most of the Punjab.

The British, however, checked Ranjit Singh's expansion to the east of the Sutlej by entering into the Treaty of Amritsar in 1809 CE, which recognized Ranjit Singh as an independent ruler of the Punjab by fixing the Sutlej as the boundary between the two powers. The *maharaja* adhered to the terms of this treaty till his death and remained friendly with the British, who in turn also remained faithful to the *maharaja* and did not disturb the Sikh kingdom during his lifetime.

After Ranjit Singh's death in 1839 CE, the Sikh state crumbled, damaged by vicious internal battles for leadership. His weak successors were unable to sustain the vast kingdom, leading to dissention among the Sikh chiefs—many of whom thought that if the powerful Sikh army was destroyed by the British, they would find it easier to establish their power in the kingdom—hence provoking the Sikh army to cross the Sutlej and attack the British forces. This was exactly what the British wanted. They were anxious to take possession of the Punjab, but did not want to take the initiative. When the Sikh army invaded British territory in 1845 CE, a war started between the Sikhs and the British forces.

The British defeated the Sikhs and laid down the terms for peace in the Treaty of Lahore in 1846 CE. According to the treaty, the British annexed the Sikh territory of the Doab between Sutlej and Beas, placing a British resident and an army in the Punjab. In 1849 CE, the Sikhs rose again against the British army positioned in the Punjab. There was another war in which the Sikhs fought bravely, but were defeated. At the end of this war, Lord Dalhousie, who was then the Governor General of India, annexed the Punjab to the British dominions.

The Sikh state was structured along the same lines as that of the Mughal state. *Jagirs* were given in lieu of salary for military service, and, in the lands which were directly taxed, official agents were appointed at the district level. Despite these administrative mechanisms, the state formed by Ranjit Singh was fragile as it was based on a system of alliances, and collapsed within a few years of his death. A dispute over regency is sometimes cited as a reason of the decline, but it appears that the state created by Ranjit Singh never really made the transition from a conquering power to a stable system of alliances formed between conflicting groups with regional interests.

The Jats

The Jats were an agricultural community settled around the regions of Delhi, Mathura and Agra. They revolted against the oppressive policies of Aurangzeb and though the Mughals were able to contain the revolt, the area remained disturbed. Under their leader, Churaman, (1660–1721 CE) the Jats rose in rebellion against the Mughals in the region. Headed by Jai Singh II, the governor of Agra, the Mughal army marched against Churaman and his forces in 1721 CE, and captured the strong fort built by him. Not able to bear the defeat, Churaman committed suicide. Thereafter, Badan Singh (1685–1756 CE), Churaman's nephew, assumed the Jat leadership. He reinforced his army and built four forts at Dig, Kumber, Ver and Bharatpur. The Mughals at this time had suffered a setback from Nadir Shah's invasion. This provided Badan Singh with an opportunity to establish his sway over the districts of Mathura and Agra, laying the foundations of the Bharatpur kingdom. Ahmad Shah Abdali was forced to accept Badan Singh as the ruler and conferred on him the epithet of 'Mahendra'. Another Jat ruler came up by the name of Suraj Mal (1707–63 CE), is credited to have further extended the boundaries of the Bharatpur kingdom by adding the adjoining the districts of Agra, Dholpur, Aligarh, Etawah, Meerut, Rohtak, Farrukhnagar, Mewat, Rewari, Gurgaon and Mathura in 1756 CE. After Suraj Mal's death in 1763 CE, there was no one to lead the Jats who then gradually withered away.

The Rajputs

The Rajputs, who had always been closely associated with the Mughals from the time of Akbar, began to feel estranged from the time of Aurangzeb and his reckless policies. They got the right opportunity in the eighteenth century to once again assert their independence and increase their influence. From the mid-sixteenth century, the Rajputs of Amber (Jaipur) and Marwar (Jodhpur) had played a significant role in Mughal politics. They had won for themselves many privileges by virtue of Akbar's favourable policies towards them, but had also alienated themselves during Aurangzeb's reign when the odds had been against them.

The Kachwahas, an important Rajput clan who controlled the Rajput principality of Amber, had remained subordinate to the Mughals from the sixteenth century, and had consequently managed to gradually consolidate their hold over the region during the seventeenth century. Members of the Rajput clan, such as Raja Man Singh, had occupied senior positions at the Mughal court. They were permitted to maintain their power over their principalities as well as a contingent for the defence of their territory.

In the early eighteenth century, the ruler Jai Singh Sawai further augmented his power by not only getting a *jagir* assigned to him by the Mughals which was in the district of his home territories, but also gained for himself the right to collect the revenues from this land. This practice gradually acquired permanence leading to the wielding of complete revenue control over the region which in turn made the Rajputs very powerful. At the time of his death in 1743 CE, Jai Singh had emerged as the single most important ruler in the region.

Relations had begun to strain between the Mughals and the Rajputs from the reign of Aurangzeb. It reached a fever pitch in emperor Bahadur Shah's reign when a campaign was led against Marwar and Ajit Singh was asked to submit in 1708 CE. In the same year, Ajit Singh formed an anti-Mughal group led by himself, Jai Singh II and Durgadas Rathor. In 1714 CE, Hussain Ali, the commander-in-chief of the Mughal forces, once again headed towards Marwar and forced Ajit Singh to agree to give one of his daughters in marriage to Emperor Farrukh Siyar.

This was a time when the Sayyid brothers were opposing Farrukh Siyar at Delhi. The Rajput chieftains of Amber and Marwar chose not to take sides to suit their interests. But the Sayyid brothers tried to win over Ajit Singh by awarding him the governorship of Ajmer and Gujarat, a position which he held till 1721 CE. Seeing this, the Mughal emperor's group appointed Jai Singh II of Amber as the governor of Agra in 1721 CE, bestowing upon him the province of Surat during the time of Emperor Muhammad Shah. Thus, the Rajputs at one point controlled the territory extending from Delhi to Surat on the western coast. However, there were so many internal conflicts within the Rajput states that they could not consolidate their position and became easy prey to Maratha intrusions.

AWADH

Awadh was one of the *subas* or provinces of the Mughal Empire, which functioned under the supervision of a *nawab* until 1819 CE. Modern Ayodhya, Banaras, Allahabad and Kanpur, along with other districts, were included in its jurisdiction. Saadat Khan, who was appointed as the *nawab* of Awadh in 1722 CE, made Faizabad near Lucknow his capital. Seeing the weakening Mughal Empire in Delhi, he declared himself independent and founded a separate kingdom at Awadh.

The wealthy kingdom of Awadh was able to maintain its independence against threats from the Marathas, the British and the Afghans. Since Saadat Khan had no successor, his nephew, Safdar Jung, who was also his son-in-law, succeeded him as the next governor. Safdar Jung was recognized as the new *nawab* by the Mughal emperor, Muhammad Shah, through a *farman* confirming his position. Safdar Jung died in 1754 CE, and was succeeded by his son, Shuja-ud-daula. The latter antagonized the British after extending help to Mir Qasim, the *nawab* of Bengal, who had turned against the British. The combined forces of Shuja-ud-Daula and Mir Qasim were defeated by the British in the Battle of Buxar in 1764 CE, after which Shuja-ud-Daula was forced to pay heavy penalties and cede parts of his territory. The British appointed a resident at Awadh in 1773 CE, and over a period of time gained control of much more territory and authority in the state. The British were not keen to openly take over Awadh as that would bring them in direct confrontation with the Marathas and the weak rulers of the Mughal Empire.

In 1798 CE, the fifth Nawab of Awadh, Wazir Ali Shah, was forced by the British to abdicate on grounds of unpopularity. The British then helped Saadat Ali Khan, a puppet king, occupy the throne. In the treaty of 1801 CE, Saadat Ali Khan ceded half of Awadh to the English East India Company, while also agreeing to disband his troops in favour of an expensive, British-run army. By the terms of this treaty Awadh became a vassal of the English East India Company, although it continued as part of the Mughal Empire only nominally till 1819 CE.

The treaty of 1801 CE benefited the English East India Company to a great extent. It authorized them to use the vast treasuries of Awadh for financing their wars with other regional powers. In addition, maintaining an army for Awadh brought them useful revenues too. The *nawabs* were more of ceremonial rulers, addicted to an elitist lifestyle of pomp and show, with hardly a say in the matters of the state. Indirect control of the British on Awadh went on till the mid-nineteenth century; however, the British became impatient with the arrangement and soon wanted direct control. To this end, they began hunting for an excuse, which the decadent *nawabs* readily provided.

In 1856 CE, the English East India Company marched onto Awadh's borders with its troops and annexed the state. Awadh was placed under a chief commissioner—Sir Henry Lawrence. Wajid Ali Shah (1822–87 CE), the tenth and last *nawab* of the kingdom of Awadh, was imprisoned and sent into exile by the British to Calcutta. Later during the Revolt in 1857 CE, the rebel Indian forces put forward his 14-year-old son, Birjis Qadr, to be crowned as ruler of Awadh, while Sir Henry Lawrence was killed in the conflict.

Bengal, Bihar and Orissa

The independent state of Bengal was founded by Murshid Quli Khan. Since Aurangzeb's reign, Murshid Quli Khan was the *diwan* and the Deputy Governor of Bengal. In 1713 CE, he was appointed Governor of Bengal and in 1719 CE, Orissa was added to his charge. Murshid Quli Khan was a capable administrator who brought about reorganization of the revenue administration, resulting in flourishing trade and commerce in the region. After Murshid Quli's death in 1727 CE, his son-in-law, Shujauddin, succeeded him. Shujauddin was given additional charge of the governorship of Bihar in 1733 CE by the Mughal emperor, Muhammad Shah, making the province of Bengal one of the largest in India. It covered the present state of West Bengal (including modern Bangladesh), Bihar, Jharkhand, Orissa and Chattisgarh. After Shujauddin's death in 1739 CE, his son, Sarfaraz Khan, succeeded him. In 1740 CE, however, Alivardi Khan, the Deputy Governor of Bihar, rebelled against his master and killed Sarfaraz Khan at Gheria, and seized power. By sending a gift of two crore rupees to the Mughal emperor at Delhi, Alivardi Khan had taken his approval for the usurpation. In 1746 CE, when the Mughal emperor wanted more money from Alivardi Khan, the latter did not oblige the emperor. As a result, the province of Bengal, Bihar and Orissa were taken back by the Mughal emperor. Alivardi Khan was not dependent upon the Mughal emperor for defending his province against the frequent raids of the Marathas. However, like the Nizam of Hyderabad and the *nawabs* of Awadh, Alivardi Khan was only trying to keep alive the aura of the Mughal emperor.

Alivardi Khan had held out long enough against the frequent Maratha incursions from Nagpur on Bengal, but had eventually grown tired of the invasions and a large part of his territory was devastated. In 1759 CE, he concluded a peace treaty with Raghoji Bhonsle of Nagpur, according to the terms of which Orissa was ceded to Raghoji and a tribute of twelve lakh a year was to be paid as *chauth.* The river Suvarnarekha was fixed as the boundary of Bengal. When Alivardi Khan died in 1756 CE he was succeeded by his grandson, Siraj-ud-daula, who was defeated by the British in the Battle of Plassey in 1757 CE—signalling the formal political entry of the British in India.

Rohilkhand

The Rohillas were the hill men, a tribe of Afghans, who migrated to India and settled in the Bareilly district to the east of Delhi. They were simple and hardworking like the Marathas and good at warfare. Their leader, Ali Muhammad, built for himself a small principality, which was recognized by the Mughal emperor, Muhammad Shah. Seizing the opportunity offered by Nadir Shah's invasion, Ali Muhammad expanded his territories, thus, including within his jurisdiction the neighbouring districts of Muradabad and Badaun. Muhammad Shah appointed Ali Muhammad as governor of all the territories under his control. After gaining control over these, Ali Muhammad made himself virtually independent. Seeing this, Muhammad Shah launched a campaign against Rohilkhand (formerly Katehr) in 1745 CE, which ended in failure; and the Rohilla state—not a state as such but more a confederacy of chiefs—continued to exist.

HYDERABAD

The independent state of Hyderabad was founded by Mir Qamaruddin Khan in the Deccan in 1724 CE. Mir Qamaruddin Khan was the viceroy of the Deccan from 1713–21 CE under the Mughals. He then held the post of the *wazir* at the imperial court at Delhi. When he became virtually independent in 1724 CE he took up the title of Asaf Jah I. He founded the Asaf Jahi dynasty in which rulers bore the title of Nizams. Despite the help received in administration from the trusted nobles and the ability of Asaf Jah I himself—who was not only a good administrator but also a seasoned diplomat—a violent power struggle ensued upon his death in 1748 CE, which became complicated due to the involvement of neighbouring and outside powers.

This was a time when wars were no longer confined to the native forces, as Britain and France had begun to fiercely compete with each other for trade and territory in India. They were ready to offer their services to any Indian kingdom that gave them the rewards they wished. In the process, numerous Hindu and Muslim *rajas* and sultans sought support from either the French or the English; and in exchange handed over territory and large reserves to them. The French and the English saw Nizam ul Mulk Asaf Jah I's death as an opportunity to make the Deccan susceptible to their intrigues and manipulations. After more than a decade of shifting military alliances and armed conflicts, Hyderabad gained internal stability during Mir Nizam Ali Khan Bahadur's reign, who was the second Nizam. Between 1765 CE and 1800 CE, he concluded several treaties with the British—the Treaty of Masulipatnam (1768 CE) and later the Subsidiary Alliance (1798 CE), which brought Hyderabad and its foreign affairs under the control of the British. Although the Subsidiary Alliance made the Nizam secure from his internal and external enemies, it was also instrumental in increasing British interference in the state's administration. Among the terms of the treaty was the positioning of a British officer or the 'Resident' within the Nizam's dominions. This development gradually led to a growing European influence in the social fabric of Hyderabad.

The period from 1803–53 CE was politically unstable for Hyderabad, when there were frequent changes of the Nizam's *diwan* or Prime Minister and an unsteady revenue administration. Law and order could not be maintained, while Arabs, Rohillas, Pathans, Sikhs, and other warlike groups demanded regular payment from their employers. The *diwan* was forced to rely on moneylenders who gave loans to the state in exchange for rights to collect revenue from districts. The insecurity of the tenure added to the exploitation of *ryots* as the assignees sought to recover their debt at the earliest. In such circumstances, besides lending money to the state, the Arabs grew in number in the Nizam's army. Most of the new regional powers that had formed at this time were military oligarchies dependent to a high degree on the support of mercenaries who were ethnically foreign or locally connected. The state of Hyderabad had allied with the British for military protection. In return for their allegiance, the fourth Nizam, Nasir ud Daulah, even supported the British in crushing whatever little uprising took place in Hyderabad in the Revolt of 1857 CE. The British felt deeply obliged to the Nizam for his support at this crucial time, and in exchange returned to him the districts of Raichur and Naldurg, conferring him with the knighthood of the most exalted order and title—Yar-o-Wafahdar or 'Faithful Ally'.

From the late nineteenth century, because of indirect rule, the state was sheltered by the British forces to a large extent. The reigns of the sixth and seventh Nizams, Mir Mahboob Ali Khan and Mir Osman Ali Khan, saw a visible cultural transformation of Hyderabad in terms of Western influence in architecture, clothing, court manners, cuisine and music. The European style adopted in the construction of the Falaknuma Palace, Mahboob Ali Khan's penchant for well-tailored suits, the holding of the English *darbars* on a regular basis by the Nizams, and the continental spread during official banquets and private parties had become popular with the elite. A large number of administrative reforms were introduced during Mahboob Ali Khan's period to improve Hyderabad's socio-economic condition.

When Mir Osman Ali Khan succeeded his father as the seventh Nizam in 1911 CE, the same socio-economic patterns were retained. The social relations, development of infrastructure, language and literature, art and architecture, education and learning, and the economic and social organization of the state represented the quintessence of the cultural traditions of his domain. Much credit goes to him for raising the status of the state of Hyderabad in myriad ways.

Karnataka

Towards the end of the seventeenth century, Aurangzeb subdued the region of Karnataka and appointed Zulfikar Ali as the nawab in 1692 CE, with the capital at Arcot. Meanwhile, Maratha power had begun to emerge strongly too. By 1677 CE, Shivaji had extended his power in the former Vijayanagar territories of Vellore, Jinji and Kurnool, while his brother had gained a firm foothold in Thanjavur by 1674 CE.

Following the death of Aurangzeb, the collapse of power in Delhi produced new changes in the southern provinces. The *nawab* of Karnataka, Saadatullah Khan (1710–32 CE), established his independence; while his successor, Dost Ali (1732–40 CE), conquered and annexed Madura in 1736 CE. Dost Ali's successors were even recognized by the Nizam of Hyderabad as *nawabs* of Karnataka. After the death of *nawab* Muhammad Anwaruddin (1744–49 CE), there was a succession dispute between Muhammad Ali and Hussein Dost Ali in Karnataka. The French and English competed for influence in this war of succession, taking opposite sides. The victory of the English established Muhammad Ali's supremacy over part of Karnataka till his death in 1795 CE.

Meanwhile, other developments in the rest of the country also had their effect on Karnataka. In 1741 CE, Madura, which Dost Ali had added to his dominions in 1736 CE, was conquered by the Marathas; and in 1743 CE Hyder Ali of Mysore occupied central Karnataka. Amidst this confusion, the British made major gains by entering into a treaty in 1801 CE, according to which all possessions of the *nawab* of Karnataka were to be transferred to them. The treaty, however, fixed that an annual revenue of several lakh pagodas was to be reserved for the Karnataka *nawab*, while the British were to maintain a military force for the protection of Karnataka in addition to taking up the responsibility for the collection of revenue. At the death of the *nawab* in 1853 CE, the decision to put an end to the nominal sovereignty of the *nawab* was taken which also allowed for an estate with funding for the royal family.

Mysore

Mysore rose as a Hindu state in the mid-seventeenth century, when rulers of the Wadeyar dynasty—Kanthirava Narasaraja and Deva Raja—embarked on campaigns to extend the Wadeyar kingdom over parts of interior Tamil Nadu. In the course of these campaigns, Dharmapuri, Salem and Coimbatore were included within Wadeyar territory, which asserted its independence during the confusion that followed the invasion of Nadir Shah. The boundaries of Mysore until the second half of the eighteenth century were such that it remained a landlocked kingdom—dependent, therefore, on trade and military supplies brought through the ports along the Coromandel Coast. Most of these ports were, however, controlled by Europeans, a fact which made Mysore less of an independent state and more vulnerable to foreign domination.

When Haidar Ali, a cavalry commander of migrant origin in the Mysore army, assumed power in Mysore in 1761 CE by reducing the Wadeyars to mere puppet kings, the tables were turned. He soon conquered the territory up to the river Krishna and extended the boundaries of his kingdom. The growing power of Haidar Ali in Mysore excited the jealousy of the Nizam of Hyderabad, the Marathas and the English. Their combined armies marched against him in 1767 CE, but Haidar Ali won over both the Marathas and the Nizam of Hyderabad before inflicting heavy losses on the English. The English had to sue for peace and a treaty was signed in 1769 CE between Haidar Ali and the English, according to which both the parties agreed to restore each other's conquered territories, while helping each other from any attack from a third party. However, the agreement between Haidar Ali and the English did not stand for long. When the Marathas attacked Mysore in 1772 CE, the English failed to come to Haidar Ali's assisstance. Annoyed with the English, Haidar Ali sought an opportunity to get even with them—which came in 1780 CE, when the English wanted to attack the French at Mahe, on the west coast. When Haidar Ali did not allow this, the English declared war on him. Though Haidar Ali inflicted heavy losses on the English, he died soon after in 1782 CE; and thereafter his son, Tipu Sultan, continued the war for two years. This war finally ended with the Treaty of Mangalore in 1784 CE, according to which both parties agreed to restore each other's conquered territories.

This treaty too proved to be short lived. In 1790 CE, Tipu Sultan launched an attack on the ruler of Thiruvitamkur, (Travancore) an

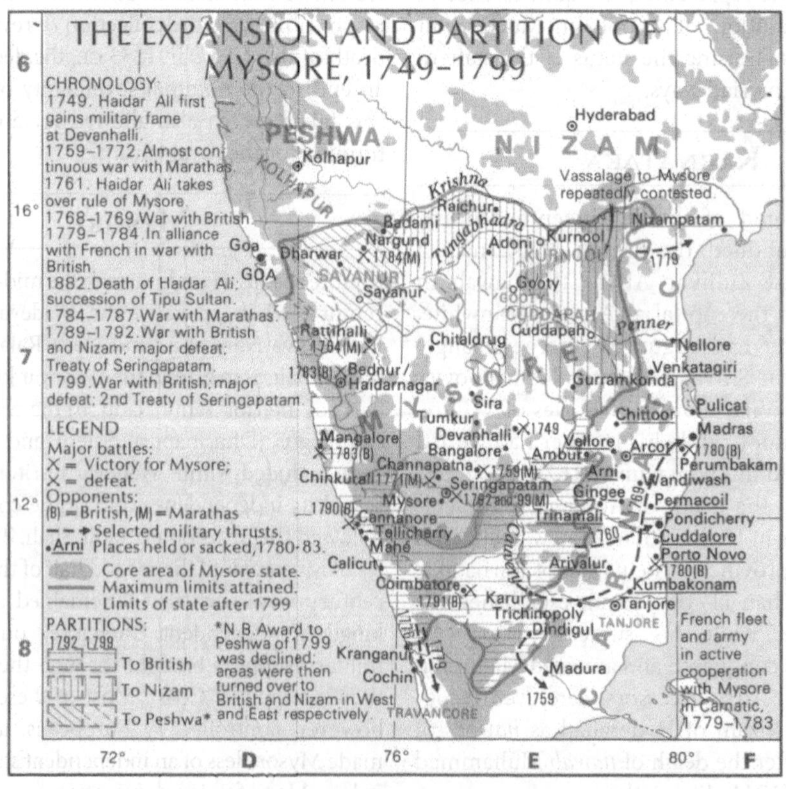

Map 28-2 *The Expansion and Partition of Mysore, 1749–1799 CE*

ally of the English—leading the English to attack Mysore and lay siege to Srirangapatnam, Tipu's capital. Tipu was compelled to sue for peace, as a result of which he surrendered half of his territory, handed over his two sons as hostages and paid a huge war indemnity to the English. Since Tipu had suffered huge losses at the hands of the English, he began to negotiate alliances with the French. It was at this juncture that Lord Wellesley asked Tipu to enter into a Subsidiary Alliance with the English; but on his refusal to do so, the English declared war on Mysore. In the ensuing battle, Tipu was killed (1799 CE) while fighting valiantly, and a large part of Mysore was annexed to the English dominions. As compensation, a small part of the territory of Mysore was returned to the erstwhile Wadeyar royal family.

Haidar Ali, followed by Tipu Sultan, made attempts to consolidate the kingdom of Mysore with access to both the coasts of peninsular India, which was achieved by stretching the boundaries of Mysore's. Tipu was also determined to completely overthrow Mughal suzerainty. The impediment for the father–son duo, however, lay in their inability to build internal accord within the Mysore nobility. They were also dependent on migrants and mercenaries to a large extent for military and fiscal services, and were always resisted by the local Poligar chiefs. By the 1770s, the English East India Company had become a great maritime enterprise with its own political ambitions. Its presence curtailed Mysore from gaining access to the rich agricultural lands and ports of the Coromandel Coast in eastern India.

Thiruvitamkur

The three regions of Kochi, Thiruvitamkur (Travancore) and Kozhikode together comprise the present state of Kerala. In the eighteenth century, the territories of a large number of chiefs and *rajas* were incorporated to form the state of Thiruvitamkur.

Thiruvitamkur gained in importance after 1729 CE, when its king, Martanda Verma, formed the southern Kerala state of Venad (Thiruvitamkur) by expanding its dominions with the help of a strong and modern army trained in European military skills and equipped with modern weaponry. The strong standing army built by Martanda Varma consisted of about 50,000 soldiers, who helped in reducing the power of the aristocracy on which the erstwhile rulers had been militarily dependent. Martanda Varma also fortified the northern limits of his kingdom along what came to be known as the 'Travancore line'. The Dutch were ousted from Kerala and feudal chiefs suppressed. Martanda Varma also extended his initiative in developing his state. Irrigation, transport and communication were greatly developed during his reign. His policies were continued in large measure by Martanda's successor, Rama Varma, who successfully defended his kingdom against a formidable rival power that had emerged in Mysore. Haidar Ali invaded Kerala in 1766 CE and annexed Malabar and Kozhikode. Thiruvitamkur, the southern most region and by far the most prominent, was spared.

Most of the regional states that rose to prominence in the latter part of the eighteenth century—with the exception of the Marathas—did not have access to the coastal areas. At a time when the English were establishing themselves as a supreme maritime power, several states made a determined attempt to consolidate their power by the use of maritime outlets so that they could participate in trading activities. The control of trade in this period was crucial, as neither the Nizam nor the *nawab* of Karnataka claimed full sovereignty, continuing to merely cast themselves as representatives of Mughal authority. In the seventeenth and eighteenth centuries, southern Indian politics, therefore, emerged as a game with many petty players on board.

SUMMARY

- The states that arose in different regions in India during 1700–1850 CE were different from each other in terms of nature, existence and wealth.
- The rise and fall of the regional states determined the historical image of the Indian subcontinent during its transition from the medieval to the modern era.
- The declining power and prestige of the Mughal Empire (on account of several factors) encouraged provincial insubordination among the governors, leading to the establishment of small semi-independent and independent states.
- The Sikhs became powerful in the Punjab in the fifteenth century. Led first by Guru Nanak, and thereafter by the nine Sikh gurus. Sikhism is based on Guru Nanak's teachings embodied in the *Guru Granth Sahib*. Banda Singh Bahadur, a militant Maratha-turned-Sikh, militarized Sikhism by extending the territorial power of the Sikh state. He was followed in his pursuits by the able Ranjit Singh, who united the *misls* into a powerful Sikh kingdom in Punjab during the first half of the nineteenth century.
- The Jats, an agricultural community, established an independent state at Bharatpur in northern India, settling around the regions of Delhi, Mathura and Agra. They revolted against the oppressive policies of Aurangzeb.
- From the mid-sixteenth century the Rajputs of Amber (Jaipur) and Marwar (Jodhpur) had played a significant role in Mughal politics. Their earlier privileges were lost during Aurangzeb's reign. Many small states came up in Rajputana to retain their Rajput identity.
- Awadh was one of the *subas* or provinces of the Mughal Empire, which functioned under the supervision of a *nawab* until 1819 CE. Saadat Khan, who was appointed as *nawab* of Awadh in 1722 CE, established his capital at Faizabad near Lucknow. Seeing the weakening Mughal Empire in Delhi, he declared himself independent and founded a separate kingdom at Awadh.
- Alivardi Khan, the governor of Bihar made himself an independent ruler of Bengal, Bihar and Orissa in 1740 CE. At about the same time, the Rohillas established an independent state in Rohilkhand.
- Hyderabad, founded by Mir Qamaruddin Khan, was a former princely state of south-central India. Mir Qamaruddin Khan was the viceroy of the Deccan under the Mughal emperors from 1713–21 CE. He founded the Asaf Jahi dynasty in 1724 CE, which ruled through seven Nizams.
- Other regional states in the Deccan and south India rose to prominence in the latter half of the eighteenth century. Principal among these were Karnataka under its *nawabs*, Thiruvitamkur in Kerala under Martanda Varma and Rama Varma, and Mysore under Haidar Ali and Tipu Sultan.

KEYWORDS

Gurmukhi	Sacha Badshah	Nizam	Subsidiary Alliance
Guru Granth Sahib	Misls	British resident	

REVIEW QUESTIONS

1. Elaborate upon the rise and growth of Sikh power under Maharaja Ranjit Singh.
2. Give an account of the rise of Awadh as an independent state in the eighteenth century.
3. Write a note on the emergence of Hyderabad State under Nizam-ul-Mulk Asaf Jah I.
4. Examine the role played by Haidar Ali and Tipu Sultan in establishing Mysore as an independent state in the eighteenth century.
5. Discuss the growth of the state of Thiruvitamkur under Martanda Varma and Rama Varma.

PART VIII–Advent of the Europeans and Establishment of British Rule in India

"Both the Spaniards and the Portuguese were cut off from trade with the East, because the Turks had taken possession of Constantinople. In consequence of this, the navigators of both countries were making earnest efforts to find a water route to India. Spain had faith in Columbus, and helped him in his plan of trying to reach India by sailing westward. But the Portuguese had a different idea. They spent their time and money in trying to sail round the African coast, in the belief that India could be reached by means of a southeast passage. This southeast passage could be found only by crossing the 'burning zone,' as the part of the earth near the equator was called; and all sailors feared to make the attempt. It was thought almost impossible to cross this burning zone, and the few navigators who had ventured as far as the equator had turned back in fear of steaming whirlpools and of fiery belts of heat.

In 1486, six years before Columbus discovered America, the King of Portugal sent Bartholomew Diaz, a bold and daring navigator, to find the end of the African coast. Bartholomew Diaz sailed through the fiery zone without meeting any of the dreadful misfortunes which the sailors so feared. When he had sailed beyond the tropic of Capricorn, a severe storm arose. The wind blew his three vessels directly south for thirteen days, during which time he lost sight of land. When the sun shone again, Diaz headed his vessels eastward, but as no land appeared, he again changed the direction, this time heading them toward the north. After sailing northward a short time, land was reached about two hundred miles east of the Cape of Good Hope. Diaz now pushed on four hundred miles farther along the coast of Africa, and saw the wide expanse of the Indian Ocean before him. Here the sailors refused to go any farther, and Diaz, although he wanted very much to go ahead and try to reach India, he was obliged to return.

On the way home, the vessels passed close to the cape which projects from the south coast of Africa, and Diaz named it Stormy Cape, in memory of the frightful storm which hid it from view on the way down. When they reached Lisbon, however, King John said that it should be called the Cape of Good Hope, because they now had hope that the southern route to India was found.

Diaz won much praise for his bravery and patience in making this voyage. He had proved that the stories about the fiery zone were false, and that the African coast had an end. It remained, however, for Vasco da Gama, then a young man of about twenty years of age, to prove that India could be reached in this way. In 1497 Da Gama sailed from Lisbon to the Cape of Good Hope, doubled the cape, and proceeded across the Indian Ocean to Hindustan. He returned to Lisbon in 1499, his ships loaded with the rich products of the East, including cloves, spices, pepper, ginger, and nutmeg. He also brought with him rich robes of silk and satin, costly gems, and many articles made of carved ivory, or of gold and of silver. The King of Portugal was greatly pleased with what Da Gama had accomplished, and his successful voyage was the wonder of the day.

The same year that Da Gama returned from India by a route around the south end of Africa, with his ships loaded with rich produce, Sebastian Cabot returned from a fruitless voyage to the strange, barren coast of North America. It was no wonder that the voyages of Columbus and the Cabot were thought unsuccessful as compared with the voyage Da Gama had just finished. No one then dreamed of a New World; all were searching for the Orient—for golden Cathay."

Source: Shaw, Edward R., 1900, *Discoverers and Explorers*, American Book Company: New York. Available at http://www.gutenberg.org/files/22116/22116-h/22116-h.htm

Image: Spanish and Portuguese Vessels, Cape of Good Hope.

CHAPTER 29

Advent of the Europeans

Review and Discussion

- Arrival of the European Trading Companies
- Anglo-French Struggle for Supremacy in the Deccan
- Reasons for the French Failure and the English Success

The arrival of the Europeans in the Indian subcontinent was an event of great significance as it revolutionized the destiny of India. Europe's interest in India dated back to the Classical or ancient age when lucrative trade was carried on between Europe and India. India had much to offer in terms of spices, textiles and other oriental products to the large consumer market in the West. Till the onset of the medieval era, trade was conducted both by sea and by land. While the sea route opened from the ports on the western coast of India and went westwards through the Persian Gulf and the Red Sea to Alexandria, the land route was traced through Afghanistan and Central Asia to the shores of the Black Sea and to Constantinople. From these two main centres of Alexandria and Constantinople, Indian trade goods found their way across the Mediterranean Sea to the commercial hubs of Venice and Genoa, from where they were then dispersed throughout the main cities of Europe.

From the ancient age down to the fifteenth century, spices formed an important part of European trade with India. Pepper, ginger, chillies, cinnamon and cloves were carried to Europe where they fetched high prices. Indian silk, fine muslin and cotton cloth too were much in demand among rich European families. Pearls and other precious stones were also highly in demand in Europe.

With the Ottoman occupation of Constantinople in 1453 CE, the flourishing trade between the Venetian and Genoese traders of Europe and the Arabs, who controlled trade between Europe and India, received a major setback as all trade routes now fell into Turkish hands. Since the Turks did not allow Christian merchants to ply their trade in Constantinople, it became necessary to discover a new trade route to the East. Several attempts were made by many European nations over the years to establish trading links with India. The period between the fifteenth and eighteenth centuries was the time of exploration and travel for the Portuguese, Spanish, English, French and Dutch who set out to discover a new world hitherto little known. This spirit of adventure and enquiry marked the beginning of a new era in Europe—of discovery, exploration, navigation and invention. Most explorers had the immediate task of finding a direct route to India and the Far East. However, when the initial period of trading and exploration came to an end, the age of European exploitation began—ultimately leading to colonialism and economic imperialism.

The Arrival of European Trading Companies

Portugal became the first European nation to make vital attempts to discover a new sea route to India. The Portuguese merchants were soon followed by the Dutch, the English and the French—among which, the last two went on to become giant maritime powers. Commanded by enterprising men and equipped with large ships with ammunition, the merchant companies of the English and the French made a heady start by building their own armies and making a debut into the territorial conquest of India.

The Portuguese

Among several efforts made by the Portuguese to discover a new trade route to India, mention must be made of the Portuguese traveller, Bartholomew Diaz, who happened to circle the Cape of Good Hope in 1487 CE and reach western tropical Africa. The discovery of Africa gave the Portuguese access to slaves to till their lands, pepper and other spices to season their food and gold to make them rich.

In 1498 CE, Vasco da Gama began his historical voyage, and after circumnavigating the Cape of Good Hope in South Africa, he reached Kozhikode (Calicut) on the Malabar Coast, where he was received cordially by the Hindu Raja who bore the hereditary title of Zamorin. Vasco da Gama carried a good cargo of spices to Portugal and made a large profit; and thereafter the Portuguese sent other expeditions to India, establishing their trading depots. They fought against the Arab merchants, who had so far contributed to the prosperity of the kingdoms of Kozhikode and Kochi (Cochin), driving them away from their territories. In 1500 CE, Pedro Alvarez Cabral arrived in Kozhikode with a huge naval fleet and began to forcibly deprive the Arabs of their commercial privileges and concessions. On being questioned by the Zamorin, the Portuguese merchants under the leadership of Cabral negotiated with the Raja of Kochi for the establishment of a shore agency. With the Raja of Kochi always seeking to gain an upper hand over the Zamorin, a Portuguese factory was soon established there. The Portuguese then went on to seize the fort of Kannur (Cannanore), strengthening it with ammunition. In 1503 CE, the Portuguese successfully resisted an attack of the Zamorin on Kochi, thereby establishing their supremacy in the region. Portuguese trade with India received a great impetus after this, allowing them to set up their own trading centres at Kozhikode, Kochi and Kannur. This led to the restoration of trade through an all-sea route between India and Europe by the Portuguese.

The Portuguese under their viceroys, Francisco de Almeida (1505–09 CE) and Alfonso de Albuquerque (1509–15 CE), went on from strength to strength by fortifying their possessions and increasing their trading network.

Francisco de Almeida, the first governor of the Portuguese in India, built strong forts around the Portuguese settlements at Kochi and Kannur. He maintained the supreme power of the Portuguese on the sea, but confined their activity to trade and commerce. He adopted a policy, wherein he believed that any attempt at territorial acquisition would not be successful in India. He felt that the Portuguese did not have sufficient manpower to maintain an empire in India and he insisted that their commercial success be based on naval supremacy. His policy was therefore called the *Blue Water* policy. He was a good administrator, interested in espousing Portuguese commerce in India. By defeating the combined fleet of the Egyptians, the Zamorin and the Sultan of Gujarat in 1509 CE, Almeida strengthened the Portuguese influence in India.

Alfonso de Albuquerque, who succeeded Almeida, was an ambitious man who secured the foundations of Portuguese authority in India by extending Portuguese territories. He conquered Goa from the Sultan of Bijapur in November 1510 CE, making it the capital of the Portuguese in India. He also added many cities belonging to the Arabs on the East Coast of Africa. He used the services of

Hindu officials in his administration, besides establishing schools for them, and was thus, found to be good with his Hindu subjects. But the same may not be said about the Muslims whom he regarded as his adversaries. He also tried to introduce social reforms in the Hindu society by legally abolishing *sati*. While encouraging inter-marriages, Albuquerque promoted Christianity by making Goa into an archbishopric. It was here that St. Francis Xavier started his activities of spreading Roman Catholicism. Even after the death of Albuquerque at Goa in 1515 CE, Portuguese power kept increasing in India. While Diu and Bassein were added in 1534 CE, Daman, Salsette, Chaul, Bombay, San Thome and Hughli were acquired in 1538 CE. That same year, they also acquired permission to build a factory at Goa. In 1545 CE, the Diu fort was attacked by the king of Gujarat, but was successfully defended. In 1571 CE, the combined efforts of the rulers of Bijapur, Ahmednagar and Kozhikode to take possession of Goa also ended in failure.

After holding forth for nearly a century, the Portuguese began to lose their maritime supremacy to the Dutch, who were fast emerging as another competent European naval power. There were several reasons why the Portuguese could not retain their commercial pre-eminence. Firstly, although the Portuguese had a strong naval fleet, they made no serious attempt to gain any inland territory. This restricted their hold along the coastline alone, leaving the hinterland practically independent. With the establishment of the Mughal Empire nearly the whole of India was unified under Mughal rule. Under these circumstances there was hardly any scope for Portuguese growth on the Indian mainland. An inland defeat would have driven them off the coast into the sea, while external aggression would have meant their total surrender. To hold such a lengthy and irregular coastland extending over 15,000 miles against all rivals made the management of logistics difficult for the small kingdom of Portugal.

Secondly, the changed political condition of India—in which the kingdom of Vijayanagar almost disappeared after the battle of Talikota—affected the prosperity of the Portuguese traders, who had so far been carrying on direct trade with Vijayanagar. Meanwhile, the Marathas, who had grown in power, plundered Goa in 1683 CE. Thirdly, the Portuguese policy of religious intolerance and forcible conversions into Christianity made them unpopular with the local population. Fourthly, the Portuguese were more dependent upon sea piracy than on regular trade, an aspect that did not hold them in good stead when it came to empire building. Lastly, when Portugal came under the control of Spain in 1580 CE, Portuguese interests were subordinated and their trading operations suffered. In such a scenario, when Brazil was discovered, Portugal turned its attention away from India and diverted most of its resources to the new land.

Though the Portuguese rule was short-lived in India, it influenced the history of southern India; and their influence may still be seen on the religious architecture of western and southern India. They were also responsible for introducing tobacco, maize and potatoes, apart from a number of fruits, such as pineapple and papaya, from the new world into India. Portuguese missionaries were sent as emissaries to the court of Akbar for interacting with clerics and sharing their religious ideas. The contribution of the Jesuit scholars to the historical and geographical literature of the world is significant for its heritage value. In fact, the greatest contribution of the Portuguese lay in the fact that they paved the way for other European powers to step in and play their roles in the political arena of India. The rise of the Dutch and the English in India eventually created strong competition for them, confining their activities only to the few ports of Goa, Daman and Diu on the west coast by the early eighteenth century.

The Dutch

After nearly a century of Portuguese maritime hegemony, the Dutch came to India. The Dutchmen were simple and adventurous people who rose to prominence in the sixteenth century when Dutch

SEAWARD VIEW OF MASULIPATNAM, *mid-17th century. Site of Dutch, British and French Factories.*

sailors ventured into the seas in quest of colonies and commerce. The Dutch Company was started in 1592 CE by a group of Amsterdam merchants. Three years later, Cornelius Houtman set out on a voyage to India and returned with a large cargo in 1597 CE—opening the gates of the Indian Archipelago to Holland. In 1602 CE, many small Dutch companies were amalgamated to form the Dutch East India Company. It was the first to break the monopoly of Portuguese trade with India. A charter was granted to the merchants of the Company that gave them monopoly of eastern trade along with the rights to wage wars, make treaties, occupy territories and build forts. But the main objective of the Dutch Company remained trade. They founded a factory at Masulipatnam in 1605 CE, and built their first fort on the mainland of India at Pulicat (Pallaicatta) in 1609 CE. They established factories along the Coromandel coast, Gujarat and Bengal. They captured Nagapattinam (Nagapatnam) on the Coromandel coast from the Portuguese in 1659 CE; and because of its proximity to the Dutch settlements in Sri Lanka (Ceylon), they established their headquarters there. Their factories in India were situated at Pallaicatta, Surat (Suryapur), Chinsurah, Kasimbazar, Patna (Pataliputra), Nagapattinam, Balasore (Baleshwar) and Kochi. The Dutch were content to evince only commercial interests in India as they were a mercantile and maritime people, with a commercial policy that was more vigorous and better supported than those of other states.

The English looked upon the rising power of the Dutch as a threat to their interests in the land. The Dutch too could not hold their ground in India for long as they turned their attention to their settlements in the islands of south east Asia. The English decided to drive them away from their Indian possessions and finally succeeded in defeating them at Bedara in 1759 CE, which weakened the Dutch position in India greatly. The Dutch possessions in India were eventually conquered by the English in 1795 CE.

The Danes

Seeing the success of other European merchants, the Danes also founded a settlement in India in 1620 CE at Tharangambadi (Tranquebar) in the Thanjavur district. They also occupied Serampore (Frederiksnagore) in 1676 CE. However, the Danes did not find a foothold in India and consequently sold their settlements to the British in 1845 CE.

The English

Bartholomew Diaz's discovery of the Cape of Good Hope in 1487 CE and Columbus's discovery of America in 1492 CE opened up new avenues for European nations; so much so that Portugal and Spain were even given the right to conduct commercial activities around the world. Rights for the eastern hemisphere went to Portugal, while the western went to Spain. For almost a century, most nations allowed Portugal and Spain to call the shots where commercial exploitation was concerned, but gradually England began to nurture the idea of discovering an alternative sea route to the East. This opportunity presented itself in the late sixteenth century when Francis Drake set out on a voyage of exploration and an English victory was scored over the Spanish Armada in 1588 CE.

England's victory over the mighty Spanish fleet provided encouragement to the maritime enterprise of the English who were keenly interested in establishing trade ties with India. English missionaries had already been visiting India and had spread reports about India's fabulous wealth. Many enterprising Englishmen like James Lancaster, Benjamin Wood, Fitch, Newberry and John Mildenhal reached India and Malaya by land and sea routes. On 31st December 1600 CE, some English merchants formed themselves into a company to trade with India. They obtained a charter from Queen Elizabeth I, and named their company 'The Company of Merchants of London Trading in the East Indies', which was to later materialize into 'The English East India Company'.

The English East India Company (Company) initially enjoyed trading links with the Spice Islands alone. It was only in 1608 CE that one of their trading vessels first reached Surat, under the leadership of William Hawkins, with the purpose of trading in silk, precious stones, indigo and sulphur. Captain Hawkins met Emperor Jahangir with a letter of introduction from James I, the king of England. Though he stayed in the Mughal court for three years, he could not get any trading concessions because of stiff Portuguese opposition to the English gaining any commercial privileges. After Hawkins left Agra to counter this Portuguese policy, Sir Henry Middleton arrived at Surat with three ships; and the very next year Captain Best arrived with two ships. It was only after the Portuguese were defeated by Captain Best in a naval attack off the coast of Surat in 1612 CE that Jahangir permitted the English to build a factory at Surat. Eager to gain a foothold in India, the English sent Sir Thomas Roe as the Company's ambassador to the Mughal court of Jahangir in 1615 CE. With his efforts, the Company was able to get permission to set up factories in several Indian towns—such as Surat, Agra, Ahmedabad and Bharuch (Broach)—that were all placed under the president and the council of the Surat factory. Surat, thus, became the English headquarters on the western coast of India. Later, an English factory was set up at Machilipatnam (Masulipatnam) for trade in cotton textiles.

In 1639 CE, Francis Day obtained the site of Chennai (Madras) from the governor of Chandragiri, Damarla Venkata (son of Chenna). In 1641 CE, the English built the Fort St. George, which was to become the headquarters of the English settlements on the eastern coast of India and laid the foundation of modern Chennai.

In 1661 CE, Charles II, the ruler of England gave permission to the Company to issue coins, build forts, maintain an army for the protection of trade interests, and to declare war or peace when the necessity arose. In 1668 CE, Charles II transferred to the Company the island of Mumbai (Bombay) which had been given by the king of Portugal to Charles II's queen as part of her wedding dowry. Bombay soon replaced Surat as the headquarters of the Company in India. In 1690 CE, Aurangzeb, gave permission to the English Company to trade in Bengal, free of all duties, in return for 3,000 rupees a year. That same year the English established a settlement in Hughli, which later on developed into the modern city of Kolkata (Calcutta). Six years later, they built Fort William, which was named after their king, William III.

Though the English did not face any serious opposition in Bombay and Madras, due to the coastal location of their settlements, in Bengal, however, when the Company's agents tried to fortify Hughli, Shaista Khan, the Mughal governor of Bengal, seized several factories and drove out the English. It was only after Job Charnock, the Company agent in Bengal, negotiated with the Mughals that the English were allowed to return to Hughli. Again when the English seized some Indian ships in the Arabian Sea, Aurangzeb ordered a general attack on all English settlements, ordering all their factories at Surat, Masulipatnam and Vizag (Vizagapatnam) to be locked up. The fort of the English at Bombay was besieged too. Later, on submission

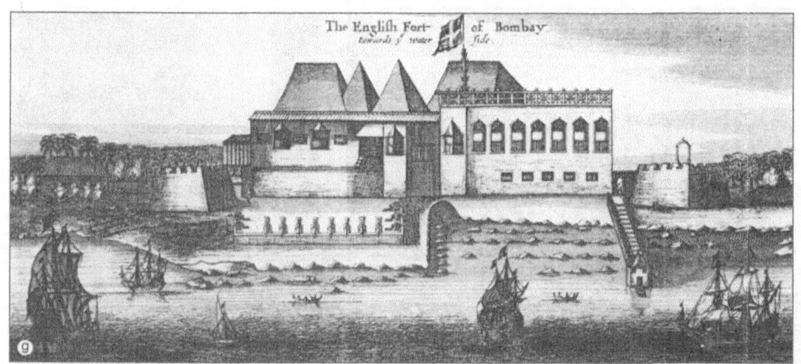

THE ENGLISH FORT AT BOMBAY,
mid-17th century.

of a humble petition, the English were allowed to resume their trade in Bengal on payment of a huge amount of indemnity, including the return of all warships. The English reorganised themselves from 1700 CE onwards, and placed their settlements in Bengal under the separate control of a president and a council.

The progress of the English East India Company was very rapid during the eighteenth century. It managed to subdue all its European rivals and also succeeded in establishing British rule in India. In 1715 CE, the Company's ambassador, John Surman, visited the court of the Mughal emperor, Farrukh Siyyar, to secure commercial privileges throughout Mughal India. Another member of the delegation, William Hamilton, who was also a physician, was able to cure the Mughal emperor of a painful disease. In gratitude, they were granted trading facilities which included the grant of certain villages near Calcutta (Sutanuti, Gobindapur and Kalikata) and Madras (Madraspatnam, Chennapatnam, Nungambakkam, etc.) as well as the right to reside wherever they chose. Following this, the English fortified Bombay to defend themselves against the Marathas and the Portuguese, increasing the number of armed ships. The position of the English was thus strengthened on the western coast, while on the eastern coast they were already in occupation of Madras. In Bengal too, the prospects of the Company looked better with the growth of trade. Thus, Bombay, Madras and Calcutta became the centres of their principal presidencies.

The French

Like their other Continental counterparts, the French too tried to establish trading ties with India and the Southeast Asian islands. Though their early efforts date back to 1604 CE they were all futile. In 1611 CE, Louis XII, the Bourbon king of France, granted the monopoly of the eastern trade to a company, which proved to be a failure. Finally, a French East India Company was formed in 1644 CE under the leadership of Colbert, the famous minister of Louis XIV with the support of the French government. This was followed by the establishment of factories at Surat in 1658 CE and Masulipatnam in 1659 CE. Their main trading centre was formed at Puducherry (Pondicherry) on the eastern coast by the French governor, Francois Martin in 1673 CE, under a grant from Sher Khan Lodi of Bijapur. In 1674 CE, the French received the site of Chandannagar (Chandernagore) on the Hughli river from Shaista Khan, the Governor of Bengal, where they built a factory. The French occupied St. Thome on the Coromandel Coast in 1672 CE, but the Dutch forcibly captured it. Dutch rivalry adversely influenced the position of the French in India. Although Pondicherry was captured by the Dutch in 1693 CE, it was handed back to the French by the treaty of Ryswick in 1697 CE. By 1720 CE, even though the French seemed to lose control over Bantum, Surat and Masulipatnam, there was a revival of fortunes with the acquisitions of Mauritius (1721 CE), Mahe (1725 CE) and Karikal (1730 CE).

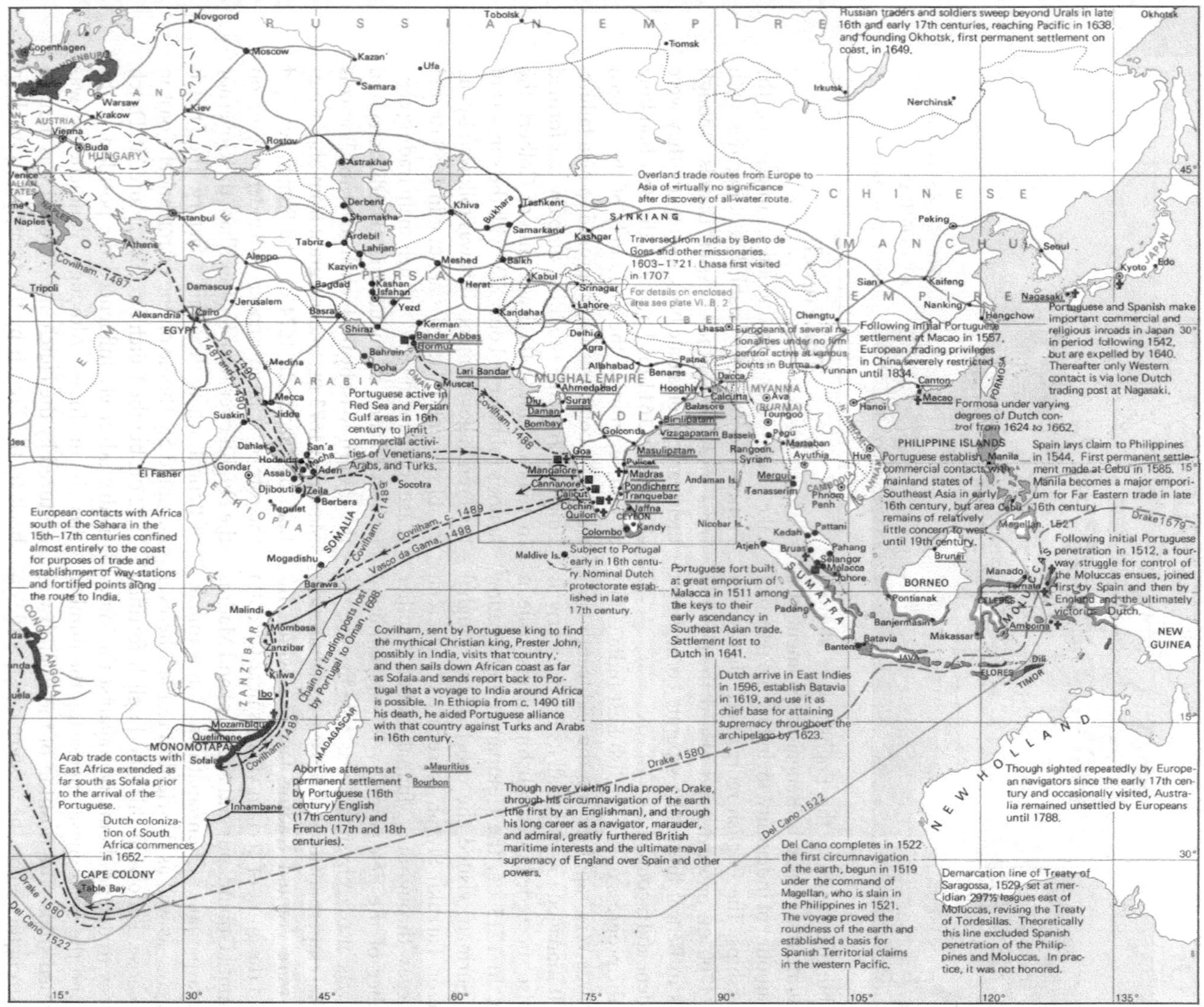

Map 29-1 *Discovery, Exploration, Trade and Colonization, 1486–1700* CE

THE EUROPEAN TRADING COMPANIES

Country	Company's Name	Year of Establishment	First Factory	First Fort/ Settlement	Major Trading Centres	Major Items of Export
Portugal	—	—	At Cannanore in 1501	At Goa in 1510	Calicut, Cochin and Cannanore	Silk, indigo and saltpetre
Dutch	The United East India Company of the Netherlands	1602 in Holland	At Masulipatnam in 1605	At Pulicut in 1609	Agra, Surat, Masulipatnam and Chinsura	Indigo, saltpetre, opium, raw silk and cotton
Danes	The Danish East India Company	1616 in Denmark	At Tranquebar in 1620	Fort Dansborg at Tranquebar	Serampore	Tea
English	The English East India Company	1600 in London	At Surat in 1613	At Madras (Fort St. George) in 1639	Agra, Surat, Ahmedabad, Calcutta, Bombay, Madras, Broach, etc.	Silk yarn, raw silk, saltpetre, indigo, etc.
French	The French East India Company was established	1664 in France	At Surat in 1667	At Pondicherry in 1674	Chandranagore, Balasore, Qasim Bazar, Mahe, Yanam, and Karikal.	Spices, raw silk, etc

The French, like the English, fostered aspirations of establishing an empire in India. Initially their ambition remained purely commercial; but as they started to make profits from the trade with India, they realised the huge potential India held in terms of wealth and began to strengthen and fortify their settlements against Indian rulers. When the French Governor, Dupleix, took to fulfilling his political mission, he faced opposition from the English—resulting in a series of armed struggles between the French and the English, which constituted a new chapter in India's history.

Anglo-French Struggle for Supremacy in the Deccan: The Carnatak Wars

Of all the rival European trading companies, the French East India Company turned out to be the most serious threat for the English East India Company in India. Their mutual rivalry lasted for a long time and was of great significance for both nations. By the mid eighteenth century, the English and the French were anxious to expand their trade in India. Their ambitious plans resulted in the three Carnatak wars (1744–63 CE) which were fought for control of trade, wealth and territory in India.

The First Carnatak War (1744–48 CE)

The First Carnatak War was the direct outcome of what was happening in Europe at the time. The English and the French were engaged in a conflict in connection with the succession of Maria Theresa to the throne of Austria. When news about this war of Austrian succession reached India, the French governor of Pondicherry was Dupleix and the English governor of Madras was Morse. Realising the naval weakness of the French, Dupleix suggested to the English governor that he remain neutral. However, more naval ships were already on the way to help the English; hence, Morse rejected the suggestion. Eager to safeguard the French, however, Dupleix requested Anwaruddin, the *nawab* of Karnataka (in whose state both the ports of Madras and Pondicherry were located) to persuade the English to change their minds.

The *nawab* asked both the English and the French to desist from fighting each other, but considering that the former paid no heed to the orders of the *nawab*, the French too began preparations for war. Dupleix also appealed to La Bourdonnais, the Governor of Mauritius, for help, who hastened to India with a fleet and reached the Coromandel Coast in July 1746 CE. After a pitched battle, the English squadron left for Sri Lanka; and maximizing on the opportunity, Dupleix asked La Bourdonnais to lay siege to Madras. The move angered the English who approached the *nawab* of Karnataka to direct the French to leave Madras. Dupleix, however, promised to hand over Madras to the *nawab*, on condition that the French be allowed to take it over again. The French eventually captured Madras in September 1746 CE, but soon differences arose between Dupleix and La Bourdonnais; the latter had accepted a bribe and restored Madras to the English for £40,000. But Dupleix recaptured Madras and the *nawab* sent an army to fight the French, who defeated the army in the battle of St. Thome (also known as the battle of Adyar).

The historic treaty of Aix La Chapelle was signed in Europe in 1748 CE which brought the First Carnatak War to a close. As a result of this treaty, the English regained Madras in India and the French Louisburg in North America. Although the treaty did not bring about any other major changes, it demonstrated the significance of naval power and displayed the superior war techniques of the Europeans in India.

The Second Carnatak War (1748–54 CE)

Not even a few months had elapsed since the First Carnatak War that the English and the French again got entangled in what came to be known as the Second Carnatak War. While the first war was the outcome of the political conditions in Europe, the second had its origin in India. The First Carnatak War had provided the Europeans with an opportunity to interfere in the political affairs of the Indian states. Succession disputes at Arcot and Hyderabad, for instance, provided Dupleix with another opportunity to counter the English. There was chaos and disorder in India in the middle of the eighteenth century with the gradual decline of the Mughal empire. Being a shrewd statesman, Dupleix foresaw the downfall of the Mughals and sought to establish a French empire in India. To this end, he began taking an active interest in the political affairs of India, pitting various regional groups against each other.

He promised to help Chanda Sahib acquire the throne of Karnataka against the ruling *nawab*, Anwaruddin. He also promised to make Muzaffar Jung, the Nizam of Hyderabad, against the ruling Nizam, Nasir Jung. Intially Dupleix was even successful in his various attempts at political interference. With the help of the French soldiers, Chanda Sahib defeated and killed Anwaruddin in the battle of Ambur in 1749 CE; and his son, Muhammad Ali, was besieged at Trichinopally by Chanda Sahib's forces. Chanda Sahib, thus, became the *nawab* of the Karnataka. Dupleix was equally successful in Hyderabad as he was able to make Muzaffar Jung the Nizam of Hyderabad. After this installation, Dupleix was appointed as governor of all the Mughal territories, south of the river Krishna. Some districts in the Northern Circars were also surrendered by the Nizam to the French; while a French army under Bussy was stationed at Hyderabad. When Muzaffar Jung was killed in January 1751 CE, Salabat Jung was placed on the throne by Bussy as the new Nizam.

The English soon realized that the rising influence of the French would go against their trade. When Muhammad Ali requested them for help, they decided to send their troops to relieve Trichinopally. This was when a young English captain, Robert Clive, made his appearance. He had come to Madras as a clerk in the service of the English East India Company, soon becoming an officer who was entrusted with the task of relieving Trichinopally. But instead of going to Trichinopally, he went to Arcot, the capital of Karnataka, and captured it. When Chanda Sahib, who was away in Trichinopally, heard that his capital had been taken, he immediately abandoned the siege of Trichinopally and rushed towards Arcot. With added reinforcements from Madras, Clive defeated Chanda Sahib and helped Muhammad Ali become the *nawab* of Karnataka. In this manner the whole of Karnataka passed into the hands of the English.

The success of the English under Clive was a great blow to Dupleix's ambition to establish French supremacy in southern India. Though he was able to establish French influence in Hyderabad only, he continued to vie for Karnataka. In the meantime, the French government recalled him to France in 1754 CE, since it did not approve the establishment of French rule in India through continuous warfare. His departure was followed by the treaty of Pondicherry in 1755 CE, which was signed by his successor, Godeheu, effectively ending the Second Carnatak War. By the new treaty, the two powers agreed not to interfere in the internal affairs of the Indian states and both retained their old positions. The English, however got a few towns in

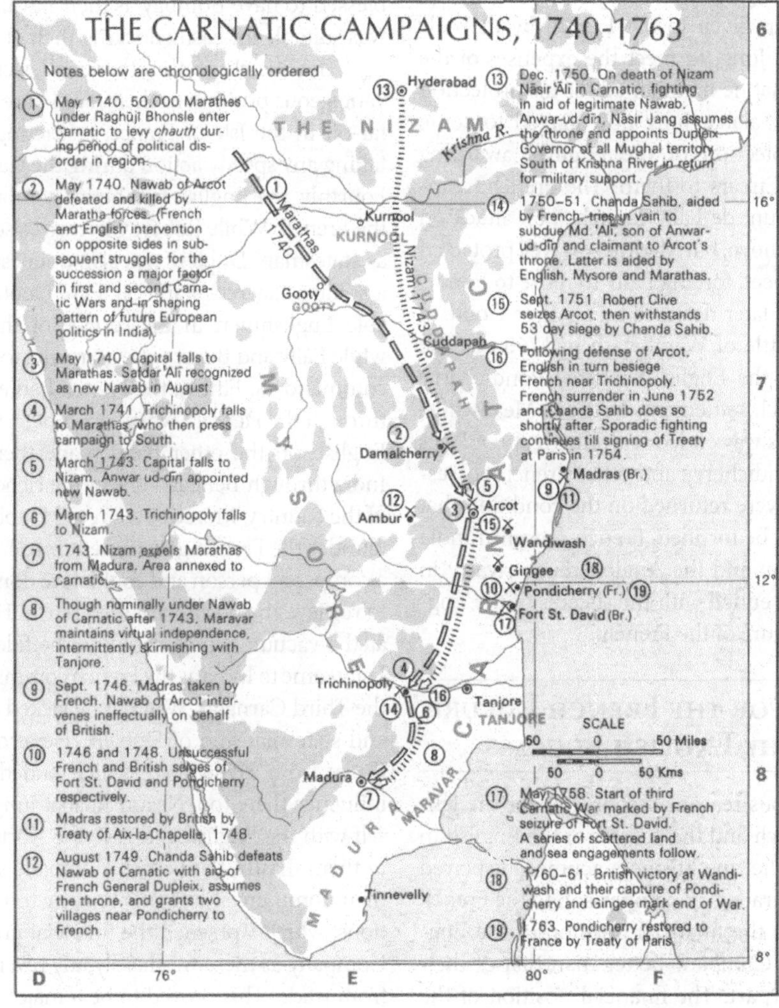

Map 29-2 *The Carnatak Campaigns, 1740–1763 CE*

the Northern Circars, while Bussy remained in the Deccan and continued to remain influential. The treaty made the English stronger in the subcontinent and also gave them the much needed respite before embarking upon the Third Carnatak War.

The Third Carnatak War (1758–63 CE)

After the departure of Dupleix, the English and the French remained in peace for nearly four years in Karnataka, till hostilities were once again resumed when the Seven Years' War broke out in Europe. In India, the English took the Northern Circars which had been given to the French by the new Nizam, Salabat Jung, to meet the expenses of the French army that he maintained for his protection at Hyderabad. Salabat Jung now agreed to come under the protection of the English, awarding the Northern Circars to them. The French, commanded by Count de Lally, launched an attack on Madras at this move; but Madras was well protected by an English fleet, forcing Lally to retire to Pondicherry. He was later defeated by Sir Eyre Coote at the decisive battle of Wandiwash in 1760 CE. The very next year the English captured Pondicherry and other French settlements in India. Meanwhile, the Seven Year's war ended with the treaty of Paris in 1763 CE. Pondicherry and other French possessions in India were returned on the condition that they would not be fortified. French power in India was thus broken and the Anglo-French rivalry in southern India ended with the success of the English and the failure of the French.

Reasons for the French Failure and the English Success

There are various reasons responsible for the failure of the French and the success of the English in India. Firstly, the fine business acumen displayed by the English traders in comparison to the French naturally made the financial position of the English East India Company better than that of their French counterpart. The financial position of the French had also worsened to such an extent that during the closing years of the Third Carnatak War, the French Company was not even able to pay their troops regularly. Secondly, the English East India Company was a private enterprise which created a spirit of self reliance among its people, with the result that the English were a more prosperous lot. On the other hand, the French East India Company was merely a subsidiary of the government, which was in the doldrums itself. Thirdly, the success of the English was due to their naval supremacy, which enabled the English to send help to India whenever it was required. The English were also blessed to have Bombay as their naval base, which was suitable for easily docking their ships.

The French, on the other hand, were in a disadvantageous position as their naval base was situated far-off in the Isle of France, restricting them from taking any speedy action during the Carnatak wars. Fourthly, the English had better commanders than the French. While Robert Clive was a soldier as well as statesman, Dupleix was also a statesman but not a soldier. Lawrence and Sir Eyre Coote were other able Englishmen in the service of the Company, while Lally and Bussy were no match for the English commanders. Fifthly, the French had entered India through the Deccan, which was not fertile land. The English on the other hand made their entry into India through Bengal—one of the richest provinces of the country. Moreover, to recall Dupleix was a big blunder the French government made. Dupleix was a competent person and could have done something to retrieve the position of the French. His recall created a vacuum which could not be filled. Count de Lally came to India as the French commander during the Third Carnatak War, but he lacked the foresight and statesmanship of Dupleix. He also called back Bussy from Hyderabad, which ended the French influence there too. Nizam Salabat Jung allied himself with the English and gave the Northern Circars to them. Lastly, the French Company subordinated their commercial interests to their territorial ambitions, which worsened the financial position of the Company as there was hardly any revenue accruing from trade. This proved to be a major impediment in extending support to Dupleix's ambitious plans.

SUMMARY

- The arrival of the Europeans in the Indian subcontinent was an event of great significance as it revolutionized the destiny of India.
- India had much to offer Europe in terms of spices, textiles and other oriental products which had a large consumer market in the West.
- Till the onset of the medieval era, trade was carried on both by sea and by land.
- With the Ottoman occupation of Constantinople in 1453 CE, the flourishing trade carried on by the Venetian and Genoese traders with the Arabs received a major setback, since the trade routes now fell into the hands of the Turks. Hence, a new trade route to the East had to be discovered.
- The Portuguese were the first to establish any European settlement in India, followed by the Dutch, the English and the French.
- From humble beginnings in trade, European trading companies began playing a dynamic role in Indian politics.
- The Portuguese followed a policy of commercial enterprise. They became the monopoly traders of India with the West. They also interfered in the political intrigues of various states of peninsular India.
- Portuguese rule was resented by the people on account of their policy of religious persecution and hostility towards other nations. The seventeenth century witnessed the gradual decline of the Portuguese who eventually got confined to Goa, Daman and Diu.
- Nearly a century after the Portuguese, the Dutch came to India for trade. But the English looked upon the rising power of the Dutch as a threat to their vested interests; and finally they succeeded in defeating the Dutch.
- The English East India Company was formed in 1600 CE. The English were able to establish their first factory at Masulipatam in southern India; and thereafter they were successful in establishing their trading settlements at Bombay and Madras.
- In Bengal, the English met with a stiff opposition from the Mughal authorities. However, the Company's struggle for exclusive rights of trade was gradually met with success. Their two European rivals, the Portuguese and the Dutch were eliminated and the Company succeeded in establishing itself in India.
- The French arrived late on the scene. Like the English, they too fostered aspirations to establish a French empire in India. Initially, the French ambition was purely commercial, but after 1742 CE, they began to entertain political ambitions. This bought them in direct conflict with the English.
- A series of armed struggles between the French and the English took place in India which came to be known as the three Carnatak Wars. Finally the supremacy of the English was established as the pre-eminent colonial power in India.

KEYWORDS

Exploration
Colonialism
Circumnavigation
Blue Water policy
Navigation
Economic imperialism

REVIEW QUESTIONS

1. Why was it important for the Europeans to find a new trade route to India after 1453 CE?
2. What were the causes for the decline of Portuguese power in India?
3. Explain the causes and consequences of the First Carnatak War.
4. Bring out the significance of the treaty of Pondicherry.
5. Enumerate the causes for the failure of the French and the success of the English in India.

CHAPTER 30

Establishment and Consolidation of British Power in Bengal

Review and Discussion

- Battle of Plassey
- Battle of Buxar
- Treaty of Allahabad
- Dual System or Dyarchy

The beginnings of British rule in India may be traced to the province of Bengal which emerged as the base from which the British first embarked on their political career that would last for almost two centuries. Bengal was the most fertile and the richest of India's provinces, where the Company had been conducting very profitable trade. It had secured valuable privileges from the Mughal emperors, who had granted the Company the freedom to export and import their goods from Bengal, without paying taxes. The English Company had founded the modern city of Kolkata and also built Fort William. The province of Bengal, which included Bihar and Orissa as well, was ruled by a *nawab*, appointed by the Mughal emperor. The authority of the Mughal emperor in the mid-eighteenth century had become nominal and the *nawab* of Bengal was virtually an independent ruler.

Battle of Plassey

After the death of Aurangzeb in 1707 CE, the Mughal Empire began to disintegrate with its acquired territories becoming independent under different regional rulers. In the case of Bengal, Alivardi Khan became the independent *nawab* of Bengal (1740–56 CE). He was able to keep the European trading companies in check by not permitting them to fortify their settlements in the region, but still managed to maintain cordial relations with the Company. While many parts of northern India were in a state of political unrest and tattered by the invasions of Nadir Shah, Bengal remained peaceful. There was a marked growth in trade, industry and agriculture. For the European traders, Bengal presented the only place where prosperity prevailed. Following the death of Alivardi Khan in 1756 CE, he was succeeded by his grandson, Siraj-ud-daula. Siraj-ud-daula was suspicious of the designs of the English and concerned that they might try to become masters of Bengal, just as they had become masters of Karnataka.

As the Seven Years War broke out in Europe, fearing an attack from each other, both the English and the French began to fortify their settlements in Bengal in 1756 CE. This made the *nawab* uneasy, and he asked them to demolish the new structures. The French carried out his orders, while the English evaded him and continued with their task which annoyed him further. Besides, the English were also misusing their trading privileges—the *dastaks* (free trade passes)—granted by the Mughal emperor, Farrukh Siyyar in 1717 CE. Added to this, the relations between the English and Siraj-ud-daula became further strained when the former supported Krishna Das, the son of Rajballabh, who was implicated by the *nawab* of maintaining fake accounts. In order to escape punishment, Krishna Das asked the English for refuge, to which the latter readily obliged. It had now become clear that the English were favouring the *nawab's* opponents. Siraj-ud-daula, therefore, wanted to curb the activities of the English in Bengal.

Siraj-ud-daula first proceeded against the English base at Kasimbazar on 4 June 1756 CE; and then attacked Calcutta with a large army, capturing Fort William on 20 June 1756 CE. The English had not anticipated these attacks. Some Englishmen, however, put up a mild resistance under the leadership of Holwell, a junior member of the council. Unable to sustain the attack for more than a few days they eventually surrendered. It is said that after capturing Calcutta, Siraj-ud-daula confined 146 English in a tiny room without any ventilation, which resulted in the death of most of them. Holwell was among the 23 who survived what came to be known as the 'Black Hole Tragedy'. While various arguments have been advanced about this incident, it must be noted that Holwell was the first to make a mention of this tragedy. The general opinion is that his facts cannot be trusted enough, and the account seems to be an exaggerated one.

Feeling complacent with his initial success, the *nawab* of Bengal exhibited an over confidence that did not take into account any effective measures to safeguard his dominions, and nor did he do anything to win the support of his people. When the news of this incident reached Madras, Robert Clive and Admiral Charles Watson were sent to Bengal with a large contingent.

This was also when the news of the outbreak of the Seven Years War in Europe reached Calcutta; and the English felt that Siraj-ud-daula might ally himself with the French and expel the English from Bengal. Watson secured the permission of the *nawab* to attack the French at their base in Chandernagore. Clive, meanwhile, reoccupied Bengal in January 1757 CE and compelled Siraj-ud-daula to restore all privileges and possessions to the Company, compensate for the losses suffered and raise no objections to the fortification of the fort at Calcutta. The *nawab* had to agree to Clive's demands, but soon sought the help of the French at Chandernagore to drive out the English from Bengal. Acting quickly, Clive at once attacked Chandernagore and took possession of it, ready to deal with the *nawab*. In the meantime, Clive received a message from Mir Jafar, the commander in chief of the *nawab's* forces, claiming that he would grant valuable privileges to the English if they helped him dethrone Siraj-ud-daula and make him the *nawab* in his place. When Clive consented, Mir Jafar assured him that in case of an attack on the *nawab*, he would not fight for Siraj-ud- daula but would instead join the English with a large army. In return for Mir Jafar being made the *nawab* of Bengal, he agreed to reward the Company with certain territories while excluding the French from the province.

Soon Clive marched towards Murshidabad, the capital of Siraj-ud-daula. He had a small garrison of 500 European soldiers, 2,100 Indian sepoys and only ten guns. Siraj-ud-daula met Clive at the battlefield of Plassey, a small village near Murshidabad. He commanded an army of about 70,000 men and had 50 guns. It was an unequal fight, but Clive's strategy and Mir Jafar's treachery decided the fate of Siraj-ud-daula. When the battle began, Mir Jafar stood aloof with about 50,000 men under his command. Siraj-ud-daula realised the breach of trust too late and lost courage.

The Battle of Plassey was fought on 23 June 1757 CE in which the *nawab's* forces were defeated. Siraj-ud-daula first ran away to Murshidabad, and from there to Patna; but he was captured and put to death by Miran, the son of Mir Jafar. Clive made Mir Jafar the new *nawab* of Bengal.

The Battle of Plassey has immense historical importance in the sense that it made the Company the virtual rulers of the rich province of Bengal. Mir Jafar remained a mere puppet in the hands of the English while the real power behind the throne remained in the hands of Robert Clive. Mir Jafar gave 24 *parganas* and one crore rupees to the Company. The Company also got minting rights, besides other privileges of free trade in Bengal. The vast resources of Bengal enabled the English to defeat their serious European rivals, i.e., the French and the Dutch. Clive launched an attack on the Dutch at Chinsurah, capturing their ships and defeating them on land. They were allowed to keep Chinsurah as a trading centre alone, and could not fortify it. The battle of Plassey, therefore, paved the way for the conquest of India by the English.

Battle of Buxar

Although Mir Jafar had accepted the tutelage of the English, he was soon dissatisfied with their continuous dominance and interference in state affairs. His coffers were emptied by the demands of the Company's officials for presents and bribes. As a result, the large sum of money that he had promised to pay to the Company could not be paid out even after three years of his accession to the throne of Bengal. He grew restless under financial pressure and the growing supremacy of the English—who had decisively eliminated all other European rivals (e.g., the French and the Dutch) by reducing them to mere traders under the governorship of Clive. After successfully laying the foundations of British rule in India, Clive departed for England in 1760 CE. Meanwhile, there was a tussle between Mir Jafar and his son-in-law, Mir Qasim, on a succession issue. Vansittart, who had replaced Clive as the Governor of Calcutta, backed Mir Qasim as his candidate to the throne of Bengal. According to a treaty signed in 1760 CE, Mir Qasim became the new *nawab* of Bengal.

Even Mir Qasim, the new *nawab*, resented the stifling control exercised by the English. He wanted to exert his own authority and improve the financial condition of his province. To this end he shifted his capital from Murshidabad to Monghyr. His felt that since he had paid the English adequately for placing him on the throne he would expect the least interference from them. The servants of the East India Company, meanwhile, were abusing their right of free trade by indulging in private trade. They were selling the rights to Indian traders whose goods were exempt from taxes. Mir Qasim tried to stop this, but when he failed to do so effectively, he abolished all duties including all transit dues on internal trade. The English resented this step as they lost out on their special advantage; and a long dispute followed between Mir Qasim and the English which lasted for two years.

The fact was that there could not be two masters in Bengal at the same time. While Mir Qasim believed that he was an independent ruler, the Company officials demanded that he be a mere puppet in their hands. A conflict erupted in which Ellis, the chief of the English factory at Patna, led the movement against the *nawab*. He forcibly occupied Patna, provoking Mir Qasim to launch an attack against Ellis, who was defeated and imprisoned by the *nawab*. This dispute eventually led to a war between Mir Qasim and the English. Mir Qasim managed to get help from Shuja-ud-daula, the *nawab* of Awadh, and the Mughal emperor, Shah Alam II. The three marched together towards Patna with their combined forces of about 50,000 soldiers. The English met them at Buxar with a small force of about 7,000 soldiers and 20 guns, under the command of Major Munro. The battle was fought on 23 October 1764 CE, in which the three combined armies of Mir Qasim, Shuja ud Daula and Shah Alam II were defeated by the English. Mir Qasim fled and was never to be seen again; while Shuja- ud-daula and Shah Alam II surrendered themselves to the English.

This victory at the Battle of Buxar was of great importance to the English as they had defeated three great rulers of northern India, including the Mughal emperor. They could now demand any terms from the *nawab* of Awadh, who had lost his throne as well as the independence of Awadh. The Mughal emperor, Shah Alam II, for his part severed his alliance with Shuja-ud-daula, and took shelter with the English. This victory demonstrated that the English were superior in military strength and capable of establishing their supremacy beyond Bengal, Bihar and Orissa.

The Battle of Buxar confirmed the position of the Company as the *de facto* rulers of Bengal. The new *nawab* of Bengal, Mir Jafar's son, Najim ud Daula, was a puppet in the Company's hands; while the *nawab* of Awadh was totally subordinated, and the Mughal emperor had become a pensioner of the English.

Treaty of Allahabad

The directors of the Company in England, meanwhile, once again appointed Clive as the Governor of Bengal; and Clive, who was then in England, was sent back to India to settle matters. He negotiated the treaty of Allahabad in 1765 CE with the powers that had been defeated in the Battle of Buxar. Clive restored Awadh (except for the districts of Allahabad and Kara) to *nawab* Shuja-ud-daula in return for 50 lakh rupees as war indemnity. Awadh was made a buffer state between the English and the Marathas. The districts of Allahabad and Kara were given by Clive to the Mughal emperor, Shah Alam II, in return for the grant of the *Diwani* of Bengal, Bihar and Orissa, as well as the right to dispense civil justice in the region. This meant that the English were granted the authority to collect revenues in these provinces and settle local issues. The English also promised to pay an annual pension of twenty six lakh rupees to the Mughal emperor.

By gaining the *Diwani* powers, the Company's position as a territorial power in Bengal, Bihar and Orissa was legalized, and it was no longer just a body of merchant adventurers. Additionally, the Mughal emperor, Shah Alam II, became completely dependent on the Company for his maintenance, since he directly came under its protection. Although Mir Jafar's son was made the *nawab* in Bengal, the English remained the virtual rulers. Later even this puppet *nawab* was deposed in 1772 CE, and the Company assumed direct control of the province of Bengal, Bihar and Orissa. As a direct result of the battles of Plassey and Buxar, therefore, the English were able to establish their rule over the richest province in India.

Dual System or Dyarchy

The *nawab* of Bengal, as the viceroy of the Mughal emperor, performed two functions—that of the *Diwani* or revenue collection and dispensation of civil justice, and of the *Nizamat* or military defence and dispensation of criminal justice. Apart from the *Diwani* powers that the Mughal emperor had bestowed on the English, the *nawab* of Bengal also granted the *Nizamat* powers in February 1765 CE, which empowered Clive to take over the state's military division after disbanding the *nawab's* army. Clive was, however, not prepared to exercise all of the Company's sovereign rights. Though the Company controlled the state's foreign policy, the army and the treasury, the duties of revenue collection and the administration of justice were entrusted to the Indian officers of the *nawab*, who were appointed with the approval of the Company. This joint exercise of power by the Company and the officers of the *nawab* is known as the dual system of government or dyarchy.

In this system of dyarchy, the respective positions of both the *nawab* of Bengal and the Company were clearly defined. This eliminated any further possibility of clashes between the two powers in Bengal. If the Company had assumed complete responsibility it would have aroused the suspicion of the Indians. This system also removed the possibility of an Anglo-Maratha clash, which could have surfaced from the Company assuming all administrative responsibilities. The system also ensured a better financial position for the Company, since it could now function as a real master without incurring any responsibilities.

During this period, however, agriculture suffered, trade and manufacturing industries declined, and there was a drain of wealth from India to Europe. The English were only thinking of making profits by exporting raw silk and were not interested in manufactured goods from India. They exported goods purchased by the revenues of Bengal and collected revenue even in the times of famine in Bengal. The *nawab* had been made totally powerless and could only remain as a mute spectator to the misery of the people. With the meagre economic resources at his disposal he failed in his administrative endeavours; besides he had no real power to enforce the law either. Without the responsibility of administration, the English had at their disposal all the economic resources of the land. Hence, the most striking drawback of this system of dyarchy was that it separated power from responsibility. This arrangement brought back old abuses, making the administration of Bengal chaotic—agriculture and trade languished, while society began to stagnate.

SUMMARY

- After the death of Aurangzeb, the Mughal Empire began to disintegrate and various parts of the empire became independent under different rulers.
- In Bengal, Alivardi Khan became the independent *nawab* of Bengal. He was succeeded by his grandson, Siraj-ud-daula, who was suspicious of the English.
- Robert Clive diplomatically entered into a conspiracy with Mir Jafar, the commander of Siraj-ud-daula's forces, who assured the former that he would not fight for Siraj-ud-daula, but would instead join the English with a large army.
- When the battle began, Mir Jafar stood aloof with about 50,000 men under his command. Siraj-ud-daul realised the breach of trust too late and lost courage.
- The Battle of Plassey was fought on 23 June 1757 CE; the *nawab* of Bengal was defeated.
- The Battle of Plassey has immense historical importance as it made the Company the virtual ruler of the rich province of Bengal.
- Although Mir Jafar had accepted the tutelage of the English, he was soon dissatisfied with their continuous dominance. The English then replaced him with his son-in-law, Mir Qasim.
- While Mir Qasim believed that he was an independent ruler, the Company officials demanded that he remain a mere tool in their hands. The dispute between Mir Qasim and the English eventually led to war.
- Mir Qasim managed to get help from Shuja-ud-daula, the *nawab* of Awadh, and the Mughal emperor, Shah Alam II. The three regents marched together towards Patna with their combined forces.
- The English met them at Buxar with a small force on 23 October 1764 CE, in which the combined armies of Mir Qasim, Shuja-ud-daula and Shah Alam II were defeated.
- The Battle of Buxar confirmed the position of the Company as the new and prominent power, which was unchallengeable.
- Clive negotiated the treaty of Allahabad in 1765 CE with the powers that had been defeated in the Battle of Buxar.
- The most important clause of this treaty was that the English got the right to the *Diwani* of Bengal, Bihar and Orissa, as well as the right to dispense civil justice in the region.
- The *nawab* granted the Company the *Nizamat* powers in 1765 CE, empowering Clive to take over the military defence of the state.
- Clive was not prepared to exercise all the rights of sovereignty conferred upon the Company. The Company controlled the foreign policy, the army and the treasury; but the duties of collecting revenues and administration of justice were entrusted to the Indian officers of the *nawab*, who were appointed with the approval of the Company.

- This joint exercise of power by the Company and the officers of the *nawab* is called the dual system of government or dyarchy, in which the English had all the power without any responsibility.
- This arrangement of dyarchy brought back old abuses, making the administration of Bengal chaotic—agriculture and trade languished, while society began to stagnate.

KEYWORDS

Dastak

De facto ruler

Dyarchy

REVIEW QUESTIONS

1. How did the Battle of Plassey pave the way for the conquest of India by the English?
2. What was the significance of the Battle of Buxar?
3. Examine the important clauses of the treaty of Allahabad.
4. Write a short note on the dual system of government introduced by Robert Clive in Bengal.

CHAPTER 31

Ideologies and Tools of Colonial Expansion

Review and Discussion

- Colonial Ideologies
- Tools of Expansion

The eighteenth and early nineteenth centuries saw the Company establishing its political hegemony in different parts of India through the pursuance of diverse policies in conquering and subjugating various Indian states. Every regime needs a rationale to carry on its domination—the purpose which determines its actions and activities. In its transformation from a trading company into a political power in India, the Company made use of a number of ideologies. Orientalists like William Jones, evangelists like Charles Grant, utilitarians like James Mill, and statesmen like Munro or Dalhousie had their different purposes for justifying British rule in India. Yet, in their diversity of ideas, Britain's overbearing mission in India provided them the required unity in action.

Colonial Ideologies

As part of their imperial ideology and spurred by the gradual development of patriotism in the eighteenth century, the British perceived the ownership of overseas territorial possessions as a magnificent and rational philosophy. In the post-enlightenment intellectual environment, the British also began to consider themselves to be 'modern' or 'civilized' in comparison to the Orientals (or for that matter to the natives of just about any of their colonies), which helped them rationalize their perspective of imperial expansion in the nineteenth century.

Orientalism

Even after establishing their political hegemony in Bengal and other parts of the Indian subcontinent, the Company did not discontinue the established practices that were hitherto followed in these regions. They thought it most prudent to continue recognizing the authority of the Mughal emperor, strike coins in his name, use Persian as the official language and enforce Hindu and Islamic laws in the courts. The dual government or dyarchy introduced by Robert Clive in Bengal only partly bestowed upon the Company the power to administer civil and fiscal matters, under which the criminal justice system remained in the hands of the officials of the *nawab*. This policy of least intervention was implemented only to avoid civil disturbances; and even when the Company had to take on added responsibilities in administering India, the process progressed gradually.

The British felt that they had stepped into a system that was decaying and needed to be regenerated through their efforts. The early image of India in the West was that it was a land steeped in a glorious heritage which had undergone degeneration in later times. Perpetuating such ideas were persons like Edward Terry and John Ovington, who had come to India as travellers (1689 CE) and described the Mughal rule as yet another example of Islamic despotism. So, the general impression that had been formed in European minds was that from the seventeenth century onwards the age-old tradition of learning and acquiring knowledge no longer existed in India. While Terry argued that the *brahmans*—the ancient repositories of knowledge—had slipped into oblivion, other signs of this degeneration were seen by the British in the rigid caste system which they equated to a rigid mind. At the same time, the early administrators were keenly aware of India's past glory. They understood that to administer this country properly a thorough knowledge of India and its past was needed.

To this end, scholars like Sir William Jones studied the Indian languages with the objective of restoring to the Indians their own forgotten heritage and culture, thus, establishing a linguistic connection between Sanskrit, Greek and Latin. Jones compared India's glorious past to that of the Classical West. This was the beginning of the Orientalist tradition that led to the founding of institutions such as the Calcutta Madrassa in 1781 CE, the Asiatic Society of Bengal in 1784 CE and the Sanskrit College in Banaras in 1794 CE. These institutions were meant to promote the study of Indian languages and scriptures. However, while discovering the glory of India's past, the Orientalist scholars defined India's traditions in a manner that served the needs of the colonial state. Thus, it is argued that, Orientalism produced knowledge of the past to meet the requirements of the present.

In its early phase, Orientalism could be seen in practice in the policies of Warren Hastings which he executed on behalf of the Company. The fundamental principle of this tradition was that the conquered people were to be ruled by their own laws. Therefore, knowledge about Indian customs and the laws of the land needed to be understood by the English for more efficient administration. It was with this political objective that Fort William College at Calcutta was established in 1800 CE to train civil servants in Indian languages and traditions. The Orientalist philosophy even went a step further by asserting a kinship link between the British and the Indians from the days of the classical past, so that it became the moral responsibility of the former to improve the lot of the Indians. In other words, after highlighting the classical glory of India, the Orientalists also emphasized the subsequent degeneration of the once magnificent civilization and the need to guide India once again towards the path of development and progress.

Evangelicalism

In the early period of establishing institutions that helped discover India's past, the stress lay more on learning about India, but with the changing needs of the British merely this idea was not enough. Now the British found India to be a lucrative market to sell their manufactured goods. For this, at least the elite in India were to be introduced to a new way of life and culture so that the new products could enter Indian markets and find acceptance. The philosophy of Evangelicalism which stressed upon the importance of personal conversion and faith as a means of salvation made its entry into India to fight the deterioration of the way of life in India. It advocated the permanence of British rule and adoption of its culture as premises that would change India for the better. The early missionaries had respected Indian traditions and merely wanted to bring about social reforms in Indian society in their quiet and steady way. But missionaries, such as Charles Grant and others, who came to India in the seventeenth and eighteenth centuries, championed the causes of social reform and Christian mission by openly encouraging conversion to Christianity. Grant surmised that not only did Indian society not acknowledge the God of Christianity and Judaism and Islam, but it was also corrupt and uncivilized. He found Indian customs such as *sati* to be repulsive social practices. He believed that it was as much Britain's duty to civilize and Christianize Indians, as it was to expand its rule in India and safeguard Britain's commercial interests. Grant, therefore, propagated the policy of the absorption of India into the great civilizing mission of Britain through the promotion of Christianity. His ideas were supported by William Wilberforce in the British Parliament, before the Charter Act of 1813 CE was passed, which allowed Christian missionaries to enter India without any restrictions.

Liberalism and Utilitarianism

Liberalism is the belief in the importance of liberty and equality. In 1815 CE, the word appeared in English for the first time and by the mid-nineteenth century, it became a fully politicized term for parties and movements all over the world. The nineteenth century was the age of British liberalism, a political orientation that favoured progress and reform. Thomas Macaulay's enunciation of the idea that the task before the British administrators was to civilize rather than conquer, set the stage for the emancipation of Indians through active governance. While serving as a member of the Supreme Council of India, Macaulay advocated freedom of the press, equality of Europeans and Indians before the law, a national system of education which was Western in outlook, and as president of a commission on Indian jurisprudence he drafted a penal code that was later to become the basis of Indian criminal law. Yet another liberal, CE. Trevelyan's idea was based on the belief that as a result of British benevolence through the implementation of British education and political institutions, social conditions in India could be bettered. It was in the midst of such ideas that utilitarianism, with all its typical authoritarian tendencies, was born. With the induction of utilitarians like James Mill to the Company's London office, India's policies henceforth came to be guided by such doctrines. Utilitarianism—as a doctrine elaborated by Jeremy Bentham and James Mill—basically believed that whatever is useful is good, with the aim of achieving the greatest happiness for the greatest number. Mill in his book, *The History of British India* (1817 CE) critiqued William Jones for emphasising India's glorious past, instead he felt what India needed for her improvement was a wise government promulgating good legislation. Keeping in line with his thought, a Law Commission was appointed in 1833 CE under Lord Macaulay, which was responsible for drawing up an Indian Penal Code in 1835 CE.

Mill also supported the restructuring of the land revenue policy in a manner that would be consistent with utilitarian economics. While on the one hand this meant direct interaction with the cultivators (as in Munro's Ryotwari settlement), on the other hand it meant taxing the landlord to such an extent that the landlord would not enjoy undue benefit at the cost of manufacture and trade just by owning the land alone. The landholder would give the state a certain proportion of the net produce as tax on land revenue—this was enforced by officers like Pringle in Bombay. Elaborate survey methods were used to calculate the net produce from land before tax rates were assessed. In practice, however, the revenue demand often went very high, sometimes as much as 50–60 sixty per cent of the produce. This form of calculation slowly gave way to more scientific methods of assessment.

The underlying authoritarianism in the English utilitarian thought developed into full-fledged despotism in colonized areas. Utilitarianism, despite being born in the tradition of liberalism, could never accept a democratic government in India. Mill, for instance, consistently opposed any form of representative government in India. Taking a cue from Mill's thought of advancing Britain's mission in India, Lord Dalhousie too created departments with single heads for Post and Telegraph Services, the Public Works Department, Irrigation Department and the Railways as part of his policy towards the Indian states. He, thus, tried to bring centralized administrative systems within the framework of a unitary British Empire in India.

Victorian Liberalism

The latter half of the nineteenth century witnessed Victorian Liberalism as the predominant policy of the British Raj. After the revolt of 1857 CE, the British increasingly felt that it was pointless to bring reforms in India. Revering Indian culture through the discovery of India's glorious heritage began to gradually get overshadowed by a celebration of the superiority of the conquering race. With studies on the racial sciences emerging as a separate discipline in Victorian England during this time, physical features were recognized over languages as the chief indicators of racial identity. Thus, the theory of the civilized, white-skinned Caucasians coming to India in the form of the Aryans and confronting the dark-skinned natives of India was given shape. In other words, the new Orientalist discourse was producing knowledge of a backward, caste-ridden Indian society, thereby further rationalising colonial rule.

However, during the first half of the nineteenth century, along with racial arrogance, another theory—that elite sections in India were developing a taste for European products and culture—was gaining currency, giving rise to a new image of the 'brown sahib'. With the crowning of Queen Victoria as the Empress of India, a new hierarchical social order was created from the common man to the native princes, among whom the viceroy was the centre of power. The Ilbert bill controversy in 1883 CE marked the ultimate victory of pompous colonial trends and racial arrogance. The bill proposed by Lord Ripon tried to give Indian judges the right to try Europeans in courts of appeal. Under pressure from the English side, it had to be remodelled since it was found to be unacceptable to the colonial settlers. It was this very attitude and such authoritarian imperial orders that Indian nationalism had to challenge in the early twentieth century.

Thus, orientalism, evangelicalism, liberalism, utilitarianism and Victorian liberalism were all theoretical concepts that reinforced the idea of the British being bestowed with the responsibility of reforming India's socio-economic order. By emphasising on factors plaguing Indian society—caste system and *sati*—and the degeneration and inferiority of the Indian mind, the British cleverly professed a need for the construction of a new social order by way of a civilizing mission. This not only provided an ideological justification for colonizing India, but also elevated the imperialist mission of the British to an exalted status, while reducing Indians to the position of the underdog. This ideological conception has popularly been termed as the 'White Man's Burden'.

Tools of Expansion

With the gradual expansion of British power in the eighteenth century, through a series of conquests and elimination of rivals, they became politically entrenched in India. The British adopted various annexation policies such as Mediatization, Subsidiary Alliance, the Policy of Subordinate Isolation, the Doctrine of Lapse, and the Policy of Masterly Inactivity to achieve this status. These tools of expansion were selectively used against the Indian states during the creation of the British Empire in India.

Lord Wellesley followed a three-pronged approach to increase the Company's power in India. Sometimes territories were annexed after conquest, such as the state of Mysore; while at other times, the administration of a particular territory was assumed by the British when there were succession disputes or a minor heir became the crown prince. In such cases, those Indian rulers remained as mere titular heads of their states. This was known as the policy of Mediatization. Another important policy adopted by the British was the Subsidiary Alliance introduced by Lord Wellesley in Awadh and Hyderabad. According to this system, the state that had accepted this particular arrangement was brought under the protection of the British, whom they recognized as the sovereign power. The princes under British protection would not have any connection with European powers other than the English, a British Resident and contingent would be stationed in the kingdom, and some territories would be granted to the British for maintaining the subsidiary force. In addition, the ruler could not take any other Europeans into service without the consent of the British, while negotiations with other Indian states could also not be carried out without consulting the English governor-general. Furthermore, the states which had accepted the Subsidiary Alliance could not interfere in the internal affairs of allied states. The Company in return promised to protect the subsidiary state against internal and external aggression. This policy enabled the British to maintain their military at the expense of the Indian states.

Through the policy of Subsidiary Alliance, the British could annex extensive regions in India; but following their territorial acquisitions the Company was not ready to accept the increasing responsibility and expenditure that came along with it. So the decision to follow a policy of non-intervention was taken for nearly eight years, during which period the Governors-General—Lord Cornwallis, Sir George Barlow and Lord Minto—maintained a low profile. This policy gave the Company the time and opportunity to organize their finances, improve their commerce and stabilize the administration of provinces under their control.

Lord Hastings became the Governor-General in 1813 CE, marking a new stage in the history of the Company. He followed the policy of Subordinate Isolation, according to which, Indian states were subordinated to the paramount British authority to the extent that the latter even controlled the foreign policy of these states, prohibited mutual alliances and even military cooperation among subordinate states, and all disputes among subordinate states were also to be settled by the British alone. This policy, therefore, went a step further than the policy of Subsidiary Alliance, giving the British unlimited control.

When Lord Dalhousie became the Governor-General, he adopted a completely different approach. Many of the states at this time were under the policy of Subordinate Isolation, which had led to a condition where no one was ready to take responsibility for running the state—leading to bad governance. Dalhousie sought a way out of this by initiating the Doctrine of Lapse. According to this principle, a subsidiary or subordinate kingdom 'lapsed' or passed over into the hands of the Company when its ruler died without a direct heir to the throne, since the claims of an adopted son were not recognized. The states that lapsed into the hands of the British included Satara (1848 CE), Jaitpur and Sambalpur (1849 CE), Baghat (1850 CE), Udaipur (1852 CE), Jhansi (1853 CE), Nagpur (1854 CE) and Awadh (1856 CE); the last being the most important case in point. This policy of annexation alarmed the ruling classes in India, when they realized that one state after another was passing off into the hands of the British. Gradually the princes began to believe that the British had adopted this policy for the lone purpose of bringing the whole of India under their rule. The absence of a direct heir was not the only pretext which Lord Dalhousie adopted to annex the state of an Indian ruler; Awadh, for instance, was annexed on the plea that the state was not being governed properly.

With the success of the British in India, many other European nations were also in search of alternative trade routes to India. Hence, in the nineteenth century the possibility of reaching India through the Northwest frontier was being seriously considered. This would mean that the intermediate territories of Egypt, Iraq, Persia and

Afghanistan would acquire a new significance for the Company. Through Afghanistan an invading army could easily conquer the Punjab, and spread into the Gangetic valley. These possibilities created new problems to the defence of India and the political relations between England and Russia also had to be taken into consideration. The absorption of the Punjab into the British Empire extended its boundary almost up to Afghanistan. Russian power, meanwhile, had been steadily expanding in the Central Asian steppes, and by 1868 CE they had reached Samarqand, which lay close to the northern frontier of Afghanistan.

Between the two expanding empires of Britain and Russia lay Afghanistan—and British foreign policy towards it naturally was of vital importance. Three lines of policies were suggested to tackle the ensuing tension in the region. The first one advocated marking the Indus as the boundary line. Opposed to this was the Forward School which favoured the conquest of the tribal zone and the formation of a frontier along the Afghan boundary. The Indian Viceroy, Lord Lawrence (1864–69 CE), followed a third policy known as the Policy of Masterly Inactivity, according to which the British maintained amity with the Afghans and refrained from interfering in their domestic affairs. Lawrence felt that this was the best possible policy under the circumstances; and besides being inexpensive and cautious, it was in keeping with the spirit of the existing treaties. He felt that every reasonable advantage could be gained by remaining politically passive, so that the Afghans would not be instigated to ally with either Russia or Persia.

SUMMARY

- The eighteenth and early nineteenth centuries saw the Company establishing its political hegemony in different parts of India through the pursuance of varied policies in conquering and subjugating Indian states.
- As part of their imperial ideology—and spurred on by the gradual development of patriotism—the British perceived the possession of overseas territorial colonies as a magnificent and rational philosophy.
- In the post-enlightenment intellectual environment, the British also began to consider themselves as 'modern' or 'civilized' in comparison to the colonized people, and this rationalized their vision of imperial expansion in the nineteenth century.
- The British felt that it was important for the European rulers to acquire the knowledge of Indian customs and laws of the land for efficient administration.
- By highlighting the classical glory of India, the Orientalists emphasized the subsequent degeneration of the once magnificent Aryan civilization and the need to improve India once again towards the path of development and progress.
- Evangelicalism—a philosophy that stressed on the importance of personal conversion and faith as the means of salvation—entered India to fight the deterioration of the way of life in India.
- The Evangelicals believed that it was Britain's duty not simply to expand its rule in India, and exploit the subcontinent for its commercial interests, but also to civilize and Christianize.
- The Liberals too saw the task before the British administrators to civilize after conquest, thus setting the stage for the emancipation of Indians through active governance.
- Utilitarianism, despite being born in the tradition of liberalism, could never accept a democratic government in India. The underlying authoritarianism in the English utilitarian thought developed into full-fledged despotism in colonized areas.
- In the latter half of the nineteenth century it was Victorian liberalism that made the policy of controlling subordinates as the dominant ideology of the British Raj.
- Revering Indian culture through the discovery of India's glorious heritage was now getting overshadowed by a celebration of the superiority of the conquering race.
- All these new theories were geared towards rationalising authoritarian colonial rule and reinforcing the theory of the 'White Man's Burden'.
- With the gradual expansion of British power in the eighteenth century, through a series of conquests

and elimination of rivals, the British got politically entrenched in India.

- To achieve political consolidation in the Indian subcontinent, the British adopted various policies such as Mediatization, Subsidiary Alliance, Policy of Subordinate Isolation, Doctrine of Lapse, and the Policy of Masterly Inactivity. All these tools of expansion were selectively used against the Indian states.

KEYWORDS

Colonial ideology	Liberalism	The white man's burden	Subordinate Isolation
Orientalism	Utilitarianism	Mediatization	Doctrine of Lapse
Evangelicalism	Victorian liberalism	Subsidiary Alliance	Masterly Inactivity

REVIEW QUESTIONS

1. What were the principles of the theory of Orientalism as enunciated by the British?
2. Give an account of how evangelicalism developed as a rationalist discourse in justifying colonial rule in India.
3. Explain how the ideas of liberalism and utilitarianism framed British imperial policy towards India.
4. Define Victorian liberalism.
5. Write an essay about the various tools of expansion used by the British in acquiring territories in India.

CHAPTER **32**

British Confrontation with Native and Neighbouring States

Review and Discussion

- The Anglo-Mysore Wars
- The Anglo-Maratha Wars
- Relations Between the British and Awadh
- The Anglo-Sikh Wars
- British Expansion in the North East
- British Relations with Central Asia

Ambitious in scope and geographical breadth, the British Empire in India was the embodiment of foreign political imperialism. Many princely states surrounded Britain's colonial possessions in the heart of the Indian subcontinent. As a result of their expansionist policies, the British often fell into confrontation with these Indian states, leading to several wars, among which the conflicts with Mysore, Awadh, the Marathas and the Sikhs are significant. To further consolidate their position, the British also felt the need to subdue and keep in check Burma and Central Asia.

The Anglo-Mysore Wars (1767–99 CE)

As discussed in Chapter 28, the state of Mysore had risen to political prominence in southern India under the leadership of Haidar Ali in 1761 CE. The wars of succession in Karnataka and Hyderabad, the conflict between the English and the French in the southern provinces, and the defeat of the Marathas in the Third Battle of Panipat (1761 CE) had all helped Haidar Ali in consolidating the kingdom of Mysore. After coming to power, Haidar Ali had to face numerous conflicts with the Marathas and the English. On one such occasion, in 1764 CE the Maratha Peshwa, Madhav Rao, defeated Haidar Ali, and a treaty was signed in 1765 CE, according to which Haidar Ali had to surrender a part of his territory to the Marathas, besides paying an annual tribute of twenty eight lakh rupees. As for the British, there were four major conflicts between them and the state of Mysore which led to the waning of the kingdom.

The First Anglo-Mysore War (1767–69 CE)

Provoked by the Nizam of Hyderabad, the British decided to subdue Haidar Ali, resulting in the First Anglo-Mysore War. While Haidar Ali desired to rid

Karnataka, and finally India, of the British, the latter always felt threatened by Haidar Ali's dynamic presence. To keep a check on his mercurial growth, a tripartite alliance was formed against Haidar Ali by the the British, the Nizam and the Marathas, but Haidar Ali succeeded in breaking the alliance and declaring war on the British. The war ended with the defeat of the British and the signing of the Treaty of Madras in 1769 CE, which called for a mutual restoration of each other's territories, and the formation of a defensive alliance between the two parties, committing the British to come to the aid of the state of Mysore in case of external attacks. The signatories to the treaty included Haidar Ali, the Company, the Raja of Thanjavur and the ruler of Malabar.

The Second Anglo-Mysore War (1780–84 CE)

The treaty of Madras was more of a truce between Mysore and the British, which gave Haidar Ali the opportunity to accuse the Company of not observing the terms of the treaty when they refused to help him against a Maratha attack in 1771 CE. In contrast, Haidar Ali found the French more helpful than the British. In 1778 CE when the British seized the French settlements—including Mahe, a port which was very crucial to Mysore for the entry of supplies into the kingdom—Haidar Ali entered into a coalition with the Nizam and the Marathas against the British. The ensuing war came to be known as the Second Anglo-Mysore War; but his untimely death in 1782 CE thrust the responsibility of continuing the war upon his son, Tipu Sultan. With success eluding both sides, the treaty of Mangalore (1784 CE) decided that the British would restore Srirangapatnam to Tipu, while Tipu would handover the fort of Badnur to the British. The two parties also agreed not to assist each other's rivals directly or indirectly, nor fight each other's allies. The trade privileges granted to the Company by Haidar Ali in 1770 CE were restored too, and Tipu also agreed to release all prisoners of war.

The Third Anglo-Mysore War (1789–92 CE)

The third confrontation between Tipu Sultan and the British continued for three years, ending in Tipu's defeat in 1792 CE. Even though Tipu fought bravely, Lord Cornwallis diplomatically isolated him by winning over the Marathas, the Nizam, as well as the rulers of Thiruvitamkur and Coorg. It was yet again proved that Indian states which trusted Europeans for the sake of temporary gains were ultimately defeated. The Third Anglo-Mysore War came to an end with the treaty of Srirangapatnam (March 1792 CE) signed between Tipu and the British in the presence of their allies, the Nizam and the Peshwa. Nearly half of the territory of Mysore was handed over to the British, including Baramahal, Dindigul and Malabar; while the Marathas acquired the territory along the Tungabhadra, and the Nizam acquired the territories between Krishna and Pennar. In addition, Tipu also had to pay a war indemnity of over three crore rupees. Two of his sons were to be detained as British hostages until the terms of the treaty were fulfilled.

The Fourth Anglo-Mysore War (1799 CE)

After his defeat in the Third Anglo-Mysore War, Tipu Sultan wanted to settle scores with the British; and went on to negotiate with the French and Zaman Shah of Kabul to help him regain his lost territory as well as to expel the British. After entering into a Subsidiary Alliance with the Nizam, Lord Wellesley expected Tipu to do the same; but upon his refusal, the British attacked Mysore in 1799 CE. The British army, under General Harris, supported by the Nizam's subsidiary force, under Arthur Wellesley, attacked Mysore from the east, while yet another British army advanced from Bombay on the west.

Tipu's forces were initially defeated by the British army advancing from the Bombay side and later by General Harris at Mallavalli. Tipu Sultan died fighting bravely at Srirangapatnam, after which an incumbent from the earlier royal family of Mysore was installed on the throne and a Subsidiary Alliance was imposed on the state. With this, Mysore lost all its former glory.

The Anglo-Maratha Wars (1775–1818 CE)

The British were in the phase of consolidating their claim over South Asia. The process, initiated with the battles of Plassey and Buxar and carried forward with the Anglo-Mysore wars, saw further consolidation with the Anglo-Maratha wars which were fought between the British and the Marathas.

The First Anglo-Maratha War (1775–82 CE)

The internal problems of the Marathas and the growing ambitions of the British was the initial cause of the power struggle between the two. The situation worsened when the British began to interfere in the internal affairs of the Marathas at Bombay. After the death of Peshwa Madhav Rao in 1772 CE, he was succeeded by his younger brother, Narain Rao. But his uncle, Raghoba, who aspired to become the next *peshwa*, had him murdered. This event unified the Maratha chiefs to take up the cause of Madhav Rao Narain, the son of Narain Rao, while Raghoba approached the British for help and signed the Treaty of Surat, hoping to gain the throne with the help of the British subsidiary troops. The treaty also specified that he cede Salsette and Bassein to the British, and refrain from making any alliances with the Company's rivals. In the ensuing war, nobody gained anything; and finally, the Treaty of Salbai was concluded in 1782 CE, according to which status quo was maintained. This gave the British 20 years of peaceful relations with the Marathas besides enabling the British to exert pressure on Mysore with the help of the Marathas in recovering their territories from Haidar Ali.

The Second Anglo-Maratha War (1803–06 CE)

The Second Anglo-Maratha war was fought when Lord Wellesley wanted the Marathas to accept his Subsidiary Alliance system. When Baji Rao II was defeated by Yashwantrao Holkar, the ruler of Indore, at the Battle of Poona in October 1802 CE, he looked to the British for support, and in December he concluded the Treaty of Bassein with them. Accordingly a subsidiary force was to be maintained at the Maratha capital in return for some territory and the *peshwa* was also to promise not to enter into a treaty with any other power. At this time the British also had to check the French influence in India.

None of the Maratha chiefs liked this arrangement and soon the Scindias, Bhonsles and Holkars together put up resistance against the British. The Scindias and Bhonsles were defeated in different battles by the British while Yashwant Rao Holkar proved more than a match for them. Wellesley was eventually recalled from India and the Company made peace with Holkar in January 1806 CE through the Treaty of Rajghat, returning many of his territories to him.

The Third Anglo-Maratha War (1817–18 CE)

The Marathas made a desperate last attempt to regain their independence and prestige in 1817 CE. A united front of the Maratha chiefs under the *peshwa* was organized to oust the British Resident who was exercising rigid control. While the *peshwa* attacked the British Residency at Poona in 1817 CE, Appa Saheb of Nagpur attacked the Residency at Nagpur and Madhav Rao Holkar helped them in their attempts. The British defeated the Maratha forces and many territories were taken away from its various members. This was accomplished by Lord Hastings in 1818 CE making the British the supreme and paramount authority in India.

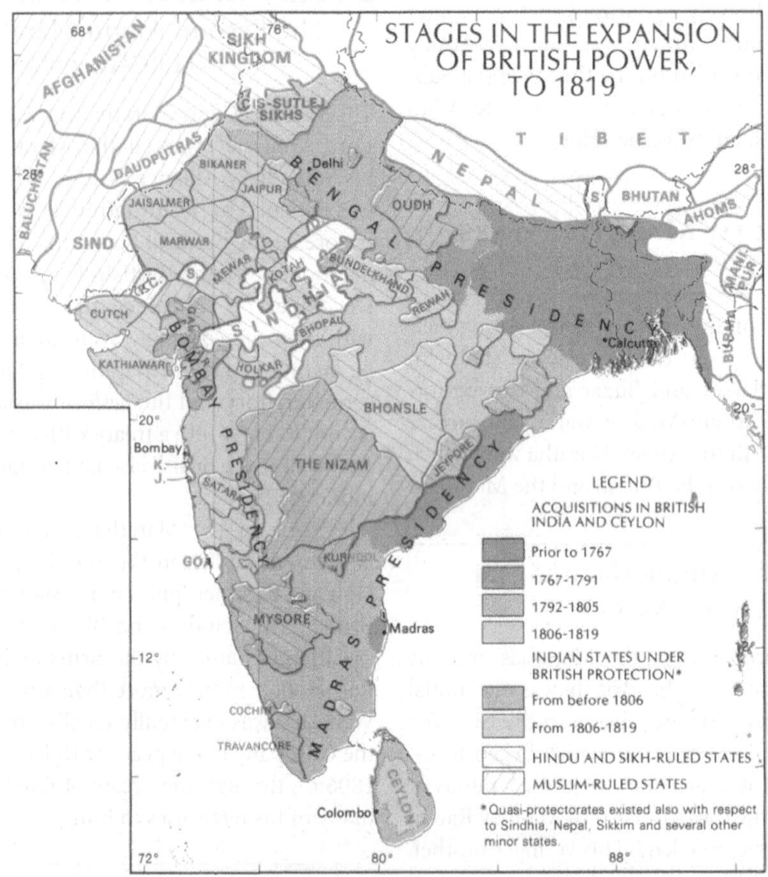

Map 32-1 *Stages in the Expansion of British Power to 1819 CE*

Relations Between the British and Awadh

Using Awadh as a buffer state against the attacks of the Marathas and the Afghans was part of the foreign policy of Lord Hastings. When Lord Dalhousie became the Governor-General in 1848 CE, he implemented the policy of the Doctrine of Lapse, through which he acquired the states of Satara, Jaitpur, Sambalpur, Baghat and Nagpur, among many others. The most important of the annexations was that of Awadh, which had been a protected state since Lord Wellesley's treaty of 1801 CE, enjoying complete independence in internal affairs. The royal court at Awadh had become a centre of decadence and vices; while state administration was neglected, adding to the misery of the people and the oppression of the *talukdars*. The British had warned the *nawab* earlier that if administration did not improve, the kingdom would be annexed to British India. But the threats proved futile, and in 1851 CE. Sir William Sleeman, the British Resident at Lucknow, reported the deplorable state of affairs and callous attitude of the government. Dalhousie initially suggested taking over the administration in Awadh, and leaving the ruler with his nominal sovereignty, but later the British decided upon annexation. When the *nawab* of Awadh was called upon to sign a treaty handing over the whole state, he refused, and the British forcibly took over Awadh.

Annexing Awadh had serious consequences for the British. The Company had benefitted from the treaty of 1801 CE and the rulers of Awadh had remained Britain's most faithful allies. Hence the annexation of the kingdom was seen as a breach of trust. Not only did the Muslim elite feel alienated with the loss of the *nawab's* power; but many in the British army's Indian troops—many of whom came from Awadh—were also antagonized because they had occupied a privileged position before the annexation and their present treatment was equivalent to a loss of prestige. Moreover, after Dalhousie's departure in 1856 CE, Awadh's landed aristocracy lost many of its privileges. As a result, there was a growing sense of discontent among many sections of the Indian society which greatly contributed to the Revolt of 1857 CE.

The Anglo-Sikh Wars (1845–49 CE)

The two Anglo-Sikh Wars were fought on separate occasions between the Sikhs and the British from 1845–49 CE. They marked the fulfilment of the British imperialist ambitions of extending the British Empire up to the natural boundary of India to the northwest.

The First Anglo-Sikh War (1845–46 CE)

The Sikh state of the Punjab had been built into a formidable power by Maharaja Ranjit Singh; but soon after his death there were a series of palace disputes and assassinations. By 1843 CE the youngest son of Ranjit Singh was placed on the throne, and his mother proclaimed queen regent. Actual power, however, rested with the army which remained in the hands of military committees. Relations with the Sikhs and the British had already become strained when the former refused to allow British troops to pass through their territory during the First Anglo-Afghan War. The Sikhs had resolved to invade British territory in India under the pretext of averting a British attack, and crossed the Sutlej in December 1845 CE. In four decisive battles fought at Mudki, Firuzpur, Aliwal and Sobraon, the Sikh forces were routed. The British annexed lands belonging to the Sikhs along the Sutlej and Beas and a British Resident was also stationed at Lahore with a contingent of British troops. Thus, as a result of the first war between the Sikhs and the British the Sikh state in northwestern India came under British domination.

The Second Anglo-Sikh War (1848–49 CE)

The Second Anglo-Sikh War resulted in the subjugation of the Sikh kingdom and the absorption of the Punjab by the British. On 19 April 1848 CE, Vans Agnew, a civil servant, and Lieutenant Anderson of the Bombay European regiment, who had been sent to take charge of Multan from its governor, Diwan Mulraj, were murdered there. Following this incident, the Sikh troops and *sardars* shortly joined together in an open rebellion. Lord Dalhousie and Sir Hugh Gough, the commander-in-chief, realized that the Company's military forces were neither adequately equipped with transport and supplies, nor prepared to launch a field attack. Besides, if the rebellion spread, it would become necessary to capture Multan and subjugate the Punjab. Dalhousie, therefore, organized a strong army and proceeded towards the Punjab. Despite the brilliant successes gained by Herbert Edwardes in the Second Anglo-Sikh War against Mulraj, and Gough's victories at Ramnagar, Sadulapur, and at the Battle of Chillianwala (13 January 1849 CE), the resistance put up by the Sikhs at Multan proved to be extremely challenging for the British. On 22 January the fortress at Multan was taken over by General Whish, who soon joined Gough at Gujarat. The British won the Battle of Gujarat (21 February 1849 CE), with the Sikh army surrendering at Rawalpindi, and their Afghan allies fleeing India. After the Gujarat victory, Lord Dalhousie annexed the Punjab for the Company in 1849 CE; while Dilip Singh, the Sikh Maharaja, was pensioned off and the Punjab put under a Board of three commissioners. The Board was later abolished, and Sir John Lawrence appointed as the Chief Commissioner of the province.

BRITISH EXPANSION IN THE NORTH EAST

The expansion of Burma had serious consequences, especially along its frontiers. As those frontiers moved ever closer to British India, there were problems both with refugees and military operations spilling over ill-defined borders. In response to the continued expansion and even direct attacks by Burma, the British and the Siamese joined forces against it in 1824 CE.

The First Anglo-Burmese War (1824–26 CE)

As part of its aggressive expansionist policy, Burma had seized Tenasserim from Siam in 1766 CE; taken over Arakan into the kingdom of Ava in 1784 CE; and conquered Manipur in 1813 CE. This advancement towards the Indian borders ruffled British feathers; but immediate conflict was avoided, since the British were involved in other areas. When the Burmese seized the Shalpuri Island near Chittagong in 1823 CE, which was owned by the Company, an Anglo-Burmese conflict became inevitable in February 1824 CE.

The British had decided to launch a sea attack against the Burmese to take over Rangoon, which lay on the banks of the Irrawadi. Thus, a joint naval and infantry expedition was organized at Port Cornwallis in the Andaman Islands, under Brigadier General Archibald Campbell and Commodore Grant. The 13th Regiment, which made up part of the 11,000-strong infantry regiment, was placed under the command of Major Robert Sale. The regiment occupied the island of Cheduba on the Arakan Coast, before attacking Rangoon and converting it into a defensive stronghold. The Burmese, however, offered stiff opposition to the British and surrounded Rangoon.

By February 1826 CE, the Anglo-Indian army had advanced towards Yandaboo, near Rangoon. The British advance on the capital caused the Burmese to flee; and the King of Ava sent out a peace treaty to British, offering to pay the expenses of the war together with a considerable part of his territory.

The Second Anglo-Burmese War (1852–53 CE)

The Second Anglo-Burmese War led to the annihilation of Burma's political independence. On 15 March 1852 CE Lord Dalhousie dispatched a force of 8,100 troops to Rangoon, under the command of General H. T. Godwin, while Commodore Lambert commanded the naval contingent. The British took over Martaban in April 1852 CE. Rangoon and the Shwe Dagon pagoda were occupied after heavy fighting, when the Burmese army retired northwards. Thereafter, Pegu was taken over after some intensive rounds of fighting around the Shwe-maw-daw pagoda. Later, the approval of the Company's court of directors and of the British government was obtained for the annexation of the lower Irrawadi valley, including Prome. Lord Dalhousie visited Rangoon and discussed the situation with the civil, military and naval authorities; and thereafter General Godwin was given the charge of occupying Prome, which was accomplished after minor resistance. Lord Dalhousie informed King Pagan that the province of Pegu would henceforth form part of the British dominions, and that if his troops resisted the measure his whole kingdom would be destroyed. The proclamation of annexation was issued on 20 January 1853 CE; and thus, the Second Burmese War came to an end without any treaty being signed.

The Third Anglo-Burmese War (1885–86 CE)

The Third Anglo-Burmese War lasted just for a year. It all began when a letter was sent by the ministerial council of Burma to the French premier suggesting teh formulation of a bilateral treaty between them. This posed a direct threat to British teak monopolies in Lower Burma. Meanwhile, the Burmese imposed a fine on the Bombay Burma Trading Corporation for under-reporting its extractions of teak from Toungoo.

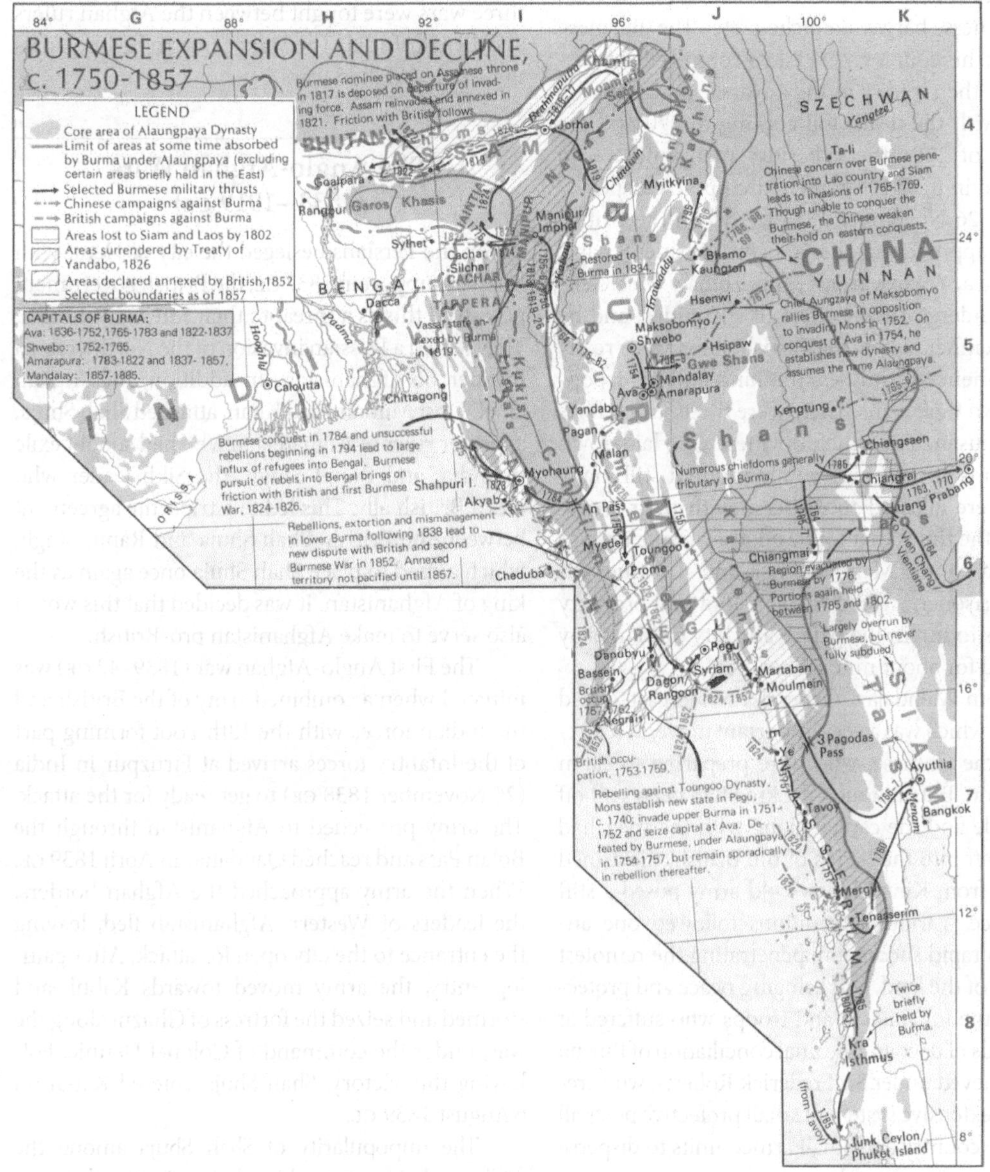

Map 32-2 *Burmese Expansion and Decline, 1750–1857 CE*

This provoked the British to occupy Mandalay and dethrone King Thibaw.

Being unfamiliar with Burmese topography, the British steamers, under the command of Major-General Prendergast, restricted their advancement to the river Irrawadi, which they had navigated earlier. The fleet consisted of no less than 55 steamers, barges, launches, etc. The Burmese king and his country were taken completely by surprise by the rapidity of the advance; and were defeated with the death toll coming to 170 and the capture of 276 others, besides many more who drowned in the river in their attempt to escape.

On 26 November 1885 CE, when the British flotilla approached the ancient Burmese capital of Ava, envoys from King Thibaw met General Prendergast with offers of surrender; and by 27 November, when the British ships were ready to commence hostilities, the king and his troops laid down their arms. There were three strong forts with thousands of armed Burmese who laid down their arms at the king's command; but still many more were allowed to disperse with their weapons. In the times that followed, they broke up into guerrilla bands. Mandalay fell, and the king was taken prisoner. All the valuable loot and property that was found in the palace and city of Mandalay was sold for about nine lakh rupees.

From Mandalay, General Prendergast seized Bhamo, which was a very important move, as it forestalled the Chinese, who were preparing to claim the region. But, although the king had been sent off into exile and the capital along with the river had passed off into the hands of the British, the armed bandits from King Thibaw's old army posed a stiff resistance. Various expeditions followed one another in rapid succession, penetrating the remotest corners of the land, and bringing peace and protection to the inhabitants and troops who suffered at the hands of dacoits. The final conciliation of Burma was achieved under Sir Frederick Roberts, who created an extensive system of small protective posts all over the country and small armed units to disperse the Burmese groups whenever they appeared.

British Relations with Central Asia

Britain's relations with Afghanistan were critical, as Russia—another strong power—was the immediate neighbour of Afghanistan. A series of three wars were fought between the Afghan rulers and British India. The wars came to be known as the Anglo-Afghan wars.

The Anglo-Afghan Wars (1838 –1919 CE)

When the Persians besieged the city of Herat with Russian support in 1837 CE, the British government perceived this as a threat to their interests in India. They feared a Russian invasion of the Northwestern frontier of Afghanistan. In addition, the Afghan chief, Dost Muhammad Khan, attacked Shah Shuja, a former ruler of Afghanistan who had sought exile in India, and Ranjit Singh, the Sikh leader who was a British ally. This led to a tripartite agreement between the British, Shah Shuja and Ranjit Singh, which aimed to place Shah Shuja once again as the king of Afghanistan. It was decided that this would also serve to make Afghanistan pro-British.

The First Anglo-Afghan war (1839–42 CE) was initiated when a combined army of the British and the Indian forces with the 13th Foot forming part of the infantry forces arrived at Firuzpur in India (26 November 1838 CE) to get ready for the attack. The army proceeded to Afghanistan through the Bolan Pass and reached Qandahar in April 1839 CE. When the army approached the Afghan borders, the leaders of Western Afghanistan fled, leaving the entrance to the city open for attack. After gaining entry, the army moved towards Kabul, and stormed and seized the fortress of Ghazni along the way, under the command of Colonel Dennie. Following this victory, Shah Shuja entered Kabul on 6 August 1839 CE.

The unpopularity of Shah Shuja among the Afghans, however, could only be offset with heavy

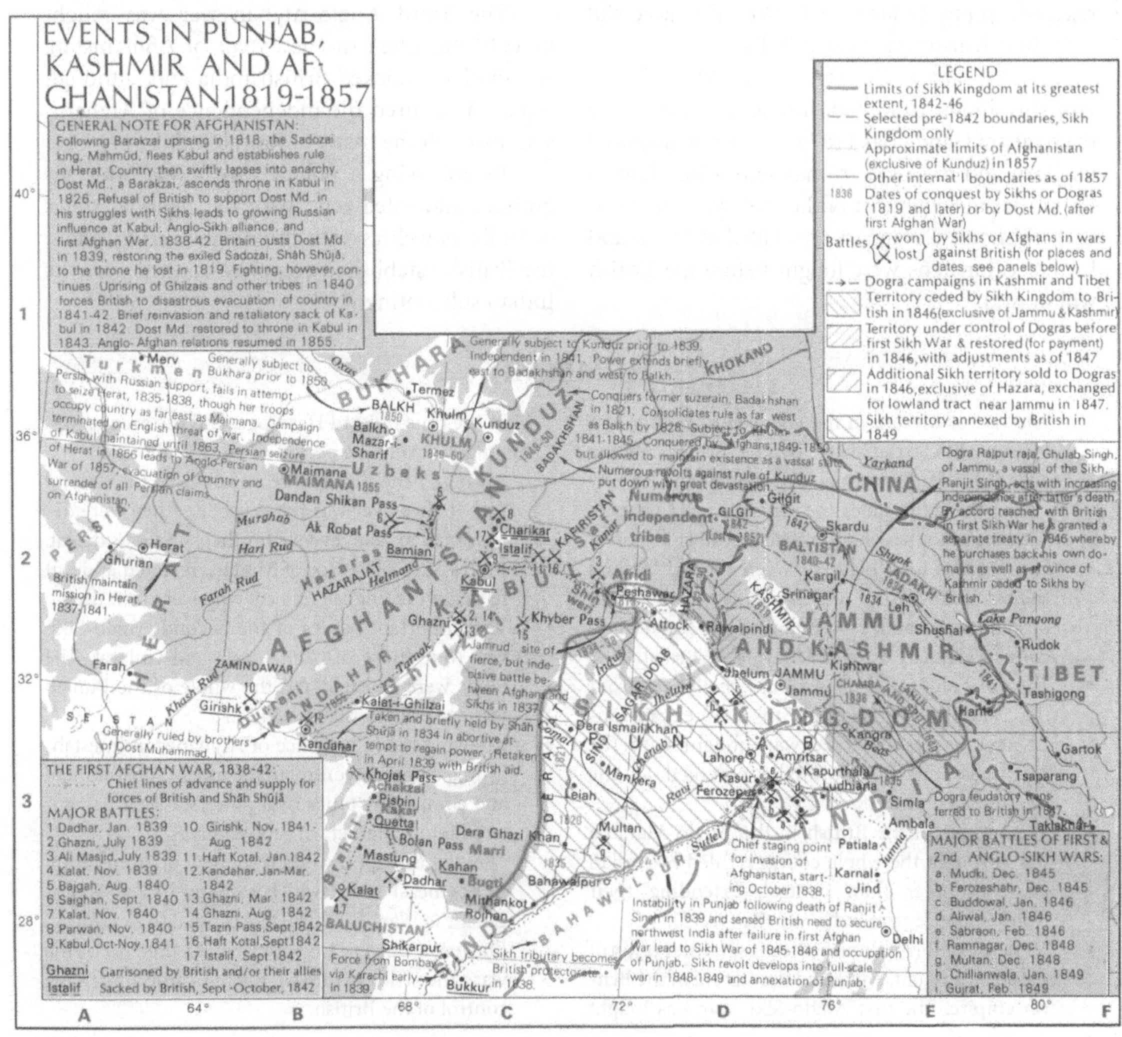

Map 32-3 *Events in the Punjab, Kashmir and Afghanistan, 1819–1857* CE

British backing. In October 1841 CE Akbar Khan, the favourite son of Dost Muhammad Khan, revolted. Khurd Kabul Pass and Gandamak became scenes of major action, resulting in an Afghan insurrection at Kabul, the overthrow of Shah Shuja, and the death of the British envoy in Afghanistan. Events took a turn for the worse, and the British army fled from Kabul with great difficulty. A relief force, led by General Pollack, was on its way, when all of a sudden an earthquake hit Jalalabad, and Pollack's force was destroyed while crossing the Khyber Pass. On 7 April 1842 CE—known in the Indo-British regiment's history as Jalalabad Day—an attack was launched on the Afghans, who were pushed back before fleeing the scene. Just a week later, General Pollack's forces reached Jalalabad, before the remaining garrisons of the army reoccupied Kabul once again. The prisoners held by the Afghans were soon released; and by 12 October 1842 CE the successful Indo-British army returned to India.

The Second Anglo-Afghan war (1878–80 CE) was also fought to exclude Russian influence. By the treaty of Gandamak (1879 CE) Britain acquired territory and the right to maintain a Resident in Kabul, but in September of the same year the Resident, Sir Louis Cavagnari, was killed in Kabul and further campaigns were fought before the British withdrawal.

The Third Anglo-Afghan war was fought in 1919 CE, when the new *amir* of Afghanistan, Amanullah, attacked British India and, although repulsed, secured the independence of Afghanistan through the treaty of Rawalpindi in 1919 CE.

By following a policy, which was both aggressive and intelligent, with the regional states of India as well as with the neighbouring states, the British established complete control over the Indian subcontinent.

SUMMARY

- The rise of Mysore in the eighteenth century was viewed with great alarm by the British. Taking advantage of the mutual dissensions and enmity among the native states, the British formed alliances with the Marathas and the Nizam against Mysore.
- Four battles took place between the British and the rulers of Mysore, which resulted in the death of Haidar Ali and Tipu Sultan, with Mysore becoming virtually a dependency of the British.
- The British faced a serious challenge from the Marathas with regard to their expansionist agenda. In the three wars fought with the Marathas, the British finally emerged as the unparalleled power.
- The success of the British in the Anglo-Maratha wars brought the whole country, ruled by Indian princes, under their control—extending their frontiers to Central India and the Deccan.
- The annexation of Punjab, the most fertile region of the subcontinent, enhanced the stature of the British empire. The first Anglo-Sikh war was fought in the time of Lord Hardinge; and the second was fought during the period of Lord Dalhousie.
- Although the Sikhs were defeated in the second war, their power was not crushed. They were determined to take revenge for their previous defeat. Mulraj, the Governor of Multan, revolted and put to death the English officers who were sent there.
- The important battles of the Second Anglo-Sikh war were those of Chilianwala and Gujarat. The Sikhs were defeated and the whole of the Punjab was annexed in March 1849 CE.
- Knowing the importance of Afghanistan in establishing complete control in the Indian subcontinent and eliminating other rival powers, the British entered into a conflict with the Afghans.
- The British applied their policy of annexation to northeast India, which resulted in the Anglo-Burmese Wars. The British intended to exclude all European powers from Burma. At the end of the wars the whole of lower Burma came under the control of the British.

KEYWORDS

Tripartite alliance　Defensive alliance　Nominal sovereignty　Bilateral treaty

REVIEW QUESTIONS

1. Examine the conflict between the Mysore state and the British.
2. What were the consequences of the Anglo-Maratha wars?
3. Write a short note on the first and second Anglo-Sikh Wars.
4. Give an account of the relations between the British and Awadh.
5. Briefly explain the reasons for the First Afghan War.

CHAPTER **33**

Eighteenth Century India: Economy and Society

Review and Discussion

- Colonial Economy
- Socio-Cultural Conditions

By the mid eighteenth century, the ruin of the Mughal Empire had led to such socio-economic conditions in India that were in stark contrast to the political unity and fair amount of peace that had been achieved by the great Mughals. At the height of their glory, the Mughals had succeeded in giving the Indian sub-continent a centralized administration, a uniform revenue policy, a network of inland trade and an expanding overseas commerce. The period between the death of Aurangzeb in 1707 CE and the Revolt of 1857 CE saw the strengthening of British influence in India—first in trade and commerce, and then in their manipulations to gain a political foothold.

After the establishment of British rule in Bengal, conditions rapidly changed in other parts of India too. The flourishing economy and export of Indian goods, especially of textiles to Europe and other countries, received a major setback. The massive demand that Indian goods enjoyed in foreign markets was no longer promoted by the British, thus, turning the system into a one-sided import-dependent one. The British similarly began to reorganize the agricultural system too. Once they started to control land revenue collection, they actively restructured agrarian policies governing the farmers and the categories of crops that were hitherto grown. Since all efforts were concentrated in making profits, these policies did not take into account the needs of the Indians. The revenue reforms brought in by the British demanded the landlords to be submissive and pay a large part of their produce as land revenue. This could only be met by producing cash crops, which the British preferred, and it turned out to be profitable. The repercussions of such policies were disastrous, leading to a massive depletion in the cultivation of food crops; and in times of famine there was no adequate storage of grains to see the people through the hard times.

Indian society was in the process of being transformed for the worse. By the time the British established their political lineage in India, many social evils, such as caste and class were gaining momentum along with *sati*, female infanticide, dowry and the sad plight of widows. By and large, the position of women was also on the ebb. These factors went into degrading the already tumultuous condition of Indians who had to cope hard to adjust with the new colonial regime.

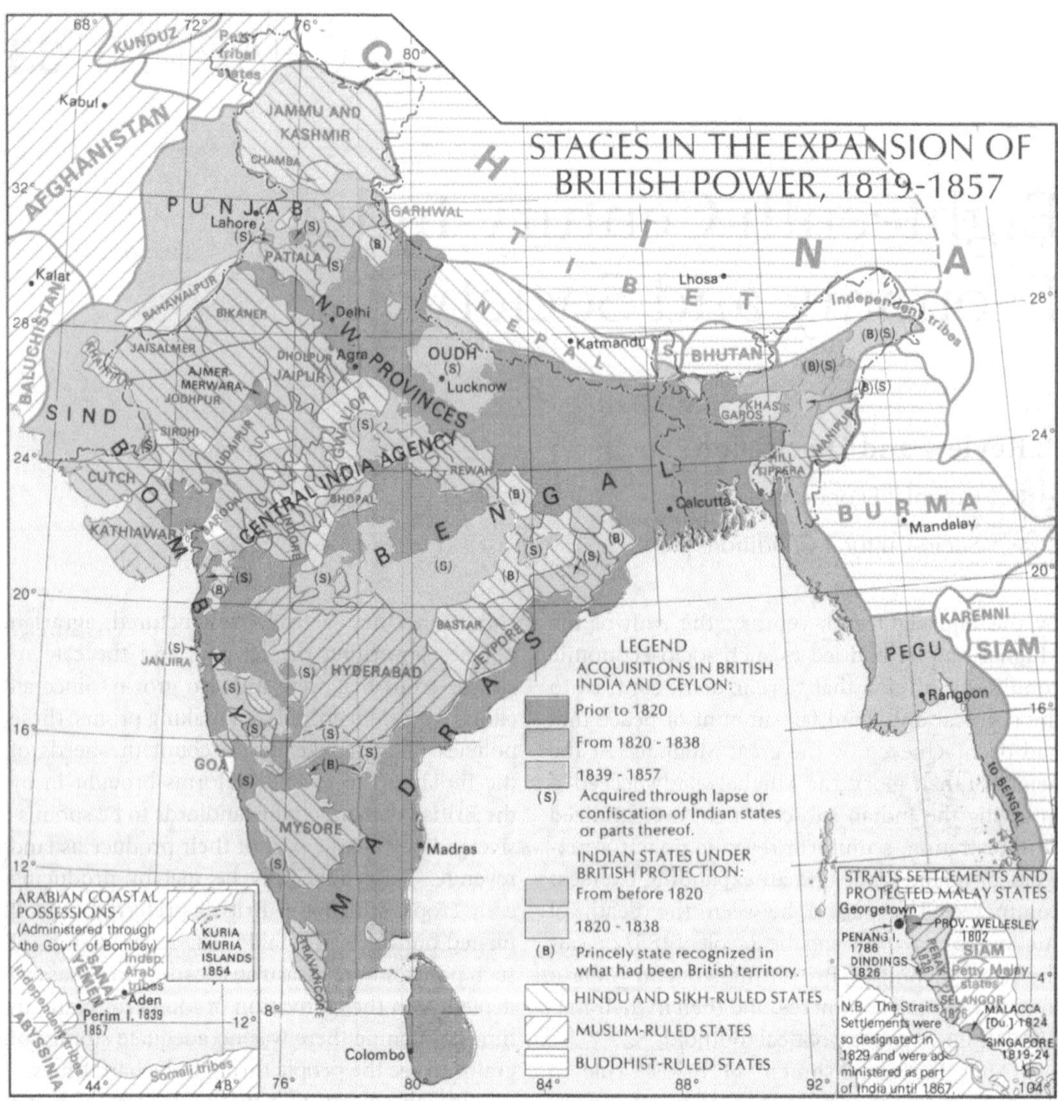

Map 33-1 *Stages in the Expansion of British Power, 1819–1857 CE*

Colonial Economy

The rise of merchant capitalism in Europe led to the formation of the East India Companies in European nations, which had as their principal endeavour, the establishment of trading ventures overseas. The East India Companies of Europe were some of the earliest joint stock companies in the world that were conferred by their respective governments with certain trade privileges. In the course of the eighteenth century, the Company and its servants acquired a monopolistic position to export commodities to some parts of India. This correlated with the increasing political hegemony and territorial expansion of the Company in India.

Land Revenue Settlements

Agriculture was always the most important economic activity of the Indians for many centuries, in turn providing rulers with the opportunity to draw a large part of their taxes from it. When the British acquired territorial control in India, they instituted various land revenue settlements which would facilitate them in imposing and collecting land taxes.

After the Battle of Plassey (1757 CE), the British did not find it necessary to replace the old system of economic administration in the province of Bengal as had been established by the *nawabs*. Rather they felt that they could collect large amounts of revenue for themselves through the established policies. However, corrupt practices among the Company's officials and their interference in the administration of the province led to chaos which was further escalated by a terrible famine in 1769–70 CE, in which it was estimated that one-third of the people of Bengal lost their lives.

Therefore, to bring reforms within the system, from 1772 CE, farming of taxes was introduced. Under this system, the government awarded the collection of land revenue to the highest bidder on a contractual basis. The bidder who offered to pay the largest amount of revenue from a certain district or subdivision within his jurisdiction was given full powers for a certain number of years. Initially the contract was awarded for a year and later increased to five years (quinquennial settlement). Holding a tenure based assignment, the revenue farmers would try to extract as much as possible during the period they held the contract. It hardly mattered to them if the people were excessively taxed or the production in the later years declined. Sometimes the revenue farmers could not collect the estimated taxes even by applying a great amount of coercion.

Permanent Revenue Settlement

In the province of Bengal, revenue collection was conducted by the *zamindars* on behalf of the Mughal emperor and his representative or *diwan* who had appointed officials especially for this purpose. According to the treaty of Allahabad (1765 CE), the Mughal emperor, Shah Alam II had given the British the *Diwani* powers over Bengal, Bihar and Orissa. This meant that the British were granted the authority to collect the revenues of these provinces. The British in turn appointed revenue farmers for land revenue collection. There was constant pressure from the Company officials to exceed the amounts to be collected and even the revenue collected was never used for social welfare. When the devastating famine in Bengal occurred, it was an eye-opener for the British who realised that it was extremely important for them to closely monitor the question of revenue collection. Hence, Warren Hastings, the British governor-general introduced a system of five-yearly inspections and collection of revenue.

But even this system was not free from defects. The appointed tax farmers took away as much money as they could earn within this five year period. When the British Parliament came to know about the corruption of the Company in 1784 CE, the British Prime Minister, Pitt the Younger, tried to improve the situation in Bengal by implementing the Pitt's India Act; and in 1786 CE Lord Cornwallis was sent to India to reorganize the economic administration of the Company and bring in revisions in the system.

In 1786 CE, the Court of Directors of the East India Company first proposed the Permanent Settlement Act only for Bengal. After many deliberations the Court of Directors passed a ten-year (Decennial) Settlement Act in 1790 CE, which finally led to the Permanent Settlement Act of 1793 CE instituted under Lord Cornwallis. It was a contract between the Company and the landholders of Bengal, according to which, the *zamindars* and independent *talukdars* were recognized as the absolute owners of landed property by the British. More so, the landholders were allowed to hold their proprietary rights at a rate that was permanent and the British government could not enhance its revenue demands on them.

The Permanent Settlement Act brought improvement of the land held by the landowners as they began to take greater interest in issues related to their lands, such as drainage and irrigation. Construction of roads and bridges was also encouraged—so far lacking in the province of Bengal. Through this settlement, the former landholders and revenue intermediaries benefitted greatly, as their proprietorship on lands was assured. Similarly, earnings for the Company were also guaranteed as *zamindars* no more defaulted on payments as a result of assured returns. As the land revenue was now fixed, the *zamindars* could invest the money saved by them without fear of tax increment. The system also ensured minimizing the fortunes made on revenues through corrupt practices by the Company officials.

Although the Permanent Settlement brought in the required reforms in revenue administration, its effects were sudden and took time for the people to understand. The tax demanded by the Company was fixed and hence the revenue collectors of the Company refused to give any consideration even during the times of drought, flood or other natural calamities when agriculturists could not pay the *zamindars*. This was an important drawback that caused many *zamindars* to fall into arrears. The Company's policy was to auction the land on which taxes were not paid. This created a new market for the land. Many Indian officials of the Company purchased the land sold through this system, thus creating a new class of bureaucrats. This led to two negative trends in the system. While the persons interested in specific lands tried to manipulate the system to have the lands they wanted listed for sale, there were others who bribed officials in order to get possession of certain lands. As a result, this class of bureaucrats became rich through unfair means. In other words, the Permanent Settlement led to commercialization of land, which had not existed in Bengal so far. It also created a new landlord class which had no connection with their lands but managed the property through managers appointed for the purpose.

The Company's goal in implementing the Permanent Settlement was to ensure that the *zamindari* class would be the source of revenue generation as well as serve as intermediaries for making British rule acceptable and protect the latter in all their interests. But the Act overlooked details regarding the use of land; it only included clauses relating to revenue collection. In order to earn more money from the land, the Company officials and *zamindars* insisted on planting indigo and cotton rather than wheat and rice. This was the cause of many famines in Bengal. Another disadvantage was the creation of absentee landlordism, a feature that led to inadequate attention paid to the improvement of lands. Thus, the *zamindari* class became more powerful than they were in the earlier Mughal period.

The Ryotwari System

Like the Permanent Settlement, the Ryotwari system was another land revenue arrangement instituted in some parts of British India to collect revenues from the cultivators of agricultural land. Both the collection of land taxes and rents came under the purview of the Ryotwari system. Under this system, every registered landowner was a proprietor who was responsible for the direct payment of land revenue to the state. The proprietor had complete power to sublet his land holdings, transfer, mortgage or sell them. He remained as proprietor until the British government wanted him to continue in this position. In case the proprietor failed to pay the state's revenue demand, he was evicted from office.

The Ryotwari system was devised by Captain Alexander Read, a British military officer, who was assisted by Thomas Munro, another military officer who was also a celebrated civil servant. It was first introduced in the Brahamahal district of Madras Presidency by Munro when he was the governor there during 1820–27 CE. Under this system, the state's demand fixed at 50 percent of the estimated produce of the fields was directly collected by the state from the individual cultivators. This system was initially implemented in many regions. But the terms and conditions of the Ryotwari system proved to be of no benefit to the tenants, farmers or the proprietors; so upon realizing its shortcomings, Munro enforced the

Ryotwari system only in those parts where the Permanent Settlement was not in operation. He also fixed a new rate of payment under the Ryotwari Settlement, according to which one-thirds of the gross produce was to be paid as land revenue. This was payable in the form of cash, and hence, did not take into consideration actual yield of the holding or the prevailing prices in the market.

In the Bombay Presidency the revenue system associated with the name of Mountsturt Elphinstone followed more or less the same features of the Ryotwari system. The initial defects were eliminated through an elaborate survey done in 1835 CE by lieutenant Wingate and Goldsmith. According to the report submitted by Wingate, the state's share of land revenue was first determined on the basis of the paying capacity of the people. Then the district's total demands were calculated by evenly dividing them among the fields which were brought under assessment. Under the new scheme, assessment of land was done on a geological basis, taking into consideration each field instead of the total holdings of a cultivator. Bringing in more flexibility, the new system permitted a cultivator to give up any field or take up another unoccupied field to till. The settlement was generally in force for thirty years.

The British tried to bring about some reforms in 1855 CE and then in 1864 CE, by conducting extensive surveys and introducing new settlement plans. Resettlement began in 1866 CE, at a time when the American Civil War had begun pushing up the demand of many commodities; and likewise the prices of Bombay cotton. With this temporary boom the survey officers got an opportunity to increase the land revenue by 66–100 percent, without giving any right to the cultivators to appeal to the court of law. The effects of this sudden increase of land revenue proved disastrous. There were agrarian riots in the Deccan in 1875 CE to which the government responded by enacting the Deccan Agriculturists Relief Act of 1879 CE. According to its provisions, the British administration provided some safeguards from moneylenders, but did nothing to restrain the excessive state demand. There was no provision for an appeal to the courts of law against over assessment. Several new rules were introduced, among which the district collector was empowered to ensure that lands were retained by cultivators according to the new rules; otherwise lands could be taken over.

The Ryotwari system, thus, had disastrous consequences—leading to the oppression of the peasantry in the form of rural indebtedness to pay the stipulated land revenue to the state. It also gave rise to a group of moneylenders, who charged exorbitant rates of interest to the farmers for borrowing money. This left them with no other option but to sink into a life of poverty. The excessive state demand with the new judicial and administrative set up turned the Indian rural economy upside down.

The Mahalwari System

The northwestern provinces and Awadh had come under British domination at different periods of time. In 1801 CE, the Company had received the districts of Allahabad and its adjoining areas from the *nawab* of Awadh which were known as the ceded districts. After the second Anglo Maratha war, the Company had acquired the territory between the Yamuna and the Ganga. These territories were called the conquered provinces. Lord Wellesley, the first lieutenant governor of the ceded districts had made a settlement with the *zamindars* and farmers for three years, according to which, the state's demand was raised—by 20 lakh rupees during the very first year—over the *nawab* of Awadh's demand. Moreover, an additional burden of 10 lakh rupees was added before the third year was out. The Company officials were also very strict in the collection of land revenue. Similar land revenue settlements were also implemented in the conquered provinces.

Mackenzie, the Secretary to the Board of Commissioners, in his Minutes of 1819 CE, highlighted the existence of village communities in northern India. In keeping with this, the Mahalwari system of land revenue was introduced in the region. The term was derived from the word *mahal*, referring to a neighbourhood. Under this system, the unit for revenue settlement was the entire village. Generally lands in the village were communally owned by the village community who were jointly responsible for the payment of land revenue, though individual responsibility also existed. The village community together owned the common land comprising the village green, forestlands, pastures, etc.

Under the Mahalwari system, the land was first surveyed, records of rights over land were prepared, and then land revenue demand in the *mahals* was fixed, and finally collected through the village headman or *lambardar*. Regulation VII of 1822 CE legalized these recommendations and fixed the land revenue on the basis of 80 percent of the rental value payable by the *zamindars*. In cases, where estates were not held by the landlords, but by the cultivators themselves, the state's demand rose up to almost 95 percent of the rental. The system broke down due to the excessive demand of the state and its rigidity in the collection of land revenue.

When William Bentinck came as the governor-general, he thoroughly reviewed the scheme and came to the conclusion that the Regulation of 1822 CE had caused widespread despair. Bentinck's government, after prolonged consultations, passed the regulation of 1833 CE, according to which the terms and conditions of the Mahalwari system were made slightly flexible. An easy procedure was adopted for preparing estimates of produce and of rents. It also introduced the fixation of average rents for different classes of soil. For the first time, field maps and field registers began to be used. This new scheme supervised by Robert Merttins Bird, a British administrator, took care that land was first surveyed by demarcating field boundaries, and the cultivated and the uncultivated parts. Assessment was then done for the whole tract followed by fixing the demand of each village. The state demand was fixed at 66 percent of the rental value and the settlement was made for a period of 30 years.

The Mahalwari system of land revenue which worked under the scheme of 1833 CE was completed under the British administrator James Thompson. Even the 66 percent rental demand formula was found to be too taxing. When Lord Dalhousie became the governor general he issued fresh directions. Under the revised Saharanpur Rules of 1855 CE, the state revenue demand was limited to 50 percent of the rental value. But the settlement officers did not implement the new rules; and as a result, the system proved to be very hard on the agricultural classes.

Other Economic Policies

Yet another innovation in India's economic policy introduced by the British was commercialization of agriculture, wherein crop production was done for the market rather than for domestic consumption. Commercialization of agriculture went against the traditional structure of the Indian village economy. The new settlements in land had already weakened the existing rural framework and now with the promotion of only cash crops—cotton, tobacco and jute instead of rice, wheat, barley—the socio-economic position of the peasantry was adversely affected.

With the introduction of different land assessment systems by the British into the Indian socio-economic setup, the Indian rural community was falling into the clutches of a new system of property rights and justice while having to work within the traditional Indian social framework. The introduction of these new systems in the traditional structures of society was difficult to resolve; and it produced tensions that over the times led to the re-orientation of social relations with the British. Most of the policies failed to promote agricultural output and even in other economic spheres there was a negative impact. There also came a time when the British could not import bullion for their purchases in Bengal, resulting in a shortage of silver, and this created immense difficulties for the peasantry, because taxes had to be paid in cash and the copper currency (the only one with which the peasant was familiar) became devalued. The situation worsened when the Company exported silver from Bengal to China for trade in tea causing a further bullion drop. There was also a drastic reduction in the export of Indian textiles after 1800 CE which impoverished the weavers. As a result, there was a mass exodus of unemployed weavers from textile-producing cities like Dhaka to other cities in search of work. Added to this was the Company's monopolistic control over textile, salt, pepper, opium, and salt industries which left the workers with no option but to accept the low wages paid by the Company, invariably forcing them take debts at exorbitant rates from moneylenders.

Thus, by mid-eighteenth century, the Company had not only come to monopolize Bengal's overseas trade, but had also replaced Indian textiles with mill-made cloth from England. As a result, the artisan-based industries in Bengal had almost lost their utility and were now restricted to cater only to the home market. The Company was operating in such a way that the Indians were being excluded from all large commercial and fiscal ventures. The situation outside Bengal was not radically different either. For example, the production of cotton, indigo, tea and opium as cash crops for export tied the Indian economy to the world market. But there was one positive feature—the banking and merchant castes in southern and western India, especially the Parsis, who were already known for their business acumen, became major participants in the new economy. Trading operations were flourishing which was also facilitated by the fact that the company-minted silver rupee became the standard currency in British India and replaced the large number of confusing currencies in circulation.

Socio-Cultural Conditions

The social structure prevalent in India at the time of the consolidation of British rule was complex and denigrated. On the one hand, many religions like Hinduism, Jainism, Buddhism, Islam and Sikhism were prevalent; while on the other hand, with the perpetuation of religious dogmas and beliefs, there was social stagnation in the common man's life, restricting his social mobility towards development. The social degeneration and backwardness that had set in was the result of many deep-rooted superstitious and rigid practices. Social rigidity and irrational religious beliefs had become the conspicuous features of eighteenth century India; and necessitated reform movements with the active participation of progressive social intellectuals. Thus, the eighteenth century was a period in which many intolerable institutions and irrational customs were prevalent—the rigid caste system, untouchability, female infanticide, child marriage, polygamy and *sati*.

The Caste System

Indian society was widely perceived as a caste-ridden society and over the centuries the history of casteism was a record of both rigidity and liberalism. There were periods of extreme caste exclusiveness, when even the shadow of a *chandala* was abominable to the *brahman*; but equally there were periods when the *chandala* and the *brahman* embraced each other. In sixteenth century India, in the heydays of the Bhakti preachers, caste rigidity had relaxed considerably and god was equally accessible through personal devotion to all sections of society, including the *shudras*. But the situation changed for the worse in the eighteenth century, when caste prejudices picked up, resulting in the formation of several hundreds of castes and subcastes. The stratification of castes was so high that it is difficult to determine the actual number of castes and subcastes prevalent in eighteenth century India.

Untouchability

The most humiliating outcome of the caste system was untouchability, a system which divided society into touchables and untouchables. Untouchability as a social inequality emanated from the rigidity in the caste system. The untouchables were denied even basic privileges necessary in life, such as access to wells, tanks, schools and temples. The untouchables were at the mercy of upper castes in society for all their needs, and had to form themselves into a separate community and live only in the peripheral areas of the cities and towns.

Seclusion of Women

Total seclusion of women was practiced in eighteenth century India, especially among the elite sections in society. The alienation of women was a cause of mental and physical degeneration, forbidding development of any sort. The *purdah* system, which was widely practised in northern and eastern India naturally forbade young women from mixing freely or attending schools. The only education in rare cases was given at home through private tutors. Thus, most Indian women were denied the opportunity to secure education. In comparison, women belonging to lower classes of society did not lead such a secluded life due to varied economic reasons. They were called upon to work in their respective caste professions or in agricultural fields; while women in cities and towns were confined to their homes. It was the complete dependence of women on men, which reduced their position to the extent of a loss of their identity and individuality. There also prevailed a system in which Hindu women were denied any right to paternal property, which made them economically dependent upon their fathers, husbands and sons. Their feeble economic status was a vital cause of their misery and suffering. In addition to this, women were also subjected to a number of unreasonable practices that made them an object of exploitation.

Female Infanticide

One of the worst practices in eighteenth century India was the killing of female children at birth. It was prevalent among the wealthier and upper caste sections in certain areas. In 1789 CE, Jonathan Duncan as the Resident of Banaras observed this practice among the Rajkumars of the place. It was also found among the Jadejas of Kathiawar and Kutch, Kachwaha Rajputs near Allahabad, Chauhan Rajputs and the Pathak Ahirs of Mainpuri. It was primarily guided by economic compulsions, such as the expenditure involved in getting young girls married off or in certain clans the dismal possibility of finding a suitable groom that led to the killing of female infants.

Child Marriage

Both Hindus and Muslims practiced the custom of child marriage. During Akbar's time attempts were made to abolish it, but to no avail. The growth of population and the physical degradation of women proceeded side by side. Motherhood at a tender age, with numerous undernourished children made Indian women lead a life of misery and distress. It also produced many other adverse effects. Depending on the depth of economic misery, parents would sell their female children as brides to those who could afford to meet their demands. There was no concept of finding suitable grooms, so in most cases young girls were married off to elderly men who died within a short period of the marriage. Naturally there were increasing number of child widows without the economic means to sustain themselves. Added to that, the lack of benevolent treatment from their relatives subjected them to suspicion and ill treatment throughout their lives.

Polygamy

Polygamy was a practice pervading both the Hindu and Muslim societies. The practice of getting married to more than one woman was confined only to the richer and higher sections of society. With their affluence and wealth, the rich could afford to become polygamous. It was neither a matter of shame nor sorrow to maintain a harem. Rather it became a matter of pride and social prestige in certain areas. In eighteenth century Bengal, polygamy was widely prevalent among the

Kulin *brahmans*, who occupied the highest social strata. The lower *brahmans* offered their daughters to them who professionalized marriage as a business. Among the Muslims, polygamy made the *purdah* system more stringent.

Celibacy of Widows

Though widows were allowed to remarry in ancient times, the custom gradually disappeared and came to be considered a sin. The forced celibacy of widows became a strict social custom, which few could defy. Society imposed a lot of restrictions on widows, as prescribed in the *Manusamhita*. There was a severe code of conduct, which the widow was supposed to follow as per the religious scriptures. Her life was regulated through a formal routine of fasting, devotion, prayer and pious works. Even little girls, who became widows early in life, had to maintain a strict life of abstinence.

Sati

The most irrational and inhumane custom widely followed in Hindu society was the custom of *sati* or the self immolation of a widow on the funeral pyre of her dead husband. The custom was appalling to many, even to some Delhi sultans and Mughal emperors, who tried to forbid it. Much before the British, Akbar had attempted to abolish the practice of *sati*. Even the Sikh Guru, Amardas, and the Maratha *Peshwas* tried to put an end to this practice. But unfortunately, this custom was so deep rooted among the orthodox Hindus that it required a serious attempt from the British in the form of legislation to bring an end to it.

There were also certain minor practices like human sacrifice or *bali*, self-torture, self-immolation, etc., which reflect the level of social standards in eighteenth century India. The deteriorating standards of Indian society proved to be advantageous to the Christian missionaries. At the beginning of its establishment in India, the Company did not interfere in the religious and social matters of the Indians; and British officers did not encourage Christian missionaries, but they did not discourage them either. The missionaries carried on their activities throughout the length and breadth of the country. They opened schools, hospitals, orphanages and also carried on humanitarian work in order to impress upon the Indians the superiority of their faith. Though they did not receive any official financial help from the Company's government, many European officers gave them money privately. Taking advantage of the situation in places where evil social customs, such as caste distinctions, *sati*, female infanticide, child marriage and the *purdah* system were prevalent, the missionaries could win over a large number of Indians to their faith. The state of affairs alarmed the educated sections and free thinkers among the Indians and they began to think of ways and means to set their house in order.

While they tried to put a stop to the rising tide of Christianity in India, the reformers of the nineteenth century began to realize that western culture was a challenge to their old traditions and beliefs. They became critical of the past and began to think of an ideal and rational social order for India. While they wanted their countrymen to get acquainted with the English language and get in touch with the values of western civilization, they did not want the Indians to ape the western culture blindly. This new awakening appeared first in social and religious reforms. Among the great social and religious reformers of the nineteenth century, the names of Raja Ram Mohan Roy, Ishwar Chandra Vidyasagar, Dayanand Saraswati, Annie Besant, Ramakrishna Paramhansa and Swami Vivekananda deserve special mention. Through their untiring efforts various reform movements emerged to restructure Indian society and rationalize religious thoughts. The preaching's of these luminaries awakened cross-sections of the Indian society and made helped them ascertain their own rights and privileges, through education and proper interpretation of Indian religious philosophies.

SUMMARY

- In order to consolidate their position, the British tried to establish their control over the administrative machinery in India.
- To hold the administrative system, the first measure, which the British adopted, was the revamping of economic policies. Therefore, they introduced different systems in assessment and collection of land revenue, which became the chief source of their income.
- Land being an important source of income, the British used it as their instrument to control the entire revenue system. They introduced several land revenue systems such as the Permanent Settlement, Ryotwari system and the Mahalwari settlement.
- Under the Permanent Settlement of 1793 CE of Cornwallis, the *zamindars* and independent *talukdars* were recognized as the absolute owners of landed property and were allowed to hold their proprietary rights at a permanent rate with the assurance that the British government would not enhance their revenue demands on them.
- Under the Ryotwari system, every registered landowner was a proprietor and was responsible for the direct payment of the land revenue to the state. The proprietor could sublet his land holdings, transfer, mortgage or sell them. He remained as proprietor until the British government wanted him to continue in this position. In case the proprietor failed to pay the state's revenue demand, he was evicted from office.
- Under the Mahalwari system, the unit for revenue settlement was the entire village. Generally lands in the village were communally owned by the village community who were jointly responsible for the payment of land revenue though individual responsibility also existed.
- Although the Ryotwari and Mahalwari systems of revenue collection improvised upon some of the mistakes made by the Permanent Settlement, they reinforced private property in land. Peasants could now be deprived of their lands for non-payment and were encouraged to produce more for the market rather than for personal consumption.
- Commercialization of agriculture made the peasants dependent on the vagaries of the market at terms unfavourable to them.
- The social structure prevalent in India at the time of consolidation of British rule was complex. With multiple religions prevailing and with the perpetuation of religious dogmas and beliefs, there was stagnation in the common man's life, restricting his social mobility towards development.
- The eighteenth century was a period in which many intolerable institutions and irrational customs were prevalent, such as a rigid caste system, untouchability, female infanticide, child marriage, polygamy and *sati*.
- The social degeneration and backwardness that had set in was the result of many deep-rooted superstitious and rigid practices.
- Social rigidity and irrational religious beliefs had become the conspicuous features of eighteenth century India, and necessitating reform movements with the active participation of progressive intellectuals in society.

KEYWORDS

Quinquennial settlement, Pitt's India Act, Ryotwari system, Mahalwari system, Permanent revenue settlement

REVIEW QUESTIONS

1. Give an account of the permanent revenue settlement of Lord Cornwallis.
2. Write a note on the Ryotwari system of land settlement.
3. Explain the main components of the Mahalwari system of land revenue.
4. Examine the general economic situation of India during the eighteenth century.
5. What were the social evils that prevailed in the eighteenth century India?

Further Readings

Agarwal, C. M. 1986. *Akbar and His Hindu Officers: A Critical Study*. Jalandhar: ABS Publications.

Ahmed, Muhammad Aziz. 1972. *Political History and Institutions of the Early Turkish Empire of Delhi (1206–1290)*. Delhi: Oriental Books Reprint Corp.

Alam, Muzaffar and Sanjay Subrahmanyam, eds. 1998. *The Mughal State (1526–1750)*. Delhi: Oxford University Press.

Alam, Muzaffar. 1993. *The Crisis of the Empire in Mughal North India: Awadh and Punjab*. Delhi: Oxford University Press.

________. 2004. *The Languages of Political Islam in India (1200–1800)*. New Delhi: Orient Longman.

Alavi, Rafi Ahmad. 1977. *History of Medieval Deccan*. New Delhi: Global Media Publications.

Alberuni and Edward Sachau. (1030 AD) 2007. *Alberuni's India*. Delhi: Atlantic Publishers and Distributors Ltd.

Ali, Athar. 1985. *Apparatus of the Empire (1574–1658)*. Delhi: Oxford University Press.

________. 2001. *Mughal Nobility Under Aurangzeb*. Delhi: Oxford University Press.

Anwar, Firdous. 2001. *Nobility Under the Mughals*. New Delhi: Manohar Publications.

Arasaratnam, Sinnapah. 1994. *Maritime India in the Seventeenth Century*. Delhi: Oxford University Press.

Ashraf , K.M. 2000. *Life and Conditions of the People of Hindustan*. Delhi: Gyan Books.

Bandyopadhyay, Sekhar. 2004.*From Plassey to Partition: A History of Modern India*. Delhi: Orient Longman.

Barnett, Richard B. 1981. *North India Between Empires: Awadh, the Mughals and the British (1720–1801)*. Berkeley, Los Angeles and London: University of California Press.

Basham, A. L. 1975. *Cultural History of India*. Great Britain: Oxford University Press.

Bawa, V. K., ed. 1975. *Aspects of Deccan History*. Hyderabad, Institute of Asian Studies.

Bayly, C. A. 1983. *Rulers, Townsmen and Bazaar*. Delhi: Cambridge University Press.

________. 1987. *The Cambridge History of India*, Vol. II, 1. 'Indian Society and the Making of the British Empire'. Delhi: Cambridge University Press.

Bernier, Francois. (1670) 1916. *Travels in the Mogul Empire (1656–1668)*. Translated by Archibald Constable. London: Oxford University Press.

Bhattacharya, Neeladri. 1986. 'Colonial State and Agrarian Society' in *Situating Indian History*. Edited by S. Gopal, S. Bhattacharya and R. Thapar. Delhi: Oxford University Press.

Bhattacharya, N. N., ed. 1989. *Medieval Bhakti Movements in India*. New Delhi: Munishiram Manoharlal.

Chandra, Satish. 2007. *History of Medieval India*. New Delhi: Orient Longman.

________. 1999. *Medieval India*, Vol II. New Delhi: Har Anand Publications Pvt. Ltd.

________. 1982. *Medieval India: Society, the Jagirdari Crisis and the Village*. Delhi: MacMillan.

________. 1972. *Parties and Politics at the Mughal Court (1707–1740)*. Delhi: Oxford University Press.

Chaurasia, Radhey Shyam. 2002. *History of Medieval India*. New Delhi: Atlantic Publishers.

Chitnis, K. N. 2002. *Socio-Economic Aspects of Medieval India*. Delhi: Atlantic Publishers.

Chopra, Pran Nath. 1963. *Some Aspects of Society and Culture During the Mughal Age (1526–1707)*. Agra: Agarwala Publishers.

Chaudhuri, K. N. 1978. *The Trading World of Asia and the English East India Company*. Cambridge: Cambridge University Press.

Das, Arbind. 1996. *Arthashastra of Kautilya and Fatwa-i-Jahandari of Ziauddin Barrani: An Analysis*. Delhi: Pratibha Publications, pp. 124–43.

Datta, Rajat, ed. 2008. *Rethinking a Millennium: Perspectives on Indian History from the Eighth to the Eighteenth Century*. Delhi: Aakar Books.

Eaton, Richard. 2002. *Essays on Islam and Indian History*. Delhi: Oxford University Press.

Farooqui, Salma Ahmed. 2005. *Islam and the Mughal State*. New Delhi: Sundeep Prakashan.

________. 2008. *Multicultural Dimensions of Medieval Deccan*. New Delhi: Sundeep Prakashan.

Fisher, Michael. H. 1987. *A Clash of Cultures: Awadh, the British and the Mughals*. Delhi: Manohar Publishers.

Frykenberg, R. E., ed. 1979. *Land Control and Social Structure in Indian History*. Manohar Publishers. Delhi.

Fukazawa, H. 1991. *The Medieval Deccan: Peasants, Social Systems and States 16th–18th Centuries*. Delhi: Oxford University Press.

Gascoigne, Bamber. 1998. *The Great Moghuls*. London: Constable and Co Ltd.

Gordon, Stewart. 1994. *Marathas, Marauders and State Formation in Eighteenth Century India*. Delhi: Oxford University Press.

Gupta, Sulekh Chandra. 1983. *Agrarian Relations and Early British Rule in India*, Bombay: Sameeksha Trust and Oxford University Press.

Habib, Irfan. 1963. *Agrarian System of Mughal India*. London: Asia Publishing House.

Habib, M. and Nizami, K.A., *Delhi Sultanate* (Vols. I and II), Macmillan, Delhi, 1970.

Hasan, Ibn. 1970. *Central Structure of the Mughal Empire and its Practical Working up to the Year 1657*. Delhi: Oxford University Press.

Hasan, Nurul. 1990. *Thoughts on Agrarian Relations in Mughal India*. New Delhi: People's Publishing House.

Hussain, Yusuf. 1971. *Indo-Muslim Polity*, Simla: Indian Institute of Advanced Studies.

________. 1973. *Glimpses of Medieval Indian Culture*. Bombay: Asia Publishing House.

Idries Shah, Sayyid. 1971. *The Sufis*. London: Anchor Publishers.

Jackson, Peter. 2003. *The Delhi Sultanate: A Political and Military History* (Cambridge Studies in Islamic Civilization). Cambridge: Cambridge University Press.

Joshi, S.K. 1985. *Defense Architecture in Early Karnataka*. Delhi: Sundeep Prakashan.

Juneja, Monica, ed. 2001. *Architecture in Medieval India*. New Delhi: Permanent Black.

Burde, Jyotsna. 1963. 'Food and Food Habits in Vijayanagara Times'. *The Journal of the Karnatak University*, Vol. VII. Dharwar: Karnatak University.

Khanna, Meenakshi, ed. 2007. *Cultural History of Medieval India*. New Delhi: Social Science Press.

Kulkarni, A. R. 1969. *Maharastra in the Age of Shivaji*. Pune: Deshmukh and Co.

Kulkarni, A. R., Nayeem, M. A., and T. R. D'Souza, eds. 1996. *Medieval Deccan History Commemoration Volume in Honour of P. M. Josh*. Bombay: Popular Prakashan.

Kulke, Hermann, ed. 1997. *The State in India 1000–1700*. Delhi: Oxford University Press.

Kumar, Sunil. 2007. *The Emergence of the Delhi Sultanate 1192–1286*. Delhi: Permanent Black.

Lings, Martin. 1999. *What is Sufism*. Cambridge: Islamic Texts Society, Cambridge University Press.

Mahalingam, T.V. 1969. *Administration and Social Life Under Vijayanagar*, Part I. Madras: University of Madras.

Majumdar R. C., ed. 1977. *The Maratha Supremacy*. Bombay: Bharatiya Vidya Bhavan.

________. ed. 2006. *The Delhi Sultanate*. Bombay: Bharatiya Vidya Bhavan.

Majumdar, Raychaudhury, and Dutta. 1988. *An Advanced History of India*. Madras: McMillan India Limited.

Marshal P. J. 1988. *The Cambridge History of India*, Vol. II, 2. 'Bengal, The British Bridgehead, Eastern India, 1740–1827'. Delhi: Cambridge University Press.

Mehta, J. L. 1996. *Advanced Study in the History of Medieval India*. New Delhi: Sterling Publishers Pvt. Ltd.

Michell, George and Mark Zebrowski. 1999. *Architecture and Art of the Deccan Sultanates* in *The New Cambridge History of India* Vol. I, 7. Cambridge: Cambridge University Press.

Moosvi, Shireen. 2008. *People, Taxation, and Trade in Mughal India*. Delhi: Oxford University Press.

Moreland, W. H. 1929. *Agrarian System of Moslem India*. Cambridge: Cambridge University Press.

Mukhia, Harbans. 1976. *Historians and Historiography during the Reign of Akbar*. New Delhi: Vikas Publishing House.

________. 1993. *Perspectives on Medieval History*. Vikas Publishing House, New Delhi,

________. 2004. *The Mughals of India*. UK: Blackwell Publishing Ltd.

Nayeem, M. A., Ray, Aniruddha and K. S. Mathew. 2002. *Studies in the History of the Deccan Medieval and Modern*. Delhi: Pragathi Publications.

Nizami, K.A. 1961. *Some Aspects of Religion and Culture During the Thirteenth Century*. Aligarh.

________. 1985. *State and Culture in Medieval India.* Delhi: Adam Publishers and Distributors.

Paes, Domingos and Fernao Nuniz. 1991.*The Vijayanagar Empire: Chronicles of Paes and Nunes.* Asian Educational Series.

Pande, Rekha. 2005. *Religious Movement in Medieval India.* Delhi: Gyan Publishing House.

________. 1990. *Succession in the Delhi Sultanate.* Delhi: Commonwealth Publishers.

Prakash, Om. 1998. *The New Cambridge History of India* Vol. II, 5 'European Commercial Enterprise in Pre-Colonial India'. Cambridge: Cambridge University Press.

Qaisar, Ahsan Jan. 1982. *Indian Response to European Technology and Culture.* Delhi: Oxford University Press.

Qureshi, I. H. 1979. *The Administration of the Mughal Empire.* Delhi: Low Price Publications.

________. 1985. *Ulema in Politics.* Delhi: Manohar Publishers.

Majumdar, R. C., ed. 1963. *British Paramountcy and Indian Renaissance*, Vol. IX, Part I. Bombay: Bharatiya Vidya Bhavan.

Richards, J. F. 1987. *Imperial Monetary System of the Mughal Empire.* Delhi: Oxford University Press.

________. 1993. *The Mughal Empire*, Vol. I, Part V, of the *New Cambridge History of India*, London: Cambridge University Press.

Rizvi, S. A. A. 1983. *A History of Sufism in India.* Delhi: Globus Media Publications.

________. 1993. *The Wonder that was India: Part II.* Calcutta: Picador India.

Sarkar, Jadunath. 1991. *Fall of the Mughal Empire*, Vols. I–II. New Delhi: Orient Longman.

Sarkar, Jagadish Narayan. 1984. *Mughal Polity.* Delhi: Idara-i Adabiyat-i Delli.

Sastri K. A. Nilakanta and G. Srinivasa Chary. 1996. *Advanced History of India.* Bombay: Allied Publishers Ltd.

Sastri, Nilakanta, K. A. 1975. *A History of South India from Pre-Historic Times to the Fall of Vijayanagar.* Delhi: Oxford University Press.

________. 1992. *Development of Religion in South India.* Delhi: Munshiram Manoharlal Publishers.

Sen, S. N., ed. 1949. *Indian Travels of Thevenot and Careri.* New Delhi: Indian Records Series.

Sewell, Robert. (1878) 2004. *A Forgotten Empire (Vijayanagar): A Contribution to the History of India.* New Delhi: Asian Educational Services,.

Sharma, K. 2002. *Bhakti and Bhakti Movement: A New Perspective.* New Delhi: Munshiram Manoharlal Publications.

Sherwani, H. K. and P. M. Joshi, eds. 1973. *History of Medieval Deccan (1294–1724)*, Vol. I. Hyderabad: Printing and Publication Bureau, Government of Andhra Pradesh.

________. 1974. eds., *History of Medieval Deccan (1294–1724)*, Vol. II. Hyderabad: Printing and Publication Bureau, Government of Andhra Pradesh.

Sherwani, H. K. 1953. *Bahmanis of the Deccan.* Hyderabad: Manager of Publications, Saood Manzil.

________. 1969. *Cultural Trends in Medieval India.* Bombay and New York: Asia Publishing House.

Sinha N. K., ed. 1967. *Economic History of Bengal*, Vol. III. Calcutta: Seagull Books Pvt. Ltd.

Srivastava, Kamal S. 2007. *A Political, Social and Cultural History of the Delhi Sultanate.* New Delhi: APH Publishing Corporation.

Stein, Burton. 1986. *Peasant, State and Society in Medieval South India.* Delhi: Oxford University Press.

________. 1998. *A History of India.* Delhi: Oxford University Press.

________. 2005. *Vijayanagara* in *The New Cambridge History of India Series.* Cambridge: Cambridge University Press.

Streusand, Douglas. 1998. *The Formation of the Mughal Empire.* Delhi: Oxford University Press.

Subrahmanyam, Sanjay. 1990. *The Political Economy of Commerce: Southern India 1500–1650.* Cambridge: Cambridge University Press.

Syed, M.H. 2004. *History of the Delhi Sultanate* Vols. I and II. Delhi: Anmol Publications.

Tripathi, R.P. 1978. *Rise and Fall of the Mughal Empire.* Allahabad: Central Book Depot.

Troll, Christain W., ed. 2003. *Muslim Shrines in India.* Delhi: Oxford University Press.

Zaehner, R. C. (1960) 1999. *Hindu and Muslim Mysticism.* London: Research Press Pvt. Ltd.

Credits

MAP CREDITS

All maps used in this book Copyright © 1978 by the Regents of the University of Minnesota, assigned 1988 to Joseph E. Schwartzberg, additional material copyright © 1992 by Joseph E. Schwartzberg.

For a detailed list of maps see Page

IMAGE CREDITS

Chapter 1

Nalanda, Manuscript Cover. Copyright © 1978 by the Regents of the University of Minnesota, assigned 1988 to Joseph E. Schwartzberg, additional material copyright © 1992 by Joseph E. Schwartzberg.

Konarak, Sun Temple. Copyright © 1978 by the Regents of the University of Minnesota, assigned 1988 to Joseph E. Schwartzberg, additional material copyright © 1992 by Joseph E. Schwartzberg.

Ellora, Kailasa Temple. Copyright © 1978 by the Regents of the University of Minnesota, assigned 1988 to Joseph E. Schwartzberg, additional material copyright © 1992 by Joseph E. Schwartzberg.

Somnathpur, Kesavara Temple. Copyright © 1978 by the Regents of the University of Minnesota, assigned 1988 to Joseph E. Schwartzberg, additional material copyright © 1992 by Joseph E. Schwartzberg.

Tamil Nadu, Shiva Nataraja. Copyright © 1978 by the Regents of the University of Minnesota, assigned 1988 to Joseph E. Schwartzberg, additional material copyright © 1992 by Joseph E. Schwartzberg.

Coins of the Reign of Akbar. Copyright © 1978 by the Regents of the University of Minnesota, assigned 1988 to Joseph E. Schwartzberg, additional material copyright © 1992 by Joseph E. Schwartzberg.

Chapter 2

Khajuraho, Kendariya Mahadeva Temple. Copyright © 1978 by the Regents of the University of Minnesota, assigned 1988 to Joseph E. Schwartzberg, additional material copyright © 1992 by Joseph E. Schwartzberg.

Thanjavur, Brihadesvara Temple. Copyright © 1978 by the Regents of the University of Minnesota, assigned 1988 to Joseph E. Schwartzberg, additional material copyright © 1992 by Joseph E. Schwartzberg.

Chapter 3

Kashmir, Avalokitesvara Image. Copyright © 1978 by the Regents of the University of Minnesota, assigned 1988 to Joseph E. Schwartzberg, additional material copyright © 1992 by Joseph E. Schwartzberg.

Bihar, Standing Vishnu. Copyright © 1978 by the Regents of the University of Minnesota, assigned 1988 to Joseph E. Schwartzberg, additional material copyright © 1992 by Joseph E. Schwartzberg.

Part II

Firuz Shah's Tomb and Adjoining Madrasa, Hauz Khas Complex, New Delhi. Courtesy: Nvvchar at en.wikipedia.

Chapter 4

The Somnath Temple. Courtesy: The Archaeological Survey of India, taken by D. H. Sykes in1869 CE.

Ayaz Kneeling Before Sultan Mahmud of Ghazni. Courtesy: British Library, London. Accessed at http://en.wikipedia.org/wiki/File:Mahmoud_and_Ayaz.jpg on 29 May 2010.

Chapter 5

The Qutb Minar, Delhi. Copyright © 1978 by the Regents of the University of Minnesota, assigned 1988 to Joseph E. Schwartzberg, additional material copyright © 1992 by Joseph E. Schwartzberg.

Chapter 8

The Defeat. Accessed at http://en.wikipedia.org/wiki/File:Timur_defeats_the_sultan_of_Delhi.jpg on 29 May 2010.

Chapter 9

The Quwwat-ul-Islam Masjid. Courtesy Salma Ahmed Farooqui.

Part III

Intricate Garuda Carving on Temple in Hampi. Courtesy Soham Banerjee; licensed under the Creative Commons Attribution 2.0 Generic license. Accessed at http://commons.wikimedia.org/wiki/File:Intricate_Garuda.jpg on 29 May 2010.

Chapter 11

Virupaksha Temple. Courtesy Salma Ahmed Farooqui

Balakrishna Temple. Courtesy Ilya Mauter. Accessed at http://commons.wikimedia.org/wiki/File:Bala_Krishna_temple_at_Hampi.JPG on 29 May 2010.

Ganesha Monolith. Copyright © Sudeshna Dasgupta.

Narasimha Monolith. Accessed at http://commons.wikimedia.org/wiki/File:Hampi3.JPG on 29 May 2010.

Lotus Mahal. Copyright © Sudeshna Dasgupta.

Stone Chariot. Copyright © Sudeshna Dasgupta.

A Beautifully Designed Step Well. Photo by Adam Jones. Accessed at http://commons.wikimedia.org/wiki/File:Temple_Architecture_Near_Hampi_-_India.JPG on 29 May 2010.

Part IV

Chand Bibi, Playing Polo, Glokonda, 1750 CE. Courtesy: National Museum. New Delhi.

Chapter 13

Tomb of Gesu Daraz, Gulbarga. Copyright © Salma Ahmed Farooqui.

Jumma Masjid. Copyright © Salma Ahmed Farooqui.

Inside Arches, Jumma Masjid. Copyright © Salma Ahmed Farooqui.

Bidar Fort. Copyright © Salma Ahmed Farooqui.

Mahmud Gawan's Madrassa. Copyright © Salma Ahmed Farooqui.

Mahmud Gawan's Madrassa. Copyright © Salma Ahmed Farooqui.

Bahmani Tombs. Copyright © Salma Ahmed Farooqui.

Solah Khamba Mosque. Copyright © Salma Ahmed Farooqui.

Elephant Supported Arches, Solah Khamba Mosque. Copyright © Salma Ahmed Farooqui.

Chapter 14

Minaret of Hayat Bakshi Begum's Masjid. Copyright © Salma Ahmed Farooqui.

Bala Hissar. Copyright © Salma Ahmed Farooqui.

Qutb Shahi Tomb. Copyright © Salma Ahmed Farooqui.

Part V

Jalauddin Rumi, Founder of the Order of the Whirling Dervishes, Showing His Love for His Young Disciple Hussam al-Din Chelebi. Courtesy: The Pierpoint Morgan Library, New York. Accessed at http://commons.wikimedia.org/wiki/File:Andr04.jpg on 29 May 2010.

Chapter 15

Tanjore Style Painting. Accessed at http://en.wikipedia.org/wiki/File:Sikh_Gurus_with_Bhai_Bala_and_Bhai_Mardana.jpg on 29 May 2010.

Govardhan, Vallabhacharya. Accessed at http://commons.wikimedia.org/wiki/File:Shrinathji_discovered.jpg on 29 May 2010.

Sri Chaitanya Mahaprabhu. Courtesy: British Library. Accessed at http://commons.wikimedia.org/wiki/File:Chaitanya_sankirtan.jpg on 29 May 2010.

Poet-Saint Tukaram. Courtesy: http://www.columbia.edu. Accessed at http://commons.wikimedia.org/wiki/File:Tukaram_print.jpg on 29 May 2010.

Chapter 16

Tomb of Qutbuddin Bakhtiar Kaki. Courtesy: Ogis. Accessed at http://commons.wikimedia.org/wiki/File:Tomb_of_Qutbuddin_Bakhtiar_Kaki,_Mehrauli.jpg on 29 May 2010.

Jahangir Preferring a Sufi Sheikh to Kings. Accessed at http://commons.wikimedia.org/wiki/File:BichitrJahangir_preferring_a_sufi_sheikh_to_kings.jpg on 29 May 2010.

Part VI

Idealized Portrait of Empress Nur Jahan (1577–1645)?, Rajasthan, Kishangarh, India, 1725–1750 CE. Courtesy: LACMA. Accessed at http://commons.wikimedia.org/wiki/File:Nurjahan.jpg on 29 May 2010.

Chapter 17

First Battle of Panipat. Courtesy: National Museum, New Delhi. Accessed at http://commons.wikimedia.org/wiki/File:Schlacht_von_Panipat.jpg on 29 May 2010.

Chapter 18

The First Rupee. Courtesy: Saithilace. Accessed at http://commons.wikimedia.org/wiki/File:Sher_shah%27s_rupee.jpg on 29 May 2010.

Chapter 19

Punishment of Adham Khan. Courtesy: V&A Museum. Accessed at http://commons.wikimedia.org/wiki/File:Akbar_orders_punishment_of_Adham_Khan,_Akbarnama.jpg on 29 May 2010.

Lord Krishna in the Golden City. Courtesy: Freer Gallery of Art, Smithsonian Institute. Accessed at http://commons.wikimedia.org/wiki/File:Dwarka.jpg on 29 May 2010.

Emperor Akbar Holds a Religious Assembly in the Ibadat Khana in Fatehpur Sikri. Accessed at http://commons.wikimedia.org/wiki/File:Jesuits_at_Akbar%27s_court.jpg on 29 May 2010.

Chapter 20

Jahangir's Dream, 1618–22 CE. Courtesy: Freer Gallery of Art, Smithsonian Institute. Accessed at http://commons.wikimedia.org/wiki/File:Jahangir%27s_dream-Abu%27l_Hasan-c.
1618-22.jpg on 29 May 2010.

Shah Jahan with Angel Musicians. Accessed at http://commons.wikimedia.org/wiki/File:Shah_Jehan_with_Angel_musicians.jpg on 29 May 2010.

Chapter 22

Administrative Organization, Mughal Empire, 1605 CE. Copyright © 1978 by the Regents of the University of Minnesota, assigned 1988 to Joseph E. Schwartzberg, additional material copyright © 1992 by Joseph E. Schwartzberg.

Chapter 23

The Razmnama or Book of Wars. Accessed at http://commons.wikimedia.org/wiki/File:Razmnama_Dronacharya.jpg on 29 May 2010.

Chapter 24

Khusrau Shah Swearing Fealty to Babur. Accessed at http://commons.wikimedia.org/wiki/File:KhusrauBabur.jpg on 29 May 2010.

The Court of Akbar. Courtesy: The Art Institute of Chicago. Accessed at http://commons.wikimedia.org/wiki/File:Court_of_Akbar_from_Akbarnama.jpg on 29 May 2010.

Sher Shah's Tomb. Courtesy: Joseph David Beglar. Accessed at http://commons.wikimedia.org/wiki/File:Sher_Shah_Suri%27s_Tomb,_Sasaram,_1870_photograph.jpg on 29 May 2010.

Diwan-i-Khas, Fatehpur Sikri. Courtesy: David Castor. Accessed at http://commons.wikimedia.org/wiki/File:Diwan-i-Khas-5.jpg on 29 May 2010.

Entrance to Jama Masjid, Fatehpur Sikri. Courtesy: David Castor. Accessed at http://commons.wikimedia.org/wiki/File:Jami_Masjid_(Fatehpur_Sikri)-7.jpg on 29 May 2010.

Panch Mahal, Fatehpur Sikri. Courtesy: David Castor. Accessed at http://commons.wikimedia.org/wiki/File:Panch_Mahal-1.jpg on 29 May 2010.

Humayun's Tomb, Nizamuddin East, Delhi. Copyright © Amarjyoti Dutta.

Akbar's Tomb, Sikandra. Copyright © Amarjyoti Dutta.

Taj Mahal, Agra. Courtesy: David Castor. Accessed at http://commons.wikimedia.org/wiki/File:Taj_Mahal-09.jpg on 29 May 2010.

Archery Competition. Coutesy: Courtesy: Freer Gallery of Art, Smithsonian Institute. Accessed at http://commons.wikimedia.org/wiki/File:Archery_Competition-Mughal-India.jpg on 29 May 2010.

Abul Hasan and Manohar with Jahangir in Darbar. Accessed at http://commons.wikimedia.org/wiki/File:Jahangir_in_Darbar,_from_the_Jahangir-nama,_c.1620.jpg on 29 May 2010.

Part VII

The Darwaja, Fort Raigad, Maharashtra, India. Courtesy: Rohit Gowaikar. Accessed at http://commons.wikimedia.org/wiki/File:Darwaja_(The_Gate).jpg on 29 May 2010.

Chapter 26

Maratha Administrative System Under Shivaji. Copyright © 1978 by the Regents of the University of Minnesota, assigned 1988 to Joseph E. Schwartzberg, additional material copyright © 1992 by Joseph E. Schwartzberg.

Part VIII

Spanish and Portuguese Vessels, Cape of Good Hope. From: Shaw, Edward R., 1900, *Discoverers and Explorers*, American Book Company: New York. Available at http://www.gutenberg.org/files/22116/22116-h/22116-h.htm. Accessed on 15 April 2010.

Seaward View of Masulipatnam. Copyright © 1978 by the Regents of the University of Minnesota, assigned 1988 to Joseph E. Schwartzberg, additional material copyright © 1992 by Joseph E. Schwartzberg.

The English Fort at Bombay. Copyright © 1978 by the Regents of the University of Minnesota, assigned 1988 to Joseph E. Schwartzberg, additional material copyright © 1992 by Joseph E. Schwartzberg.

Index

B

C

S